2 CORINTHIANS

A Commentary in the Wesleyan Tradition

*New Beacon Bible Commentary

2 CORINTHIANS

A Commentary in the Wesleyan Tradition

Frank G. Carver

BEACON HILL PRESS
OF KANSAS CITY

ISBN 978-0-8341-2396-0

Printed in the United States of America

Cover Design: J.R. Caines
Interior Design: Sharon Page

Library of Congress Cataloging-in-Publication Data

Carver, Frank G.
2 Corinthians / Frank G. Carver.
p. cm. — (New Beacon Bible commentary)
Includes bibliographical references.
ISBN 978-0-8341-2396-0 (pbk.)
1. Bible. N.T. Corinthians, 2nd—Commentaries. I. Title.

BS2675.53.C37 2009
227'.307—dc22

2009012502

10 9 8 7 6 5 4 3 2 1

DEDICATION

To Betty, my loving and loyal wife of over sixty years,
and to Mark and Carol, our children of whom I am proud.

COMMENTARY EDITORS

CONTENTS

GENERAL EDITORS' PREFACE

The purpose of the New Beacon Bible Commentary is to make available to pastors and students in the twenty-first century a biblical commentary that reflects the best scholarship in the Wesleyan theological tradition. The commentary project aims to make this scholarship accessible to a wider audience to assist them in their understanding and proclamation of Scripture as God's Word.

Writers of the volumes in this series not only are scholars within the Wesleyan theological tradition and experts in their field but also have special interest in the books assigned to them. Their task is to communicate clearly the critical consensus and the full range of other credible voices who have commented on the Scriptures. Though scholarship and scholarly contribution to the understanding of the Scriptures are key concerns of this series, it is not intended as an academic dialogue within the scholarly community. Commentators of this series constantly aim to demonstrate in their work the significance of the Bible as the church's book and the contemporary relevance and application of the biblical message. The project's overall goal is to make available to the church and for her service the fruits of the labors of scholars who are committed to their Christian faith.

The *New International Version* (NIV) is the reference version of the Bible used in this series; however, the focus of exegetical study and comments is the biblical text in its original language. When the commentary uses the NIV, it is printed in bold. The text printed in bold italics is the translation of the author. Commentators also refer to other translations where the text may be difficult or ambiguous.

The structure and organization of the commentaries in this series seeks to facilitate the study of the biblical text in a systematic and methodical way. Study of each biblical book begins with an ***Introduction*** section that gives an overview of authorship, date, provenance, audience, occasion, purpose, sociological/cultural issues, textual history, literary features, hermeneutical issues, and theological themes necessary to understand the book. This section also includes a brief outline of the book and a list of general works and standard commentaries.

The commentary section for each biblical book follows the outline of the book presented in the introduction. In some volumes, readers will find section ***overviews*** of large portions of scripture with general comments on their overall literary structure and other literary features. A consistent feature of the commentary is the paragraph-by-paragraph study of biblical texts. This section has three parts: ***Behind the Text***, ***In the Text***, and ***From the Text***.

The goal of the ***Behind the Text*** section is to provide the reader with all the relevant information necessary to understand the text. This includes specific historical situations reflected in the text, the literary context of the text, sociological and cultural issues, and literary features of the text.

In the Text explores what the text says, following its verse-by-verse structure. This section includes a discussion of grammatical details, word studies, and the connectedness of the text to other biblical books/passages or other parts of the book being studied (the canonical relationship). This section provides transliterations of key words in Hebrew and Greek and their literal meanings. The goal here is to explain what the author would have meant and/or what the audience would have understood as the meaning of the text. This is the largest section of the commentary.

The ***From the Text*** section examines the text in relation to the following areas: theological significance, intertextuality, the history of interpretation, use of the Old Testament scriptures in the New Testament, interpretation in later church history, actualization, and application.

The commentary provides ***sidebars*** on topics of interest that are important but not necessarily part of an explanation of the biblical text. These topics are informational items and may cover archaeological, historical, literary, cultural, and theological matters that have relevance to the biblical text. Occasionally, longer detailed discussions of special topics are included as ***excurses.***

We offer this series with our hope and prayer that readers will find it a valuable resource for their understanding of God's Word and an indispensable tool for their critical engagement with the biblical texts.

Roger Hahn, Centennial Initiative General Editor
Alex Varughese, General Editor (Old Testament)
George Lyons, General Editor (New Testament)

ACKNOWLEDGMENTS

The majority of the research and writing of this commentary took place in a quiet semi-office in the Wesleyan Center for Twenty-First Century Studies at Point Loma Nazarene University. My expression of appreciation for this privilege goes first to Maxine Walker (1995-2007) and then to Mark Mann (2008-), directors of the center, for their gracious hospitality. The friendliness and helpfulness of staff members Sharon Bowles, Robin Evans, and Jennifer Rogers added to the welcome I felt in this environment.

Just outside the door to the Wesleyan Center is the University Library. Head librarians, first Jim Newburg and then Frank Quinn, have been encouraging friends in this more than three-year journey. Librarians and staff who have been most helpful include Sandy Casto, Doug Fruehling, Denise Nelson, Beryl Pagan, and the early morning "Buenos Dias" and "¿Como esta usted?" from Patrica Salas.

Among those who have read and commented on the writing along the way, first mention goes to my wife, Betty, who has proofread the entire manuscript. Others who joined in this process are our daughter, Carol, and Donna Tyler. Premier mention goes to the members of the "Come and Go" Sunday School class at San Diego First Church of the Nazarene, who have endured many lessons taken directly from the commentary-in-progress. They have made a unique contribution to the project. Affirming me all along in this endeavor has been my pastor, Selden D. Kelley III, who has afforded me feedback from time to time.

My gratitude goes to two special friends of many years who have functioned as dialoguing partners in the research and writing process. Philosopher-theologian Herbert L. Prince, coteacher of "Come and Go," has allowed me over and over to run by him my ventures into theological areas as well as the appropriateness of my language. Robert W. Smith, fellow NT exegete, has always been available for questions and to read my exploration of a passage. He has afforded me invaluable advice, as well as indispensable encouragement.

Last but not least are the long hours of meticulous work put in by my section editor, George Lyons, a general editor of the NBBC series. Although in his words, he is not "fixing" the commentary, I am deeply grateful for his suggestions and needed contributions to the comprehensiveness and quality of its content. His editorial touch has improved its readability and clarity. Enjoyable, too, has been the not-so-subtle pressure he has kept on me to complete the commentary on schedule.

ABBREVIATIONS

With a few exceptions, these abbreviations follow those in *The SBL Handbook of Style* (Alexander 1999).

General

A.D.	anno Domini
ACCS	Ancient Christian Commentary on Scripture
B.C.	before Christ
BDF	Blass, Debrunner, Funk (1961)
ch	chapter
chs	chapters
Did.	*Didache*
EDNT	*Exegetical Dictionary of the New Testament*, edited by Balz and Schneider (1990–93)
ed.	edited by
e.g.	*exempli gratia*, for example
esp.	especially
etc.	*et cetera*, and the rest
i.e.	*id est*, that is
ktl.	etc. (in Greek transliteration)
LXX	Septuagint (Greek translation of the OT)
n	note
n.d.	no date
MT	Masoretic Text (Hebrew OT)
NT	New Testament
OT	Old Testament
s.v.	*sub verbo*, under the word
vol.	volume
v	verse
vv	verses

Modern English Versions

GNT	Good News Translation
JB	Jerusalem Bible
KJV	King James Version
NASB	New American Standard Bible
NEB	New English Bible
NIV	New International Version
NRSV	New Revised Standard Version
REB	Revised English Bible
RSV	Revised Standard Version
TLB	The Living Bible
TM	The Message
TNIV	Today's New International Version

Print Conventions for Translations

Bold font	NIV (bold without quotation marks in the text under study; elsewhere in the regular font, with quotation marks and no further identification)
Bold italic font	Author's translation (without quotation marks)

Behind the Text:	Literary or historical background information average readers might not know from reading the biblical text alone
In the Text:	Comments on the biblical text, words, phrases, grammar, and so forth
From the Text:	The use of the text by later interpreters, contemporary relevance, theological and ethical implications of the text, with particular emphasis on Wesleyan concerns

Old Testament

Gen	Genesis
Exod	Exodus
Lev	Leviticus
Num	Numbers
Deut	Deuteronomy
Josh	Joshua
Judg	Judges
Ruth	Ruth
1–2 Sam	1–2 Samuel
1–2 Kgs	1–2 Kings
1–2 Chr	1–2 Chronicles
Ezra	Ezra
Neh	Nehemiah
Esth	Esther
Job	Job
Ps/Pss	Psalms
Prov	Proverbs
Eccl	Ecclesiastes
Song	Song of Songs / Song of Solomon
Isa	Isaiah
Jer	Jeremiah
Lam	Lamentations
Ezek	Ezekiel
Dan	Daniel
Hos	Hosea
Joel	Joel
Amos	Amos
Obad	Obadiah
Jonah	Jonah
Mic	Micah
Nah	Nahum
Hab	Habakkuk
Zeph	Zephaniah
Hag	Haggai
Zech	Zechariah
Mal	Malachi

(Note: Chapter and verse numbering in the MT and LXX often differ compared to those in English Bibles. To avoid confusion, all biblical references follow the chapter and verse numbering in English translations, even when the text in the MT and LXX is under discussion.)

New Testament

Matt	Matthew
Mark	Mark
Luke	Luke
John	John
Acts	Acts
Rom	Romans
1–2 Cor	1–2 Corinthians
Gal	Galatians
Eph	Ephesians
Phil	Philippians
Col	Colossians
1–2 Thess	1–2 Thessalonians
1–2 Tim	1–2 Timothy
Titus	Titus
Phlm	Philemon
Heb	Hebrews
Jas	James
1–2 Pet	1–2 Peter
1–2–3 John	1–2–3 John
Jude	Jude
Rev	Revelation

Apocrypha

APOT	*The Apocrypha and Pseudepigrapha of the Old Testament*, edited by R. H. Charles, 2 vols. (Oxford, 1913)
Bar	Baruch
Add Dan	Additions to Daniel
Pr Azar	Prayer of Azariah
Bel	Bel and the Dragon
Sg Three	Song of the Three Young Men
Sus	Susanna
1–2 Esd	1–2 Esdras
Add Esth	Additions to Esther
Ep Jer	Epistle of Jeremiah
Jdt	Judith
1—2 Macc	1—2 Maccabees
3—4 Macc	3—4 Maccabees
Pr Man	Prayer of Manasseh
Ps 151	Psalm 151
Sir	Sirach/Ecclesiasticus
Tob	Tobit
Wis	Wisdom of Solomon

OT Pseudepigrapha

Ahiqar	*Ahiqar*
Apoc. Ab.	*Apocalypse of Abraham*
Apoc. Adam	*Apocalypse of Adam*
Apoc. Dan.	*Apocalypse of Daniel*
Apoc. El. (H)	Hebrew *Apocalypse of Elijah*
Apoc. El. (C)	Coptic *Apocalypse of Elijah*
Apoc. Mos.	*Apocalypse of Moses*
Apoc. Sedr.	*Apocalypse of Sedrach*
Apoc. Zeph.	*Apocalypse of Zephaniah*
Apocr. Ezek.	*Apocrypon of Ezekiel*
Aris. Ex.	Aristeas the Exegete
Aristob.	Aristobulus
Artap.	Artapanus
As. Mos.	*Assumption of Moses*
2 Bar.	*2 Baruch (Syriac Apocalypse)*
3 Bar.	*3 Baruch (Greek Apocalypse)*
4 Bar.	*4 Baruch (Paraleipomena Jeremiou)*
Bk. Noah	*Book of Noah*
Cav. Tr.	*Cave of Treasures*
Cl. Mal.	Cleodemus Malchus
Dem.	Demetrius (the Chronographer)
El. Mod.	*Eldad and Modad*
1 En.	*1 Enoch (Ethiopic Apocalypse)*
2 En.	*2 Enoch (Slavonic Apocalypse)*
3 En.	*3 Enoch (Hebrew Apocalypse)*
Eup.	Eupolemus
Ezek. Trag.	Ezekiel the Tragedian
4 Ezra	*4 Ezra*
5 Apoc. Syr. Pss.	*Five Apocryphal Syriac Psalms*

Dead Sea Scrolls

1Qap Gen^{ar}	*Genesis Apocryphon*
1QH^{a}	*Hodayot*^{a} or *Thanksgiving Hymns*^{a}
1QIsa^{a}	Isaiah^{a}

1QIsa^{b}	Isaiah^{b}
1QM	*Milkamah* or *War Scroll*
1QpHa^{b}	*Pesher Habakkuk*
1QS	*Serek Hayakad* or *Rule of the Community*
CD	Cairo Genizah copy of the *Damascus Document*

Josephus

Vita	*Vita*
Life	*The Life*
C. Ap.	*Contra Apionem*
Ag. Ap.	*Against Apion*
A.J.	*Antiquitates judaicae*
Ant.	*Jewish Antiquities*
B.J.	*Bellum judaicum*
J.W.	*Jewish War*

Greek Transliteration

Greek	***Letter***	***English***
α	*alpha*	*a*
β	*bēta*	*b*
γ	*gamma*	*g*
γ	*gamma nasal*	*n* (before γ, κ, ξ, χ)
δ	*delta*	*d*
ε	*epsilon*	*e*
ζ	*zēta*	*z*
η	*ēta*	*ē*
θ	*thēta*	*th*
ι	*iōta*	*i*
κ	*kappa*	*k*
λ	*lambda*	*l*
μ	*my*	*m*
ν	*ny*	*n*
ξ	*xi*	*x*
ο	*omicron*	*o*
π	*pi*	*p*
ρ	*rhō*	*r*
ρ	initial *rhō*	*rh*
σ/ς	*sigma*	*s*
τ	*tau*	*t*
υ	*upsilon*	*y*
υ	*upsilon*	*u* (in diphthongs: *au, eu, ēu, ou, ui*)
φ	*phi*	*ph*
χ	*chi*	*ch*
ψ	*psi*	*ps*
ω	*ōmega*	*ō*
ʽ	rough breathing	*h* (before initial vowels or diphthongs)

Hebrew Consonant Transliteration

Hebrew/ Aramaic	***Letter***	***English***
א	*alef*	’
ב	*bet*	*b*
ג	*gimel*	*g*
ד	*dalet*	*d*
ה	*he*	*h*
ו	*vav*	*v* or *w*
ז	*zayin*	*z*
ח	*khet*	*ḥ*
ט	*tet*	*ṭ*
י	*yod*	*y*
כ/ך	*kaf*	*k*
ל	*lamed*	*l*
מ/ם	*mem*	*m*
נ/ן	*nun*	*n*
ס	*samek*	*s*
ע	*ayin*	‘
פ/ף	*pe*	*p*
צ/ץ	*tsade*	*ṣ*
ק	*qof*	*q*
ר	*resh*	*r*
שׂ	*sin*	*ś*
שׁ	*shin*	*š*
ת	*tav*	*t*

BIBLIOGRAPHY

Achtemeier, Paul J., Joel B. Green, and Marianne Meye Thompson. 2001. *Introducing the New Testament: Its Literature and Theology.* Grand Rapids: Eerdmans.

Ahern, Barnabas Mary. 1960. "The Fellowship of His Sufferings (Phil 3:10): A Study of St. Paul's Doctrine of Christian Suffering." *Catholic Biblical Quarterly* 12:1-32.

Baird, William. 1960. *Paul's Message and Mission.* Nashville: Abingdon.

________. 1964. *The Corinthian Church: A Biblical Approach to Urban Culture.* New York: Abingdon.

Balz, Horst Robert, and Gerhard Schneider, eds. 1990-93. *Exegetical Dictionary of the New Testament.* Translated by Virgil P. Howard, James W. Thompson, John W. Medendorp, and Douglas W. Stott. 3 vols. Grand Rapids: Eerdmans.

Barclay, William. 1956. *The Letters to the Corinthians.* 2nd ed. Daily Study Bible. Philadelphia: Westminster.

Barnett, Paul. 1997. *The Second Epistle to the Corinthians.* The New International Commentary on the New Testament. Grand Rapids: Eerdmans.

Barrett, C. K. 1970. *The Signs of an Apostle.* London: Epworth.

________. 1973. *Commentary on the Second Epistle to the Corinthians.* Harper's New Testament Commentaries. San Francisco: Harper and Row.

Bauer, William, Frederick W. Danker, W. F. Arndt, F. Wilbur Gingrich, and Frederick W. Danker. 2000. *A Greek-English Lexicon of the New Testament and Other Early Christian Literature.* 3rd ed. Chicago: University of Chicago Press. Cited as BDAG.

Beale, G. K. 1989-90. "The Old Testament Background of Reconciliation in 2 Corinthians 5-7 and its Bearing on the Literary Problem of 2 Corinthians 6.14-7.1." *New Testament Studies* 35:550-81.

Beardslee, William A. 1961. *Human Achievement and Divine Vocation in the Message of Paul.* Naperville, Ill.: Allenson.

Belleville, Linda L. 1991. *Reflections of Glory: Paul's Polemical Use of the Moses-*Doxa *Tradition in 2 Corinthians 3:1-18.* Journal for the Study of the New Testament: Supplement Series 52. Sheffield: Sheffield Academic Press.

Bengel, John Albert. 1895. *Gnomon of the New Testament.* 6th ed. Vol. 3. Translated by James Bryce. Edinburgh: T. and T. Clark.

Bernard, J. H. 1987. The Second Epistle to the Corinthians. Pages 3-119 in vol. 3 in *Expositor's Greek Testament.* Edited by W. Robertson Nicoll. New York: Hodder and Stoughton, 1897. Repr. Grand Rapids: Eerdmans.

Best, Ernest. 1987. *Second Corinthians.* Interpretation. Atlanta: John Knox.

Betz, Hans Dieter. 1972. *Der Apostel Paulus und die sokratische Tradition. Eine exegetische Untersuchung zu seiner "Apologie" 2 Korinther 10-13.* BHT 45. Tübingen: Mohr.

________. 1973. 2 Cor 6:14—7:1: An Anti-Pauline Fragment? *Journal of Biblical Literature* 92:88-108.

________. 1975. *Paul's Apology: II Corinthians 10-13, and the Socratic Tradition.* Berkeley, Calif.: Center for Hermeneutical Studies in Hellenistic and Modern Culture.

________. 1985. *2 Corinthians 8 and 9: A Commentary on Two Administrative Letters of the Apostle Paul.* Hermeneia. Philadelphia: Fortress.

Bjerkelund, Carl J. 1967. *PARAKALŌ: Form, Funktion und Sinn der parakalō-Sätze in den paulinischen Briefen.* Oslo: Universitetsforlaget.

Blaiklock, E. M. 1965. *Cities of the New Testament.* Westwood, N.J.: Fleming H. Revell.

Blass, F., A. Debrunner, and Robert W. Funk. 1961. *A Greek Grammar of the New Testament and Other Early Christian Literature.* Chicago: University of Chicago Press. Cited as BDF.

Bray, Gerald, ed. 1999. *1-2 Corinthians.* Ancient Christian Commentary on Scripture. New Testament. Vol. 7. Edited by Thomas C. Oden. Downers Grove, Ill.: InterVarsity Press. Cited as ACCS NT 7.

Brower, Kent E. 2006. *Living as God's Holy People: Pauline Perspectives on Christian Holiness.* H. Orton Wiley Lecture Series, February 27—March 1, 2006. San Diego: Point Loma Nazarene University.

Bultmann, Rudolf. 1985. *The Second Letter to the Corinthians.* Translated by Roy A. Harrisville. Minneapolis: Augsburg.
Burke, Tevor J., and J. Keith Elliott, eds. 2003. *Paul and the Corinthians: Studies on a Community in Conflict. Essays in Honour of Margaret Thrall.* Leiden: Brill.
Caird, G. B. 1956. *Principalities and Powers: A Study in Pauline Theology.* Oxford: Clarendon Press.
Calvin, John. 1964 (=1547). *The Second Epistle of Paul the Apostle to the Corinthians and the Epistles to Timothy, Titus and Philemon.* Calvin's Commentaries 10. Translated by T. A. Smail. Edited by David W. Torrence and Thomas Torrence. Grand Rapids: Eerdmans.
Carson, D. A. 1984. *From Triumphalism to Maturity: An Exposition of 2 Corinthians 10-13.* Grand Rapids: Baker.
Carver, Frank G. 1987. *The Cross and the Spirit: Peter and the Way of the Holy.* Kansas City: Beacon Hill Press of Kansas City.
Cassian, John. 1958. *Conferences.* Conference 9. Paragraph 4. *Western Asceticism.* Edited by Owen Chadwick. Library of Christian Classics. Philadelphia: Westminster.
Clarke, Adam. 1854. *The New Testament of Our Lord and Saviour Jesus Christ: A Commentary and Critical Notes.* Vol. 2. New York: Carlton and Phillips.
Collins, John N. 1990. *Diakonia: Re-interpreting the Ancient Sources.* New York: Oxford University Press.
________. 1992. *Are All Christians Ministers?* Collegeville, Minn.: Liturgical Press.
Crafton, Jeffrey A. 1991. *The Agency of the Apostle: A Dramatic Analysis of Paul's Responses to Conflict in 2 Corinthians.* Journal for the Study of the New Testament: Supplement Series 51. Sheffield: Sheffield Academic Press.
Cranfield, C. E. B. 1965. "Minister and Congregation in the Light of II Corinthians 4:5-7." *Interpretation* 19:163-67.
Culbertson, Paul T. 1966. *More like the Master: How to Develop a Christlike Personality.* Kansas City: Beacon Hill Press of Kansas City.
Cullmann, Oscar M. 1958. *Immortality of the Soul or Resurrection of the Dead? The Witness of the New Testament.* Translation of a study published in *Theologische Zeitschrift.* London: Epworth.
________. 1959. *The Christology of the New Testament.* Translated by Shirley C. Guthrie and Charles A. M. Hall. Philadelphia: Westminster.
Curtis, Olin Alfred. 1905. *The Christian Faith Personally Given in a System of Doctrine.* New York: Methodist Book Concern.
Daiches, David. 1975. *Moses: The Man and His Vision.* New York: Praeger.
Davies, W. D. 1962. "Conscience." Pages 671-76 in vol. 1 of *The Interpreter's Dictionary of the Bible.* New York: Abingdon.
Deissmann, G. A. 1901. *Bible Studies.* Translated by A. Grieve. Edinburgh: T. and T. Clark.
________. 1927. *Light from the Ancient East.* Translated by L. R. M. Strachan. New York: Harper and Brothers.
Denney, James. 1943. The Second Epistle to the Corinthians. Pages 715-809 in vol. 5 in *The Expositor's Bible.* Edited by W. Robertson Nicoll. Repr. of 1894 ed.
deSilva, David A. 2004. *An Introduction to the New Testament: Contexts, Methods and Ministry Formation.* Downers Grove, Ill.: InterVarsity.
Doty, William G. 1973. *Letters in Primitive Christianity.* Philadelphia: Fortress Press.
Douglas, Deborah Smith. 2008. "Thanks Be to God: Gratitude as Prayer of Adoration." *Weavings* 23, 2:6-12.
Dunn, J. D. G. 1975. *Jesus and the Spirit.* Philadelphia: Westminster.
________. 1998. *The Theology of Paul the Apostle.* Grand Rapids: Eerdmans.
Ellis, E. Earle. 1957. *Paul's Use of the Old Testament.* Grand Rapids: Eerdmans.
________. 1959-60. "II Corinthians v. 1-10 in Pauline Eschatology." *New Testament Studies* 6:211-24. Also in E. Earle Ellis. Pages 35-48 in *Paul and His Recent Interpreters.* Grand Rapids: Eerdmans, 1961.
________. 1970-71. "Paul and His Co-Workers." *New Testament Studies* 17:437-52. Also in E. Earle Ellis. Pages 3-22 in *Prophecy and Hermeneutic in Early Christianity.* Grand Rapids: Eerdmans, 1978.
________. 1977. "How the New Testament Uses the Old." Pages 199-219 in *New Testament Interpretation Essays on Principles and Methods.* Edited by I. Howard Marshall. Grand Rapids: Eerdmans.

________. 1993. "Coworkers, Paul and His." Pages 183-88 in *Dictionary of Paul and His Letters.* Edited by Gerald F. Hawthorne, Ralph P. Martin, and Daniel G. Reid. Downers Grove, Ill.: InterVarsity.

Fee, Gordon. 1994. *God's Empowering Presence: The Holy Spirit in the Letters of Paul.* Peabody, Mass.: Hendrickson.

Filson, Floyd. 1953. The Second Epistle to the Corinthians (Exegesis). Pages 263-425 in vol. 10 of *The Interpreter's Bible.* Edited by George A. Buttrick and others. New York: Abingdon-Cokesbury.

Fitzmyer, Joseph A. 1971. "Qumran and the Interpolated Paragraph in 2 Cor 6:14—7:1." Pages 205-17 in *Essays on the Semitic Background of the New Testament.* London: Chapman.

Flemming, Dean. 2009. *Philippians.* New Beacon Bible Commentary. Kansas City: Beacon Hill Press of Kansas City.

Forbes, Christopher. 1986. "Comparison, Self-Praise and Irony: Paul's Boasting and the Conventions of Hellenistic Rhetoric." *New Testament Studies* 36:1-30.

Forsyth, P. T. 1907. *Positive Preaching and the Modern Mind.* Lyman Beecher Lectures on Preaching, Yale University. New York: A. C. Armstrong and Son.

Furnish, Victor Paul. 1981. "Glory Reflected on the Face of Christ (2 Cor 3:7—4:6) and a Palestinian Jewish Motif." *Texts and Studies* 42:630-44. Reprinted as pages 64-79 in *According to Paul: Studies in the Theology of the Apostle.* New York: Paulist Press, 1993.

________. 1984. *II Corinthians.* Vol. 32A of The Anchor Bible. Garden City, N.Y.: Doubleday.

Garland, David E. 1999. *2 Corinthians.* Vol. 29 in the New American Commentary. Nashville: Broadman and Holman.

Gaster, Theodore. 1957. *The Dead Sea Scriptures.* New York: Doubleday.

Georgi, Dieter. 1992. *Remembering the Poor: The History of Paul's Collection for Jerusalem.* Translated by John Bowden. Nashville: Abingdon Press. German, 1965.

Gorman, Michael J. 2001. *Cruciformity: Paul's Narrative Spirituality of the Cross.* Grand Rapids: Eerdmans.

Greathouse, William M., with George Lyons. 2008. *Romans 1-8.* New Beacon Bible Commentary. Kansas City: Beacon Hill Press of Kansas City.

Green, Joel B. 2004. "Is There a Contemporary Wesleyan Hermeneutic?" Pages 123-34 in *Reading the Bible in Wesleyan Ways: Some Constructive Proposals.* Edited by Barry L. Callen and Richard P. Thompson. Kansas City: Beacon Hill Press of Kansas City.

Greenberg, Moshe. 1960. *nsh* in "Exodus 20:20 and the Purpose of Sinaitic Theophany." *Journal of Biblical Literature* 79:273-76.

Hafemann, Scott J. 1990a. "'Self-Commendation' and Apostolic Legitimacy in 2 Corinthians." *New Testament Studies* 36:66-88.

________. 1990b. *Suffering and Ministry in the Spirit: Paul's Defense of His Apostolic Ministry in 2 Corinthians 2:14-3:3.* Grand Rapids: Eerdmans.

________. 1995. *Paul, Moses, and the History of Israel: The Letter/Spirit Contrast and the Argument from Scripture in 2 Corinthians 3.* Tübingen: J. C. B. Mohr (Paul Siebeck).

________. 2000. *2 Corinthians* in the NIV Application Commentary. Grand Rapids: Zondervan.

Hamilton, Elizabeth. 1982. *The Life of Saint Teresa of Ávila.* Wheathampstead, U.K.: Anthony Clark.

Hanson, Anthony Tyrrell. 1974. *Studies in Paul's Technique and Theology.* Grand Rapids: Eerdmans.

Hanson, R. P. C. 1954. *The Second Epistle to the Corinthians.* Torch Bible Commentaries. London: S.C.M.

Harink, Douglas. 2003. *Paul Among the Postliberals: Pauline Theology Beyond Christendom and Modernity.* Grand Rapids: Brazos Press.

Harris, Murray J. 2005. *The Second Epistle to the Corinthians: A Commentary on the Greek Text.* New International Greek Testament Commentary. Grand Rapids: Eerdmans.

Hays, Richard B. 1989. *Echoes of Scripture in the Letters of Paul.* New Haven, Conn.: Yale University Press.

________. 1996. *The Moral Vision of the New Testament: A Contemporary Introduction to New Testament Ethics.* San Francisco: HarperSanFrancisco.

________. 2005. *The Conversion of the Imagination: Paul as an Interpreter of Israel's Scripture.* Grand Rapids: Eerdmans.

Hickling, Colin J. A. 1974-75. "The Sequence of Thought in II Corinthians, Chapter Three." *New Testament Studies* 21:380-95.

Hill, David. 2001. *Greek Words and Hebrew Meanings: Studies in the Semantics of Soteriological*

Terms. Society for New Testament Studies Monograph Series 5. Eugene, Oreg.: Wipf and Stock.
Hinson, E. Glenn. 2008. "Impasse and the Sufficiency of Grace." *Weavings* 23, 1:35-43.
Hock, Ronald F. 1980. *The Social Context of Paul's Ministry: Tentmaking and Apostleship.* Philadelphia: Fortress.
Hodge, Charles. 1866. *An Exposition of the Second Epistle to the Corinthians.* New York: Robert Carter and Brothers.
Hodgson, Robert. 1983. "Paul the Apostle and First Century Tribulation List." *Zeitschrift für die Neutestamentlische Wissenschaft und die Kunde der Älteren Kirche* 74:59-80.
Hoffmann, E. 1978. "Promise." Pages 68-74 in vol. 3 of *The New International Dictionary of New Testament Theology.* Edited and translated by Colin Brown and others. Grand Rapids: Zondervan.
Holladay, William M. 1988. *A Concise Hebrew Lexicon of the Old Testament.* Grand Rapids: Eerdmans.
Hughes, Philip Edgcumbe. 1962. *Paul's Second Epistle to the Corinthians.* The New International Commentary on the New Testament. Grand Rapids: Eerdmans.
James, M. R. 1924. *The Apocryphal New Testament.* Oxford: Clarendon Press.
Jeremias, Joachim. 1958. *Unknown Sayings of Jesus.* Translated by R. H. Fuller. London: S.P.C.K.
Jones, L. Gregory, and Kevin R. Armstrong. 2006. *Resurrecting Excellence: Shaping Faithful Christian Ministry.* Grand Rapids: Eerdmans.
Kavanaugh, Kieran, and Otilio Rodriguez, trans. 1991. *The Collected Works of St. John of the Cross.* Washington, D.C.: Institute of Carmelite Studies.
Kay, James F. 2001. 2 Corinthians 4:3-6 through 2 Corinthians 6:1-13. Pages 243-64 in vol. 2 of *The Lectionary Commentary: Theological Exegesis for Sunday's Texts. The Second Readings: Acts and Epistles.* Edited by Roger E. Van Harn. Grand Rapids: Eerdmans.
________. 2007. *Preaching and Theology.* St Louis: Chalice Press.
Kennedy, George A. 1984. *New Testament Interpretation Through Rhetorical Criticism.* Chapel Hill: University of North Carolina Press.
Kim, C.-H. 1972. *Form and Structure of the Familiar Greek Letter of Recommendation.* Missoula, Mont.: Scholars.
Kittel, Gerhard, and Gerhard Friedrich, eds. 1964-76. *Theological Dictionary of the New Testament.* Translated and edited by Geoffrey W. Bromiley. 10 vols. Grand Rapids: Eerdmans.
Knox, R. A. 1944. *The New Testament.* New York: Sheed and Ward.
Koehler, Ludwig, and Walter Baumgartner. 1994. *The Hebrew and Aramaic Lexicon of the Old Testament.* Translated and edited under the supervision of M. E. J. Richardson. 4 vols. Leiden: Brill.
Kolodiejchuk, Brian M. C. 2007. *Mother Teresa, Come Be My Light: The Private Writings of the "Saint of Calcutta."* New York: Doubleday.
Kruse, Colin G. 1987. *The Second Epistle of Paul to the Corinthians: An Introduction and Commentary.* Vol. 8 in Tyndale New Testament Commentary. Grand Rapids: Eerdmans.
Kümmel, Werner Georg. 1963. *Man in the New Testament.* Philadelphia: Westminster.
Lambrecht, Jan. 1978. "The Fragment 2 Cor vi 14—vii 1: A Plea for Its Authenticity." Pages 143-61 in *Miscellanea Neotestamentica.* Edited by T. Baarda and others. Novum Testamentum Supplement 47. Leiden: Brill. Repr. as pages 531-49 in *Studies on 2 Corinthians.* Edited by Reimund Bieringer and Jan Lambrecht. Bibliotheca Ephemeridum Theologicarum Lovaniensium 125. Leuven: Leuven University Press/Peeters, 1994.
________. 1983. "Structure and Line of Thought in 2 Cor 2,14—4,6." *Biblica* 64:344-80. Repr. as pages 257-94 in *Studies on 2 Corinthians.* Edited by Reimund Bieringer and Jan Lambrecht. Bibliotheca Ephemeridum Theologicarum Lovaniensium 102. Leuven: Leuven University Press/Peeters, 1994.
________. 1996. "Paul's Appeal and the Obedience to Christ: The Line of Thought in 2 Corinthians 10, 1-6." *Biblica* 77:398-416.
________. 1999. *Second Corinthians.* Vol. 8 in Sacra Pagina. Collegeville, Minn.: Liturgical Press.
Leivestad, Ragnar. 1965-66. "The Meekness and Gentleness of Christ": II Cor. X. 1. *New Testament Studies* 13:156-65.
Lenski, R. C. H. 1937. *The Interpretation of St. Paul's First and Second Epistle to the Corinthians.* Columbus: Wartburg Press.
Lewis, C. S. 1945. *The Great Divorce: A Dream.* New York: Macmillan.

________. 1961. *The Screwtape Letters.* New York: Simon and Schuster.
________. 1967. *Letters to an American Lady.* Edited by Clyde S. Kilby. Grand Rapids: Eerdmans.
Lightfoot, J. B. 1895. *Notes on Epistles of St. Paul from Unpublished Commentaries.* New York: Macmillan.
Lincoln, A. T. 1978. "Paul the Visionary: The Setting and Significance of the Rapture to Paradise in II Corinthians XII. 1-10." *New Testament Studies* 25:204-20.
________. 1981. *Paradise Now and Not Yet: Studies in the Role of the Heavenly Dimension in Paul's Thought with Special Reference to His Eschatology.* Society for New Testament Studies Monograph Series 43. Cambridge: Cambridge University Press.
Luti, J. Mary. 1991. *Teresa of Avila's Way: The Way of the Christian Mystics 13.* Edited by Noel Dermot O'Dionoghue. Collegeville, Minn.: Liturgical Press.
Lyons, George. 1985. *Pauline Autobiography: Toward a New Understanding.* Society of Biblical Literature Dissertation Series 73. Atlanta: Scholars Press.
McCant, Jerry W. 1988. "Paul's Thorn of Rejected Apostleship." *New Testament Studies* 34:550-72.
________. 1999. *2 Corinthians.* Readings: A New Biblical Commentary. Edited by John Jarick. Sheffield: Sheffield Academic Press.
________. 2006. "Cruciform Ministry: Paul's Vision in 2 Corinthians." Pages 47-59 in *The Wise Shepherd: Biblical and Theological Resources for the Pastoral Task.* Edited by Brad Kelle. San Diego: Point Loma Press.
Martin, Ralph P. 1986. *2 Corinthians.* Vol. 14 in Word Biblical Commentary. Waco, Tex.: Word.
________. 1989. *Reconciliation: A Study of Paul's Theology.* Rev. ed. Grand Rapids: Zondervan.
Martyn, J. Louis. 1997. *Theological Issues in the Letters of Paul.* Nashville: Abingdon.
Matera, Frank J. 2003. *II Corinthians: A Commentary.* The New Testament Library. Louisville, Ky.: Westminster John Knox.
Merton, Thomas. 1961. *New Seeds of Contemplation.* New York: New Directions Publishing.
Metzger, Bruce M. 1994. *A Textual Commentary of the Greek New Testament.* 4th ed. New York: United Bible Societies.
Metzger, Bruce M., and Bart D. Ehrman. 2005. *The Text of the New Testament: Its Transmission, Corruption, and Restoration.* 4th ed. New York: Oxford University Press.
Mitchell, Margaret M. 2003. "The Corinthian Correspondence and the Birth of Pauline Hermeneutics." Pages 17-54 in *Paul and the Corinthians: Studies on a Community in Conflict. Essays in Honour of Margaret Thrall.* Edited by Tevor J. Burke and J. Keith Elliott. Leiden: Brill.
Moore, Frank. 2005. *The Power to Be Free: Discovering Life in the Spirit of Christ.* Kansas City: Beacon Hill Press of Kansas City.
Morgan, G. Campbell. 1946. *The Corinthian Letters of Paul: An Exposition of I and II Corinthians.* New York: Fleming H. Revell.
Morón-Arroyo, Ciriaco. 1984. "I Will Give You a Living Book": Spiritual Currents at Work in the Time of St. Teresa of Jesus. Pages 95-112 in *Carmelite Studies: Centenary of St Teresa.* Edited by John Sullivan. Washington, D.C.: Institute of Carmelite Studies.
Moulton, James Hope. 1908. *A Grammar of New Testament Greek.* Vol. I: Prolegomena. 3rd ed. Edinburgh: T. and T. Clark.
Moulton, James Hope, and G. Milligan. 1949. *The Vocabulary of the Greek New Testament.* Grand Rapids: Eerdmans.
Mounce, Robert H. 1960. *The Essential Nature of New Testament Preaching.* Grand Rapids: Eerdmans.
Munck, Johannes. 1959. *Paul and the Salvation of Mankind.* Translated by Frank Clarke. Richmond, Va.: John Knox.
Murphy-O'Connor, Jerome. 1991. *The Theology of the Second Letter to the Corinthians.* Cambridge: Cambridge University Press.
Nickle, Keith F. 1966. *The Collection: A Study in Paul's Strategy.* Studies in Biblical Theology 48. Naperville, Ill.: Allenson.
O'Brien, Peter Thomas. 1977. *Introductory Thanksgivings in the Letters of Paul. Supplements to Novum Testamentum,* Supplement 49. Leiden: Brill.
Ogilvie, Lloyd John. 1981. Reading for June 13 in *God's Best for My Life.* Eugene, Oreg.: Harvest House.
Opperwall, Nola J. 1979. "Conscience." Pages 761-65 in vol. 1 of *The International Standard Bible Encyclopedia.* Edited by Geoffrey W. Bromiley. Grand Rapids: Eerdmans.

Outler, Albert E., ed. 1985. "The Scripture Way of Salvation." Pages 34-70 in vol. 2 of *Sermons. The Works of John Wesley.* Nashville: Abingdon.

Peterson, Brian K. 1998. *Eloquence and the Proclamation of the Gospel in Corinth.* Society of Biblical Literature Dissertation Series 163. Atlanta: Scholars Press.

Peterson, Eugene H. 2006. *Eat This Book: A Conversation in the Art of Spiritual Reading.* Grand Rapids: Eerdmans.

Plummer, Alfred. 1915. *A Critical and Exegetical Commentary on the Second Epistle of St. Paul to the Corinthians.* International Critical Commentary. Edinburgh: T. and T. Clark.

Powell, Samuel M. 2008. *Discovering Our Christian Faith: An Introduction to Theology.* Kansas City: Beacon Hill Press of Kansas City.

Powers, Daniel G. 2001. *Salvation Through Participation: An Examination of the Notion of the Believer's Corporate Unity with Christ in Early Christian Soteriology.* Leiden: Brill.

Rad, Gerhard Von. 1965. *Old Testament Theology:* Vol. II, *The Theology of Israel's Prophetic Traditions.* Translated by D. M. G. Stalker. New York: Harper and Row.

Reed, Oscar. 1976. *Corinthians.* Beacon Bible Expositions. Kansas City: Beacon Hill Press of Kansas City.

Robertson, A. T. 1934. *A Grammar of the Greek New Testament in the Light of Historical Research.* Nashville: Broadman.

Sampley, J. Paul. 1988. "Paul, His Opponents in 2 Corinthians 10—13, and the Rhetorical Handbooks." Pages 162-77 in *The Social World of Formative Christianity and Judaism.* Edited by Jacob Neusner, Ernest S. Frerichs, Peder Borgen, and Richard Horsley. Philadelphia: Fortress Press.

________. 2000. "The Second Letter to the Corinthians: Introduction, Commentary, and Reflections." Pages 2-180 in vol. 11 in *New Interpreter's Bible.* Nashville: Abingdon.

Schlatter, Adolf. 1956. *Paulus, Der Bote Jesus, Seine Deutung Seiner Briefe an die Korinther.* Stuttgart: Calwer.

Schneemelcher, Wilhelm. 1965. "Acts of Paul." Pages 322-90 in vol. 2 of *New Testament Apocrypha.* Translated by R. McL. Wilson. Philadelphia: Westminster.

Schniewind, Julius, and Gerhard Friedrich. 1964. *epangellō, ktl.* Pages 576-86 in vol. 2 in *Theological Dictionary of the New Testament.* Edited by Gerhard Kittel and Gerhard Friedrich.

Schweizer, Eduard. 1965. *The Church as the Body of Christ.* London: S.P.C.K.

Shillington, V. George. 1998. *2 Corinthians.* Believers Church Bible Commentary. Edited by Elmer Martens and Willard M. Swartley. Scottdale, Pa.: Herald.

Stowers, Stanley K. 1986. *Letter Writing in Greco-Roman Antiquity.* Philadelphia: Westminster.

Strack, Herman L., and Paul Billerbeck. 1926. *Die Briefe des Neuen Testaments und die Offenbarung Johannis* in Kommentar zum Neuen Testament aus Talmud und Midrash. Vol. 3. Munich: C. H. Beck'sche.

Teresa of Avila. 1980. "The Interior Castle." Pages 281-452 in vol. 2 of *The Collected Works of St. Teresa of Avila.* Translated by Kieran Kavanaugh and Otilio Rodriguez. Washington, D.C.: Institute of Carmelite Studies.

________. 1987. "The Book of Her Life." Pages 53-365 in vol. 1 of *The Collected Works of St. Teresa of Avila.* 2nd ed. Translated by Kieran Kavanaugh and Otilio Rodriguez. Washington, D.C.: Institute of Carmelite Studies.

Thielicke, Helmut. 1965. *The Trouble with the Church: A Call for Renewal.* Translated by John Doberstein. New York: Harper and Row.

Thornton, L. S. 1950. *The Common Life in the Body of Christ.* 3rd ed. London: Dacre.

Thrall, Margaret E. 1994. *A Critical and Exegetical Commentary on the Second Epistle to the Corinthians.* Vol. 1: *Introduction and Commentary on II Corinthians I-VII.* International Critical Commentary. Edinburgh: T. and T. Clark.

________. 2000. *A Critical and Exegetical Commentary on the Second Epistle to the Corinthians.* Vol. 2: *Commentary on II Corinthians VIII-XIII.* International Critical Commentary. Edinburgh: T. and T. Clark.

Tillich, Paul. 1957. *Dynamics of Faith.* New York: Harper and Row.

Turner, Nigel. 1963a. *Grammatical Insights into the New Testament.* Edinburgh: T. and T. Clark.

________. 1963b. *Syntax.* Vol. 3 of *A Grammar of New Testament Greek.* Edited by James Hope Moulton. Edinburgh: T. and T. Clark.

The United Methodist Hymnal. 1989. Nashville: United Methodist Publishing House.

Unnick, W. C. van. 1962. *Tarsus or Jerusalem, the City of Paul's Youth*. Translated by George Ogg. London: Epworth.
Wall, Robert W. 2004a. "Facilitating Scripture's Future Role Among Wesleyans." Pages 107-20 in *Reading the Bible in Wesleyan Ways: Some Constructive Proposals*. Edited by Barry L. Callen and Richard P. Thompson. Kansas City: Beacon Hill Press of Kansas City.
Wall, Robert W. 2004b. "Toward a Wesleyan Hermeneutic of Understanding." Pages 39-55 in *Reading the Bible in Wesleyan Ways: Some Constructive Proposals*. Edited by Barry L. Callen and Richard P. Thompson. Kansas City: Beacon Hill Press of Kansas City.
Weima, Jeffrey A. D. 1994. *Neglected Endings: The Significance of the Pauline Letter Closings*. Journal for the Study of the New Testament: Supplement Series 101. Sheffield: Sheffield Academic.
Welch, Reuben R. 1982. *We Really Do Need Each Other*. Grand Rapids: Zondervan.
________. 1988. *Preaching from Second Corinthians 2 Through 5*. Kansas City: Beacon Hill Press of Kansas City.
Wesley, Charles. 1991. *Hymns for the Nativity of Our Lord*, with Introduction and Notes by Frank Baker. Madison, N.J.: Charles Wesley Society. A facsimile of the first edition. London: William Strahan, 1745.
Wesley, John. 1950. *Explanatory Notes on the New Testament*. London: Epworth.
________. 1979. *The Works of John Wesley*. 3rd ed. 10 vols. Edited by Thomas Jackson. 1872. Repr. Grand Rapids: Baker.
________. 1984. *Sermons I, 1-33* in *The Works of John Wesley*, Vol. 1. Edited by Albert C. Outler. Nashville: Abingdon.
________. 1985. *Sermons II, 34-70* in *The Works of John Wesley*, Vol. 2. Edited by Albert C. Outler. Nashville: Abingdon.
Whitmire, Catherine. 2001. *Plain Living: A Quaker Path to Simplicity*. Notre Dame, Ind.: Sorin.
Windisch, Hans. 1924. *Der Zweite Korintherbrief*. Göttingen: Vandenhoeck and Ruprecht.
Witherington, Ben, III. 1995. *Conflict and Community in Corinth: A Socio-Rhetorical Commentary on 1 and 2 Corinthians*. Grand Rapids: Eerdmans.
________. 2001. *The Paul Quest: The Renewed Search for the Jew of Tarsus*. Downers Grove, Ill.: InterVarsity.
Yabroff, Jennie. 2007. "A Year of Selling Books." *Newsweek* 84. October 1, 2007. Quotes Ron Hogan in his publishing-industry blog Galleycat.com.
Young, Frances, and David F. Ford. 1987. *Meaning and Truth in 2 Corinthians*. Grand Rapids: Eerdmans.
Zmijewski, Josef. 1990. *kauchaomai, ktl*. Pages 276-79 in vol. 2 of *Exegetical Dictionary of the New Testament*. Edited by Horst Balz and Gerhard Schneider.

2 CORINTHIANS

INTRODUCTION

A. A Personal Letter

C. S. Lewis, writing from Oxford to an American lady on April 1, 1956, recommended that she read 2 Corinthians. "About prayer (for others)," he wrote, "and suffering for others there's a lot scattered through 2d Cor which is well worth meditation" (1967, 52). What C. S. Lewis felt has been echoed down through the centuries by countless folk who have been comforted and challenged by what Paul wrote. In this letter, the apostle bares his heart to those he loved deeply. On behalf of the gospel of Christ and in the sight of God, for these "others"—the recalcitrant church at Corinth, he prayed much and suffered more. New problems have arisen since the writing of 1 Corinthians.

Only in 1 and 2 Corinthians among all Paul's correspondence can we observe such a long relationship with a people to whom he has given birth "in Christ." None of Paul's other letters to the churches carries us so profoundly into the heart of the man and the minister as his second letter to the church at Corinth. Here, mused R. P. C. Hanson long ago, "broken sharply off, with none of the jagged edges filed down, is a chunk of Paul's life—authentic, uncensored, bewilderingly complicated, but amazingly interesting" (1954, 7-8). The apostle expresses his love for a church that has misunderstood him in a tone Frank J. Matera describes as both "compassionate and defensive, reconciling and provocative, forgiving and threatening, joyful and complaining" (2003, 1).

As Philippians amazes us with its unveiling of the quality of Paul's commitment as a Christian, 2 Corinthians astounds us by its revelation of the radical caliber of his commitment as a servant and apostle of Christ. Open to view in this letter is the heartthrob of that gospel ministry that belongs to every member of Christ, clergy and laity alike—its life commitment, its divine resources, and its cross/resurrection character. Witness is borne to the inescapable truth that the mission of the church as the body of Christ is to carry on the self-giving, sacrificial, and suffering ministry of Jesus.

What Paul writes in this letter has much to do with the internal life of the Christian community in Corinth. This is a church at odds with the apostle. So he designs this letter to complete his personal reconciliation as the spiritual father with his impertinent children in the faith. Many in the church have been taken in by severe criticisms leveled at Paul. Some outsiders have entered their midst and challenged the integrity and authority of Paul's apostolic ministry. To meet this attack on his personal calling he appeals to the character of the gospel he brought them, "the word of reconciliation" (5:19 NASB).

This is in contrast to Paul's tactics in his letter to the Galatians. To them, when some had attempted to attach a legalistic compromise to the gospel of grace, Paul argued from the divine origin of his apostolate to the integrity of his gospel. To the Corinthians, he proceeds in reverse. He moves from the nature of the gospel of Christ to the character of his apostolic calling.

For Paul, the message of the gospel and the manner of its proclamation were inseparable. The character and methods of an apostolic ministry were determined by the nature of the message. So as Paul defends his stewardship of the gospel we are confronted with a challenging and potentially transforming witness to the reality and import of the coming of God into the world "in Christ."

Apart from the more personal passages (1:1-11; 6:11—7:16; 13:11-14) and his concern for the collection project (8:1—9:15), the letter falls into two main sections. The first (1:12—6:10) contains Paul's defense of his apostolic integrity—his motives and methods of operation in relation to the Corinthians. The second (10:1—13:10) deals with the vindication of his apostolic authority in the light of the attacks made against it.

The necessity of defending the integrity of his conduct as an apostle in such personally excruciating circumstances reveals the fundamental drives of the man Paul. Out of this situation has come to us a penetrating witness to the all-pervading dynamic of the gospel of Christ in the life of this minister of God. To the contemporary church this letter raises questions about the shape of its message and the nature and style of its ministry. The theological dimension of the letter is of crucial significance for the self-understanding of the church in today's world.

To appreciate rightly and fully the above glimpse at the letter, several questions need to be considered. What kind of a city was Corinth and what was the church there like? How often was Paul there, what letters did he write to it, and when? Did he write the entire letter? Did he write it all at one time? How is the letter to be described as a literary document? What theological themes permeate the letter? What interpretive problems are involved in its proper understanding?

B. Destination

1. The City of Corinth

Ancient Corinth was situated on the Isthmus of Corinth under the shadow of a 2,000 foot outcrop of rock. It overlooked two nearby seaports—Cenchrea to the east and Lechaion to the west. This location allowed it a command of a major trade route between the Aegean and Ionian seas.

Map of Achaia

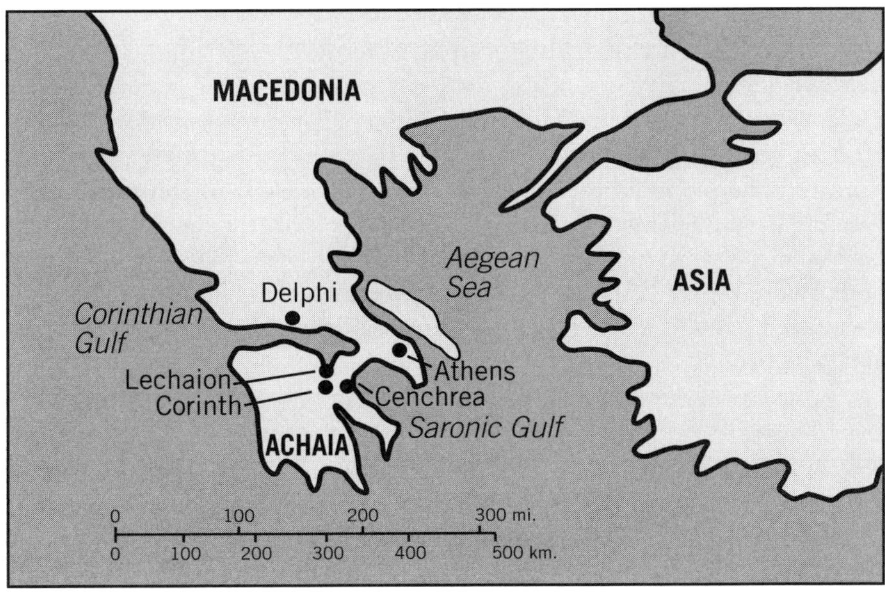

The economic benefits of Corinth's location were considerable. The Greek city of Corinth had existed as a political entity since the eighth century B.C. Its population reached nearly 100,000 by 400 B.C. A major interruption in its prominence and prosperity came with the ruthless destruction of the city by the Romans in 146 B.C. The Roman consul with 32,000 troops devastated the city, massacred the men, and sold the women and children into slavery. For a century the site lay in ruins (Blaiklock 1965, 56-59).

In Paul's day, the rebuilt city was the capital of the Roman province of Achaia. It was reestablished as a Roman colony by Julius Caesar in 44 B.C. It was renamed *Colonia Laus Julia Corinthiensis* in his honor. Roman laws were adopted, Latin became the official language of public inscriptions, and Roman organization and planning were in evidence throughout the design of the city. Corinth was governed by a proconsul appointed by the Roman Senate.

When Paul arrived in Corinth it was the third most important city in the Roman Empire, surpassed in status only by Rome and Alexandria. Its population had reached 80,000, with an additional 20,000 in the surrounding rural areas (Hafemann 2000, 23). An influx of Greeks from the neighboring areas made Greek the prevalent spoken language.

Corinth was a prosperous commercial city, probably the wealthiest in Greece. Through it passed the mainland route for the trade between east and west as well as its several sea routes. It was situated in a significant position between the Peloponnese to the south and the rest of Greece to the north. Its people were a multicultural mix of Greeks, Orientals, Jews, soldiers, a large slave population, and Roman freedmen (former slaves). All had come there because of the opportunities for economic and social advancement afforded by the newly founded city. Local craftsmen gathered together in *collegia*, social fraternities organized around devotion to a patron deity.

Corinth was a city obsessed with upward mobility. Within its prevailing honor-shame society, social status and its accompanying benefits were all-important. For some, success came by birth into the hereditary patrician class. For others it was determined by newly acquired wealth. The most prominent citizens were the recently rich. They were "those most likely to affect culture by entertaining the Sophists, preferring their more popular rhetoric of display and entertainment to serious discourse" (Witherington 1995, 24). Elite families of both groups provided the networks of power, influence, and patronage. Their wealth and power created a great gap between them and the masses of miserable poor people.

The city became a pluralistic melting pot of diverse nationalities, subcultures, lifestyles, and religions. Many had severed their traditional local ties and were searching for new ideas and loyalties. They were self-promoters, thirsty for honor and recognition. Sincere itinerant philosophers and unscrupulous charlatans proclaimed their messages side-by-side on Corinth's street corners. Corinth was a "boisterous, brawling, bustling" city open to new philosophies in a way that more traditional cities were not (Murphy-O'Connor 1991, 6). Yet as a recently founded city of uprooted people hungry for status and security, the atmosphere was that of spiritual emptiness.

Corinth was famous as a city with a culture of constant entertainment. There was a prominent place for the arts and a love of public rhetoric and human achievement. The theater in Paul's day held 14,000 to 18,000 people and the concert hall held 3,000. Sports were represented by the isthmian games held every other year, second only in size and prestige to the Olympics (Hafemann 2000, 24).

As a metropolitan center with a seaport city teeming with tourists and travelers, Corinth was no stranger to immorality and vice. The comic playwright Aristophanes (450-385 B.C.) coined the term *korinthiazō*, "act like a Corinthian, that is, commit fornication." Ancient Corinth had this reputation. The evidence for Corinth being an exceptionally licentious city applies to the earlier Greek city, rather than to the later Roman. By Paul's time, new Corinth was probably no more filled with vice and licentiousness than any other seaport and commercial center of the time.

Central to the life of the city was the worship of Aphrodite, the goddess of love, beauty, and fertility. Numerous temples were erected in her honor. But the earlier prevalence of sacred prostitution in the Greek city has not been supported by historical and archaeological investigation for the Roman city of NT times. Nevertheless, one should not underestimate the role of sexual expression in both pagan religious festivals and in some pagan temple precincts (Witherington 1995, 13).

Religiously, Corinth was thoroughly pluralistic. As Paul wrote earlier of Corinth, "Indeed there are many 'gods' and many 'lords'" (1 Cor 8:5). The Romans incorporated Greek gods and goddesses into their religious practices, often doing little more than changing their names. These and the omnipresent Roman imperial cult existed alongside the mystery religions. Greco-Roman pagan religion was essential to political stability, economic prosperity, and civil order. It undergirded most aspects of ancient society; there was little distinction between religion and secular life (deSilva 2004, 558). There is archaeological evidence excavated from the ruins for at least thirty-four different deities worshipped in Corinth. In addition to Aphrodite, there are temples or shrines to Fortune, Neptune, Apollo, Venus, Octavia, Asclepius, Demeter, Core, and Poseidon. But in popular practice, superstition and magic ruled the day (Witherington 1995, 12-18).

2. The Church at Corinth

To this strategic urban center of Corinth, Paul the apostle came on his second missionary journey following a somewhat disappointing visit to Athens (Acts 15:36—18:22). Acts 18:1-18 reports that he made his home in Corinth with Aquila and Priscilla. They were exiles as a result of the expulsion of Jews from Rome by Claudius (in A.D. 49). Together they plied their common trade of tentmaking. Every Sabbath, Paul was in the synagogue attempting to persuade both Jews and Greek proselytes that Jesus was the Christ.

Opposition to Paul's preaching soon arose from the Jews. So he turned to the pagan Gentiles, continuing his evangelistic activity in the house of Titius Justus next door to the synagogue. Crispus, the leader of the synagogue, along with many of the Corinthians, believed in the Lord. Thus, the church was composed of both Gentile and Jewish believers. Both Silas and Timothy were coworkers with Paul in Corinth (2 Cor 1:19).

During his eighteen-month stay in Corinth, Paul was brought by the Jews before the Roman proconsul Gallio (Acts 18:12-16). Gallio was the older brother of the more famous Roman politician and writer Seneca. According to an inscription preserved at the ancient shrine of Delphi, Gallio held office from July A.D. 51 to June 52. He refused to indict Paul. This effectively secured Paul from further open attacks from the Jews. His encounter with Gallio allows us to date Paul's stay in Corinth from the spring of A.D. 50 to the late summer of A.D. 51. God encouraged Paul to remain in Corinth for a year and a half and to establish the church there (Acts 18:9-11). When the apostle left Corinth, he returned to Antioch of Syria by way of Ephesus, making no contact with the Corinthian church except by letter until after his three-year mission in Ephesus during his third missionary journey (Acts 19:1—41).

The church in Corinth was a cross-section of its inhabitants, differing in social strata, and affected by the cultural and religious atmosphere of its environments. Paul spoke of them as not "wise by human standards; not many were influential; not many were of noble birth" (1 Cor 1:26). Paul's "not many" may indicate that there were perhaps a few in the church who might be classified as "wise," "influential," and "of noble birth." Yet, the majority of the membership was of lower socioeconomic status. They possessed little wealth or power but offered a new and group identity that transformed aspects of their former class-consciousness (Young and Ford 1987, 189).

The church members in Corinth along with those in the surrounding area met in small groups in various house churches (1 Cor 16:19; see 14:23). No doubt, they met in the houses of the more well-to-do. Meeting in different locations of necessity made it difficult for the church to speak with one voice. Their relative isolation from one another inevitably encouraged divisions and differences.

It is understandable that this church gave Paul more problems and severely anxious moments than any other church. In his extant letters then, as Paul deals with their internal problems (1 Corinthians) and his own relation to them (2 Corinthians), we are afforded a rare glimpse into the life and heart of a primitive Christian community.

But to reconstruct the sequence and nature of the apostle's subsequent visits and correspondence with the Corinthian church is problematic. The order listed, the number of letters (four to seven), and the composition especially of 2 Corinthians can be disputed. Beyond, however, the above sketch of Paul's founding visit (Acts 18:10), there is solid textual evidence for:

- a previous letter now lost (1 Cor 5:9-13)
- 1 Corinthians carried by Timothy from Ephesus (1 Cor 4:17; 16:10-11)
- a painful visit from Ephesus (2 Cor 2:1; 13:2; see Acts 20:18, 31)
- a sorrowful letter now lost (2 Cor 2:3-4), variously called the letter of tears, severe, or painful letter (2 Cor 8:6, 16-18, 22-24), and
- a third anticipated visit (2 Cor 1:15-16; 12:14; 13:1-2; Acts 20:2-3)

Various partition theories divide 2 Corinthians into from three to five letters, each sent separately (Harris 2005, 26). Such hypotheses are based on conjecture alone, since there is no surviving manuscript evidence of another version of the letter than the familiar canonical form. We cite two recent analyses of 2 Corinthians as a composite of several dispatches, brought together by a later editor. Both build on earlier proposals:

First, Margaret E. Thrall (2004, 77) makes a case for dividing 2 Corinthians into three letters, sent in the following order:

1. 1:1—8:24
2. 9:1-15
3. 10:1-13

More recently, Margaret M. Mitchell's 2003 essay (21), based on the research of earlier Corinthian scholarship, analyzes the constituent letters making up 2 Corinthians in this order of dispatch:

1. 8:1-24
2. 2:14—7:4 (minus 6:14—7:1, treated as an interpolation)
3. 10:1—13:10 (= the sorrowful letter mentioned above)
4. 2:1-13; 7:5-16; 13:11-13 and
5. 9:1-15

We will give these partition possibilities more detailed consideration later. For now we offer a tentative reconstruction of Paul's relations and contacts with the church at Corinth based on the solid textual evidence listed above, suggesting alternative possibilities as we proceed.

Following his year-and-one-half stay in Corinth (Acts 18:1-18), Paul returned to Ephesus (Acts 18:18-21). From there he sent a letter back to Corinth alluded to in 1 Cor 5:9. This has been designated the "previous letter," now lost, though some scholars believe that 2 Cor 6:14—7:1 is a fragment of it. In this "previous letter," Paul warned the Corinthians not to associate with immoral persons within the fellowship of the church. They took such instructions as entirely impractical, misconstruing—whether deliberately or innocently—Paul to prohibit contact with immoral people in general (1 Cor 5:10-11). Due, perhaps, to the repetition of its substance in 1 Corinthians, the letter was not preserved.

A second letter, our 1 Corinthians, was written in response to this misunderstanding as well as to several other matters. Paul had heard of their divisiveness from members of "Chloe's household" (1:11) and had received oral reports from others regarding "sexual immorality" (5:1-2) and lawsuits (6:1-8) within the church. Also a letter had come to him, brought perhaps by a delegation (16:17), asking for his guidance on marriage (7:1), meat sacrificed to idols (8:1), spiritual gifts (12:1), and the resurrection (15:l-58). This letter seems to have been sent in the spring of A.D. 55 or 56. Those who identify 2 Cor 8:1-24 as a separate letter place it here, as a follow-up fund-raising letter (Mitchell 2003, 21-23).

First Corinthians did not produce the results Paul desired. Borne possibly by Timothy (4:17), the report came back that conditions in the church were actually worse. Paul abandoned his work at Ephesus and paid them what he describes as a "painful visit" to Corinth (2 Cor 2:1; 1:15-16; 13:2), to deal with the issue in person. Not much is known about what happened during this visit. But it appears that some ringleader rose up in arrogant defiance of Paul (2:5-8; 7:12). The church sided with the attacker. Paul hastily returned to Ephesus, humiliated by the Corinthians' response. There, in great distress over the condition of the church, he puzzled over how best to respond. This was probably not simply a retreat by a Paul cowed before opposition (10:2).

Second Corinthians gives evidence that the Corinthian polemic against the apostle only increased after his departure. The charges and slurs against his person and office were many. Paul carried no letters of recommendation (3:1-3). When he wrote to them he did not make his meaning clear (1:12-13), but used his "weighty and forceful" letters to intimidate them into submission (10:9-10). Paul was insincere (1:12), lorded it over their faith (1:24), and was inferior in knowledge and eloquence to the newcomers, who only egged on the criticism. Paul, they alleged, lacked ability as a public speaker (10:10; 11:6). Furthermore, they charged, he had wronged the church by refusing to receive financial remuneration from them (11:7, 9; 12:13). Yet he had authorized his agents to raise an offering from the Corinthian church, undoubtedly intending to divert some of it for himself (12:17-18; 1:16; 1 Cor 16:6).

Thus, the integrity of Paul's motives, his character, his behavior (2 Cor 10:11), and even his courage (10:1) were all brought into question in Corinth. Most crucial of all, the legitimacy of his apostolic ministry (12:11-12) was under attack (Harris 2005, 69-70).

On returning to Ephesus from the "painful visit," Paul wrote the "sorrowful letter" (see 2:3-4). He dispatched Titus (7:6) to take it to Corinth and to attempt to restore the church to Paul (for a discussion of the historical issues involved, see Harris 2005, 54-64). Mitchell (2003, 21) and some others take this letter to be 2 Cor 10:1—13:10. This, she supposes, was followed by an "apologetic letter" (2 Cor 2:14—7:4, less 6:14—7:1). After Titus's departure, Paul's troubled state would not allow him to keep his mind on his work. So he proceeded to Troas (2:12) and on to Macedonia (2:13; 7:5) to await the return of Titus. When Titus came with word that the church had dealt with the offender and that it had resubmitted itself to the authority of the apostle, Paul was comforted (7:6-12).

So from Macedonia, within a year (8:10; 9:2) after the writing of 1 Corinthians, Paul wrote 2 Corinthians to the church of God in Corinth. He included "all the saints throughout Achaia" (1:1) in his address and asked them to prepare for his third visit (2 Cor 1:15-16; 12:14; 13:1-2; Acts 20:2-3). In the letter he expressed his relief at the general success of Titus's mission of reconciliation and answered the derogatory charges of his critics. With the restoration of normal relations Paul was also anxious to reactivate the collection project and carry it to completion (1 Cor 16:1-6; 2 Cor 8:1—9:15).

Throughout the entire letter, but especially in chs 10—13, he found it necessary to defend the legitimacy and authority of his apostleship. Apparently, in a pause in writing or dictation of some, perhaps even lengthy, extent between chs 9 and 10—13, Paul received disturbing news that the situation at Corinth had deteriorated. This caused him to change to a more stern and defensive tone. Although proper relations between the apostle and the majority of the church had apparently been restored, some severe opposition to Paul obviously still remained in Corinth. Reconciliation had only been partially achieved. Paul hoped with this letter to fully heal the situation there.

When Paul visited Corinth for the third time (12:14; 13:1-2), he spent the winter (1 Cor 16:6) before continuing on to Jerusalem with the offering for the poverty-stricken Christians there. Thrall proposes that 2 Cor 10:1—13:10 was sent as a separate letter before this third visit (2004, 77).

The vexed question as to precisely "who" were Paul's opponents in Corinth remains. Scholarly hypotheses seem endless. Interpreters use the device of "mirror reading" to induce the nature of Paul's opponents based on his rhetoric. His apparent charges and answers to charges have led to imaginative guesses as to what prompted them. These have been highly speculative, leading some to question their plausibility (Lyons 1985, 75-122).

As many as nineteen suggestions as to the nature of Paul's opposition have been made (Harris 2005, 79-80). Harris reduces them to four: "Hellenistic Jewish propagandists, pneumatics, Gnostics, and Judaizers" (2005, 80). Hafemann suggests three: gnostics, legalistic Judaizers, and super-charismatics (alleged "divine men") who "represented a mixture of legalistic and pneumatic elements of various persuasions" (2000, 33). McCant, who is skeptical of "mirror-reading," insists that since pastoral concerns permeate 2 Corinthians, Paul's focus is throughout on the church as such, certainly a troublesome lot, who are not to be considered strictly as "opponents" (1999, 18). He feels the door on all discussions about opponents at Corinth should be closed.

Yet two facts or considerations persist. First, the only available evidence is what the two Corinthian letters provide. Thus, the attempt to interpret what the biblical text suggests about Paul's critics is imperative. Second, 2 Cor 11:4 and 11:22-23 appear to refer to strangers who have entered the church from outside. So the nature of Paul's opposition or even "opponents" in Corinth remains a valid and significant question.

The most recent critical and comprehensive discussion of this issue is that of Harris (2005, 71-87). Working with evidence from both extant letters to Corinth, he identifies them as probably Jews from Judea (Jerusalem?). They came to Corinth as self-appointed agents of a Judaizing program, one not identical to that which plagued the churches in Galatia. Claiming to be Christian and presuming to possess the authority of the Twelve, they joined in uneasy alliance with a group of Corinthian "proto-gnostics" in an attempt to undermine Paul's apostolic ministry (2005, 87).

The Corinthian opposition to Paul and his ministry, which Harris terms "proto-gnostic," were unduly influenced by their Hellenistic heritage. They possessed several characteristics in common with the heresy of Gnosticism, which became a serious threat to Christianity as a whole during the second century:

- They denied a future bodily resurrection (1 Cor 15:12; 2 Cor 5:2-4). They believed that the only resurrection was spiritual, accomplished by baptism, and, therefore, lay in the past.
- They were either libertines or ascetic in their morality. Sexual permissiveness probably persisted among some in the church (1 Cor 6:18; 2 Cor 7:1; 12:21). The transition from 1 Cor 6:12 to 7:1 and following indicates the ascetic bent of others. These two superficially opposite ethical stances arose from a common Hellenistic assumption.

Gnostics emphasized that the material world was contemptible, including the human body. This arose from their emphasis on the radical transcendence of God. Consistent with this, some chose abstinence, to deprive their despicable bodies the fleshly delights they craved. Others, persuaded that all material things were destined to perish anyway, simply indulged. Two radically different ethical codes resulted, asceticism and libertinism. Both groups took pride in their superior *gnosis* or "knowledge," which put them above the naive, ordinary believers (Harris 2005, 80-84).

Harris labels the Palestinian intruders who infiltrated the Corinthian church "Judaizers." They considered themselves "Christian," a claim Paul was uncomfortable with (10:7; 11:13, 23). These "Judaizers" differed from those in the background of Galatians in their *modus operandi*. There is no indication in 2 Corinthians of any controversy concerning circumcision, food laws, and the observance of Jewish festivals. Nevertheless, they probably shared with their Galatian predecessors the ultimate goal of bringing all Gentile churches into submission to the mother church in Jerusalem. But the Corinthian Judaizers were likewise seeking to impose Jewish practices on the Gentile church as conditions either for salvation or for Christian fellowship.

So in reality Paul faced two sets of opponents in Corinth: Corinthian "proto-gnostics" and Palestinian "Judaizers." Despite their differences, they had temporarily closed ranks in their shared opposition to Paul (Harris 2005, 85-86).

Harris's reconstruction may reason a bit beyond the evidence. Still, we find the essence of his analysis both helpful and convincing. Our reading of 2 Corinthians assumes that Paul was dealing with Palestinian opponents of his mission and apostolic dignity who had joined themselves with the gnostic-like opposition to Paul already evident in 1 Corinthians. A "Corinthianization" of the intruding Judaizers appears to explain best the coming together of otherwise incompatible traits that surface in 2 Corinthians (Murphy-O'Connor 1991, 15). The influence of culture at Corinth was both subtle and strong.

"How does one participate fully in the power of the Spirit?" This may well have been a question asked by the Corinthians. It arose from both their Hellenistic worldview and the concerns of the Palestinians of Jewish heritage. Both believed that their perspective provided a more powerful experience of the Spirit than that found in Paul's gospel. They emphasized what has been called "a theology of glory." Paul counters this with a presentation of the relationship between the power of the Spirit and suffering in his apostolic ministry (Hafemann 2000, 34).

Further Reading on Corinth

Engels, Donald. 1990. *Roman Corinth.* Chicago: University of Chicago Press.

Meeks, Wayne A. 1983. *The First Urban Christians.* New Haven, Conn.: Yale University Press.

Murphy-O'Connor, Jerome. 1983. *Saint Paul's Corinth: Texts and Archeology.* Wilmington, Del.: Michael Glazier.

_________. 1992. "Corinth." Pages 1134-39 in vol. 1 of *The Anchor Bible Dictionary.* Edited by David N. Freedman. Garden City, N.Y.: Doubleday.

Theissen, Gerd. 1982. *The Social Setting of Pauline Christianity: Essays on Corinth.* Philadelphia: Fortress.

Winter, B.W. 2001. Pages 7-22 in *After Paul Left Corinth.* Grand Rapids: Eerdmans.

Witherington, Ben, III. 1995. Pages 5-35 in *Conflict and Community in Corinth.* Grand Rapids: Eerdmans.

C. Integrity

1. Authorship and Authenticity

Along with 1 Corinthians, 2 Corinthians claims in its salutation to come from the hand of Paul: "Paul, an apostle of Christ Jesus . . . To the church of God in Corinth" (2 Cor 1:1). All literary indications within the letter, both stylistic and doctrinal, confirm this claim. The historical attestation for 1 Corinthians is as early as Clement of Rome in A.D. 95 or 96. But the attestation for 2 Corinthians is ambiguous until mid-second century. In A.D. 62-64, Polycarp of Smyrna, in his letter to the *Philippians*, may allude to 2 Cor 3:2; 4:14; 5:10; and possibly 6:7 and 8:21. Irenaeus of Lyons, writing toward the end of the second century, both quotes from the letter and names it. So the letter was widely known by the second half of the second century. It finds its place in both the Marcion's Canon (140) and in the Muratorian Canon (late second century). As a result, the genuineness of the Pauline authorship of 2 Corinthians and its rightful place in the Pauline corpus remains undisputed in the main in contemporary critical scholarship (Plummer 1915, xi-xii; Thrall 2004, 2-3; Harris 2005, 1-3).

The only exception to the consensus that 2 Corinthians is an authentic Pauline letter concerns 2 Cor 6:14—7:1, which some consider a non-Pauline interpolation into the letter. Its distinct vocabulary and subject matter convince some that it derives from a Jewish source, perhaps influenced by the Qumran documents (Hafemann 2000, 31). Since the problems concerning this passage belong to the question of the unity of 2 Corinthians, we discuss them in more detail below.

2. Unity

In considerations of the unity of the letter, 6:14—7:1 is not the only problem. Although there is no supporting evidence in the history of the transmission of the text, many scholars hold that 2 Corinthians is a collection of letters or fragments of letters written by the apostle to the Corinthian church at various times. The manuscript evidence knows no exception to the present content and order of the material in canonical 2 Corinthians.

So the question of the unity and integrity of the letter is an exegetical one. That is, decisions are based on subjective assessments of the internal evidence. On the one hand, a convincing motive for a secondary combination must present itself before the assumption of the unity of the letter is abandoned. On the other hand, in order to defend the unity of the letter, the difficult transitions at each point call for a credible explanation. These transition issues will be noted in the process of our commentary on the text.

Partition theories of 2 Corinthians have become increasingly complex across the years. We can address the unity problem by considering the four passages that have become the focus of scholarly dispute: *(a)* 2:14—7:4; *(b)* 6:14—7:1; *(c)* 8:1—9:15; and *(d)* 10:1—13:14. Below, we define the issues in each passage and present the main reasons given for them following the order of the canonical text.

(a) We begin with 2:14—7:4, neglecting 6:14—7:1 for the moment. Is this segment, with its internal literary unity, a separate letter of defense (as Mitchell [2003, 21] alleges)? Or, is it a digression in which Paul pauses to de-

fend more directly his apostolic ministry? That is, it is an integral part of chs 1—7 (Harris 2005, 14).

The main reason given for considering 2:14—7:4 a part of a separate letter are the abrupt transitions from 2:13 to 2:14 and from 7:4 to 7:5. The transition from 2:13 to 7:5 seems smooth, if 2:14—7:4 is left out.

First, the subject matter is continuous; there is no abrupt change of topics or tone. Paul has described his anxiety while awaiting the return of Titus from Corinth in 2:12-13: "I still had no peace of mind" (see 9:5). But he breaks off the travel narrative until 7:5-16, in which he describes the comfort brought by the return of Titus: "But God, who comforts the downcast, comforted us by the coming of Titus" (7:6). Other reasons may explain this, primarily that Paul may not have intended to give a continuous account of the events concerning the reception of the sorrowful letter (Thrall 2004, 21-24).

Second, there is discontinuity in the language at the two transition points, 2:13-14 and 7:4-5. In the first transition, the text shifts abruptly from a conciliatory to an argumentative tone, from a biographical report to a thanksgiving: "But thanks be to God." In the second, there is another change in tone from 7:4 to 7:5, from "I am greatly encouraged" to "this body of ours had no rest."

The opposing consideration to the first transition contrasts the weakness of the human instrument (2:12-13) with the power of God that "leads us in triumphal procession . . . everywhere" in the proclamation of the gospel (2:14). This contrast is inherent to the thought of the letter.

The argument concerning the second transition is countered in the minds of many by the verbal similarities between 7:4 (*kauchēsis, paraklēsei, chara, thlipsei*) and 7:5-16 (Harris 2005, 12-13; see 7:5, 6, 7, 9, 13, 14).

The shift from 2:13 directly to 7:5 remains an awkward shift. So the probability supports the canonical evidence that 2:14—7:4 belongs to its present literary context. To make it an interpolation does not satisfy the two tests for unity suggested above.

(b) The passage (6:14—7:1) is considered by many to be an interpolation of non-Pauline material, either by a later redactor or by Paul himself. Its rightful place in its canonical context is questioned because it appears to create an abrupt interruption of the thought connecting 6:13 and 7:2. "Open wide your hearts also" ends 6:13 and "make room for us in your hearts" begins 7:2.

It can be claimed that to connect 6:13 with 7:2 makes for a rough transition. This is because 7:2 reads like a resumption of an appeal after an interruption. Harris sees a confirmation of this in the chiastic structure of 6:11-13 and 7:2-4. That is, 7:2-4 takes up the thought of 6:11-13 in reverse order, a conscious rhetorical device (Harris 2005, 16-17).

The passage (6:14—7:1) is also questioned because the subject matter allegedly does not fit the context. Some consider it an interpolated fragment of an earlier letter (the "previous letter"; 1 Cor 5:9) that warns against fellowship with a fornicator "who calls himself a brother" (1 Cor 5:11). Here, however, the warning is against being "yoked together with unbelievers" (2 Cor 6:14).

But connections can be found between every verse in 6:13—7:1 and the preceding sections of the letter, which similarly call for a clear-cut distinction between believers and unbelievers (Thrall 2004, 27-28).

If the passage is simply a digression, Paul paused to warn the Corinthians, after asking them to open their hearts to him. A warning against dangerous compromises with paganism was not uncalled for.

This is not the only place in his letters where the apostle tends to digress. Here, it may be due to the necessity of writing the letter at several sittings. McCant explains this paragraph as an epideictic digression in which Paul goes on the offensive (McCant 1999, 63-64; see Witherington 1995, 402, as well for the function of digression in rhetorical discourse).

A more serious question is the Pauline character of the passage. Is this Paul's own composition? Did he write it specifically for 2 Corinthians? Or, was it inserted by him from an earlier homily? Some of the vocabulary of the passage is not typical Pauline vocabulary or common Pauline words employed in non-Pauline ways.

Does the fact that some of the vocabulary has clear affinities to Qumran language and thought forms indicate that it is a piece of Christianized Essene theology used in the church as baptismal liturgy (so Fitzmyer 1971, 25-217)? But there are similarities between Qumran and many other NT passages, particularly in Paul (Harris 2005, 19-20). These include such things as the dualism of light and darkness and the saved community as the temple of God.

Thrall asserts that there are enough genuine Pauline characteristics present in 6:14—7:1 that it cannot be proved conclusively that Paul did not write the passage (2004, 34-35). Harris concludes that despite its non-Pauline features, its uncontestable Pauline characteristics and its place in a genuine Pauline letter 6:14—7:1 "stem *in toto* from Paul's own hand" (2005, 25). He concedes that Paul may have composed it at an earlier time under Essene influence and incorporated it "as a digressive appeal to the Corinthians to sever all their ties with paganism and thereby become fully reconciled to their father in the faith" (Harris 2005, 25).

We suggest that whether or not Paul wrote it, it belongs to the time and process of the composition of 2 Corinthians by the apostle (see McCant 1999, 62-64). In making such a controversial decision, we are led to examine the text more closely than we otherwise might have in the process of the exegesis that follows (see the sidebar on Further Reading on 2 Cor 6:14—7:1, p. 221).

(c) When it comes to 8:1—9:15, the partition theories are bewilderingly varied in Pauline scholarship. A recent reconstruction may serve as a typical example. Mitchell considers 8:1-24 and 9:1-15 as separate letters. Chapter 8 was sent as a fund-raising letter to follow up 1 Corinthians. Chapter 9 was a final fund-raising letter sent to Achaia after the remainder of 2 Corinthians

(which she conceives as four separate letters; 2003, 21). Thrall conceives of ch 8 as belonging to chs 1—7. But ch 9, on her reading, is a separate letter sent later, before chs 10—13 (2004, 38-43; see Betz 1985, 3-41, 129-45, for a detailed treatment of two separate letters). Still other interpreters put chs 8 and 9 together as a unified but separate letter.

In summary, the issues can be viewed as two: Do chs 8 and 9 belong together? And, are the two chapters an integral part of the larger letter?

The reasons for separating chs 8 and 9 include content—redundancy and discrepancies—and a change in atmosphere. Nevertheless, there is a network of specific links between the two chapters. And the differences can be satisfactorily accounted for (Harris 2005, 37-38; see McCant 1999, 75-77, for a detailed refutation of Betz's proposal).

In relation to the larger letter, Mitchell calls attention to the parallelism in both content and expression between 12:17-18 and 8:6, 18. The relationship to the coming of Titus to Corinth provides strong evidence that the fundraising letter (at least ch 8) was received by the church before his writing and their reception of chs 10—13 (2003, 22). In her view, ch 8 is an earlier letter that contributed to the deterioration of the relationship between Paul and the Corinthians (2003, 23).

It is probable that 8:6 refers to an early visit by Titus to prepare the way for the collection. Thus, 8:18 and 22 refer to the visit that carries the appeal of chs 8 and 9. The reference in 12:17-18, then, is to the earlier visit reported in 8:6.

The troubling transition from chs 1—7 to chs 8—9 is understandable as a move from apology to exhortation. This is consistent with such a change of subject and purpose. Reconciliation with the majority of the church had taken place, as reported by the coming of Titus to Paul. Now Paul takes up the task of reviving the collection project at Corinth. His reconciliation with them affords an effective base from which to launch his appeal.

If chs 8 and 9 belong together, there is little difficulty in seeing them as a proper addition to chs 1—7. Almost all scholars who keep the chapters together do not separate them from chs 1—7 (Harris 2005, 29).

(d) The most likely partition hypothesis proposed by many scholars is that chs 10—13 should be considered a separate letter. Among scholars, this has assumed two forms.

One form assumes that chs 10—13 were written earlier than chs 1—9 and constitute the "sorrowful letter" (see 2:3-9). This letter was written "out of great distress and anguish of heart and with many tears" (2:4). It appears to have brought about the reconciliation of the church as a whole with Paul (7:6-16). A classic defense of this view is that of Plummer (1915, xxvii-xxxvi).

A second form of this hypothesis is defended more widely in recent scholarship. It sees the four-chapter letter as the last of five letters written to the church at Corinth, after 2 Cor 1—9. Apparently, as these chapters seem to indicate, the situation at Corinth took a turn for the worse with the coming of the "intruders" into the church.

News of this development led Paul to write a more hard-hitting letter in preparation for his forthcoming visit to Corinth (13:2, 10). A classic recent defense of this view is that of Thrall (2004, 5-20, 77). Since nothing is said in chs 1—9 about the reaction of the congregation to the polemic against the false apostles of Christ in chs 10—13, we consider this second form of the hypothesis the more viable of the two.

The essential partition issue is the separation of chs 10—13 from chs 1—9. To maintain that the two parts originated in the same letter-writing situation presents serious challenges to interpreters. The most difficult is the change from a sense of an accomplished reconciliation in chs 1—9 to a renewed attack against "some" launched in 10:2 and Paul's accusation that some in the church are "false apostles" (11:13). Reconciliation seems inconsistent with Paul's fears that when he comes he will not find them as he would like (12:20). Nor does it fit with his threat that he "will not spare" the unrepentant (13:2). Futhermore, the general tone and attitude of chs 1—9 and 10—13 seem incompatible. How are we to account for this different attitude and situation in Corinth, the abrupt transition from chs 8—9 to 10:1? How are we to explain that the imminent visit promised in 12:14 and 13:1 is not even intimated in the earlier chapters (Thrall 2004, 5-6; Harris 2005, 29-33)?

The decisive question is whether or not it is possible for chs 10—13 to have stood in the same epistle with chs 1—9. Some basic considerations may remove the supposed impossibility of the two sections standing together:

First, although Paul appears to change his position with respect to the church in chs 10—13, there are indications in the previous chapters that all is not well with the church. Among the hints are Paul's defenses against a misinterpretation of the conduct of his ministry (4:2-6; 5:11-15; 7:2) and his polemic against other traveling preachers (2:17—3:1; see 4:2-5).

Second, the polemic of 2:17 is expanded in chs 10—13. In the latter, Paul indicates that it is only specific persons in the church who are attacking him (10:2; 11:5; 12:15, 21; 13:2). Paul may address the majority, who are reconciled with him, in order to support their discipline of the dangerous minority, at whose center are the "false apostles" (11:13).

The increased antagonism to Paul evidenced in chs 10—13 may indicate that there was a lapse of time between the writing of the first and second sections. This time would allow for the deterioration to take place (Harris 2005, 38-39). Witherington, however, does not see the need of postulating a significant time gap between chs 1—9 and 10—13 to account for the sudden shift in tone and atmosphere. He explains these by appeal to the change in rhetorical conventions Paul is following (1995, 431; see 429-32).

Third, the theme of strength through weakness pervades the whole of 2 Corinthians. The entire argument for the genuineness of Paul's apostolic authority is bound up in this theme: "It is by the amazing contrast between his own frailty and the all-conquering strength of God manifested through him that his apostleship is unshakably authenticated to the world" (Hughes 1962, xxx). Matera comments that Paul could not have written as he did in chs 10—13 if he had not laid the theological foundation in 2:14—7:4, which he calls "the heart and soul of 2 Corinthians" (2003, 66).

After examining the arguments for and against treating chs 10—13 as part of Paul's original letter, Young and Ford conclude that ultimately "the only serious argument is the psychological one" (1987, 31). Finally, a defense of the unity can be made from the viewpoint of ancient rhetoric. Second Corinthians is to be taken as a compositional whole as an example of forensic or judicial rhetoric (Witherington 1995, 333-36; McCant 1999, 13-15).

In conclusion, the evidence and arguments for considering chs 10—13 a separate letter, written and sent later than chs 1—9, are fully convincing for many. Thrall, for example, concludes her very detailed analysis by saying that there seems to be no decisive reason to reject viewing chs 10—13 as a separate letter (2004, 20). Yet those who hold to the unity of 2 Corinthians find explanations for the textual data and considerations used to deny its unity (Harris 2005, 29-51).

The letter may well have been written in three stages (chs 1—7, 8—9, and 10—13). We leave the issue of the writing of chs 10—13 open in theory. We interpret the text, however, on the assumption that chs 10—13 are later than chs 1—9 *and* that the letter makes sense in its canonical form.

3. Purpose

The apostle states his general purpose in writing 2 Corinthians in 12:19: "Everything we do, dear friends, is for your strengthening." To this Paul adds in 13:9 that his "prayer is for your perfection." He writes to aid in building them up (*oikodomēs*) in the faith and in their maturation (*katartisis*) as Christians—in how they live in relation to God and to one another. The three well-defined sections of the letter (1:1—7:16; 8:1—9:15; 10:1—13:14) reflect the perspective of the apostle in the successive phases of his relations with the church. Each prepares for the next.

As Paul writes 1:1—7:16, he reflects back on the history of his relationship with Corinth. This explains his defense of the legitimacy of his apostleship and his anxiety and relief in connection with the mission of Titus to deliver Paul's "sorrowful letter."

The next section, 8:1—9:15, reflects Paul's present position in relation to Corinth. Thus, he seeks to motivate their generosity, so they will complete what they promised for the collection before his next visit.

The final section, 10:1—13:14, looks ahead to some problems that threaten the future relations between the apostle and the church at Corinth. Some disruptive matters still need attention in the church. Thus, Paul seeks to help them recognize the criteria for authentic apostleship and concludes with words of exhortation and encouragement.

All these parts, suggests Harris (2005, 52-53), serve Paul's overarching specific purpose of preparing the way for an enjoyable and successful third visit by the apostle. And it appears from Acts 20:2-3 that Paul's third visit to Corinth was successful. That Paul appears to have written his letter to the Romans from Corinth just prior to delivering the collection to Jerusalem also suggests the same (see Rom 16:1; see 1 Cor 16:3-4).

D. Literary Features

1. Genre

The quest for the literary genre of 2 Corinthians is most interesting. Obviously, it is related to the Greco-Roman letters of the Hellenistic period. This is seen by the similarity of the salutation (1:1-2) and the closing (13:11-14) to the conventions of Hellenistic letters (see Doty 1973, 27-42, and commentary on these verses). Second Corinthians is a genuine occasional letter. That is, it was written to a designated people and directed to a specific situation. The letter was written to serve as a surrogate for Paul's personal presence, as what he would say if he were present speaking to them. It was intended to be read aloud to the church as a whole—and probably more than once—for the instruction and admonition of the congregation.

Paul adapted and expanded the various elements of the traditional letter form to suit his pastoral—ethical and theological—concerns as an apostle of Christ. Thus, in form the letter stands somewhere between a private letter and the more literary epistle—a sent treatise. From the standpoint of its letter—or epistolary—form, 2 Corinthians can be analyzed as follows:

1:1-2	Salutation
1:3-11	Blessing
1:12—13:10	Body
13:11-14	Closing

Paraenetic or ethical advice appears at various points throughout the letter. Other literary forms or subgenres may also be noted in the course of the interpretation of the text.

The question of the literary genre of 2 Corinthians does not end, however, with its obvious similarity to the ancient Hellenistic letter. Young and Ford, for example, suggest that the closest analogy to 2 Corinthians is an apologetic speech purportedly written by Demosthenes in epistolary form (1987, 37). This raises the question of the relation of 2 Corinthians to Greek rhetoric. The judgment of Young and Ford, and of others examining 2 Corinthians from the standpoint of classical rhetoric, is that the letter makes ample use of forensic or judicial rhetoric. This does not assume that Paul knew the writings of

Demosthenes or others like him, though he may have been aware of the rhetorical handbooks.

As an educated person of the first century, Paul would "have been hard put to escape an awareness of rhetoric as practiced in the culture around [him] for the rhetorical theory of the schools found its immediate application in almost every form of oral and written communication" (Kennedy 1984, 10).

The three species of rhetoric employed were *judicial, deliberative,* and *epideictic.* The most common of these, *judicial* or *forensic,* was aimed at persuading an audience to make a judgment about past events. Rhetoric was *deliberative* when it sought to persuade the audience regarding some future action. And it was *epideictic* when it attempted to persuade to praise or blame someone as to actions in the present (Kennedy 1984, 19; Harris 2005, 106).

The classical rhetorical handbooks present the six expected parts of a judicial speech (as outlined by Harris 2005, 106):

1. The *exordium* (introduction) establishes the speaker's (or writer's) good moral character (*ēthos*) and seeks to ensure the audience's receptivity.
2. The *narratio* (narration) states the agreed facts of the case.
3. The *propositio* (proposition) sets out the basic facts to be proven true or false and areas of agreement or disagreement with opponents.
4. The *probatio* or *argumentatio* (proof) gives the reasoning (*logos*) in support of the speaker's case.
5. The *refutatio* (refutation) disproves or impairs the opponents' arguments. And
6. The *peroratio* (conclusion) sums up the case and seeks to arouse the audience's sympathetic emotions (*pathos*).

Several analyses have been proposed in the scholarly literature on 2 Corinthians. In the course of the present commentary, we refer often to the analysis of Ben Witherington III (1995, 335-36). Thus, we offer here his rhetorical analysis as one example:

Epistolary prescript (1:1-2)
Epistolary thanksgiving and *exordium* (1:3-7)
Narratio (1:8—2:16)
Propositio (2:17)
Probatio and *refutatio* (3:1—13:4), which includes:

a. Paul's characterization of his ministry (3:1—6:13)
b. a deliberative digression (6:14—7:1)
c. Paul's defense of the severe letter (7:2-16)
d. a largely deliberative argument concerning the collection (chs 8 and 9), and
e. a rhetorical *synkrisis* (comparison) of Paul and his competitors in Corinth, the false *apostoloi,* with a strong emotional appeal (10:1—13:4)

Peroratio or conclusion (13:5-10)

Closing epistolary greetings and remarks (13:11-13 [14])

Harris (2005, 107-8) presents several analyses including that of Kennedy (1984, 87-91; see also Young and Ford [1987, 38-40]).

To what extent should we view the genre of 2 Corinthians through the lens of judicial rhetoric? Young and Ford, for example, conclude that "2 Corinthians was self-consciously conceived as an apology according to the norms of the day" and "that the thrust of Paul's argument is clear, provided we take the text as a unity, and understand its genre as that of an apologetic letter" (1987, 43, 54-55; see also McCant [1999, 13-16], who sees the letter as "a parody of defense"). Harris, however, sounds some warnings.

Paul negatively assesses (especially) the ornamental rhetoric of his day (see 1 Cor 1:20). His argument in 2 Cor 10—13 against the rhetorical skills of his opponents in Corinth indicates that, in his presentations, he had confidence in the truth, in rational appeal, and in the persuasiveness of the Holy Spirit. He disparages dependence on mere rhetorical skill: "form was always secondary to content; style was invariably the servant of substance" (2005, 109). Harris's conclusion is cautious but helpful:

First, it is doubtful that the apostle "would have consciously developed his argumentation in accordance with the successive divisions of forensic or deliberative or epideictic rhetoric."

Second, any document as lengthy as 2 Corinthians "that is (1) written by a highly educated person, (2) apologetic in character, (3) logical in presentation, and (4) aimed at winning over an audience and influencing their way of thinking and acting is likely to display the basic ingredients of forensic, deliberative, or epideictic rhetoric" (2005, 108-10). Regardless of the precise relation of 2 Corinthians to the apologetic or forensic speech, attention to the rhetorical background will help us appreciate and understand more accurately how Paul pours out his apostolic heart to the Corinthians.

2. Content Analysis

The Apostle Paul writes this letter to alleviate the troubled aspects of his relationship with the church at Corinth. This concern leads him to appeal to the conduct and character of his ministry that had come under fire in the church. Paul defines his apostolic ministry in terms of the gospel he preached to them—the gospel of the cross and resurrection of Christ. This gospel they had received gladly when the church was born in Corinth. The Corinthians themselves then, as his children in the faith, are living proof of his ministry. As such they should respond to his care and love for them and fully reconcile with him. Some in the church, unfortunately, have listened to intruding "preachers," who are seeking to undermine Paul's standing with the Corinthians.

Paul introduces his letter (1:1-11) with a Christianized form of the standard Hellenistic greeting (1:1-2). As "an apostle of Christ Jesus by the will of

God" (v 1) along with his coworker Timothy, he addresses the Christians in Corinth and the surrounding area. The greeting is followed by a benediction-like blessing (1:3-7), which strikes a key theological note of the letter. Paul blesses "the God of all comfort" (1:3) for his comfort, with which the apostle in turn can comfort the Corinthians. This comfort he knows through his troubles suffered in a ministry that he identifies with "the sufferings of Christ" (1:5).

Paul testifies out of his own experience in a time of deadly peril (1:8-11). His participation in the sufferings of Christ gives rise to hope in the God "who raises the dead" (1:9). God has delivered him and will continue to deliver him with the aid of the Corinthians' prayers, for which he gives thanks. Thus, Paul defines his ministry as a sharing in the sufferings of Christ.

In the first major section of the letter, the apostle seeks to justify the conduct of his ministry in relation to the church at Corinth (1:12—7:16). The issue prompting his defense is his travel plans, which he has felt necessary to change (1:12—2:13). For this Paul is accused of vacillation, of possessing a "'Yes' and 'No'" (1:18) character. His first response is that his conduct and his correspondence have been sincere in the grace of God (1:12-14). Furthermore, his decisions are grounded in the character of God as revealed in the gospel he preaches (1:15-22).

Paul does not lord it over their faith, for it was out of love and care for them that he did not come as planned (1:23—2:13). It was to spare them and him more pain like that caused by his painful visit and the "sorrowful letter" it prompted. Paul explains his movement to Troas, where the Lord had facilitated his preaching. But he found no peace of mind there, for he did not find Titus. So he proceeded on to Macedonia.

The second issue Paul faced is the crucial one. It concerns the very nature of his apostolic ministry. This he next seeks to defend (2:14—6:10). As he begins to expound on the character of his calling, he pauses to thank God for leading him as a triumphal prisoner, spreading everywhere he goes "the aroma of Christ" (2:14-17; quotation from v 15). His apostolic ministry possesses the power of life and death. With divine integrity Paul carries the message of "the word of God" (v 17), a task to which he is not equal.

Revealing his heart about his apostolic calling, Paul attempts to lead the Corinthians into an understanding of his ministry that will contribute to their reconciliation. To do this he presents his ministry as "a ministry of the Spirit" (3:1—4:6), "a ministry of suffering" (4:7—5:10), and "a ministry of reconciliation" (5:11—6:10).

As Paul commends his ministry as one empowered by "the Spirit," Paul anticipates and answers the charge that he is engaging in self-commendation (3:1-3). On the contrary, he insists that he needs no letters of commendation, because the Corinthians themselves are his letter of commendation written on his heart.

The apostle defines his ministry as that of a new covenant. Its adequacy is not one of the letter but of the life-giving Spirit (3:4-6). Paul uses the example of the fading radiance on the face of Moses as he came down from Mount Sinai (Exod 34:29-35) to illustrate how the glory of the new covenant exceeds that of the old covenant (2 Cor 3:7-11). Such a ministry brings a new freedom, a new boldness in proclamation, and new possibilities for transformation (3:12-18). The new liberty of the Spirit makes for a lifelong conversion of life and character into the likeness of Christ. This is possible for those privileged by the Spirit to see the glory of the Lord as in a mirror. Thus Paul, having such a "Spirit ministry," is encouraged. He is encouraged because his ministry is open to everyone's inspection in the sight of God. It is hidden only to the unbelieving, who are perishing (4:1-6). Paul's is a servant ministry possessed by "the knowledge of the glory of God in the face of Christ" (4:6).

Paul continues his presentation of "this ministry" (4:1) as he characterizes his new covenant ministry as one of "suffering" (4:7—5:10). As a "treasure in jars of clay" (4:7), his suffering in the conduct of his ministry is one that participates in the dying of Jesus. As it does so, it releases the resurrection life of Jesus into the lives of the Corinthians (4:7-15).

The fruit of Paul's ministry is hope in the future resurrection for both Paul and the Corinthian believers. Consequently, all can be encouraged. For as the outward life declines, the inward life is on the increase (4:16-18). Thus, he insists: "what is seen is temporary, but what is unseen is eternal" (4:18). This affirmation leads Paul into an exposition of the Christian's hope for the heavenly home (5:1-10). It is a hope that by faith, possessed of the Spirit, seeks to live pleasing to Christ in anticipation of the judgment.

Jolted back to reality by his mention of the final judgment, Paul returns to his concern for reconciliation with the Corinthians. For "this ministry" (4:1) is supremely one of reconciliation (5:11—6:10). The apostle explains that his motives in ministry are grounded in his fear of the Lord, the love of Christ, and the meaning of Christ's death (5:11-15). Thus, "those who live should no longer live for themselves" (5:15).

This central conviction moves Paul into the very heart of his gospel message, the "God . . . in Christ" event of reconciliation (5:16-21). From this vantage point, all is now viewed. From it come both the ministry and the message ("word") of reconciliation: "Be reconciled to God" (5:20).

Paul urges his readers to receive God's grace. He concludes his third presentation of his ministry with a description of his ministerial life (6:1-10). Expressed paradoxically, the life of a true apostle is one of ironic suffering: "having nothing, and yet possessing everything" (v 10).

In a new section, Paul resumes the matter of his relationship with the Corinthians. He reaffirms his love for them with an appeal based on his "great confidence" (7:4, 16) in them (6:11—7:16). For some reason the apostle interrupts his call for renewed mutual affection (6:11-13; 7:2-4) with an exhortation to separated living (6:14—7:1). In relation to unbelievers the Corinthians are to maintain holiness of life by a clear separation from all that is evil. This is appropriate to their being the temple and family of God.

Paul then returns to his call for mutual affection with an intense affirmation of his love for them: "you are in our hearts to die together and to live together" (7:3 NASB). The apostle concluded this section with a report of Titus's role in the reconciliation of Paul with the church at Corinth (7:5-16; see 2:12-13).

With what feels like a digression, Paul brings up the matter of the collection that he has been promoting among his missionary churches in Galatia, Achaia, Asia, and Macedonia for the aid of the poor in the Jerusalem Christian community (8:1—9:15). He obviously viewed the collection as a significant aspect of his ministry, for reasons that are not entirely obvious to us. Paul presents the offering as an opportunity for the Corinthians to demonstrate their genuineness and their confidence in him by completing their promised participation.

Paul encourages the Corinthians to contribute toward the collection by appealing, first, to the example of the liberality of the Macedonians (8:1-7). Only after that does he challenge them by appeal to the liberality of Christ (8:8-15): "For you know the grace of our Lord Jesus Christ, that though he was rich, yet for your sakes he became poor" (v 9).

To complete the offering with delicate care he assigns the task to a delegation of Titus and companions and prepares to send them on their way. Their task is to facilitate his own subsequent visit to Corinth (8:16—9:15).

With 10:1—13:14 comes a new and final section of the letter. Apparently the situation in the church has deteriorated since he completed the writing of chs 8—9. In the final four chapters of the letter, he concentrates more on vindicating his apostolic authority. This has been undermined by intruding "false apostles" (11:13) and their negative influence on the church. As Paul deals with this, he is concerned, as well, to prepare the way for his third visit to the Corinthians. In the process the character of a true apostolic ministry is clearly exposed.

These four chapters fall into three discernible parts. In 10:1-18 Paul answers his opponents in Corinth, by defending his integrity as an apostle. In 11:1—12:13, he plays the role of a fool to indulge in mock boasting. Finally in 12:14—13:10, anticipating his third visit, Paul exhorts the church to set itself in order and mend its ways so that he will not be required to resort to severe discipline when he comes. An exhortation and a theologically rich benediction conclude the letter in 13:11-14.

Paul answers the opposition in Corinth, probably invading Judaizers. In 10:1-18 he asserts, first, that the methods of his apostolic ministry are spiritual, not carnal (10:1-6). He has no interest in coming to Corinth as a disciplinarian, unless it is absolutely necessary. His "weapons . . . are not the weapons of the world." His weapons "have divine power to . . . demolish arguments and every pretension that sets itself up against the knowledge of God" (10:4-5). Therefore, Paul's conduct and his letters, that is, his two primary means of exercising apostolic authority, are totally consistent. Together, they show who he is as one belonging to Christ (10:7-11).

The boasting Paul is compelled to do in the defense of his ministry is more legitimate than that of his opponents (10:12-18). Contrary to their measuring of "themselves by themselves" (10:12), Paul will not boast beyond the proper limits God has assigned to him.

With 11:1—12:13 Paul sharpens his polemic in his "fool's speech." He becomes more specific in his boast. Yet he uses it to reveal the heart of who he is as an apostle in likeness to his crucified and risen Lord. The apostle appeals to the Corinthians to put up with his foolishness for two reasons (11:1-6). First, because of his urgent concern for their spiritual welfare; and, second, because he needs to show that he is in no way inferior to the intruding "super-apostles" (11:5).

The "super-apostles" used Paul's refusal to accept financial support from the Corinthians against him. Thus, he defends his true motives for doing so, in the face of their perverse explanation of his motives (11:7-15). He insists that his motives are pure, whereas those of his accusers are actually deceptive. He severely labels them "deceitful workmen," indeed, "false apostles" (11:13).

Because Paul has reluctantly been forced to adopt the boastful tactics of the intruders, he renews his appeal for the Corinthians to bear with him. His mock boasting shows how foolish such boasting is (11:16-21*a*). But, after all, he writes, "You gladly put up with fools" (11:19). His description of the abusive tactics of the interlopers in Corinth calls attention to the real fools. He sarcastically and ironically apologizes for being so weak by comparison to the "super-apostles."

So, "like a madman" (11:23 NRSV), Paul launches his boast (11:21*b*—12:10). It takes two forms. First, Paul boasts of "the things that show my weakness" (11:30). To do so he catalogs the suffering and humiliations he endures in the course of his apostolic ministry (11:21*b*-33).

Second, Paul's "foolishness of boasting" turns to "visions and revelations from the Lord" (12:1-10). He begins these with a report of a heavenly experience, about which he refuses to boast so that no one might think more of him than what they can actually hear or see in him (12:1-6). He then moves on to an account of his thorn in the flesh. This leads him to confess that his apostolic ministry is one of power made perfect through weakness (12:7-10): "Therefore I will boast all the more gladly about my weaknesses, so that Christ's power may rest on me" (12:9).

Before moving on to his final concern, his plans for a third visit (12:14—13:10), Paul brings his "fool's speech" to a conclusion. He adds one last word about his conduct in Corinth (12:11-13). Again, mentioning his foolishness, he asserts anew his equality with his rivals, emphasizes the authenticity of his ministry in Corinth, and reminds the Corinthians that he did not mistreat them in sparing them his financial support.

As Paul approaches the end of his letter to the Corinthians, the apostle prepares the way for his third visit (12:14—13:10). "Now I am ready to visit you" (12:14). And they, too, must prepare for his coming. To this end Paul returns to his financial policy in relation to the church at Corinth (12:14-18). He has not taken advantage of them in any way, for he loves them sacrificially. His concern is for their welfare. But he is fearful as to the spiritual and moral condition in which he may find them, to his sorrow (12:19-21).

Putting words to his fears with a final warning, Paul seeks to encourage the unrepentant Corinthians to change their behavior. When he comes the third time he will be as firm in his discipline as their situation demands (13:1-4). He will give them the proof that Christ is speaking in him by appealing to Christ crucified and risen!

Paul's theme of weakness has come to its final expression. After that he challenges them for proof of their Christian faith. He has some confidence that the Corinthians will be able to correct their situation so that he will not have to deal too severely with them (13:5-10). His prayer remains for their perfection in the faith.

Paul brings his letter to a close with an appropriate conclusion. It contains an exhortation, a greeting, and a benediction (13:11-14). Reflecting back on what he has written, he Christianizes his final greeting that contains one last appeal for their spiritual welfare (13:11-13). Paul's desire for their full enjoyment of the full blessing of God comes to expression in a concluding "Trinitarian-like" benediction (13:14). Paul's concerns for the church permeated every facet of his closing words, even the benediction: "May the grace of the Lord Jesus Christ, and the love of God, and the fellowship of the Holy Spirit be with you all."

3. Text

The transmission of the Greek text of 2 Corinthians is so trouble-free that few critical commentaries even discuss it. Significant variants will be discussed briefly as they appear in the course of our commentary on the text. Approximately 5,700 Greek manuscripts exist that contain all or part of the NT from which the original text of 2 Corinthians can be established.

Witnesses to the text include the Greek papyri, Greek majuscule manuscripts, Greek minuscule manuscripts, and ancient versions of the NT. The more important of these are listed below in each of these categories, with a (parenthetic) note concerning their most likely date of origin, and an indication of the extent of their inclusion of the text of 2 Corinthians (see Metzger 2005, 52-134; Plummer 1915, liii-lv).

Greek Papyri

p^{46} a Chester Beatty biblical papyrus (about A.D. 200), all of 2 Corinthians

Greek Majuscule Manuscripts
ℵ Sinaiticus (fourth century), all of 2 Corinthians
A Alexandrinus (fifth century), missing 4:13—12:6
B Vaticanus (fourth century), all of 2 Corinthians
C Ephraemi (fifth century), missing 10:8—12:14
D^p Claromontanus (sixth century), all of 2 Corinthians
H^p Coislinianus (sixth century), contains only 4:2-7 and 10:18—11:6
Greek Minuscule Manuscripts
33 "the queen of the cursives" (ninth century), all of 2 Corinthians
Ancient Versions (known from differing manuscripts)
Peshitta/Syriac Vulgate (fifth century), all of 2 Corinthians
Old Latin versions (third century), a few fragments of 2 Corinthians
Latin Vulgate (fourth century), all of 2 Corinthians
Coptic Sahidic (third century), only fragments
Coptic Boharic (late?), only fragments

E. Theological Themes

> For God, who said, "Let light shine out of darkness," made his light shine in our hearts to give us the light of the knowledge of the glory of God in the face of Christ. But we have this treasure in jars of clay to show that this all-surpassing power is from God and not from us. (4:6-7)

The theology imbedded in 2 Corinthians is simply Christology, the mysterious and profound deed of Christ crucified and risen. Christology functions for Paul both as a telescope and a microscope. He looks through them at everything involved in his apostolic calling. This is true whether his gaze is lifted up to God the Father or brought down to the humiliations, hardships, and dangers he encounters in the course of his ministry. Every aspect of his ministry takes on the meaning only in relation to Jesus the Christ. Whether Paul is probing the grandeur of the work of the Holy Spirit or defining his ministry to those who look upon it with disdain, the key to each is the person of the Christ.

Real to his life and thought with implications for the gospel he preaches, for the nature of the church, and for the life of the Christian is the dying of the Jesus who yet lives by the power of God. Such a Christology radically transforms all it touches. This is the distinctive contribution of 2 Corinthians to the theology of the NT. From Paul's christological perspective we will examine briefly the themes of God, the gospel, and the ministry. We presuppose the interpretation of the texts employed as set forth in the commentary.

1. God

By definition theology begins with God. To say (*logos*) anything about God (*Theos*) is to do theology. And for Paul thinking about "the living God" (3:3) requires looking first into "the face of Christ," where "a human face [is] united with the being of God" (Young and Ford 1987, 255). There one sees fully "the glory of God." In "the face of Christ," the Creator-God, who said, "Let light shine out of darkness," shines into human minds and hearts to give the "light of the knowledge" of himself. What did Paul understand about his *Theos*? What kind of God revealed himself to Paul in the face of his Lord?

Paul attributes his calling to be an apostle of Christ Jesus to the "will of God" (1:1). For him God is the One, above all, who actively determines his life in Christ. It is just as the Macedonians first gave themselves to the Lord and then to the apostles—"in keeping with God's will" (8:5).

Thus, all believers and all Christian communities belong to God as "the church of God" (1:1). To all these the apostle sends his greeting of "grace and peace from God our Father and the Lord Jesus Christ" (1:2). The greeting originates from God *and* Jesus, as both are inherent to the very being of the church and its apostle.

Paul's first description of God to the church at Corinth is as "our Father" (1:2). Understood in the context of his Jewish background and the traditions of the earthly Jesus, God is first a Father (1:2, 3). It was Jesus first who taught his disciples to pray "Father" (Luke 11:3; Matt 6:9; see Matt 11:25-27). With this heritage, God became for the apostle primarily and preeminently the "Father of our Lord Jesus Christ" (2 Cor 1:3; 11:31).

Paul can speak of "the Son of God, Jesus Christ" (1:19; see 1 Cor 1:9; only here in the Corinthian letters but frequently in Romans). As Father and Son, each defines the other. They are the single source of all that Paul sees and receives from God. Thus, God *and* Christ are to be blessed or praised (2 Cor 1:3). To God, both thanks (2:14; 8:16; 9:11-12, 15) and prayers (13:7, 9; see 1:11; 9:14) are to be directed.

In 2 Corinthians, Paul identifies God's character, first, as "the Father of compassion and the God of all comfort" (1:3). Paul uses the attribute "compassion" (*oiktirmōn*), literally "mercies" (NRSV), elsewhere both of God (Rom 12:1) and of Christ (Phil 2:1). Divine blessing, salvation, calling, and life all flow out from them. As "the God of all comfort" (*paraklēseōs*) or "encouragement" (Young and Ford 1987, 262), God (1:4) and Christ (1:5) are the source of the apostles' comfort in all their troubles (see also 7:6).

On this basis, the apostles can comfort/encourage the Corinthians with "the comfort we ourselves have received from God" (1:4). Significantly their ability to comfort others with the comfort of God is due to "the sufferings of Christ" (1:5) overflowing into their ministries (1:7). With such a source, the theme of mutual comfort flows through the entire letter (*paraklēseōs*—1:5, 6, 7; 7:4, 13; *parakaleō*—1:4, 6; 2:7; 7:7, 13).

Central to Paul's faith in God is the God "who raises the dead" (1:9). Spoken in the throes of a deadly trial from which he was delivered, the phrase reaches to the height of NT faith. For the God "who raises the dead" is precisely the God "who raised the Lord Jesus from the dead" (4:14). Had Paul not written to the Corinthians earlier that "if Christ has not been raised, your faith is futile; you are still in your sins" (1 Cor 15:17)? It is this very life-giving character of God that allows Paul to affirm that God "will also raise us with Jesus and present us with you in his presence" (2 Cor 4:14). Such a God is the guarantee that "we have a building from God, an eternal house in heaven" (5:1) in which to "appear before the judgment seat of Christ" (5:10).

The God who raises the dead (1:9) is the kind of God who is at work in the ministries of his servants. With Christ, who now "lives by God's power," Paul writes, also "by God's power we will live with him to serve you" (13:4). Paul conducts his ministry in a manner that shows that "this all surpassing power is from God and not from us" (4:7; see 6:7). The resurrection power of God in Christ applies not only to our deaths but also to our lives and ministries (7:3). God is the God of the resurrection, an essential dimension of the story of God.

For Paul, God is the One whose "grace" thoroughly characterizes his ministry (1:12). The "holiness and sincerity" that rules his conduct in the world and with the Corinthians are from God (1:12). His message to them is a "Yes" (1:19), precisely because "God is faithful" to him (1:18). God is known to be faithful because "the Son of God, Jesus Christ" (1:19) whom Paul and his companions preached in Corinth is a "Yes" to the "many promises of God" (1:20). "In Christ" God has made them all "stand firm," for he has "anointed" those who believe, "set his seal of ownership" on them, "and put his Spirit" in their "hearts as a deposit, guaranteeing what is to come" (1:21-22; see 5:5). God's action by his Spirit in the ministry of his apostles is in and through his Son, Jesus.

As is already obvious, Paul attributes his ministry directly to God. It is God "who always leads us in triumphal procession" (2:14); and it is "the word of God" (*ton tou logon Theou*—2:17; 4:20; see 5:19) that he proclaims. Yet his apostolic triumph is only and comprehensively "in Christ" (2:14; 5:19). That is, he triumphs by identifying with Christ's suffering and death, *and* in the power of his resurrected life. In this manner Paul was "to God the aroma of Christ" to all who came in contact with his ministry, to both "those who are being saved" and to "those who are perishing" (2:15).

It was "to God" to whom Paul was supremely accountable, for it was in Christ that he and his coworkers spoke "before God with sincerity, like men sent from God" (2:17; see 5:10). Their "confidence" as apostles was "through Christ before God" (3:4). Their "competence" as "ministers of a new covenant" came "from God" (3:5-6). In a real sense "through Christ before God" was their core definition, as self-acclaimed "servants of God" (6:4). As such Paul limits his ministerial activities "to the field God has assigned to us" (10:13), which included Corinth.

With the term "grace" (*charis*) central to his theological vocabulary, God was for Paul supremely a God of grace. Grace came, wrote Paul, "from God our Father and the Lord Jesus Christ" (1:2). It comprehended God's "unsought and unmerited benevolence" (Harris 2005, 192), which expresses itself in no longer "counting men's sins against them" (5:19). God extends this grace to all humanity in the person and work of Christ: "For you know the grace of our Lord Jesus Christ, that though he was rich, yet for your sakes he became poor, so that you through his poverty might become rich" (8:9; see 12:9; 13:14).

This grace of God determined Paul's conduct in ministry (1:12). Through his ministry and that of his coworkers, God's grace reached out to "more and more people" (4:15), including the response of the Macedonians to the collection out of their severe trials and "extreme poverty" (8:2). As a "surpassing grace" (9:14), God caused it to abound to the Corinthians so that they, having all that they need, "will abound in every good work" (9:8). For all these reasons and more, Paul urged them "not to receive God's grace in vain" (6:1).

The God of grace was the author and the foundational source of the reconciliation "through Christ." As recipients of this reconciliation, Paul, his coworkers, and the Corinthians were given by God "the ministry of reconciliation." It consisted of "the message of reconciliation," the revealing word (*logon*) that "God was reconciling the world to himself in Christ." God made Christ, "who had no sin to be sin," so that "the righteousness of God" might be extended to all who will receive it. In this ministry the apostles were "Christ's ambassadors," spokespersons through whom Christ was making his reconciling appeal to the world (5:18-21).

God is One who loves the church and its people. The apostle expresses this grand assumption in benedictory terms: "the God of love and peace will be with you" (13:11) and "the love of God will be with you all" (13:14; see 5:14). An inherent part of God's love in this final benediction is "the grace of . . . Christ" and "the fellowship of the Holy Spirit." This forms "the most developed *trinitarian affirmation* in the NT" (Harris 2005, 116).

When theology is applied to the more mundane context, Paul seeks to motivate meaningfully the church with the reminder that "God loves a cheerful giver" (9:7). The benedictory "God of . . . peace" along with the salutary "peace to you from God our Father and the Lord Jesus Christ" (1:2) conveys the comprehensive biblical *shalom* in a familiar Pauline characterization of God (Rom 15:13; Phil 4:9; 1 Thess 5:23; see 2 Thess 3:16; Heb 13:20).

One fascinating feature of theology in 2 Corinthians is the expression "the glory of God" (1:20; 4:6, 15). Its implications penetrate Paul's entire presentation. For now we note only that this characterization of God focuses on "the glory of Christ, who is the image of God" and in whose face God has shown "the light of the knowledge" of his glory (4:6). This is the God whom Paul defines in the proclamation of his gospel.

2. The Gospel

Paul's gospel is supremely "the gospel of Christ" (2:12). Four of the eight appearances of the term "gospel" (*euangelion*) in 2 Corinthians identify "Christ" as its content (2:12; 4:4; 9:13; 10:14; see the commentary on 2:12). Once in the phrase "the gospel of God" (11:7; the cognate verb *euēngelisamēn* occurs here as well as in 10:16), Paul names God as the source of the gospel that is Christ. In 4:3, "our gospel" is the gospel Paul preaches. And in 11:4, "a different gospel" is an ironic reference to the message preached by Paul's rivals in Corinth. Paul can also speak simply and grandly of simply "the gospel" (8:18).

The crucial question is: What is the content of Paul's gospel? For Paul that content not only is Christ but also is expressed as "the glory of Christ, who is the image of God" (4:4). Interestingly, this is the "light of the gospel" that he defines in 4:6 as "the light of the knowledge of the glory of God in the face of Christ." With Christ as "the image of God," Paul means that it is "in the face [*prosōpōi*, ***person***] of Christ" that God makes known his glory (see the commentary on 4:4-6).

"Glory" belongs uniquely to God, and ultimately transcends human comprehension. The extensive use of the terminology of "glory" (both noun and verb) in 3:7-18 has the fiery, blinding presence of God on Sinai as its background.

Yet the "glory" can be known! God can be known and the most that can be known of him is seen in the human face of Jesus—in his person and work. It is in Christ—in his life, death, and resurrection—that God comes to humankind in the fullness of his revealing and saving presence. Christ is the "***Yes***" to the ***many promises of God,*** for ***through him is the "Amen" to God for glory through*** the ministry of the apostles (1:20; see the commentary on this verse). The content of Paul's gospel is ultimately "the glory of God." It is his hidden mystery and his revealed holiness, as he shares in John's witness to Jesus the Christ (see John 1:14, 18).

Given the unity of the Son with the Father Paul takes for granted, we may further explore Paul's gospel in his presentation of the one he calls the Christ. All-important and all-consuming is the death and resurrection of Christ viewed as one continually present event. The risen Christ remains the crucified one and the crucified Christ remains the risen one (McCant 1999, 162). Integral to this presentation are "the sufferings of Christ" (1:5) in his life and death.

The first and basic consequence is that Christ "died for all" so that all humans may "live . . . for him who died for them and was raised again" (5:15). Guaranteed with Christ's resurrection is that the God who "raised the Lord Jesus from the dead will also raise us with Jesus and present us . . . in his presence" (4:14). Further, the redemptive core of Christ's death "for all" is that "God made him who had no sin to be sin for us, so that in him we might become the righteousness of God" (5:21). In that act, "God was reconciling the world to himself in Christ" (5:19). The redemptive, saving, action and presence of God in his world is in the deed of the glorified cross, in Christ's death and resurrection.

This redemptive event is the content of Paul's gospel. At its heart is the "message of reconciliation" (5:19), which is then the very "word [*logon*] of God" (2:17; 4:2). To receive this message as true for oneself is to be "in Christ . . . a new creation" (5:17), to be with him who is "the image of God" (4:4). In union with this Christ, crucified and risen, God's servants are entrusted with "the ministry of reconciliation" (5:18) as his "ambassadors" (5:20). They possess this "treasure in jars of clay"—as lowly human instruments, for the "all-surpassing power" of the gospel is "from God," not from his messengers (4:7).

This leads to a second and equally important consequence of the significance of "the sufferings of Christ" (1:5) in the theology of this letter. We will consider this under the heading "The Ministry" below. Paul's gospel and his ministry are so intimately interrelated that it is difficult to discuss the two separately. Just as Paul's gospel determines his ministry, so his ministry reveals his gospel. Accordingly, some themes treated below could just as appropriately have been considered under the heading "The Gospel."

For example, Paul accuses some Corinthians of receiving from his rivals "another Jesus," "a different spirit," and "a different gospel" (11:4 NRSV) than those on which the church at Corinth was founded. At issue in the three closely related charges is the person and work of Christ and the relation of his sufferings/death to his resurrection. Put in Pauline terminology, it is the relation of power to weakness that constitutes the ministry of Jesus and the ministry of his apostles: "For to be sure, he was crucified in weakness, yet he lives by God's power. Likewise, we are weak in him, yet by God's power we will live with him to serve you" (13:4). Thus we arrive at the all-permeating theme of the ministry of Paul given to him by his risen Lord, "power is made perfect in weakness" (12:9).

3. The Ministry

At a significant transition point in his argument, Paul asserts for himself and his coworkers that "we have this ministry" (4:1). This ministry, which he first defines as "the ministry of the Spirit" (3:8), he later sums up grandly as "the ministry of reconciliation" (5:18), as has already been noted.

The apostle's concern for the apostolic and Christian ministry is seen in his frequent use of the terminology of ministry throughout 2 Corinthians. This is translated by the NIV as either "ministry" (seven times) or "service" (five times, including 11:8: "to serve"). The Greek noun *diakonia* occurs twelve times (3:6, 7, 8, 9; 4:1; 5:18; 6:3; 8:4; 9:1, 12, 13; 11:8). The verb form (*diakoneō*), which appears twice, is rendered by the NIV as "the result of our ministry" (3:3) and "we administer" (8:19) in reference to the collection. The abstract noun *diakonia* (***ministry***) is similarly treated in 8:4; 9:1, 12, 13; 11:8. The cognate noun form (*diakonos*), ***servant*** or ***minister,*** is translated four times as "ministers" (3:6; 11:15 [twice], 23) and once as "servants" (6:4) by the NRSV. Both the NRSV and NIV use "ministers of a new covenant" for *diakonous kainēs diathēkēs* in 3:6.

a. A ministry of the Spirit. The first specific characterization of Paul's apostolic and Christian ministry is "the ministry of the Spirit" (3:8). Constituting this ministry is the fact that God "has made us competent as ministers of a new covenant" in which "the Spirit gives life" (3:6). The new covenant is in contrast to the old Mosaic covenant. The old covenant was made with Israel through Moses in the majestic thunder and lightning of Mount Sinai (Exod 18—20). It "came with glory," but it was "engraved in letters on stone" and, as such, was a "ministry that brought death" (3:7).

In contrast, Paul's new covenant ministry is "written . . . with the Spirit of the living God . . . on tablets of human hearts" (3:3). The apostle's prime example was the Corinthians themselves. They were Paul's letter of recommendation, which Christ wrote by the Spirit (3:2-3). That is, the Spirit of Christ made them the new persons they became when they accepted Paul's gospel message. The old covenant of "the letter kills," but the new covenant of "the Spirit gives life" (3:6). The new possesses the glory of "the ministry that brings righteousness" (3:9).

The face of Moses as he descended from Sinai illustrates the glory of the old covenant. His face was so radiant "that the Israelites could not look steadily at" his face, "because of its glory, fading though it was" (3:7). The old was indeed "glorious" (3:9), but it was fading away in comparison to "the surpassing . . . glory of that which lasts" (3:10-11). The new ministry of life rather than death, of righteousness rather than condemnation (3:9)—"the ministry of the Spirit"—has come to stay! It possesses "an eternal glory" (4:17).

The Spirit as the dynamic of this ministry is given to the apostles and to all believers "as a deposit, guaranteeing what is to come" (1:22; 5:5). With this hope comes a boldness, a new openness (3:12). The difference, the superiority, the "surpassing glory" is that now the old veil over human hearts is taken away in the person and work of Christ (3:14-16). Christ, by his death and resurrection, is of the essence of "the ministry of the Spirit." For "the Lord is the Spirit, and where the Spirit of the Lord is, there is freedom" (3:17). Therefore, Paul's ministry is "in the Holy Spirit" (6:6).

The resultant character of this ministry of the Spirit for individual believers and the corporate church cannot be described in any better way than Paul does: ***We all with unveiled face, seeing as in a mirror the glory of the Lord, are being transformed into the same image from glory to glory, just as from the Lord who is the Spirit*** (3:18; see the commentary on 3:17-18). The ministry of the Spirit is the power of the resurrected Christ, who brings the glory of God into human lives. This is the God proclaimed in 2 Corinthians; this is Paul's "gospel of the *glory* of Christ, who is the image of God" (4:4, emphasis added); this is our glorious privilege in ministry.

So Paul can say, "since through God's mercy we have this ministry, we do not lose heart" (4:1). How does this ministry work? Since Christian ministry is "the ministry of reconciliation," the redemptive work of God in Christ is its starting point. We have noted that Paul's theology of suffering (1:3-11) is grounded in "the sufferings of Christ." He applies this as a "treasure in jars of clay" (4:7) to his own ministry of the gospel of Christ in a penetrating paradox (4:8-12).

b. A ministry of suffering. Paul in his ministry is "hard pressed on every side, but not crushed; perplexed, but not in despair; persecuted, but not abandoned; struck down, but not destroyed" (4:8-9). Theologically put, Paul sees his apostolic life as one of carrying about ***the dying of Jesus*** in order that "the life of Jesus" might "be revealed" in and through it (4:10). In his words, "For we who are alive are always being given over to death for Jesus' sake, so that his life may be revealed in our mortal body" (4:11). This is the theological heart of a Christian ministry, "death is at work in us, but life in you" (4:12 NRSV). This "death" is sharing in the "sufferings of Christ." And this "life" is sharing in the sustaining and empowering presence of the resurrected and living Christ.

The evident anointing of God on the ministry of Mother Teresa surely tapped into this theological dynamic. Her spiritual power was grounded in her unique faith identification with Christ crucified and risen. In Mother Teresa's devotion to the passion of Christ, suffering was taken by her as a means in her vocation. Her career-long experience of interior "darkness" appears related. In the poor, the sick, and the dying to whom she ministered in the slums, she met Christ. She "grasped the depth of Jesus' identification with each sufferer and understood the mystical connection between the sufferings of Christ and the sufferings of the poor" (Kolodiejchuk 2007, 43). In her words, "Suffering in itself is nothing; but suffering shared with Christ's Passion is a wonderful gift" (Kolodiejchuk 2007, 146).

What Paul identifies as "the sufferings of Christ" in his ministry he describes in a second paradoxical list in 6:4-10. This list, commending himself that his "ministry will not be discredited" (6:3), comes to an ironic summary climax: "having nothing, and yet possessing everything" (6:10). In 11:23-29, in the context of his boasting as a fool (11:1-21), comes a final list (but not the final mention) of his apostolic sufferings. This list, set against the boast of his rivals in pedigree, in trouble-free triumphal ministry, and in ecstatic experiences, concludes with a vivid expression of the theme of power through weakness. This theme has woven itself throughout the entire letter. If Paul has to boast in defense of his ministry, he will only boast, he writes, "of the things that show my weakness" (11:30).

The apostle's christological understanding of specifically "Christian" ministry comes to profound clarity as he speaks of "visions and revelations from the Lord" (12:1 in 12:1-10). Of no value to anyone but himself are Paul's ecstatic or high spiritual moments (12:2-6). Rather, he was graced with "a thorn in my flesh . . . to torment me" (12:7). His plea for deliverance from it was refused. Then came the revelation from the Lord that forever defines his apostolic ministry and all future truly Christian ministry: "My grace is sufficient for you, for power is made perfect in weakness" (12:9 NRSV). This is how Paul's ministry takes place "in the power of God" (6:7). In his suffering, he is nonetheless sustained.

Here is where the apostle most deeply saw "the light of the gospel of the glory of Christ" (4:4). For he concludes: "Therefore I will boast all the more gladly about my weaknesses, so that Christ's power may rest on me. . . . For when I am weak, then I am strong" (12:9). Paul indeed saw "the glory of God in the face of Christ" (4:6). So can we! No wonder he declares that God leads Christian ministers "in triumphal procession in Christ" and makes them "to God the aroma of Christ" everywhere (2:14-15). But the sobering fact is that Christian ministers are at once "the smell of death" to some, and "the fragrance of life" to others (2:16). With Paul, we must ask, "who is equal to such a task?"

Yet on this somber note, can we not conclude from 2 Corinthians that the ultimate expression of the glory of God is in the Christian ministry? Is it not in the witness of his people, the leaven of Christ's church in the world? Paul's language suggests as much. In the administration of the collection for the saints in Jerusalem, "administration" translates the cognate verb for doing ministry, *diakonoumenēi* (8:19). The offering is being administrated "for the glory [*doxan*] of the Lord himself" (NRSV). In 8:23, those who administer the offering are "the glory [*doxa*] of Christ" (NRSV). And in 9:13, ***people will glorify*** [*doxazontes*] ***God*** for the Corinthians' ministry (*diakonias*) of "generosity in sharing with them and with everyone else."

In the ministry of the gospel of Christ we "are being transformed into his likeness with ever-increasing glory," into "the *glory* of Christ, who is the image of God" (3:18; 4:4, emphasis added). As we serve with our eyes fixed on "the face of Christ" (see Heb 12:2), we witness in our hearts "the light of the knowledge of the glory of God" (4:6). The theology of 2 Corinthians is brought to a succinct yet comprehensive summary in Paul's unique Trinitarian benediction (13:14):

May the grace of the Lord Jesus Christ,
and the love of God,
and the fellowship of the Holy Spirit
be with you all.

Following the order of Christian experience:

1. "The grace of the Lord Jesus Christ." In his life, death, and resurrection, Christ brought into being the gospel and its ministry. These are inseparably intertwined. Both take the shape of his cross and resurrection life.
2. "The love of God." Paul knows God the Father as the source of all life and hope.
3. "The fellowship of the Holy Spirit." The common sharing in the divine life that constitutes the church is the divine gift that is the Spirit. He transforms every life and empowers the ministry of the people of God.

F. Hermeneutical Issues

ou grammatos alla pneumatos
"not of the letter but of the Spirit" (3:6)

"Now the Lord is the Spirit, and
where the Spirit of the Lord is, there is freedom" (3:17).

1. An Apostolic Hermeneutic

The Apostle Paul lived in the Scriptures as known to him primarily in the Greek translation of the OT (the LXX). In 2 Corinthians, his quotations from and seemingly limitless allusions to OT texts make this obvious. As a result, Paul possessed a "biblical spirituality" (Young and Ford 1987, 62). His reading and pondering of his Bible shaped his understanding of both himself and the nature of the situation in the church at Corinth. Young and Ford observe that Paul "has 'lived in the Bible' to the point where the Bible has formed his whole outlook on how the world is and what his place in it might be" (1987, 63).

One can trace the influence of Paul's Bible throughout the whole of the letter. The whole range of Scriptures we call the OT—the Law, the Prophets, and the Writings—impacted his mind and heart. The language of the Psalms was in his bloodstream. From the psalms of lament and other psalms come his sense of confidence and hope in the midst of affliction. Direct quotations appear in 4:13 (Ps 116:10) and 9:9 (Ps 112:9).

Most significant were Paul's allusions to Ps 116, focused on the quotation of 116:10. He alludes as well to the surrounding psalms, 112—117. These are the Hallel (praise) psalms, used in synagogue worship on the occasion of the great festivals. The Psalms were, no doubt, his lifelong prayer book and hymnbook. As such, they were instrumental in molding his spirituality (see Young and Ford 1987, 63-69).

The prophets represented in 2 Corinthians by direct quotations are Isaiah (49:8 and 52:11 in 2 Cor 6:2; 6:17*a*), Jeremiah (9:24 in 2 Cor 10:17), and Ezekiel (37:27 and 20:34 in 2 Cor 6:16-17). Again the allusions are multiple. With and beyond these linguistic links, however, was Paul's assimilation of and dependence upon the substance of their message and prophetic perspectives. He interpreted his prophetic vocation in the light of the call of Jeremiah and the way he lived out his prophetic office. Furthermore, Jeremiah furnished Paul with his key text on boasting (9:24) as well as the terminology of the new covenant (31:31-34; 2 Cor 3:6; see Ezek 37:26-28).

Ezekiel's stress on the glory of God (1:28; 3:23; 39:21: 43:1-5), the importance of the Spirit (2:2; 37:1-10), and the human need for a new heart and spirit (11:19; 18:31) were all in the background of Paul's understanding. Other connections abound. Aspects of and allusions to the vision of Isaiah (chs 1—66) all made their impact on Paul's prophetic perception. From these prophets he learned to see God's dealing with his people in historical perspective. The prophets were examples of despair and warning as well as of hope and encouragement. Paul sought to carry on their vision of redemptive purposes as the ambassador of a new covenant to the Gentiles (see Young and Ford 1987, 69-78).

The Wisdom literature furnished Paul with ample illustration of his boasting theme. Other themes such as singleness of heart, trust in affliction, divine counsel, and the aroma of wisdom are also present in 2 Corinthians. Allusions from Proverbs appear in chs 8 and 9 and may appear elsewhere. Significant, too, are Paul's quotations from Lev 26:12 (2 Cor 6:16), 2 Sam 7:8, 14 (2 Cor 6:18), Exod 16:18 (2 Cor 8:15), and Deut 19:15 (2 Cor 13:1; see the commentary on these passages).

Most important, however, for an appreciation of Paul's biblical hermeneutic is his interpretation of Exod 34:29-35 in 2 Cor 3:7-18 (see Hays 1989, 122-53). Here scriptural exegesis constitutes the method of his argument. He appeals to the Law, the Torah, the basic and most authoritative portion of Scripture for the Jewish community. From the prophets Paul understood the historical failure of the old covenant, a covenant that indeed possessed God's glory. He saw the consequences of destruction, death, and the exile for the people of God.

Paul understood the need of the prophetically promised new covenant (Jeremiah and Ezekiel) and its fulfillment in a new covenant of the Spirit. With a dynamic hermeneutic of the Spirit he interpreted the realization of the covenant as coming to completion in the person and work of Christ. In Paul's view, "the entire history of God's dealings with mankind could be summed up by the formula 'God in Christ'" (Hanson 1974, 241).

The word of God overwhelmed the apostle with transforming insight into Christ, "the Lord, who is the Spirit." Caught up in the raptured creativity of fulfillment, he writes with fresh boldness, "Now the Lord is the Spirit, and where the Spirit of the Lord is, there is freedom. And we . . . are being transformed into his likeness with an ever-increasing glory" (3:17-18; see 3:12; 12:2-4). Richard B. Hays comments: "Paul provides us with a model of hermeneutical freedom" (1989, 186).

E. Earle Ellis terms Pauline biblical exegesis as "grammatical-historical plus." By this he means that Paul's interpretation pursues the grammar and historical meaning according to the accepted methods of his day. But his exegesis "in its essential character, begins where grammatical-historical exegesis ends" (1957, 147). Paul has soaked himself in the whole of Scripture. He submits his mind and heart to the Spirit of God and hears the biblical witness to its ultimate end and meaning in Christ.

Paul knows the Scriptures, but he also knows full well the situation in Corinth. In this matrix, listening to the Spirit and to the needs of the church, he understands anew the Scripture in relation to the condition of the recipients of his apostolic labors in Corinth. This is the witness, the understanding of Scripture that he brings to bear on the world of his day.

To what extent does Paul point the way for the role of the church's sacred text in the lives of God's people in the world of our day? How is 2 Corinthians divinely designed to function for us in our personal reading, in the preaching task, and for our understanding of our calling to be witnesses and ministers? Can a "rich, alive, personally revealing God as experienced in Father, Son, and Holy Spirit, personally" address "us in whatever circumstance we find ourselves" (Peterson 2006, 28)? Can the Spirit give us a transforming word from the biblical text for our people?

Further Reading on Pauline Hermeneutics

Ellis, E. Earle. 1957. *Paul's Use of the Old Testament.* Grand Rapids: Eerdmans.

Hanson, Anthony Tyrrell. 1974. *Studies in Paul's Technique and Theology.* Grand Rapids: Eerdmans.

Hays, Richard B. 1989. *Echoes of Scripture in the Letters of Paul.* New Haven, Conn.: Yale University Press.

_________. 2005. *The Conversion of the Imagination: Paul as an Interpreter of Israel's Scripture.* Grand Rapids: Eerdmans.

Young, Frances, and David F. Ford. 1987. *Meaning and Truth in 2 Corinthians.* Grand Rapids: Eerdmans.

2. A Biblical Hermeneutic

Volumes dealing with the question of biblical interpretation could fill a library. We cannot write another book! I will attempt merely to articulate in a few paragraphs what my mind and heart grasps as basic in light of 2 Corinthians. I write inescapably as a Wesleyan (see Green 2004, 124) mining from Paul "a biblical hermeneutic" for the role of Scripture in the church of our day.

We start with a faith declaration: the key to our reading of Scripture is Scripture! Why could not the starting point of our instruction for the proclamation of the message of Scripture be Scripture?

Our approach to the biblical text begins with a twofold assumption. The first is the appropriate role of the grammatical or literary-historical method. The second is the nature of Scripture as "God-breathed" (2 Tim 3:16): "when he, the Spirit of truth, comes, he will guide you into all truth" (John 16:13).

The Bible is at one and the same time a "human" book and a "Holy Spirit" book. The Bible is literature, written in an ancient language according to the literary conventions of its day. It was written at specific times in history, at specific geographical locations, in specific ancient languages, and within specific cultures far removed from our postmodern times.

In the progress of God's redemptive action in regard to his people, he has in his providence given to the church the biblical canon of the Old and New

Testaments. God by his Spirit was involved in its writing, its tradition history, its preservation, its collection, and in its canonical formation. Throughout the history of the church, the Holy Spirit has spoken to the people of God through its sacred texts, interpreting them for Christian faith, life, and ministry.

Hays observes, "The Holy Spirit is not a theological abstraction but the manifestation of God's presence in the community, making everything new" (1996, 45). Thus, the Bible divorced from the Spirit of God and read apart from a heart and mind open to the Holy Spirit is hardly the Christian Scriptures. It is merely a collection of ancient documents of historical interest and literary inspiration: "an anthology of ancient literary art, a record of historical events, or a depository of universal wisdom" (Wall 2004a, 109). The Bible is the Word of God for human lives only in dynamic union with the Living Word: "The Lord is the Spirit" (3:17).

With these two assumptions, one historical and the other of faith, our hermeneutic centers in the character and function of Holy Scripture as a "witness to faith." As the church's normative rule of faith, this is its divinely intended function. Simply put, the scriptural canon consists of prophetic prewitness (the OT) and apostolic postwitness (the NT) to Jesus Christ the incarnate Son of God.

The character of this witness can be fully clarified by literary and historical questioning. The function of this witness can be effectively known only by a hearing of mind and heart in the lives of individuals and in the work of the church. So our attempt is to sum up a biblical hermeneutical approach to 2 Corinthians as a "christological witness."

First, we listen to Scripture as a witness, as an inspired testimony to what God is up to. As did Paul in writing 2 Corinthians, we set Scripture in the context of the age-long history of the people of God witnessed to by the Law, the Prophets, and the Writings. Paul included in this history of salvation the coming of the Christ; so we include the NT and the centuries-long history of Christ's church. We need to see the biblical text in the light of what God in Christ has been doing redemptively in the ages-long life of the people of God. Within that perspective the primary question is "Who is Christ?"

How does Paul understand Christ? What is the essence of his work? What is Paul's basic Christology? How did Paul experience Jesus the Christ? Then, as we grasp Paul's witness in its linguistic, historical, and theological form, we listen for the Spirit's witness in and for our concrete human situation: "the Spirit will take from what is mine and make it known to you" (John 16:15).

Robert W. Wall writes, "The Spirit of God is at work" in the "Scripture's performance as the Word of God" in "the interplay of biblical text and social context" (2004a, 117-18). Within the worshipping community, we encounter in our own particularity of life the crucified and risen Christ in whose face we see "the light of the knowledge of the glory of God" (4:6; see 5:14, 15, 21).

Our hermeneutic is first to hear and share in a witness! For the church it starts with what God has done "reconciling . . . in Christ" (5:19). It begins as a "listening" hermeneutic!

Second, our hermeneutical approach to 2 Corinthians is christological. As best we can, having understood Paul's Christ in his life, death, and resurrection, we follow Paul in the application of his faith in Christ. In 2 Corinthians Paul's Christology informs and shapes everything about his apostolic life and work. His message, his gospel, was simply "the gospel of Christ" (2:12) and profoundly "the gospel of the glory of Christ" (4:4).

Paul's ministry, as "the ministry of reconciliation" (5:18), fully partook of Christ's ministry: "We always carry around in our body the death [***dying***] of Jesus, so that the life of Jesus may also be revealed in our body" (4:10; see vv 11-12; 1:5; 6:3-10; 11:21—12:10; 13:4). As "Christ's ambassadors," God was "making his appeal" through the apostles (5:20). The most fundamental form of ministry is "the life of Jesus" as it highlights the effect of the present reality of grace in the personality of the minister (Murphy-O'Connor 1991, 145).

Paul viewed the Corinthians as the church through a christological lens; they were promised in marriage to the "one husband, to Christ" (11:2). The conduct of their lives was to be determined by their "sincere and pure devotion to Christ" (11:3; 12:20-21; 13:11). The ethics of the Christian community and of individual Christians were to be "Christ-ethics." The norm for ethics is more than a predetermined set of rules for conduct, "right action must be *discerned* on the basis of a christological paradigm, with a view to the need of the community" (Hays 1996, 43, see 18, 39-45).

To sum up, a contemporary hermeneutical approach to 2 Corinthians centers on Paul's Spirit-empowered witness to the person and work of Christ. That is, it focuses primarily on ***God in Christ reconciling the world to himself.*** This witness as received is, then, under the same Spirit's guidance, worked out in every aspect of the life of the church, its ministry, and in the individual lives of its people in obedience to the revealed and living Christ. In the language of the Fourth Gospel: the Spirit, the Advocate, makes known to us what is Christ's (John 16:15). The Spirit will guide us "into all truth" and tell "what is yet to come" (John 16:13). He will inspire us to know what Jesus means for us now, where we are in life and community. Thus the Scriptures as the Word of God face us with "the arduous task of interpretation" (Kay 2007, 120).

Paul asserts: "the Lord is the Spirit, and where the Spirit of the Lord is, there is freedom" (2 Cor 3:17). This "freedom," as 2 Corinthians shows in nearly every line, involves inherently a christological-ethical imperative. Paul's "mode of hermeneutical freedom" is a model of hermeneutical responsibility: "Aim for perfection, listen to my appeal, be of one mind, live in peace. And the God of love and peace will be with you" (13:11).

In the FROM THE TEXT sections of this commentary I attempt to employ prayerfully the hermeneutic set forth here. As the exegetical disciplines were applied to the text of 2 Corinthians, the presence and mind of the Living Christ were sincerely sought. My own mind and heart yearned for the witness of the Spirit speaking through the inspired text to Christ, to see "the light of the knowledge of the glory of God in the face of Christ" (4:6). The goal was to articulate the witness of the Living Word through the written Word for my own life and for that of the church I love. I am hopeful that a fresh vision of Christ crucified and risen is faithfully applied to Christian ministry and life.

Perhaps a personal example will help at this point. Recently, I was asked to give the scriptural meditation at the memorial service for the wife of a colleague of over four decades (09/03/08). I felt drawn to 2 Cor 4:7—5:10 as I searched for the voice of the Living Lord for my friend and his family. I wanted to proclaim the gospel as we had shared it over the years in this time of great loss. For forty-eight years we had been united in our love of Scripture and had exchanged our "penetrating" insights.

Another text from Paul's letter to Corinth leaped out at me as well. The apostle's word to a troubled church was: "I do not say this to condemn you, for I said before that you are in our hearts, to die together and to live together" (2 Cor 7:3 NRSV). Speaking this text directly to my friend and his two children on behalf of myself and the gathered congregation, I made use of the FROM THE TEXT section on 2 Cor 4:7—5:10.

The approach to the text for this occasion was as follows:

> Plainly and directly Paul understands his present life as one characterized equally by both the "dying of Jesus" (NASB) and the "life of Jesus" (4:10). This transforms both his present and his future life. Such is the nature of the Pauline gospel, and by the grace and providence of God, our gospel, our good news, as well. So as we listen with our hearts to this inspired text, keep in mind that "you are in our hearts, to die together and to live together."
>
> The apostle would have us today center the understanding of our lives in the death and the resurrection of Jesus. For as we, with Paul-like confidence (4:1, 16; 5:6, 8), attempt to face the "expected" and the "unexpecteds" of our earthly course as Christians, we discover three profound affirmations about our faith

I proceeded to unpack the following affirmations of biblical faith in the face of the loss of a loved one.

> Scripture tells us that we are able to face the crucibles of life *because:*
>
> 1. *We center our faith in the cross and resurrection of Jesus* (4:7-15).
> 2. *We live by faith in the unseen* (4:16-18). And
> 3. *We possess a confident faith in the future* (5:1-10).

The concluding word was twofold, first to the family, "This is our privilege, our hope, our fountain of courage! We are grateful!" And then a prayer, **"Lord, we hear your word"!**

Gebraucht das Gebet als einen Bohrer und
die Quellen lebendigen Wassers werden
aus dem Wort Gottes fließen!
Use prayer as a drill and
springs of living water will flow
from the word of God!

Further Reading on a Wesleyan Hermeneutic

Bassett, Paul M. 1978. "The Fundamentalist Leavening of the Holiness Movement, 1914-1940. The Church of the Nazarene: A Case Study." *Wesleyan Theological Journal* 13:65-85.

Dunning, H. Ray. 1988. Pages 55-76 in *Grace, Faith, and Holiness*. Kansas City: Beacon Hill Press of Kansas City.

Green, Joel B. 2004. "Is There a Contemporary Wesleyan Hermeneutic?" Pages 123-34 in *Reading the Bible in Wesleyan Ways: Some Constructive Proposals*. Edited by Barry L. Callen and Richard P. Thompson. Kansas City: Beacon Hill Press of Kansas City.

Peterson, Eugene H. 2006. *Eat This Book: A Conversation in the Art of Spiritual Reading*. Grand Rapids: Eerdmans.

Wall, Robert W. 2004a. "Facilitating Scripture's Future Role Among Wesleyans." Pages 107-20 in *Reading the Bible in Wesleyan Ways: Some Constructive Proposals*. Edited by Barry L. Callen and Richard P. Thompson. Kansas City: Beacon Hill Press of Kansas City.

_________. 2004b. "Toward a Wesleyan Hermeneutic of Understanding." Pages 39-55 in *Reading the Bible in Wesleyan Ways: Some Constructive Proposals*. Edited by Barry L. Callen and Richard P. Thompson. Kansas City: Beacon Hill Press of Kansas City.

Wiley, H. Orton. 1940. Pages 135-43 and 166-84 in *Christian Theology*, Vol. 1. Kansas City: Nazarene Publishing House.

Wiley, H. Orton, and Paul T. Culbertson. 1945. Pages 40-55 in *Introduction to Christian Theology*. Kansas City: Beacon Hill Press.

COMMENTARY

I. AN APOSTOLIC INTRODUCTION: 2 CORINTHIANS 1:1-11

Second Corinthians 1:1-11 comprise the first of the three major parts of the letter, setting the stage for the main body of the letter (1:12—13:10). The letter concludes with a brief conclusion (13:11-13). The words of Paul's introduction to this intensely personal letter to the church at Corinth in 1:1-11 reflect his central concern.

Even as Paul greets the church (1:1-2) and pauses to give praise to God (1:3-11), he touches the nerve that sensitizes the entire letter—the actuality, the integrity, and the character of his apostolic ministry in relation to the Corinthians. The composition of the salutation (vv 1-2), the exchange of the usual or expected thanksgiving for a benediction (vv 3-7), and a report of God's deliverance of Paul in Asia (vv 8-11) have in mind his strained relationship with the church at Corinth that Paul seeks to reconcile. Thus, the salutation (vv 1-2) already leads us into the substance of the letter as Paul defends his apostleship among them.

A. Paul Greets the Church (1:1-2)

BEHIND THE TEXT

Paul's salutation, **Paul . . . To the church . . . Grace and peace,** is rooted in Near Eastern epistolary traditions. He follows the form of ancient letter writing prevalent in his day. Paul, however, uses nouns rather than verbs, differing from Greek conventions. The form names the writer, those addressed, and follows with the greeting proper. A typical example of the letter opening appears in a letter recorded in Acts 23:26-30: "Claudius Lysias, To His Excellency, Governor Felix: Greetings" (v 26; see Acts 15:23).

Paul's letter to Corinth has an intensely personal tone. But, like all of his letters, it is a communal letter, intended for public use in a religious gathering. That is, his letters were intended to be read when the church met as a community. And not just once; they were to be read time and time again for the instruction and admonition of the congregation (Doty 1973, 24).

The apostle in his letters expands the form of the salutation used in the Greco-Roman period with a distinctly Christian accent (see Rom 1:1-7 and 1 Cor 1:1-3). The Christianized salutation appears throughout the larger Pauline corpus.

The blessing, **Grace and peace to you from God our Father and the Lord Jesus Christ,** is somewhat uniform (Rom 1:7; Gal 1:3; Eph 1:2; Phil 1:2; 2 Thess 1:2; 1 Tim 1:2; 2 Tim 1:2; Phlm 3). The only exceptions are Col 1:2, which has "God our Father" only, and 1 Thess 1:1, which uses simply the invocation, "Grace and peace to you."

IN THE TEXT

■ **1** The name **Paul** as the writer of the letter appears only once more in the letter at 10:1, "I appeal to you—I, Paul." Acts 13:9 refers to "Saul, who was also called Paul." **Paul** (*Paulos*), as used throughout the NT, is the Greek form of his original Hebrew name "Saul" (*Saulos*).

Born a Hebrew, Paul was from the tribe of Benjamin (Phil 3:5). He enjoyed the rare privilege of Roman citizenship (see Acts 16:37). This latter status gave him an elite standing in Greco-Roman society. Likewise, as a Pharisaic Diaspora Jew, Paul belonged to the elite of Jewish society (see Greathouse and Lyons 2008, 37-39).

Timothy (see Acts 16:1-3; 17:14-15; 18:5) **our brother** (*ho adelphos*) is named as the cosender, not necessarily coauthor, of the letter as in other Pauline correspondence (Phil 1:1; Col 1:1; 1 Thess 1:1; 2 Thess 1:1; Philemon). The presence of the definite article (*ho, **the***) may indicate Timothy's status as a missionary colleague. The Greek *adelphos* (**brother**) was used in Paul's time as a mutual designation by members of any select community. This usage was a figurative extension of its meaning as a male from the same "womb" (= *delphys*). In the early church, it replaced the term "disciple" (*mathētēs*), used in the Gospels to identify the followers of Jesus.

Other fellow workers like **Timothy,** also named as such, were Sosthenes (1 Cor 1:1) and Silas (1 Thess 1:1). Paul customarily mentioned cosenders in his salutations. He did this partly from courtesy (Phil 1:1; Col 1:1; 1 Thess 1:1; 2 Thess 1:1; Phlm 1). Timothy was a valued colleague, a Christian **brother,** both of himself and of the Corinthians (1 Thess 3:2). **Brother** for Paul designated a special relationship of respect, support, and care. (In Phlm 16, Paul refers to Onesimus "no longer as a slave, but better than a slave, as a dear brother.") Paul's sense of camaraderie with **Timothy** was so strong that he even calls him "my son [*teknon*] whom I love" (1 Cor 4:17; see Phil 2:22; 1 Tim 1:1; 2 Tim 1:2).

Timothy was the son of a Greek father and a Jewish mother. After meeting him during his ministry at Lystra, Paul made Timothy's Jewish status official by circumcising him (Acts 16:1-3). Timothy had worked with him in Corinth in the early days of the church's existence (Acts 18:5; 1 Cor 4:17; 16:10-11; 2 Cor 1:19). Now Paul reassures the Corinthians that Timothy shares fully in his pastoral concern for them. He identifies with the apostle in his teachings and admonitions. Timothy's ministry among them is validated, backed as it is by Paul's own apostleship.

Even as Paul greets the church **in Corinth** (vv 1-2; see 1 Cor 1:1-9; Phil 1:1-11) he plunges into the major issues of his letter. He takes his stance in the very first phrase, **an apostle of Christ Jesus by the will of God.** Paul's self-designation as an **apostle** (*apostolos*) is a pivotal term in the letter, both positively and negatively (11:13; Martin 1986, 2).

Here Paul focuses his readers' attention affirmatively on his office as **an apostle of Christ Jesus.** His role came **by** (*dia*) or ***through*** the efficient cause of **the will of God.** This is phrased exactly as in Col 1:1 (BDAG 2000, 224). The office of apostle, according to Mark 6:7, originated in the decision of Jesus to select twelve of his disciples for a special mission. These "he sent . . . out" (*apostellein*) as bearers of his own authority to preach and to heal (Matt 10:1-7; Mark 6:7-30; Luke 6:13; 9:1-6).

Jesus sent these apostles out as his representatives, indeed as himself: "He who listens to you listens to me; he who rejects you rejects me; but he who rejects me rejects him who sent me" (Luke 10:16). Apostles serve as trusted "ambassadors" (2 Cor 5:20) with the full authority of the one they represent. Their dignity and worth lay not in themselves but in the one who sent them (Barrett 1970, 13). In the background is the OT "sending" (Exod 3:10; Judg 6:8, 14; Isa 6:8; Jer 1:7; Ezek 2:3). The Jewish aphorism, "The one sent by a man is as the man himself" (Hafemann 2000, 44) reflects a Hellenistic-Jewish background for the Christian apostolate.

In the NT, there is a sense of identity between Jesus and those he commissions. They both do God's will and act in behalf of God. When they proclaim the gospel in Jesus' name they actualize his presence. Following the death and resurrection of Jesus, the apostolic office was renewed with the gift of the Spirit. As witnesses to Jesus and the resurrection, apostles totally relied upon the Holy Spirit first given at Pentecost (Acts 1:6-8, 15-26; 2:4, 32-33; 4:33; 5:29-32). Paul uses the term "apostle" to refer to the original Twelve and to his own sense of calling. He also extends the designation to include others of God's honored envoys—missionaries, "those sent on a mission," whose authority depended on the churches that sent them.

Paul, who feels a need to assert his credentials in **Corinth,** "was deeply, thoughtfully, and passionately convinced of his call to be an apostle" (Barrett 1970, 35). Paul knew himself to be **an apostle.** He fails to designate himself an apostle only in the prescripts of 1 Thess 1:1; Phil 1:1; and Phlm 1. But he uses the term five times more in 2 Corinthians (8:23; 11:5, 13; 12:11, 12). He grounds his claim to the title by virtue of his personal encounter with the risen Lord. He equates the appearance of the Lord to him with the appearances of the risen Lord to the other apostles (1 Cor 9:1-2; 15:5-8).

Paul was convinced that he had been directly commissioned by Jesus to bear witness to the Gentiles (Acts 9:1-9, 15-16; 22:12-21; 26:15-18, 22-23; 1 Cor 15:9; Gal 1:15-16). He describes himself as "set apart for the gospel of God" (Rom 1:1). He validates his apostleship by appeal to his role in founding the Christian community in Corinth: "you are the seal of my apostleship in the Lord" (1 Cor 9:2).

It appears that Paul viewed God's call to him as "a renewal of God's will for the salvation of the Gentiles, giving him a place in the history of salvation" in continuity with Isaiah and Jeremiah (see Gal 1:15-16 with Isa 49:1-6 and Jer 1:4-5; and Acts 26:12-18 with Jer 1:7-8; Isa 42:6-7, 16; and 61:1. Munck 1959, 24-27). Paul's apostleship has an eschatological (i.e., related to the end times) dimension; his ministry belongs to God's future kingdom action that was inaugurated by the life, death, and resurrection of Jesus.

Although Paul was not a witness of the earthly life of Jesus in exactly the same sense as the Twelve (Acts 1:21-22; Luke 1:2), he had entered wholeheartedly into the stream of early Christian tradition concerning Jesus (1 Cor 11:2,

23; 15:1-11). **Paul** took care to live in fellowship with the apostles of Jerusalem in order to protect the authenticity of the churches he founded (Gal 2:1-10). He became one with the original apostles in their shared commitment to the story of Jesus as the only foundation and content of his preaching.

Thus, Paul's apostleship was unique in character: "one abnormally born . . . the least of the apostles" (1 Cor 15:8-9). His apostolic sense of mission originated solely in **the will of God** (2 Cor 1:1; Eph 1:1; Col 1:1; 2 Tim 1:1; see Gal 1:1). Paul saw himself as a "chosen instrument" (Acts 9:15) whose call came by divine revelation uncorrupted by human initiative (see Gal 1:11-17).

If Paul's apostolic authority was questioned, he saw the issue as not about his own person but about the cause of God, who commissioned him "by Jesus Christ" (Gal 1:1). As **an apostle** Paul was the servant of his message—"the message [*logos*] of the cross" (1 Cor 1:18). So whenever Paul found it necessary to speak authoritatively to his churches, he stressed his apostolic authorization by the Lord as he began his letters. Paul's apostolate, as evidenced by his correspondence, consisted in a twofold task. His primary function was to found churches. His secondary responsibility was the pastoral care of these churches (Thrall 1994, 80).

Paul identifies those addressed in this letter as "the church of God in Corinth" (1 Cor 1:2; 12:13-27). This community of Christian believers was the localized manifestation of the body of Christ, the Universal Church. **Church** (*ekklēsia*) in its other eight appearances in 2 Corinthians is used in the plural (8:1, 18, 19, 23, 24; 11:8, 28; 12:13). This seems to indicate that the various local gatherings of believers somehow belong together. Here Paul combines the local (1 Thess 1:1) and the generic (1 Cor 10:32) uses of the word **church.** That it is **the church of God** separates it from the Greek political assemblies, which also called themselves *ekklēsia*. This modification of the standard, everyday use of the term, identifies the **church** as belonging uniquely to **God.** With **the church of God** Paul gives the church at Corinth the same title of honor that he gave the church at Jerusalem (1 Cor 15:9; Gal 1:13).

The letter address also mentions **all the saints** in the independent senatorial province of **Achaia.** This province was established in A.D. 27 under the Roman emperor Augustus (Harris 2005, 133). This Roman province comprised the whole of ancient Greece. Thus, Paul's address embraced believers not only in **Corinth,** in the port of Cenchrea, and in Athens, but probably also other believers living beyond the environs of these cities (see 9:2; 11:10; Rom 15:26; 1 Cor 16:5).

All the saints (*tois hagiois pasin*) or ***all the holy ones*** indicates simply "all Christians," the believers throughout or "in the whole" (*en holēi*) of the area. The NT never uses this expression to refer to a spiritual elite within the church. This NT meaning of **saints** (Acts 9:13; Heb 6:10) was particularly characteristic of Paul (Rom 8:27; 1 Cor 6:1). The traditional Pauline corpus contains thirty-six of the term's fifty-two NT occurrences. Interestingly, "saint"/"holy one" is never used in the singular to refer to an individual Christian. In the singular it refers only to the person of Jesus (Mark 1:24; Luke 1:35; 4:34; John 6:69; Acts 3:14; 4:27, 30; 1 John 2:20; Rev 3:7). Only together can believers be called **saints.** The **saints** are the church as called by God and set apart for his service, and thus they are God's ***holy ones.***

The Corinthian readers are not called **saints** because they have realized the full implications of the name. They are so designated simply because they authentically belong to Christ as a body of believers. In the NT the term designates those who belong to the new covenant community by virtue of the sacrificial death of Christ (Heb 13:12). They are a holy people only "in Christ Jesus" (1 Cor 1:2, 30; Phil 1:1). Their vocation is to belong wholly to God (Rom 1:7) and to serve him unreservedly (Rom 12:1-2). The effective agent of this life is the Holy Spirit (Rom 15:16; 1 Cor 3:16-17; 1 Pet 1:2). It is their possession by the indwelling presence of God that marks them as his people.

The Holy

The roots of the language of the holy are in the OT. Israel is first called a holy people as a nation set apart by divine election. That is, God called them, distinguishing them from the rest of the peoples of the ancient world. The second reason Israel is called a holy nation arises from their national life, whose mission is to be a distinctive witness to God (Martin 1986, 3).

The first emphasis of "the holy" is on purity of relationship with God in Christ. But essential to it is ethical action. The two go together in the actual lives of those who belong to God. This is because the ethical quality of their relationship to God must answer to the character of the God to whom they belong (1 Thess 2:10-12; 1 Pet 1:14-16). So in the view of the church, to be "saints," God's holy ones means nothing less than to be like Christ (1 John 2:6; 3:2-3).

■ **2** The greeting proper, **Grace and peace to you from God our Father and the Lord Jesus Christ** (v 2), is Paul's favorite. Paul exchanges the colorless Greek greeting *charein* (Acts 15:23)—"Hello"—for the rich *charis*—**grace.** He unites this allusion to God's gracious initiative in Christ (see 2 Cor 8:9) with **peace,** the customary Jewish greeting (see 2 Sam 18:28). Paul immerses both traditional greetings in Jesus Christ (Martin 1986, 4; Harris 2005, 135).

In the Greek OT, the LXX, **peace** (*eirēnē*), translates *shalom* (Dan 4:1, "May your peace abound," NASB). The basic sense of the Hebrew term is comprehensive well-being, seen as a gift of God. Paul uses the Greek equivalent to describe the spiritual well-being of believers (see Rom 5:1-2; Phil 4:7).

Paul clearly indicates the Christian overtones of his twofold greeting by stressing the singular origin as **God our Father and the Lord Jesus Christ.** It is significant that Paul does not repeat the preposition **from** (*apo*). Its omission indicates that **God our Father and the Lord Jesus Christ** jointly form a single source of divine grace and peace (Harris 2005, 136).

The phrase **our Father** may allude to the Lord's Prayer (Matt 6:9). The title **Lord** (*kyrios*) frequently identifies Jesus in the letters of Paul. Importantly, it is the word consistently used in the LXX as the equivalent for the covenant name of Israel's God, Yahweh.

FROM THE TEXT

The opening verses of the letter assume the form of a greeting and certainly function as such. In an encouraging manner, *Paul loads his "Hello" to the church with spiritual freight.* With a play on words, the apostle has replaced the everyday greeting (*charein*) of Greek culture with the most magnificent of all Christian words, "grace" (*charis*). To top it off, from his Hebrew culture he adds the greeting "peace," a wish for spiritual blessing.

In our current competitive, "big ego" culture, with its partisan bickering and destructive enmity, Christians are graced with the ability to "bless" in the most informal and casual of human contacts. Because of who we are—people who live in obedience to the indwelling Spirit of Christ—our "Hello, how are you?" need not be a merely superficial courtesy. We can bring with it the full meaning of the gospel, even the presence of Christ! This is our privilege. Let us exploit it in the spirit of prayer even as we sign the credit slip at the checkout counter.

In the content of Paul's greeting, he reveals to us authentic insights into the essential character of (1) *God's messenger,* (2) *God's people,* and (3) *God's message.*

First, *we are God's messengers.* Although we are not first-century apostles, we, too, by our Christian confession are "sent" into the culture of our time as the incarnated presence of the risen Christ. By the grace of God and the gift of the Holy Spirit, our presence becomes *his* presence! This is "the will God" for us, by God's intention our lives are "purpose driven." As called by God, we are not self-made men and women. Here is both the starting point and the goal of our very existence, a divine calling that holds us steady through the beguiling soft breezes and oppressive hard winds of life. We do possess authority, but one not inherently ours. It is the Holy Spirit at work in and through our lives bearing witness to Jesus (John 16:14-15; 20:21-23).

Second, *we belong to God's people.* We are bound together with the folk in Corinth and beyond as people of the same God (1 Cor 8:6). As a family first before we are an institution, we belong to each other. As my longtime colleague Reuben Welch put it in his popular 1982 book on 1 John, *We Really Do Need Each Other!*

As those who live under one Lord (Eph 4:4-6), our differences do not divide us. The course of centuries, the geography that puts great distances between us, the diversity of cultures, our racial peculiarities, and even our treasured denominations dare not essentially divide us. As people of the same unchanging God, we are united, local, universal, and historical. Or, as the Nicene Creed puts it, we are "one holy catholic and apostolic church."

Simply because we belong to this holy God, we are a holy people "in Christ." We are "saints," as Paul calls us. We are literally "the holy ones." This is not because each of us as individuals has fully grown up into Christ. But when we are all added up together, we exhibit "the whole measure of the fullness of Christ" (Eph 4:13) to all who have eyes to see! (Ps 135:16; Isa 6:10).

Third, *we possess God's message.* Paul's greeting, his prayerful wish for his readers, sums up the Christian message with two of the grandest terms in all of Scripture. When we translate **grace** and **peace** into theology, they speak to us of our "justification" and our "sanctification."

Grace speaks of our reconciliation to God "in Christ." It underlies the whole of our Christian existence. **Peace** holds out the promise of the wholeness that is the goal of reconciliation. Together they comprehend life's ultimate purpose and fulfillment. "Grace," wrote James Denney, "is the first and last word of the Gospel, and peace—perfect spiritual soundness—is the finished work of grace in the soul" (1943, 5:721; see Col 3:15).

B. Paul Praises God for His Comfort (1:3-11)

BEHIND THE TEXT

According to the pattern of the Hellenistic letter, a thanksgiving or prayer to a deity usually follows the opening salutation. Here in vv 3-11 the thanksgiving takes the form of a blessing (v 3, *eulogētos ho Theos*). Thus, Paul begins: **Praise be to the God** or "Blessed be the God" (NRSV).

Berakah Benedictions

The introductory words and structure differ from the usual thanksgiving. Some interpreters call it a benediction, or a doxology, referring more strictly to vv 3-7. A more precise suggestion is the designation of a "congratulatory benediction." Here speakers praise God and congratulate the recipient of the gift (as in Exod 18:10; McCant 1999, 29-30). Another designation, stressing its background, calls it "a synagogue benediction." An example is "Blessed art thou, O Lord our God and God of our fathers, God of Abraham, God of Isaac, and God of Jacob" (Barnett 1997, 67).

Paul's *berakah/eulogētos* language and the content is influenced by OT worship and Jewish liturgy (O'Brien 1977, 11, 233-38). Perhaps, this is due to the expectation that the letters would be read in the Christian congregation assembled for worship (Martin 1986, 7). But here the Jewish *berakah* is obviously Christianized.

Comparing Paul's benediction with contemporary Greek rhetorical discourses, it corresponds in form and function to the introduction, the *exordium*. In forensic (legal/judicial) rhetoric, this addresses the judge, not the spectators in the audience or even the jury. Similarly here, the apostle addresses God. He is the true judge of Paul's apostolic conduct, not the Corinthians. Of course, Paul must ultimately convince the jury as well, here the Corinthian Christians (Witherington 1995, 356).

Although it differs from them substantially, Paul's blessing or *berakah* in 2 Corinthians begins with language identical to the "blessings" in Eph 1:3-11 and 1 Pet 1:3-12: **Praise be to [*blessed be*] the God and Father of our Lord Jesus Christ.** Customarily, in Paul's letters a thanksgiving appears instead of the blessing (Rom 1:8-15; 1 Cor 1:4-9; Phil 1:3-11; 1 Thess 1:2-10; Col 1:3-11).

The typical thanksgivings in Paul's letter openings serve in several ways. They introduce epistolary (letter) and pastoral/apostolic concerns. They offer didactic (instructive) and paraenetic (directive) guidance. They set the tone and themes of what is to follow (O'Brien 1977, 13-15, 262-63). Galatians is unique, having neither a thanksgiving nor a blessing following the salutation.

IN THE TEXT

Paul's carefully crafted literary opening (1) introduces the main topic of this letter to the church at Corinth, (2) expresses the letter's controlling perspective, and (3) appeals to the readers to share Paul's convictions. It is far more than a mere "spontaneous outburst of unreflected piety" (Hafemann 2000, 59).

The blessing/*berakah* was more suited than a thanksgiving to Paul's intentions in his introduction. It was more expressive of the profound effect his apostolic troubles had on him and of the intensely personal nature of the letter (O'Brien 1977, 257). There is a significant difference between Paul's earlier thanksgiving in 1 Corinthians (1:4-9) and the blessing here. In 2 Corinthians, when Paul uses **Praise be to [*eulogētos*] the God,** he includes what God has done for him within the scope of God's blessing.

In Paul's other thanksgiving sections (which begin with "I/We thank God . . ." [*eucharistō/eucharistoumen*]), he offers thanks for God's work in the lives of his addressees (O'Brien 1977, 239). In 1 Corinthians Paul speaks of the Corinthians' rich experience of the grace of God in Christ Jesus. But here his thoughts flow from a perilous personal experience in Asia (vv 8-11) to the role of the **troubles** or ***affliction*** (*thlipsei*) he endured during his ministry to them as an apostle (vv 3-11).

The unifying theme of 2 Cor 1—9 is launched in the *berakah*/blessing. Many of the key terms appearing here recur with varying nuances throughout these chapters.

The NIV translates the Greek cognates *thlipsis* and *thlibō* throughout this passage as **troubles, trouble, distressed,** and **hardships.** Paul uses these words thirty-one times (Rom 2:9; 5:3; 8:35; 12:12; 1 Cor 7:28; 2 Cor 1:4, 6, 8; 2:4; 4:8, 17; 6:4; 7:4, 5; 8:2, 13; Eph 3:13; Phil 1:17; 4:14; Col 1:24; 1 Thess 1:6; 3:3, 4, 7; 2 Thess 1:4, 6, 7; 1 Tim 5:10)—more than all other NT authors combined (twenty-four times).

This word group refers to any kind of trouble that inflicts distress, oppression, affliction, or tribulation (BDAG 2000, 457). Paul's praise focuses on what God has accomplished for him and through him via his **troubles.** The apostle's words evidence the depth of his devotion to the Corinthians. But they also suggest the place of suffering in the lives of genuine apostles of Christ.

In his opening benediction, Paul praises God as the source of **comfort** in the midst of his suffering. The cognates *paraklēsis* and *parakaleō* (**comfort**) appear here twelve times and eighteen times subsequently in the letter (2:7, 8; 5:20; 6:1; 7:4, 6 [2x], 7 [2x], 13 [2x]; 8:4, 6, 17; 9:5; 10:1; 12:18; 13:11). They occur forty-four times in Paul's other letters and sixty-four times elsewhere in the NT.

1. Comfort Through Christ (1:3-7)

In vv 3-7 Paul's theme is "comfort through Christ." Typical of Paul (see Rom 15:1-7; 1 Cor 1:18-31; 4:9-10; Phil 2:5-11), **comfort** is used to render *parakaleō* and *paraklēsis*. In vv 3-7 the two words are used ten times (vv 3, 4 [4x], 5, 6 [3x], and 7). Inherent in the verb is the idea of calling for help or encouraging (BDAG 2000, 764-65; the cognate noun *paraklētos* in John 14:16, 26; 15:26; 16:7; and 1 John 2:1 is variously translated "Comforter" [KJV], "Helper" [NASB], "Counselor" [NIV], and "Advocate" [NRSV]).

Particularly characteristic of this letter (4:7-12; 6:4-10; 7:5-7; 11:30; 12:5-10; 13:2-9) is the interchange of opposite experiences in Christ. Here the interchange of **comfort** and **trouble** permeates Paul's words of praise. Linking the two opposites is **the sufferings of Christ** (v 5). Paul describes his own sufferings as an apostle in relation to those of Jesus. He claims that **the sufferings of Christ flow over into our lives** or "are abundant for us" (v 5 NRSV). Christ was the greatest of sufferers. Now Paul is "overwhelmed by the same stream" as his Lord. The suffering Christ functions here as the middle term between Paul's ministry and **the God of all comfort** (Shillington 1998, 36).

■ **3** The noun **praise** (*eulogētos*) has no accompanying verb. This raises the question: Is Paul's blessing a wish that God might be praised or an affirmation that God is worthy of praise? Either way, it "amounts to praise or thanksgiving" (Harris 2005, 141). Paul praises **the God and Father of our Lord Jesus Christ** as the **Father of compassion** or "mercies" (NRSV; Ps 103:13; Rom 12:1) **and the God of all comfort.** Paul emphasizes this new understanding by an inverted repetition (*chiasmus* in the Greek structure) of **God** and **Father** as at the heart of his concept of deity.

■ **4 The Father of compassion** as **the God of all comfort,** constantly and predictably (indicated by the Greek present tense) **comforts** Paul. This enables him to **comfort** others (v 4). This God is **the God and Father** of Christ. His **sufferings . . . flow over into our lives** (v 5). Because they are linked by a single article, **the** (*ho Theos kai patēr*), the **Father** is identical with **the God** of **our Lord Jesus Christ** (v 3).

Since Jesus became as genuinely human as we are (John 1:14; Heb 2:14), he depended entirely upon God for spiritual strength and direction (Mark 15:34; John 20:17; Heb 10:7). **Jesus Christ** as the divine Son lived in perfect obedience to **God** the **Father** (see John 5:30). The key to Paul's perspective is the Son of God's actual obedience. He shares our common humanity even to the acceptance of suffering and death for all humanity (Phil 2:8; Heb 5:8).

■ **5** Paul's **troubles** or ***afflictions*** are so vitally related to **the sufferings of Christ** that **also through Christ** Paul's **comfort overflows** to the Corinthians. Paul discerns a divinely ordered correspondence "between the intensity of his suffering and the adequacy of God's comfort" (Harris 2005, 145). Both Paul's experiences of being **distressed** and of being **comforted** are for the sake of the Corinthians (4:15; 12:15).

■ **6-7** The Corinthians, in turn, are granted patience to endure **the same sufferings** Paul **suffers** (v 6). Thus, they are ***partners*** (*koinōnoi* occurs once in v 7 but is represented twice by **share in**) in **sufferings.** They are ***fellow participants*** with Paul in pain. They **share in** a common bond, rooted in these **same sufferings.**

Paul's **hope for** them **is firm.** Just as they **share in** the **sufferings** that are his lot as an apostle of Christ, he is confident that they will be enabled to **share in** his **comfort** (v 7). The two go together. Their comfort—which encourages, strengthens, and spiritually renews them—finds its source in God through **the sufferings of Christ** (vv 4-5). Comfort is mediated to them through the apostolic ministry of Paul, "the middle man" (Harris 2005, 144).

FROM THE TEXT

At the heart of Paul's understanding of the gospel and its ministry vibrates "A Theology of the Cross." We see it in these verses for the first time, but it is a theology that is penetratingly alive throughout the letter (see 1:5 and 13:4).

Paul finds the source of mutual comfort in the character of God as revealed in Jesus Christ. For Paul the sufferings of the church—apostle and people—are united with **the sufferings of Christ.** But upon what theological basis can Paul make this identification? What precisely does he mean by it?

Paul's identification of **the sufferings of Christ** and the church is more than just similar or even "for Christ's sake." Far more deeply, this identification arises out of the Christian's redemptive participation in the life and death of Christ (Rom 6:5). For Paul, this mutual participation is at the heart of being "in Christ."

Messianic afflictions (Mark 13:19, 24) featured prominently in the earthly ministry of Jesus culminating in the cross. Paul linked these with the life of the Christian in Rom 8:17-18. The sufferings of Christians can partake of Christ's sufferings because they are united with Christ in both his death and life (Rom 5:10). The atoning sacrifice of Christ, although complete in the sense of sufficiency for salvation, continues in kind in the ongoing mission of the church to the world (Col 1:24).

Paul identified his troubles with **the sufferings of Christ.** His sufferings in their behalf mediated the comfort of the resurrection to the Corinthians. Paul considered his afflictions as an apostle a divinely ordained vehicle for releasing God's presence in the lives of his people. He saw the connection between suffering and comfort as corresponding to the earthly career of Jesus. After suffering on the cross, he rose from the dead releasing his own resurrection life into the life of the church.

Paul understood his participation in the afflictions/tribulations of this age as messianic sufferings. Sharing in Christ's suffering is an indispensable part of the ongoing life of the church (Acts 14:22; Rom 8:17-18; Phil 1:29-30).

Even discipleship during Jesus' lifetime led to the disciples' sharing in his life and ministry, in his Servant destiny. By divine necessity, Jesus' own way led to rejection, suffering, and death, and only then to glory. So must it be for his disciples (see Matt 16:21; Mark 8:31-38; 10:35-45). Paul appears to have found in the Suffering Servant songs of Isaiah the pattern for his own ministry (compare Phil 2:8 with Isa 49:4; Rom 10:15 with Isa 52:7 and 53:1; 2 Cor 5:20 with Isa 52:7; Acts 26:12-18 with Isa 41:1-16).

Paul believes that most specifically his own afflictions were a necessary part of God's redeeming activity. He considered such sufferings an integral part of Christian service in general and an essential element of his apostolic ministry in particular (Acts 9:15-16). Paul writes to the Colossians that through his own bodily afflictions he is "completing what is lacking in Christ's afflictions for the sake of his body, that is, the church" (Col 1:24 NRSV). Thus, he views his own sufferings as a real participation in the sufferings of Christ. This is because they are endured both for Christ's sake and in vital fellowship with him. The Spirit of Christ is the life principle of Paul's service for Christ, crucified and risen.

In Phil 3:10-11, participating in Christ's suffering is an essential part of the perfecting path that leads to the resurrection from the dead. These sufferings, including the actual afflictions of Paul's life, comprehend the lifelong state of death ("becoming like him in his death" [Phil 3:10; see 4:11-12; Rom 8:36]), inaugurated through the power of the Spirit.

Thus, through the bond of the spirit of the resurrection, Paul can call his sufferings **the sufferings of Christ.** At the heart of the sharing in these sufferings lies the experience of union with Christ in his death and resurrection. In Denney's words, "to partake in His sufferings is to be united to *Him;* and to be united to Him is to partake of His *life*" (1943, 5:722).

Paul's intimacy with his Lord was so close that he regarded his apostolic career as an inner participation in the redemptive ministry of Christ. Paul's comfort and the comfort of the Corinthians is the presence of Christ in the heart through his Spirit. His perception of the unseen and the eternal gave him a conviction of divine love that could not be shaken (Denney 1943, 5:723).

IN THE TEXT

2. Affliction and Deliverance (1:8-11)

■ **8** In vv 8-11, Paul includes an autobiographical account of his affliction and deliverance experienced **in the province of Asia.** The opening idiomatic expression, **We do not want you to be uninformed,** functions rhetorically as a disclosure formula. Such expressions are often used in Paul to signal the introduction of a new thought (see 8:1; Rom 1:13; 11:25; 1 Cor 10:1; 1 Thess 4:13; Phil 1:12). Some scholars think it marks the beginning of a new section.

But here, its connection with what has gone before in vv 3-7, indicates that Paul uses it to call attention to a second reason for praising God. This is demonstrated by the Greek conjunction *gar* (***For,*** left untranslated in the NIV). It begins the sentence: ***For we do not want you to be ignorant*** ("unaware," NASB). This formulation indicates the apostle's intention that his afflictions will be a major topic in his defense to follow (McCant 1999, 31). The way Paul shapes the narrative of his ministry forms a picture of himself designed to win the sympathy of his audience. He prepares for the argument to follow (Shillington 1998, 40), appealing to the rhetorical argument of *pathos* (emotion).

As the blessing continues, Paul refers to an incident of extreme personal peril that occurred in the Roman **province of Asia.** This experience of affliction and deliverance enabled Paul to encourage the Corinthians in the manner that he did (vv 3-7). He reports it in the first person plural (we/our/us) in vv 8-10. As he often does in 2 Corinthians, Paul is probably using the editorial first person plural when he has in mind the first person singular (I/my/me). Here it is possible, however, that at least Timothy (1:1) may be included as well (see the commentary on 1:18).

The reference to **hardships** [*thlipseōs*] **suffered in the province of Asia** is obscure both as to place and kind. Paul relates it primarily as an occasion of divine deliverance for which he can testify to the mercies of God.

Paul does not say where in Asia he had this experience. Some interpreters speculate that Paul alludes to the mob violence in Ephesus described in Acts 19:23-41. Harris argues for Troas (see Acts 16:8, 11; 20:5; 2 Cor 2:12) as the place, thus eliminating the discrepancies between the two accounts (2005, 154). But the strength of his conjecture depends entirely on the argument from silence.

Many suggestions have been made as to the nature of Paul's ***affliction.*** The two most likely are either an unknown occasion of extreme external physical danger or a severe life-threatening, perhaps recurring, bodily illness (see 11:23-29). Probability favors the latter (Harris 2005, 154, 164-82). We will consider its possible relation to Paul's thorn in the flesh (12:7) later. Paul's purpose, however, in mentioning it was not to specify the precise kind of mortal peril he faced but its impact in relation to his ministry as an apostle to the Corinthians.

The **hardships** were so great, writes Paul, that **we were under great pressure, far beyond our ability to endure.** He writes literally, "we were burdened excessively, beyond our strength" (NASB). Paul claimed to have **despaired even of life.** That is, he had surrendered even the prospect of physical survival. The verb Paul uses for his despair (*exaporeō*) occurs only here and in 4:8 in the NT. It appears once in the LXX of Ps 88:15 in the psalmist's lament for a deep psychological loss (BDAG 2000, 345; see 2 Cor 7:5-7).

■ **9** As far as Paul could see, like Isaac of old (Heb 11:17-19), he had received **the sentence of death.** Paul dramatically depicts his feelings, **in our hearts we felt,** literally, ***within ourselves*** [*en heautois*] ***we had the sentence of death.*** The aorist (*eschēkamen*) may have a perfective force here: ***We have received and still possess*** this death sentence.

Some interpreters take the term **sentence** (*apokrima*) as signifying a judicial decree. But there are no contemporary instances of *apokrima* (a *hapax legomenon* [occurring once] in biblical Greek) referring to the results of a legal proceeding (Harris 2005, 155). In secular Greek *apokrima* refers rather to a verdict or decision made in response to a petition by an ambassador (Witherington 1995, 361). Paul's **sentence of death,** when viewed as an answer that Paul had received from a petition he had made to God, fits Paul's situation. Paul's prayer for deliverance was both answered and unanswered as the tense of *eschēkamen* appears to indicate. The meaning of Paul's "answer of death" may be unclear, but its purpose is not (Garland 1999, 79).

It is clear that the divine purpose (*hina*, **that**) was not to kill Paul. It was rather that Paul learn from his deep despair to trust God more fully and rely less on himself. He must have needed such a new understanding of himself. For this lesson required Paul first to be convinced of his own helplessness. He learned, like Abraham (Rom 4:17), to rely completely **on God, who raises the dead.** This permanent characteristic of God, common in Jewish liturgy, strikes a chord that reverberates throughout the entire letter underlying all that Paul writes (2 Cor 2:13-14; 4:7-12, 16; 12:7-10; 13:4).

■ **10-11** In v 10 Paul reflects on the further implications of his hard-learned lesson. God had **delivered** Paul in Asia **from such a deadly peril.** And he had **set** his **hope** on this God for future deliverance. The God who raised Jesus from the dead (v 9; see Rom 1:4; 8:11; 1 Cor 15; Eph 1:19-20) was also able to spare from death.

Emphatically, Paul defines the content of his hope: God **will . . . deliver us.** He does not presume that he will never die. But he is convinced that God

will continue to deliver [him]**, as** [the Corinthians] **help** [him] **by** [their] **prayers** (vv 10-11). Pelagius (359/354-420/425) remarked on this passage: "Death itself teaches us that all human help is inadequate and that our only hope is to rely on him who can raise us from the dead" (ACCS NT 7:197).

In v 11 Paul concludes his benedictory blessing with thanksgiving and praise to God, returning to the mood of v 3. The goal of his ministry is thanksgiving and praise to God. The apostle's hope for continuing divine deliverance is intimately related to human intercession.

Paul employs the characteristics of an introductory thanksgiving form in a remarkable way. The Corinthians now, instead of Paul, are the ones who will give thanks (O'Brien 1977, 250-51). Thus, involved in the **gracious favor** (*charisma*) of God's deliverance are the intercessory **prayers** of the Corinthians for Paul. He asks that they continue to intercede in his behalf that **many will give thanks on our behalf.**

Paul takes for granted the Corinthians' ongoing spiritual involvement in his ministry. The expression translated **many** is literally "many faces" ("many persons," NASB; see 4:15; 9:11-12). Although it is God who freely delivers, Paul values highly the intercessory prayers of other Christians. The function of such prayers is twofold. They emphasize the dependence of the Christian and the sovereignty of God. Both express and promote the fellowship of the saints.

Paul has now fulfilled the fourfold purpose of his opening blessing—the epistolary, pastoral, didactic, and paraenetic functions of the literary form (O'Brien 1977, 261-63). Paul (1) has made it clear that the comfort of God in the midst of affliction is a main theme of the letter. He (2) has demonstrated his care for the church. He (3) has stated the thesis that paradoxically his suffering is the means by which God's comfort is mediated to others, indeed legitimizing his apostleship. Therefore, Paul (4) appeals to the Corinthians to join him in thanking God for his suffering and deliverance by the God who raises the dead (Hafemann 2000, 65).

FROM THE TEXT

In his opening blessing (vv 3-11) Paul graces us with an encouraging witness springing from his own ministry: **the God and Father of our Lord Jesus Christ** (v 3) is the God **who comforts us** (v 4) and the **God, who raises the dead** (v 9). Both affirmations contain a timeless present participle and express permanent attributes of God. Together they stagger human thought.

Empowering to the Christian is Paul's insight that the connection between the two aspects of God's character is **the sufferings of Christ,** a connection so real and so significant for the apostle that he proclaims to the Corinthians that the "Savior claims as his own the sufferings which the dynamic presence of his Spirit occasions in his members" (Ahern 1960, 32). This news is so good that our minds cannot fully grasp its implications for our faith. As one many decades ago has noted, Paul sets our afflictions before us as a school of *sympathy* (v 4), of *encouragement* (v 5), and of *hope* (v 10, Plummer 1915, 19).

What the apostle witnesses to is now possible for our own lives and ministries. Paul opens to us a view of our afflictions or **troubles** that grants us (1) *a profound understanding of God* (vv 3-5, 8-10), (2) *an effective power to comfort others* (vv 4-7), and (3) *an enticing call to intercessory prayer* (v 11).

First, *we understand who* ***the Father of compassion and the God of all comfort*** *is primarily from the perspective of the reality of the cross and resurrection of Jesus in our lives.* What God has done for us redemptively in Christ now fully characterizes us as Christians. This is who we are "in Christ."

Not only have the cross and resurrection become the very essence of our relation to God, but they also permeate the quality of our living. They are to determine the manner of our personal relationships and our ministry to others; they are cruciform in character. As we serve, we identify by faith with the cross in order that resurrection life might be released in the lives of others. As Paul comments later in the letter, "so then, death is at work in us, but life is at work in you" (4:12). Therefore, all that we endure in life for Christ and his ministry can be seen in the light of the faith that "the sufferings of Christ are ours" (1:5 NASB). We are "in Christ." We are with him in all that he experienced as the incarnate Son of the Father on our behalf—in the revelation of God himself to us in Christ. Thus, our **troubles,** what we bear in relation to family and friends and in service to others, can be an occasion for the power of the resurrection in their lives.

Second, *we are enabled to help others in their* ***troubles*** *with a power that is not of ourselves.* This **comfort** "is more than consolation in sorrow or trial; it includes encouragement, and implies the divine gift of strength to meet and master life's crises" (Filson 1953, 280). We are able to sympathize with others out of our common experience. But more importantly, the Holy Spirit is able to work through us to bring encouragement to others. **Just as the sufferings of Christ flow over into our lives, so also through Christ our comfort overflows** to those who are likewise suffering. We have released the power of the resurrection into their lives. They are enabled to rely not on themselves, as is our natural tendency, **but on God, who raises the dead.** As Ogilvie reminds us:

> there is a joy to be experienced when we care deeply about people and their needs. This joy comes when we let our hearts mourn over the things which bring grief to the heart of God. When we are involved with God in caring for people, we are also recipients of God's comfort. (Ogilvie 1981, reading for June 13)

Third, *we are invited into the spiritual reality and the fellowship of intercessory prayer.* Intercessory prayer *does* make a difference: **you help us by your prayers. . . . the gracious favor granted us in answer to the prayers of many.** Paul was fully convinced of the power of the intercessory prayer of others in his life: **He has delivered us.**

We are called to share this confidence in relation to our lives and the needs of others. Concretely, it *helps* to pray. At the same time, significantly, intercessory prayer is a fellowship, those for whom we pray and those who pray for us are by this means with us and we with them. Prayer means we need never be alone, not only in relation to God, but also in relation to others, whatever our physical circumstances.

Regardless of distance and time, we are never separated from a loved one or friend. Space and time have no power over the things of the spirit: Muhammad said that "everyone is with the one they love." We can visit them every day! Intercessory prayer means they still belong to us, and we to them. We can "attend" to them; we can "hold" them in our prayers. Our "care" for them springs from the presence of Christ within us. As I once heard the Carmelite sisters put it, through our prayers we bring the world into the monastery.

In the light of these privileges "in Christ," our **troubles** undergone in relation to others in all spheres of our lives are (1) *a school of sympathy* because we are able to understand, feel, and enter into the sufferings of others; (2) *a school of encouragement* because we are present with them in the same kind of experiences that we can identify as **the sufferings of Christ;** and (3) *a school of hope* because hope is contagious in that the Holy Spirit, the Spirit of the resurrection of Christ, is at work in all of our lives, in them and in us!

My editor and friend George Lyons suggests a fourth effect of the witness of Paul for our lives and ministry: Paul opens to us a view of our afflictions that grants (4) *a new understanding of ourselves.*

It is noteworthy how Paul claims to have acquired a new understanding of himself in this passage. He had been a Christian for nearly twenty years when he experienced the despair he describes here. Nevertheless, he says he learned from this anew not to rely any longer on himself.

Is there any other way to learn to rely on God completely? Must we learn to despair of inordinate self-confidence by coming again and again to the limits of our own resources? So why do we regard failure, defeat, and disappointment as enemies? How else will we learn to swallow our pride and acknowledge our humanity, especially our mortality? How are we to realize that unlike God we have limits?

Physical illness, unjust persecution, the threat of death, misunderstanding, the impending failure of his work in Corinth—all of these were among the causes that led to the breaking down of a man. Yet, if anyone had reason for confidence in himself, it was Paul (Phil 3:4; 2 Cor 11:22-23; Acts 14:22; Barrett 1973, 66).

Paul understood his painful experience as instructive. It taught him not to rely on himself but to rely on God (v 9). As James Denney observed over a century ago (1894), it is natural "for us to trust in ourselves. It is so natural, and so confirmed by the habits of a lifetime, that no ordinary difficulties or perplexities avail to break us of it" (1943, 5:724).

The good news of the gospel is not that we have been set free by Christ to love ourselves, but that we have been set free from obsession with ourselves. But sooner or later, we must learn, often the hard way, to acknowledge our utter dependence on God. There comes a tremendous sense of relief with the discovery that the security and acceptance we were struggling to earn has been given to us freely by the One whose love and acceptance matter most!

Paul's revised understanding of himself certainly would have contributed to his appreciation of his own sufferings as partnership in Christ's sufferings. Paul was no morbid masochist seeking out suffering wherever he could find it (see 1 Thess 4:11-12). Not all our sufferings are a sharing in the suffering of Christ, that is, the sufferings that come to us because we are partners with him in his mission in the world. Some suffering is the result, not of our sanctity, but of our stupidity, the natural consequence of our wrong decisions and sinful actions.

Paul, however, came to interpret his experiences of persecution and the senseless and undeserved pain that life in a fallen world sometimes brings as participation with Christ in the cross. He saw that the death of Christ in God's saving action led to the resurrection of Christ.

Through this Paul learned that God's comfort depended on the acceptance of suffering. He gained a new appreciation of the God of all comfort. The God from whom all blessings flow did not spare his Son. Nor will he spare us from death. Yet, he is the God who raises the dead, the God on whom we have set our hope (vv 9-10).

Paul gained from his near-death experience a new ability to comfort those who are in affliction. He comforted others, not through his strong personality, but through the comfort with which he himself was comforted by God (v 4).

What Paul learned from his personal cross and the experience of God's comfort was to be shared with others: "If we are distressed, it is for your comfort and salvation; if we are comforted, it is for your comfort" (v 6). The benefit from his experience of despair went beyond himself. Again, in Denney's apt words,

> We are selfish, and instinctively regard ourselves as the centre of all providences; we naturally seek to explain everything by its bearing on ourselves alone. But God has not made us for selfishness and isolation, and some mysteries would be cleared up if we had love enough to see the ties by which our [lives are] indissolubly linked to others. (1943, 5:723)

Paul "gained a new power at a great price" (Denny 1943, 5:723). He learned that sharing our lives with others is what it means to serve, and service is what it means to be a Christian.

II. AN APOSTOLIC MINISTRY: 2 CORINTHIANS 1:12—7:16

Paul opens this first part of the main body of the letter with a brief defense of his conduct in relation to the Corinthian church (1:12—2:17). This moves him to discuss at length the character of his apostolic ministry (3:1—6:10). A few words about his attitude toward the church and his relationship to them concludes the section (6:11—7:16). Paul's aim in this first part is to restore his warm relations with the church caused in part by a harsh letter he sent in place of an expected visit.

A. Paul Reveals His Intentions (1:12—2:13)

Paul begins the body of the letter with a narrative of past events. Paul's conduct in regard to his travel plans and the situation surrounding the repentant offender has come under critical scrutiny by many in the Corinthian church. In question is not only his integrity as a person but also the authenticity of his apostolic calling. Thus Paul's first concern in this portion of the letter as he clarifies his motives and explains his conduct to the Corinthians is to assure them that **the holiness and sincerity that are from God** has characterized his **relations** with them. He has been sincere in intention and his behavior has been consistent with **God's grace** (1:12-14). Paul was neither simply fickle nor duplicitous. The reason that he did not come as planned (1:15-22) was out of consideration for them (1:23—2:4) and for the one whom they are to forgive and restore to fellowship (2:5-11). He did, in fact, come as far as Macedonia (2:12-13). Paul seeks, second, throughout his defense to demonstrate his pastoral concern and fatherly love for the Corinthians.

It will help here to sketch briefly our view (see Introduction) of the contacts between Paul and the Corinthians reflected in this passage. After sending the letter we call 1 Corinthians from Ephesus (1 Cor 16:8), word came to Paul there that the situation in the Corinthian church had deteriorated in relation to him. To address this, Paul returned to Corinth. During this second, "painful visit" (2:1) he endured a personal attack by someone in the church (2:5-11). No one in the church apparently took Paul's side at the time (10:1, 10-11; 13:2). He then returned to Ephesus (for a discussion of the historical issues involved, see Harris 2005, 54-64).

From there he sent Titus to Corinth with a sorrowful letter (2:4; 7:6-9). After Titus's departure, Paul's troubled concern would not allow him to continue his work, so he proceeded to Troas (2:12) and on to Macedonia (2:13; 7:5) to anxiously await the return of Titus with a report of its reception. The news was encouraging. In response to this report, Paul began the letter we call 2 Corinthians.

Apparently, before the "painful visit," Paul had intended to visit the Corinthians twice, both going to and coming from Macedonia (1:15-16). But the turn of events during the visit and Paul's humiliating departure from Corinth called for a change of plans. The present passage is Paul's attempt to explain why he changed plans. As he writes 2 Corinthians, Paul is planning a third visit to Corinth (13:1, 21).

BEHIND THE TEXT

Rhetorically, 1:12—2:13 with its apparent "defensive" mood belongs to the larger genre of forensic or judicial rhetoric whose setting is the law court and is focused on the past. Chapters 1—7 and 10—13 partake of this genre.

Our specific text is designed to explain some of the background facts that occasioned the letter and here climaxes with a thanksgiving and transition (Witherington 1995, 333-36). Paul, of course, has adapted the rhetorical form to his particular needs in relation to the Corinthians.

IN THE TEXT

1. The Sincerity of His Correspondence (1:12-14)

■ **12** Verses 12-14 function as a transition to what follows (1:16—2:17) as Paul begins to defend himself against criticism and hopes for an improved relationship between himself and the church. Martin designates them an *apologia* (1986, 19).

Now translates the Greek conjunction *gar*, "for" (NASB) or "you see," is used as a marker of clarification (BDAG 2000, 189). In the previous verse (1:11), Paul had asked for the Corinthians' help in the form of prayers in his behalf. He could do this, because, contrary to the accusations of his opponents, his life has been pure and his purposes transparent among them. Paul's assertion of integrity of motive and action leads into the further defense of his conduct in the paragraphs that follow.

Paul here first employs his **boast** or "proud confidence" (NASB) language (*kauchēma* along with the verb *kauchaomai*), which he uses as often in this letter as in all his other letters combined (29 of 59 occurrences). Here, the language of boasting defends his apostleship and will be used significantly as such later in the letter. Although boasting can be negative and tactless (1 Cor 1:29; 3:21; 4:7; 5:6), here it is used positively. In 1:14, he will boast of the Corinthians.

The basis for Paul's exultant confidence in his apostolic integrity is "the testimony" (NRSV; *to martyrion*, "witness" or "proof") of his own **conscience.** The term *syneidēsis* (**conscience**) denotes one's moral consciousness or a person's ability to pass judgment on his or her own acts and attitudes. It appears frequently in Paul's letters (20 times compared to 10 times in the rest of the NT; see Rom 2:15; 9:1; 13:5; 1 Cor 8:7, 10, 12; 10:25, 27, 28, 29; 1 Tim 1:5, 19; 3:9; 4:2; 2 Tim 1:3; Titus 1:15). Paul will use it again in 2 Cor 4:2 and 5:11. The general idea of conscience was a widespread popular idea in Greek culture and apparently a favorite concept in Corinth.

Conscience

The noun form *syneidēsis* (**conscience**) is thought to have developed in everyday Greek usage from the verb *synoida* ("know in common with"). It is found as early as Democritus (625-595 B.C.E.) and is subsequently found in both Greek and Latin authors. The reflexive form of the verb, *synoida emautōi* ("I know with myself") is close to the meaning of the noun. Here the one who knows and the one who bears witness to it are the same person. The noun comes to mean "the self that knows with itself." The term *syneidēsis* is then another self within

> the self or an agent that observes one's own person and then testifies to what it sees. Self-awareness was basic to the concept. This was a faculty, implanted in every human being as a part of his very nature, often traced to God.
>
> In secular Greek usage conscience included self-awareness in the broader sense as well as a moral meaning. They understood the conscience possessed the capacity to inflict inward pain and remorse on those who reject its testimony. Conscience was more, however, a positive rather than a negative element in human nature. One should live in such a way as to be on good terms with one's conscience. (See Opperwall 1979, 762-63)

In Paul's usage, the criteria or norm for the witness of his conscience goes far beyond his own self-awareness; it depends on his reception of the gospel, for the conscience must be educated. That our conscience does not accuse us, does not give a "cast-iron guarantee that we are right" (Best 1987, 16). John Wesley, however, suggests that in Paul "we may understand by conscience a faculty or power, implanted by God in every soul that comes into the world, of perceiving what is right or wrong in his own heart or life, in his tempers, thoughts, words, and actions" (1984, 302).

The **boast** to which Paul's **conscience testifies** concerns his habitual manner of life. **We have conducted ourselves** translates the Greek verb *anestraphēmen* (see Eph 2:3; 1 Tim 3:15; Heb 10:33; 13:18; 1 Pet 1:17; 2 Pet 2:18). The cognate noun *anastrophē* describes a person's characteristic behavior or way of life (see Gal 1:13; Eph 4:22; 1 Tim 4:12; Heb 13:7; Jas 3:13; 1 Pet 1:15; 2:12; 3:1, 2, 16; 2 Pet 3:11; BDAG 2000, 73).

Paul proudly claims that his lifestyle **in the world** (*en tōi kosmōi*) and **especially** in relation to the Corinthians was **not according to worldly wisdom** (*en sophiai sarkikēi*, "in fleshly wisdom," NASB). That is, his conduct was not dominated by typical human motives and values (1 Cor 1:20; 2:6; see 3:1-3). Rather he routinely lived **in** (*en*) the realm of/by means of **God's grace.**

God granted Paul the ability to live **in the holiness and sincerity that are from God.** The textual evidence is divided between reading *hagiotēti* (**holiness**) or *haplotēti* ("simplicity"). If we read "simplicity" or "frankness" (NRSV), the reference would be to the absence of any duplicity or deviousness on Paul's part (Harris 2005, 185). **Holiness,** on the other hand, would refer to Paul's moral purity in an all-character sense. In part, this the Corinthians had questioned (7:2).

Paul does not use *hagiotēti* elsewhere in his letters. But he does use *haplotēti* (in Rom 12:8; 2 Cor 8:2; 9:11, 13; 11:3; Eph 6:5; Col 3:22). (Thus, a scribe might have been more inclined to conform this unique term to Paul's usual vocabulary, rather than vice versa.) Both internal considerations and the external evidence tip the scale slightly in favor of *hagiotēti* (so Thrall 1994, 133; Harris 2005, 183-84). To live in **holiness** is to behave so as to reflect one's possession by a holy God.

Both the adjectives **holiness** and **sincerity** seem to be qualified by *tou theou* ("of God"). If so, the expression has the force of a subjective genitive, indicating their source as **from God.** But if *tou Theou* is a genitive of quality, it modifies only **sincerity** and would be translated as "godly sincerity" (as in the NRSV). **Sincerity** indicates that Paul's behavior lacked pretense or hidden motives. His lifestyle transparently (2:17; see 1 Cor 5:8; Phil 1:10) revealed his pure inner motives. The popular etymology of the Greek term translated **sincerity,** *eilikrineia* (*helē* ["sun"] + *krinō* ["I judge"]), as "judge in the light of the sun," may be dubious (BDAG 2000, 282). Nonetheless, such **sincerity** entails a "what you see is what you get" kind of moral integrity.

We have conducted ourselves (*anestrephēmen*), viewed as a constative aorist, no doubt comprehends the whole of Paul's life as a Christian in a single glance. There is no contrast between his behavior among people in general and among the Corinthians. In fact, he has been **especially** careful in his **relations** with them. His pastoral care of the church gave them a unique opportunity to observe his way of life. They knew the integrity of his conduct. So Paul's appeal to his own conscience essentially becomes an appeal to the Corinthians' conscience (Harris 2005, 186).

The words **We have done so** in the NIV have no Greek equivalent. They are added in order to make two sentences out of an over-long Pauline sentence.

Worldly (*sarkikēi*) is literally "fleshly" (NASB; see 1 Cor 3:3) or "earthly" (NRSV). The adjective has the connotations of Paul's view of "flesh" as a mind-set (*sarx*, Rom 8:3-9; 2 Cor 1:17; 10:2; Gal 5:13, 16, 17, 19; Eph 2:3). In Rom 8:3-9 and similar contexts *sarx* is best translated literally as "flesh," as in NRSV. The translation of *sarx* as "sinful nature" (NIV) can be more seriously misleading theologically than flesh (see Greathouse and Lyons 2008, 218).

To describe **wisdom** (*sophia*) as fleshly certainly gives it a negative connotation. Paul's point is not that such wisdom is sensual or even base. As "fleshly" it is merely the "conventional wisdom" of unaided human speculation. The opposite qualification describes Paul's modus operandi as **according to God's grace.** His conduct relies on divine grace. (See 1 Cor 1:18—2:16 for Paul's lengthy discourse on the contrast between human wisdom and divine power.)

The repeated expression **according to** translates the preposition *en* as instrumental. The objects of the two prepositions, **worldly wisdom** and **God's grace** contrast two potential modes of living, as Paul describes his conduct **in the world** (Harris 2005, 186). The former serves as merely the foil for the latter. Paul's life is not worldly-wise; it is divinely empowered.

■ **13** Paul claims that his sincerity and transparency extend also to the letters he has written to the Corinthians. What they **read** (*anaginōskete*) from him is consistent with what they should **understand** (*epiginōskete*) him to be. His colorful play on words insists that he means exactly what he says. There are no hidden undertones in his letters. The plain sense of Paul's words is their meaning. He may be misunderstood at times, yet he never intended to mislead or deceive (Best 1987, 15).

■ **14** Paul is convinced that the Corinthians have already **understood** [him] **. . . in part.** But he hopes they **will come to understand fully** (*heōs telous*, literally "understand until the end," NRSV; v 13).

What had they partially misunderstood? He could refer to any of three letters. Was it the "previous" letter (1 Cor 5:9), the "severe" letter (2 Cor 2:3-4), or what we call 1 Corinthians? Possibly some were critical of all that Paul had previously written them. Paul explicitly indicates that they had somewhat misunderstood the (apparently now lost) first letter (1 Cor 5:8-13). And he was certainly concerned with how the church was dealing (perhaps misdealing) with a certain member who had figured in the "severe" letter (2 Cor 2:5-11).

Paul wants the Corinthians to be as proud of him as he is of them. That is, he wants them to be able to **boast** of him as he **will boast** of them. He anticipates that this mutual exchange of honor will occur **in the day of the Lord Jesus** (see Phil 2:15-16; 1 Thess 2:19-20). For Paul, this seems to be the NT equivalent (1 Cor 5:5; 1 Thess 5:2) of the OT Day of the Lord (Isa 13:9; Jer 46:10; Ezek 30:3; Joel 1:15; 2:1, 11, 31; Amos 5:18; Zech 14:1; Acts 2:20). The idea of judgment is retained in the NT **day of the Lord Jesus** (1 Cor 4:4-5; 2 Cor 5:10). But more often hope is emphasized, as here (1 Cor 1:8; Phil 1:6, 10).

Paul's main concern is to remove any reason they may have for finding fault with his ministry among them. He believes he can answer their criticism by clearing up their confusion about his true motives. Thus, their knowledge of him might be such that they may become as proud of him in the present as he will be of them at the Parousia. At the second coming, "the Lord . . . will bring to light what is hidden in darkness and will expose the motives of men's hearts," for "at that time each will receive his praise from God" (1 Cor 4:5).

What presently divides Paul and his Corinthian detractors is their failure to recognize fully the authentic nature of Paul's apostleship. They fail to appreciate his role as the founder of their church. His ministry among them (1 Cor 3:9-10; 4:14-15) mediated to them their status as Christians. Paul has contributed to their expected approval by God on **the day of the Lord Jesus.** Paul hopes this reminder of his role in their future destiny will penetrate, even alter their present thinking about him.

Paul rests the general defense of his personal integrity in these verses. First, his defense is on the witness of his conscience as to his conduct in Corinth (v 12). Second, as a result, Paul expects the Corinthians fully to acknowledge the genuineness of his apostolic ministry among them (vv 13-14). Rhetorically speaking, these verses formally introduce the purpose (Latin: *causa*) he intends to achieve in the body of the letter. They explain why Paul writes the letter. They function as an exordium that announces a theme central to Paul's defense.

2. The Integrity of His Travel Plans (1:15-22)

Paul had failed to carry through his announced travel plans (1 Cor 4:19; 16:5-6). This was apparently a major issue for certain of the Corinthians. They challenged the apostle's integrity because of the change. Paul insisted that his conscience was clear, his motives sincere, and his behavior pure (1:12-14). Nevertheless, he was well aware that his changed travel plans opened him up to questions about his integrity. Paul denies that he made his plans like a fickle man of the world (1:15-17). But his thoughts quickly turned from a vindication of his character to the foundation of his integrity—the character of God (vv 18-22).

Before Paul explains the actual reason for the change of plans, he first denies the charge of fickleness (v 17). Then he proceeds to ground his integrity as a minister of Christ in the integrity of God himself: **God is faithful** (v 18). Paul's defense is, therefore, first and foremost theological.

■ **15-16** Paul's plans were made on the basis of the confidence he expressed in 1:12-14. That is, he took for granted their mutual recognition and appreciation. On the basis of this (mistaken) assumption, Paul **planned** [*eboulomēn*, "I wanted," NRSV] **to visit** the Corinthians **first,** both on the way to and on the way from **Macedonia** (v 16). He hoped next to be sent by them on his **way to Judea.**

The adverb **first** (*proteron*), following the verb "wanted," could be taken as to mean "earlier" or "formerly" (BDAG 2000, 888). On this interpretation, it would refer to Paul's planning stage between the sending of 1 Corinthians and his "painful visit" (Thrall 1994, 136). But v 16 (and the textual variants that reflect this understanding) lead most interpreters to take it as referring to Paul's desire to come **first** of all to Corinth (Harris 2005, 192).

Paul seems to have had two travel plans. The first he announced in 1 Corinthians; and the second, here. Apparently, when Paul wrote 1 Cor 16:2-8, he had planned to go from Ephesus to Macedonia, then to Corinth, and on to Jerusalem. But by the time he wrote 2 Cor 1:15-16, the intended route had been changed. After leaving Ephesus, Paul wanted to go twice to Corinth, on the way to and returning from Macedonia en route to Judea (Harris 2005, 59-64).

Paul's stated reason for the double visit was **so that you might benefit twice.** The expression is literally ***a second grace*** (*deuteron charin*). *Chara* ("joy"; thus "a double pleasure," RSV; see Phil 1:26) is almost as well-attested in surviving manuscripts as *charin.* Both terms come from the same cognate family. And they are not always clearly distinct in meaning. As the more difficult reading, *charin* is probably to be preferred.

What does Paul mean by this peculiar use of *charis*? How can he use one of the great words in his theological vocabulary in such a mundane way? Among several options, two are the most feasible.

First, as a bearer of divine grace (see Rom 1:11; 15:29), the apostle's visit both going and coming, would allow the Corinthians "twice [to] receive a blessing" (NASB). A second option would be to take it as "a double favor"

(NRSV) or a "second proof of [Paul's] goodwill" (BDAG 2000, 1080). Both nuances are probably comprehended in the NIV translation **benefit** (Harris 2005, 193).

Paul insisted that his change of plans was not due to a defect in his personal integrity but rather to his deep concern for the Corinthians. Far from slighting them by his changed plans, Paul was sparing them another "painful visit" by writing instead. His integrity was not inflexible. It was tempered by the undergirding motive of love and the desire that the mutual sorrow created by their misunderstanding might be replaced by mutual joy.

Paul also insists that his conduct was consistent with the character of God. Paul assumes throughout that our character is transformed by that to which we give ourselves. Thus, he claims that his integrity, which seemed to be challenged by his changing plans, was nonetheless consistent with the integrity of his Lord.

Following his unfulfilled second visit, Paul had wanted the Corinthians to **send** [him] **on** [his] **way.** That is, he hoped that they would support his journey to Judea "with food, money, by arranging for companions, means of travel, etc." (BDAG 2000, 873; see Acts 15:3; Rom 15:24; 1 Cor 16:6, 11). His unannounced early visit to Corinth, however, did not go well.

Apparently, there was an ugly scene, prompted perhaps by some extremely unpleasant disciplinary action required by certain unnamed wrongdoers in the church (see 1 Cor 4:17-21; 2 Cor 1:23; 2:2; 12:20, 21; 13:1, 2, 10). Was Paul too forceful or too lenient in carrying out his written threats in 1 Corinthians (see 2 Cor 10:1-11; 11:21*a;* 12:19-21; 13:1-4, 10)? We cannot be sure. Someone apparently greatly wronged Paul during this visit, and no one came to his defense (2:3, 5; 7:11, 12). Whatever exactly occurred, the unfortunate development during this unannounced stop caused Paul to abandon his twice announced visit on returning from Macedonia (2:1). We can conjecture the possibility that this set of circumstances plunged Paul into the deep depression and despair he mentions in 1:8-10.

■ **17** Paul's "painful visit" (2:1) to the church led him to alter his itinerary (v 17). Paul does not dispute the fact that he changed his plans. But he insists, perhaps in response to the allegations of Corinthian critics, that he did not do so **lightly.** The underlying Greek term *elaphriai* has the connotation of acting frivolously or irresponsibly, an indication of a character prone to vacillation or levity (BDAG 2000, 314).

The formulation of Paul's first question "invites a negative response" (BDAG 2000, 649 s.v. *mēti*): "I was not vacillating when I intended to do this, was I?" (NASB). The apostle emphatically denies as incredible any inference that he was motivated by "momentary expediency and self interest" (Thrall 1994, 140).

His second rhetorical question is also an implicit denial: **Do I make my plans in a worldly manner so that in the same breath I say, "Yes, yes" and "No,**

no"? (see Matt 5:37; Jas 5:12). The translation, **so that in the same breath I say,** is a paraphrase. Literally, Paul wrote "that it may be with me" (*hina ēi par' emoi*). The NIV along with the NASB and NRSV take the meaning to be that it rests on Paul to say **"Yes, yes" and "No, no"** in regard to his travel plans. This puzzling expression can also be taken to mean that it does not rest on Paul but on God ultimately to say "'yes' and 'yes', or 'no' and 'no'" (NEB). Paul implicitly denies that his change of travel plans is arbitrary. Rather, the decision is God's, for the focus is not so much on Paul's reliability as on God's reliability (see Young and Ford 1987, 100-103; Harris 2005, 197).

To alter one's plans on a whim is to make decisions (*bouleuomai . . . bouleuomai;* see BDAG 2000, 181) **in a worldly manner** (*kata sarka,* "according to the flesh," NASB; see 5:16; 10:2; 11:18). To change one's mind for self-centered reasons would be in direct opposition to Paul's life **according to God's grace** (v 12). It would be contrary to life "according to the Spirit" (Rom 8:4-8). Such would be a denial of Paul's character, a contradiction of the person the church knew him to be (1:13-15).

■ **18** Ultimately, Paul bases the integrity of his relations with the Corinthians on a theological appeal to the integrity of God himself. **But as surely as God is faithful, our message to you is not "Yes" and "No."**

Paul does not claim that he is as trustworthy as God. But the analogy does imply that he assumes the reliability of God should be reflected in the character of his preachers whose ministries are enabled by the Spirit of God.

The confessional formula, **God is faithful,** is found elsewhere in Paul (1 Cor 1:9; 10:13; see 1 Thess 5:24; 2 Thess 3:3). But only here is it followed by the conjunction *hoti* ("that"; **surely**). This turns it into an oath-formula. Paul solemnly invokes the trustworthiness of God himself to serve as a witness guaranteeing that he speaks the truth. Elsewhere, Paul calls upon God to witness to the truth of his claims (see 2 Cor 1:23; 11:31; Rom 9:1; Gal 1:20; Phil 1:8; 1 Thess 2:5, 10) only when it is impossible to validate them otherwise. God alone can vouch for the purity of his motives (see 2 Cor 12:19).

Paul often uses the editorial first person plural (we/our/us) in 2 Corinthians when his focus is actually on the first person singular (I/my/me). Here, however, **<u>our</u> message** (*logos hēmōn,* "our word"; emphasis added) must include not only Paul but also Silas and Timothy (see v 19).

Their "word" includes all their spoken and written words, comprehending Paul's letters and informal speech. But its primary reference is to their preaching and teaching of the gospel, to which the Corinthian church owes its very existence. Paul insists that any change of plans is more a display of God's faithfulness than an expression of his vacillating character.

■ **19** Paul's underlying assumption is that a person's character is transformed by that to which one gives his or her life. For Paul, it was **the Son of God, Jesus Christ,** who was the content of his gospel, ensuring its reliability. And thus the more faithful Paul is to that gospel, the more reliable he is.

The christological title **Son of God** is comparatively rare in Paul's letters (15 times compared to about 200 references each to "Christ" and "Lord"). In Paul's use, the title emphasizes the unique relationship of Jesus to God. Here it implies that there was an implicit likeness or identity of character between Father and Son (Thrall 1994, 146).

The **Son of God** is the one Paul **preached among** the Corinthians. But Paul was not the only intermediary **by** or through (*dia*) whom Christ was preached. Paul mentions also **Silas** (see Acts 15:22-40; 16:19-29; 17:4—18:5; 1 Thess 1:1; 2 Thess 1:1; 1 Pet 5:12] **and Timothy** (see Acts 16:1-3; 17:14-15; 18:5; 19:22; 20:4; 1 Cor 4:17; 16:10; 1 Thess 1:1; 3:2, 6; 2 Thess 1:1). His two associates are named here perhaps as witnesses validating Paul's message (Deut 19:15).

Jesus Christ had proved to be (*egeneto*) utterly reliable, **not "Yes" and "No,"** in his earthly ministry and had become once and for all (*gegonen*) the grand **"Yes"** of God (Heb 13:8). Paul's integrity, the reliability of his "word" (*logos;* see v 18) to them, is that of his gospel whose content is Jesus Christ. He is the Son of the faithful God, whom Paul and his missionary colleagues preached.

Paul's daring claim is that the very presence of the life of this risen Son of God determines the character of his emissaries. And it was the Corinthians' faith in the message brought by them that made them Christians. Paul's proclamation of the Christ constituted who he is as an apostle of the Son of the faithful God.

■ **20** This verse contains no explicit verbs. Greek authors routinely omitted the verb "to be" and other verbs that might be inferred from the preceding context. In order to make English sense, translators are compelled to add implied verbs. The NIV inserts **has made, they are,** and **is spoken.** It also renders *en autoi* ("in him") **in Christ** to eliminate any antecedent confusion. A more literal translation would be: ***For however many promises of God there are, in Christ are Yes. Therefore, also through him is the Amen to God for glory through us.***

It is not perfectly clear why the NIV (so also NASB and NRSV) resorts to paraphrase and separates the Greek dative indirect object, "to God" (*tōi Theōi*), from **the "Amen"** and places it with the prepositional phrase **to the glory** (*pros doxan*). Did Paul mean that we say **the "Amen"** "to God for his glory" (Harris 2005, 203) or **the "Amen" is spoken by us to the glory of God**? The Greek word order favors the former. But regardless of the precise grammatical structure, Paul appears to mean that ***God affirms all of his promises in Christ. So, also through Christ we agree with God to his glory.***

Clearly, Paul had in mind the Hebrew origins of **the "Amen"** (*to amēn*). Its Hebrew root, *ʿmn,* means "to be firm or faithful." In the OT **"Amen"** acknowledges a preceding statement as valid and binding (see Deut 27:15; 1 Chr 16:36; Neh 5:13; Ps 106:48; Jer 28:6). In Jewish synagogue worship it was the expected congregational response to expressions of praise and benediction. The NT similarly uses **"Amen"** as a liturgical response in Christian worship (1 Cor 14:26; Rev 5:14; 7:10-12; 19:1-4; Thrall 1994, 149).

In v 20, Paul argues that God's **"Yes"** is what he proclaims in Christ. Christ is the **"Yes"** to all the **promises God has made.** They are all fulfilled in the person of Jesus Christ, as the worshipping church affirms (Rev 1:7; 22:20).

Promises

What did Paul mean by his reference to God's **promises**? The underlying Greek term, *epangelia,* which appears 26 times in Paul's letters, is found in the LXX only in Esth 4:7, where it translates a Hebrew word meaning an exact statement or information. The term in the sense of promise first appears within the biblical tradition in Hellenistic Judaism (see 3 Macc 2:10-11; *Ps. Sol.* 12:6; *T. Jos.* 20:1).

Although a precise term for promise is otherwise absent from the OT, the concept is not. Our English versions show this when they translate the Hebrew text with "promise" in noun form (e.g., Josh 23:15; 1 Kgs 2:4; 2 Chr 1:9; Jer 29:10; 33:14; 34:4) and more often in verbal form (e.g., Gen 18:29; 21:1; Exod 12:25; 33:1; Num 11:12; 32:11). Gerhard von Rad, characterizing "Israel's whole existence before God," has attempted to show that "from Abraham to Malachi, Israel was kept constantly in motion because of what God said and did, and that she was always in one way or another in an area of tension constituted by promise and fulfillment" (1965, 371). Josephus in Paul's century refers to the promises (*hai epangelei*) from God that Moses received on behalf of the people (*A. J.* III.i.5. Paul wrote to the Roman church about "the people of Israel" in his day who possessed "the promises" (9:4).

Although we cannot know with certainty what specific OT passages Paul may have had in mind among God's **many promises** in 2 Corinthians, what he intended can be safely assumed from what he wrote later to the Romans (4:13, 14, 16, 20; 9:4, 7, 8, 9; 15:8), Galatians (3:14, 16, 17, 18, 21, 22, 29; 4:23, 28), and to the Ephesians (1:13; 2:12; 3:6; 6:2). Surely in his mind was at least God's covenantal agreement with Abraham and his descendants in Gen 15 and the new covenant prophecies of Ezek 36 and Jer 31. Paul would understand all of these passages as references to the Messiah, the age of the Spirit, and the inclusion of the Gentiles in God's saving purposes (see Hoffmann 1978, 68-74; Schniewind and Friedrich 1964, 2:578-84).

For this reason (*dio*), or so **through him the "Amen" is spoken by us to the glory of God.** This sentence is difficult to interpret precisely. A probable solution links **through him** (*di' autou*) with **the "Amen"** (*ta amēn*) and refers to the corporate worship of the Corinthian believers. They must have learned from Paul during his apostolic ministry in Corinth to pronounce the Hebrew word **to the glory** of God. Thus, Corinthian worship validated Paul's ministry among them. Their ability to say **the "Amen"** was due to his influence (1 Cor 1:6; 2 Cor 3:2-3).

The phrase **by us** (*di' hēmōn*, "through us," NASB) then goes with both **the "Amen"** and **the glory** (Harris 2005, 203-4). The Corinthians' **"Amen"** attests to the trustworthiness of God. So how can they suspect the trustworthiness of the apostle who taught them to say "Amen"? Paul subtly reminds the Corinthians of their inconsistency! Denney suggests that Paul's argument in vv 18-20 "might be *repeated* by a hypocrite, but no hypocrite could ever have *invented* it" (1943, 5:78).

■ **21-22** This is the final phase of Paul's affirmation of the integrity of his travel plans. He appeals to a present, progressive experience confirmed by three prior decisive and simultaneous acts of **God** in his life. Paul's use of the first person plural (**us**), however, identifies these as experiences he and his coworkers shared with the Corinthians. The focus is not on their experiences, however, but on God as the one responsible for them. Placed last in the first clause, **God** is in an emphatic position. This is "one of the most God-centered, God-focused paragraphs in the Pauline Corpus" (Fee 1994, 289).

The Greek sentence is structured around a present participle followed by three aorist participles: *bebaiōn . . . chrisas . . . sphragisamenos . . . dous*. God is the implied subject of each of these: ***establishing*** . . . ***having anointed*** . . . ***sealed*** . . . ***given.*** Paul grounds his reliability as an apostle in his **God**-graced, intimate, and dynamic union with **Christ.** It is **in** (*eis*) their shared relation with **Christ** that **God** continuously **makes both** Paul and the Corinthians **stand firm** (1 Cor 1:8-9; see Col 2:7; Heb 13:9) in their faith.

Makes . . . stand firm (*bebaiō*) or "establishes" (NRSV) was a legal term used to express a guaranteed security, such as a seller's guarantee against any third party claims (Deissmann 1901, 104-9). With this background, Paul affirms that God has placed believers in a legally indisputable relationship to **Christ** that is constantly being confirmed and strengthened. Perhaps Paul also implies that both he and the Corinthians, as united together to **Christ,** find the quality of their lives being transformed by Christ's life (3:18). The term is possibly used here in the same religious sense as in 1 Cor 1:8-9, where Paul assures the Corinthians that Christ "will also confirm you to the end, blameless in the day of our Lord Jesus Christ" (v 8 NASB).

Paul applies the decisive action of **God** expressed by the three aorist participles—**anointed . . . set his seal . . . put . . . as a deposit**—first to his own calling and commission (Acts 9:15-18). But also in view were Paul's fellow workers as well as his Corinthian hearers, as the threefold use of the first person personal pronoun implies: **us . . . us . . . our.**

First, being **anointed** (*chrisas*) by **God** has its background in the OT practice of anointing with oil. By this means, priests (Exod 29:7; Lev 8:12; 16:32), prophets (1 Kgs 19:16), and kings (1 Sam 9:16; 15:1, 17; 16:12) were consecrated to their office. Jesus was considered the model "Anointed One" (*Christos*, "Christ") in the early church (Isa 61:1-3; Mark 1:10-11; Luke 4:18-19; Acts 4:27; 10:38; Heb 1:9). This probably plays a role in the understanding here. The anointing to divine service, carrying with it the concepts of authenticity and reliability, implied the gifts necessary for the tasks (see 1 John 2:20, 27).

Second, they were "sealed" (NASB). In antiquity seals served as marks of identification, authentication, and security. This is reflected in the NIV paraphrase: **God** has **set his seal of ownership on us.** In the LXX sealing refers primarily to the legal validation of documents (Esth 3:12; Jer 32:10-14). The sealing in Rev 7:2-8 and 9:4 reflects the biblical idea of placing a protective mark on someone (Cain in Gen 4:15; on the righteous in Ezek 9:6).

Third, the apostle writes, God has "given the earnest of the Spirit in our hearts" (KJV). The NIV helpfully paraphrases: **God** has **put his Spirit in our hearts as a deposit** [*arrabōna*, ***earnest***]**, guaranteeing what is to come** (see 5:5; Eph 1:14). The imagery is drawn from the worlds of law and commerce. The gift of the Holy Spirit (Acts 2:38; 15:8-9) is compared to a "first installment, deposit, pledge, down payment" (BDAG 2000, 134). The Spirit is a portion of the purchase price paid in advance, guaranteeing the full payment. Agricultural imagery makes a similar point in the expression, "the firstfruits of the Spirit" (Rom 8:23). An aspect of the anticipated future age has already become a present reality. The Spirit serves as the pledge that all God has promised for the future will be ours.

By the use of the term *arrabōna*, Paul links the Spirit to the fulfillment of God's promises (v 22), to the resurrection life of the redeemed (5:5), and to the inheritance of redemption (Eph 1:14). By the very acceptance of the **deposit,** the recipients receive the gift of the Spirit. The gift of the Spirit comes not only as a *privilege* to enjoy and a *hope* to revel in but also as *an obligation* to fulfill. As we shall see, the Spirit will play a crucial role in Paul's presentation of the ministry of the new covenant (3:2-18; see 13:14).

Paul's case for the integrity of his intention as an apostle of Christ is now complete. The faithfulness of God (v 18) certified by Christ (vv 19-20) is verified in his life and ministry by the Spirit (vv 21-22). Indeed, it was Paul's own ministry that mediated God's presence and power to the Corinthians in life-changing ways in their experience as a people of God.

The integrity of God has been realized in both the apostle and the church. Paul is confident that surely they can see how groundless their accusations are. To doubt Paul's motives would be to cast doubt on the reality of their own life in Christ (Hafemann 2000, 86).

3. The Reason He Did Not Come (1:23—2:4)

Paul now returns to his original intention to visit Corinth (1:15-16). He explains why he changed his plans. This was due, not to a defect in his personal integrity, but to his deep concern to spare them grief. Instead of making **another painful visit** (2:1), he had written them a sorrowful letter (2:3; see 7:8-13). His change of plans was motivated by his love for them (2:4) and his hope to rekindle their common joy (2:3).

■ **23** The apostle affirms the truth of this explanation with an oath formula: **I call God as my witness** (see Rom 1:9; 1 Thess 2:5, 10). The Greek *epi tēn emēn psychēn* ("upon my soul," KJV; "against me," NRSV) means "on my own life." God is both his witness and his judge (Harris 2005, 212). Paul is willing to stake his own life on the truth of his witness. He calls upon God to support his claim (see the commentary on 1:18). For God to add his witness to Paul's conforms to the scriptural principle that an unsupported testimony does not stand (see John 5:31-37; Deut 17:6).

In 2 Cor 1:19 Paul named two witnesses besides himself—Silas and Timothy. But only God could vouch for his motives. He is conscious of God's scrutiny of the secrets of his heart and dares not lie (see 11:31; 12:19; Gal 1:20).

The reason Paul **did not return to Corinth** was to **spare** them. But to spare them from what? From an unpleasant application of his apostolic authority and the mutual pain this would bring them (1 Cor 4:21)? From the shame of his presence and the accompanying sorrow? Both? We cannot be certain. Certainly his overriding purpose was their mutual "joy" (1:24; 2:3).

■ **24** Perhaps Paul feared that the Corinthians might mistake his explanation for a veiled threat. So he hastens to assure them that he does not **lord it over** them in regard to their faith and conduct (see 4:5). Had someone charged that Paul was overly domineering?

Paul insists that faith by its very nature is free: it recognizes no human master. He and his colleagues are coworkers (*synergoi*) with the Corinthians for their **joy** ("the kingdom of God is . . . joy in the Holy Spirit," Rom 14:17).

Furthermore, Paul has no need to intimidate or dominate them. For (*gar*, **because**) they already **stand firm** on their own **by** or better "in" (NRSV) **faith** (*tēi . . . pistei*). Here (as in 1 Cor 15:1; 16:13; and Rom 5:2; see Greathouse and Lyons 2008, 154), Paul refers to **faith** as a sphere, a metaphorical room into which one may enter. He does not (as in Rom 6:17 and 1 Thess 2:15) mean "in the faith," as in full compliance with apostolic teaching. Paul's stance was simply that **we work with you for your joy.**

■ **2:1** It was not only to spare them but also to spare himself that Paul **made up** his **mind** not to **make another painful visit.** The expression with the aorist tense connotes the decisiveness of his decision. Paul ***determined for himself*** (*ekrina . . . emautōi*, "for my own sake," NASB; see 1 Cor 2:2).

Paul decided "not to come again" (*to mē palin . . . elthein*) to Corinth. He refers to a second visit, following his founding visit recorded in Acts 18. This visit, made previous to this writing, is not mentioned in Acts. All we know of it depends on Paul's passing references to it in 2 Corinthians. We can only guess what happened, why, and how. Both Paul and the Corinthians knew all too well. And he seems reluctant to reopen this unpleasant chapter in their shared experience.

The visit he had planned as a surprise gift to them had turned into a painful experience for both Paul and the church. He has no desire to precipitate such a situation again, no disposition to **grieve** them unless apostolic duty absolutely demanded it.

■ **2-3** Paul was convinced that a prime function of his apostolic ministry was the promotion of mutual joy (see 1:24; 2:3). He could take no satisfaction in grieving his Corinthian friends, whom he longed to make glad. How could his heart be cheered except by those whom he had **grieved**? They were the very source of his happiness. So, he asks rhetorically, **who is left to make me glad but you . . . ?**

When Paul refers to the church as a community, he moves easily back and forth between singular (**who . . . whom;** *tis ho . . . ho*) and plural (**you . . . you . . . you;** *hymas . . . hymas . . . hymōn*) pronouns. The church could be conceived as both a collection of individuals and a unified body.

As the spiritual father of the Corinthian church (1 Cor 4:14), why should Paul **be distressed by those who ought to make** him **rejoice** (v 3)? The words in 2:1-7 translated **painful, grieve, grieved, distressed, grief,** and **sorrow** are all derived from the same Greek root (see BDAG 2000, 604-5 s.v. *lypeō* and *lypē*).

■ **4** Rather than visit the Corinthians at such an inopportune time, instead Paul **wrote as** he **did** (*touto auto, **this very thing***). What he wrote was a sorrowful letter, written **out of great distress and anguish of heart and with many tears.** Any grief the letter might cause was to be transcended by its intentions. Paul's ultimate design was the prompting of joy in both apostle and people.

Paul wrote with the **confidence** that his **joy** would be the joy of the Corinthians. He stresses the only valid basis for his authority over them as an apostle. This was the **depth** ("special quality/quantity"; "abundant," NRSV) of his **love** for them. The word order of Paul's Greek construction emphatically emphasizes this. Literally he wrote: "the love [*tēn agapēn*], in order that you may know that [*hēn*] I have especially [*perissoterōs*] for you." Paul lays bare his motives, granting his readers a revealing insight into the heart of a true apostle. This is the heart of anyone who would minister in the name of Christ.

4. Forgiveness for the Offender (2:5-11)

Paul's sorrowful letter to the church was occasioned by the offense of a particular member of the church at Corinth. That he or she was a native Corinthian rather than an intruder (11:4, 20) is indicated by the way the church dealt with him or her. Some have identified this offender with the incestuous man of 1 Cor 5:1-5. But this does not suit the situation well.

Most modern interpreters identify the offending member as one who was guilty of a personal affront to Paul. This probably took place during Paul's "painful visit" to the church. Harris, however, argues for a "verbal assault on Paul's person and authority" that took place sometime between the "painful visit" and the sorrowful letter (2005, 226-27). The incident was distressing for Paul personally and diminished his standing in his relation to the church (2:1).

In vv 5-11, Paul urges all the Corinthians freely to forgive the offender. Paul, with a pastoral heart, has a delicate regard for the dignity and feelings of the individual; he does not name either the offender or the offense. He says only what is needed for his relations with the church. The Corinthians knew what he meant, but it is difficult for us to be certain.

■ **5** Paul refuses to consider the offense on a personal level. As a modern paraphrase renders the verse, "I want you to know that I am not the one injured in this as much as, with a few exceptions, all of you" (TM). If the offense had been just against Paul, he would probably have followed his own advice in 1 Cor 6:7 and prefer "rather [to] be wronged" than to pursue personal vindication. Further, the extent to which Paul is the one wronged is an open question.

Certainly the integrity of the congregation was at stake. Paul has already argued that the legitimacy of the Corinthians is inextricably bound up with that of the apostle (1:18-22; see 3:1-3). So it was a matter with which Paul needed to deal (see 2:3-4 and 1 Cor 4:14-21; Hafemann 2000, 88).

The most probable force of the words **to some extent** (*apo merous*, "in some degree"; BDAG 2000, 633) is to limit the extent to which the **grief** was felt by **all** of the Corinthians. But it may indicate that not everyone in the church shared in the **grief.** If so, did a minority feel that the "punishment" (v 6) inflicted was too harsh; or was it not harsh enough?

Satan: The Accuser

In Job 1:6 the Satan came along with the sons of god to present themselves to the Lord (see Job 1:6-12; 2:1-7 and commentary on 6:14 in regard to "Belial"). As a member in good standing in the Heavenly Council, the Satan was asked by the Lord to give an account of his activities. His answer was, "From roaming through the earth and going back and forth in it" (Job 1:7). The divine response seems to indicate that he was only doing his job. He is pictured as the eyes and ears of the divine monarch. His special function was to investigate things on earth.

G. B. Caird goes so far as to say that, as one who has the right of access to the heavenly court, the Satan's role was to serve as the public prosecutor of wrongdoers (1956, 32). But to identify the Satan here as a "public prosecutor" is not yet fully evident in the OT presentation. In this scene he acts at least as a troublemaker, a disturber of the kingdom.

The Hebrew expression for "Satan" is literally "the satan" (*hassatan*), "the accuser" or "the adversary" (Holladay 1998, 350). It functions as a title rather than a personal name in Zech 3:1 (see Ps 109:6). Here the Satan's function as a prosecuting attorney becomes clear. The verb "to accuse" is the same Hebrew root (*stn*) as Satan. In the NT the Greek word for "the devil" (e.g., Matt 4:1) is *ho diabolos*. Its basic meaning is "one who engages in slander." It is derived from the verb *diaballō*, "to make a complaint about a pers[on] to a third party, *bring charges*" (BDAG 2000, 22).

Consider Rev 12:10:

"Now have come the salvation and the power and the kingdom of our God,
and the authority of his Christ.
For the accuser [*ho katēgōr*] of our brothers,
who accuses [*ho katēgorōn*] them before our God day and night,
has been hurled down."

Here the verb *katēgoreō* is used with the meaning of "the satan" in the OT: "*to bring charges* in court" (BDAG 2000, 533). As suggested by this language, the satanic figure is the consummate legalist! He is the accuser on the basis of absolute justice—no mercy!

The Satan's role as the tempter to evil is a secondary development in the OT, only unquestionably evident in 1 Chr 21:1: "Satan [*satan*] rose up against Israel and incited David to take a census of Israel." We read the NT as well in the light of these primary and secondary meanings for "throughout the NT period Satan retains his juridical duties" (Caird 1956, 33, see 31-53).

Illuminating is the way Thomas Merton picks up on the legalistic character of the biblical satanic figure with what he calls "The Moral Theology of the Devil" in which

> the important thing is to be absolutely right and to prove that everybody else is absolutely wrong. . . . The Cross, then, is no longer a sign of mercy (for mercy has no place in such a theology), it is the sign that Law and Justice have utterly triumphed. . . . The theology of the devil is for those who . . . because they have come to an agreement with the Law, no longer need any mercy. . . . That is why God Himself is absent from hell. Mercy is the manifestation of His presence. (Merton 1961, 96, 91-92)

The parenthetical phrase, **not to put it too severely,** seems to mean "in order not to say too much" (NASB; i.e., not to "exaggerate"). This favors the former interpretation of the previous phrase. That is, Paul was concerned with the degree to which the Corinthians were grieved by the matter.

■ **6** The church in response to Paul's now lost severe letter had taken steps to punish the offender. So Paul pleads for mercy to be offered the man who had caused the affront (v 6). ***This*** [*hautē;* **The**] **punishment** (*epitimia*) refers to the discipline that had already been dispensed. The expression occurs only here in the NT. We can only guess what form of church discipline Paul had in mind. Was it exclusion from the Lord's Supper and the social life of the church (see 1 Cor 5:2, 5, 13; see 1 Thess 5:14; 2 Thess 3:6-15)?

Whatever the discipline exacted **by the majority,** Paul considered it **sufficient** for the situation and to be discontinued. Paul's mention of **the majority** could imply that a minority disagreed. If so, it is also unclear whether they disagreed with the leniency or severity of the disciplinary measures. In any case it seems clear "that the exercise of church discipline was a function of the local church," not just of an apostle (Harris 2005, 228).

■ **7-8** Paul considered the offender's sorrow evidence of his repentance. Thus, the church could now turn from discipline and **forgive** (Col 3:13) and **comfort** ("console," NRSV) the man. The goal of discipline was not vengeance but restoration. The offender (**him,** *tounantion,* ***such a one***) was to be reinstated before his **excessive sorrow** overwhelmed him. Despair could lead him to fail to return to the redeeming fellowship of the church.

Consequently, Paul's urgent plea was that they **reaffirm** their **love for him** (*auton,* v 8). This would allow him to know that he was forgiven. **Reaffirm** (*kyrōsai*) is a technical term meaning to "confirm, ratify, validate, make legally binding" (BDAG 2000, 579). Here, it may indicate a formal congregational resolution reinstating the offender to the love and fellowship of the church. In Gal 3:15, the only other use of the word in the NT, the verb refers to the ratification of a will: "no one can set aside or add to a human covenant that has been duly established" (*kekyrōmenēn*). Paul does not command forgiveness on the basis of his apostolic authority, but he urges it as a fellow Christian in keeping with the character of Christian love.

■ **9** Paul had written the sorrowful letter (v 9) for just such a demonstration of love through discipline. A third reason for writing (see 2:3 and 2:4) **was to see if you would stand the test.** That is, literally, ***so that I might know the proof*** [*dokimēn*] ***of you.*** This is to test your character to see **if you** are (*este*) **obedient in everything** (7:15; 10:6; see Phil 2:12; 2 Thess 3:14; Phlm 21).

At stake in their response to his letter was the proper recognition of Paul's apostolic authority. This was the test of their legitimacy as a "church of God" (1:1). As a representative of Christ, Paul is to be obeyed. His apostleship requires the acceptance of his authority. In Corinth, this involved both the imposition of discipline and the eagerness to forgive once the offender had repented (2:7, 10).

■ **10** Since the Corinthians had joined Paul in the verdict to punish the offender, he joins them in the verdict of forgiveness: **If you forgive anyone, I also forgive him. And what I have forgiven—if there was anything to forgive—I have forgiven in the sight of Christ for your sake.** The second **forgive** and **have forgiven,** while not in the original text, translators add as intended by the Greek syntax.

The hypothetical **if** is a touch of pastoral grace rather than an indication that forgiveness was unneeded. Paul indicates the depth of his Christlike spirit, since forgiveness was his object from the first. Paul forgave the offender **for** the **sake** of the well-being of the church as one who was fully aware that he lived in **the sight of Christ** (2:17; 4:2). **Sight** translates the Greek word *prosopon,* literally "face." By the figure of speech metonymy, it means "in the presence of Christ" (NASB). This was, no doubt, influenced by the Hebrew idiom *lifnē* (see Prov 4:3 and 25:7), which can express either sense. Paul is confident that the ever-present Christ is aware of Paul's forgiveness. And he approves.

■ **11** Here Paul offers a second reason for the necessity of forgiveness (see

1:7). He also clarifies why it was necessary precisely "for your sake" (v 10). They must all forgive **in order that Satan might not outwit us** (v 11). **Satan** (4:4; 6:15; 11:3; 12:7) is the accuser and adversary of the church. If Paul and the church were to withhold forgiveness from the offender, **Satan** might take advantage of the situation. He could gain control of their Christian brother through his "excessive sorrow." A harsh, unforgiving spirit would harm the church. By such a spirit Satan could defraud the church of their "joy and peace in believing" (Rom 15:13 NASB) and of the bond of love (Col 3:14). They would cease to be a saving fellowship.

For such an outcome, they would be personally accountable to Christ. For Christ is the all-comprehending motive for the exercise of forgiveness (Matt 5:12, 14-15; 18:23-25). Paul was fully aware that the enemy would "take advantage" (7:2; 12:18) of the situation. A strict or vindictive sense of justice or a legalistic attitude of superiority on the part of the church may be destructive (see Gal 6:1-5). Likewise, the excessive sorrow of the repentant man could be counterproductive (see 2 Cor 7:8-12).

Therefore, Paul warns, **we are not unaware of his** [i.e., Satan's] **schemes** ("designs," NRSV). Paul would say, "Let us not be hesitant with our forgiveness and assurances of love, lest Satan use what is our good against us for evil." To promote discord within the congregation is one of Satan's chief strategies for thwarting God's purposes in and through it. Recall that, in 1 Corinthians, the unity of the church was throughout a significant issue (1:10; 3:1-3; 4:14, 16; 5:4-8; 6:1-20; 8:9-13; 10:14; 11:33-34).

FROM THE TEXT

For Paul in 2:5-11, "Forgiveness Is a Must" in the context of the health of the church. He offers at least three reasons: (1) for the sake of the one who does wrong (vv 5-7); (2) for the spiritual well-being of those whose part it is to forgive (vv 8-10); and (3) for the integrity of the fellowship of the church (v 11).

IN THE TEXT

5. The Trip to Troas and Macedonia (2:12-13)

■ **12** Paul's rhetorical strategy reaches its climax in the pathos (emotional argument) of vv 12 and 13 (Matera 2003, 65). Here Paul returns to the theme of his itinerary, interrupted in 1:17—2:11, by his explanation of his change of plans. These transitional verses also introduce the lengthy exposition of his apostolic ministry in 2:14—7:4. This exposition interrupts again the story of his travels relevant to the Corinthians. He will return to them in 7:5.

Here Paul concludes his self-defense. He provides the Corinthians with further proof that his change of plans did not indicate a vacillating character or a lack of love for them. Paul went from Ephesus to **Troas** in Asia Minor primarily **to preach the gospel of Christ.**

This is the first of Paul's eight explicit references to the noun **gospel** (*euangelion*) in 2 Corinthians. **The gospel** is the "good news" (from the prefix *eu-*, "good," and *angelia*, "message") of God's saving intervention in human history in **Christ.** Only in 8:18 does the word stand alone.

Here, as in 9:13 and 10:14, Paul further identifies it with a genitive modifier, as **the gospel of Christ.** In 4:4, he calls it "the gospel of the glory of Christ." In 11:7, he identifies the message he preached (*euēngelisamēn*, the verbal cognate, also appears in 10:16) in Corinth as "the gospel of God" (NRSV: "I proclaimed God's good news"). This is a genitive of *source*—God is the source of the good news, but its content is **Christ.**

In 4:3, Paul refers to "our gospel." By this, he clearly means ***the gospel we preach*** (a subjective genitive). In 11:4 he refers ironically to the message of the so-called "super-apostles" (11:5) as "a different gospel" (see Gal 1:6-9), because they preached "a Jesus other than the Jesus we preached."

The word **gospel** is not to be equated simply with the Christian message. It is not the human activity of preaching the story of Jesus that saves those who believe it. It is the events the preaching proclaims that make universal salvation possible—the powerful activity of God in Christ (see Rom 1:16-17). And it is the Holy Spirit who powerfully persuades those who hear the proclaimed message, which announces this good news (see 1 Thess 1:5)—not the rhetorical cunning of those who preach.

Paradoxically, the power of the Triune God announced in the gospel appears strangely weak, shameful, scandalous, and even foolish. Central to Paul's understanding of the gospel is Christ's violent death on the cross. His death is not "good news" in itself, nor did it become good simply because of his subsequent resurrection. The gospel is not only the account of how God turned tragedy into triumph. The message of the cross is good news because through it God has chosen to save those who believe (see 1 Cor 1:18—2:1-5).

Some interpreters think that when Paul mentioned going **to Troas to preach the gospel,** he referred to the region of **Troas** or the Troad, not the city. But his secondary motive for going to **Troas** was to meet his associate Titus. Paul had sent Titus with the sorrowful letter to Corinth (see 1:3-4; 7:5-12). Paul would have been more apt to intercept Titus in a city than in a region (Harris 2005, 236).

A church had probably already been established in **Troas** (Acts 16:8-11; 20:5-12). Paul was hoping to expand the work geographically. On his arrival, Paul discovered that in his providence **the Lord had opened a door** (v 12; see 1 Cor 16:9; Col 4:3; Acts 14:27; Rev 3:8) of evangelistic opportunity for him. He considered openness to gospel-preaching the work of God (see 1 Thess 2:1-6).

John Wesley probably drew on his own experience as an itinerate evangelist to explain Paul's metaphor: "There was free liberty to speak, and many were willing to hear" (1950, 648). Augustine (354-430) comments that this is "a most manifest demonstration that even the very beginning of faith is the gift of God." Paul's expression contains the phrase ***in the Lord*** (*en kyriōi*). There is a linguistic if not conceptual link to Paul's theologically significant "in Christ" (see the commentary on 5:17).

■ **13** Paul intended to occupy himself with this mission until **Titus** returned from Corinth with the news of the situation there (7:6-15). He describes this younger colleague in ministry as his **brother** (v 13; see 1:1). Not literally related to Paul, Titus was a Greek (Gal 2:3). More than merely a fellow believer, he was Paul's "partner and fellow worker" (8:23). He plays a prominent role in the letter (7:6-7, 13-14; 8:6, 16, 23; see Gal 2:1; 2 Tim 4:10; Titus 1:4). Remarkably, Titus is never mentioned in Acts.

Paul was preoccupied with the welfare of the Corinthians and anxious to learn their response to his sorrowful letter. Overwhelmed by these concerns, he found no **peace of mind** in Troas, despite his success there (2:4, 12).

Paul describes his anxiety twice. Here he literally writes, I had "no rest for my spirit" (NASB; *anesin tōi pneumati mou*). But in 7:5, he will say, "this body of ours had no rest" (literally, "our flesh [*anesin hē sarx hēmōn*] had no rest," NASB). This undermines any notion of a Platonic mind-body dualism in Paul's thought. It indicates that he has his whole person is in mind, whether viewed from the inward or outward perspective. The emotional and spiritual dimensions of human existence are not easily distinguishable from physical frailty and vulnerability.

The Greek word translated **peace** is not Paul's usual term (*eirēnē*, in 1:1; 13:11; and 41 times elsewhere in his letters). It is instead *anesin*, which entered English as the brand name of the pain reliever "Anacin." In each of its Pauline uses (2 Cor 2:13; 7:5; 8:13; and 2 Thess 1:7), it refers to relief from something **"onerous or troublesome"** (BDAG 2000, 77).

Distracted by anxiety over Titus and the precarious situation in Corinth, Paul sought relief in Macedonia. Paul **said** a public and formal **good-by** to the believers in Troas and proceeded **to Macedonia.** Evidently, he knew Titus's travel plans and hoped to meet him there or on the way.

So profoundly felt was Paul's suffering on behalf of the Corinthians that he abandoned a promising missionary opportunity in Troas. How could the Corinthians now question his attachment to them? He had deprived others out of concern for them.

Paul was not an insensitive Stoic with a calm spirit that nothing could disturb. He was a fully human person, a Christian who for the sake of a troubled church got emotionally involved. Paul experienced grief, shed tears, and was overtaken by deep anxiety. This experience in Troas was part of the hardest suffering Paul had to bear as an apostle (Hafemann 2000, 106).

In 1:12—2:13 Paul defends his intentions to the Corinthians. He offers as evidence of his integrity: (1) his own conscience (1:12); (2) his conduct when among his converts (1:13-14); (3) the character of the God whom he proclaims (1:15-22); (4) and his concern for those whom he serves in the gospel (1:23—2:13). Obviously, his concern was not to demonstrate that he was a true apostle. This, he and his Corinthian readers took for granted. It was, instead, to provide them with evidence as to the kind of apostle he was.

FROM THE TEXT

The human issue that drives 2 Cor 1:12—2:13 is Paul's defense of his personal integrity as an apostle. He may have felt obliged to respond to accusations made against him by some in the church at Corinth. He insists, however, that his conscience is clear. Can we learn anything from Paul about self-defense in the face of misunderstandings and false accusations?

If we follow his example, we will steadfastly resist the temptation to move ourselves to the center when we are forced to defend ourselves. As Christians we may explain our actions when circumstances justify it. That is, if, like Paul, in doing so we exult in the gospel and do not just defend our wounded egos. Self-defense is not the place for "spiritual" arrogance! Perhaps the "right" circumstances are crucial.

Paul offers a Christian way to defend ourselves. His self-defense was essentially theological. This was because his faith and calling motivated and controlled the whole of his life. Paul was an apostle of the Son of God, who was the "Yes" of the faithful God (1:18-19).

Paul begins his defense by calling attention to the Corinthians' own reception of the gospel. He reminds them that they received the life-changing gospel from him. The gospel defines the character of both the Corinthians as a church and Paul as an apostle. They are one "in Christ." Paul's authenticity as an apostle is one with their authenticity as Christians!

Jesus' silence at his trial (see, e.g., Mark 14:60-61; 15:1-5) has led some to imagine that Christians are denied the right to defend themselves. Does Paul's theology of self-defense offer a model we can imitate? What Pauline faith-perspectives can assist us in the face of misunderstanding and unjust accusations? When we are convinced that we have acted consistently with faithfulness to what the gospel demands, may we defend ourselves? When we as Christians find ourselves in circumstances similar to Paul's, how should we for the sake of the gospel defend ourselves?

A look at the theology implicit in 2 Cor 1:12—2:13 reveals the importance and power of our personal faith-convictions.

First, *it is in the ordinary events of life where the spiritual realities are lived out*. Paul is simply talking about his travel plans in relation to the Corinthians. Thus with Paul all of life, even our conduct in the menial and ordinary tasks and activities, are part of who we are as Christians. It is here that our supposed secular witness has its effect, much more so than in the ephemeral area of signs and wonders—in the so-called charismatic!

Paul's presence alone would be a grace: **I planned to visit you first so that you might have benefit twice** (*charis,* 1:15). What Christians do day after day, week upon week, fulfilling their responsibilities to others—family, friends, and colleagues—matters. Our entire lives as believers are caught up in the gospel and reveal the genuineness and power of our faith. As Paul put it: **we do not write you anything you cannot read or understand** (1:13). At this most basic level of life, the gospel makes its real difference.

Paul's integrity as an apostle, his view of himself, the Corinthians' view of him, and the genuineness of his faith and mission were all involved in his change of travel plans. Thus, he could insist: **When I planned this, did I do it lightly? Or do I make my plans in a worldly manner so that in the same breath I say, "Yes, yes" and "No, no"?** (1:17).

Second, we understand with Paul that as Christians *our integrity is grounded primarily in the nature of the gospel of Christ,* not in ourselves.

1. We are formed and characterized by what or to whom we give our lives. So, our very acceptance of the Christian message indicates that *who* we are and *what* we are is defined by Christ. In his incarnate and resurrected life **the Son of God, Jesus Christ** (1:19) is the content of the gospel. As such, he is the supreme **"Yes"** of God to us in relation to all that God is; therefore, all of God's promises **are "Yes" in Christ** (1:20).

In Jesus we know what God is really like: **God is faithful** (1:18). So the more faithful we are in life to God in Christ, the more we are not "yes" and "no" people. Our character does not vacillate between integrity and undependability. We are, instead, the kind of people for whom "being 'in Christ' makes caprice impossible" (Reed 1976, 193). This is who we are, who we can be, and who we are called to be. So with Paul, "Let us be what we are!" Our conduct will then be **in the holiness and sincerity that are from God, . . . not according to worldly wisdom but according to God's grace** (1:12).

2. This we can know by experience in mind and heart because of God's "establishing" presence in our lives. God has made both Paul and the Corinthians to **stand firm in Christ** by his threefold work—**He anointed us, set his seal of ownership on us, and put his Spirit in our hearts as a deposit, guaranteeing what is to come** (1:21-22).

Our "anointing" speaks of vocation, our authority and equipping for the task of service to Christ. Chrysostom (344/354-407) puts it plainly: "Through the chrism the cross is stamped on you" (ACCS NT 7:202). Our "sealing" brings with it our identification, authenticity, and security as those belonging to Christ. The presence of the indwelling Spirit is God's pledge for our certain future in his kingdom. For the divine "not yet" is "already" the "first installment" (NRSV) that guarantees the full payment. Augustine (354-430) suggests that "we receive a little of it in this life as a pledge to make us learn how to long for its fullness" (ACCS NT 7:203).

New Testament faith says that God's future has effectively invaded our present. The kingdom of God is already arriving when we choose to live in a manner consistent with its arrival. What a privilege! But also, what an obligation! For by our acceptance of the Spirit we pledge ourselves henceforth to live in the Spirit, to walk worthy of our calling: "The Spirit has, as it were, a lien upon us" (Lightfoot 1895, 324).

3. *As Christians our common faith binds us to each other.* In keeping with the creed, *"one* holy catholic and apostolic *church,"* Christians *as Christian* are concerned for each other's spiritual welfare. We take pride in each other's faith. Christians love and forgive one another. And we are confident of our joint future in the faith, especially in anticipation of the day of Jesus Christ the Lord.

Paul struggled with the problems affecting his relationship with the church at Corinth. Nevertheless, his hope was that they would be able to **boast of** him and his coworkers at the Parousia. For his part, he insisted, **we will boast of you in the day of the Lord Jesus** (1:14).

Paul changed his travel plans **in order to spare** (1:23) the Corinthians. His intent was to **work with** [them] **for** [their] **joy** in order that they **would all share** [his] **joy** (1:24; 2:3). But even the noblest intentions may be misunderstood. Grand expectations are sometimes followed by disappointing experiences. What Paul had planned to bless his friends, became a disaster. Then, what he did to avert another disaster only made matters worse. Deeper misunderstanding and distrust brought Paul to the brink of despair.

Paul wrote **out of great distress and anguish of heart and with many tears, not to grieve** [the Corinthians] **but to let** [them] **know the depth of** [his] **love for** [them] (2:4). Why does he tell them this? Because he believes they share in his grief over the situation in Corinth.

But the most significant evidence of the church's real "oneness" was their practice of mutual forgiveness. In the church forgiveness is an absolute necessity. The church cannot be the church unless members forgive one another for Christ's sake. As Paul puts it: **what I have forgiven . . . I have forgiven in the sight of Christ for your sake.**

Forgiveness is the decisive test of the integrity of the church *as church.* The *church prays,* "Forgive us our sins, for we also forgive everyone who sins against us" (Luke 11:4). It is impossible to explain all that forgiveness means in human relationships. But the definition of the Quaker writer Joyce Sams is helpful: "forgiveness is giving up the right to hurt someone for the hurt they've done to you" (Whitmire 2001, 158).

How do we understand what God has done in Jesus the Christ? How do we perceive our Christian faith? Our deeply held personal theological convictions form us. They determine how we live and act in the crucible of human relationships and in the life of the church.

Second Corinthians 1:12—2:13 tells us that: (1) our faith must work in the most ordinary details of life; (2) who we really are bottom-line is determined by the Christ whom we serve; and (3) fundamentally and practically "we are one in the bond of love."

Theology is important not only for the issues of life and death but also for everything else about our lives. It is far more than a classroom exercise or a professional game that scholars play. Theology defines *us!*

God grades us on the cross, not the curve!

B. Paul Characterizes His Ministry (2:14—6:10)

This new section is marked by an apparently abrupt transition from 2:13 to 2:14. Here begins what has been called "the great digression," which extends through 7:4. It is not a distinct letter (see Introduction).

Paul has placed a defense of his ministry within the framework of apostolic suffering, between 2:12-13 and 7:5-16. In 7:5 Paul resumes the narration of his anxiety (2:13) concerning the Corinthians. Here, for the first time he reports that it was relieved by the coming of Titus with news from Corinth (7:5-7).

Apparently evoked by the mention of Macedonia (2:13), Paul's dictation begins to burst out enthusiastically in praise to God. As he contemplates what God has accomplished by means of an instrument as feeble as he, he celebrates the irony (2:14-17).

We have this ministry (4:1) is Paul's theme. He proceeds to delineate its character more precisely as:

- a ministry of the Spirit in a new covenant (3:1—4:6)
- a ministry of suffering in the service of the God who raises the dead (4:7—5:10) and
- a ministry of reconciliation with himself as an ambassador of Christ (5:11—6:10)

The apostle seeks to lead the Corinthians into an understanding of his ministry that will contribute to the restoration of right relations. This would lead the Corinthians to boast in him rather than criticize him.

In this passage Paul opens his heart about his apostolic calling. He presents us with one of the most profound portrayals of authentic Christian ministry to be found anywhere in Scripture. It is particularly "striking in its Christological intensity" (Murphy-O'Connor 1991, 28).

1. Thanksgiving for Triumph in Christ (2:14-17)

Paul breaks into praise or **thanks** to **God** at the thought of God's presence and power manifested through his apostolic ministry. This outburst interrupts the narrative as it begins the long digression. Its soaring insights, however, provide living flesh for the structural bones of Paul's theology of ministry. It presents ministry shaped by the crucified Christ as characterized by **the smell of death** for some and **the fragrance of life** for others. Paul was awed by the privilege and accompanying accountability: **who is equal to such a task?** Such is Paul's introduction to his larger discussion of his apostolic ministry.

BEHIND THE TEXT

In contrast to the "congratulatory benediction" in 1:3-7 (McCant 1999, 29-30), the literary genre of 2:14-16 is clearly "thanksgiving." The first thanksgiving in the letter, it functions as a transition to the *propositio* (2:17). The purpose of the *propositio* in forensic writings is to state the basic facts under dispute in the argument (Witherington 1995, 335). As such, it prepares the way for what follows.

In this text, Paul takes three images from his world and uses them metaphorically to illustrate Christian ministry.

The *first* is the Roman triumph. This took the form of a triumphal procession, following the return from battle of the victorious Roman legions. This parade in Rome was the highest honor that could be given a commanding general.

The Roman triumph is described in various ancient authors (see *J.W.* VII, v, 4-6). These were lavish military parades consisting of state officials and the senate at the head of the procession. They were followed by trumpeters and those carrying spoils of war. These included pictures of the conquered land and models of conquered citadels and ships. Next came flute players leading white oxen that were to be sacrificed. Next there were representatives from the conquered country, dignitaries, generals, and significant warriors. These were all sober and sullen. Not only defeated, some were destined for execution. They walked in chains as prisoners of war. Then, preceded by the lectors bearing the official insignia, were musicians and priests, swinging their censers filled with burning sweet-smelling incense. These preceded the ornate chariot in which the honored general or the Caesar himself rode, followed by his family. At the end of the procession came shouting, exultant, and victorious soldiers, wearing all their decorations and garlands, home at last (Barclay 1956, 205). It was a triumphal spectacle!

The *second* of these pictures is the OT sacrifices. From these came the sweet smell of burnt offerings ascending pleasingly to God. The Wisdom figure who "gave forth perfume [*osmē*]" and "spread forth my fragrance [*euōdia*]" (Sir 24:15, NRSV) may be related. Some suggest here the influence of the general idea in antiquity that fragrance was a sign of the presence of deity.

More likely **fragrance** (*osmē*) reflects the burning of incense in Roman processions, which signaled the approach of the procession (Thrall 2004, 197; McCant 1999, 34). The aroma from the priests' swinging censers announced joy, triumph, and life to the victors. At the same time, it reminded the captives of their execution and death (Barclay 1956, 205).

The *third* picture is that of a retailer or petty-merchant. It is inherent in the verb *kapēleuō*, which occurs only here in the NT (the cognate noun, *kapēlos*, however, appears twice in the LXX, Isa 1:22 and Sir 26:29). The verb could have a neutral or negative nuance. Its negative, pejorative force could have either of two senses.

First, it came to be used for the activities of peddlers. As "middlemen," their only concern seemed to be profit. They did not hesitate to adulterate their goods or give short measure. In short, they were cheats.

Second, it came to be applied to itinerant teachers who "traded" in ideas. More showmen than philosophers, they would *"huckster"* (BDAG 2000, 508) their intellectual wares for personal gain. Playing to the crowd, they adulterated the truth. Chrysostom (344/354-407) dubbed them "wretched sophists" (Furnish 1984, 168).

IN THE TEXT

■ **14 Thanks be to God** (*tōi . . . Theōi charis*) was a normal Greek expression, used often by Paul (Rom 6:17; 1 Cor 15:57; 2 Cor 8:16; 9:15). The word *charis* ("grace") is a key concept in the letter. With this thanksgiving, Paul identifies with his readers' worlds. He unites two metaphors to depict the pervasive spread of the gospel through the apostolic ministry: **Thanks be to God, who . . . through us spreads everywhere . . . the knowledge of him.** Paul expresses gratitude to God for the privilege granted him and his fellow apostles of disclosing (*phanerounti*) the message about Christ ***in every place*** (*en panti topōi*).

The first metaphor, **God . . . always leads us in triumphal procession in Christ,** builds on his audience's knowledge of the Roman triumph. This was the victory parade of triumphant Roman generals on the return of their armies to Rome (see BEHIND THE TEXT). Here, for Paul, the **triumphal procession** is God's parade. He takes part in the cause of and in union with **Christ** (*en tōi Christōi*).

It is difficult to determine how Paul applies the metaphor. With what precise sense does Paul use the verb *thriambeuonti* (**leads . . . in triumphal procession**)? Where do Paul and his partners in ministry (*hēmas*, **us,** and *di' hēmōn*, **through us**) fit into this parade? The scholarly suggestions are many and varied. The general sense is clear enough. The glory of the divine victory is the primary point. Yet, how far can one push the metaphor?

How is Paul being led in the triumphal procession? Does he picture himself in a place of honor or as a conquered captive in the procession? The sense of "causeth us to triumph in Christ" (KJV), favored by the older commentators, is not supported by the linguistic evidence (Thrall 2004, 192). Some contemporary scholars see Paul as among the victorious soldiers following their general, a partner "collaborating with God" (Barrett 1973, 98). Most, however, see him among the captives as God's conquered prisoner of war. The force of the language is paradoxical, of course. Paul was "a willing and privileged captive" (Harris 2005, 245).

Even if Paul employs a metaphor of shame (McCant 1999, 34), the nature of his captivity is in some deep paradoxical sense also Paul's triumph. After all, it is God who triumphs over him! That is his boast. The victory of the gospel is Christ's, and it is his privilege as an apostle to share in it. Paul would certainly identify with the lines of George Matheson,

Make me a captive, Lord,
And then I shall be free.
Force me to render up my sword,
And I shall conqueror be.
—*Sacred Songs*, 1890
The United Methodist Hymnal, 1989, 421

■ **15** The second metaphor in v 15 is of an offering burning on an altar of sacrifice. The process was well known in Jewish and pagan practice. It resulted in the sending up of an aroma considered pleasing to the deity (see Gen 8:20; Exod 20:18; Ezek 20:41; Mal 3:4; Eph 5:2; Phil 4:18).

The term **fragrance** translates the word *osmē* in vv 14 and 16 (twice). There it refers to the quality of something that stimulates the sense of smell, whether pleasant or unpleasant (BDAG 2000, 728). In contrast the term **aroma** (*euōdia*) in v 15 is always pleasant, "a fragrant odor" (BDAG 2000, 417). The **fragrance** (*osmēn*) that permeates the atmosphere **everywhere** through the apostolic ministry is **the knowledge of** Christ, which is the **aroma of Christ** (v 15). Again "the Son of God, Jesus Christ" (1:19) is what the gospel is all about, the essence of the apostolic message.

The cause of (*hoti*, **For**) this sweetening of the atmosphere is Paul and his fellow workers. As Paul moves his imagery from the *osmē* of the Roman procession to the *euōdia* of the OT sacrifice, he declares them to be **the aroma** [*euōdia*] **of Christ** (Harris 2005, 248). Their "scent" is pleasing **to God** both **among those who are being saved and those who are perishing.**

The present tenses, *sōizomenois* (**being saved**) and *apollymenois* (**are perishing**), stress present realities for those so indicated, both of which are in process (see 1 Cor 1:18). The first of the passives may be viewed as in part a divine passive implying that God is doing the saving. The second passive, **are perishing,** should be seen in a similar way. Certainly such are living under God's wrath (Rom 1:18), yet the "why" is not stated as with **are being saved.** Verse 16 makes it clear, however, that the difference is made by the impact of the **aroma of Christ** on each group. Paul thus does not appear to be implying any divine decree in effect as to who is saved and who is lost. He is rather describing their respective life responses to the preaching of the gospel (see the commentary on 4:3-4).

Being "in Christ" characterizes the apostolic ministry and message. Whether people received or rejected the gospel they proclaimed, it remained

the aroma of Christ! Within this metaphor, Christ is pictured as the sacrifice; and Paul, as the aroma that arises from it. This is because "the knowledge of God manifest in the cross of Christ is now being revealed through Paul's suffering among those to whom he is sent" (Hafemann 2000, 111). Here, as in 2:14, Paul's theme remains God's paradoxical power, displayed through human weakness. In fact, this theme is evident throughout the letter (see 12:9).

■ **16** The effect of Paul's ministry was twofold, again exhibiting its paradoxical nature. Those who resisted the message of Paul and his coworkers found them to be **the smell of death.** By rejecting the apostolic gospel, its messengers became for them ***a stench from/of death leading to death*** (*osmē ek thanatou eis thanaton*). On the other hand, those who responded favorably to the preaching of Paul and his fellow workers discovered them to be **the fragrance of life.** As with the former, Paul's description is more literally ***a fragrance from/of life leading to life*** (*osmē ek zōēs eis zōēn*).

The context certainly justifies translating the neutral term, *osmē*, differently in its two appearances in v 16 (see the commentary on vv 14 and 15). The contrasting terms **smell/*stench*** and **fragrance** correctly indicate that the same odor is for some unpleasant and for others pleasant.

More debatable is the question whether the prepositions *ek* and *eis* should be assigned separate meanings? If so, does *ek* suggest the source (***from***) or nature (***of***) and *eis* indicate the result (***to***)? If the prepositions are construed together (as in the NIV) the emphasis is merely rhetorical. They intensify by repetition of the noun the progression from one stage of death/life to another (for similar grammatical constructions using these two pronouns, see Rom 1:17; John 5:24; 12:27; Luke 10:7; 17:24).

A similar rabbinic concept views the Law as a drug, the effect of which can be either fatal or vitalizing. If the Law is studied for its own sake, it is a life-giving medicine. But if one does not study the Law for its own sake, it is a deadly poison (Strack and Billerbeck 1926, 3:498).

Just so, Paul views the ministry of the gospel of grace as inevitably a sentence of death to some and an opportunity of life for others (see 2 Cor 4:3; Luke 2:34; John 5:19-30; 1 Cor 1:18; Phil 1:28). The same saving activity of God in Christ that destroyed death for **those who are being saved** brought death to **those who are perishing.**

The responsibility entailed in the proclamation of the gospel of Christ, which would be "from beginning to end" (Denney 1943, 5:741) an occasion of death or life, overwhelmed Paul. He could only utter, "Who is adequate for these things?" (v 16 NASB). What kind of ministry could be ***sufficient*** (*hikanos*)—**equal to such a task**?

In light of the subsequent contrast between the old and new covenants in 3:4-18, it seems probable that Paul's question echoes Moses' profession of inadequacy for the call of God in Exod 4:10. The LXX translates Moses' objection, *ouch hikanos eimi*—"I am not adequate."

What answer did Paul presume for his question, **And who is equal to such a task?** If the intertextual echo of Exod 4:10 was self-conscious, his implied answer is, "We are!" It seems unlikely that his question was merely rhetorical, implying only, "No one is **equal to such a task"** (see 3:5).

■ **17** In v 17, Paul substantiates his implicit claim that the Spirit of God had made him competent to minister (see 3:4-6). ***For*** [*gar*] **unlike so many, we do not peddle the word of God for profit.** The figure Paul appropriates here may be that of a tavern keeper. The LXX translation of Isa 1:22 (see also Sir 26:29) uses the noun form (*kapēlos*) of the verb **peddle** (*kapēleuō*) Paul uses in v 17. "The tavern-keepers [*hoi kapēloi*] mix wine with water" to increase their profit margin.

The Word of God

The NT use of *logos* (**word**) in relation to the coming of Jesus as the Son of God into the world is varied and rich. In the Fourth Gospel it is employed for the preexistent Son of God who entered the world as fully human. John writes that "in the beginning was the Word [*logos*], and the Word [*logos*] was with God, and the Word [*logos*] was God. . . . The Word [*logos*] became flesh and made his dwelling among us. We have seen his glory, the glory of the One and Only . . . full of grace and truth" (John 1:1, 14). In John's first letter the expression *peri tou logou tēs zōēs* ("concerning the Word of life") appears to include both the person of the incarnate Jesus and the apostolic message concerning him.

Acts frequently uses *logos* ("word") to refer to the message of the gospel of Christ (4:29; 6:4; 8:4; 14:25; 15:7 ["the message of the gospel," *ton logon tou euangeliou*]; 16:6; 17:11; 18:5). Also appearing in Acts are the phrases "the word of the Lord [*ton logon tou kyriou*]" (8:25; 11:16; 12:24; 13:48-49; 15:35-36; 16:32; 19:10) and "the message of his grace [*tōi logōi tēs charitos autou*]" (14:3; 20:32).

Occurring most often for the message and proclamation of the gospel is the phrase Paul uses twice in 2 Corinthians, *ton logon tou Theou* ("the word of God," 2:17; 4:2). This designation is found eleven times in Acts (Acts 4:31; 6:2, 7; 8:14; 11:1; 13:5, 7, 44, 46; 17:13; 18:11), and in Paul's canonical writings eight more times (Rom 9:6; 1 Cor 14:36; Eph 6:17; Phil 1:14; 1 Thess 2:13; 1 Tim 4:5; 2 Tim 2:9; Titus 2:5). Paul also qualifies the *logos* as message by "faith" (Rom 10:8), "Christ" (Rom 10:17; Col 3:16), "cross" (1 Cor 1:18), "reconciliation" (2 Cor 5:19), "truth" (2 Cor 6:7; Col 1:5; 2 Tim 2:15), and "life" (Phil 2:16). To complete the picture, Paul also frequently makes use of the unqualified *logos* for the message and preaching of the gospel (Rom 10:8; 1 Cor 15:2; Gal 6:6; Eph 5:26; Col 4:3; 1 Thess 1:5-6; 2 Tim 4:2; Titus 1:3, 9).

As seen in the life of the early Christians, not only in Acts but also in Hebrews (4:12; 6:5; 11:3; 13:7), 1 Peter (1:23), 1 John (2:14), and Revelation (1:2, 9; 6:9; 19:13; 20:4), "the word of God" as used by Paul in 2 Corinthians was familiar usage throughout the first-century church. All this should make it clear that the NT never uses the expression as modern Christians are inclined to do, as equivalent to the Bible.

Paul contrasts himself and his ministry with those who **peddle the word of God for profit.** They are only hucksters of the gospel in both intention and method. He maligns these anonymous gospel-hawkers with the designation *hoi polloi*—**so many.** The expression "hoi polloi" entered English in the early nineteenth century. In both languages, it refers pejoratively to the masses, people in general (BDAG 2000, 849).

Paul does not imply that all or even most other Christian ministers are frauds. He seems to have in mind the supposed "super-apostles" (11:5), who are actually "false apostles" (11:13). Thus, Paul contrasts his ministry, in both motive and manner, to that of these intruders in Corinth. Here, he implies that they made the ministry a business for personal gain. To do so, they adulterated the gospel with more palatable demands and limited perspectives to further their own interests.

Paul implies that one leads to the other. To approach supposedly Christian ministry with motives of personal profit, ambition, or vanity is already to adulterate it. Some so-called apostles made their message serve their advantage, rather than being subject to it. Such perverse motives changed the very character of the gospel.

Paul refused to water down the gospel (see 4:1-2) to suit himself or his audience. **On the contrary,** Paul insists, **in Christ we speak before God with sincerity, like men sent from God.** Paul refused to play to the crowd. It was an audience of One he tried to please (see Gal 1:10). Paul's claim to **speak before** [*katenanti*]
God (see 12:19) implies that he stands under God's jurisdiction. He was ***accountable to God*** alone (BDAG 2000, 530), as defined **in Christ** (see 1:21; 5:17). 2:17

The phrase **like men sent from God** is, literally, ***as from God*** (*hōs ek Theou*). Certainly, God had called him to be an apostle (see Gal 1:1, 15-17). Not only was he a person sent by God, but the source of Paul's proclamation is God. God bears witness to his work. And it is to God alone he must answer. His ministry was performed in life union with the risen Christ. All of these convictions motivated Paul to **speak . . . with sincerity** (*ex eilikrineias;* see 1:12).

Paul's ministry partakes of the life and ministry of Christ himself. In this lies Paul's sufficiency as an apostle (see 3:5-6), which he will soon expound more fully (3:1—6:10). The gospel of the crucified Christ characterizes both the inspiration and the technique of Paul's apostolic ministry. With the metaphors of the triumphal procession and the aroma of incense and sacrifice, Paul has presented the character of his life-and-death ministry. The negative metaphor of the unscrupulous wine merchant serves to distinguish his ministry from that of his opponents, who are mere peddlers of the word of God.

FROM THE TEXT

Paul's thanksgiving functions as an apology (i.e., a rhetorical defense) for Paul's ministry. It takes us to the heart of authentic ministry. Its insights apply equally to a first-century apostle, a contemporary ordained minister, or the life and witness of any serious believer in the contemporary world. Who are we as Christians in our homes, workplaces, in the larger world, and even in church? What can we learn about ministry from these few verses?

From Paul's experience we see that authentic ministry (1) *is a sovereign God at work* (v 14); (2) *inescapably results in life or in death* (vv 15-16), and (3) *partakes of the character of its message* (v 17).

First, *ministry is a sovereign God at work.* **God . . . leads us in triumphal procession in Christ** (v 14). Like Paul, those in Christ's ministry are conquered prisoners, yet gladly marching in God's victory parade. God is sovereign over all the circumstances of their lives, even over the sufferings and disappointments they endure in the course of their service to Christ. The triumph belongs to **God . . . in Christ**. The ministry is God's; it is God who is **always** at work in the lives of his servants, for they are only paraded as captives of the Christ of the cross.

A fascinating image expresses how this occurs. As those who minister we are **the fragrance of the knowledge of him** (v 14). By our faith identification in life and ministry with Christ in his sufferings (1:3-7), wrote Clement of Alexander (150-215), "the suffering of the Lord, indeed, has filled us with its fragrance" (ACCS NT 7:210). Although not always visible to human eyes, the presence of Christ can be recognized by the fragrance of our lives: "the knowledge of God [is] an aroma. Its presence is sensed rather than seen" (Pelagius [354-420], ACCS NT 7:210). And it is through the fragrance of such lives that "the providential unseen hand of God often works quietly in the shadows of our world" (Moore 2005, 56-57). The hidden Christ makes known the crucified and risen Christ, in whom the knowledge of the invisible God is understood.

Second, *ministry inescapably results in life or death.* The presence of the Christian minister in the broadest sense is paradoxical. On the one hand it is the presence of life; and, on the other, the presence of death. The **aroma** of the crucified and risen Christ rises up from the sacrificial altar of our lives. This becomes at one and the same time **the smell of death** to some and **the fragrance of life** for others. We have no control over its effect.

Paul uses the same Greek word for both **smell** and **fragrance,** for **the aroma of Christ** can be experienced as either death or life by the recipient. Some receive, while others reject, the life that confronts them in the atmosphere of our presence, work, and words. The ones who open their hearts to the crucified God we represent are in the process of **being saved.** The ones whose hearts remain closed to God **are perishing.**

What men and women do with **the fragrance of the knowledge** of the cross of Christ, invisibly present in the grace that goes before, determines their response to the Christ visible in the Scriptures. With Paul, we cannot help but cry out, **and who is equal to such a task?** (v 16). So, with Origen (185-254), we must keep "an altar of incense in" our "innermost heart" (ACCS NT 7:210).

Third, *ministry partakes of the character of its message.* Unlike some high-profit offshore investment schemes, a truly Christian ministry passes the "smell" test. It goes beyond the merely legal. With the apostle in ministry and witness, we conduct ourselves in a twofold manner consistent with our message: (1) **we do not peddle the word of God** in *motive,* for **in Christ we speak** "from sincerity . . . as from God" (NASB).

Beyond just compensation, a ministry that is Christian does not "trade in" the gospel for personal gain. To compromise purity of motive in presenting the gospel is to change it. The message is no longer the same. Even in his day John Chrysostom (344/354-407) wrote that "corruption occurs when one sells for money what one ought to give freely" (ACCS NT 7:211).

Just as importantly (2) **we do not peddle the word of God** in *method,* for **we speak *in the sight of God in Christ.*** To do "gospel" is to be faithful to, not compromise, its content. We do not mix the message with something else in order to secure a more friendly reception. To do so changes its character. It becomes "a different gospel," perhaps "really no gospel at all" (Gal 1:6).

Recall the demonic advice of C. S. Lewis' Screwtape to his nephew:

> Once you have made the World an end and faith a means, you have almost won your man, and it makes very little difference what kind of worldly end he is pursuing. Provided that meetings, pamphlets, policies, movements, causes, and crusades matter more to him than prayers and sacraments and charity, he is ours—and the more "religious" (on those terms), the more securely ours. (Lewis 1961, 39)

Our sense of accountability to God is to stand guard against merchandising the gospel. As our lives are united with the risen Christ, our ministry becomes at once his ministry. Therefore, our adequacy for the task is not *of* ourselves. It is in the nature and power of our message. It is in the gospel of the crucified Christ as empowered by the presence of God through the Spirit.

2. A Ministry of the Spirit (3:1—4:6)

Paul's impressive description of his ministry could very well have prompted the charge that he was engaged in sheer self-promotion. But he insists that the nature of his apostolic ministry among the Corinthians was such that he needed no fresh introductions or letters of recommendation either from or to the Corinthians. Their very existence as Christians was recommendation enough (3:1-3).

The apostle's ministry was one of a new covenant.

- Its adequacy is found in the life-giving Spirit (3:4-6).
- Its glory surpasses that of the old covenant (3:7-11).
- And its liberty is from the transforming Spirit of the Lord (3:12-18).

A ministry thus grounded in the mercy of God is completely open to the conscience of everyone and conducted in the sight of God (4:1-6). In these verses Paul continues his theological reflection on the nature of his apostolic ministry. He lays a theological foundation for the rest of the letter and for all who are in Christian ministry.

BEHIND THE TEXT

Second Corinthians 2:17 functions rhetorically as the *propositio*. That is, it states the basic facts under dispute in the argument. Its apologetic rhetorical objective calls for a reference to letters of commendation or recommendation (*systatikē epistolē*) in 3:1. Such letters of introduction were common in antiquity. They normally commended the bearer to the recipient, requesting help, hospitality, instruction, or even employment. The letters indicated that their bearers were in good standing with their senders. Their recipients, as friends or patrons, were expected to comply with such requests. The cultural atmosphere of the day considered such recommendations as important, and weight was given to them. An example from A.D. 6 reads:

> Apollonius to Serapion the strategus and gymnasiarch, many greetings and good health always. Isidorus, the one who is delivering this letter, is from my household. I ask you to consider him as introduced to you, and if he come to you for anything do it for him for my sake. If you do this, I will be indebted to you. Whatever you wish to signify I will do without delay. Take care of yourself so that you will be in good health. Farewell. (Quoted in Stowers 1986, 157; see Thrall 2004, 219, n 219)

Paul had carried such letters in his pre-Christian days as a persecutor of the first Christians (Acts 9:2; 22:5). He often recommended his associates in his letters, as in Rom 16:1-2:

> I commend to you our sister Phoebe, a servant of the church in Cenchrea. I ask you to receive her in the Lord in a way worthy of the saints and to give her any help she may need from you, for she has been a great help to many people, including me. (See also 1 Cor 16:1-2; 2 Cor 8:22-23; Eph 6:21-22; Col 4:7-8, 10; Phlm 10-12, 17-19.)

The use of such letters was widespread in the NT church (see Acts 15:25-27; 18:27). Philemon and 3 John are often considered letters of recommendation (Witherington 1995, 335, 276-378; Stowers 1986, 153-56; see Thrall 2004, 218-19, n 219).

In the background of 3:1-18 stands the theologically rich narrative in Exod 32—34. Paul clearly echoes the account in 34:29-35. The OT setting places the Israelites at the foot of Mount Sinai (Exod 19:1). There they awaited the terms of the covenant with Yahweh (19:4-6). The revelation at Sinai included the giving of the Ten Words (19:1—20:21), the Book of the Covenant (20:22—23:33), and the ratification of the covenant (24:1-18). After this, Moses went up the mountain for forty days and nights to be with the Lord. There he received instructions for building the tabernacle and "the two tablets of the Testimony, the tablets of stone inscribed by the finger of God" (25:1—31:18; see 2 Cor 3:3).

While Moses was away, the Israelites became impatient with his absence. They persuaded Aaron to make them a golden calf and proceeded to worship it in a riotous manner (32:1-6). Their worship reflected the debauchery commonly associated with the fertility gods, whom they imagined brought them up out of Egypt (v 8). This was a "second fall"!

Israel's apostasy led to a profound series of intercessions, as Moses sought to turn away the anger of God from the destruction he threatened to bring upon his people (32:7—33:23). Moses' intercession was heard, and the Lord renewed his covenant by giving Moses two new stone tablets containing "the words of the covenant—the Ten Commandments" (34:1-28).

Paul mentions these "tablets of stone" in 3:3. At this point in the Exod narrative (34:29-35), Moses came down from Mount Sinai with the two tablets in his hands unaware that "his face was radiant because he had spoken with the LORD" (34:29). When the people saw Moses' radiant face, they were afraid to approach him. At his invitation, however, Aaron and the leaders came back; and Moses "gave them all the commands the LORD had given him on Mount Sinai" (34:32). "When Moses finished speaking to them, he put a veil over his face" (34:33). He removed it when he went into the tent of meeting to enter "the LORD's presence to speak with him" (34:34). But whenever Moses came out to speak to the Israelites, he kept the veil over his face.

Paul alludes to these incidents in 2 Cor 3:7-18. In light of his free and reflective use of this OT account, it should be noted that Paul "lived in" his Bible. As Young and Ford remark, Paul used the Scriptures "in study, devotion and prayer, to the point where certain features of the scriptural material had come to mould his self-understanding and his discernment of what was going on in the conflict between himself and the church at Corinth" (1987, 80, see 80-84).

IN THE TEXT

a. Paul's Letter of Recommendation (3:1-3)

Paul begins this section mentioning "letters of recommendation" (v 1). He poses two rhetorical questions to open the issue of self-commendation. He concedes that he has, in some sense, been commending himself (1:12—2:17). This is demonstrated by his use of the word **again.**

Yet the formulation of his questions shows that Paul expected a negative answer to his question: "Surely we do not need, as some do, letters of recommendation to you or from you, do we?" (v 1 NRSV). Paradoxically, Paul then insists that the Corinthians are themselves his letter of commendation to them (v 2). The church in Corinth constitutes his credentials!

How can Paul here so disparage self-commendation, when he later will indulge in it openly? In 4:2 he will write, "we commend ourselves to every man's conscience in the sight of God." And in 6:4 he will add, "as servants of God we commend ourselves in every way."

More than a century ago (1897), J. H. Bernard distinguished between two types of statements in Paul's usage in this regard (1987, 3:52). When Paul speaks negatively about self-commendation he writes, *heautous synistanein* (3:1; see 5:12; 10:12, 18). But when he speaks positively, he reverses the Greek word order, writing *synistanein heautous* (see 4:2; 6:4; 7:11; 12:11). The different positions of the pronoun *heautou* (**ourselves**) apparently matters.

The first phrase in v 1 has *heautous* (**ourselves**) in an emphatic grammatical position. This seems to refer to praising oneself without supporting evidence. The second formulation, in 4:2, places *heautous* in a secondary position. Paul appeals to the work of God through his servant to God's glory (Harris 2005, 259).

This "solution" may be too simple (see 5:12). But, at least, it helps us recognize how Paul understands self-commendation. This is a delicate subject in any culture, both in a good and a bad sense. Whether or not self-commendation is offensive depends on its manner and the circumstances occasioning it (see Witherington 1995, 376, 385).

Verses 1-3 look back to 2:17 and anticipate 3:4-6. They are transitional and openly introduce Paul's defense of his apostolic ministry: his person, his office, and his message. His defense here, more clearly than earlier in the letter, states that the essential commendation of his ministry is simply the evident Christian character of the Corinthians themselves. Their very existence as Christians affirmed the power and authority of the apostle. Even in 1

Corinthians Paul had written to the Corinthians, "you are the seal of my apostleship in the Lord" (9:2). The Corinthians as a body of believers are, in fact, a letter written by Christ himself with Paul as the scribe and courier in the founding of the church at Corinth.

■ **1** Paul fears that the insistence on his sincerity (2:17) would be again turned into an accusation of self-praise by his enemies. He deftly fields the anticipated charge with a question phrased to anticipate a negative answer: ***We do not need, do we*** [*ē mē chrēizomen*]**, like some people, letters of recommendation to you or from you?** With neat, almost sarcastic irony Paul returns the charge to his detractors. **Some people** (*tines*), no doubt, refers to the same people identified as the "many" in 2:17. They may be the false apostles (11:13) who had invaded the Corinthian church on the strength of **letters of recommendation.**

Hughes describes these letters as "bills of clearance for the profitable marketing of their merchandise in spiritual things" (1962, 85). Such **letters,** current in Paul's day, were also widely used in the early church. While they were easily abused, they were a necessity, especially for church leaders who needed to travel between churches as it rapidly expanded geographically.

■ **2** Paul, however, had no need to flourish letters written on parchment or papyrus to the Corinthians. Rather, the Corinthians themselves constituted his apostolic credentials: **You yourselves are our letter, written on our hearts, known and read by everybody.**

Some interpreters instead of **our** (*hēmōn*) are open to the possibility of the textual variant "your" (*hymōn*). In this instance, the **hearts** would belong to the Corinthians, who are Paul's letter of recommendation (Thrall 2004, 224; Martin 1986, 44). Although "your" (*hymōn*) may fit the context better, the external evidence along with the judgment of other translators (NASB and NRSV), favors the NIV's choice of **our hearts** (see Harris 2005, 257). Paul is their father in the faith (1 Cor 4:15) and as his children they are in his heart (2 Cor 7:3).

Paul refers to the "heart" as the center of the human personality—the whole person feeling, thinking, and willing. Both here and in v 3 the expression **tablets of human hearts** has a rich OT background (Jer 31:33; Ezek 11:19; 36:26-27).

The unmistakable transformation that had occurred in the lives of the Corinthians through the power of the gospel (see Acts 4:13-16) continually evidences to all who know them the genuineness of Paul's apostleship: "you are the seal of my apostleship in the Lord" (1 Cor 9:2).

This knowledge is stressed by the two participles, **known and read** (*ginōskomenē kai anaginōskomenē*). Their present tense indicates that this metaphorical **letter** was always open for careful examination. The qualifying phrase **by everybody** is literally ***by all men*** (*hypo pantōn anthrōpōn*), here meaning ***people.*** The perfect participle **written** (*engegrammenē*) refers to the present state resulting from a past event. Paul came to love his Corinthian converts. And he continues to have a deep, personal, and enduring love for these folks (2:4; 6:11-13; 7:2-3). He carries them always with him in his heart.

Everybody stands in contrast to **some people** (v 1) whose ministerial motives were highly questionable (2:17; 11:13). Paul considered sincere motives and an intense concern for people indispensible to authentic ministry.

■ **3** With this verse Paul begins to base the validity of his apostleship specifically on the presence and power of the Spirit in his ministry (see 1:22). In a startling metaphor, the Corinthians ***are shown in reality*** (*phaneroumenoi*) to be **a letter from Christ.** Christ is the letter's source or its author (a subjective genitive). Paul's description of how this has taken place is theologically illuminating.

First, Paul insists, **you are . . . the result of our ministry** or "you are . . . cared for by us" (NASB). The Greek phrase *diakonētheisa hyph' hēmōn* ("ministered by us" [KJV]), carries the full authority of the apostolic ministry (see Mark 10:45).

The use here of the **letter** metaphor, however, allows for such translations as "delivered by us" (RSV) and "prepared by us" (NRSV) to complete the picture. Harris suggests the translation "we transcribed." Paul presents himself as the scribe or amanuensis of the letter of Christ, which is, of the Corinthian church (2005, 263). He acted as a representative of Christ in founding the church. Significantly, this verb anticipates Paul's use of "ministers" (*diakonous*) in v 6 and "ministry" (*diakonia*) in vv 7-9 (see 4:1; 5:18). Thus, the controlling concepts are "ministers of a new covenant" (3:6) and "the ministry of the Spirit" (v 8).

Second, consistent with Paul's imagery, the letter was **written not with ink but with the Spirit of the living God.** As the first of two telling contrasts, the transition from the inanimate (**ink**) to the animate (**Spirit**) is unexpected and, therefore, dramatic (Harris 2005, 264). The transforming reception of the gospel in Corinth was not simply a matter of human agency. It was the work of the Spirit.

The phrase **the Spirit of the living God** occurs only here in Scripture, whereas the component phrases—"the living God" (Rom 9:26) and "the Spirit of God" (Rom 8:9)—are both found in Paul and elsewhere in the NT. With this phrase the apostle introduces a key concept in his understanding of the new covenant ministry, which he will more fully develop in 3:4-18.

Third, the second contrast with which Paul describes his ministry is **not on tablets of stone but on tablets of human hearts.** Paul has moved from a contrast between two *means* of writing to a contrast between two writing *materials*. One is "stony" and the other is "human." He contrasts the writing of the old covenant on **tablets of stone** (*lithinais*) with the new covenant written on ***tablets of flesh*** (*sarkinais*). His imagery combines the language of Exod 31:18, "tablets of stone inscribed by the finger of God" (see Deut 9:10), with that of the major prophets Jeremiah and Ezekiel.

Jeremiah wrote of a time when Yahweh "will make a new covenant," one in which he will write his law "on their hearts" and "be their God, and they will be my people" (31:31, 33). Paul's language is even more similar to
3:3 Ezekiel's. In Ezek 11:19, Paul's **human hearts** (*kardiais sarkinais*) reflects Ezekiel's "heart of flesh" (see 36:26 LXX: *kardian sarkinēn*). Also significant for our passage is the promise of the Spirit in Ezekiel's context. Yahweh will give his people "a new heart" and a "new spirit" as a result of his promise: "I will put my Spirit in you" (36:26, 27).

Paul's rich imagery exposes the inner character of his apostolic commission (see 3:6). This **letter** is no literal epistle. The spiritual experience of the Corinthians themselves is its content. The presence of the Spirit in their lives is undeniable as Paul seeks their spiritual encouragement along with his own defense. Written on Paul's heart by Christ, the Corinthians are his letter of commendation. Their own Christian standing is at stake in his apostleship. The church in Corinth legitimates his apostolic standing.

Thrall points out that people in the ancient world considered the inner memory and mind to be superior to literal inscriptions. The oral was preferred to the written. **Written** suggests that letters of recommendation would be a less persuasive, substitute source of credibility (2004, 227).

Ultimately, what commends the apostle is his divine commission within the new covenant. Paul proceeds to enlarge upon the ministry of the Spirit, written first on his own heart and then delivered to others. In these verses with their unique vocabulary, Paul laid the foundation for the comparison of this ministry with that of Moses, which follows in vv 4-18.

b. The Adequacy of the New Covenant Ministry (3:4-6)

Paul's presentation of the ministry of the new covenant continues to guard against a misinterpretation of the triumphal description of his apostolic ministry (2:14-17). Paul's motives were pure. He had no need to commend himself to the Corinthians (3:1-3).

In vv 4-6 he insists that the ground of his **confidence** is not in himself. God has made him adequate as a minister of **a new covenant.** This is already intimated by Paul's imagery in v 3. As a ministry of the Spirit and not of the letter, the ministry of the new covenant transcends that of the old covenant (see the commentary on 3:14).

Paul will demonstrate this in 3:7-11. There he will appeal to the shine on Moses' face, which Moses covered with a veil. He did so on account of the people as he returned to them from Mount Sinai (Exod 34:29-35).

■ **4** The words **such confidence** referred to the apostle's conviction concerning the Corinthians themselves. They constituted an irrefutable witness to the validity of his apostolic calling. Included as well in **such confidence** was the character of Paul's own ministry as God's agent and its effectiveness in the founding of the church. Paul's use of the term **confidence** (*pepoithēsin*) is unique to his letters in the NT. It appears six times in this letter (1:15; 3:4; 8:22; 10:2) and twice in others (Eph 3:13; Phil 3:4).

Paul possessed **such confidence** only **through Christ before God.** Above all for him, it was **through** [*dia*] **Christ** (see Eph 2:18). This **confidence** Paul possessed in the presence of or in relation to **God.** He looked to **God** as its ultimate source. His was not a mere human confidence. It was a **confidence** in a sense spoken face-to-face (*pros*) with God. It could survive the test of divine scrutiny (see 5:10).

■ **5** Paul's explanation continues, motivated by his concern to avoid being misinterpreted. He insists that it is **not that we are competent** [*hikanoi*] **in ourselves** or have any inherent ***adequacy.*** Rather, as new covenant ministers, we do not **claim anything for ourselves.** We do not ***consider*** [*logisasthai*] ***anything as coming from ourselves*** [*ex heautōn*]. ***On the contrary*** [*alla*, **but**], **our competence** [*hikanotēs;* only here in the Greek Bible] **comes from** [*ek*] **God** (see 4:7; 5:18; 6:4; 7:5-6; 11:23; 12:9-10; 13:3-4; 1 Cor 15:10).

Paul's grasp and mastery of apostolic ministry did not stem from his own human resources. He lays no personal claim to his ***adequacy*** in the gospel, as he rejects all false self-commendation. He uses the same terminology with which he first raised the question in 2:16, ***who is adequate for these things?*** Paul develops his answer in vv 5-6. Significantly for Paul's language, Ruth and Job (LXX) several times described God as *ho hikanos*, the "Sufficient One" (Ruth 1:20, 21; Job 21:15; 31:2; 40:2). Is Paul saying that "our adequacy comes from the only Adequate One"?

With the language of adequacy, Paul again compares his call to that of Moses (2:16; see Exod 4:1, 10, 13). To do so he evokes the OT prophetic call narratives that follow a similar pattern (Isa 6:1-8; Jer 1:4-10; Ezek 1:1—3:11; see Judg 6:11-14). All the prophets were insufficient in themselves. Yet they were made sufficient by God for their task. Paul as an apostle of Jesus Christ (1:1) understands his ministry as like that of an OT prophet. With this allusion to his call (Acts 9:3-18; 22:14-16; 26:16-18; see 1 Tim 1:12-14), Paul insists that **our competence** [*hikanotēs*] **comes from God.**

■ **6** He reinforces this point in v 6. God **has made us competent as ministers** [*diakonous*] **of a new covenant** (v 6; 1 Cor 11:25; Jer 31:31-34).

The Greek word for **ministers,** *diakonous* (see 3:3), is used by Paul to describe his function as an authoritative spokesman for God. His appointed role was to be an apostolic "medium" of God's revelation and glory (esp. 2 Cor 2:14—6:13; Collins 1990, 202-3). The aorist tense of the verb, **made us competent** (*hikanōsen*), suggests that Paul refers back to the event of his conversion-call.

Covenant, which translates the Greek *diathēkēs,* is its normal translation in the NT. One exception is Heb 9:16-17, where "will" (NIV, NRSV) or "testament" (KJV) is preferred. In the LXX it translates the Hebrew *brith.* Thus, *diathēkē* carries with it the broad connotations of the OT concept of "covenant" from the ministry of Moses to that of Jeremiah.

Covenant throughout the Bible refers to an agreement, not between equals, but between God and his people. God graciously offers his saving presence. This invitation is confirmed by the grateful response of his people in their fulfillment of their **covenant** obligations. Paul received the expression **new covenant** from the early Christian Last Supper tradition (1 Cor 11:25; Luke 22:20; see Matt 26:27-29; Mark 14:24-25). He was probably aware that it came ultimately from Jer 38:31 (LXX; see Jer 31:31-34; Heb 8:6-13; 9:15; 12:24; CD 6:19; 8:21).

Paul saw himself as a minister of a **new covenant** in some significant sense as contrasted to "the old covenant" (3:14; see Exod 24:3-8; Gal 4:24). Its newness (*kainēs*) was, first, one of time. It belonged to a new era in the history of God's salvation purposes. It was a **covenant** inaugurated by Jesus in his life, ministry, death, and resurrection: "the new covenant in my blood" (1 Cor 11:25; see Luke 22:20).

The covenant's newness was, second, one of kind. Paul described it as **not of the letter but of the Spirit** (v 6; see Rom 2:28-29). With this statement, Paul moves from describing himself as a "minister" to a description of the nature of his ministry. He proceeds to elucidate his ministry in the verses that follow.

By **letter** (*grammatos*)**,** Paul views the old covenant as set down in an outward or written code of Law (see 3:7). By **Spirit,** he characterizes the era of the new covenant Christ inaugurated in terms of its inner, divine dynamic. It consists of the Law written "on their hearts" (Jer 31:33). It is the presence of God's Spirit involved in a new way.

The contrast is not between a literal (material) and an allegorical (intellectual) or "spiritual" interpretation of Scripture as beginning with the church father Origen (185-254; ACCS NT 7:216). The contrast is between a covenant viewed as external commands to be obeyed inscribed on stone tablets and a covenant characterized by the Spirit of God living in the human heart eliciting a response of life (3:3). Hafemann expresses this contrast as between "the law itself without the Spirit" as "experienced by the majority of Israelites under the Sinai covenant" and *"the law with the Spirit"* as "now being experienced by those under the new covenant in Christ" (2000, 133).

This is seen in the contrasting results of the two covenants. Paul sets these in bold relief. The glory (see 3:7-11) of the ministry of the new covenant is "the ministry of the Spirit" (v 8). This distinction between the old and the new consists in light of the declaration that **the letter kills, but the Spirit gives life** (see Rom 7:6).

The letter refers to God's will expressed or conceived only in the form of written prohibitions. These could incite and condemn sin (see Rom 7:7-25). But they were powerless, due to human weakness ("the flesh" in Rom 8:3 NRSV). Thus, the old covenant became a "ministry that brought death" (v 7; see 1 Cor 15:56). But "the Spirit of life in Christ Jesus" (Rom 8:2 NASB; see 3:17; 1 Cor 15:45) is able to engrave the will of God on human hearts (see Acts 15:9). That is, the Spirit enables believers actually to fulfill the righteous requirements of a holy God (Rom 8:4).

Nevertheless, the Law of Moses remains valid, for "the law is holy" and "spiritual" (Rom 7:12, 14). Far from being invalidated, it is established (Rom 3:31) or fulfilled (Rom 13:8-10; Gal 5:14) by the Spirit. By the power of the constant presence of the Spirit of Christ (Rom 8:2-9), faith operates through love (*agapē*). The Spirit empowers believers to attend to the ethical concerns of Christians (Gal 5:6). The sufficiency of Paul's calling is that it is anchored in a superior ministry. His ministry does not depend on impotent external commands, but on the effective inner working of the transforming Spirit (3:18).

c. *The Glory of the New Covenant Ministry (3:7-11)*

In vv 7-11, Paul moves to a description of the glory of the new covenant. He clearly elaborates on what he has previously only alluded to by means of the terms **letter** and **Spirit** (3:3, 6). The contrast between the ministries of the old and new covenants is focused on the ministries of Moses the lawgiver and Paul the apostolic messenger. Paul views both of these eras of ministry in the history of salvation in their wholeness.

Paul composes his remarks in vv 7-11 around three carefully structured comparisons (vv 7-8, 10, 11). Each uses the rabbinic argumentative style known as *qal wahomer* (Hebrew: "the light and the heavy"). His argument moves from "the lesser to the greater" (Latin: *a minori ad maius*). It argues from what is generally accepted as "true" to the **how much more** (v 9; note: **even more glorious** in v 8 and **how much greater** in v 11) of "what is even more certainly true" (Harris 2005, 279).

■ **7** To do this, Paul interprets the story of Moses in Exod 34:29-35 in homiletical fashion. He opens his first comparison with a rhetorical question (vv 7-8). Unlike the rhetorical question in 3:1, here he expects a positive answer: ***The ministry empowered by the Spirit will be even more glorious, will it not?***

Paul refused to let "the letter kills" (v 6) have the last word about the old covenant. True, the ministry of Moses was ***a ministry of death engraved in letters on stone*** (v 7; see 3:3). And it was **fading** (vv 7 and 11). But it also **came with glory** (vv 7 and 11). That is, it was ***attended by radiance.***

To validate this claim, Paul recalls the radiance on Moses' face as he came down from the mountain "with the two tablets of the Testimony in his hands" (Exod 34:29). The result was that **the Israelites** [*huious Israēl,* ***sons/children of Israel***] **could not look steadily** [*atenisai*] **at the face of Moses because of *the glory of his face,* fading though it was.** The aorist verb *atenisai* suggests that the people could not keep their gaze focused on the shining brilliance of Moses' face.

The word **glory** (*doxan;* see *doxēi* in vv 8, 9, and 11; *doxa* in v 9; *dedoxastai* and *dedoxasmenon* in v 10; *doxēs* in vv 10 and 11) reflects LXX terminology (*dedoxastai* in Exod 34:29-30, 35). Significantly, *doxa* translates the Hebrew *kabod* in Exod 24:16-17: "and the glory of the LORD settled on Mount Sinai. . . . To the Israelites the glory of the LORD looked like a consuming fire on top of the mountain" (see Exod 40:34-35). Here **glory** (*kabod*) describes the awful holiness of the Divine Presence as unapproachable light.

Moses' Horns

Michelangelo's colossal statue of Moses in San Pietro in Vincoli, Rome, represents Moses just after his descent from Mount Sinai, when he finds the Israelites worshipping the golden calf. Moses is seated, heavily bearded, and draped. In his right hand he holds the tables of the Law. Those who have seen the image cannot help but be struck by an unexpected feature. Moses has two horns protruding from his upper forehead. This statue, crafted between 1513 and 1516, climaxed a two hundred year medieval tradition of the depiction of this scene in statuary.

The tradition of Moses' horns arose from the Latin Vulgate, the official biblical translation of medieval Christendom. In Exod 34:29-30 and 35 the MT uses the Hebrew verb *qaran* ("shine, be radiant"). Moses' "face was radiant" as he came down from the mountain. Literally, it says that "the skin of Moses' face shone with horn-like rays." The Hebrew noun *qeren* can mean "horn" or "ray of light." The Vulgate mistakenly took *qaran* to mean that Moses had acquired horns: "his face was horned" (Daiches 1975, 228, 243; Harris 2005, 283).

Jewish tradition was familiar with this splendor of the Shekinah of God on Moses' face as he came down from the mountain (Thrall 2004, 242-43). But it knew nothing of Paul's interpretive addition: **fading though it was.** The adverbial participle, *katargoumenēn*, has a concessive force (**though**). It is from the verb *katargeō*, meaning "to cause something to come to an end or to be no longer in existence" (BDAG 2000, 525; see Rom 6:6; 1 Cor 6:13; 13:11). Here, in the passive voice, it has the intransitive meaning *"cease, pass away"* (BDAG 2000, 525; see 1 Cor 3:18). The NRSV translates it as "a glory now set aside." Hafemann interprets the participle to mean that the veil rendered the impact of the glory on Moses' face inoperative. Otherwise, it would have destroyed Israel because of their rebellion (Exod 33:3, 5; Hafemann 2000, 147-49; see Harris 2005, 284 n 43; and 298 n 23).

■ **8** An awareness of all this gives Paul's rhetorical question a striking force. "The ministry that brought death" involved only letters engraved on stone tablets. If it came with such splendor, is it not more than obvious (*ouchi*), asks Paul, that **the ministry of the Spirit** (v 8), who "gives life" (v 6), should **be even more glorious?**

Paul contrasts two ministries (*diakonia*). One denoted the old system of the Mosaic law; and the other, the new covenant in Christ. The earlier one was passing away; the other, possessing the future (*estai*, **will . . . be**). The comparison opposes ***the ministry of death*** (v 7) and **the ministry of the Spirit** (v 8).

The two genitives (*thanatou*, **of death,** and *pneumatos*, **of the Spirit**) could be interpreted as adjectival. As such, it would characterize the two ministries as deadly vs. spiritual. Or, the genitives could be treated as objective genitives. That is, the words **death** and **Spirit** function as implied direct objects of the verbal noun **ministry.** The one **ministry** leads to **death;** the other, to **the Spirit,** who is the source of "life." The former is more probable.

■ **9** In the second phase of the first contrast, Paul explains: ***For if glory is with the ministry of condemnation, how much more does the ministry of righteousness abound with glory*** (see Deut 27:26; Gal 3:10; Rom 1:17; 5:17; 8:1-4; 1 Cor 1:30). ***Condemnation*** (*katakriseōs*) is best taken as an objective genitive expressing what the old **ministry** did (thus, the NIV): **the ministry . . . condemns men.**

John Calvin comments that Paul considered "the function of the Law" in Israel's history to be "to show us the disease without offering any hope of cure." By way of contrast, "the function of the Gospel [was] to provide a remedy for those in despair" (1547, 45).

"The ministry of the Spirit" (v 8) exceeds the ministry of the old covenant. This is because it is a greater matter to acquit sinners than to condemn them. The one takes only the letter of the Law on stones; the other, the Spirit of Christ, who is able to transform human hearts.

The **righteousness** on which Paul bases the superiority of the new covenant ministry is *"the* righteousness of God" revealed in "the gospel" (Rom 1:16-17 NASB; see Rom 3:24-26; 2 Cor 5:21). This "righteousness" the apostle expounds in terms of justification by faith and the sanctification of life in Rom 3:31—8:39. It is the new **righteousness** of a "right" relationship with God in

Christ. This, of course, issues in a life made "right," because it has been transformed by the Spirit of Christ.

■ **10** In this verse, Paul has created a striking oxymoron or paradox: "what has had splendor has not had splendor" (Furnish 1984, 204). Paul's substantive adjectival participle, **what was glorious** (*to dedozasmenon*), refers primarily to the Mosaic covenant as a whole. But it may also allude to Moses' countenance as he returned to the Israelites (LXX, Exod 34:29, 30, 35).

The apostle presents the contrast between the old and new ministries as a radical one. The old covenant ***once had glory*** (*to dedozasmenon*). It was, after all, the instrument of God's self-revelation. Compared to the new covenant, however, the old ***has no glory*** (*ou dedozastai*). This is ***on account of the glory*** of the second ministry, which so far ***surpasses*** it (see John 1:17; Rom 10:4; Gal 3:21-26). The splendor of the old covenant as a whole has now become comparatively dim. It is like the light from a lamp when the splendor of dawn appears. "The greater light swallows up the less" (Wesley 1950, 650).

■ **11** Paul has reached the decisive third stage of his argument (vv 7-8, 10). ***For*** [*gar*] **if what was fading away came with glory** [*dia doxēs*], **how much greater is the glory** [*en doxē*] **of that which lasts!** One should probably not distinguish between the force of the propositions *dia* and *en*, since *en doxē* qualifies both covenants in vv 7-8. Both prepositional phrases describe the glorious circumstances attending each covenant.

The final point of contrast concerns the radiance of Moses' face "because he had spoken with the LORD" (Exod 34:29). This **glory** Paul interpreted as fading away even as Moses was coming down from Mount Sinai. This was indicative of the transitory nature of the covenant that Moses represented. It was a vanishing order, which began to fade soon after its inception. Paul contrasts the ephemeral character of the old order with the permanency (*to menon*, **which lasts**) of the dispensation of the Spirit (see John 1:33). Paul's reasoning depends on his assumptions about religious history in light of Christ (Harris 2005, 291).

In these verses, Paul affirms the adequacy of his apostolic ministry in a theologically rich series of contrasts. He is convinced that his ministry is superior to that of the old covenant, because his is a ministry of a new covenant. That is, it is a ministry of the Spirit rather than of the letter. It is superior (1) as life is more glorious than death, (2) as righteousness is more glorious than condemnation, and (3) as the permanent is more glorious than the transitory. Paul does not denigrate the old covenant, for it, too, was a covenant of God's glory. The Spirit of the Lord (3:18), seen through the lens of the incarnation and the cross, makes the new covenant unique.

d. The Liberty of the New Covenant Ministry (3:12-18)

With such a ministry, Paul, even in the face of accusations, freely speaks out openly. He conceals nothing, as he articulates the liberty characteristic of the new covenant ministry. His ministry, unlike that of Moses, who personifies the old covenant, is transparent. It possesses the liberty of the Spirit of the Lord. The Spirit enables all to behold the glory of the Lord in a life-transforming manner. In 3:7-11, the apostle commented on Exod 24:29-30. In 3:12-18 he depends more on Exod 34:33-35 to make his point. He also moves from comparison to differences as he puts his argument to work.

In 3:7-18 Paul highlights three things not explicit in the Exodus narrative:

- the inability of the Israelites to gaze intently at Moses' face (see 3:7)
- the fading radiance of Moses' face (see 3:7) and
- the reason why Moses intentionally veiled his face

Paul employs the imagery of veiling to explain Israel's continued imperceptive understanding of **Moses.** In v 15, **Moses** refers to the Law/the Scriptures, not to the person. To unbelieving Israel's **dull** reading of the Scriptures (v 14) Paul contrasts the unveiled understanding of the people of the new covenant. The latter **are being transformed** into the **likeness** of **the Lord, who is the Spirit** (v 18).

■ **12** Paul may be implicitly responding to criticism. What are his intentions (see 1:13, 17), is his message clear (4:3), and are his motives pure (4:2)? **Therefore** (*oun*), Paul insists, **since we have such a hope,** in our ministry "we act with great boldness" (v 12 NRSV). His "great boldness" is based on the **hope** he has. He refers back to the characteristics of his new covenant ministry spelled out in 3:4-11. First, his **hope** is based on its permanence (*to menon en doxē*, v 11). It has a future (*estai*, v 8) that will not be superseded or surpassed. Second, it is a **hope** because God's glorious future age is already authentically present in the ministry of the Spirit (1:21-22; see Rom 8:24).

Such an adequate **hope** allows, indeed demands, a ministry that is courageous and plainspoken. This is indicated by the Greek term *parrēsiai*, translated **bold** or "boldness" (NASB, NRSV). The term belonged to the political arena, where it indicated the freedom to speak one's mind. Its application to openness and frankness in speech came eventually to characterize the whole of one's conduct as courageous and forthright (Harris 2005, 295; see Mark 8:32; John 7:4; Acts 4:29, 31; 28:31; Col 2:15; Heb 4:16; 10:35). Paul will employ the identical phrase, *pollē parrēsia* (= **very bold**), in 7:4 ("great confidence") to describe his frank speech toward the Corinthians (Thrall 2004, 485).

■ **13** To illustrate this assertion of the openness and boldness of his ministry, Paul returns to compare and contrast his ministry with that of Moses. Moses' ministry, he suggests, was characterized by concealment. But Paul insists, **We are not like Moses** in this respect.

Here we must deal with two somewhat different questions concerning Paul's reading of Exod 34:29-35 in the LXX. Here, the Greek translation does not differ in any significant detail from the Hebrew text. First, what does Exod 34:29-35 say about the experience of Moses and the Israelites on his second descent from Mount Sinai to the people? Second, how does the apostle use or interpret the Exodus narrative for his argumentative purposes?

First, these are the pertinent points from Exod 34:29-34: (1) When the people saw that Moses' face was radiant as a result of speaking with the Lord, they became afraid to approach him. (2) Moses called them to come to him. And he gave them all the commandments the Lord had given him with his face still unveiled. (3) When Moses finished speaking, he put a veil over his face. And he removed it whenever he reentered the presence of the Lord. (4) Moses returned to the people from time to time from the Lord's presence and told them whatever the Lord had commanded.

Exodus 34:35, instead of continuing the sequence of events, appears to summarize 34:29-34. It says that because the people saw the radiance on Moses' face, Moses veiled his face until he went again to speak with the Lord. Paul reinterprets this for his purposes. His focus is on (1) the people's looking/not looking at Moses' shining face, and (2) Moses' veiling his face.

Second, how does Paul reinterpret these two facets of the OT narrative? The apostle had said in 3:7 that "the Israelites could not look steadily [*atenisai*] at the face of Moses because of its glory, fading though it was." Now in 3:13 Paul says that Moses put ***a veil over his face so that*** [*pros to*] ***the Israelites would not look intently*** [*atenisai*] ***at the end*** [*to telos*] ***of what was fading away.***

Paul's use of an iterative imperfect tense (*etithei*), Moses ***used to put,*** here reflects the threefold use of the tense in the LXX of Exod 34:34. But Paul's point seems to be that the veil was employed not so much to conceal the intimidating radiance of Moses' face as to keep the Israelites from seeing *to telos* (= ***the end***) of its dimming radiance. Paul's interpretation does not seem to be the most natural reading of Exod 34:29-35.

The major exegetical problem of the passage is this: What does Paul mean by ***the end*** [*to telos*] ***of what was fading away***? Many proposals have been offered in answer to this question (see Thrall 2004, 259-60; and Harris 2005, 297-98, for a survey of the range of opinion).

Moses veiled his face ***so that the Israelites would not look intently*** [*atenisai*] ***at the end of what was fading away.*** Apart from its two occurrences in 3:7 and 13, the verb *atenizō* in its fourteen NT appearances always indicates physical sight rather than mental recognition.

Harris suggests that the Israelites' initial fear of Moses turned to amazement at the repeated sight of his radiant face. Paul understood Moses as seeking to prevent Israel from being preoccupied with the outward glory of the Sinai revelation reflected in Moses' face.

Paul inserted *to telos* (= ***the end***) to interpret the **fading away** as a demonstration of the temporary character of the whole Mosaic system of Law and covenant (Harris 2005, 298-300). In v 7 Paul stressed the glory of the Mosaic dispensation. But in v 13 he stresses its impermanence, perhaps interpreting v 7. When "Paul says that the law was fading way . . . he means that it was coming to an end in Christ" (Theodoret of Cyr [393-466], ACCS NT 7:222).

■ **14** We come now to Paul's use of the veil imagery (vv 14-15) in Exod 34:33-35. First, in the case of the original Israelites, he interprets **their minds** as being ***hardened*** (*epōrōthē*). Exodus 32:1—34:9 depicts the entire wilderness generation as ***hardened***—stubborn, rebellious, and spiritually insensitive. Moses' intercessions for Israel (32:11-13, 31-32; 33:12-20; 34:8-9) acknowledged their obstinance. "O Lord, if I have found favor in your eyes, . . . then let the Lord go with us. Although this is a stiff-necked people, forgive our wickedness and our sin, and take us as your inheritance" (34:9; see 33:3, 5).

Second, Paul had two veils in mind as he read the Exodus passage. Of course, he recognized the physical one Moses used to cover his face. But of greater concern to him was the metaphorical veil covering Israelite/Jewish hearts (Harris 2005, 302). This prevented them from recognizing the glory of the new covenant message of Christ.

Just as the Israelites of Moses' day were blinded by the glory, so their contemporaries in Paul's day were oblivious to the new thing God had done in Christ. Paul applies the veil imagery to the spiritual condition of the **hearts** of the present old covenant generation. Thus, he claims that **the same veil remains** [*menei*] **when the old covenant** [*tēs palaias diathēkēs*, only here in the Greek Bible] **is read.**

Paul's use of the terminology of ***hardened*** or **made dull** along with **veil** perhaps echoes Isa 29:10. There the covering of the seers' heads was linked with the divine hardening of Israel (see Isa 6:9-10; Deut 29:4). Paul's phrase ***until this very day*** (*achri . . . tēs sēmeron hēmeras*), recalls the similar phrase in Rom 11:7-8. There he describes unbelieving Israel as "hardened . . . to this very day [*hēs tēs sēmeon hēmeras*]." The words appear in an apparent citation of Deut 29:4 (*hōs tēs hēmeras tautēs*) and Isa 29:10.

God hardened Israel, but not without its willing cooperation. As in Pharaoh's case, "hardening" always includes a human element (see Exod 7:13; 8:32; see Acts 28:24-28). That is, Israel's unbelief is fundamentally a moral issue, as Paul goes on to indicate. It is not a matter of a sovereign decree rendering faith impossible. In the remainder of vv 14-15 Paul both explains (*gar* = ***for***) what he means and verifies his claim of Israel's self-determined dullness. And he does so by appeal to the present behavior of the non-Christian Jewish community.

Continuing his explanation of the "hardening" of Israel, Paul adds one final reason why unbelieving Israel does not read their Bibles as Christians do. He explains that **only in Christ is** [the veil] **taken away.** The English word **only** is not explicit in the Greek, but it is implied.

The Greek verb translated **taken away** (*katargeitai*, see vv 11-12) is in the present tense. Paul refers to what is now occurring in Christ, in the new covenant community. **In Christ,** Paul claims, Christians have been given the interpretive key to the OT. That is, from his perspective, the Christian reading of the OT does not impose something on the text that was not there. Rather, it sees with clarity what was obscured prior to the coming of Christ.

■ **15** Verse 15 serves as Paul's summary restatement of what he has said in vv 13-14. Like v 14, v 15 begins with an emphatic adversative conjunction, *alla*. In v 14 it is translated **But.** In v 15 in the NIV, it is entirely omitted. The NRSV translates it "Indeed."

Paul's mention of **Moses** being **read** here, of course, refers to the reading of the Pentateuch (i.e., **the old covenant** in v 14) in synagogue worship. Reading aloud was normal practice in antiquity, even with private reading. The verb translated **is read,** *anaginōskētai*, is derived from the intensive prepositional prefix *ana-* ("up," "among," "again"; BDAG 2000, 60) and the verb *ginōskō* ("know"). Readers acquire again the knowledge inscribed by authors. That is, unless something prevents them from grasping the message.

Paul seems to use **minds** in v 14 as roughly equivalent to **hearts** in v 15. If there is a difference, it is that the latter refers to the whole inner person, emotions as well as intellect. The slightly different wording of v 14—**a veil remains**—compared to v 15—**a veil covers their hearts**—may suggest that Paul thought conditions had deteriorated from Moses' day to his. Nevertheless, Paul maintains that **a veil** hindered the comprehension of all the generations from Moses to his day.

Paul never identifies the literal counterpart to the image of the **veil**. But his point is clear enough: Something has prevented unbelieving Jews from grasping the true significance of their own Scriptures. Paul assumes that a proper reception of the message of Moses would have prepared the way for a believing reception of Christ (see John 5:46-47). But that a **veil remains** (v 14) was obvious. Witness the fact that the present Israel was not turning to Christ in any great numbers. (See Greathouse and Lyons 2008, 41-122, for a discussion of Paul's anguished struggle over this in Rom 9—11.)

■ **16** In v 16 Paul returns to the OT basis for his analogy, specifically Moses' removal of the veil. What was once true of Moses only, in Christ may now be the experience of all God's people. **But whenever anyone turns to the Lord, the veil is taken away.** This assertion he based on Exod 34:34: "But whenever Moses entered the Lord's presence to speak to him, he would take off his veil until he went out" (LXX). The similar vocabulary and word order of the two verses indicates a dependent relation rather than a direct citation. Paul makes only general use of the scene as he applies it to the issue at hand. The major similarity is that Moses removed the veil in the presence of the Lord.

Moses' experience in Paul's mind is a kind of "prototype" (Hafemann 2000, 159) of anyone who now **turns to the Lord.** Paul applies Moses' repeated removing of his veil to the experience of conversion under the new covenant. The expression **turns to the Lord** in the LXX (e.g., Deut 4:30; 2 Chr 24:19; 30:9; Isa 19:22) became part of the missionary language of the church (1 Thess 1:9; Acts 9:35; 11:21; 14:15; 15:19; 26:20).

In Exod 34:34, the iterative imperfect *eiseporeueto*, "kept entering," describes Moses' repeated entrance into the Lord's presence. In Paul's appropriation, it is replaced with an aorist verb, *epistrepsēi pros*, **turns.** This change allows for its application to Christian conversion. This one-time event applies to those who have and will subsequently turn to the Lord. Paul certainly hoped this would include many of those currently unbelieving Jews whose "minds were made dull" (v 14; see Rom 11:7-32; esp. vv 7 and 25).

Whereas Moses removed his own veil, Paul sees the "veil" over the "hearts" (v 15) of unbelieving Jews as **taken away . . . whenever anyone turns to the Lord.** The verb **is taken away** (*periairetai*), only here in Paul's writings, is probably a divine passive. That is, **the Lord** removes the **veil** that covers their minds **and hearts.**

The question remains, however: Who is **the Lord** in vv 16-18? In his letters, except when he is referring to a text from Scripture, Paul uses **Lord** to mean Christ (Furnish 1984, 211; see 4:5). Even here, where Exod 34:34 echoes in the background, contextually **Lord** (v 16) seems to refer to Christ as in v 14.

This raises a secondary question: What did Paul mean by the title **Lord**? In Greco-Roman practice it was used to refer to human masters as well as divine beings. The Aramaic prayer, *Marana tha*, **"Come, O Lord!"** (cited in 1 Cor 16:22), suggests that Jesus was first addressed as Lord among Jewish, not Greek-speaking Christians. The LXX use of *kyrios* to translate the divine name of Israel's God—Yahweh—certainly facilitated the development of the church's exalted Christology. To apply a passage like Exod 34:34 to Christ strongly suggests that Paul thought of Jesus in divine terms.

Undoubtedly, Paul recalled his own personal experience as "a Hebrew of Hebrews" (Phil 3:5). When he met the risen Jesus on the Damascus road, he began to see the true significance of the new covenant as fulfilled in Jesus Christ (Acts 10:4). It was there that the veil was removed from his spiritual understanding, and the cross of Jesus, once so utterly despicable to him, became bathed with the very glory of God himself.

But is Paul's thinking in this text (vv 16-18) specifically christological (Hafemann 2000, 160)? That is, does he refer here to the confession of the early church that "God has made this Jesus, whom you crucified, both Lord and Christ" (Acts 2:36; see Ps 110:1; Mark 12:35)? Is Paul here identifying the resurrected and exalted Jesus with Yahweh (*kyrios*, "LORD" in the LXX)? Was the preincarnate Christ the God who appeared to Moses (see Rom 10:9; 1 Cor 12:3; Phil 2:9-11)?

■ **17** Verses 12-18 are considered one of the most difficult passages in 2 Corinthians to understand precisely. And v 17, although linguistically simple, is one of the most debated sentences in the NT. The question: Who is **the Lord** in vv 16-18? becomes crucial in v 17. Here Paul makes the simple assertion that **the Lord is the Spirit** (*ho . . . kyrios to pneuma estin*).

Two interpretations prevail. Both raise what appears to be a simple question: What does **is** (*estin*) mean? That is, how does **the Lord** relate to **the Spirit**? Both views have their attractions. The most widely held view is that Paul identifies **the Lord** here as the church's risen Lord, Jesus Christ. If so, the identity cannot be personal, that is, a direct equation, but rather a dynamic unity in which **the Spirit** mediates the presence and power of the risen, exalted Lord and Christ.

The second view, increasingly popular with recent interpreters, is that what God or Yahweh was to Moses in the old covenant, now **the Spirit** is to the new covenant person. That is, "the Lord" or Yahweh of Exod 34:34 becomes in the present era **the Spirit** of 3:6 and 8 (see v 3). The verb **is,** then, is understood possibly as "means" or "refers to."

Paul's emphasis is essentially theological, the contrast between dispensations, the superiority of the new over the old. Ellis calls this *charismatic* or *eschatological exegesis* in continuity with Qumran *pesher.* In the Christian context this kind of exegesis allows the new age of the Spirit to give new meaning to an ancient text (Ellis 1977, 207, 214; Martin 1986, 60).

The significance of the difference between the two views concerning "Who is the **Lord**?" in vv 16-18 is primarily in the precise movement of Paul's argument in these verses. Its effect is minimal in their ultimate significance for the experience and understanding of the new covenant church. In both views, the total benefits of the new covenant are communicated by **the Spirit.** And where the Spirit is, in Paul's theology, there is Christ. Paul's conception of the Spirit is christocentric. It has been determined by his faith in Jesus Christ. And his experience of the Spirit has convinced him of the spiritual nature of the new covenant ministry (3:3). For Paul, as with John, the Spirit is self-effacing in his presentation of Christ, so as not to detract from our Lord (John 15:26; 16:13).

Paul expresses the early Christian conviction that what God the Father accomplished in Jesus Christ has been experienced through the gift of the Spirit. His concern here is not to explain Christ's preexistence and incarnation, the activity of the Holy Spirit in the OT era, or inter-Trinitarian relationships.

As a monotheist, Paul certainly did not think in terms of three gods. The God of Israel has acted in Christ to bring about human redemption in the power of the Spirit. Paul virtually identified the experience of the Spirit with the indwelling Christ. For all its risk of hopelessly confusing the members of the Holy Trinity, this saves Christians from falling into a magical conception of the supernatural in human experience. Of course, it was centuries before the ecumenical creeds articulated a fully nuanced doctrine of the Trinity. This passage and others made the extended debates, which led to the orthodox consensus, a necessity.

Paul's stress in this passage is on the power of the Spirit. That is, the redemptive activity of the Spirit is what supremely characterizes the new era begun with the coming of Christ. Paul emphasizes the work of the Holy Spirit in order to clarify more fully the basic character of his ministry as one "not of the letter but of the spirit" (v 6). This contrast is essential for understanding Paul's self-conception of his ministry as an apostle.

Paul can boldly assert that **where the Spirit of the Lord is, there is freedom.** Paul's language implies that **freedom** (*eleutheria:* "liberty," KJV, NASB) is to be defined contextually and in contrast to the spiritual state of affairs sketched in Exod 34:29-35 (see chs 32—34).

Therefore, the **freedom** Paul speaks of is first and above all like that of Moses. It is the liberty of being in the presence of **the Lord** (Exod 34:34), because of the new covenant presence of **the Spirit.** It is a freedom "from" the letter of the Law, the liberty "to" read Scripture for its life-giving purpose. It is freedom "from" the hardness of mind and heart, the liberty "to" be open and bold in the divine presence without fear. It is freedom "from" the limitations of the old covenant (see Rom 7:5-6; Gal 4:5-6; 5:1); it is the liberty "to" enjoy the full glory of the new covenant.

Freedom "from" the letter of the law of Moses is effected by the life-giving presence of the Holy Spirit. In Paul's larger theological perspective, this comprehends freedom from sin (Rom 6:6-7), from death (Rom 6:21-23; 7:10-11), and from condemnation (Rom 8:1, 17-21, 28-39): "There is therefore now no condemnation for those who are in Christ Jesus. For the law of the Spirit of life in Christ Jesus has set you free from the law of sin and of death" (Rom 8:1-2 NRSV). Freedom is the liberty "to" be the children of God (Rom 8:14-16), who are in possession of the prospect of the future "glorious freedom of the children of God" (Rom 8:21). In sum, it is the freedom and liberty of the "unveiled" in the lifelong, thrilling process of moral and spiritual transformation that Paul goes on to develop in v 18. This life has as its destiny "to be conformed to the image of his Son" (Rom 8:29 NRSV).

■ **18** In v 18 Paul crowns the contrast (*de,* "Now" [v 17] or ***But***) between Moses' ministry of the old covenant and his own ministry of the new covenant. But this is not his experience alone. He exults in the privilege of **all** (*pantes*) Christians, apostles and people alike.

We all have the privilege formerly reserved for representative leaders like Moses. Every Christian enjoys the presence of God ***with unveiled face.*** We see ***as in a mirror the glory of the Lord.*** Does this suggest that it is not only God's glory we witness? Are we able to see our own increasingly Christlike lives reflect his glory, just as Moses' face radiated from his intimate encounter with God? This sanctifying process is the work of the Holy Spirit. We ***are being*** progressively ***transformed into the same image from glory to glory, just as from the Lord who is the Spirit.*** Formerly, only Moses could look openly upon the glory of the Lord. Direct access to God was limited to Moses alone. As Paul interprets it, even Moses used a veil to hide his own fading reflection of God's glory from the people of Israel (vv 13-15).

In contrast to the old covenant, among the privileges of the new covenant community are **unveiled faces.** The veil of confusion has been removed from the minds and hearts of all who turn to the Lord. **We . . . all,** like Moses, are able to gaze on ***the glory of the Lord.*** In the middle voice as here, the verb *katoptrizomenoi* may mean merely "to look at something as in a mirror" or to *"contemplate"* (BDAG 2000, 535). Or, it may mean simply "to reflect like a mirror" (see Harris 2005, 314; Thrall 2004, 290-95; Young and Ford 1987, 93). The NRSV stresses the first meaning while retaining the mirror imagery: "And all of us . . . [see] the glory of the Lord as though reflected in a mirror." Christians certainly enjoy the freedom throughout their lives to contemplate ***the glory of the Lord.*** But they may also reflect that glory in their own lives, as the word ***image*** (*eikōn*) implies (see 4:4). In the background of Paul's thinking is the "radiance" (v 13) that shone on Moses' face as he spoke with the Lord.

As in v 17, the first reference here of ***the Lord*** is to the God—Yahweh—of the old covenant, now experienced in the new covenant as ***the Spirit.*** As a result, in this age of the Spirit, Christians are progressively ***being transformed into the same image*** [*eikona*] ***from glory to glory.*** For Paul, of course, "Christ . . . is the image [*eikōn*] of God" (4:4; see 4:6; Col 1:5; Gen 1:26-27). And so transformation ***into the same image*** is ultimately into the likeness of Christ (Rom 8:29; 1 Cor 15:49; Col 3:10).

The **glory** of God is supremely revealed in Christ (4:4). But what is the meaning of the phrase ***from glory to glory***? Several modern translations tend to paraphrase it. The NIV translates it **with ever-increasing glory;** the NRSV, "from one degree of glory to another." Biblical parallels suggest that this may be the correct approach:

3:18
- Ps 84:7*a* — The righteous "go from strength to strength."
- Jer 9:3*c* — The unrighteous "proceed from evil to evil" (NASB).
- Rom 1:17*a* — ***The righteousness of God is revealed in the gospel from faith to faith.***
- 2 Cor 2:15-16 — "We are a fragrance of Christ to God among those who are being saved . . . an aroma from life to life," but to "those who are perishing . . . an aroma from death to death" (NASB).

In contrast to the fading radiance on Moses' face (3:7, 11), the **glory** of the Christian life is always on the increase (see 4:16-18). This proceeds from the glory seen to the glory reflected. Progressive glorification begins with the initial glory received at conversion and continues to the final glorification of believers at the Parousia (see Rom 8:18, 21, 30; see Harris 2005, 316). Paul may also have had in mind the idea of our increasing capacity to give glory to God.

The present tense of *metamorphoumetha* stresses the lifelong, ongoing transformation (see Matt 17:2). It penetrates to the inner life (3:3; see Rom 12:2; Heb 4:12-13). And it will not cease until we see God "face to face" (1 Cor 13:12). Then "we shall be like him, for we shall see him as he is" (1 John 3:2; see Rom 8:18).

Just as a mirror reveals our physical features in order that we may be properly groomed (see Jas 1:22-25), so our constant faith vision of ***the glory of the Lord*** reveals the shortcomings of our Christian character. But it also inspires and enables us to make the necessary adjustments in our thoughts and behavior. This is transformation into the likeness of Christ (Eph 4:13). The new covenant liberty of the Spirit not only includes the crises of forgiveness of sins and the cleansing of our hearts but also stresses the possibility of progressive and comprehensive sanctification. It affects every dimension of our lives (7:1; 1 Thess 5:20-23; Heb 12:14). This process reaches completion only at glorification, as we come to full conformity to the image of the Son of God (Rom 8:28-30).

The transformation of life that takes place in the continuing experience of ***seeing . . . the glory of the Lord*** is by the agency of **the Lord who is the Spirit,** or ***from the Lord, the Spirit*** (*apo kyriou pneumatos*). This spiritual liberty can be the privileged experience of all who turn to the Lord. The Spirit is the power of God's magnificent future already at work among us in the ministry of the new covenant. The new covenant, inaugurated in the person and work of Jesus Christ, will reach its culmination in his second coming.

The effective presence of the Holy Spirit at work in Paul's ministry moves him to speak of his ministry as "a hope" (v 12). This makes for openness in his access to God in Christ, and bold confidence in his proclamation of the gospel. In the gospel of Christ there is a liberty (1) actually present among us, (2) penetrating to the core of our personality, and (3) promising in its future perspectives. Paul Tillich calls Paul's "description of the Spirit the answer to the question and the fulfillment of the dynamics which drive the history of faith" (1957, 71). Paul will explain next how all this works out in the paradoxical experience of suffering in his apostolic ministry (4:7—5:10).

Further Reading on 2 Cor 3:1-18

Belleville, Linda L. 1991. *Reflections of Glory: Paul's Polemical Use of the Moses-Doxa Tradition in 2 Corinthians 3:1-18.* Journal for the Study of the New Testament: Supplement Series 52. Sheffield: Sheffield Academic Press.

Fitzmyer, J.A. 1981. "Glory Reflected on the Face of Christ (2 Cor 3:7—4:6): Palestinian Jewish Motif." *Theological Studies* 42:630-44. Repr. as pages 64-79 in *According to Paul: Studies in the Theology of the Apostle.* New York: Paulist Press, 1993.

Hafemann, Scott J. 1955. *Paul, Moses, and the History of Israel: The Letter/Spirit Contrast and the Argument from Scripture in 2 Corinthians 3.* Tübingen: J. C. B. Mohr (Paul Siebeck).

_________. 1990. *Suffering and Ministry in the Spirit: Paul's Defense of His Apostolic Ministry in 2 Corinthians 2:14-3:3.* Grand Rapids: Eerdmans.

Hickling, Colin J. A. 1974-75. "The Sequence of Thought in II Corinthians, Chapter Three." *New Testament Studies* 21:380-95.

Lambrecht, Jan. 1983. "Structure and Line of Thought in 2 Cor 2,14—4,6." *Biblica* 64:344-80. Repr. as pages 257-94 in Reimund Bieringer and Jan Lambrecht. *Studies on 2 Corinthians*. Bibliotheca Ephemeridum Theologicarum Lovaniensium 102. Leuven: Leuven University Press/Peeters, 1994.

Stockhausen, Carol Kern. 1989. *Moses' Veil and the Glory of the New Covenant: The Exegetical Substructure of II Cor 3,1-4,6*. Analecta biblica 116. Rome: Pontifical Institute.

e. *The Openness of the Apostolic Ministry (4:1-6)*

With a transitional declaration (v 1), which both concludes and introduces, Paul turns now to the openness of the apostolic ministry. He employs the literary device of "ring composition." This allows him to close the unit, 2:14—4:6, with remarks reflecting the statements about the integrity of his ministry with which he began it. A circle of ideas is now completed with a reminder of the language in 2:14-17 (Martin 1986, 75). This rhetorical device, sometimes called *inclusio*, functions much like matched literary bookends.

With thoughts flowing from 3:7-18, Paul asserts the integrity of his apostolic ministry against those who would discredit it. Paul elaborates upon the theme of 3:12 with direct application to the practical character of his ministry—the transparent character of his proclamation of the gospel.

A boldness and openness issuing from the new covenant ministry of the Spirit (3:4-18) characterizes Paul's ministry. As in the preceding verses (3:12-18), Paul has three subjects: (1) the splendor of the new covenant ministry as the reason for his courage and conduct (vv 1-2), (2) the spiritual condition of those who are unable to see that splendor (vv 3-4), and (3) the divine source of the splendor of the gospel of Jesus Christ as Lord (vv 5-6). Thus, Paul's unique exposition of the new covenant and its ministry, set against Moses' experience in Exod 34:29-35, is framed by two affirmations of confidence in his apostolic ministry (2:14-17; 4:1-6).

■ **1** Paul's **Therefore** (*Dia touto*) looks forward to **this ministry** (*tēn diakonian tautēn*). But it also looks back to the new covenant ministry he has just described, climaxing in 3:18. It is in the caliber of this ministry that he roots his courage as an apostle. He has just described this ministry as a ministry of life, of righteousness, of liberty, and of glory (3:6-18).

On the basis of **this ministry** (see 3:6-10), Paul himself has ***received mercy*** (*ēleēthēmen;* see 1 Cor 7:25; 15:9-10; Gal 1:15; 1 Tim 1:16). The aorist tense of the *ēleēthēmen* points back to the historical moment of Paul's conversion-call to the apostolic ministry (see 1 Tim 1:12-13, 16; see Acts 9:15-16; 1 Cor 15:9-10). Its passive voice presumes God as the source of the mercy he received. The first person plural (**we**) allows his Corinthian audience to identify with him in their own experience of God's mercy.

And ***just as*** [*kathōs*] ***we have received mercy,*** it is only to and by that

mercy as the essence of his life that Paul bears witness in his preaching. His integrity as a minister is the integrity of mercy, the mercy of God that undergirds the entirety of his own existence. Mercy is his only boast, his only ground of confidence as an apostle (see 3:4).

Based on this experience of mercy alone, Paul writes, **We do not lose heart** (*enkakoumen*). This verb, found in Koine Greek, outside the NT has only the meaning "to behave badly" or "to be remiss" (Thrall 2004, 299). Barrett translates "we do not neglect our duty" (1973, 126). This meaning is possibly supported by the fact that some ancient scribes inserted the variant *ekkakoumen*, clearly meaning "to lose heart," perhaps to simplify the difficult reading. But it is equally possible that the scribes were attempting only to clarify the correct understanding of *enkakoumen* ("lose heart," BDAG 2000, 303).

Most translators, in the light of its NT contexts, have presumed the derivative meaning of losing one's motivation in relation to a chosen path of conduct. That is, Paul's experience of mercy explains why he has not lost his enthusiasm or been discouraged (BDAG 2000, 272; see Luke 18:1; Gal 6:9; 2 Thess 3:13; 2 Cor 4:1, 16; Eph 3:13) in his ministry. Some interpreters, however, suggest that in 2 Cor 4:1, 16; and Eph 3:13 the verb means "to be afraid in the face of great difficulty" (BDAG 2000, 272). Garland contends that "to be cowardly or timid" best fits the present context (1999, 204).

Thrall suggests that the meaning of the term outside the NT is also appropriate in 4:1. She suggests that the Corinthians were more apt to accuse Paul of being lax in his duties than with being tired or despondent (2004, 299-300). But it is far from obvious that Paul's every denial responds to an accusation from his opponents. Furthermore, Harris notes that weariness and despair, which lead to a decreasing effort, are ways of "conducting oneself remissly" (2005, 323). Nonetheless, the translation **lose heart** (NIV, NRSV, NASB) expresses well the antithesis of Paul's outspokenness (3:12) and his compulsion for unceasing activity in behalf of the church at Corinth (4:7-15). The heart of and motivation for his ministry from every perspective was the mercy of God.

■ **2** The phrase **Rather** [*alla*], **we have renounced** points emphatically to what is excluded from Paul's ministry. New covenant ministry is deeply grounded in the grace of God and characterized by the Spirit. When Paul became an apostle, he disowned once and for all any method that would be unworthy of his calling. This is not to suggest that he considered his preconversion behavior as characterized by **secret and shameful ways.** True, he had "persecuted the church" (1 Cor 15:9; see Gal 1:13, 23). But at the time, he did so with a clear conscience, considering himself "as to righteousness under the law, blameless" (Phil 3:6 NRSV). Furthermore, there is no reason to think that his denial reflects the charges of his opponents. On the contrary, it may indirectly accuse the false apostles with practicing cunning and deceit (see 2:17; 11:1-15).

The aorist tense of the verb **renounced** (*apeipametha*) probably has a timeless (gnomic) force. It does not of necessity refer to some decisive change of Paul's behavior, but may merely characterize the disposition of his ministry. Interpreters who see it as parallel to ***received mercy*** (v 1), however, presume it refers to some renunciation at a particular moment in Paul's past.

The behaviors Paul identifies as unworthy of his new covenant ministry, and, therefore, summarily **renounced,** are **secret and shameful ways** (*ta krypta tēs aischynēs*). These are literally ***the secret things of shame.*** This genitive phrase has been taken in a variety of ways (see Thrall 2004, 303). It certainly includes shameful or disgraceful conduct that is deceitfully hidden (BDAG 2000, 29-30).

This apostolic renunciation is twofold, defined specifically by Paul with two negatively framed participial phrases. First, literally, ***not walking in craftiness.*** That is, **we do not use deception.** Paul never had conducted his ministry, nor does he now conduct it, in a merely pragmatic or opportunistic manner. Both means and ends mattered. Pure motives did not justify deceitful methods. The Greek term translated ***craftiness*** (*panourgia:* "cunning," NRSV) or "trickery," appears always in the bad sense in the NT (Luke 20:23; 1 Cor 3:19; 2 Cor 11:3; Eph 4:14; see 2 Cor 12:16). It means basically "the readiness to do anything" (BDAG 2000, 754). Paul was not, like Satan and his ministers (2 Cor 11:14-15; 12:16), ready to adopt an "anything goes" policy as the means to achieve his ends.

The second defining participial phrase, ***distorting*** or ***adulterating*** **the word of God.** The **word of God** can refer to the OT Scriptures. But the ex-
4:2 pression **word of God** elsewhere in the NT refers to either the "words God spoke" (subjective genitive) or the "words humans speak about or in behalf of God" (objective genitive). Here, it most likely refers to the Christian proclamation; that is, Paul's message (see 2:17; 4:3). It was not Paul's practice to adulterate or "falsify" (NRSV) his message, writes John Wesley, "by any additions or alterations, or by attempting to accommodate it to the taste of the hearers" (1950, 652). Inseparably linked together for Paul and all ministers are integrity in ministerial methodology and honesty with **the word of God.**

Paul now turns to a positive description of his ministry. Far from distortion and deceit, **On the contrary** (*alla*), his approach above all was characterized **by setting forth the truth plainly.** The verb *phaneroō,* **set forth . . . plainly,** is derived from the adjective *phanerōs,* which referred to things that were evident, obvious, visible, and clearly seen (BDAG 2000, 1047). The cognate noun *phanos* refers to portable lights—lamps and lanterns (BDAG 2000, 1049). Paul uses words from this cognate family ten times in 2 Corinthians (2:14; 3:3; 4:2, 10, 11; 5:10, 11 [twice]; 7:12; and 11:6), nearly one-third of all its appearances in all his letters (Rom 1:19 [twice]; 2:28 [twice]; 3:21; 16:26; 1 Cor 3:13; 4:5; 11:19; 12:7; 14:25; Gal 5:19; Eph 5:13, 14; Phil 1:13; Col 1:26; 3:4 [twice]; 4:4; 1 Tim 3:16; 4:15; 2 Tim 1:10; Titus 1:3).

The **truth** Paul declared openly he identifies in v 4 as "the gospel of the glory of Christ." He further defines this message in vv 5-6. Paul claimed that by this forthright approach **we commend ourselves** [*synistanontes heautous*] **to every man's conscience in the sight of God.** With a reversing of the word order from 3:1 (*heautous synistanontes*), the expression now has positive rather than negative implications (Hafemann 2000, 176; see Harris 2005, 259). Paul commended himself to every human conscience. That is, he made himself and his message open to everyone's assessment. He had nothing to hide from anyone. Moreover, as indicated in 1:12; 2:10, and 17, his preaching is also **in the sight of God.** That is, it is subject to the divine verdict (see 5:11; 6:4). He implicitly invites God to testify to the transparency of his inner motives.

Paul seeks simply to make the truth known, for he dares to believe that the saving truth of God needs no spin to achieve its ends (see Jer 23:29). It is unnecessary to "market" the gospel. To be persuasive the "gospel" (v 3) does not require cleverness, but the transparent honesty of those who preach it. Paul submits his claim not only to his human hearers but also to God. He acknowledges that his ministry not only depends on the mercy of God (v 1) but that God scrutinizes **every . . . conscience** (see Heb 4:13; see the sidebar on "conscience" with the commentary on 1:2).

Paul's appeal has reached a climax. This verse appears to some extent to answer the muffled accusations of his detractors (see 2:17). Thus, it prepares the way for the sustained polemic in chs 10—13.

■ **3** Had some objected that if Paul's proclamation was so transparent, why was his **gospel** still **veiled** to so many of his hearers (see 3:15)? The words **and even if** (*ei de kai*, "yet if in fact" [Harris 2005, 326]) reflect Paul's admission that for some it is veiled. But **it is veiled** only in the case of **those who are perishing** (see the commentary on 2:15).

Paul continued to use the imagery of the veil that covered Moses' face, which he employed to explain the hard heart of Jewish hearers (see 3:14-15; 2:16). Was he responsible for their rejection of the gospel, because he had veiled the gospel by hiding it in a crucified Christ (1 Cor 2:2; see 1:22-24)? Did the centrality of the cross explain the "weakness" of his ministry (4:7-12; see 13:4)? Did his critics consider his gospel to be at fault? What did the veiling have to do with their rejection? Was the veil caused by their unbelief, or was it the cause of their unbelief?

■ **4** Paul's answer to these questions seems simple: "In their case the god of this world has blinded the minds of the unbelievers" (v 4 NRSV). Unbelief unquestionably does have its irrational or "demonic" side; it "does not simply yield to reason and understanding" (Best 1987, 38). Yet, Paul also expresses himself as in v 3. There it is "to those who are perishing" that "our gospel is veiled." It is **the minds of unbelievers** that **the god of this age has blinded.** It appears that "the fault that leads to their destruction is also their own" (Barrett 1973, 131), for "those who are perishing" *are* **unbelievers**—those who refuse to believe!

Paul makes no clear statement as to cause and effect. Can people's minds believe what their wills have already chosen not to believe? Surely, our inner moral choices (in response to God's prevenient grace operative in the Spirit) affect our outward or cognitive beliefs. Jesus said to his Jewish hearers, "If you [had] believed Moses, you would believe me, for he wrote about me" (John 5:46).

The expression **the god of this age** (*aiōnos*) is without parallel in the NT. Thus, some have insisted that "Paul meant God when he said God" (Young and Ford 1987, 116; see Thrall 2004, 306-8). But Paul was aware of the widely held apocalyptic conviction that Satan (see 2:11; 1 Cor 5:5; 7:5; Rom 16:20) had usurped God's rule over "the present evil age" (Gal 1:4; see Matt 4:8-9; Rom 12:2; 1 Cor 1:20; 2:6, 8; 3:18; Eph 2:2).

Paul did not refer to Satan's dominion over the physical world as such (*kosmos*), but to the present **age** in contrast to the age to come. John refers to Satan as "the prince of this world [*kosmos*]." But he uses "world" in a distinctive sense. And the Fourth Gospel insists that "the prince of this world will be driven out" (John 12:31), "is coming" (14:30), and "now stands condemned" (16:11). First John 5:19 claims that "the whole world [*kosmos*] is under the control of the evil one."

Satan's present rule is qualified supremely by the consummation of the kingdom of God, which is already in progress (1 Cor 15:20-28). Standing in the background of Paul's thought is the apocalyptic dualism of Judaism, which in Paul is primarily temporal and ethical. He contrasts life as it is in the world apart from Christ with life in the new age.

The two ages, though qualitatively distinct, overlap in time in the NT. In **this age,** by his opposition to God, Satan exercises a very real rule, yet one limited and temporary—this is a "passing age" (REB; see Luke 10:18; Rev 12:7-9). Paul was convinced that "the time is short"; that "this world [*tou kosmou toutou*] in its present form is passing away" (1 Cor 7:29, 31). Satan's dominion in the present age extends only over those who choose to give their allegiance to causes that compromise God's eternal purpose of grace.

Paul claimed that "the rulers of this age" had "crucified the Lord of glory" (1 Cor 2:6 and 8). A "crucified . . . Lord of glory" might seem paradoxical. But Paul was convinced that in Christ the victory that belongs in its fullness to the future age had already decisively broken into this present age. Paul's gospel announced the cross as the secret plan of God to recover his usurped rule (see Young and Ford 1987, 124-26).

The result (*eis to*, **so that**) of this coexisting moral and spiritual condition of "unbelieving" and "blinding" is that **they cannot see the light of the gospel of the glory of Christ.** Usually the articular infinitive (here, *eis to mē augasai*, **so that they cannot see**) signifies purpose. But the two categories are closely related, "for a purpose is an anticipated result and a result is an achieved purpose" (Harris 2005, 330). Thus, the expression is ambiguous here.

In the NT, the verb *augazō* appears only here; and the noun *phōtismos*, only here and in v 6. The verb can be read as either transitive (**see**) or intransitive (***"shine forth"***) (BDAG 2000, 149). As a transitive verb, the accusative noun *ton phōtismon* (**the light**) must be the direct object of the infinitive verb *augasai*. This would call for the translation: ***so that they might not come to see the light*** (presumed in the NIV). But accusative nouns frequently serve as functional "subjects" of infinitives. This would call for the translation: ***so that the light might not shine on them*** (following the textual tradition behind the KJV). But the latter reading requires the pronoun "them [*autois*]," absent in the better manuscripts of v 4.

The noun *phōtismon* is used figuratively here to mean ***"enlightment"*** (BDAG 2000, 1074). When it is used in an astronomical sense, it refers to a reflected light, such as the moon's radiance from the light of the sun. Paul's pile-up of three genitive phrases—**of the gospel of the glory of Christ** (see 1 Cor 2:8)—complicates interpretation.

It appears that **the gospel** is the source of the figurative **light.** And **the gospel** proclaims **the glory** that **Christ** possesses. He is at once the content **of the gospel** message and the very **image of God.** See the commentary on 2:14 for a full discussion of **the gospel.**

By naming **Christ** as **the image of God** (see 3:18), Paul now scales the commanding summit of the passage. Here is **the glory of Christ.** By nature Christ is the visible "image of the invisible God" (Col 1:15; see 1:19). He radiates the very glory of God (see Heb 1:3; John 12:45; 14:9). Paul emphasizes the equality of **the image** (*eikōn*) with the original (see Phil 2:6). An *eikōn* is not a feeble copy of something; it illuminates its inner essence. Christ both shares and expresses God's nature. Christ fulfills in himself the creative destiny of the image of God in humankind (Gen 1:26; see Heb 2:6-9). Paul seems to have known Wis 6:26-27, in which the *eikōn* of God, divine wisdom, mediates the knowledge of God to humanity.

Christ, who embodies God's very nature and reveals his character, is the image and likeness of what all those who are "being transformed into the same image from glory to glory" (3:18 NASB) will become (Rom 8:29). In Christ Christians are being restored to the image of God (2 Cor 5:17). Paul is now prepared to make very clear, possibly with his critics in mind (see 3:1), what he meant by "setting forth the truth plainly" (v 2).

■ **5** With such a "gospel" (v 4), **we do not preach ourselves,** that is, a gospel about ourselves. Paul's ministry may have more glory than that of Moses. But neither his message nor his ministry is about his own glorification, his ideas, his eloquence, or his gifted personality. This is because (*gar*, **For**) Paul preaches only two things, **Jesus Christ as Lord, and ourselves as your servants for Jesus' sake.**

Simply put, the content of Paul's gospel is **Jesus Christ.** The earliest church confessed that "God has made this Jesus . . . both Lord and Christ" (Acts 2:36). Paul's key confession as he preached "Christ crucified" (1 Cor 1:23; 2:2) was "Jesus is Lord [*kyrios Iēsous;* 1 Cor 12:3]." For Paul, this Jesus, who became "obedient to death—even death on a cross" God "exalted to the highest place." And God has determined that to him "every knee should bow" and "confess that Jesus Christ is Lord" (Phil 2:8-11; see Rom 10:9). This lordship of Jesus as the crucified Christ radically governed the methodology of Paul's ministry (2 Cor 1:24; 1 Cor 2:2).

Therefore, the only legitimate self-proclamation worthy of the apostolic ministry according to Paul is **ourselves as your servants for Jesus' sake.** Paul's thought moves naturally from lordship to its antithesis—slavery, as he returns to his own essential role in ministry. In the language of the Jewish faith, to be a servant meant to be one chosen by God (Martin 1986, 80). **Servants** is actually the Greek *douloi*. This refers to ***slaves*** who were owned, rather than servants hired by their masters in the first-century socioeconomic context.

Elsewhere in his letters, Paul describes himself and his coworkers as ***slaves*** obligated to serve other Christians (Rom 1:1; Gal 1:10; Phil 1:1). Here, however, he identifies mutual enslavement as the calling of all Christians (see 1 Cor 7:22-23). As a slave, Christ "emptied himself" (Phil 2:7). As a slave to the Corinthians, Paul vowed, "I will very gladly spend for you everything I have and expend myself as well" (2 Cor 12:15).

If only the Corinthians could have grasped this, their attitude toward him might have been different. Paul's lowly service was motivated (5:14) and characterized by that of his Lord. Christ left his exaltation to God (Phil 2:7; see Mark 10:45; John 13:2-5; 1 Pet 2:23; 5:6).

4:5-6 Yet, Christians, laypeople and ministers (to use the terms anachronistically), do not actually *own* each other. We have no rightful claim on each other. Rather the service all of us render is **for Jesus' sake** (see 1:24; Mark 10:45). Only Jesus Christ is Lord! The Christian community functions as such "only when each behaves as slave to all the others (see Mark 10:42-44)" (Best 1987, 39).

■ **6** Paul now explains why (*hoti*, **For/*Because***) he preaches "Jesus Christ as Lord" (v 5). It is because ***the God who said, "Light shall shine out of darkness," . . . has shone in our hearts*** (v 6). Paul is responsible to share the light (v 4) he has received (v 5). With allusions to Gen 1:3-4 and Isa 9:1, Paul affirms that he belongs to a new creation (see 5:17).

The apostle's conversion-call encounter with the risen Christ excluded self-exaltation from the gospel ministry. In that experience, Paul met the Creator, who by a word had dispelled the darkness with the light. In the revelation of the exalted Jesus, his life had been interrupted by the God whose glory "shone on the face of Moses" (John Chrysostom [344/354-407], ACCS NT 7:230). The God of creation and revelation had illuminated Paul's darkened understanding.

The aorist verb *elampsen* (**made his light shine**) has a constative force here. That is, Paul referred to an accomplished event. The similarities in wording and concept between v 6 and the Acts accounts of Paul's conversion (Acts

9:3-19; 22:2-18; 26:13-19; see Gal 1:15-16) make a reference to his conversion likely.

The plural **our hearts** suggests that Paul, while referring primarily to himself, views the coming of light into the darkness as a paradigm for Christian conversion in general. The dispelling of darkness by light is a frequent theme in the NT (Acts 26:18; Eph 5:8; Col 1:12-13; 1 Thess 5:4-5; 1 Pet 2:9).

In an antithetical parallel to v 4, Paul expresses the substance of the gospel given to him by God. The God of new creation had shined **the light of the knowledge of the glory of God in the face of Christ. Light** here is *phōtismon,* as in 4:4. But now **knowledge** takes the place of "gospel [*euangelion*]."

As in v 4, Paul piles up a string of three genitival phrases. **Light** is the source of **the knowledge. Glory** is the object and content of this **knowledge.** And **God** is the One to whom **the glory** belongs. Barrett, however, sees the first genitive construction as appositional. That is, "illumination . . . consists in the knowledge" (1973, 134).

Paul sees all of this, with an "unveiled face" (3:18), **in the face of Christ** (see 4:4). This embraces "the whole gospel." Accordingly, the present passage can be viewed as "the theological heart of the letter" (Young and Ford 1987, 249; see 248-52). Denney observes, "in that light which God flashed into his heart, [Paul] saw the face of Jesus Christ, and knew that the glory which shone there was the glory of God" (1943, 5:754).

In the abiding reality of his conversion-call experience lay Paul's unique qualification to be a minister of Christ. The light of God illumined his life so that he might illumine others (Acts 26:16-18) with the knowledge of God's glory in the face of Jesus the Christ. The apostle's message and ministry were certainly not about himself. Thus, Paul was not discouraged.

The bold confidence of Paul's apostolic ministry, received from God through Christ (Gal 1:1), is seen in its methodology. Paul's ministry was, first, utterly open to both human and divine scrutiny. Second, he sought to manifest Jesus Christ alone as its supreme content. Christ is the ultimate measure of both the preacher and the hearer of the gospel, for God can be adequately known only in him. To refuse the light of the gospel of the glory of Christ is to invite spiritual darkness. To exalt self in the presentation of Jesus is to betray the ministry.

Paul grounded the integrity of his ministry in its basically spiritual character:

- Its *proof* is in transformed people (3:1-3).
- Its *dynamic* is the ministry of the Spirit as the life-giving quality of the new covenant (3:4-11).
- Its *boldness* resides in the transforming presence of the Spirit of the Lord (3:12-18).
- Its *openness* flows out of the fullness of the revelation of the glory of God in Christ as received by the apostle (4:1-6).

FROM THE TEXT

Paul's personal defense of his apostolic ministry began formally in 1:12. It now takes the form of a presentation of the new covenant ministry. He both compares and contrasts it to the ministry of Moses. The comparison particularly concerns the narrative of the second giving of the Mosaic law in Exod 34:29-35. The apostolic **ministry** is Paul's theme as indicated by his sixfold use in various cognate forms of the term in our passage (3:3, 6, 7, 8, 9; 4:1). Paul sought biblical support for his affirmations of confidence (v 3) and hope (v 12) in his new covenant ministry. The term **ministry** (*diakonia*) here and elsewhere in the NT generally refers to the "called" ministry.

As authentic members of the historic Christian Church, we live in the spiritual era Paul calls the new covenant **ministry** (3:6; see Collins 1992, 1-13, 44-50). We are partakers of a new epoch in the history of salvation. This "present evil age" (Gal 1:4) exists in dynamic tension with the "old age."

Paul further characterizes this ministry as a ministry of "righteousness" (2 Cor 3:9). But, most significantly in this passage, it is for him a "ministry of the Spirit" (3:8). It is a ministry that becomes increasingly and thoroughly christological, for in "the face of Christ" we know **the glory of God** (4:6). This is where we live and serve as Christians.

So, what is this "new covenant ministry of the Spirit"? How do we understand the privileged life of the church in the NT age, this era of prophetic fulfillment? What is this "new covenant ministry"?

First, this "new covenant ministry" is *a ministry whose credibility is validated by the changed lives of the people who make up the church* (3:1-3). "You are a letter from Christ . . . written . . . with the Spirit of the living God . . . on tablets of human hearts" (3:3). As the ancient church fathers understood our text, "the Corinthians themselves are all the recommendation Paul needed. They are like a personal letter from Christ, written with the Spirit of God" (ACCS NT 7:212).

We can consider three implications of this here:

1. As "a letter from Christ," our changed lives in the church and the world recommend our pastors to all who care to read us. We are affirming their ministry. Chrysostom (344/354-407) commented centuries ago that "the virtue of disciples commend the teacher more than any letter" (ACCS NT 7:213).

2. As "a letter from Christ," we, by our words and deeds in our community, recommend our church to all who observe us. Like a store, the church is known by its products and its services.

3. As "a letter from Christ," most significantly, we are recommending Jesus by the radiance emanating from our living and loving.

To paraphrase William Barclay, every Christian, like it or not, is an advertisement for Christ, the Church, and Christianity. Their honor is in the hands of Christ's followers. We judge shopkeepers by the kinds of goods they sell. We judge craftsmen by the kinds of articles they produce. We judge a church by the kind of people it creates. Just so, the world judges Christ by his followers (1956, 208-9). Attractive Christians "are not made with *ink, but by the Spirit of the living God;* for the gifts and graces that constitute the mind that was in Christ are produced in you by the Holy Ghost" (Clarke 1854, 2:323).

Second, the "new covenant ministry" that defines us as Christians is *a ministry whose confidence does not come from any human competence, but from God* (3:4-6). It is only "ours through Christ before God . . . [whose] Spirit gives life" (3:4, 6). The apostle bases his confidence in relation to his ministry to the Corinthians in his call and the reality of the Spirit.

Like Paul, our confidence as Christians does not have its ultimate source in ourselves. Our faithfulness to God and our adequacy as representatives of our Lord in our workplace, among our friends and family, and in the world testify to the Spirit's activity in our lives.

Paul identified the old covenant as being "weakened as it always was by fractured human nature" (Rom 8:3 TM). We have all discovered, to our dismay, that our intellect and moral stamina do not always suffice for our obedience to God and our faithful witness in the world. Neither talent nor learning, neither position nor prowess can in themselves make for spiritual competence. Rather, whatever confidence and competence in ministry we have come from the presence of God in the new covenant through Christ.

The intent of the old covenant is now fulfilled as we walk according to "the Spirit of life in Christ Jesus" (Rom 8:2 NASB). The Spirit does not discourage or kill but "gives life" (see Rom 8:11). The Spirit enables us actually to live a moral and spiritual life. And the Spirit speaks through our presence to others in Christ's behalf. For like Paul, we live "through Christ before God." We are people through whom the graces of the Spirit radiate.

Third, the "new covenant ministry" that defines us as Christians in the world is *a ministry whose splendor transcends that of the old covenant* (3:7-11). "Will not the ministry of the Spirit be even more glorious?" (3:8). Paul turns to the Scriptures in reliance on the Spirit. And he seeks the Scriptures' intention in its original context for the foundation of his defense. With John Chrysostom (344/354-407), this "does not disparage the Old Testament but highly commends it, since comparisons are apt to be made between things which are basically similar in kind" (ACCS NT 7:220). So, in what did the splendor of the old covenant consist?

1. The shine on Moses' face (4:7, 13; see Exod 34:29-35) speaks of the "awe-full" majesty of Sinai where the old covenant was made (Exod 19:16-19; 20:18-19; 24:1-18). To the Israelites the glory of the Lord looked like a consuming fire on top of the mountain (Exod 24:17; see Ps 18:7-15). Centuries later the writer to the Hebrews described Sinai as "a mountain that can be touched and that is burning with fire; to darkness, gloom and storm; to a trum-

pet blast or to such a voice speaking words that those who heard it begged that no further word be spoken to them" (12:18-19).

2. At the heart of the old covenant was the twofold giving of the Ten Words (*haddbarim*) or Ten Commandments (Exod 34:28; see 20:1-21; 34:1-28). These are spiritual and moral behaviors that have not lost their relevance. The Decalogue is neglected by much of human society to its sorrow, self-destruction, and despair. As originally intended, the Ten Words were a means of grace. They were given to mediate the presence of God to the lives of the people. "God has come to test you" or that you may have experience of him, "so that the fear of God will be with you to keep you from sinning" (Exod 20:20; see Greenberg 1960, 275). "I am the LORD, who heals you" (Exod 15:26) was the earlier stated purpose of the giving of the Law, as a careful examination of the terminology in vv 25-26 reveals.

But, sadly, we read that "the people remained at a distance while Moses approached the thick darkness where God was" (20:21). The splendor of the old covenant was that even then the people were called to and offered the opportunity of enabled lives in the presence of God. Tragically, however, they preferred the letter to the spirit. This left them vulnerable to the idolatrous condition of the Israelites described in Exod 32—33. This is akin to the picture of veiled hearts of the Jewish people Paul painted in our text, appealing to Exod 34:29-35.

The covenant mediated by Moses with the people of Israel was the first of the two most momentous moments in all of human history. They are, first, the revelation of God through Moses in the giving of the Law; and, second, the divine revelation of God in the incarnate Jesus of the Gospels.

The splendor of the new covenant is the accomplishment or fulfillment of the original design of the old. Augustine (354-430) saw this clearly: "How does the Spirit give life? By causing the letter to be fulfilled, so that it may not kill" (ACCS NT 7:217).

Fourth, the "new covenant ministry" that defines us as Christians in the world is seen best as *a ministry whose freedom liberates its recipients to a lifelong transformation of moral and spiritual life* (3:12-18). ***All of us, with unveiled face, seeing as in a mirror the glory of the Lord, are being transformed into the same image from glory to glory; just as from the Lord, the Spirit*** (3:18).

Ironically, a passage that is so difficult to interpret technically clearly opens up to the Christian possibilities of the transformation of moral character and spiritual life beyond the ability of human language to describe. We expect this, for with the age of the new covenant, God's time of consummation has entered qualitatively into our broken and complex times. James B. Chapman, an early leader in the Church of the Nazarene, suggested that "there is no 'ceiling' for us. The topless heaven above beckons us on to everlasting progress" (cited in Culbertson 1966, 165).

This reminds us of John 14:2 where Jesus described to his disciples the life that would be possible with the soon coming of the Paraclete, the Holy Spirit (see John 14:16-18; 15:26-27; 16:7-11). He promised, "In my Father's house are many rooms" (14:2). These are not to be thought of as heavenly mansions. They refer to the richness and variety of possibilities available to disciples when the Spirit comes; for the Father "gives the Spirit without limit" (3:34). The picture is of an ancient castle with endless unexplored rooms that will take a lifetime of delightful discovery to enter and enjoy. In her classic work on prayer, *The Interior Castle* (1577), Teresa of Avila (1515-82) imagines "our soul to be like a castle made entirely out of a diamond or of very clear crystal, in which there are many rooms." Her seven dwelling places of *The Interior Castle* "are not seven, but a million"! (Morón-Arroyo 1984, 110). J. Mary Luti, interpreting Teresa at this point, writes:

> We are invited to seek within the companionship of God and Christ, to glimpse within the beauty and worth of our humanness, to cherish within the dignity of our having been created in God's image and redeemed by Christ's love, and to experience at every turn the invitation to ever-increasing intimacy. (1991, 88)

In another idiom, "This is truly perfection: never to stop growing toward what is better and never placing any limit on perfection" (ACCS NT 7:226). This is the vision of the Cappadocian father Gregory of Nyssa (335-394). This takes place as we gaze intently upon "the glory of the Lord as though reflected in a mirror" (2 Cor 3:18 NRSV). In classical writers mirror imagery conveys three ideas: purity as a mirror's clean surface, self-knowledge (Jas 1:23), and indirect knowledge (1 Cor 13:12; Harris 2005, 315).

To gaze lifelong at the glory of God in the face of Christ who is the image of God (1) purifies our motives and perspectives in the light of the holy, (2) grants to us a knowledge of ourselves in comparison with the incarnate Jesus (see 1 John 2:6; 3:3; 4:17), and (3) allows for an unseen working of the Spirit in our innermost beings that only others can observe.

All this is involved in Paul's admonition to the Philippians to "continue to work out your salvation with fear and trembling, for it is God who works in you to will and to act according to his good purpose" (Phil 2:12-13; see Rom 12:1-2). Discipline and grace go together as we are being transformed "with ever increasing glory, which comes from the Lord, who is the Spirit" (2 Cor 3:18). Thus, the psalmist exhorts, "Look to him, and be radiant" (Ps 34:5 NRSV).

As privileged Christians of the new covenant, we have open access to (1) the presence of God, (2) the deep needs of our own hearts, and (3) the sure hope of the glory of God forever (see Rom 5:1-5). We sing with W. D. Longstaff the text's admonition to us:

Take time to be holy. The world rushes on;
Spend much time in secret with Jesus alone.
By looking to Jesus, like Him thou shalt be;
Thy friends in thy conduct His likeness shall see.

No wonder then, as Paul returns to the conduct of his own apostolic ministry, that he declares that "new covenant ministry" is finally *a ministry whose confidence is fully in the gospel that is proclaimed* (2 Cor 4:1-6). "By the open statement of the truth we commend ourselves to the conscience of everyone in the sight of God . . . who has shone in our hearts to give the light of the knowledge of the glory of God in the face of Jesus Christ" (4:2, 6 NRSV).

Authentic ministry focuses on "the truth," which is "the gospel of the glory of Christ." It is further defined as "the knowledge of the glory of God in the face of Jesus Christ." For those called to minister and for all ordinary Christians who share in their ministry, the implications are life-determining:

First, we need not surrender to deep discouragement. After all, we are dealing with "the truth" of God as revealed to us in Jesus the crucified and resurrected Son of God. We are dealing with the full and final revelation of God to humankind. Here our faith says that the ultimate meaning, the baseline reality of the earth and the cosmos, of all history and eternity without end, is seen in the face of Christ. "He is before all things, and in him all things hold together" (Col 1:17; see vv 15-20; Eph 1:3-23). All this belongs to the gospel we know and share.

Second, the methods we use to share the gospel are never deceptive, nor do we "distort the word of God" (2 Cor 4:2*a*). Instead, "by the open statement of the truth we commend ourselves to the conscience of everyone in the sight of God" (4:2*b* NRSV). In every way in our relation to the gospel of Christ, we are transparent. John Wesley wrote that it was never Paul's practice to "falsify" (4:2*a* NRSV) his message "by any additions or alterations, or by attempting to accommodate it to the taste of the hearers" (1950, 652). Integrity in one's ministerial methodology and honesty with the message we preach always go together (see 2:17).

Third, therefore, the gospel is not about us; and our confidence is not in ourselves. We, like Paul, "do not preach ourselves, but Jesus Christ as Lord." New Testament scholar and preacher C. E. B. Cranfield, commenting on our text in 1965, left us words that are as penetratingly relevant now as they were then:

> Of the various temptations which beset the Christian minister, one of the chief and deadliest is the temptation to preach himself. It is an extremely insidious tendency, and none of us can claim that he has never yielded to it. . . . Many of us are sensitive enough to recognize when a colleague succumbs at all obviously to it; but to notice when one yields to it oneself is very much harder. And usually when we succumb to it, we are quite unaware of what is happening. . . . It is possible to preach oneself quite blatantly, as, for example, when a preacher makes no really serious attempt at all to expound the Scriptures, offering to his congregation his own ideas, opinions, and prejudices. But more often the preaching of oneself is decently disguised and, indeed, unconscious—all

the more dangerous because it is not at all obvious. There is the temptation to exploit the gospel, to exploit its drama, pathos, solemnity, and majesty, for the display of one's own powers, one's ability, eloquence, humor, learning, gifts of popular exposition. . . . To this temptation every minister without exception yields to some extent. . . . Congregations are apt to put a stumbling block in a minister's way, in relation to this temptation, and to encourage him to yield to it. For they are prone to like to be entertained and to enjoy a minister's self-exhibition. They are prone, too, to indulge in a personality cult. **But this is the unkindest thing that a congregation has in its power to do to its pastor, for it tempts him to betray his ministry.** (1965, 163-64)

3. A Ministry of Suffering (4:7—5:10)

Paul continues with the theme of his "ministry" begun in 4:1. Here he moves on from "a ministry of the Spirit" (4:1-6) to an exposition of the apostolic ministry as "a ministry of suffering." He delves more deeply into his profound vision of the new covenant ministry.

Here, Paul seems to engage in a "running debate" (Martin 1986, 84) with his critics. They apparently thought that an apostle should be one whose power and presence they could respect and admire. Paul turns from the sublimity of his mission to the actual misery of his physical existence. The frail apostle was continually exposed to suffering and death (1 Cor 4:11-13; 2 Cor 1:8; 6:4-5; 11:23-27).

But Paul's suffering released the resurrection life of Jesus into the lives of the Corinthians (4:7-15). With this claim Paul answers their question, Where is the glory of the new covenant? The apostle declares that even in the midst of outward decay, he experiences inner renewal (4:16-18). The sure hope of the heavenly home is at work in his life (5:1-10). The weakness of the ministers of the new covenant enhances rather than hampers the boldness of their ministry (see 13:4). Two issues are foremost in his mind: the relationship between suffering and ministry, and the prospect of death (Murphy-O'Connor 1991, 44).

Paul uses the literary plural throughout this section. His "we" refers primarily to himself, in light of the criticisms he had received. But no doubt in view as well are those who are aligned with him in ministry. And certainly what he says is applicable to the life and work of all believers (Matera 2003, 105-6). This is especially true concerning what he says about the resurrection. The basic pattern of "this treasure in earthen vessels" (4:7 NASB) is what characterizes all Christians.

BEHIND THE TEXT

Paul's use of the apologetic rhetorical structure continues in 4:7—5:10. It begins with what has been variously called a tribulation/hardship list or a catalog of affliction/suffering. Stoic and Cynic sages used such catalogs, common in antiquity, most notably to demonstrate their superiority over circumstances. Epictetus and Seneca contain lists in many ways similar to the NT catalogs. Epictetus views tribulation as sent by God, which affords sufferers an opportunity to demonstrate moral character (Witherington 1995, 388).

Eight of these lists or catalogs appear in Paul's writings. "Simple lists" are found in Rom 8:35; 2 Cor 6:4-5; 11:23-29; 12:10. "Antithetical lists" appear in 1 Cor 4:10-13; 2 Cor 4:8-9; 6:8-10; Phil 4:12 (Hodgson 1983, 66-67).

In antiquity, lists were composed as individuals and nations suffered misfortunes of various kinds. Such catalogs of hardships afforded a widespread literary background from which Paul drew. He was undoubtedly, whether consciously or unconsciously, influenced by such lists. (See Harris 2005, 341; and Hodgson 1983, 67-80; for the striking parallels in the preserved writings of Greco-Roman philosophy and a wide range of Jewish literature.)

Paul's style in 4:8-9 reflects the influence of the Cynic-Stoic diatribe in its antithetical structure, linked by paronomasia (= wordplay; Bultmann 1985, 113; Martin 1986, 83). The parallels are merely formal; for the material content and functions differ. The Stoic or Cynic sage presented himself as self-sufficient and strong. Unlike them, Paul is sustained by the power of God. He "is God-reliant and God-confident" (Witherington 1995, 388).

The rhetorical function of such catalogs was to establish the trustworthy character of the philosopher. In an obviously countercultural move, Paul establishes his credibility in defense of his apostleship with a paradoxical appeal to his human weakness. Precisely his *inadequacy* is the occasion for the manifestation of divine power. Thus, Paul's use of antithetical structure characterizes much of 4:16—5:10 (McCant 1999, 43, 48).

Particularly in 4:13-15 Paul indicates his OT and Jewish assumptions. These provide the context for his reflections on the tradition of the righteous sufferer whom God does not abandon. In addition to his quotation of Ps 116:10, other passages in 2 Corinthians reflect this tradition. For example, behind 1:3-11 stands Ps 71:20-21:

> Though you have made me see troubles, many and bitter,
>   you will restore my life again;
> from the depths of the earth
>   you will bring me up.
> You will increase my honor
>   and comfort me once again.

In addition to 2 Cor 1:3-11 and 4:7-18, Paul reflects this tradition in 6:1-10 and 8:9 (see Hafemann 2000, 187 n 16). Paul's spirituality was biblical. As one who has "lived in the Bible," the Bible formed his worldview and sense of place in the world (Young and Ford 1987, 62-63; see Thrall 2004, 357-59, for other possible parallels to Greek and Jewish literature in 5:1-10).

IN THE TEXT

a. The Life of Jesus as Revealed in Affliction (4:7-15)

Paul turns to face the human realities of his apostolic ministry that he had previously touched on (in 1:8-9), exploiting new imagery. With **treasure in jars of clay,** Paul further explores an essential aspect of his ministry: How is the life of Jesus revealed in the suffering of his ministers?

With the rhetoric of paradox, Paul writes of power in the midst of weakness (4:7-9), life in the midst of death (vv 10-12), and of faith leading to speech (vv 13-14; Harris 2005, 338). The apostle is concerned to show the Corinthians the intimate relationship between his new covenant ministry and his human sufferings (Matera 2003, 105).

From Paul's perspective, suffering and glory belong inseparably together in a kind of polar tension (see already 1:3-10; 2:14). The glory of Christ was revealed in his passion and death. Must not the glory of the apostolic office also be revealed through suffering? Paul's gospel was "the message of the cross" (1 Cor 1:18). In his ministry he was "resolved to know nothing . . . except Jesus Christ and him crucified" (1 Cor 2:2). His testimony was that above all he wanted "to know Christ and the power of his resurrection and the fellowship of sharing in his sufferings, becoming like him in his death" (Phil 3:10). Thus, the very "act of God which the gospel is, is an act of suffering" (Baird 1960, 68).

Paul was convinced that, through his actual physical hardships and dangers as an apostle, he reenacted the sufferings of Christ (2 Cor 1:5). His apostolic suffering confronted his audience with the resurrection power of the living Christ. Here in the letter we meet a second interchange of opposite experiences (1:3-7), now the interchange of life and death.

■ **7 We have this treasure in jars of clay.** The verb *echomen,* **We have,** is used by Paul significantly throughout the discussion of his apostolic ministry (3:4, 12; 4:1, 7, 13; 5:1; 6:10; 7:1).

Treasure (*thēsauron*) can refer either to a place where valuables are stored for safekeeping (Matt 2:11; 13:52) or to what is stored (Matt 6:21; Luke 12:34; BDAG 2000, 456). Paul uses it here as a metaphor either for his gospel (Thrall 2004, 322) or his ministry (McCant 1999, 42). In fact, for Paul, the two are inseparable. His ministry incarnates his message. Ambrosiaster (ca. 366-384) was the "name given by Erasmus to the author of a work once thought to have been composed by Ambrose." He refers to the **treasure** with the inviting and illuminating phrase, "the sacrament of God in Christ" (ACCS NT 7:231, 325).

Note the parallel phrases in the preceding verses:

- "this ministry" (4:1)
- "our gospel" (4:3)
- "the light of the glory of the gospel of Christ" (4:4)

- "the light of the knowledge of the glory of God in the face of Christ" (4:6)

Paul uses **treasure** here to image the gospel of God's glory as revealed in Christ (BDAG 2000, 456 s.v. *thēsauros*). The content of Paul's ministry is preaching the glorious gospel of Christ. His point is that **this treasure** is to be found in fragile, ordinary earthenware containers, **jars of clay.**

Paul does not use **jars of clay** as a negative reference to the body as the contemptible receptacle for the divine soul as some thought in Paul's day. Rather, Paul's life and ministry, which were characterized by suffering, is compared to a common and fragile clay vessel (4:16; 5:1). The imagery was used as a metaphor for human existence in the OT (Job 10:9; Ps 31:12; Isa 29:16; 30:14; 64:8; Jer 18:6; 19:11) and in the writings from the Dead Sea Scrolls (1QS 11:22; 1QH[a] 1:21-22; 3:20-21; 4:29). These references suggest that Paul's point is the apparent insignificance and destructibility of the **jars.**

Paul's imagery alludes to earthen jars in which precious treasures were often stored in antiquity. These were hidden or carried as containers for valuable coins, sometimes in triumphal processions (2 Cor 2:14). The imagery highlights the contrast between the ordinary, inexpensive container and its priceless contents.

Paul acknowledges that human ministers possess a mortal frailty that embraces their total person. The apostolic life was vulnerable (see 1:8; 7:5). Yet this fragile life only magnifies the power inherent in the apostolic ministry (see 12:9). The purpose (*hina,* **that**) of his paradoxical expression, writes Paul, is "that it may be made clear that this extraordinary [*hyperbolē*] power belongs to God and does not come from us" (NRSV). The genitive phrase, *tou Theou* (**from God**), and the prepositional phrase, *ex hēmōn* (**from us**), may both be treated as possessives or as subjective genitives as in the NIV. In the true apostle, God's power is "transcendent" (RSV) even in the midst of mundane hardships and dangers.

■ **8** Paul begins the first of his four catalogs of hardships in the letter (4:8-9; 6:4-10; 11:23-29; 12:10). With it he illustrates from the trials experienced in the course of his ministry (see 6:4-5; 11:23-27; 1 Cor 4:11-13) how the excess of power in his ministry is clearly God's (2 Cor 8—9).

Paul expresses this in four adversative contrasts. These balanced antitheses consist of eight nominative plural present participles, all stressing continuous action. Frequent use of antithesis is a distinctive feature of Paul's writings. The "attentional novelty" of antithesis appeals to the emotions of his audience. Simultaneously, its paired elements are mutually interpretive, encouraging their assent (McCant 1999, 44).

The four participles could be linked back to *echomen* in 4:7. We could read ***we have, . . . being hard pressed,*** and so forth. Most translations, however, treat the participles as syntactically independent, taking the place of the indicative. Thus, the NIV starts a new sentence: **We are hard pressed.** The first element in each antithesis illustrates a human weakness. The second element, more intense than the first, indicates the divine deliverance from it: **hard pressed on every side, but not crushed.**

The qualifying adverbial phrase, **on every side** (*en panti:* "in every way," NASB) in v 8, seems to belong with all four of the antitheses. Thus, it forms an *inclusio*—literary bookends, so to speak—with "always" (*pantote*) in v 10.

Participles, like other nonindicative verbs, are routinely negated with some form of the particle *mē* in the Greek NT. The negative particles here are instead forms of *ou*. This is best explained either as negating a single idea in the four antitheses (BDAG 2000, 733; BDF 1961, §430.3) or as the proper negative "of a downright fact" (Moulton 1908, 1:232).

This unusual use of the negative particle expressing what is "clear cut and decisive" (Robertson 1934, 1137-38) is sometimes translated "never" (e.g., JB, NEB): ***afflicted . . . , but never crushed*** (Harris 2005, 343). The net effect is to stress the redeeming factor of God's presence (see Matt 28:20) in the apostolic suffering.

The first of the apostle's four antitheses describe Paul and his associates as **hard pressed** [*thlibomenoi*] **on every side, but not crushed** (v 8). The same verb, *thlibō*, is translated "distressed" in 1:6. The plural form of the cognate noun *thlipsis* in 1:4 is rendered "troubles"; and in 1:8, "hardships."

The second, negated participle, *stenochōroumenoi*, **crushed,** also has a general meaning. It reflects the imagery of confinement in a narrow space—crowded, cramped, restricted, compressed (BDAG 2000, 923). They are in a situation from which there is no way to escape, humanly speaking.

The second antithesis employs a play on words visible only in Greek. They are **perplexed** [*aporoumenoi;* see Gal 4:20], **but not in despair** (*exaporoumenoi*). Paul admits to feelings of despair in 1:8; but here, from the standpoint of faith, he insists that there was no reason for despair. Several interpretive attempts have been made to represent Paul's wordplay in English: "sometimes in doubt, but never in despair" (GNT); "confused but not confounded" (Hughes 1962, 138); "at a loss, but not lost" (Harris 2005, 343).

■ **9** The third antithesis, **persecuted** [*diōkomenoi*], **but not abandoned** (*enkataleipoumenoi*), employs the imagery of pursuit as in a hunt or battle. Forms of the first verb (*diōkō*) are used mostly of persecution in Paul's letters (see 1 Cor 4:12; Gal 1:13, 23; Phil 3:6).

Abandoned looks to the future divine deliverance Paul expects (see 1:10). In the LXX, the passive form of this verb presumes that God is the unfailing friend who will never forsake his people (Gen 28:15; Deut 31:6, 8; 1 Chr 28:20; Pss 16:10; 37:25, 28). Thus, Barclay paraphrases: "We are persecuted by men, but never abandoned by God" (1956, 220). The root verb appears in Jesus' familiar cry from the cross, "My God, my God, why have you forsaken [*engkatelipes*] me?" (Matt 27:46; Mark 15:34; citing Ps 22:1 LXX). Does this suggest that Paul subordinates his story to the story of Jesus? (so McCant 2006, 48).

The fourth and final antithesis, **struck down, but not destroyed,** employs the imagery of physical combat, the figure applied to wrestling, boxing, and military combat. Acts 14:18-20 records an instance in which Paul was attacked in Lystra, dragged out of the city, and left for dead. But with the aid of his disciples he was able to get up and, miraculously, went on to Derbe the next day. In 1 Thess 2:2 Paul wrote: "We had previously suffered and been insulted in Philippi, as you know, but with the help of our God we dared to tell you his gospel in spite of strong opposition."

The four antitheses of the hardship/suffering catalog in 2 Cor 4:8-9 speak of a life of daily endurance. In the midst of adversity, Paul depends, not on his human virtue and character, but on the "extraordinary power" (NRSV) of God.

■ **10** Following directly on this series of antithetically paired participles, and within the same Greek sentence, is yet another participle: ***carrying about*** (*peripherontes*). In vv 10-11 Paul offers a christological interpretation of his experiences described in the antitheses of vv 8-9. The interpretation of his experiences in terms of the death *and* resurrection of Jesus indicates Paul's specific understanding of his apostolic sufferings.

Paul presents the four aspects of suffering as a vicarious participation in **the death of Jesus,** or as ***the dying of Jesus*** (BDAG 2000, 688). Likewise, the four aspects of deliverance are interpreted as **the life of Jesus** (v 10), anticipating his share in Christ's resurrection.

It is unclear, however, whether the phrase **the death** [*nekrōsin*] **of Jesus** refers to the process of dying or the state of being figuratively dead. The first option would stand in synonymous parallelism with "always being given over to death" in v 11. But to **carry around . . . the death of Jesus** could mean instead to be metaphorically dead, as in Rom 4:19, Paul's only other use of the word. The immediate context favors the former translation—***the dying of Jesus*** (see Rom 8:36; 1 Cor 15:30-31). Barrett defends this reading, translating the phrase "the killing of Jesus" (Barrett 1973, 139-40).

On this view, the apostle's point is that ministers of the gospel live in the constant awareness that they are in the same process of dying, which culminated in the passion of Jesus. As an apostle, Paul not only preached the gospel, but his suffering played an integral part in the revelation of the paradoxical good news that life comes by way of death (see Gal 4:14; 6:17). Perhaps he suggests that like Christ, he suffers vicariously for the Corinthians (see Col 1:24).

But more than suffering and death, the apostolic gospel proclaimed the resurrection of Jesus. That same resurrection life, **the life** [*zōē*] **of Jesus,** is now **revealed** (*phanerōthēi;* see 2 Cor 2:14; 4:2, 11) in Paul's **body.** True, he bore on his "body the marks of Jesus" (Gal 6:17). And he could claim, "I have been crucified with Christ and I no longer live [*zō*]." But he could also add, "but Christ lives [*zēi*] in me. The life I live [*zō*] in the body, I live [*zō*] by faith in the Son of

God, who loved me and gave himself for me" (Gal 2:20-21). Because the apostle shares in "the death that Jesus died" he shares also in "the life that Jesus lives" (NEB). In the words of Chrysostom (344/354-407): "It is the daily deaths which they died, by which the resurrection also was shown" (ACCS NT 7:233). The emphasis in both experiences is on the paradoxical present existence of the apostle, not on Paul's actual physical death and future resurrection.

■ **11** In v 11, Paul explains (*gar*, **For**), restates, and clarifies his assertions in v 10.

First, *aei* (**always**) is used here rather than *pantote* (**always,** used in v 10). The two adverbs are essentially synonymous, but *aei* is used infrequently in Paul (3 times: here; 6:10; Titus 1:12 vs. 27 times for *pantote*). *Aei* stresses continuous duration rather than repeated occurrences. And it is emphatic, appearing first in the Greek sentence.

Second, **we** is implicit only in the verb ending in v 10. In v 11 it is expanded and emphatic: **we who are alive** (*hēmeis hoi zōntes*). Thus, Paul highlights the life-death paradox already central in vv 10-12 (Harris 2005, 347).

Third, in v 11 **we . . . are . . . being given over** [*paradidometha*] **to death** [*thanaton*] **for Jesus' sake** clarifies what Paul meant by "carry[ing] around in our body the death [or ***dying***] of Jesus" in v 10. The verb *paradidōmi* is "intimately linked with the passion of Jesus" (McCant 1999, 46). For example, in Mark 9:31; 10:33; 14:10, 11, 18, 21, 41, 42, 44; and 1 Cor 11:23 it refers to Judas' betrayal of Jesus. In Mark 15:1, 10, and 15 it describes the actions of the officials, who handed Jesus over to be crucified. In Gal 2:20 it describes Jesus' voluntary self-surrender to crucifixion: "the Son of God . . . gave [*paradontos*] himself for me."

Fourth, Paul's suffering was ***on account of*** [*dia*] ***Jesus*** or **for Jesus' sake.** Remarkable and atypical for Paul is the fourfold recurrence or anaphoric use of the name of **Jesus** rather than the royal title "Christ" in 2 Cor 4:10-11 (see vv 13-14). It indicates how closely Paul linked the career of Jesus with his own. He was a servant of the Servant. The two were bound together by a solidarity in suffering and dying.

Fifth, Paul continues to stress his identity with Jesus in his suffering by replacing "in our body" (*sōmati*) in v 10 with ***in our mortal flesh*** (*thētēi sarki*) in v 11. The final position of this clause in v 11 makes it particularly emphatic.

Paul's rhetoric, with its rhythmic pattern and repetition, infuses passion into his exposition of his paradoxical ministry. Thereby, he seeks to compel his readers to hear what he says with sympathy. He attempts to persuade them that suffering is as essential to his ministry as it was to the ministry of Jesus (McCant 1999, 46).

The **life** of Jesus is inevitably **revealed** in the ***mortal flesh*** of the minister who so fully identifies with Christ's death (vv 10-11). The union between Christ's death and resurrection is absolute. Paul considers them equally inseparable in both the life of the Christian and in the pattern of Christian ministry (see Rom 6:4, 8, 17; Gal 2:20; Phil 3:10). Participation in one presumes participation in the other.

So the life of Jesus presented by the life of the apostle to the Corinthians is the resurrection life of the crucified Jesus (see Acts 2:42). It is the life that the once earthly Jesus now lives at God's right hand, made effective in the church through the presence of the Holy Spirit (2 Cor 1:22; 5:5). The Spirit, in turn, communicates the resurrection life of the Lord Jesus to his subjects (3:17; Rom 1:4).

■ **12** With a strong conclusion (*hōste*, **So then** or ***Therefore***), Paul wraps up his thoughts in vv 8-11. He addresses any who might be tempted to despise his ministry, which includes the experience of suffering. **So then, death is at work in us, but life is at work in you.**

The first clause repeats in summary form the essence of vv 8-9, 10*a*, and 11*a*. The second clause is literally ***but life in you;*** the verb *energeitai* is not repeated. It shifts the perspective to the experience of the Corinthians.

Paul establishes a reciprocal connection between the continuing process of ***the dying of Jesus*** in Paul's ministry and the enjoyment of "the life of Jesus" by the Corinthians (v 10). Paul exposes himself to the forces of death so that the Corinthians might be exposed to the force of life. What is in him the sign of the cross is in them the sign of the resurrection!

Paul insists that the mark of a true apostle is that "he is, like Jesus, a suffering and dying figure, whose work and power and victory arise from his weakness and infirmity and defeat" (Munck 1959, 184). Thus, in the apostle as in his Lord, "the tension between this age and the age to come shows itself at its sharpest" (Beardslee 1961, 114). In these verses Paul furnishes the theological basis for his conviction that his suffering, like "the death of Jesus," mediates to others the resurrection power of God, that is, "the life of Jesus" (Hafemann 2000, 184).

■ **13** A literal translation of v 13 would be: ***But*** [*de*] ***having the same spirit of faith in accordance with what is written, "I believed, so I spoke," we also believe, so we also speak.*** The adversative particle *de*, ***But*** or "Yet," connects vv 8-12 with 13-14. A single sentence in Greek, vv 13-14 not only complete what precedes it but also anticipate Paul's presentation of the future hope in 4:16—5:10.

The transitional function of 4:13-14 is probably best conveyed by understanding the adverbial present participle *echontes* (***having***) with a causal force. The participial phrase in the present context sums up what has gone before (see 3:4, 12; 4:1, 7). Thus, an interpretive translation would be: ***Because we have the same spirit of faith . . .***

Paul could endure the continual suffering that accompanied his cruciform ministry (described in vv 7-12) only because of the particular character of his faith. He professes **that same spirit of faith** as the author of Ps 116. The psalmist illustrated his faith when he spoke out his experience of suffering: **I**

believed; therefore I have spoken (2 Cor 4:13). The Psalms were doubtless Paul's lifelong prayer book. So when he quotes only an excerpt from Ps 116:10, he was surely aware of the larger context:

You, O LORD, have delivered my soul from death,
. . . that I may walk before the LORD
in the land of the living.
I believed; therefore I said,
"I am greatly afflicted." (Ps 116:8-10)

Paul believed the psalmist's God was working in his own life.

Paul's favorite formula for introducing OT quotations is *kathōs gegraptai*, "just as it is written" (Rom 1:17; see Rom 2:24; 3:4, 10; 4:17; 8:36; 9:13, 33; 10:15; 11:8, 26; 15:3, 9, 21; 1 Cor 1:31; 2:9; 2 Cor 8:15; 9:9). The formula *kata to gegrammenon*, "according to what is written" (NASB), appears only here in the NT. Paul quotes the LXX of Ps 116:10, rather than the Hebrew text behind our English translations. In the LXX, the next line of the quote reads, "I was exceedingly humiliated [*etapeinōthēn*]." The Hebrew of Ps 116:10 can be translated: "I kept my faith, even when I said, 'I am greatly afflicted'" (NRSV).

By **spirit** (*pneuma*), Paul may have had in mind the Holy Spirit (so NASB; see 1:22; 5:5). No provision existed in antiquity to distinguish proper nouns by capitalization, as in modern English. Nevertheless, the form of Paul's expression and his stress on **faith** suggest that he referred instead to a particular attitude—a shared spiritual state or disposition of faith. Paul uses the term "spirit" elsewhere in this descriptive sense (see, e.g., 1 Cor 4:21; Gal 6:1; Eph 4:23).

Paul quotes a psalm of thanksgiving for deliverance from deadly peril (see 2 Cor 1:10). By doing so, he places himself in the OT tradition of the righteous sufferer. He affirms his religious continuity in spiritual life with Israel's saints of ages past (see Hafemann 2000, 187 n 16).

Paul uses Ps 116:10 to bring the import of the whole psalm—the experience and testimony of the psalmist—to bear on his own declaration. Paul used the psalm as a lens through which to interpret and articulate his experience in Christ, who was supremely *the* suffering Righteous One. It is out of this self-understanding that Paul bears his apostolic witness: **We also believe and therefore speak.**

The shift of person from the first person singular (**I**) to plural (**we**) and from the aorist past to the present tense is noteworthy. The apostle's sustained faith is such that he must keep on speaking. And he does so with confidence (see 4:2, 5). He cannot keep silent.

■ **14** The "faith" (v 13) that transformed Paul's present and sustained his ministry is focused on the hope of the final resurrection. The translation **Because we know** reflects the certainty of Paul's hope. It interprets the adverbial participle *eidotes* (literally, "knowing") as presuming a causal force. Paul believed that the God **who raised the Lord Jesus from the dead will also raise us with Jesus.**

Recent commentators, against most modern translations (NASB, NEB, NIV, NRSV), prefer the shorter reading, **Jesus,** to **Lord Jesus.** This preference is due, in part, to the slightly stronger manuscript evidence. But it also reflects the clear tendency of scribes to add divine names to the texts they received. Furthermore, the unmodified name **Jesus** is predominant in the immediate context (see vv 10-11, 14*b;* Thrall 1994, 342; Harris 2005, 339). The NIV adds the words **from the dead,** which have no basis in Greek, to clarify the meaning of *ho egeiras*. The NRSV translates the fuller reading literally: "the one who raised the Lord Jesus."

The content of Paul's faith is the certainty of the future resurrection from the dead as guaranteed by the prior resurrection of Jesus (see 1 Cor 15:1-8). This arose from his conviction that Jesus was "the firstfruits of those who have fallen asleep" (1 Cor 15:20), "the firstborn among many brothers" (Rom 8:29), and "the firstborn from among the dead" (Col 1:18; see Heb 1:6).

As a pre-Christian Pharisee, Paul expected the final resurrection at the end of time. According to Jewish apocalyptic assumptions, the resurrection of Jesus was an anomaly, unexpectedly out of sequence. A resurrection had occurred, while the old age of suffering and death persisted. That there had been a resurrection, however, announced the dawning of the new age. The rapidly approaching end of the old age, it was presumed, would soon effect the final resurrection of all the dead.

Paul's resurrection hope was sealed by two irrefutable proofs:

4:14
- First, the presence of the Holy Spirit in the church. Israel's prophets had associated the coming of the Spirit with the eschaton (see Ezek 36:22—37:14; Joel 2:28-32).
- Second, his conversion-call, in which God had revealed the risen Jesus to him (see 1 Cor 15:3-8; Gal 1:13-17).

Beyond the momentary event that changed the direction of his life, he continued to experience the power of the resurrection life of Jesus. The Spirit was an ongoing reality in his own life and in the lives of his converts (2 Cor 1:22; 5:5; 13:14; Rom 8:11; Phil 3:10-11).

Believers will be raised up to be **with Jesus** (*syn Iēsou*) in the resurrection glory that is already his (see Rom 8:17; Col 3:3-4; 1 Thess 4:14, 17; 5:10). The resurrection of Jesus is the pledge or guarantee of their resurrection. In this sense they already "share in his resurrection" (see Rom 6:5).

Following the future resurrection, Paul adds, God ***will present us with you.*** The NIV adds, **God will . . . present us with you in his presence** (emphasis added; so also NRSV; see Eph 5:26-27). The Corinthians were clearly on the apostle's mind as he wrote. Paul, of course, took for granted the solidarity of all Christians **with Jesus.** Furthermore, he presumed that participation in life **with Jesus** applied to all the decisive moments in Christ's given life—his death, resurrection, and final triumph.

Union **with Jesus** convinced Paul that God would present him, his coworkers, the Corinthians—all believers—approved before the throne of God (see 2 Cor 5:10; 11:2; Jude 24). By its explicit reference to the resurrection, v 14 furnishes the bridge connecting this section (vv 7-15) with the paragraphs that follow (4:16—5:10).

■ **15** Paul's conviction of the certainty of a triumphant future, no doubt, sustained him in his perilous and demanding calling (v 14; Filson 1953, 321-23). He cites three other bases for his hope:

- The reassurance of the psalmist (v 13).
- His concern for his converts held him steady (v 15). His claim, **all this is for your benefit,** in v 15 explains Paul's addition of "with you" in v 14. **All this** looks back to the resurrection-faith that compelled him to "speak" in vv 13-14. Paul's suffering was a gift and calling that he shared with the Corinthians (see 1:3-6).
- His absorption in the execution of God's purpose for the world gave him hope. God ultimately intends for all humanity gratefully to recognize him as God. Paul's calling was to take the gospel to those who had never heard (see Rom 15:17-21). He felt compelled to reach **more and more people** with the message of God's **grace.** Success in doing so would **cause thanksgiving to overflow to the glory of God.** The **grace** of God through Paul's ministry, by **reaching more and more people,** would enable many more thanksgivings to rise to the greater glory of God.

As with 1:11, the precise translation of this verse is difficult, but its point is clear enough (see Thrall 1994, 344-47; Harris 2005, 355-57). The NIV, NRSV, and NASB all agree on this understanding of the flow of Paul's thought. The NEB renders the meaning of the verse clearly: "As the abounding grace of God is shared by more and more, the greater . . . the chorus of thanksgiving that ascends to the glory of God." Paul is assured of the effective power of grace (see v 7) in the lives of people though his ministry.

Paul's presentation of the gospel and its ministry as a treasure in earthen vessels in vv 7-15 is illuminating. The weakness of the human vessel demands the intervention of divine power for the very preservation and usefulness of the vessel (vv 7-12). Furthermore, the character of that intervening divine life convinces those who share it of the resurrection perspective of the gospel (vv 13-15). From the vantage point of convinced faith, Paul was willing to suffer, first "for Jesus' sake" (v 11), then for the ***sake*** of the Corinthians (v 15), but ultimately for the eternal **glory of God** (v 15).

b. Outer Decay but Inner Renewal (4:16-18)

Paul continues to stress his courageous spirit (see 4:1) as he begins to speak more directly of the future. He writes of present inner renewal accompanying his outer decay. Verses 16-18 are a transitional passage that looks backward and forward. It bridges the gap between "life in the midst of death" in vv 7-15 and "life after death" in 5:1-10.

At work in Paul's thinking is "the tension between the old age persisting and the new age dawning" (Young and Ford 1987, 131). The apostle's use of antithetical pairs continues through 5:10.

An inferential conjunction, *dio,* **therefore,** connects 4:16-18 with what preceded in 4:7-15. Likewise, the reiteration of the phrase **we do not lose heart** reaches all the way back to where Paul began in 4:1. There he expressed his confidence in the integrity of his ministry, despite his suffering (4:1-2). Beginning with 4:16, Paul turns to the ground of his courage, even as he faces the depletion of his physical and mental resources occasioned by the hardships of his ministry (see 4:8-12).

■ **16** Verse 16 begins with the words, **Therefore we do not lose heart.** Paul's repetition of these words from 4:1 brings his argument full circle back to where he began. His emphasis shifts from a commendation of the cruciform character of his ministry to an expression of his confidence in the resurrection hope that sustains him in his suffering (see the commentary on 4:1).

Paul used the categories of ***outer*** and ***inner self*** to connect with his Hellenistic readers. But he did not share the Platonic-dualistic body-soul dichotomy often associated with the terminology (Thrall 2004, 347). Rather, he contrasts his total personal existence from the physical perspective with his whole person in relation to Christ (see 5:17).

The words ***but even though*** (*all' ei kai*) indicate that Paul does **not lose heart** despite the deadly processes at work **outwardly.** The Greek words *exō anthrōpos,* literally, the ***outward human,*** refer to his "outer nature" (NRSV) or ***outer self.*** John Calvin suggests that Paul intended by this expression not only bodily existence but also "everything that has to do with this present life." (1964, 10:63). This ***outward human*** is thus not to be identified as the "old man" (KJV) or "old self" (NRSV) of Rom 6:6; Eph 4:22; and Col 3:9.

The emphatic contrast is continued by **yet** (*all',* ***but***), which introduces the next clause. This stresses that, ***even though*** **outwardly** (*ho exō . . . anthrōpos*) Paul's life is in decay, **yet inwardly** (*ho esō*) he is **being renewed day by day** (*hēmerai kai hēmerai*) or "day after day" (Harris 2005, 359). The word *anthrōpos* is not repeated with *esō,* but may be presumed on the basis of ellipsis (BDF 1961, §479).

Paul views the contrast between the ***inner self*** and the ***outer self*** in terms of daily renewal. Despite his outward circumstances as a suffering apostle, he is being daily transformed into the likeness of Christ. The expression **day by day** and the present tense of the contrasting verbs indicate two simultaneous, continuing processes. Paul is supremely optimistic. His life in relation to Christ consists of the reception of fresh spiritual resources each day (3:18; see Rom 12:2). Inward waxing and outward waning proceed apace. Although the one process must inevitably end in death, the other will just as certainly result in life that is eternal.

■ **17** To substantiate what is introduced by "therefore" (*dio*) in v 16, Paul explains his paradoxical affirmation with a series of even more startling contrasts. This he does with the first of six uses of the explanatory conjunction *gar* (**For;** 4:17, 18; 5:1, 2, 4, 10).

Paul's **troubles,** borne "for Jesus' sake" (4:11) are actually producing a "glory beyond all measure" (v 17 NRSV; see v 7). In comparison with the **troubles** that are **light and momentary,** the **glory** is **eternal** and **far outweighs them all.** Paul's expression is more literally ***an eternal weight of glory beyond all comparison*** (*kath' hyperbolēn eis hyperbolēn aiōnion baros doxēs*). This can be translated *"beyond all measure and proportion"* (BDAG 2000, 1032). Paul's rhetoric hyperbolically intensifies both elements.

In 1:8 Paul used the verbal form of ***weight*** (*baros*) to describe his tribulations (*thlipseōs,* **troubles,** "affliction," NRSV). "We were burdened [*ebarēthēmen*] excessively . . . [despairing] even of life" (NASB). But now he describes the hardships of his life **outwardly** as ***weightless*** or *"insignificant"* (*elaphron,* **light;** BDAG 2000, 314) compared to the ***weight*** of the **eternal glory.**

Paul's second contrast is between **troubles** that are **momentary** and **glory** that is **eternal.** The contrast is not between "present" and "future" but between "transient" and "permanent." The glory he experiences not only is in the future (see 3:18; 4:18) but originates in the eternal order.

It is interesting and probably significant to note that the Hebrew word *kabod,* often translated "glory" in the OT, can also mean "weight." Paul's point is that in God's economy, suffering actually produces glory (see Rom 5:1-5). Therefore, what he now endures as an apostle is both of little significance and brief in comparison with the glory "beyond all measure" (NRSV) he is now accumulating (see Rom 8:17-18).

■ **18** Paul's transition to a further explanation of his apostolic perspective on his "troubles" (v 17) employs a present adverbial participle clause. In the absence of an explicit particle or conjunction such as *dio* (v 16) or *gar* (v 17), its precise function in relation to v 17 is a matter of interpretation.

The NASB translates it as a temporal clause: "while we look not at the things which are seen." It might serve as merely an attendant circumstance: ***And we keep our eyes not on****. . . .* The NIV treats it as a result: **so we fix our eyes** (*skopountōn*). The NRSV reads it with a causal force: "because we look not."

The NIV, perhaps, does the greatest justice to the sense of fixed attention Paul calls for here. And it recognizes the causal force of the final clause in v 18: **For [*gar*] what is seen is temporary, but what is unseen is eternal.** But v 18 as a whole seems to explain why Paul regards his troubles as he does according to v 17, favoring the NRSV translation. Paul's paradoxical perspective is effective in the lives of the apostle and his coworkers "because" they pay careful attention "not at what can be seen but at what cannot be seen" (NRSV).

The contrast between the **seen** and **unseen** is not one of philosophical subtlety. Paul recognizes the existence of realities human eyes cannot see, because of their physical limitations and temporality. The contrast has an eschatological dimension. That is, it partakes of the Pauline tension between "the already" and the "not yet" (Rom 8:23-25; 1 Cor 12:12).

Paul continues his conclusion, **For** [*gar*], **what is seen is temporary, but what is unseen is eternal.** It has the form of an aphorism based on faith in the resurrection (Matera 2003, 116). Again, the **seen** is both temporal and transitory (*proskaira*), while the **unseen** is permanent. One ends; the other does not. Paul can undergo the sufferings attending his apostolic ministry because the unseen is more real and relevant to him than the seen (see Rom 8:38-39).

So, what does it matter if Paul's life of daily deliverance from death should in some moment end in death? He possesses a certain future beyond death, a future that has broken into his present with assurance (see 4:14; 5:1, 5). He focuses on the things that are **unseen,** that is, on (1) his continuing, Spirit-enabled participation in the image of God that will (2) culminate in his final transformation into the likeness of God in Christ (3:18; 4:4, 6; Hafemann 2000, 191). Paul narrows the gap between his individual and corporate existence as he progressively actualizes in the present what he already *is* "in Christ."

c. The Hope for the Heavenly Home (5:1-10)

All of this leads into the hope for the heavenly home, showing to us Paul's overall orientation (Witherington 1995, 391). Modern chapter divisions are purely arbitrary—convenient for locating a passage, but not usually helpful in defining thought units. This paragraph expands and reinforces the theme of 4:16-18. So it belongs more to what precedes than to what follows after 5:11.

The Greek conjunction *gar*, ***For*** or ***because***, begins the paragraph in v 1. It reaches back to v 16 to introduce Paul's further treatment of "what is unseen" (4:18). It explains the reason why he refuses to be discouraged and offers the basis for his confidence.

We know, an apostolic plural (see 4:1, 16), indicates the certainty of Paul's future hope, which he shares with the other apostles, the Corinthians, and all Christian believers. His courage, as he faces failing faculties and the inevitability of suffering and death, is to be found in his assurance of the unseen and the eternal (4:18), that is, in the certainty of his **eternal house in heaven** (5:1).

■ **1** The contrast between the fleeting "seen" and the lasting "unseen" is now expressed in terms of **the earthly tent we live in** vs. **a building from God, an eternal house in heaven** (v 1). The phrase translated **we live in** is literally ***our house*** (***our,*** understood as a subjective genitive). Thus, the contrast is between our present and future "houses"—modes of existence.

What is "seen" is only an **earthly tent.** What is "unseen" is **a building from God . . . in heaven.** Paul exploits the familiar metaphor of a tent, a transitory dwelling. The **tent** characterizes the apostle's physical life on earth—that is, his *sōma* or body (see Rom 6:12; 4:19). A tent may be dismantled at any time (see Heb 11:8-10; 2 Pet 1:13-14; Isa 38:12 LXX; Wis 9:15). Paul takes for granted that he will die at some uncertain time in the future. His **earthly**

tent will be "taken down" (BDAG 2000, 522) or **destroyed.** Then Paul will possess **a building from God** (*oikodomēn ek Theou*).

We have (*echomen*) probably expresses no more than the apostle's faith that after this life, whenever and however the transition occurs, a heavenly body is prepared for believers. Paul described this in his earlier letter to Corinth as a "spiritual body" (*sōma pneumatikon;* 1 Cor 15:44). Interpreters have attempted to be more specific in their reading of Paul's mind. Thrall lists nine ways of understanding **a building from God** (2004, 363-67; see Harris 2005, 371-72). Harris examines five ways of interpreting **we have** (Harris 2005, 374-80; see Thrall 2004, 368-70).

We settle on a view that seems most natural to the context. Paul has in mind primarily the resurrection body individuals will possess at death, either in full reality or only potentially (with the full possession of the spiritual body coming at the Parousia; see 1 Cor 15:35-57). Verses 1-10 are among the most thoroughly studied and hotly disputed verses in 2 Corinthians (see Further Reading on 5:1-10).

At the very least, Paul believed he even now possessed **by faith** (5:7) this **eternal house in heaven,** one **not built by human hands** (*acheiropoiēton,* 1 Cor 15:40; see Col 2:11; Heb 9:11, 24). Perhaps he understood it as already prepared in heaven, waiting for him. In Gal 4:25-26, Paul contrasts "the present city of Jerusalem" with "the Jerusalem that is above." Did he similarly conceive of the **eternal house in heaven** as already present "above" and not just future?

The language of Mark 14:58 is amazingly similar: "We heard him say, 'I will destroy [*katalyso*] this man-made [*cheiropoiōton*] temple and in three days will build [*oikodomēsō*] another, not made by man [*acheiropoiēton*].'" To this statement of Jesus', John's Gospel adds, "The temple he had spoken of was his body" (2:21). Paul links the resurrection of Christ with the church as the body of Christ (Rom 7:4; 1 Cor 6:14-15; Col 1:18; Eph 1:18-23) and uses temple imagery for the body (2 Cor 6:16; 1 Cor 3:16).

Therefore, **a building from God** (see 1 Cor 3:9; Eph 2:21; 4:12, 16) and a **house . . . not built by human hands** reflects a similar thought. Paul's hope falls within the larger framework of the "corporate solidarities which inhere . . . in Christ . . . in whom the new aeon has been fully actualized and who alone is individually present in the heavenlies" (Ellis 1959-60, 217-18).

Ellis suggests that the threefold description—**a building from God, an eternal house in heaven,** and a house **not built by human hands**—is a comprehensive description of Paul's future hope. He looks forward as well to the Parousia for the full actualization of the hope that is already his "in Christ" and that awaits him immediately following his death. This actualization is the "eternal weight of glory" (4:17 NASB).

■ **2 Meanwhile** (*kai gar*), or better, ***For also,*** introduces another reason for Paul's assurance of his future "house in heaven." Because "in this tent" (*toutōi,* NRSV), that is, in this present life we live with limitations and imperfections.

We continue to **groan, longing to be clothed with our heavenly dwelling** (see v 4; Rom 8:23).

Groaning probably has both positive and negative connotations. It expresses the tension Paul and all Christians experience between suffering and hope (see Rom 5:1-5). Paul creates "a bizarre metaphor" (McCant 1999, 49) as he mixes the metaphorical use of **dwelling** (*oikētērion;* see *oikia* and *oikodomēn* in v 1) with that of clothing. This enables him to speak of putting on (*ependysasthai*) the heavenly existence over (not in place of) the old existence, as if it were an outer garment.

■ **3** Paul's note of confidence continues in v 3, as he explains why "we groan" (v 2). It is **because** [*ei ge kai;* "if indeed," NRSV] **when we are clothed, we will not be found naked** (v 3).

A textual variant explains the differences between the NIV and NRSV at this point. The NRSV translates *ekdysamenoi* "when we have taken it off." The NIV translates *endysamenoi,* **when we are clothed.** Both internal coherence and external manuscript evidence favor the NIV reading (Harris 2005, 368). The verb translated **will . . . be found** often refers to the results of a judicial investigation. Here it appears to point ahead to the judgment scene in v 10 (McCant 1999, 50).

Crucial to understanding the passage is our answer to the question: What does Paul mean by **naked** (v 3)? Since **naked** is obviously related to **unclothed** in v 4, it may also reflect the judgment theme. Traditionally, interpreters have taken **naked** as a reference to an intermediate, temporary state of incompleteness between the death of Christians and their bodily resurrection at the end. In Greek philosophical terminology, however, **naked** referred to disembodied souls, stripped of their earthly bodies. This was thought to be the mode of existence in the afterlife. If so, Paul rejects such a view: **we will not be found naked.** Was he challenging a view espoused by Gnosticizing Corinthians who idealized a permanently disembodied postmortem state (so Harris 2005, 386)?

But was Paul even thinking here about bodily vs. disembodied existence in the afterlife? In light of v 10, some think the judgment scene is in view here. If so, then **naked** and **unclothed** would function like "shame" in both the OT (Gen 3:10; Isa 20:4; Ezek 16:37, 39; 23:26, 29; Hos 2:3) and NT (Rom 10:11; 1 John 2:28; Rev 3:17-18). To be **naked** would be to stand guilty before "the judgment seat of Christ" (Ellis 1959-60, 220-21; Hafemann 2000, 211-14). If this is Paul's understanding, to be **naked** metaphorically describes one unprepared for the eternal order.

To have no **heavenly dwelling** after death (vv 1-2) would then be comparable to having no "wedding clothes" at the eschatological banquet (Matt 22:11). It would be to be "disqualified for the prize" in the Christian race (1 Cor 9:24-27). It would be to have no "spiritual body" (1 Cor 15:44, 53-54). Paul is certain that such will not be his state, irrespective of when he dies. He is confident he will participate in the resurrection life in the eternal age to come, as 2 Cor 5:4 affirms.

■ **4** Is the final judgment the key issue in Paul's mind as v 4 expands and restates v 3? Paul reinforces **we groan** (*stenazomen*) with ***we* are burdened** (see 1:8). He attaches a purpose clause to complete the sentence: **so that** [*hina*] **what is mortal may be swallowed up by life.** Paul explains why he is intensely **burdened** with the following causal clause: **because** [*eph hōi*] **we do not wish to be unclothed but to be clothed with our heavenly dwelling.**

If Paul was rejecting a mistaken view of the afterlife, then there was a positive reason for his burdened sighing. It was not so much a fear of judgment as a longing for the full deliverance his future **heavenly dwelling** would bring. He longs for a body free from the limitations of the **earthly tent** (see 4:7-12), for a life fully responsive to the Spirit, and suited for the heavenly realm (Harris 2005, 387-88).

The purpose clause, **so that what is mortal may be swallowed up** [*katapothēi*] **by life,** probably has the same meaning as 1 Cor 15:53. There Paul wrote, "The perishable must clothe itself with the imperishable, and the mortal with immortality." Paul expected this to occur at the Parousia. Death itself is neither the end nor a redeemer. Death will, after all, be "swallowed up in victory" (1 Cor 15:54).

Swallowing Death

The ornamented stone casket used as a burial box in antiquity was known as a sarcophagus. The natural processes of decomposition following death probably account for the designation, which in Greek means literally, "flesh eater." The OT frequently uses the imagery of death swallowing its victims (see Pss 49:14; 69:15; 141:7; Prov 1:12; 27:20; 30:15-16; Isa 5:14; Hab 2:5). But Isa 25:8 announces an ironic reversal: At the great eschatological banquet of final salvation, Death, the great swallower, will be swallowed (*katepien* in the LXX) by Yahweh. In 1 Cor 15:54-55; Rev 21:4-5; and probably in the present passage, this prophecy provides the imagery describing resurrection hope.

Irrespective of whether or not he died before the Parousia, Paul longed for full and final redemption. In Rom 8:23 he wrote: "We ourselves, who have the firstfruits of the Spirit, groan inwardly [*stenazomen*] as we wait eagerly for our adoption as sons, the redemption of our bodies" (see Phil 3:10-14). Paul groaned along with the rest of creation as he anxiously awaited the final actualization of the new creation at Christ's coming. Paul was convinced of and longed intensely for the transformation of his mortal body by immortal life. No doubt, he would have preferred the Parousia over death for this transition (Thrall 2004, 398).

■ **5** Paul offers another reason for the certainty of his hope: the gift of the Holy Spirit. **God,** of course, is the One who initiates this gift. Paul emphasizes

God's role by assigning the word an emphatic position in the sentence. He has already stressed God's active role in the letter (1:4, 9-10, 21-22; 2:14; 3:5-6; 4:6-7; 5:1). It is "God, who raises the dead" (1:9). **It is God,** as the "creator and consummator of all things" (Harris 2005, 392), **who has made us for this very purpose** (*eis auto touto*, "for this very thing," NRSV).

The purpose Paul refers to here is all that he has described to this point—"a building from God," "an eternal house in heaven" (v 1), "our heavenly dwelling" (v 2), "clothed" (v 3), and "clothed with our heavenly dwelling . . . mortal . . . swallowed up [*katapothēi*] by life" (v 4). The gift of the Spirit guarantees the final swallowing up of what is mortal by eternal life.

The two aorist participial expressions, **God who has made us** (*ho . . . katergasamenos hēmas*; see 4:17) and **God who . . . has given us** (*ho . . . dous hēmin*) refer back to the historic events: the coming of Christ and the gift of the Spirit to the church. The gift of the Spirit clinches Paul's point. **God . . . has given us the Spirit as a deposit** [*arrabōna*], **guaranteeing what is to come** (see 1:22).

Paul describes the Holy Spirit as an *arrabōna*. That is, the Spirit is the ***"first installment, deposit, pledge, down payment"*** (BDAG 2000, 134) of the consummation of his purpose of transformation for Christians (see Phil 1:6; 1 Thess 5:24). As the empowering presence of God, the Spirit anticipates our future dwelling with God and guarantees what is only hope for the present. "If the Spirit of him who raised Jesus from the dead is living in you, he who raised Christ from the dead will also give life to your mortal bodies through his Spirit, who lives in you" (Rom 8:11; see Eph 1:13-14, 19-20).

The Spirit represents the continuity between the redemptive activity of God already begun and its consummation in the age to come. The Spirit is "the firstfruits" (Rom 8:23) who guarantees the coming harvest of final salvation. Paul now possesses in mortal life the authentic beginning of that perfect life (Phil 3:12), which will comprise the totality of his existence at the end of the age.

The connection is real, personal, and spiritual. His longing is no illusion, for he grounds it in God's own work in his own present life and in the lives of the Corinthians. There is no delusion, for Paul's hope gives certainty! Present life in the Spirit affords security; and this security *is* to be found in the ongoing divine work of sanctification (Rom 8:1-39)!

With v 5, Paul composes a climactic summary to 5:1-4 and prepares for a shift in style at 5:6. The stance from which he views his life and ministry is now clear. It flows from a divine future that God has initiated in the present "in Christ" and possessed "in the Spirit." The first installment of the future inheritance was "the Spirit of sonship" (Rom 8:15).

■ **6** Paul's mood and style appear to change as he begins to draw conclusions from his certainty about the future. He becomes more positive. Because of the Spirit's presence, his longing for the future encourages him in the present: **Therefore we are always confident** (see 4:1, 16).

The metaphors Paul used for **the body** in 4:16—5:5 are now abandoned. Here he refers explicitly to the term **body** (*to sōma*) itself (6 times in vv 6-10). In view is **the body** as the sphere of one's physical life on earth with all of its frailties (see Rom 6:12; 12:1). For Paul a mortal body is not incompatible with life "in Christ" (2 Cor 5:17; Gal 2:20).

Paul continues to use the architectural imagery of 5:1-2. The metaphors of being **at home** (*endēmeō*) and "away from our home" (*ekdēmeō*, Furnish 1984, 253) are obviously related to the earlier terminology of "tent," "building," and "house." Paul's imagery should be recognized for what it is: imagery. He is not dreaming of a "Mansion over the Hilltop."

Earthly existence in the physical body means for Paul that "we are exiles from the Lord" (NEB). That is, although we are "in Christ" we are not yet "with Christ" (Phil 1:23). **We . . . know** [*eidotes*] **that as long as we are at home in the body we are away from the Lord.** We are not yet in our eternal residence with the risen Christ.

■ **7** Verse 7 is a broken construction (= an anacoluthon: it does not follow grammatically). Paul has shifted from the grammatical structure he will resume in v 8. So he inserts a clarifying parenthetical clause, **We live by faith, not by sight** (see Rom 8:24; 1 Cor 13:12). This reflects the "seen . . . unseen" contrast of 4:18. Paul says literally that ***we walk*** (*peripatoumen*). The Greek verb here employs the typical Jewish imagery of walking as a metaphor for the way we conduct our lives morally. In the Talmud, rabbinic discussions of legal matters related to appropriate and inappropriate behaviors and lifestyle fall under the heading of Halakah (Hebrew: "walk"). Thus Paul claims, **we live** our lives in (*dia*) the realm of **faith,** not in (*dia*) the realm of **sight** (Harris 2005, 397).

Who or what is it that we do not see, but only trust for the present? It is, of course, the heavenly Christ. On earth Christians live in relation to the Lord, not by what is seen (*eidous*) visibly (see 5:16). Our relationship is a matter of **faith** in "what is unseen" (4:18; see Heb 11:1).

In Rom 8:24*b*-25 Paul will write about the groaning of Spirit-filled Christians for the future "redemption of our bodies" (Rom 8:23). "Hope that is seen [*blepomenē*] is no hope at all. Who hopes for what he already has? But if we hope for what we do not yet have, we wait for it patiently" (see Greathouse and Lyons 2008, 265-66).

Paul is painfully aware that earth is not heaven, and that a faith vision of Jesus is not to be compared with the direct vision of the Lord in his glory (Rom 8:16-18; see 1 John 3:2). "Faith is our guide, we do not see him" (NEB).

Paul was perhaps correcting a triumphalist misperception of what it meant to be "in Christ." Against those who felt they had fully arrived spiritually (see 1 Cor 4:8; 15:12), the apostle is prepared to discuss the issues of ethical accountability and moral transformation that will occupy him later in the letter.

■ **8** Paul begins again where he left off in v 6*a*. With **we are confident, I say** he resumes and reformulates vv 6-7. The conjunction *de,* left untranslated in the NIV, has the resumptive force reflected in the NRSV: "Yes, we do have confidence." As Paul reiterates his courageous stance, in vv 8-9 he exposes more fully what it means to remain "away from the Lord" and yet to live "by faith."

He reverses the order of the terms used in v 6 to write: ***We prefer rather* to be away from the body and at home with the Lord** (v 8*b*). The verb translated ***prefer*** (*eudokoumen*) with (*mallon*, ***rather***) indicates the deliberate choice of what is better (BDAG 2000, 404 s.v. *eudokeō*). Paul prefers sight to faith. That is, he would rather be in heavenly residence with the Lord than to continue in his earthly residence, that is, "in the body" (5:6).

Paul would prefer (see 5:1-4) the manner of life he will possess when faith becomes sight (see 1 Cor 13:8-12). For then he will fully realize the consummation of the justification, sanctification, and redemption (2 Cor 3:18; 1 Cor 1:30) that are now his "in Christ." Although Paul looks finally to the resurrection of the body (1 Cor 15:42-48), he insists that with death he will be **at home with** [i.e., ***face to face with***, *pros*] **the Lord.** A temporary, disembodied state between death and the Parousia does not appear to be in view here.

■ **9** This preference rules all of Paul's circumstances. He is encouraged (4:1, 16; 5:6, 8). And because of this, he writes: ***Therefore*** [*dio*, **So**] **we make it our goal to please** [*euarestoi*] **him, whether we are at home in the body or away from it** (v 9). It is Paul's **goal** or ***ambition*** to be always pleasing to his Lord. In fact, he considers it an honor to do so (BDAG 2000, 1059 s.v. *philotimeomai*).

Paul's letters frequently use the adjective *euarestos* to describe human behavior that is "acceptable" or "well-pleasing" to God (see Rom 12:1, 2; 14:18; Eph 5:10; Phil 4:18; Col 3:20). Pleasing Christ was the all-consuming passion of Paul's life (see v 14) and the overall objective of his apostolic ministry. This was true, as the present tenses indicate, whether he lived on in a vulnerable human frame or whether he died and was **away from** his bodily home on earth. The nature of the future, Paul's destiny of residence with the Lord (v 8), and the necessity of appearing before him for judgment (v 10), all motivated him to please the Lord.

■ **10** The conjunction **For** (*gar*) introduces this last noted motivation for Paul's honorable aim to please the Lord. He recognized his approaching final and absolute accountability to God: **For we must all appear before the judgment seat of Christ** (v 10). This brings to bear "an explicit warrant for moral action" (Hays 1996, 39).

The infinitive *phanerōthēnai* (**appear**) is a constantive aorist, indicating a one-time event. It can also mean to ***be made manifest.*** The final judgment will publicly expose us for what we really are (1 Cor 4:5; see Heb 4:13). This is consistent with the verb's meaning twice in 5:11: "we are made manifest" (NASB). The judicial context of a court appearance and Rom 14:12 ("each of us will give an account of himself to God"), however, favors the translation **appear** in v 10 (NIV, NASB, and NRSV).

The **judgment seat** (*bēma*) indicates a platform or Roman tribunal bench on which an official sat to render judgment in legal cases (Acts 25:6, 10, 17). Paul expected that he, his coworkers, the Corinthians, and indeed all Christians would face final judgment (Rom 14:10, 12; 1 Cor 3:10-15; 4:5). At the eschatological judgment the true reality of one's moral character will be openly and fully revealed.

The purpose of judgment is that each of us **may receive** a recompense (*komisētai;* BDAG 2000, 557) for **the things done *through* the body** (*ta dia tou sōmatos*). The verb **done** here actually belongs in the following prepositional phrase: ***in accordance with what one has done*** [or ***accomplished;*** *pros ha epraxen*], **whether good or bad.**

Paul usually contrasts **good** (*agathon*) and "bad" (*kakon;* see, e.g., Rom 2:7-10; 3:8; 7:19; 12:2, 9, 17, 21; 13:3, 4, 10; 16:19). Implied in this different word for **bad** (*phaulon;* contrasted with *agathos* only in Rom 9:11; 2 Cor 5:10; and Titus 2:5) is the thought of behaviors that are worthless or "inferior in quality" (BDAG 2000, 1050). Reward, not status, is in view. The English translations of this colloquial Greek sentence are necessarily periphrastic. They must express the content of divine judgment in general terms (see, e.g., the NRSV: "recompense for what has been done in the body").

Perhaps Paul's intention is more specific. Although Christians are saved by free grace (Eph 2:8), their reward at the judgment *is* the resultant quality of their own lives viewed as a unity (Eph 6:8; Rom 2:2-11). The aorist tense of ***what one has done*** (*epraxen*) conceives of the idea of judgment as a whole. The bottom line is simply that we receive at the judgment the kind of person we have chosen to be! Thus, Paul sought to eliminate the worthless in his life of service to Christ. He was convinced that there is a direct and definite continuity between earthly existence and the eternal one to come.

Christians are accountable to God for the quality of their lives of faith and moral action in the present. Paul viewed the judgment of God on his own life as totally just and impartial. God's judgment would be in no way arbitrary. Rather, it would involve natural retribution (see 11:15; Ps 81:12). The punishment of the godless is fundamentally that they will receive what they have become (see Gal 6:7-8). They are sentenced to live throughout eternity as the persons they have become!

Hell

It is noteworthy that the word "hell" nowhere appears in Paul's letters. Nevertheless, 2 Thess 1:6 identifies God's retributive justice in these terms: "He will pay back trouble to those who trouble you." In 2 Thess 1:8-9, he says that "those who do not know God and do not obey the gospel . . . will be punished with everlasting destruction and shut out from the presence of the Lord and from the majesty of his power." In Rom 2:5, Paul claims that the stubborn and unrepentant are "storing up wrath against [themselves] for the day of God's wrath, when his righteous judgment will be revealed." In vv 8-9, he adds that "those who are self-seeking and who reject the truth and follow evil" will experience God's "wrath and anger" in the form of "trouble and distress."

We are free to choose in life who we are and, thus, the kind of people we will be in eternity. C. S. Lewis's allegory of heaven and hell was on target. In the words of the Teacher, George Macdonald, "There are only two kinds of people in the end: those who say to God, 'Thy will be done,' and those to whom God says, in the end '*Thy* will be done.' All that are in Hell, choose it." (1945, 69)

Paul was passionately courageous in the face of a ministry that entailed suffering. His ministry, characterized by the dying of Jesus in his body (4:10), is doubly motivated:

First (vv 1-5), he was sure that at the end of his earthly life he would be ushered into a fully redeemed existence. The flesh and the power of death will have lost its grasp even on the outer person, as it had already over the inner person. He was convinced that all will be made new by the Spirit of the Lord.

Second (vv 6-10), Paul was intensely concerned to be pleasing to the Lord, both now and then. He was convinced that how well-pleasing he would be "at home with the Lord" was in continuity with how pleasing he was now "at home in the body." He would not be satisfied merely to "make heaven."

The apostle had an insatiable longing to possess fully all the privileges of heaven. In his present life he was passionately preoccupied with pleasing the Lord with the positive quality of his character and service. This explains why
5:10 Paul's credentials as an apostle were not found primarily in "what is seen" but in "what is unseen." He lived "by faith, not by sight" (McCant 1999, 51). Biblically, eschatology is always connected with ethics.

Paul gladly accepted his ministry of suffering (4:7—5:10), not because he was a masochist but because:

1. The afflictions he courageously endured as he proclaimed the gospel partook of the nature of the sufferings of Jesus. Accordingly, they had been broken into by the power of the resurrection of Jesus (4:7-11).
2. The resurrection life of Jesus imparted by the inward presence of the Spirit was the dynamic of Paul's ministry, authentically confronting men and women with Jesus (4:12-15).
3. Paul's continued courage arose from his being prepared (4:16-18) for the full consummation of his heavenly hope with the Lord (5:1-10). For Paul "faith is the state of being ultimately concerned" (Tillich 1957, 4).

The Intermediate State

Some interpreters have seen in the "unclothed" and "naked" language of 2 Cor 5:2-3 what theologians have called "the intermediate state." If so, how is what Paul wrote in 1 Thess 4:13-18 to be reconciled with what he wrote in 2 Cor 5:1-

10? What did Paul mean when he referred in 1 Thess 4:14 to those who have "fallen asleep" in Jesus? What is the state of the believer between the death of the body and the final resurrection? (see Cullmann 1958, 10-11, 48-57).

The Greeks saw death as the great liberator and thought of the afterlife as the escape of the soul/spirit from the body. Thus, their hope was an otherworldly immortality of the soul. From the second century B.C. onward, the Jewish conception of life after physical death involved bodily life on a renewed earth. For those Jews who believed in an afterlife, it included the body. In the NT, redemption includes the "whole person," body and spirit (1 Thess 5:23) in continuity with Jewish conceptions. Body and soul/spirit were not considered opposites. Both will partake of the resurrection.

Interpreting these and other biblical hints, theological reason has posited a mode of existence between the death of the individual and the resurrection of the body that theologians designate "the intermediate state." What this might be like is a matter of speculation.

In 2 Cor 5:1-10 Paul speaks of death as followed immediately by being "at home with the Lord" (v 8). And he appears to identify this as being "clothed with our heavenly dwelling" (v 4). To the Philippians he wrote of departing from this life to "be with Christ" (Phil 1:23). If there is such a state between death and resurrection, an "in between" mode of existence, Paul does not define it. It seems unlikely that he even had such a thing in mind. He is absorbed with being at home with Christ at death.

A classic theological presentation of the intermediate state is that of Olin Alfred Curtis in his *Christian Faith Personally Given in a System of Doctrine,* published in 1905. For further reading from the perspective of biblical scholarship, see:

Craig, William L. 1988. "Paul's Dilemma in 2 Corinthians 5.1-10: A 'Catch 22.'" *New Testament Studies* 34:145-47.

Cullmann, Oscar. 1958. Pages 48-57 in *Immortality of the Soul or Resurrection of the Dead: The Witness of the New Testament.* London: Epworth Press.

Ellis, E. Earle. 1959-60. "II Corinthians v. 1-10 in Pauline Eschatology." *New Testament Studies* 6:211-24.

_________. 1961. "The Structure of Pauline Eschatology (II Corinthians v. 1-10)." Pages 35-48 in *Paul and His Recent Interpreters.* Grand Rapids: Eerdmans.

Hanhart, K. 1966. *The Intermediate State in the New Testament.* Franeker: Wever.

_________. 1969. "Paul's Hope in the Face of Death." *Journal of Biblical Literature* 88:445-57.

Harris, Murray J. 1974. "Paul's View of Death in 2 Corinthians 5:1-10." Pages 317-38 in *New Dimensions in New Testament Study.* Edited by R. N. Longenecker and M. C. Tenney. Grand Rapids: Zondervan.

Lincoln, A. T. 1981. Pages 55-70 in *Paradise Now and Not Yet; Studies in the Role of the Heavenly Dimension in Paul's Thought with Special Reference to His Eschatology.* Society for New Testament Studies Monograph Series 43. Cambridge: Cambridge University Press.

FROM THE TEXT

As Paul continues to defend his apostolic ministry, he is confident. Some may have disparaged his ministry because of its vulnerability to humiliation and affliction. Paul himself describes it as "a ministry of suffering" (4:7—5:10). How can he keep up his courage in the face of all the difficulties? Paul sees the life of Jesus revealed in his afflictions (4:7-15). He knows his life is one of outer decay but inner renewal (4:16-18). And in it all he realizes the hope for a heavenly home (5:1-10).

To put it succinctly, Paul understands his present life as one characterized equally by both the "dying of Jesus" (NASB) and the **life of Jesus.** Both transform his present and future. Paul's witness challenges us to ask, *What should be our perspective as we seek to live as Christians and serve others in a world like ours?*

Paul's answer for our day is simple yet profound. Profoundly put, he would have us center our self-understanding in the death and resurrection of Jesus. We may, with Paul-like courage, confidence, and uplifted spirits (4:1, 16; 5:6, 8), face the "unexpected" in our earthly course as Christians.

Paul's description of his ministry leads to three profound affirmations about the nature of our faith. We can face the crucibles of life because (1) *we center our faith in the cross and resurrection of Jesus,* (2) *we live by faith in the unseen,* and (3) *we possess a confident faith in the future.*

4:7—5:10 Paul applies his daring affirmation of "the knowledge of the glory of God in the face of Christ" (4:6) to the hard realities of his ministry. With Paul *we center our faith in the cross and resurrection of Jesus* (4:7-15). Paul describes his ministry with the metaphor, a "treasure in jars of clay." He lists its difficulties in antithetical prose, **hard pressed . . . perplexed . . . persecuted . . . struck down,** on the one hand. But it is not **crushed . . . in despair . . . abandoned . . . destroyed** (vv 7-9) on the other. William Barclay calls these "the great paradoxes of the Christian life" (1956, 223). How can both be true?

The apostle's suffering was real; but it did not spell defeat. Rather Paul saw it as carrying around in his body **the death of Jesus** (v 10). In the midst of the hardships of life and ministry, Paul identified with the worldly weakness displayed in the cross of the earthly Christ.

Truly Christian faith sees all of life taken up into the pattern of the earthly life and death of Jesus. The ministry to the poor and dying—a resurrection ministry—of Mother Teresa had its root in her early and joyful identification with the sufferings of Jesus. On February 8, 1937, she wrote a letter, after her special call but before her lifelong ministry to the "poorest of the poor" began. In it she wrote: "Now I rejoice with my whole heart that I have joyfully carried my cross with Jesus. There were sufferings—there were moments when my eyes were filled with tears—but thanks be to God for everything" (Kolodiejchuk 2007, 20). The harsh realities of life need never be meaningless for any of us, for they partake of the redemptive presence of God in Christ in the world. How can this be?

Paul's faith saw in his human weakness an opportunity for God. Just so, by faith we can open our lives to the resurrection life of Jesus. **So that the life of Jesus may also be revealed in our body** (v 10; see v 11) are the apostle's words. This is "the vocation and job description of the church" (Hays 1996, 197). The cross of Jesus *entails* the resurrection of Jesus. In the crucible of life our faith is not in a half but in a whole Christ, a Jesus both crucified *and* risen! We cannot separate the two—in either Jesus' life or ours.

The apostle declared to the Corinthians that in his ministry to them, **death** [was] **at work in us, but life** [was] **at work in you** (v 12). Such is the nature of Christian life and witness in the world. With Chrysostom (344/354-407), "we bear about the power of his dying that the power of his life may be manifest" (ACCS NT 7:211).

As a result, Christians may experience a freedom to be and a release to speak. Paul quoted the psalmist in difficult circumstances (Ps 116:10). He was convinced that they shared the **same spirit of faith.** Thus, he could affirm: **we also believe and therefore speak** (v 13). G. Campbell Morgan wrote: "Faith creating testimony . . . is one secret of power . . . in the Christian ministry" (Morgan 1946, 239). From the biblical perspective, preaching partakes of the character of witness, which, by its very nature, demands authenticity.

Helmut Thielicke reminds us that "people today are not generally asking the question: 'Where shall I learn to believe?' . . . People are rather asking, 'Where can I find credible witnesses?'" (1965, 15). Authentic faith works in our present lives as it reaches out to the future. We can, like Paul, **know that the one who raised the Lord Jesus from the dead will also raise us with Jesus** (v 14).

Part of the unified package of "Cross and Resurrection" faith is the certainty of future life. This may be true, not only for us, but also for those to whom we minister. Thus, Paul wrote, **All this is for your benefit, . . .** [for he will] **present us with you in his presence** (vv 15, 14). The power of the resurrection did not end with Jesus. It reaches to all who by faith conduct their vulnerable earthly lives in light of the cross. Otherwise life can be simply tragic, suffering without purpose or meaning.

All this connects us intimately with God's ordained future for us. Paul describes how this may already be so in this life as *we live by faith in the unseen* (4:16-18). Paul contrasts the present life with life after death, the visible with the invisible dimension of human existence.

Therefore, Paul did "not lose heart" (see 4:1). His present existence was marked with suffering and was gradually "wasting away." But his true life was not slipping out of his grasp. Even so, like Paul, our lives in relation to Christ "are being renewed day by day" (4:16) with ever-increasing spiritual resources available (3:18; Rom 12:2).

With this perspective, our "troubles" in this life can be seen as "light and momentary." This is because we realize that they "are achieving for us an eternal glory that far outweighs them all." This, however, remains "unseen." The future, full, and final transformation of our lives in Christ may be seen only with the eyes of faith. By faith "we fix our eyes" on the invisible, as we make our way through the unpredictable paths of the present.

Nevertheless, the "glory" is not all future, for we *are* on a path "like the first gleam of dawn, shining ever brighter till the full light of day" (Prov 4:18). We already possess the deposit of the Spirit (2 Cor 5:5). So we are inescapably involved in a moral and spiritual process that affects our "outlook on life and what the body *does,* not what the body *is,* this latter awaits the resurrection" (Ellis 1959-60, 213). As John expresses it, "all who have this hope in him purify themselves, just as he is pure." Eschatological conviction motivates ethical seriousness. This is because "when he is revealed, we will be like him, for we will see him as he is" (1 John 3:3, 2 NRSV).

As Paul continues his sketch of the future life, he turns to the consequences for faith. *We have confidence for the future* (5:1-10). The theme of assurance of the future life permeates the whole of the paragraph. Paul writes with certainty: "we know" and "we are always confident." No matter when in God's scheme of things it all will take place, Paul is sure that he has "an eternal house in heaven" and will be fully "clothed with a heavenly dwelling." That is, he will be "at home with the Lord." This, too, may be our assured hope. We, like Paul, believe that God "has given us the Spirit as a deposit, guaranteeing what is to come."

At funerals and memorial services those who have lost loved ones have the right to expect the scriptural proclamation of the certainty of life after death in the presence of Christ. "The fruit of the Spirit" (Gal 5:22), evident in the life of the departed, is its God-given guarantee. Because of our hope, "we make it our goal" in this present life "to please him." This is not an empty ambition; by the gift of the Holy Spirit whom God has given us (see Rom 5:5), we can realize this aspiration. As always the glory belongs to God (4:6, 15, 17; see 10:17-18), for "we live by faith, not by sight"! With John Wesley, "They that *live* by faith, 'walk by faith'" (1985, 54).

What can we learn from this passage about what life after death is like? With his metaphors, Paul paints three pictures hanging on the wall in our gallery of faith, as prime exhibits in the museum of life. Each picture displays an illuminating contrast.

In the first picture on the left we see human life on earth as a temporary dwelling, a tent like those Paul made for a livelihood. A tent is an earthly, transitory, impermanent, and insecure dwelling. Tents are easily moved and destroyed. In juxtaposition to the tent Paul pictures a building. He describes this building as eternal, as a house in heaven, as a dwelling received from God, not made with human hands. The future life is permanent, indestructible, "God-made, not handmade" (5:1 TM). And it is where God dwells.

In the picture hanging in the center, Paul pictures life after death as being fully clothed. He thought of being found naked in public a nightmare. To be properly clothed was to have this present mortal life "swallowed up," fully transformed by resurrection life. It was not to be left in some "naked," transitory, "halfway state." It was to be immediately accepted into the heavenly dwelling without shame. The future life, as Paul pictures it, is full, complete, and again where God dwells.

Looking to the picture on the right, Paul presents us with the most heartwarming contrast of the three. This present life is to be "at home in the body"; the future life, to be "at home with the Lord." As we say, "home is where the heart is." And in metaphor, "the hearth warms both body and soul."

How "at home" are we "in the body"? To what extent are we prepared to feel "at home with the Lord"? Obviously, this may depend on how old we are. But as the years go by, the question becomes: Do we more and more "live by faith, not by sight"?

Whatever we trust for the future has its inevitable impact on how we conduct ourselves in the present. Paul's aim to please the Lord whether "at home in the body or away from it" was doubly motivated. Not only did he expect life after death, but he had an intense longing to be "at home with the Lord" (vv 2, 4, 8). Why do we not hear more in today's church culture about the "expectation" or "intense longing" for our heavenly home, or indeed about the future judgment? Are these themes not relevant for today's "spirituality"?

Paul's ambition to please the Lord led him to consider the reality of "the judgment seat of Christ." He was convinced that what we take away from the judgment will be precisely what we bring to it. Our heavenly reward, Paul says, is literally *"the things"* we have done *"through the body."* Spiritual reality is that our life and our holy character, formed through living in the Spirit, are their own reward in the presence of a holy God. What more could God give us in the end than a life like his? After all, this is what he has been working in us all of our lives in our earthly tent. In marketplace terms, our investment in a life of integrity and a holy character pays dividends. It is "worth it all." Our living is being transformed by the "unseen" reality on which we have fixed our lifelong gaze. "We live by faith, not by sight."

I have heard of a land on the far away strand,
'Tis a beautiful home of the soul;
Built by Jesus on high, where we never shall die,
'Tis a land where we never grow old.

Never grow old, never grow old,
In a land where we'll never grow old;
Never grow old, never grow old,
In a land where we'll never grow old.
—James C. Moore (1888-1962), *circa* 1914

As graced partakers of the new covenant ministry, we Christians are involved in a ministry empowered by the Spirit. But according to Paul, our spiritual power is in inverse proportion to our weakness (2 Cor 11). Thus, Paul is committed to a "ministry of suffering." Such a ministry the apostle describes as a life of service to others that faces head-on this world's harsh realities, a ministry that:

- centers its faith in the cross and resurrection of Jesus (4:1-15)
- lives by faith in the unseen (4:16-18) and
- possesses a confident faith in the future (5:1-10)

Further Reading on Life After Death

Alcorn, Randy. 2004. *Heaven.* Wheaton, Ill.: Tyndale House.

Kreeft, Peter. 1980. *Heaven: The Heart's Deepest Longing.* San Francisco: Harper and Row.

Walls, Jerry L. 2002. *Heaven: The Logic of Eternal Joy.* New York: Oxford University Press.

Wright, N. T. 2008. *Surprised by Hope: Rethinking Heaven, the Resurrection, and the Mission of the Church.* New York: HarperOne.

4. A Ministry of Reconciliation (5:11—6:10)

Paul continues to unpack his conviction that "we have this ministry"
(4:1). His reference to evaluation at the final judgment of one's earthly con-
5:11—6:10 duct jolts his mind back to the situation at Corinth (see 4:1-6). With this Paul
comes to the third characteristic of his ministry, that of reconciliation. Here he proceeds to reassert the moral and spiritual quality of his labors among the Corinthians (see 1:12; 2:17; 4:2). Both the fear of the Lord and the love of Christ (5:11-15) guarantee the selflessness of his motives.

As Christ's ambassador, Paul's message is one of reconciliation to God in Christ (5:16-21). Therefore, his manner of life as an apostle is consistent with that message (6:3-10). Both 5:11-21 and 6:1-10 defend Paul's integrity and appeal for reconciliation. The second passage draws out the consequences of the first. The controlling theme of both is the death of Christ by which God reconciled the world to himself (Matera 2003, 127). Both present the answer the Corinthians should give those who would impugn the authentic character of Paul's ministry. A correct understanding of his ministry remains his major concern throughout both passages. But Paul articulates it in such a way that it serves as a paradigm for the behavior of all Christians (Murphy-O'Connor 1991, 55).

BEHIND THE TEXT

The apostle continues the apologetic rhetorical structure. His stated intent remains "to persuade men" (v 11). This indicates that he writes within the tradition of Greco-Roman rhetoric. At its heart was the art of persuasion.

As an ambassador (v 20), he would use the three species of rhetoric prevalent in his culture. An ambassador would use epideictic rhetoric to praise those to whom he was sent. He used deliberative rhetoric to argue for a particular course of action. And he employed forensic rhetoric to defend the policies of the one who sent him or to bring accusations of misconduct (Witherington 1995, 392).

BEHIND THE TEXT in the previous section (4:7—5:10) describes the rhetorical form of hardship catalogs, which Paul uses again in 6:4-10. Verses 8-10 are an example of the antithetical list. These catalogs functioned to demonstrate one's superiority over circumstances. The literary background of such lists ranges from Greco-Roman philosophy to Jewish literature. In contrast to Cynic and Stoic sages, Paul uses such lists to defend his apostleship. But his defense illustrates how divine power is manifested through human weakness. In 6:4-10 Paul uses the catalogs not to communicate new information but to reorient the Corinthians' view of his apostleship (McCant 1999, 60).

IN THE TEXT

a. The Fear of the Lord and the Love of Christ (5:11-15)

Some at Corinth seem to think otherwise. But Paul insists that he is neither self-seeking nor unscrupulous in his labors among them. Rather, the fear of the Lord and the love of Christ motivate him. He is accountable to God for the quality of his ministry. The very nature of Christ's love for him excludes unworthy motives. Paul is consistent with the whole biblical tradition when he insists that reverence for God and his love for all people determine human behavior toward others.

■ **11** Paul continues to have the reality and the character of the judgment in mind as he writes. One could translate the link between vv 10 and 11: ***Therefore, because we know . . .*** Paul is fully conscious of his awesome responsibility to God. God is the Judge for the conduct of his life and ministry. Paul defines his consciousness of responsibility before God as ***the fear of the Lord*** (*ton phobon tou kyriou*). The genitive here is objective, as in the NIV translation: **we . . . fear the Lord.**

The phrase comes out of the OT wisdom tradition: "the fear of the LORD is the beginning of knowledge" (Prov 1:7; Job 28:28; see Pss 2:11; 111:10; Isa 2:10). At issue is an appropriate respect and reverence with a touch of holy terror (see Heb 10:31; 12:25-29).

Therefore (*oun*) in the light of his responsibility to Christ, Paul's ministry aimed to persuade people. He sought to persuade them of both the truth of the gospel and of the integrity of his apostolic credentials and conduct.

We try to persuade men ("others," NRSV) translates the present tense (*peithomen*) as tendential. It refers to an action begun or attempted but not fully accomplished. His work is not yet done. As the Genevan reformer sums it up: "It is as if he had said, 'My mouth speaks to men, but my heart speaks to God'" (Calvin 1964, 10:72).

But (*de*), continues the apostle, **what we are is plain to God.** He resumes the theme of openness broached in 3:12, 18; and 4:2. The Corinthians' security against any insincerity on Paul's part is to what God knows about him, which is everything (see Heb 4:12-13). This must be the basis of Paul's appeal, since only God can know for certain what is hidden in his **heart** (see v 12).

The first person plural pronouns (**we**, **ourselves**, **us**, **our**) in vv 11-14 have primary, but not exclusive reference, to Paul. But in the last clause of v 11, he shifts to the first person singular (**I**). Perhaps he wants to make a more personal appeal: **I hope it is also plain to your conscience** (see the commentary on 1:12). Has not Paul been as transparent with them as he has been with God in the manner of his ministry?

Paul appeals to their moral consciousness (1:12; 4:2; 5:11), not to their proud intelligence (see 1 Cor 1:18-31). The apostle believes that in their hearts the Corinthians know he is genuine.

Paul changes from the aorist tense in v 10 (*phanerōthēnai*) to two perfect tense verbs in v 11 (*pephanerōmetha . . . pephanerōsthai:* "are well known . . . are . . . well known," NRSV; **is plain . . . is . . . plain**). This puts the stress on his existing condition. That is, "his character has been, and still is, laid bare" (Plummer 1915, 169) before God and the Corinthians.

■ **12** Lest his adversaries interpret this affirmation of openness as arrogant boasting, Paul hastens to clarify his meaning. He is not beginning to **commend** himself **again** to them (see 3:1). Rather, Paul's purpose is to give them **an opportunity to take pride** [*kauchēmatos:* "boast," NRSV] **in** him.

In the NT, the word *aphormēn*, **opportunity,** is found only in Paul's letters (Rom 7:8, 11; 2 Cor 5:12; 11:12; Gal 5:13; 1 Tim 5:14). The term refers to an operational base or the resources needed to carry through an undertaking (BDAG 2000, 158). With a firsthand knowledge of his life and ministry, Paul wants to furnish the Corinthians with reasons to be proud of him.

But he also offers them the resources they need to respond adequately to those who attack him. He equips the Corinthians to defend their apostle, as they ought to do (see 1:14). He offers his apology, he writes, **so that you can answer** these critics. Modern English translations supply the word **answer** to complete the thought of the Greek verb *echēte*, literally, ***you may have.***

Paul describes his critics as **those who take pride** [*kauchōmenous:* "boast," NRSV] **in what is seen rather than in what is in the heart**. **What is seen** translates *prosōpōi* (literally, ***the face***), indicating one's visible presence with another, the "outward appearance" (NRSV; see 4:18; 5:16). In Gal 2:6, Paul insists that God does not judge people on the basis of "external appearance [*prosōpon:* ***the face***]." That is, "God shows no partiality" (NRSV). Paul's critics, however, judge him prejudicially and unfairly. They ignore the crucial issue of his character. Paul uses *kardiai* (**heart**) to describe "the *whole* man to his very depths" (Kümmel 1963, 171). He contrasts **heart**—inward character, which is "unseen" (see 4:18)—and the superficial facade. This may be an intertextual echo of 1 Sam 16:7 (LXX), where the contrast between *prosōpon* and *kardia* first appears in the biblical tradition: "Man looks at the outward appearance, but the LORD looks at the heart."

The superior claims of Paul's opponents, whatever they may have been, were only a false front, designed to impress and gain advantage. That they cared little or nothing for the true realities of the ministry was evident from their opposition to Paul as a suffering apostle. Their "pride is all in outward show and not in inward worth" (NEB). Margaret Thrall, referring back to ch 3, suggests that his critics "perceive Paul's lack of outward 'Mosaic' glory and fail to recognize his credentials in the form of the community he has founded" (2004, 405).

■ **13** With a connecting ***for*** (*gar*) Paul continues to explain why the Corinthians can defend his sincerity as an apostle. Self-interest is overcome in the life of Paul, for his ministry stands under a twofold rule. It is ***for God*** (*Theōi*) and ***for you*** (*hymin*): **If we are out of our mind, it is for the sake of God; if we are in our right mind, it is for you.**

Paul's essential point, his denial of self-interest, is obvious enough. But what is behind the contrast, especially the suggestion that **we are out of our mind,** is not clear. The verb *exestēmen*, "we are beside ourselves" (NRSV), occurs only here in Paul. But the same verb occurs in a similar context in Mark 3:21. There it refers to Jesus: "He is out of his mind." It indicates that those so described have experienced a loss of normal rational powers, if they are not insane.

The parallel between the two datives of advantage (*Theōi* . . . *hymin*) suggests that whatever the charge against him, Paul takes it as positive: **it is for the sake of God.** Chrysostom (344/354-407) commented, "Even if people think he is mad, everything he does is for the glory of God" (ACCS NT 7:245).

Two basic directions of explanation are feasible. Are they criticizing Paul for "the presence" or for "the absence" of certain behaviors? If "the presence," no doubt it is the maniacal manner (see Acts 26:24) in which he went about his ministry. His passionate drive made him seem to less intense souls to be a man possessed. Or, he could refer to the constant spiritual tension in which he lived and worked. That he persisted in his mission, despite its attendant humiliation, weakness, and suffering, suggested than an "unearthly flame . . . burned unceasingly in his bosom, . . . a kind of sacred madness" (Denney 1943, 5:764). Some interpreters suggest that Paul's ecstatic experiences as observed by the Corinthians (1 Cor 14:2, 18; 2 Cor 12:1-7; see Acts 22:17-21) may stand behind the charge that he was **out of** [his] **mind.**

But the reason for the question concerning Paul's sanity may have been "the absence" of expected behaviors. Was he deficient in charisma, rhetorical gifts, or demonstrable spiritual powers that some thought should characterize the ministry of a true apostle?

Either charge could have come from **those who take pride in what is seen rather than in what is in the heart** (v 12). In fact, the two accusations may go together as two sides of one coin. Paul acknowledged that the essential nature of his apostleship flowed compulsively from both the cross and the resurrection of Jesus (see 4:7-18; 13:4). He insists that the true character of his apostleship and persona, and the behaviors that go with them, are God's concern, they are ***for God.***

On the other hand, when Paul's behavior seems prudent, when it appears to conform to acceptable standards of rationality, or when he seems normal and ordinary (*sōphronoumen: **"of sound mind," "reasonable, sensible"*** [BDAG 2000, 986]), it is **for** the Corinthians. Therefore, contrary to his critics, in his ministry Paul totally restrains himself from self-seeking conduct. He assures the Corinthians: When my manner of life does not make sense—insane, **it is for the sake of God;** when it does make sense—sane, **it is for you.**

■ **14** Paul now gives the reason why (*gar,* **For**) he has committed his life "for others." He builds a bridge to the essential nature of the redemptive action of God in Christ. He can live this way because **Christ's love compels us** ("the love of Christ controls us," NASB).

This raises two questions: (1) Does Paul refer to his love for Christ (objective) *or* Christ's love for him (subjective genitive)? (2) Does the "love of Christ" constrain him *to* pursue selfless motives *or* restrain him *from* self-seeking in his ministry?

1. The genitive construction, *agapē tou Christou* ("love of Christ"), is considered by most interpreters to be subjective (Rom 8:35, 39; see Gal 2:20; 2 Cor 13:13). The immediately following reference to Christ's death (**one died for all**) supports this reading. So the NIV translates the construction as **Christ's love.** Some believe Paul intended both senses here, but that is not likely in this context.

2. Does Christ's love for Paul positively compel him to continue his ministry for God and others? Or, does it negatively hold him back from adopting a self-indulgent life? The verb *synechō* has the basic meaning "hold together" (BDAG 2000, 970-71). It allows for either translation: "constrained to" or "restrained from." The NASB has "controls us," which maintains the ambiguity—***holds us in check*** or **compels us** ("urges us," NRSV). Regardless, the ruling power of Christ's love for Paul leaves him with no option but to live for God (v 13)/for Christ (v 15). Two convictions follow in vv 14-15.

Paul explains why God's love for him in Christ (Rom 5:8) has such a controlling grip on his motives. On this basis, he reached some vital conclusions—**we are convinced.** The aorist participle phrase *krinantas touto* literally means, "having made this judgment" or "having resolved this." Paul refers to a decisive and conscious decision he had made in the past. It was a theological decision about the saving significance of the death and resurrection of Christ (see v 15): That Christ **died for all** convinced him that God loved him (Rom

5:8). The certainty that he was loved by God in Christ, validated by the gift of the Spirit (Rom 5:5), held Paul captive. This love originates and ends with the Triune God (see Rom 8:28-30).

■ **14-15** In vv 14-15 Paul expresses two convictions (**we are convinced**) based on Christ's vicarious death (*hyper pantōn apethanen,* he **died for all**). The first is the conclusion: **therefore** [*ara*] **all** [*hoi pantes*] **died** (v 14). The second explains the purpose/result of Christ's death: **that** [*hina*] **those who live should no longer live for themselves but for him who died for them and was raised again** (v 15).

The preposition **for** (*hyper*) in **one died for all,** provides an insufficient basis for defending any full-fledged atonement theory. Scholars generally hold, however, that it includes the ideas of both substitution and representation or participation.

Daniel Powers, however, argues persuasively that *hyper* does not have the sense of substitution here. It is difficult to carry this meaning into the following phrase, **therefore all died** (Powers 2001, 54-58). Paul certainly says that Christ acted on our behalf in his self-offering. And the word **all** in **for all** and in **all died** obviously indicates everyone (v 15; see Rom 5:12-19).

When Christ died, all the descendants of Adam—the entire human race—were involved. In some real sense, he took us all with him to his death. "Everyone [is] in the same boat" (TM). We were all with him there, sharing responsibility for his death. We were all in desperate need of the redemption he accomplished by his death. We did him in, and we died with him, as he died **for** us.

The preposition **for** (*hyper*) means not only that we identified with Christ in what he did for us but that we **died** as well. And in that same event he identified himself with us. He participated in the full extent of our sinfulness and alienation from God (2 Cor 5:21; see 1 Pet 2:24): "Mercy there was great, and grace was free" (William R. Newell, "At Calvary").

In view of Christ's death, we all *are* dead in respect to any spiritual self-sufficiency. As Paul confirms in what follows, the death of Christ constitutes the fundamental criterion of human existence (Murphy-O'Connor 1991, 58). He articulates this perspective more fully in Rom 5:12-19.

Paul's second conviction explains why/how the death of Christ works on behalf of **all. He died for all, that those who live** in the world **should no longer live for themselves but for him who died for them and was raised again** (v 15; see Rom 14:7-9; 1 Cor 3:21-23; Gal 2:20).

The participial phrase **those who live** (*hoi zōntes*) could refer either narrowly to those who are "alive to God in Christ Jesus" (Rom 6:11) or broadly to all those who live in the natural sense (Thrall 2004, 412). The immediate context favors the latter. Thus, in the new era inaugurated by the death of Christ, "the *living* should never again *live* to themselves" (Plummer 1915, 175). Grace, prevenient grace, opens the door to **all** to share in the benefits made available by Christ's death.

Most importantly for Paul, the resurrection and the crucifixion are inseparably joined in the atoning work of Christ (Rom 4:25; 5:10; 1 Cor 15:17) making for a new way of life (see 2 Cor 3:18) and a new way of knowing (5:16). As flip sides of the same coin, our identification by faith with Christ in his death inherently involves our participation in his resurrection life (Powers 2001, 62). Union with him in one is at the same time union with him in the other (Rom 5:10). The old life (Rom 6:6; Eph 4:22; Col 3:9) with self as the focus of interest is transformed into a new life centered on the One who **died for them and was raised again.** Christ enters into our experience that we may enter into his.

Justification reaches out to involve sanctification. In Paul's own words written later to the church in Rome:

> Our old self was crucified with him . . . that we should no longer be slaves to sin. . . . Now if we died with Christ, we believe that we will also live with him. . . . The death he died, he died to sin once for all; but the life he lives, he lives to God. In the same way, count yourselves dead to sin but alive to God in Christ Jesus. (Rom 6:6, 8, 10-11)

For Paul, "to live is Christ" (Phil 1:21). In such a life there remains no room for self-centered living (see Phil 2:5-18). Paul's ethics are totally christocentric.

Paul never seeks merely to exalt and advance himself for two reasons:

1. He is transparent to God, to whom he must give an account for the integrity of his ministry. His real self is open to his converts (2 Cor 5:11) in contrast to the duplicity of his critics (v 12).

2. The amazing reach of Christ's love for him holds him in check. This love, effected in Christ's death on his behalf, radically controls his motives. Paul offers two explanations why this is so:

   1. He is aware of the desperate helplessness of the death from which it has delivered him (v 14).
   2. He is captured by the transcendent quality of the life it has set him free to live (v 15).

Paul is constrained by his awesome responsibility to God and by his gratifying life in Christ. His personal integrity is undergirded by Christ's love manifested in his saving death (Matera 2003, 132).

b. The Perspective of Reconciliation (5:16-21)

Paul's reflections on the heart of the gospel lead him into a passage of "lyrical grandeur, cosmic scope, theological depth, and emotional appeal" (Shillington 1998, 126). The key word here is **reconciliation**—the process by which sinners are brought into a relationship of friendship with God. Reconciliation is the central object of Paul's Christian life and ministry.

The very character of the message Paul proclaims supports his claim to sincerity. God's reconciling act in Christ (vv 18-19) has furnished the final criterion for the way he views Christ and others (v 16). A new order of life in Christ is already a present reality (v 17). The ministry of reconciliation (vv 18-

20) makes possible a new relationship to God (v 21). God no longer counts the sins of humanity against them (v 19), thanks to the life-giving fountain of the death and resurrection of Christ.

■ **16** Paul begins with a negative consequence of the death of Christ for all (5:14-15). His way of looking at humanity is not the same as it once was. His outlook on other people as well as on Christ is different. His way of knowing on the human level has been transformed: ***for this reason*** [*hōste*] **we regard no one from a worldly point of view.**

Since the death of Christ and his discovery of its significance with his conversion-call on the road to Damascus—**from now on**—Paul does not know or understand anyone merely "according to the flesh" (*kata sarka,* NASB; see 1:17; 10:2; 11:18). His new perspective is not in terms of a relationship purely of this world or "from a human point of view" (NRSV). As Paul sees it, the opposite of knowing *kata sarka* is knowing *kata stauron* ("according to the cross"; Martyn 1997, 109).

The expression "according to the flesh" refers to the typical external distinctions of human society—national origin, wealth and power, social status, intellect, physical characteristics, and charismatic endowments. All of these are ways by which we humans often estimate the worth of one another. The values of Paul's critics were no doubt somewhat similar (v 12). But Christ's death and resurrection had robbed such standards of significance for Paul, for they were contrary to the resultant reality of life in the Spirit (5:14-15; 3:18; see Rom 8:2-11).

Paul confirms this perspective as he particularizes his previous general statement in v 16*a*. He concedes (*ei kai,* **Though;** BDAG 2000, 278 s.v. *ei*) that he had **once regarded Christ *according to the flesh,*** but he **no longer** regards him ***according to the flesh.*** To avoid repetition, the NIV translates the second *kata sarka,* **in this way.**

We can take this phrase in either of two ways. We can take it with **Christ.** This assumes that Paul once knew Christ in the historical sense as merely a human being. Or we can take it with the verb, **regarded . . . in this way.** That is, Paul once knew Christ through worldly, merely human eyes. Pauline word order and usage prefer this latter sense (Harris 2005, 428).

Paul is most probably speaking about a real rather than a hypothetical situation. That is, Paul as a Pharisee before his conversion did evaluate Jesus, whom Christians considered the Christ, by the fleshly criteria of his culture (Phil 3:4-6; see Gal 1:13-14). This led him both to judge Jesus' claim to messianic sonship as blasphemous and to persecute his followers (1 Tim 1:13).

But Paul does **so no longer,** for now he knows Jesus as he really is—the incarnate Christ who died and was raised for all (Phil 2:5-11). James F. Kay sees here "the futility of all quests for the 'historical Jesus,' in so far as these *kata sarka* reconstructions proclaim as 'saving' one known apart from his cross and resurrection" (2001, 258).

With his new way of knowing, Paul views all humanity through this transforming lens. In question is not whether or not Paul had any contact with Jesus during his earthly ministry. Nor is he saying that knowledge about the historical Jesus is now irrelevant for faith. The object of his evaluation has not changed; only his approach to evaluating others has been altered.

Paul has not simply exchanged the "historical Jesus" for a "kerygmatic Christ" (see Kay 2007, 102-3). The former cannot be divorced from the latter, both are essential to NT faith. Paul's point is simply that his value system in relation to God and humankind has been fundamentally changed, turned upside down by his encounter with the living Christ (see Gal 3:28). Paul no longer uses his understanding of fallen humanity to view Christ. Rather he uses his new understanding of Christ as the new Adam to reveal what true humanity is (see Rom 5:12-19; 1 Cor 15:45).

■ **17** Paul proceeds to state, second, the positive consequences (*hōste* [v 16] . . . *hōste* [v 17]) of vv 14-15. Verse 17 is one of the more fascinating verses in the letter. Its "grandiose anticipation" of **a new creation** results from being **in Christ.** Out of the death and resurrection of Christ has risen a new life that we may live for the Lord. This new life is set in a renewed religious or spiritual context, which Paul describes by his characteristic phrase **in Christ.**

English usage requires a verb to be supplied in the first and third clauses of v 17. Most translations presume that a form of the verb "to be" has been ellipsed from these clauses. Adding *estin* . . . *estin* results in the usual translation:

Therefore, if anyone is in Christ, he is a new creation, or better: "so if anyone is in Christ, there is a new creation" (NRSV; see Rom 5:12-21).

Central to Paul's theological understanding and significant for his thought here is his phrase **in Christ** (*en Christōi*). With its parallels, it occurs over 160 times in his writings. In these, it has both individual and corporate references.

With the phrase **in Christ,** Paul vividly portrays his conviction that only in an intimate and personal relationship with the risen Christ may we continually realize the salvation of God. To be **in Christ** is to be taken up into the sphere of God's total redemptive activity (2 Cor 5:21; 1 Cor 1:30). This results from a realistic identification or union in faith with the person of Christ, both crucified and risen. Paul can speak of dying and rising with Christ (Rom 6:1-12; Gal 2:20).

The concept is social as well as individual (1 Cor 1:2). To be **in Christ** is a sharing together (*koinōnia*) in Christ (1 Cor 1:9). It is to be incorporated into the body of Christ (1 Cor 12:12-13, 27; Rom 12:4-5), that is, into the church.

Paul conceives of Christ by virtue of the resurrection as the second Adam (Rom 5:12-21; 1 Cor 15:45). As such, he is the head of a new humanity. That is, he was the "firstfruits" (1 Cor 15:20, 23), the "firstborn among many" (Rom 8:29; Col 1:18), and the "life-giving spirit" (1 Cor 15:45). He was first to experience fully all God intends for all humanity. As all humanity *was* "in Adam," so *now* all Christians are **in Christ.**

To be **in Christ** is to be **a new creation** (Gal 6:14-15). The adjective **new** (*kainē*) refers to what is new in nature replacing the old as obsolete. Therefore, the new is "superior in kind to the old" (BDAG 2000, 497). The concept of "newness" is characteristic of Paul's thought (Rom 6:4; 7:6; 1 Cor 11:25; 2 Cor 3:6; Eph 2:10; 4:24; Col 3:10) and of the NT generally. This is summed up by the voice from the throne in Rev 21:5: "Behold, I am making all things new" (NASB; see Mark 2:22; Luke 22:20; John 13:34; Heb 8:8; 1 John 2:8; Rev 5:9; 21:1-2). Here Paul expands upon his earlier new covenant terminology (2 Cor 3:4-6), announcing with it the advent of **a new creation** in the apostolic gospel.

Like **in Christ,** the term **a new creation** appears to have both individual and corporate connotations: "the old things passed away; behold, new things have come" (NASB). The background of Paul's thinking here may be found in the themes of Isa 40—66. The similarity of terminology is particularly impressive in Isa 43:18-19:

Do not call to mind the former things,
Or ponder things of the past.
Behold, I will do something new [*kaina*, LXX],
Now it will spring forth;
Will you not be aware of it?
I will even make a roadway in the wilderness,
Rivers in the desert. (NASB)

The setting in Isa 43:1-21 and 65:17-25 (see 66:22) is the return of Israel from exile. The prophet pictures this as a kind of second exodus, through 5:17
startling new creation imagery. Paul considers Isaiah's promise of Israel's restoration from the alienation of exile as now being fulfilled in the gospel he proclaims (Beale 1989-90, 556; see Hafemann 2000, 243-44). Paul sees the complete eschatological (end-time) expectation of Isa 40—66 as comprehended by his term **new creation.** Some would place the immediate background of Paul's thinking in later or apocalyptic Judaism undoubtedly familiar to Paul (Furnish 1984, 314-15; Thrall 2004, 421-22).

The Christ event has created a *new* situation, **a new creation.** A *new* order of humanity has come into being, bringing with it a *new* kind of person, God's future kind of people. Paul stresses the renewal of individuals that prefigures the renewal of the cosmos (Matt 19:28; Rom 8:19-23). Christians are distinctively **a new creation** by virtue of their new relationship with God. All the former attachments and behaviors ***according to the flesh*** (*kata sarka*) are **gone,** for "behold, new things have come" (NASB). **The old** (*ta archaia*) points to the former state of things, the old Mosaic order.

"Behold" (*idou;* "see," NRSV) is not translated by the NIV. It is an interjection calling attention to an unusual moment or deed (McCant 1999, 54).

The creative process that is underway is redemptive, not destructive. The new creation re-creates the old as seen through "the lens of the crucified Christ" (Shillington 1998, 131). The apostle is jubilant at the thought. He bases his ministry on the conviction that the old order of salvation has been superseded. Everything converges on the singular perspective of the new order from now on.

■ **18** As we come "to the quintessence of this stately creedal paragraph" (Martin 1989, 103), Paul probes more deeply into this new order. In this order we display a new attitude and constitute a new creation in Christ due to God's creative act (see 4:6; Rom 3:25; 11:36) of **reconciliation** (2 Cor 5:18-19). John Calvin writes that here, "if anywhere in Paul's writings, we have a quite remarkably important passage" (1964, 10:77). **All this** Paul has been talking about in vv 14-17 is from God. This is because he has **reconciled us to himself through Christ.**

Paul's **us** (*hēmas*) is an apostolic plural referring primarily to Paul himself. In a letter that Paul writes to celebrate the reconciliation of the Corinthian community to their apostle, he aptly uses the term **reconciliation** as the central concept of his formulation of the gospel in 5:18-19.

Reconciliation and its cognates (*katallagē, katallassō apokatallassō*) appear only in Paul's writings in the NT (Rom 5:10 [twice], 11; 11:15; 1 Cor 7:11; 2 Cor 5:18 [twice], 19 [twice], 20; Eph 2:16; Col 1:20, 22). Some interpreters consider it the key concept in Paul's theological thought (Martin 1989, 46).

The basic meaning of **reconciliation** (*katallagē*) is "exchange," particularly of merchandise or money. Metaphorically, the meaning depicted the exchange of peace for war or of friendship for enmity (Harris 2005, 436-37). In Paul's writings the meaning centers on the "reestablishment of an interrupted or broken relationship" (BDAG 2000, 521), as in a marriage separation (1 Cor 7:10).

Primarily in view in the apostle's use of the terminology is the overcoming of the alienation of humankind from God through the death of Christ. This is an objective change in the situation: "When we were God's enemies, we were reconciled to him through the death of his Son" (Rom 5:10; Col 1:20-22). We were formerly enemies (Rom 5:10; Col 1:21) of God and hostile to him (Eph 2:16). As a result of this reconciling act of **God . . . in Christ,** we enter into a new condition of peace (Eph 2:12-17; Col 1:20; see Rom 5:1, 6-11). Reconciliation is the restoration of a proper relationship to God, and fellowship with him.

In our passage, Paul has two concerns: (1) God's act of reconciling the world through Christ and (2) The ministry of reconciliation entrusted to Christ's ambassadors. In Paul's concept of reconciliation, God is the chief actor. It is the world, not God, that needs to be reconciled, for God does the reconciling. Reconciliation involves the issue of the wrath of God against human sinfulness (Rom 1:18; 2:5). The wrath of a holy God against all human "godlessness and wickedness" (Rom 1:18) makes sin a deadly serious matter. Otherwise, God would not count their "sins against them." Humans can do nothing to take away God's wrath. They cannot, by offering their lives to God, "make atonement" (Exod 32:32; Lev 4:26), as the Maccabean martyrs thought (2 Macc 7:37-38; 12:45; 4 Macc 17:21-22).

But God himself in holy love took the initiative and became the aggressor **through Christ** (*dia Christou*). He invaded estranged human life with his forgiving love: "God has poured out his love into our hearts. . . . While we were still sinners, Christ died for us" (Rom 5:5, 8). The aorist participial construction, **God, who reconciled us** (*tou Theou tou katallaxantos hēmas*), in 2 Cor 5:18, indicates that our reconciliation took place in the Christ event. We *were* reconciled there and then! It was then that God effected a dramatic change in human nature and life.

The Christian church has never reached consensus on a single theory of the atonement. Biblical interpreters continue to debate precisely how and why the Christ event effected human redemption. Paul emphasizes certain aspects of what came to be known as the doctrine of "propitiation." Divine justice demands that sin's alienating effects on humanity be taken seriously, adequately addressed, and resolved, not merely glossed over. But Paul does not picture God as a peeved and vindictive deity whose wrath can be satisfied only by killing someone. Nor does God play a trick on himself. Atonement requires more than mere "expiation," a self-deceptive covering of sins. And Christ's death is more than a noble example of selfless love, as in modern versions of the "moral influence" theory. (See Greathouse and Lyons 2008, 128-30.)

Paul insists that what God has done in Christ adequately dealt with human sin (vv 19 and 21). Christ set humanity free from sin's devastating effects (Rom 7:5-25; 8:2) without compromising either the holiness or the justice of God (Rom 3:21-26).

Not only did God take the initiative in reconciliation, but he is its primary goal as well. He has **reconciled us to himself.** For Paul and the Corinthians reconciliation is an accomplished fact. The way into a right relationship with God is now open to all. God has granted to the apostle **the ministry** [*diakonian*] **of reconciliation** (2 Cor 4:18; see 3:4-18)—announcing God's open invitation for all to become his friends. Here is the climax of the passage and the final reason Paul cannot live for himself alone (vv 13-15): his apostolic commission.

■ **19** The apostle affirms what he considers the essential significance of the Christ event: "The ministry of reconciliation" consists in proclaiming **the message** [*logon*] **of reconciliation.** Paul's ministry is a ***Word*** (*logos*)! His task is to announce the news: **God was reconciling the world to himself in Christ.** "Compare the entire mystery of the evangelical faith with these words!" wrote Hilary of Poitiers (315-67; ACCS NT 7:251).

The opening words in the Greek text of v 19 are *hōs hoti*. The NIV translates them as merely a discourse content marker: **that.** Some interpreters understand them to have a causal force: "because." But it is probably best to take them as introducing a restatement of what Paul had already said in v 18.

Thus, they have the force of "to the effect that" (Turner 1963b, 137; so NEB: "what I mean is, that," and NRSV: "that is").

Historically, v 19 has often been interpreted as placing the stress on the incarnation. The Greek word order certainly allows for the KJV punctuation: "God was in Christ, reconciling . . ." (*Theos ēn en Christōi . . . katallasson*). On this reading, the imperfect verb **was** (*ēn*) stands alone; and the participle is adverbial.

Recent translations, however, understand the participle as a periphrastic imperfect (i.e., predicate adjectival). Thus: **God was reconciling . . . in** [*en*] **Christ** (NIV; see NASB, NEB, NRSV). On this reading, the prepositional phrase has an instrumental force roughly parallel with "through Christ" (*dia Christou*) in v 18.

That Paul opts for *en* with the dative instead of *dia* with the genitive allows for both senses (see v 17). Powers notes that "reconciliation to God not only takes place through the agency of Christ, but through incorporation 'in Christ' as well" (2001, 70-71). If the periphrastic construction is a "disguised aorist," the emphasis is on the reconciling event as a whole rather than as a continuous process. As John Calvin insists, "the meaning is fuller and richer than that" (1964, 10:78)—that is, than the periphrastic imperfect.

These considerations lead Murray Harris to suggest five considerations that favor the KJV punctuation. His concern is not to validate the divine nature of Christ. That "God was in Christ" refers to the entire life and ministry of Christ on earth, not to the moment when "The Word became flesh" (John 1:14). Harris insists that "a functional Christology presupposes, and finds its ultimate basis in an ontological Christology" (2005, 441-43). Paul's point, on any reading, is what God did in Christ. This implies a unity of Father and Son in redemptive activity as the essence of Paul's message.

The **world** as the object of reconciliation refers to the created world and everything that belongs to it as hostile to God and lost in sin (BDAG 2000, 562; see Rom 1:20; 8:19-22; 1 Cor 3:22). Perhaps it even reaches to the cosmic proportions of "all things," as in Col 1:20: "God was pleased . . . through him to reconcile to himself all things, whether things on earth or things in heaven, by making peace through his blood, shed on the cross" (1:19-20; see 1:16; 2:15). The 2 Corinthians context, however, summarizes the application of reconciliation with the phrase "not counting their trespasses against them" (NRSV). This seems to limit Paul's intention here to the human world (see 1:12), to the world of personal relationships.

The first consequence of reconciliation is that God is no longer **counting** their **sins against them. Counting** (*logizomenos*) is an accounting term (see Rom 4:8; Ps 32:2). The Greek word translated **sins** here is *paraptōmata*, ***trespasses. Harmartias*** is the term usually translated "sins" (see v 21) in the NT.

Trespasses refer to the false steps and, thus, the lost footing of humanity—to their violation of God's moral standards (BDAG 2000, 770). The terms

trespasses (v 19) and **sin** (v 21) bring out the link between reconciliation and justification (see Rom 5:1, 9-11; 4:3-8) as forgiveness grounded exclusively in the death of Christ.

This leads to the second consequence of reconciliation, the apostolic task of proclaiming it. God **has committed to us** [*en hēmin*] **the message of reconciliation.** Proclaiming the **message of reconciliation** is the essence of the "ministry of reconciliation." Preaching is not separate from, but part and parcel of God's work of **reconciliation.** God has placed into the hands and hearts of the apostles ***the Word of reconciliation*** as a privilege and an obligation.

Although adequately translated as **message** here, it must be emphasized that *logos* in Scripture is associated with revelation. As in John 1:1 and 14, according to Oscar Cullmann, in 1 Cor 1:18 and 2 Cor 5:19 "Logos is the final definitive revelation as such" (1959, 261). In this sense, the **message** as ***Word*** qualifies all phases of apostolic ministry. Christian ministry (*diakonia*) does not merely give good advice. Rather, it communicates the startling good news of what God has done **in Christ** for **the world.**

■ **20** The apostle must be the servant of his message. As **Christ's ambassadors** (see Isa 52:7; Eph 6:20), Paul and his helpers serve *hyper Christou*. That is, they serve on behalf of and as representatives of Christ. His commission as an apostle is like that of the powerful legate of an ancient emperor. His dignity and authority are those of his Sovereign.

Apostles do not *pretend* to speak for God; they actually do. Thus, the translation **as though** (*hōs*) should not be taken to mean "under the pretence of" (Turner 1963b, 158). Rather, it means "seeing that" (Plummer 1915, 185), "with the conviction that" (BDF 1961, §220), or "since God is making his appeal through us" (NRSV; see 1 Thess 2:13). "Where Paul speaks, God speaks" (Barrett 1973, 178). God himself speaks in Christian proclamation. "Preaching is not talking *about* God; it is allowing *God* to talk" (Mounce 1960, 154).

This is the basis of Paul's urgent, passionate appeal: **We implore** [*deometha*, "we beg" (NASB); "we entreat" (NRSV); "we plead" (GNT)] **you on Christ's behalf** [*hyper Christou*]: **Be reconciled to God.** Not only is Paul an ambassador *hyper* **Christ**, but he entreats people *hyper* **Christ.** He speaks as Christ's representative.

The once-for-all, completed reconciliation (vv 18-19) is incomplete until the invitation, **Be reconciled to God** (v 20), is accepted. The force of the aorist passive imperative verb, *katallagēte*, **Be reconciled,** merits careful analysis. The imperative mood indicates that reconciliation requires a favorable, individual human response. The passive voice implies, however, that the human response is possible only because of the divine initiative. Therefore, the apostle calls for surrender to God's terms for reconciliation. The aorist tense calls for a decisive, one-time response.

But who does Paul invite to **be reconciled to God**? Does he address his appeal to the unconverted world or to the Christian community in Corinth?

Rudolf Bultmann takes Paul to speak in a "missions style," appropriate to eschatological preaching. That is, by using *deometha*, Paul appeals for a decision that must be always carried out anew (1985, 164). More likely, the apostle is speaking generally of the proclamation of his apostolic message, centered in the deed of Christ. He has in mind any audience that he and others might address in their role as ambassadors for Christ (so Thrall 2004, 438; and Harris 2005, 448).

In vv 18-20, we see the transcendent value and the contemporary dynamic of Christian ministry. By the Spirit of Christ, God stands behind the preaching of his ministers and actually speaks through them. Their words (*logoi*) *are* God's Word (*logos;* see 1 Thess 2:13). For "to say that God simultaneously instituted the deed and the word of reconciliation is to claim that Jesus Christ is savingly present whenever the word announcing his cross and resurrection as God's act on our behalf is proclaimed" (Kay 2001, 260). These verses present us with a theology of preaching as well as a theology of Christian ministry (see Heb 4:12-13).

■ **21** Arising from this context, v 21 brings us to one of the most profound sentences in the whole of Scripture. Here Paul addresses the mystery of the atoning work of God in Christ. He expands v 19*ab* to state "how" the reconciliation of God with alienated humanity is possible.

Reconciliation has two efficient causes: (1) What God has done in Christ; and (2) What, as a result, Christ means for us. So far as English usage allows, Paul writes literally: ***The one*** [Christ] ***who knew no sin, he*** [God] ***made to be sin for our sake, so that we might become the righteousness of God in him*** [Christ].

First, behind the translation **him who had no sin** is the participial form of the verb "know" (*gnonta*). Behind the Greek term, Paul takes for granted its Hebrew meaning (*yada'*), based on LXX usage (see Hill 2001). To know sin would be to have personal, experiential knowledge of it (see Gen 4:1; Matt 1:25; Rom 7:7). Paul concurs with the uniform testimony of the NT as to the sinlessness of Christ. Jesus lived in unfailing obedience to the Father, free from sin during his entire earthly life (see Rom 5:19; Phil 2:8; John 7:18; 8:46; Acts 3:14; Heb 4:15; 7:26; 1 Pet 1:19; 2:22; 3:18; 1 John 3:5).

The assertion that **God made him . . . to be sin for us** opens up Paul's understanding of atonement. Two questions are basic. (1) Did the identification of Christ with **sin** take place in the incarnation, that is, in the entire earthly life of Jesus, or only in his crucifixion? (2) In what sense did God make Christ **to be sin**? A third arises from these: (3) Do the two occurrences of **sin** (*harmartian*) in v 21 carry the same meaning? We will consider question 3 first.

Some say the meaning of **sin** in the phrase **sin for us** is different than in the phrase **had no sin.** They understand *harmartia* in the first instance in terms of the OT "sin offering" (see Lev 3; Isa 53:9-11, esp. v 10). *Harmartia* may mean "sin offering" in the LXX (Exod 29:14; Lev 4:24; Num 18:9) and in Heb 10:26. For Pauline parallels they appeal to two passages. Rom 8:3: "God . . .

[sent] his own Son . . . to be a sin offering [*peri harmartias*]." And, Gal 3:13: "Christ redeemed us . . . by becoming a curse for us."

This correlation of passages has a long interpretive tradition behind it. Nevertheless, this translation of Rom 8:3 is uncertain; and nowhere else in Paul does *harmartia* mean "sin offering." This is not to say that he does not use sacrificial language in connection with the death of Christ (see Rom 3:25; 1 Cor 5:7).

This meaning for *harmartia* in the phrase **sin for us** would limit the reference to the crucifixion of Jesus (in answer to question 1 above). But what if the two occurrences of **sin** in v 21 are essentially identical in meaning? This allows that Paul's reference applies to the whole incarnate life of Jesus. This would support an understanding of atonement primarily in terms of personal and interrelational categories. The terminology of "reconciliation" in the passage would lend support to this interpretation. Paul's point would then be that Christ participated with us in our alienation from God because of our sin. This alienation pertained throughout his historical and incarnate life, not only as it climaxed in his death and resurrection.

Thus, the phrase **made . . . to be sin for us** was not a matter of the administration of an abstract justice—an impersonal imposition of the death penalty. His identification with us would be, instead, a personal identification with us in our lot, in which he "became obedient to death—even death on a cross!" (Phil 2:8).

Did Christ not only represent sinners but also fully participate in the reality of sin in some sense beyond our comprehension? But how could one "who knew no sin" (NRSV) yet participate in sin? James Denney proposes that "there is something in God as well as something in man which has to be dealt with" (1943, 5:769). God treated Christ as **sin,** aligning him so completely with sin and its consequences that, from the divine perspective, Christ became indistinguishable from sin itself (Harris 2005, 454). We stand ultimately before a mystery!

Johannes Bengel (1687-1752) suggests that Christ "was made *sin* in the same way that we are made *righteousness.* Who would have dared speak thus, if Paul had not led the way?" (1895, 3:385).

The phrase **in him** (*en autoi*) corresponds with **for us** (*hyper hēmōn*), thus aiding in the understanding of both phrases. Both we and Christ embrace what is not inherently or deservedly theirs. Christ, who "was innocent of sin" (NEB), entered a sphere utterly alien to him, away from home. He did this that we might enter that sphere from which we have alienated ourselves, our true home—***the righteousness of God in him*** (Thornton 1950, 45).

Christ, an absolute Stranger to any rebellion against the Father (John 8:46; Heb 4:15; 1 Pet 2:22), made himself fully responsible for the world's rebellion against God (Isa 53:6; 1 Pet 2:24). Christ as the representative of God suffered what God does to sin. He makes visible what happens when we have God against us (Schlatter 1956, 569). Christ became "a curse for us" (Gal

3:13; see Deut 21:23; Isa 53:12; Luke 22:37; Rom 8:2). He "came to stand in that relation with God which normally is the result of sin, estranged from God and the object of his wrath" (Barrett 1973, 180). **God made him** indicates the full unity of the Father and Son in the identification with sin (see John 10:30). If Trinitarian theology is correct, God himself accepted the divine judgment for sin we deserved. In the ultimate sense, God, for the sake of forgiving love, suffers within himself the consequences of human sin.

From a description of identification, Paul goes on to elucidate the phrase in terms of exchange in the second half of the verse: **so that in him we might become the righteousness of God.** Because of our relationship with Christ (*en autōi*), God exchanges our old sinful situation for a new situation. Paul describes this as **the righteousness of God** (*dikaiosynē Theou*).

In the present context, which emphasizes personal reconciliation, the result is forgiveness in the fullest sense. It is the restoration of a right relation to God. It is deliverance from the power and consequences of sin and a new quality of life, which our new status requires. Paul's language here is forensic, that of courtroom justification (see Rom 5:19). But the exchange takes place "in Christ"; that is, in union with his personal being. It is not a matter of any imputed or alien righteousness. We actually share in Christ's experience of becoming the righteousness of God in his death and resurrection.

The **righteousness of God** is not so much a thing as an activity of God (Rom 1:17). It is the vindication of God's cause and the accomplishing of
5:21 God's purposes in the world. Stemming from God as righteous, it is a regal act. It is not merely acquittal, but pardon (Rom 3:24-26). Justification in Paul is not merely a bookkeeping concept. It is not only a divine pronouncement, although it is that. To be declared right by God presumes that what God says is a performative word, not just descriptive. When God speaks, things happen. The word of God works effectively within us and creates new life. We are taken up into **the righteousness of God,** into a new way, into a new kind of life (vv 15, 17). This is not our doing (see Eph 2:1-10). Our only merit is what Christ has done. We are able to do right only because of the indwelling Spirit of Christ.

The resultant righteous character is that of the *rightness* of our new relation to God (Phil 3:9). It is the consequence of our possession of that *right* Spirit, the transforming Holy Spirit (2 Cor 3:18). He is God's poured-out expression of love, freely given to us (Rom 5:5).

Paul does not say that the church is to know about, to believe in, or even to receive **the righteousness of God.** He says that it is God's purpose (*hina,* **so that**) that we should **become the righteousness of God.** We are to incarnate the reconciling love of Christ present in the world as God's new creation (Hays 1996, 24).

Once again justification reaches out to involve sanctification, for it is a righteousness "in Christ" (2 Cor 5:17) who has become to us "righteousness, holiness and redemption" (1 Cor 1:29*b*). "It is because of him [God] that [we] are in Christ Jesus" (1 Cor 1:29*a*). And it is the sanctifying Spirit of Christ, who is the divine agent, effecting these changes within us (Rom 8:1-11).

Paul's ministry consists in proclaiming the advent of the new creation "in Christ" (2 Cor 5:16-21). This entails the dramatic recovery of this alienated and dislocated world by God. He has acted eschatologically (i.e., in these end times) in Christ and placed the world under his rule (Martin 1986, 104). Paul approaches his ministry supremely "in Christ":

1. As a new creation "in Christ," Paul looks out on the world of humankind (vv 16-17). As such
2. He has been entrusted with the message of God's reconciling act "in Christ" (vv 18-19), in order that
3. He might offer us the free opportunity "in Christ" to become the righteousness of God (vv 20-21).

c. *The Life of an Apostle (6:1-10)*

Paul continues his defense of his ministry from the standpoint of his conduct and experiences as an ambassador of Christ. He turns now to a description of his life as an apostle. He opens with a transitional word of appeal (vv 1-2). It introduces the new topic, while forming a practical conclusion to his presentation of the new order of salvation in Christ (5:17-21). The thought of 5:20 continues with an added nuance. The verbal linkage is significant. There God was "making his appeal" (*parakalountos*) through Paul. Here Paul directly appeals (*parakaloumen*, **we urge**) to his readers. He is concerned that his conduct not discredit his ministry of reconciliation (6:3-10). Explaining what his ministry involves, he seeks to validate it as one of a suffering and, therefore, a true apostle. That Paul needs to make such an appeal and claim indicates that all is not yet well in Corinth (see 6:11—7:4).

■ 1 The opening adverbial participle, *synergountes*, ***working together***, stands alone, unqualified in the text. But the preceding verses make it probable that Paul refers to God as the One with whom he cooperates in ministry. As Christ's ambassador, Paul and God are coworkers (5:18, 20; see 1 Cor 3:9). Beardslee suggests, however, that the apostle speaks cautiously of God working with humans. It would be truer to Paul's thought to say that all real human work is God's work than to say simply that God and humans work together (1961, 60). He follows Isaiah in this: "O LORD, . . . all that we have done, you have done for us" (26:12 NRSV).

Paul appeals to the Corinthians (**you,** *hymas*) **not to receive God's grace in vain.** "The grace of God" (NRSV) summarizes the gospel of salvation (see *sōtērias* in 6:2), particularly in light of the emphases of 5:16-21. No doubt, there are implications in the exhortation for the Corinthians' relation to their apostle. The aorist tense of the infinitive **to receive** (*dexasthai*) refers to an unspecified time, probably here looking forward to future acts of receiving, viewed as one act (Harris 2005, 458).

Paul encourages the Corinthians never **to receive God's grace in vain** (see Gal 2:2; Phil 2:16). That is, they must allow **grace** to achieve its intended saving effect now and always. Paul fears they will resist God's efforts to produce among them the holy lives the death of Christ demands (2 Cor 5:14-15). Only such lives can face the judgment unashamed (5:10; see 1 Cor 3:10-15). The new relationship with God created by Christ does not maintain itself automatically. Paul urges his audience not to "let it go for nothing" (NEB). The exhortations, God's as well as Paul's, involve the Corinthians' reconciliation with their apostle as well as with God. Failure to reconcile with God's messenger amounts to receiving **God's grace in vain** (McCant 1999, 54-55).

■ **2** Some interpreters consider v 2 a parenthesis within Paul's argument. But it reveals a fundamental assumption of his gospel. It reinforces his appeal in v 1 with a prophetic word quoted from Isa 49:8: **"In the time of my favor I heard you, and in the day of salvation I helped you."** In the second of Isaiah's four "Servant Songs" (Isa 49:1-12), the Lord calls upon his Servant to restore the nation from their exile in Babylon (Isa 49:6). In the verse Paul quotes, God promises the Servant help in that day of Israel's salvation from exile.

Using the Jewish interpretive method known as *pesher,* Paul applies the Isaiah quotation to his contemporary situation: ***Behold, now*** [*idou nyn*] ***is the favorable time; behold, now is*** **the day of salvation.** The Greek terms for **favor** in the LXX of Isaiah (*dektōi*) and ***favorable*** (*euprosdektos*), in Paul's reinterpretation, may both be translated "acceptable" (NRSV), as in a welcome situation (BDAG 2000, 411). Paul has changed Isaiah's word to a strengthened form by adding two prefixes (*eu-* ["good"] with *pros-* as an intensifier). He emphasizes that what the Corinthians experienced through his proclamation is the actual fulfillment of Isaiah's prophecy.

The twofold ***Behold, now*** . . . ***behold, now*** stresses that the prophetic future is the present time. God's final salvation action is taking place in the present. The last days are not a far-off event; they have finally arrived. The gospel era is the crisis moment in salvation history. It is the unique time accepted/favored by God for all to respond to his invitation to reconciliation in Christ. Paul's preaching is part of the eschatological event itself as it announces the word of the cross. It creates a crisis that demands a response. Will those who hear the message welcome the age initiated with the resurrection of Christ (see 2 Cor 5:16; Martin 1986, 169)? The Corinthians must recognize that Paul's preaching encounters them as God's eschatological message (McCant 1999, 55). Paul's role in the history of redemption is strategic.

■ **3** The exhortation of Paul and his associates is consistent with the quality of their apostolic ministry. Their conduct conforms to the nature of the gospel. This continuity would be strengthened grammatically, if v 2 were taken as parenthetical. On this reading, the participles ***giving*** (*didontes*) and ***commending*** (*synistantes*) in vv 3 and 4 are, like "working together" (NASB; *synergountes*) in v 1, dependent on the main verb **we urge** (*parakaloumen*) of v 1. Most translators, however, treat *didontes* as if it were a finite verb (so NIV). On this reading, it starts a new sentence: **We put [*didontes, giving*] no stumbling block in anyone's path, so that our ministry will not be discredited** (v 3; see 8:20).

However we understand the relation of vv 3 and 4 to v 1, these verses restate the point of 5:12. Apparently, someone has attempted to discredit the apostle's ministry. In response, Paul goes on the offensive, making the polemical claim that he has done nothing to discredit his ministry (McCant 1999, 56). His conscience is clear.

Paul's conduct has provided no *proskopēn*, ***"occasion for taking offense"*** (BDAG 2000, 882). No legitimate basis can be found for rejecting his apostolic message. Although Paul has written simply "the ministry [*hē diakonia*]" (NASB), the context supports the meaning **our ministry,** rather than the apostolic ministry in general.

■ **4** Paul's Corinthian detractors apparently felt that the honor of an apostolic appointment by God meant success and preeminence. So Paul felt he needed **Rather** (*all'*), or ***on the contrary,*** to point out that even his sufferings were demonstrations of the genuineness of his apostleship (vv 4-5).

"In all circumstances" or **in every way,** Paul and his fellow laborers were ***commending*** (see 3:1; 4:2; 5:12) themselves as ***ministers/*servants** [*diakonoi*] **of God** (see 3:6; Matt 20:26; Mark 10:43). As in 4:2 and 5:12 (as opposed to 3:1), the word order here is *synistantes heautous* rather than *heautous synistanein*. Paul's consistent usage here suggests that his apostolic self-commendation is not illegitimate self-praise. It is wholly justified because it leads to the praise of God exhibited through human weakness (Harris 2005, 470). Paul stresses this by the design of what follows. All the conditions mentioned in vv 4-10 provide a platform for the display of God's grace in the lives of his servants.

Beginning in v 4 Paul employs a lyrical rhetorical structure with its lists of hardships, virtues, vicissitudes, and antitheses (McCant 1999, 56). Paul's first phrase descriptive of his conduct, **in great endurance,** has a general rather than specific reference. This and other considerations lead most interpreters to take it as a heading for (at least) vv 4*b*-5.

Paul organizes the structure of vv 4*b*-10 beginning with the repeated use of three prepositions:

- three triads of phrases introduced by ***in*** (*en*), naming hardships (vv 4*b*-5)
- eight phrases introduced by ***in*** (*en*), listing virtues (vv 6-7*a*) and
- three phrases introduced by ***by*** (*dia*), referring to life's vicissitudes (vv 7*b*-8*a*)

It concludes with seven antitheses (vv 8*b*-10) introduced by ***as*** (*hōs*).

Keeping as closely as possible to the NIV wording, the rhetorical character appears as follows:

in great endurance;
in troubles, ***in*** hardships, and ***in*** distresses;
in beatings, ***in*** imprisonments and ***in*** riots;

in hard work, ***in*** sleepless nights and ***in*** hunger;
in purity, ***in*** understanding, ***in*** patience and ***in*** kindness;
in the Holy Spirit and in sincere love;
in truthful speech and in the power of God;
by weapons of righteousness in the right hand and in the left;
by glory and dishonor, ***by*** bad report and good report;
as imposters, yet [*kai*] genuine;
as unknown, yet [*kai*] known;
as dying, yet [*kai*] ***behold*** we live;
as beaten, yet [*kai*] not killed;
as sorrowful, yet [*de*] always rejoicing;
as poor, yet [*de*] making many rich;
as having nothing, yet [*kai*] possessing everything.

Paul's elevated style is most likely his own artistry. He uses the catalog form to point to the paradoxical, yet authentic, character of his ministry.

An overarching characteristic of Paul's apostolic ministry is that he has conducted it **in great endurance. Endurance,** greatly stressed by Jesus (Matt 10:22; Luke 8:15; 21:19) and certainly significant for Paul (2 Cor 1:6; 11:23-30; Rom 5:3-4; 1 Thess 1:3), is placed at the head of three triads of difficult circumstances.

The first triad, climactic in order in v 4, presents Paul's sufferings in general terms. These appear to refer to those hardships independent of human
6:4-7*a* agency. Included are ***afflictions*****/troubles** (see 2 Cor 1:3-10; 2:4; 4:8, 17; 6:4; 7:4; 8:2, 13; Acts 14:22; 20:23). All these are experiences of physical, mental, or spiritual pressure that might be avoided. However, **hardships**/calamities could not be evaded. And no escape was possible from **distresses**/"dire straits" (NEB; see 4:8).

■ **5** The second triad (v 5) specifies particular sufferings inflicted by others. Paul commends himself as a true servant of God, by showing the utmost patience amid **beatings** (11:23-25; Acts 16:23), **imprisonments** (Acts 16:23-40; "far more imprisonments" in 2 Cor 11:23 NASB), and **riots** (Acts 13:50; 14:19; 16:19; 19:29; 21:30).

The third triad consists of those disciplines that Paul imposed upon himself in the furtherance of his mission: **in hard work, *in* sleepless nights and *in* hunger.** This hardship list presupposes the one in 4:8-10 and anticipates the one in 11:23-29.

■ **6-7*a*** Having catalogued the nine conditions illustrating his apostolic endurance, Paul takes a breath, so to speak. He next enumerates eight spiritual characteristics introduced by ***in*** [*en*]. These recount the means by which God enabled him to endure as a minister of Christ (vv 6-7*a*).

These are, first, a life of **purity.** He can make this claim for he has kept his motives single and his behavior aboveboard. Second, Paul possesses an **understanding/*knowledge*** of what God had done in Jesus Christ (see 8:7; 11:6; 1

Cor 2:6-16) both in his own life and in its implications for all humanity. Third, with God-given **patience**/forbearance he could endure the injuries, insults, stubbornness, and stupidity of people without responding in anger or revenge (see Rom 12:19; Col 3:12). Fourth, Paul exhibited **kindness;** he was sweet-tempered in his sympathy with such people (see Luke 6:35; 1 Cor 13:4; Gal 5:22; Eph 4:32).

Next in Paul's list of instrumental means is **in the Holy Spirit**/"holiness of spirit" (NRSV). Paul could use *pneuma* to refer to the human spirit (7:1, 13, 34; 1 Cor 2:11). But he never adds the adjective *hagios* when he intends this meaning. Furthermore, when he does apply the adjective in the expression *hagios pneuma,* his reference is usually to the Holy Spirit (e.g., Rom 9:1; 14:17; 15:16; 1 Cor 6:19; 12:3; 2 Cor 13:14; 1 Thess 1:5-6; 4:8).

Nevertheless, finding **the Holy Spirit** mentioned in the midst of a list of moral qualities is startling this side of the ecumenical creeds. We might at least expect this at the end or beginning, in an emphatic position. Here the phrase could be shorthand for the "gifts of the Holy Spirit" (NEB; see Gal 5:5).

Paul considers the divine **Spirit** the inner dynamic of all the virtues listed. Such virtues are evidence of the Spirit's inner operation. Paul earlier identified his own ministry as a "ministry of the Spirit" (*diakonia tou pneumatos* in 3:8; see 1 Cor 2:4; 1 Thess 1:5). In it these virtues were on display. The premier fruit of the Spirit is, of course, **sincere love** (Gal 5:22-23; see Rom 12:9; 1 Tim 1:5; 1 Pet 1:22). **Love** (*agapēi*) reflects the attitude of Christ (see 2 Cor 5:14; 1 Cor 13:1-13) in the life of the apostle. The adjective **sincere** (*anypokritōi*) describes this love as "without pretense" (BDAG 2000, 91). It was not the performance of an actor (*hypokritēs*).

Paul concludes his list of eight virtues that have sustained him as an apostle (see vv 4-5) with two more: **in truthful speech** and **in the power of God** (v 7*a*). Another possible translation of **in truthful speech** (*en logō alētheias*) is ***in the word of truth.*** In the first instance *alētheias* would be understood an attributive genitive. In the second, as an objective genitive, Paul means that the message he preaches is the truth.

In 4:2, Paul places "the word of God" in parallel with "setting forth the truth plainly." In this light, the objective genitive translation appears preferable here. Therefore, we take the expression "in the technical sense to denote the gospel" (Bultmann 1985, 172). That is, the gospel Paul proclaims is ***the truth*** (Eph 1:13; Col 1:5; 2 Thess 2:12; see 2 Cor 5:19).

Paul's virtuous ministry and endurance under difficult circumstances were possible only **in the power of God** (see 4:7-11; 12:9-10; 1 Cor 2:3-5). His ministry is the very activity of God himself (2 Cor 5:20), as is any truly Christian ministry. But ministry is a matter of obedience and faith, not of presumption!

■ ***7b-8a*** With a change in prepositions (*dia* replacing the *en* of vv 4-7*a*), perhaps to break the monotony, Paul states in a formal unity three more characteristics of his apostolic ministry (vv 7*b*-8*a*).

The first is instrumental, that is, **with weapons** (emphasis added; see 10:4). Paul wields these metaphorical implements of battle **in the right hand and in the left.** These doubtless include armor (see Isa 59:17; Rom 13:12; Eph 6:13-17; 1 Thess 5:8), which consists of **righteousness** (see Rom 6:13), an epexegetic genitive. As a subjective genitive, Paul might have in mind the **weapons** provided by the divine **righteousness** (see 2 Cor 5:21).

Either way, from the resources of his relationship with God, Paul is fully equipped. Following the conventions of his day, he carries offensive weapons **in the right hand** and a defensive shield **in the left.** In Ephesians the imagery is expanded to include explicit mention of "the sword of the Spirit" (Eph 6:17) and "the shield of faith" (Eph 6:16). Paul makes frequent use of military metaphors elsewhere (2 Cor 10:3-4; Rom 5:13; 6:13; 13:12; 1 Thess 5:8; Phlm 2).

The second two characteristics introduced with *dia* may be best translated by **through.** They describe some of the varied responses to his ministry Paul encountered:

a **through glory and**
    b [through] **dishonor,**
    b' ***through*** **bad report and**
a' [through] **good report.**

Paul uses the rhetorical device of the chiastic (i.e., X-shaped) construction (abb'a') to reinforce his point. He was held in high esteem by some and treated with contempt by others. He endured the vicissitudes of both disrepute and good repute. In sum, he knew both success and failure in the reception of his ministry (see Isa 6:8-10).

This is the only place in Paul's letters that he uses *doxa* in the secular Greek sense. Here **glory** refers to his own reputation. Elsewhere, he follows the LXX use of **glory** to refer to the praiseworthy reality of God. Some interpreters think **glory** represents a main theme in the letter—the glory of God and the reputation of Paul (Young and Ford 1987, 12).

■ **8*b*-9** Paul now lists seven antitheses or contrasting conditions that he suffers cheerfully for the sake of his calling (vv 8-10). All are introduced by ***as*** (*hōs*). The formal structure is clear in the NASB:

as deceivers	and yet [*kai*]	true
as unknown	yet [*kai*]	well-known
as dying	yet [*kai*]	behold, we live
as punished	yet [*kai*]	not put to death
as sorrowful	yet [*de*]	always rejoicing
as poor	yet [*de*]	making many rich
as having nothing	yet [*kai*]	possessing all things

This is the third interchange of paradoxical experiences in Christ that Paul has listed in the letter (1:3-7; 4:7-12; see 7:5-7; 11:30; 12:5-10; 13:2-9). These opposed pairs in Paul's apostolic life illustrate two central themes in the letter: life in the midst of death and the power of God in the midst of human weakness. The same paradox of humiliation and glory that characterized the career of Jesus is an integral part of Paul's ministry. This is already evident in the nature of the message committed to Paul and known by the Corinthians.

In the first two sets of contrasting realities, the apostles are **regarded as impostors** or ***deceivers*** by some (see 1:15—2:1; 7:2; 12:17). Nonetheless, they are ***true*** or **genuine** (v 8) by others. They are **regarded as unknown** (v 9) in the human world (and particularly among Paul's rivals). But they are truly **known** by some in the church, and certainly by God (1:1; Gal 1:1; 2:7, 9, 20).

In the second pair of paradoxical experiences Paul alludes to Ps 118. This serves as the climax of the Egyptian Hallel (Pss 113—118), sung at the great Jewish religious festivals. As worshippers celebrated a God-given military victory, there were "shouts of victory and joy." This was because "the LORD's right hand has done mighty things" (Ps 118:15-16). Then the psalmist adds,

> I will not die but live,
> and will proclaim what the LORD has done.
> The LORD has chastened me severely,
> but he has not given me over to death. (118:17-18)

Although frequently exposed to death (2 Cor 1:8-9; 1 Cor 15:30), surprisingly (*idou*, ***behold***), Paul exults: **we live on.** His language seems to echo that of Ps 118:17 in the LXX.

In the next contrast—***as*** [*hōs*] **beaten** [*paideuomenoi*], **and yet not killed** —*paideuomenoi* has the sense of ***punished,*** as in "disciplined," like the psalm. Although humanly administrated (2 Cor 11:23), Paul sees the hand of God in it (see 1 Cor 11:32). Discipline is evidence of God's loving care (see Prov 3:11-12; Heb 12:4-11).

■ **10** The paradox, ***as*** [*hōs*] **sorrowful, yet always rejoicing** (v 10), characterizes his ambivalence in the midst of the events of his ministry. This is perhaps best illustrated in his letter to the Philippians.

As [*hōs*] **poor, yet making many rich** refers, no doubt, to Paul's frequent experience of material poverty, even by ancient standards (see 2 Cor 11:9, 27; 1 Cor 4:11-12; Phil 4:10-13). The positive antithesis may be to the Corinthians' spiritual enrichment in Christ (1 Cor 1:5) as a result of his ministry to them (see Prov 13:7). In this, Paul followed the example of Christ: "For you know the grace of our Lord Jesus Christ, that though he was rich, yet for your sakes he became poor, so that you through his poverty might become rich" (2 Cor 8:9).

With ***as*** [*hōs*] **having nothing, and yet possessing everything,** Paul brings his antitheses to a climax in a rhetorical flourish. Referring back to the previous contrast, Paul suggests that, paradoxically, his poverty was actually an asset. It truly was "more blessed to give than to receive" (Acts 20:35).

At first glance, this contrast appears merely to be a repetition. But the striking wordplay—*echontes . . . katechontes*—is more comprehensive: ***as having nothing, yet really having all things.*** It indicates a summary-like contrast between a simple and temporary possession on the one hand, and a secure and permanent possession on the other. The first is literal, this-worldly, and the second reaches out to take in all things real and worthwhile, **everything** of eternal value (2 Cor 4:18; 1 Cor 3:21-23; Phil 3:7-8; Rom 8:17).

There are Stoic and Cynic parallels to the idea that having no material goods frees one to possess everything in a higher sense (Furnish 1984, 348; Thrall 2004, 457-68). Paul may have Christianized a familiar philosophical motif. On this high note, Paul has defined and commended his ministry to the Corinthians with lists of his apostolic hardships and triumphs (Harris 2005, 485-86).

In summary, Paul characterizes his ministry in 2:14—6:10:

1. He begins with thanksgiving. Although he is like a captive in chains, his ministry is one of triumph in Christ (2:14-17).
2. This ministry is supremely one of the Spirit because of the presence and work of the Holy Spirit (3:1—4:6).
3. It is guaranteed because all that Paul endures for Jesus' sake is the dying of Jesus. This releases into the lives of his hearers the Spirit—the resurrection life of Jesus. Already in this life both Paul and they fully share in the future (4:7—5:10).
4. These characteristics of the apostle's ministry are true only in that Paul's ministry consists of God's act of reconciliation in Christ for the world (5:11—6:10).

FROM THE TEXT

6:10

In the past several decades, many have had much to say about the Christian ministry, its nature and its task. Extensive research, detailed how-to books, and high-powered seminars have penetrated the life and work of busy pastors. Models of the minister are appealed to—shepherd, rancher, CEO, therapist, coach, among others. How *do* we define what the ministry is in a day like ours with its complicated demands? Where do we turn to find a model relevant, or better, sufficient for a postmodern world with its new age ethos? What most of all is to determine our model?

Where do we look first? To the tastes of popular culture? To the demands of the marketplace? To the success techniques of the corporate world? To the secular healing professions? To the managerial skills of winners in the world of sports? To the modus operandi of the political world? To the assured views of the academic elite? All these certainly have their value. So where do we find a model ultimately trustworthy for ministry and for the minister, a model that is fully in touch with the reality of a world defined by confrontation with the gospel of Christ?

Can we learn anything from Paul's apologia of his ministry as a ministry of reconciliation (5:11—6:10)? He considers his ministry as always open to the judgment of Christ (5:10). In this light he seeks to reflect on (1) the *motive,* (2) the *message,* and (3) the *manne*r of his apostolic ministry. In the process, he lifts up a model of Christian life and service, which, although often neglected and forgotten, has served the church well for over two millennia. As Paul analyzes his own ministry, he takes us to the very heart of the Christian ministry and, indeed, to what our everyday lives are about as Christians.

1. *Motive.* We start with Paul's attempt to articulate *the motive of Christian life and service* (5:11-15). He knows "what it is to fear the Lord." He fully realizes that his motives are well known to God. And, he hopes the consciences of the Corinthians are likewise aware of them. As he seeks "to persuade" people to believe, Paul is drawn like a magnet to a more profound motivation: "Christ's love compels us."

An adequate motive for Christian life and service is simple and single, the love that Christ has for us: "Faith arises when God's love is encountered at the Cross" (Welch 1988, 59). Love motivates us, God's love for us as revealed in the life and ministry of the Son of God. When all has been said and done, that is what makes us tick. We are controlled by Christ's love for us. This inner constraint has both "kept him from" self-preoccupation and "held him to" his life of service. Paul would say, "Christ's love has moved me to such extremes. His love has the first and last word in everything I do" (5:14 TM).

This means that some folks will always misunderstand us. They will be incapable of grasping what drives our attitudes and conduct, considering us a little weird or even insane. But we are willing to be perceived as "out of our mind" (5:13) for God, because "the world does not know us" (1 John 3:1; see John 15:18-19). They do not know the inner secret of our living. Many cannot understand our spirit of forgiveness, our willingness to deny ourselves for others, and our giving of our time and talents to the scandalous institution called the church—those crazy, misguided, even dangerous Evangelicals!

Yet, if our lives are motivated and controlled by God's love for us in Christ, "we are in our right mind" (2 Cor 5:13)—for others, for the needs of those around us, and for the kind of world in which we live. How can such a life be—it hardly seems natural or even human? It can be, for it is patterned after and enabled by a mystery Paul attempts to put into words: "We are convinced."

What is this thing—"Christ's love" (5:14)—that we have put our faith in for life and eternity? It is twofold. We are convinced, not only that Christ died for all of us, but that when he died we also died.

First, therefore, Christ died "for all"—even as we shared in putting him on the cross. He died "for all" as sinful and alienated from God. We are in desperate need of what Christ accomplished in his death.

Second, not only did we do him in as he died "for us," but we also are all dead with him. Human life itself has changed because God died in Christ. The death of Christ redefines us all; the cross of Christ has become the fundamental criterion of who we are as God's creatures, whether we are with faith or apart from faith.

With faith, it is not only his death but also his resurrection from the dead that defines us all. For as Paul put it, "he died for all, that those who live should no longer live for themselves but for him who died for them and was raised again" (5:15). This in a nutshell is the Christian gospel. Our identification by faith with Christ in his death involves us inherently in his resurrection life. We are set free to live love-controlled lives, because he lives (Rom 6:6-11; Gal 2:20; Phil 1:21; 2:5-18). It is not our doing that causes our lives to be grounded in the mystery of grace, in the cross and resurrection of Christ. It is his. In sum, "To live *for* Christ is to live *like* Christ" (Hafemann 2000, 241).

2. *Message.* Motive settled, Paul leads us forthrightly into *the message of Christian life and service* (5:12-21). As those who have received "the ministry of reconciliation" our message is "the message of reconciliation." What all does this involve?

At the heart of it all is Christ, "who had no sin," whom God made "to be sin for us, so that in him we might become the *righteousness* of God" (5:21, emphasis added).

This once-for-all event means, *first,* that we view everyone and all things, not "from a worldly point of view" (5:16). Our new perspective is from Christ's cross and resurrection. This perspective turns our old human, this-worldly values upside down. When we were guided by worldly distinctions, we knew only a few people, and those by what was superficial in their nature. All such distinctions died with Christ in his death. And to look at others in relation to Christ is to know everyone, not merely on the surface, but to the heart (Denney 1943, 5:768). Who and what Christ is now determines both what and who we are.

Involved *second* in this message of reconciliation is a new order of human existence. We participate already in **"a new creation"** formed, rather "transformed," "in Christ." We are new persons living as members of a new society on earth. We are the body of Christ (Rom 12:4-5), a human community that belongs to and experiences the end-time expectations of the whole of Scripture. We are part and parcel of God's final purposes in Christ. This is the church!

Third, as those entrusted with the message of reconciliation, God is actually making his appeal to the world through us. We are "Christ's ambassadors." By virtue of our participation in the resurrection life of Christ, we live, possessed by the Spirit of Christ, as God's agents. God actually and continually speaks to those around us in our world through us. Our invitation to "be reconciled to God" (5:20) is at the same time God's! This is inherent in who and what we are.

For the preaching ministry, this means that God discloses himself in the act of preaching, "for revelation and proclamation partake of the same nature" (Mounce 1960, 152). P. T. Forsyth wrote over a hundred years ago that preaching "is the Gospel prolonging and declaring itself" (1907, 5). More recently, James F. Kay expresses a similar point: "in Paul's letters faith in Jesus

Christ and faith in the word (or kerygma or gospel) proclaiming him are one and the same" (2001, 260).

Our congregations need more than our human assurances; they need a convincing touch from Someone beyond us, for our message to be vital. In 1566, the reformer Heinrich Bullinger (1504-75) gave us what "may be the most influential theological sentence ever written about preaching" (Kay 2007, 8). In a famous marginal heading, the Second Helvetic Confession declares: "The Preaching of the Word of God Is the Word of God" (Kay 2007, 7).

Further Reading on Theology and Preaching in Historical Perspective

Forsyth, P. T. 1907. *Positive Preaching and the Modern Mind.* The Lyman Beecher Lectures on Preaching, Yale University. New York: A. C. Armstrong and Son.

Kay, James F. 2007. *Preaching and Theology.* St. Louis: Chalice Press.

Wright, John W. 2007. *Telling God's Story: Narrative Preaching for Christian Formation.* Downers Grove, Ill.: IVP Academic.

Fourth, the message of reconciliation draws us inevitably back to the One who does the reconciling. We are reminded that "God was in Christ reconciling" (5:19 NASB). How did God do it? God "made Him who knew no sin *to be* sin on our behalf" (5:21*a* NASB). Again we bow in faith at the foot of the cross of Christ. There we can declare to all that "in him" they may "become the righteousness of God" (5:21*b*). That is, they may be fully restored to fellowship with God. Their sin and alienation can be taken into the suffering in God's own being. Entering the sphere of such faith in Christ brings us in touch with the holy, into "the sanctuary of life" (Tillich 1957, 12).

Paul has interpreted the death of Christ as the fundamental criterion of human life. If he is correct, how should the cross and resurrection of Christ together constitute the "first" model of the Christian minister entrusted with a ministry of reconciliation? And how much more should it constitute the basic paradigm for the whole of a truly "Christian" life? In Christian faith and ministry, "any acceptance of Jesus as the Christ which is not the acceptance of Jesus the crucified is a form of idolatry." Therefore, "the ultimate concern of the Christian is . . . the Christ Jesus who is manifest as the crucified" (Tillich 1957, 98). The cross—and resurrection—of Jesus is the final criterion by which Christian ministry and life are now to be measured.

3. *Manner.* This cross/resurrection perspective determines *the manner of Christian life and service* (6:1-10). Our ministry is properly defined as "together" with God. That our works are God's doing has penetrating and profound implications. Ministry is "God at work" in the power of Christ's death and resurrection through human lives. Thus, it is a "grace" that by its very nature transforms life and character, *"minds* and *manners"* (Clarke 1854, 2:337).

Therefore, no one can ever truly receive grace "in vain," that is, without its changing the recipient. This is the nature and power of Christian life and service—the ministry. This places a heavy and urgent responsibility on those who hear our message. Both the message and the messenger make the end-times announcement: "see, now is the day of salvation!" (6:2*d* NRSV). Now is God's time for us, "the time of God's favor" (6:2*c*).

No wonder Paul muses, with such a life and witness, "who is adequate for these things?" (2:16 NASB). Therefore, we seek to walk in step with the gospel we profess. And we seek to live in humble dependence on the Spirit of Christ, lest we become a "stumbling block" to others and our witness "be discredited."

How do we do that? Paul describes in lyrical form the manner of life, the ministry, that is fully consistent with the gospel of Christ. What commends a Christian life is that it partakes of the cross and resurrection of Christ. Our ministry must at once embrace both Good Friday and Easter Sunday.

Such a ministry, in the midst of normal and abnormal hardships, displays "great endurance" as the virtues of the gospel grace such a ministry (see 6:4-6). Such a ministry is open to unexpected circumstances, both positive and negative, both uplifting and depressing (see 6:7-8*a*). Most significantly, such a life and witness are penetrated by the paradoxes of the incarnate life and earthly ministry of the resurrected Christ (6:8*b*-10).

There is a profound sense in which our Christian lives and witness, a truly Christian ministry, if you please, can be poured into Paul's final antithesis: "as having nothing, and yet possessing everything." In his "Sketch of Mount Carmel," the poetic lines of John of the Cross (1542-91) seem certainly to have been inspired by the great apostle (Kavanaugh 1991, 111):

> To come to possess all
> desire the possession of nothing.

Now to return to our initial question: Where can we find a model for the ministry in our day in a world for which Christ died? Is it too simple, or is it profoundly attractive though unsearchable and unfathomable (Rom 11:33) to find our model in our Lord Jesus himself—the incarnation, the life and ministry, the crucifixion and death, and the resurrection of Jesus as the Christ?

In 2001, Duke Divinity School invited a group of pastors, lay leaders, and theological educators to join a Colloquium of Excellence in Ministry. This was part of a Pulpit and Pew research project on the lives and work of American Christian pastoral leaders. This was a diverse group—lay and ordained, of various races, of both genders, of numerous denominations, of a wide range of theological backgrounds, and of a multitude of assigned functions in the work of the larger church.

After many months of scriptural study, reading of classical and contemporary writers, exposure to Pulpit and Pew research data, and extended conversations, they published the results of their work in the book *Resurrecting Excellence: Shaping Faithful Christian Ministry* (2006).

With Phil 2:6-11 as a focal text, they took the life, death, and resurrection of Jesus as both the basis and the goal of their summons to excellence. They "glimpsed in the stories of the pastors and their congregations the cultivation of . . . a common life marked by Christ's dying and rising." Intersections were discovered that are often turned "into false alternatives—youth and age, strength and weakness, joy and suffering, abundance and sacrifice, tragedy and hope, community and solitude, church and world." In conclusion, they report their conviction that "resurrecting excellence is fundamentally shaped by a lifelong attentiveness and obedience to the life, death, and resurrection of Christ" (Jones 2006, 3, 19, 29, 176).

C. Paul Has Confidence in the Church (6:11—7:16)

As indicated by his direct address to the **Corinthians,** Paul begins here a new section of his letter. He has finished for the present the characterization of his ministry, which has occupied his attention since 2:14. In the process he has probed its implications for the integrity of his attitude toward his converts.

Here Paul resumes the matter of his relationship with the Corinthians. He reaffirms his love for them with an appeal based on his "great confidence" (7:4; see 7:16) in them. For some reason the apostle interrupts the call for renewed mutual affection (6:11—7:4) with an exhortation to separated living (6:14—7:1). The section closes with a consideration of the effect of Titus's role in the reconciliation of Paul with the church at Corinth (7:5-16; see 2:12-13).

BEHIND THE TEXT

Perhaps in order here is a quick look at 6:14—7:1 as "a six verse conundrum" (Sampley 2000, 1001). At first glance, this passage appears inappropriate to the immediate context. Rhetorically, it appears as an epideictic or deliberative digression. This was normal in ancient rhetorical discourse. It expresses greater vehemence and freedom of speech than the surrounding argument (Witherington 1995, 402; Quintilian, *Institutio oratoria* 4.3.12, 15). Its rhetorical questions cause it to resemble the Hellenistic-Roman diatribe (McCant 1999, 64). The goal of epideictic rhetoric was to strengthen existing adherence to shared values. Deliberative rhetoric calls for a change in future behavior, involving rebuke, admonition, and indignation.

Consistent with its context, 6:14—7:1 appears to be a deliberative digression inserted here by Paul. He wrote to reconcile with the Corinthians. To achieve this end, he needed to defend his ministry and warn his readers against behaviors and alliances that might alienate (or may already have alienated) some of them from him (Witherington 1995, 402-4; Quintilian, *Institutio oratoria* 4.3.15-16).

Paul probably composed the contents of these verses himself. Perhaps, he wrote them earlier for another purpose and inserted them here. Or, he may have formulated them only as he wrote this letter (see Introduction). Bultmann suggests that it reflects typically Jewish parenesis that Paul has Christianized (1985, 180). Hans Dieter Betz goes so far as to identify 2 Cor 6:14—7:1 as an anti-Pauline fragment secondarily interpolated into the letter (1973).

IN THE TEXT

1. An Appeal for Fellowship (6:11-13)

Following his exhortation to the Corinthians "not to receive God's grace in vain" (6:1), Paul lists the hardships he endured fulfilling his ministry. He shared with them his circumstances, feelings, and desires concerning his ministry in behalf of the gospel and for them (6:4-10). The apostle appears surprised at himself for having so frankly revealed to the Corinthians the scars he bears from his life as an apostle. He, therefore, attempts to capitalize on his frankness by making explicit what he has already expressed only subtly and indirectly. He bares his heart, affirming his affection for them and his desire for them to respond in kind. As Matera comments, "from a rhetorical point of view, they should be well disposed to his appeal" (2003, 161).

■ **11** Deeply affected by what he has just dictated, in rare fashion in his letters, Paul addresses his converts directly: **you, Corinthians**. He becomes intensely personal as he indicates his feelings toward his children in the faith (see 6:13). Besides here, Paul addresses a congregation by naming their city or province only in Gal 3:1 and Phil 4:13. In Galatians, he is alarmed by the Galatians' perversion of the gospel. In Philippians, he is warmly appreciative of their ongoing support of his ministry. But 2 Cor 6:11 begins a section that "is wrapped in a blanket of warm affection without equal in the letters" (Shillington 1998, 148).

Our mouth is open to you is a common Hebrew idiom for speaking (Judg 11:35-36; 1 Sam 2:1; Ezek 29:21; Rom 3:19). The NIV translates it, **We have spoken freely to you.** The expression often refers to a weighty and solemn utterance (Job 3:1; Matt 5:1; Eph 6:19). That Paul's ***mouth*** stands so ***open***—that he has spoken so openly and so frankly—should be evidence to the **Corinthians** that Paul's **heart** is also **opened wide** to them.

The verbs translated "open" in the two phrases are different. In the first, *aneōigen* meant open as accessible, open as opposed to closed, candid as opposed to coy (BDAG 2000, 84-85). In the second, *peplatyntai* means opened in the sense of broadened or enlarged (BDAG 2000, 823; KJV: "our heart is enlarged"). In Ps 119:32, the LXX uses this same verb to express the psalmist's praise to God: "you have set my heart free." The perfect tense of the verb indicates that Paul's heart has and will continue to have room to embrace the Corinthians.

Paul speaks candidly to the Corinthians. His heart expands to make full room for them. Such spontaneous and uninhibited expression flows only from a warm, trusting, and wide-open heart: "For the mouth speaks out of that which fills the heart" (Matt 12:34 NASB).

■ **12** Paul insists that the problem in their relationship is not on his part but on theirs. He continues to use the imagery of space, but in an opposite way. To make the Greek expression clear we translate expansively: ***You are not without room in us, but you are allowing little room in your affections for us.***

The verb *stenochōreisthe* is a compound of *stenos*, "narrow," and *chōros*, "space." It means **"to confine or restrict to a narrow space"** (BDAG 2000, 942).

Paul's term for **affection** (*splanchnois*) denotes "inward parts." It is often used as a synonym for **heart** (*kardia*), and like **heart** is used to denote the seat of the emotions. The term refers broadly to the vital organs—the heart, liver, spleen, and lungs—the upper, in distinction from the lower, viscera (Harris 2005, 490). But here the meaning is perhaps narrower than **heart**, denoting the self as moved by love (McCant 1999, 61). The Corinthians, not Paul, are the ones cramped or restricted in their affections. The NIV does not translate literally. But it renders Paul's meaning clearly: **We are not withholding our affection from you, but you are withholding yours from us.**

■ **13** The apostle concludes his thought with an appeal to the Corinthians to respond to him with an "affection" equal to his. He writes: *"in the same way in exchange"* (BDAG 2000, 90), ***you also*** **open wide your hearts.** The word for **exchange** (*antimisthian*), expresses both recompense and identity. Paul seeks a mutual relationship of the same degree and kind. He repeats the verb he used in v 11*b*: **open wide** [*platynthēte*] **your hearts also.** Paul uses the emphatic pronoun subject *hymeis*, ***you***, omitted in the NIV. This highlights the contrast between him and the Corinthians. But he ellipses the implied object, **hearts**, which the NIV adds for clarity.

Paul appeals to them as his **children** in the faith. In 1 Cor 4:14-15, he wrote: "my dear children, . . . I became your father through the gospel." He frequently addresses his converts in this way (see Gal 4:19; 1 Thess 2:7-8). As their spiritual father, Paul reminds the Corinthians of their special relationship with him. On this basis he asks them, as he has made room for them in his heart, that they in return treat him with the same love and openness. Paul challenges them to demonstrate their reconciliation to God in a full reconciliation to him (see 5:20; 6:1). The two cannot be separated.

By his language (2:14—6:10), the apostle has put his heart into his mouth for the Corinthians. This (1) indicates the largeness of his love for them and (2) furnishes an adequate motivation for them to remove all restraints from their attitude toward him. There must be this openness of love and confidence between minister and people for the free operation of the grace of God among them.

2. An Exhortation to Holy Living (6:14—7:1)

Abruptly following the apostle's burst of affection for the Corinthians in 6:11-13, he makes an equally impassioned appeal for them to break their ties with evil. His admonition calls for radical ethical separation of the church from its pagan environment. This call is not totally unanticipated, although it seems to interrupt the flow of thought, which resumes in 7:2.

This exhortation was foreshadowed in the appeal in 6:1: "we urge you not to receive God's grace in vain." Paul calls for "covenantal exclusiveness" (Shillington 1998, 153). The basis for this lies in the Corinthians' identity as a new covenant people (see 3:6). They are to maintain the holiness of life appropriate to their calling to be the temple and family of God, the church.

Some in Corinth were slow either to understand or to embrace the social implications of being "in Christ." Their reconciliation to God and, therefore, to Paul implied the necessity of forsaking entangling, competing alliances, which may have lingered for years (see 1 Cor 8—10).

Paul's ethical advice, expressed in the classic form of a relevant digression, is not inappropriate between 2 Cor 6:11-13 and 7:2. Rather, it functions as a "carefully structured, closely argued, and theologically rich climax" to the argument Paul began in 2:14 (Hafemann 2000, 277).

The paragraph opens with a thematic exhortation, a second person plural ("you all") imperative. Following in turn are five rhetorical questions, an affirmation, a list of OT texts, and a closing twofold exhortation in the first person
6:14 plural ("let us") based on the preceding promises.

The appearance in the digression of vocabulary new to Paul is consistent with his rhetoric. This abrupt change has its desired effect here, as in other places in his writings (see 2 Cor 4:7-13; 6:3-10; and 11:22-29). The Greek orator Demosthenes, in his speech *On the Crown*, similarly uses a significant number of words for rhetorical effect that he employs nowhere else (McCant 1999, 66).

■ **14** This exhortation calls for the Corinthians to take the opposite stance toward evil that they are to take toward Paul. Closely connected to his previous exhortation, "open wide your hearts" (6:13), Paul exhorts: **Do not be yoked together with unbelievers.** Reconciliation between people, as well as with God, has ethical implications. Reconciling with Paul means rejecting his critics. More is involved than hurt feelings over Paul's changed travel plans and his harsh letter (Matera 2003, 160). This exhortation states the basic moral claim of the passage. At the same time it sets the stage for Paul's leading exhortations to holiness of life in 6:17 and 7:1.

This leading exhortation is a periphrastic construction. The present tense of both the main verb (*ginesthe*, "become") and the participle (*heterozygountes*, "mismated") emphasize the durative force of the appeal. This increases its rhetorical power by calling attention to a continuing action to be avoided (McCant 1999, 67).

Perhaps Paul appeals to a metaphor from the OT here. There with similar terminology, the Law prohibits the crossbreeding of animals of different kinds (Lev 19:19 LXX). Although Deut 22:10, "You shall not plow with an ox and a donkey together" (NASB), does not refer to a "yoke," Paul may take it for granted.

But who are these **unbelievers** (*apistois*)? Who are those with whom the Corinthian Christians are not to ***"be unevenly yoked"*** (BDAG 2000, 399) in a close relationship? Paul has already used *apistois* in 2 Cor 4:4 to refer to those whose eyes Satan has blinded to the light of the gospel. In 1 Corinthians, Paul uses the term eleven times to refer to non-Christians (1 Cor 6:6; 7:12-15; 10:27; 14:22-24). Thus, it might seem unlikely that Paul has in mind the false apostles of chs 10—13. But in light of the polemical context, Hafemann holds that Paul indeed labels those who oppose him **unbelievers** (2000, 279-80). In 2 Cor 11:13-15 Paul calls the false apostles deceivers, servants of Satan masquerading as servants of righteousness.

Significantly, the term *apistois* does not appear in chs 10—13. In Paul's rhetorical question in v 16 he asks: "What agreement is there between the temple of God and idols?" This appears to echo Paul's discussion in 1 Cor 8—10, where he discusses the issues faced by the church in "eating food sacrificed to idols" (1 Cor 8:4). This was symptomatic of Paul's problems with the Corinthian church as it related to its pagan environment. Implicit in the sweep of his metaphor are all the ethical problems dealt with in 1 Corinthians (6:5-10; 10:14; 14:24). Wesley suggested that it might also advise against mixed marriages of believers and unbelievers (1950, 660). But in 1 Corinthians, Paul advised married couples to remain together, even if one was an unbeliever (1 Cor 7:12-15).

Paul's admonitions are applicable to any association involving idolatry and its often-accompanying immorality. But his call to separation is selective rather than exclusive. That is, the Corinthians are to avoid only those close relationships and partnerships that compromise the integrity of the Christian faith and its moral standards (see 1 Cor 5:9-13). For the sake of evangelism, Paul was willing to conform to the pattern of the culture in which he found himself (1 Cor 9:19-23), but never at the expense of the church's witness in the world.

With the rhetoric of a preacher, Paul reinforces his initial injunction with a series of five antithetical questions, all anticipating a negative answer. The five contrasting questions, each with a different verb (2 Cor 6:14-16), illustrate the opening umbrella exhortation: **Do not be yoked together.** Each question "highlights 'belief-unbelief' as the fundamental issue" (Murphy-O'Connor 1991, 68). The first four antitheses (vv 14-15) are arranged in pairs. The last question concludes the series and states the premise for what follows. The antitheses illustrate the absolute incongruity of believers entering or maintaining compromising relationships with unbelievers.

First, there can be no partnership (*metochē*) between the moral **righ-**

teousness of the Christian (5:21; see 6:7; 11:15; Rom 6:13-19; 14:1, 7; Phil 1:11) and the **wickedness** or "lawlessness" (NRSV, *anomiai*) characteristic of the pagan world (see Ps 45:7; Heb 1:9).

The second contrast is between the realm of **light** and the realm of **darkness** (2 Cor 4:4-6; Rom 13:12; Eph 5:7-14; 1 Thess 5:5). This antithesis is common in the Dead Sea Scrolls (1QS 3:3, 2-21, 25; 1QM 1:11; 13:5, 15) as well as in the NT. Prohibited by this contrast is no **fellowship** (*koinōnia*) or close sharing in common interests (1 Cor 1:9; 10:16).

■ **15** The second series of contrasts is more concrete and personal. First, Paul contrasts the leaders of the two realms, **Christ** and **Belial.** Then, he contrasts their respective subjects, **believer** and **unbeliever.** In **Christ** "the interest of holiness is gathered up" and in **Belial** "the interest of evil . . . , and they have nothing in common" (Denney 1943, 5:777).

Belial, occurring only here in the NT, is the Greek transliteration of a Hebrew word (*bĕlêyyʿal*). It is used twenty-seven times in the OT as a descriptive adjective, as in the phrase "some worthless men" (Deut 13:14 NASB; see Judg 19:22; 20:13; 1 Sam 2:12).

In later Jewish literature, the word **Belial** appears as a personal name for the devil/Satan/Antichrist (see BDAG 2000, 173; and Martin 1986, 200, for the primary sources). In the Dead Sea Scrolls **Belial** designates the angel of darkness in charge of the powers of evil as opposed to God (1QM 1:1, 5, 13; 4:2; 11:8; 13:2, 4-5, 11-12; 14:9; 15:3; 18:1, 3; 1QH^{a} 6:21; 1QS 2:2, 5; see Martin 1986, 199-200).

Paul's usual word for the supreme demonic power is "Satan." Here he may well have picked up the term **Belial** to stress the total lack of **harmony** (*symphōnēsis*) between Christ, the one in whom righteousness now centers, and Belial, the embodiment of evil. There can be nothing essential **in common** between their respective subjects, the **believer** and the **unbeliever.** Neither can have ***a part*** (*meris*) in that which is peculiar to the other.

Again, the antithesis is selective and not exclusive of the concerns of common humanity. **Believer** is the adjective *pistos*, which is used as a noun elsewhere in Paul only in the Pastoral Epistles (1 Tim 4:10, 12; 5:16; 6:2).

■ **16** The fifth and final antithetical question is, **What agreement** [*synkatathesis*] **is there between the temple of God and idols?** Paul appeals to Judaism's complete break with idolatry (see Rom 2:22) that the Gentile believers are to emulate (see Acts 15:20; 1 Cor 6:9; 10:14; 1 Thess 1:9). The Corinthians must break with the cultic practices associated with idol worship. This is ***because*** (*gar*), as Paul's use of **we** indicates, the church is **the temple of the living God.** The "Spirit of the living God" (3:3) dwells in the church.

The image of **temple** here is corporate as in 1 Cor 3:16-17. The local gathering of believers is where God dwells. In Eph 2:21 the metaphor is extended to the universal church. But Paul can apply temple imagery to individual Christians (1 Cor 6:19). This was its use in Hellenism (see Thrall 2004,

476, for the primary evidence). The metaphorical use of **temple** occurs in the Dead Sea Scrolls, where the Qumran community saw itself as a holy temple in opposition to the compromised Jerusalem temple (see 1QS 2:11; 1QH[a] 4:19; CD 20:9). The emphatically placed participial adjective **living** (*zōntos*) highlights the contrast between the true God and the idols pagans worshipped, which Jews and Christians considered "lifeless"!

In the NT, the term **temple** (*naos*) usually refers to the inner part of the sanctuary in distinction from the entire temple complex of buildings (*hieron*). In the *naos* the Divine Presence was especially manifest. The NT church as the temple of God is a familiar figure (1 Cor 3:16-17; Eph 2:20-22), related to the church as the body of Christ. This stands in the background of 5:1-4. Paul's use was related to Jesus' own use of "temple" for his body, which was to be resurrected (John 2:21; see Acts 6:13; 7:48; 17:24). Christians are "a spiritual house to be a holy priesthood, offering spiritual sacrifices acceptable to God by Jesus Christ" (1 Pet 2:5; see Exod 19:6).

Paul views the ethical response of Christians in terms of presenting themselves "as living sacrifices, holy and pleasing to God." Paul describes this self-offering of believers as their "spiritual act of worship" (Rom 12:1). The writer to the Hebrews spoke of ethical integrity as "a sacrifice of praise—the fruit of lips that confess [God's] name." "To do good and to share with others" are the "sacrifices" with which "God is pleased" (Heb 13:15-16). The Qumran community used similar imagery. They refer to "the oblation of the lips" as a "pleasant savor on the altar." And they considered themselves "a true and distinctive temple—a veritable holy of holies— . . . a true and distinctive synagogue made up of laymen who walk in integrity" (1QS 9:3-6 from Gaster 1957, 57). Paul's temple imagery vividly sets the stage for his concluding exhortation in 7:1.

Paul highlights his point with an OT quotation that conflates Lev 26:12 and Ezek 37:27. He perhaps alludes to the Law and the Prophets, to promises designed to inspire and sustain obedience. Paul varies the formulas with which he introduces OT quotations. Here, **As God has said,** is unique in the NT (but see 4:6). Paul views the whole of Scripture as the word of God.

The expressions **among them** and **they will be** come from Ezekiel. The verb *emperipatēsō* (**I will . . . walk**) is from Leviticus. Both OT passages contain the covenantal formula **I will be their God, and they will be my people** (see also Jer 32:38). In Leviticus, it recalls the constitution of Israel as a people after their Exodus from Egypt. In Ezekiel the covenant formula looks forward to the reconstitution of the nation after their return from exile in Babylon, viewed as a second Exodus (see Ezek 27:11-14, 21).

Paul sees the ancient promises that describe God's presence with his people and his covenant relationship with them throughout their history as being fulfilled in the present new covenant community. Restoration is taking place now. The church in Corinth is a living part of the **people** of God in whom **the living God** dwells.

The continuing promises of God to them are fourfold: **I will live . . .** [I will] **walk . . . I will be . . . they will be.** In this light, any compromise with idolatry and its attendant moral corruption are utterly irreconcilable with the life of the church as **the temple of the living God,** the place where the presence of God is uniquely found (see 1 Cor 3:16-17).

■ **17** In the NT generally and in Paul's writings in particular, the privilege of grace always leads to ethical consequences. So Paul's next word is **Therefore** (*dio*). Significantly, even his conclusion in vv 17-18 is expressed in the language of Scripture. It consists of a threefold call to separation with an accompanying assurance of divine acceptance. The words are adapted from Isa 52:11 and Ezek 20:34 (LXX).

Isaiah 52:11 is a call to the Jews in exile in Babylon to "depart, depart, go out from there! Touch no unclean thing! Come out from it and be pure, you who carry the vessels of the LORD" (see Ezra 1:7-11; Jer 51:45; Rev 18:4). In view, in contrast to "the vessels of the LORD," were probably religious objects associated with Babylonian idol worship, now given a general application by Paul (see 1 Thess 5:22).

Ezekiel 20:34 was a promise to those called out of an idolatrous land, which God would judge and purify. Paul selects only the assurance, "I will welcome you" (NRSV), for his purposes. The aorist tense of the three imperative verbs indicates that the break with pagan practices Paul calls for is to be decisive: **come out . . . be separate . . . touch no.** The promise, expressed in the future tense, is that from now on God **will receive** them.

■ **18** In v 18, Paul rewrites the promise to David of a royal dynasty in 2 Sam 7:14 (see 2 Sam 7:8-16). He probably is also thinking here of Isa 43:6. There the promise of a second exodus for a captive people is applied to both sons and daughters (see Isa 49:22; Hos 2:1). This may explain Paul's addition of **daughters** to his quotation from 2 Sam 7:14. Paul is egalitarian in his desire to be reconciled with the women as well as the men of the church at Corinth. With God as their **Father** and the Corinthians as his **sons and daughters,** the church is now a family as well as a temple. But more importantly, Paul's quotations, linking the eternal Davidic covenant and the postexilic restoration of the nation of Israel, apply these promises to the church. Paul announces God's invitation to the Christian men and women of Corinth to participate in the fulfillment of God's end-time promises.

Paul takes the ascription **says the Lord Almighty** from the beginning of the Nathan oracle in 2 Sam 7:8. In the NT, the title *pantokratōr*, the ***"All-Powerful, Omnipotent (One)"*** (BDAG 2000, 755), is used only here and in Revelation (1:8; 4:8; 11:17; 15:3; 16:7, 14; 19:6, 15; 21:22). This inspires confidence in God's ability to fulfill His promises.

Paul's loose quotations, with variations in the text in 6:16-18, reflect the methods used in the Jewish interpretive method known as *Midrash pesher.* He incorporates his contemporary interpretation into the text itself to reapply the ancient prophecies to the messianic age. He applies (1) the original command to Israel regarding Babylon to the relation of Christians to unbelievers and (2) the promise given to David and his line to the church as the body of Christ (Ellis 1957, 144, see 90, 139-49). Paul's fusing of the various references into one citation indicates that for him and his readers "it was more important to understand that these imperatives and promises were the very words of God than to know from where they came" (Matera 2003, 165).

■ **7:1** Paul brings his "relevant digression" to a close with an exhortation in 7:1. Its opening inferential particle, *oun*, ***Therefore*** (omitted in the NIV), indicates that it sums up the preceding appeals (6:14, 17; see 6:1).

On the basis of **these** great **promises,** Paul reformulates and expands the command of 6:14. Here he addresses the Corinthians as his **dear friends** (*agapētoi*, ***beloved***). ***Beloved*** is an address frequently used by Paul for those with whom he enjoys a close and congenial relationship (2 Cor 12:19; Rom 12:19; 1 Cor 15:58; Phil 2:12; 4:1; BDAG 2000, 7).

Paul supports his opening and closing exhortations in 6:14 and 7:1 with intervening arguments constructed loosely from various passages of Scripture. The key imperative is imbedded in 6:17. One could say that there is really one exhortation, given in three forms. Together these apply the OT injunction "Touch no unclean thing" to the life of the church.

Paul's call for ethical living employs a hortatory aorist subjunctive: **Let us purify ourselves** (see Eph 5:26; Titus 2:14). Such exhortations are less forceful than commands (in the imperative mood). They invite the audience to join the author in pursuing the shared expectation.

The term *katharisōmen* (**purify** or ***cleanse***) originated in cultic settings (see Mark 7:19; Acts 10:15; 11:9). It is used in the Gospels for the healing of leprosy (Matt 8:2-3; 11:5; Mark 1:42; Luke 4:27). But here its scope is extended to include moral cleansing (BDAG 2000, 488-89; see Jas 4:8; 1 John 1:7; Heb 9:14). For this cleansing of life to occur presumes "the requisite grace" (Clarke 1854, 2:344) of the transforming Spirit (see Rom 8:1-4 and 12:2). Only in this sense are they responsible for its doing. The ethical cleavage between their old pagan way of life and their new way of life in Christ is to be both decisive and comprehensive (see Rom 13:13).

Let us purify, as a constative aorist, looks to a decisive course of action characterizing life as a whole. Thus, it should apply to "every defilement of body and of spirit" (NRSV). "Defilement" (*molysmou*), used only here in the NT, refers to the moral and spiritual contamination that results from participation in pagan practices.

The terms **body** (*sarkos*, ***flesh***) and **spirit** (*pneumatos*), in the expression "every defilement of body and of spirit" (NRSV), are objective genitives. Thus, the NIV paraphrases: **everything that contaminates body and spirit.**

Here, Paul does not use ***flesh*** and **spirit** as opposing ethical principles, as he does in Romans (e.g., 8:1-11) and Galatians (e.g., 5:16-24). Instead, he uses them in a popular manner to comprehend the whole person viewed physically and spiritually. Paul calls for a thorough moral cleansing that will affect the Corinthians' entire existence (see 1 Cor 7:34; 1 Thess 5:23). John Wesley speaks of sanctification as cleansing from all outward and inward sin (1950, 661).

Paul's point is that Christians must make and sustain a clean break from any activity or association that would defile them. All acts and attitudes that might compromise the singleness of their devotion to the will of God are to be avoided. The decisive break from defiling pagan associations (6:17) is to characterize all of their living (see Rom 12:1-2).

Paul further interprets his primary exhortation in the aorist tense—**Let us purify ourselves**—with a circumstantial adverbial participle in the present tense. It is literally: **perfecting holiness out of reverence for God.** Nevertheless, its circumstantial relationship with the main verb gives it the force of a secondary exhortation: ***Let us perfect holiness in the fear of God.***

The term **perfecting** (*epiteLountes*) involves bringing **"about a result according to plan or objective"** (BDAG 2000, 383). The durative force of the present tense of the participle points to repeated actions viewed holistically. The break with defiling influences must be decisive. But the process of cleansing is ongoing. Christians cleanse themselves effectively when, in every opportunity that presents itself, they turn from what contaminates **body and spirit.** This entails seeking moment by moment to attain the goal of an appropriate ethical response to a holy God (Phil 3:14).

For Paul the **perfecting** of **holiness** is the purpose of the Christian life (see Rom 6:19). Adam Clarke defines this unending process as "getting the whole mind of Christ brought into the soul." This is "the grand object of a genuine Christian pursuit" (Clarke 1854, 2:344).

The term **holiness** (*hagiōsynēn*) is used elsewhere by Paul only in Rom 1:4 and 1 Thess 3:13. It refers to a quality of ethical and moral life resulting from reconciliation with God in Christ (2 Cor 5:18-21). Its cognate term *hagiasmos,* more frequent in the NT, is normally translated "sanctification" (see 1 Cor 1:30 NASB). It indicates a "sanctifying action" with an ethical force (Rom 6:19, 22; 1 Thess 4:3-4, 7; 2 Thess 2:13; 1 Tim 2:15; Heb 12:14; 1 Pet 1:2).

In 2 Cor 7:1, the present participle **perfecting** emphasizes the need for continuous and practical ethical progress toward full Christlikeness (3:18; see 1 John 3:2). This is a constant aim in the daily lives of those who live **out of reverence for God** or "in the fear of God" (NRSV).

Murray Harris suggests that the preposition "in" (*en*) could have causal (i.e., ***because of the fear of God***) or circumstantial (i.e., ***while fearing God***) force. But here it is best taken as instrumental (i.e., ***with the fear of God***). Of course, "fear" here is not about fright or terror at the thought of God or impending judgment. It concerns an appropriate **reverence for** a holy God (see 2 Cor 5:10-11). This is basic and essential to the pursuit of **holiness.** Christian ethics needs the sanction of the holy! (Harris 2005, 514).

There is a paradox here. Those who have been brought definitively into a sanctified relationship to God in Jesus Christ (1 Cor 1:2, 30; see Heb 2:11; 10:10, 14, 29; 13:12) must ever be reaching for the ethical ideals consistent with that relationship. Holiness is both a gift and a task. We are to become what we are. We are to be who we can be, thanks to God's empowering presence in our lives. Such an actualizing attitude to life (see Phil 3:12-15) is the respect and reverence owed a holy God by the community that is both his temple (1 Cor 3:17) and his people (2 Cor 6:16; Lev 19:2).

The Scottish Presbyterian scholar James Denney wrote over a century ago: "the prompt decisive side" of a holy life is represented in ***let us cleanse ourselves.*** But its patient, laborious side is represented in ***perfecting holiness in the fear of God*** (1943 [repr.], 5:776).

FROM THE TEXT

The focus of Paul's appeal in 2 Cor 6:14—7:1 is not on a "second crisis" moment of entire sanctification. It is on the actualization of the holiness ethic—actually living as holy people. But it certainly presupposes a crisis moment at a definitive point along the Christian journey.

To be holy means first and foremost that we belong to God. Our conception of God and the extent of our surrender to God's enabling power in our lives determine the moral and ethical character of our relationship with him. At some stage in our Christian journey, we face the issue of total surrender to God. Our surrender must be decisive and clear. We must fully repent of our self-sufficiency in things spiritual. The "crisis" moment will come when we finally allow grace to be truly grace in our living, whether or not we are fully aware of it.

In this passage Paul has made an impassioned outcry against worldliness of every form in the body of Christ. A church conformed to the world can never lead it. If the church is to be truly in the world ministering to human needs, it must cleanse itself from the spirit of the world inside and out. This cleansing must extend even to the weapons of its warfare (2 Cor 10:4). The threefold call of 2 Cor 6:14—7:1 (see 6:17-18) presents us with both (1) the necessity and (2) the motivation for that quality of life that is actually **perfecting holiness out of reverence for God.**

Further Reading on 2 Cor 6:14—7:1

Betz, Hans Dieter. 1973. "2 Cor 6:14—7:1: An Anti-Pauline Fragment?" *Journal of Biblical Literature* 92:88-108.

Fee, Gordon D. 1976-77. "II Corinthians vi.14—vii.1 and Food Offered to Idols." *New Testament Studies* 23:140-61.

Fitzmeyer, Joseph A. 1971. "Qumran and the Interpolated Paragraph in 2 Cor 6:14—7:1." Pages 205-17 in *Essays on the Semitic Background of the New Testament.* London: Chapman.

Lambrecht, Jan. 1978. "The Fragment 2 Cor vi 14—vii 1: A Plea for Its Authenticity." Pages 143-61 in *Miscellanea Neotestamentica*. Vol. 2. Edited by T. Baarda, A. F. J. Klign, and W. C. van Unnik. Supplements to Novum Testamentum 47. Leiden: Brill. Repr. as pages 531-49 in Reimund Bieringer and Jan Lambrecht. 1994. *Studies on 2 Corinthians*. Bibliotheca Ephemeridum Theologicarum Lovaniensium, 102. Leuven: Leuven University Press/Peeters.

_________. 1983. "Structure and Line of Thought in 2 Cor 2,14—4,6." *Biblica* 64:344-80. Repr. as pages 257-94 in Reimund Bieringer and Jan Lambrecht. 1994. *Studies on 2 Corinthians*. Bibliotheca Ephemeridum Theologicarum Lovaniensium, 102. Leuven: Leuven University Press/Peeters.

McCant, Jerry W. 1999. Pages 62-68 in *2 Corinthians*. Readings: A New Biblical Commentary. Edited by John Jarick. Sheffield: Sheffield Academic Press.

Thrall, M. E. 1977-78. "The Problem of II Cor. vi.14—vii.1 in Some Recent Discussion." *New Testament Studies* 24:132-48.

3. Renewed Appeal for Fellowship (7:2-4)

BEHIND THE TEXT

In 7:2-4 Paul returns to his call for renewed mutual affection begun in 6:11-13: **Make room for us in your hearts** (v 2). Thus 6:11-13 has its reprise in 7:2-4, as Paul reiterates his plea of 6:13, "Open wide your hearts also" (6:13, see 6:11). Together these verses are an affectionate appeal without equal in the NT (Shillington 1998, 151).

What 7:2-4 means is made clear as Paul seeks to complete his reconciliation with the Corinthians. He appears to recognize questions in their minds about his conduct, for he insists with a threefold statement that he mistreated no one in Corinth. As a pivotal passage in the letter it looks both forward and backward. Second Corinthians 7:2-4 concludes Paul's lengthy digression on the nature of his ministry and its defense that began in 2:14. And it leads into the resumption of his account of his meeting with Titus in Macedonia begun in 2:12-13.

IN THE TEXT

■ **2** To the appeal, **Make room for us** (*chōrēsate hēmas*), most translations add the words **in your hearts** to make clear that Paul is picking up where he left off in 6:11: "our heart is wide open" (NRSV). The Corinthians must reciprocate if there is to be reconciliation. Genuine fellowship (*koinōnia*) in the faith requires sharing and mutuality. Paul is open to this display of mutual affection. And he urges them to respond in kind. He insists that he has never at any time **wronged, corrupted,** or **exploited** any of them. Whether or not they had accused him of being guilty of any of these, Paul clears the air.

The first verb, **wronged** (*ēdikēsamen*), is a general term for wrongdoing involving injury or unjust treatment (7:12; see 2:5-11). It is to do the exact opposite of what is right (*dikaios*). The timeless aorist tense implies that Paul never acted unjustly toward the Corinthians.

The second aorist verb, **corrupted** (*ephtheiramen*), has to do with morals or doctrine. Paul denies that he had ever corrupted the gospel by his preaching.

The third aorist verb, **exploited** (*epleonektēsamen*), means **"to take advantage of, *exploit, outwit, defraud, cheat*"** (BDAG 2000, 824). Paul uses the verb twice in 12:17-18 (see 2:11), where he denies taking from them financially.

The rhetorical effect of the three verbs in the aorist tense along with the threefold emphatic repetition of **no one** (*oudena*) makes the denial general rather than specific. It is possible that he responds to particular charges made against him (Harris 2005, 517), but this remains purely speculative. Paul insists upon his innocence to make a plea for mutual trust (Bultmann 1985, 177).

■ **3** Paul wants to avoid any possible misunderstanding with the Corinthians. So, he assures them: **I do not say this to condemn you** (see 6:11-13). On the contrary, his desire for mutual love and confidence is so intense that he can say to them, "you are in our hearts to die together and to live together" (NASB; see 1:6-7; 3:2; Phil 1:7). This is the key to all that follows.

The NIV translation reverses the Greek word order: **we would live or die with you.** It presumes, with most interpreters, that Paul is simply using a conventional expression of the inviolable bonds of loyalty between friends (see 2 Sam 15:21; Mark 14:31; John 11:16; Bultmann 1985, 178; see Furnish 1984, 367; and Martin 1986, 219, for secular parallels). Some interpreters, however, see an allusion to the death (aorist tense) and life (present tense) of Christ that is integral to Paul's understanding of his ministry, and in which the Corinthians are to participate (4:7-14).

The two meanings are hardly exclusive. The original word order (which mentions death first), as well as Paul's view of the gospel, of his apostolic ministry, and of life itself make a christological allusion likely. But the present context certainly stresses friendship (Matera 2003, 169-70; see Lambrecht 1999, 119, 125-27). Like a true friend, Paul insists that he is willing to share either life or death with the Corinthians. But can he even conceive of death and life apart from the death and resurrection of Christ?

■ **4** Verse 4 forms a transitional bridge to what follows. Paul's word choices take us back to the early chapters of the letter. And they point ahead to themes that will surface later in the letter. The terms ***comfort*** (*paraklēsei*), **joy** (see 7:7, 9, 13), and **troubles** (see 7:5) are particularly noteworthy. As in 1:3-8, the word and the theme ***comfort*** permeate the following paragraph (7:5-13, see vv 6, 7, 13). Its appearance in 7:13: "In this we find comfort" (NRSV), forms an *inclusio* with v 4. That is, the term ***comfort*** holds together this section of the letter, like literary bookends at its beginning and end.

Rather than condemn the Corinthians, Paul has **great confidence** (*pollē*

. . . *parrēsia*) in them. As in 3:12, he uses *parrēsia* to mean frank speech or "candor" (Furnish 1984, 385; see 3:12). From his open heart and candid speech Paul expresses his **great pride** (*pollē . . . kauchēsis*) in them (1:12-14; 7:14; 8:24; 9:2-4). The term *kauchēsis* ("boasting" [NASB]) can refer either to the act or the object of boasting or both (BDAG 2000, 537). Paul openly communicates his **great confidence** in the Corinthians to them. And he is equally open in his expressions of **great pride** in the Corinthians to others (Harris 2005, 520).

Thanks to the news Titus delivered (7:5-7), Paul is **greatly encouraged** about the situation in Corinth. Literally, he writes: ***I am filled with comfort.*** The perfect tense of the verb *peplērōmai* refers to the enduring result of a past event, here the coming of Titus (7:6). From the depths of despair, the good news buoys Paul's spirit to exuberance. His **joy** is ***overflowing*** (*hyperperisseuōmai*), even in all his **troubles** or ***affliction*** (*thlipsei*). As we have seen, at the heart of the letter is the vital relation between Paul's **great pride** and the sufferings of Christ (1:3-10; 4:8, 17; 6:4; see 7:5). Therefore, his **troubles** as well are open to the power of Christ's resurrection.

An inescapable link exists between Paul's two claims: **in all our troubles my joy knows no bounds** (v 4) and **we would live or die with you** (v 3). The apostle has kept the door open wide to full personal reconciliation by (1) the integrity of his behavior (v 2), (2) the depth of his affection (v 3); and (3) his positive attitude toward the Corinthians (v 4). Paul loves them with a love

that "bears all things, believes all things, hopes all things, endures all things" (1 Cor 13:7 NRSV).

4. The Coming of Titus (7:5-7)

In vv 5-7 Paul resumes the account of his travels in relation to the church in Corinth. These had occupied him in 1:12—2:13. But he left the story unfinished, turning to a lengthy parenthesis about his ministry in 2:14—7:4.

After his "painful visit" (see 2:1 and Introduction, "Paul's Relationship to the Church at Corinth"), Paul did not return to Corinth. Instead, he sent Titus from Ephesus to Corinth with the sorrowful letter. He hoped it would be well received, but feared it would not. Paul had traveled to Troas, where "the Lord had opened a door" for his ministry and expected to meet Titus, returning with news from the church. Titus, however, was not there. Restless, Paul moved on to Macedonia anxiously to await the return of Titus. There, he left his readers also waiting, breaking off his travel narrative to yield to an irresistible urge to give praise to God for his apostolic ministry (2:14—7:4).

We can only guess precisely what motivated Paul to break off his narrative to discuss the character of his apostolic ministry. This long digression (2:14—7:4) suggests that Paul wrote spontaneously. We can be grateful for this; his digressions elsewhere have resulted in some of our richest biblical treasures (e.g., 1 Cor 13; Phil 2:5-11). These verses (2:14—7:4) are remarkable in their theological insight as they give expression to the presence and work of God in Paul's ministry and the life of the Corinthian community (Matera 2003, 173).

■ **5** **For when** or ***For even when*** (*kai gar*) introduces Paul's explanation of what he has just said. He describes his anxiety on not finding Titus in Macedonia: **this body of ours had no rest.** Like "spirit" (*pneuma*) in 2:13 (see 7:13), **body** (*sarx: **flesh***) here refers to his entire person. His word choice perhaps emphasizes his human vulnerability, both psychical and physical.

Paul continues to describe his ***restless flesh*** in terminology reminiscent of 1:3-10 and 4:8: "we were afflicted in every way" (NRSV) or "on every side" (see v 4). He specifies his troubles (*thlibomenoi: **we were troubled***) as **conflicts on the outside, fears within.** He refers to his sufferings and anxious concern for the safety of Titus and the welfare of the church. Genuine concern, such as Paul had for Titus and the Corinthians, increases the capacity for suffering. The apostle, as human as any of us, was open to emotional agitation and inner fears. Tranquillity was not always his lot!

■ **6** Yet Paul does not stop here. With the strong adversative **But** (*alla*), he affirms the consolation of God in his life (v 6). His own experience taught him that God was "the Father of compassion and the God of all comfort" (1:3; see v 4). Now he describes God as the one **who comforts the downcast** ("the lowly"; BDAG 2000, 989). Perhaps his terminology was influenced by Isa 49:13 (LXX), where the prophet speaks of "the day of salvation" (Isa 49:8) as a new creation (see Isa 49:8-13). Recall that Paul quoted from this Servant Song in 6:2 (see the commentary).

Paul's word order in Greek places **God** in the emphatic final position. Literally, he wrote: ***But the one who comforts the lowly comforted us—God, by the presence of Titus.*** God is defined as the comforter. Paul's combination, **But God,** reminds us of his significant use of the expression "but now" (*nyni de*) in similar contrasts (e.g., Rom 3:21; 7:6; 1 Cor 13:13; 15:20; Gal 5:9; Col 3:8). God turned Paul's restless despair into boundless joy. But he did it **by the coming** [*parousiai*] **of Titus.**

■ **7** The ***arrival and resulting presence*** (*parousiai;* BDAG 2000, 780) of **Titus** meant more to the anxious Paul than just reunion with a beloved companion. With him came comforting news from Corinth, which rejuvenated the apostle.

Titus was anxious too. Paul's comfort came **not only by his coming.** It **also** came from "the comfort with which he [i.e., Titus] was comforted" (NASB). Paul's colleague in ministry shared in the apostle's joy. He was as anxious as Paul to see the Corinthians reconciled to Paul's mission. It was apparently their repentance (see 7:8-13, esp. v 13) that was the source of **the comfort** [they] **had given him.**

As in 1:3-7 the fourfold use of the Greek verb for "comfort" (*parakaleō*) in vv 6 and 7 is rhetorically striking. Both Paul and Titus were "comforted" by news Titus brought of the Corinthians' **longing, . . . deep sorrow,** and **ardent concern for** the apostle.

It was not only the coming of Titus, the news he delivered, or the comfort of Titus that comforted Paul. As he writes, he refers emphatically to <u>**your**</u> **longing . . .** <u>**your**</u> **deep sorrow,** <u>**your**</u> **ardent concern** (emphasis added). The threefold repetition of *hymōn*, **your,** focuses Paul's appreciation on the tangible expressions of the Corinthians' love for him (*hyper emou*, **for me,** is mentioned only once, despite the NIV translation). The church was reciprocating Paul's love for them.

Paul understood all of this human activity from a theological perspective as ultimately the work of the "God, who comforts" (v 6). Whatever the ultimate and intermediate causes, all this caused Paul's **joy** to be **greater than ever** ("I rejoiced still more," NRSV).

These verses reveal (1) that human affairs had the power to depress the apostle. But (2) the God who has "compassion on his afflicted ones" (Isa 49:13) was (3) in his sovereign power able through human agency to lift his depression: "Praise be to . . . the God of all comfort" (2 Cor 1:3).

5. The Repentance of the Church (7:8-13*a*)

In vv 8-13*a* Paul delicately attempts to complete his reconciliation with the church by recounting recent events well known to the Corinthians. If all the misunderstandings and suspicions are to be removed from their relationship, the past must be opened up, not covered over, only to rise again in some future quarrel. In these verses Paul:

- commends them for their response to his sorrowful letter
- assures them of their innocence in the matter and
- establishes Titus with the Corinthians as a reliable and effective representative of both them and the apostle

In the process Paul deals theologically with the pain and sorrow he caused them in terms of their relation to God and personally in their relation to him. He proves that he does indeed have the Corinthians in his heart "to die together and to live together" (7:3 NASB).

■ **8-9*a*** In v 8 Paul begins to explain (*hoti*, ***because***) his renewed and boundless joy (7:7). He wrote the **letter** that **caused** them **sorrow** "out of great distress [*thlipseōs*] and anguish of heart" (2:4, see vv 3-11). And after he sent it, he ***regretted*** (*metemelomēn*) it.

Paul does not mention or explain here his canceled visit (see 1:23; 1:15-17), but only this **letter.** This letter had caused them pain and grief. Paul had sent it with Titus that the Corinthians might know the extent of Paul's love for them (2:4). But despite his best intentions, there were moments before Titus's return that the apostle **did regret** sending the letter. But now that the letter has achieved its desired end, he does **not regret it.**

What Paul means in vv 8*b*-9*a* seems clear enough. But his Greek syntax is difficult. With the exception of the omission of ***for*** (*gar*) in ***for* I see** (*blepō gar*), the NIV gives an acceptable solution: **Though I did regret it—I see that my letter hurt** [*elypēsen, **made . . . sorrowful***] **you, but only for a little while—yet now I am happy** (*chairō, **I rejoice;*** vv 8*b*-9*a;* see Harris 2005, 534-35; Thrall 2004, 491). Paul did not **regret** sending the letter, because the **sorrow** (*elypēsa, **I made . . . sorry***) it caused was not permanent. It was **only for a little while.** Paul did the right thing. But while their reception of the letter hung in the balance, he ***was regretting it.***

The verb *metamelomai* appears just twice in Paul's letters, both in v 8. It appears once in the present (**I do . . . regret**) and once in the imperfect (**I did regret**) tense. Both tenses emphasize a continuous or repeated activity—one in the present, the other in the past.

■ **9*b*** Paul can ***now rejoice,*** not because he made them sorrowful, but because of the fruit of their **sorrow:** it **led** [them] **to repentance.** The rare noun *metanoia,* **repentance,** appears only four times in Paul's letters (vv 9-10; Rom 2:4; 2 Tim 2:25). The verb form occurs just once (2 Cor 12:21).

Both *metamelomai* and *metanoia* refer to a change of mind. The distinction between them here is that the former indicates a change of mood and the latter a change of view. The first entails only a change of feelings—remorse or regret; the second, a change of heart—repentance, a turning in attitude and behavior. Thus, repentance is a spiritual more than an emotional change (Denney 1943, 5:779). The translations represent this distinction well.

Rather than **repentance,** "faith" was Paul's preferred word to describe one's turning to God in the Gentile world. The early church in its Jewish environment favored the term "repentance" (Matt 3:11; Luke 24:27; Acts 2:38; 3:19; 5:31; 11:18). Both here and in 12:21, Paul uses the terminology of repentance to describe what Christians do to remedy their wrong choices. In Paul's usage, repentance is for those in the church, not for unbelievers outside.

The Corinthians' **sorrow** was *kata Theon,* **as God intended**—"according to the will of God" (NASB; see Rom 8:27). It was a "godly grief" (NRSV). The same expression appears in vv 9, 10, and 11. The Corinthians **were not** permanently **harmed in any way** by Paul's letter. No loss was suffered by them in the realm of grace.

■ **10** ***For*** (*gar*), as Paul writes again in v 10, their pain was a **godly sorrow** (*kata Theon*). This is because it produced the kind of **repentance that leads to salvation.** It was a **repentance *without* regret** (*ametamelēton*). A "repentance . . . not to be repented of" (KJV) would seem to be an oxymoron. But perhaps Paul intended ***without regret*** (*ametamelēton*) to modify the whole of the preceding expression—a **repentance that leads to salvation,** instead of simply the word **repentance.** But the meaning is hardly different. Their **repentance,** their change of heart, was a sign that the Spirit of God was at work in them (see Acts 11:18) in both his short- and long-range goals of **salvation** (see Rom 8:18-25).

Remorse vs. Repentance

In Matt 27:3, the verb *metamelomai* describes the remorse of Judas Iscariot following his betrayal of Jesus and before his suicide. It appears elsewhere only in Matt 21:30, 32; 2 Cor 7:8; and Heb 7:21. The cognate adjective *ametalmelētos* (**no regret**) appears only in 2 Cor 7:10 and Rom 11:29.

Peter's bitter tears after denying Jesus three times (Matt 26:75) were turned into joy and worship following the resurrection of Jesus (Matt 28:8, 17). Sadly, Judas's remorse over his betrayal of Jesus did not lead him to repent, but to hang himself (Matt 27:3-10). Paul puts it this way: "Godly sorrow brings repentance that leads to salvation and leaves no regret, but worldly sorrow brings death" (2 Cor 7:10).

Paul contrasts the Corinthians' **godly sorrow** (*kata Theon lypē*) with **worldly sorrow** (*tou kosmou lypē*). The former **sorrow** was within the realm and will of God. He used it to achieve his saving ends. The latter is a **sorrow** within the sphere of the world (*tou kosmou*). Both in the present and in the future it ultimately produces only **death**.

The contrast is between spiritual health and a deadly spirit—peace and joy over against resentment and bitterness. The real difference is not the character or source of the pain or sorrow. The difference is in how it is endured, *kata Theon* or *tou kosmou*.

The NIV translates two slightly different verbs in v 10 identically: **brings**
7:10-11 [*ergazetai*] **repentance . . . brings** [*katergazetai*] **death.** The difference may be merely stylistic. But Paul may have intended a distinction in emphasis between the *process* and the *result* of the two different kinds of **sorrow—godly** and **worldly.** This would be consistent with his use of two slightly different words describing a change of mind in vv 8-10.

■ **11** The apostle expresses his joy at the Corinthians' response with considerable rhetorical flourish. **See** (*idou, **Behold!***) is a call to give close consideration. It introduces seven nouns Paul says verify the genuineness of their repentance. It **produced** (*kateirgasato;* note the same verb in v 10) "this very thing, this godly sorrow" (NASB).

All seven nouns are emphatically introduced by a repeated **what.** In Greek the first is *posēn,* literally ***how great***. Its intensive force is carried through with a sixfold repeated *alla*. This adversative particle is usually translated "but." Here, in this emphatic series, however, it indicates "yes, indeed" (BDAG 2000, 45).

The first exclamation, **what earnestness** or ***eagerness,*** is linked closely to the verb **produced** (*posēn kateirgasato hymin spoudēn*). It may be intended as a comprehensive term to be illustrated by the six terms that follow (see NASB).

The Corinthians are now eager to deal with the problems in their church (see v 12). Indeed, Paul writes, you possess an **eagerness to clear your-**

selves (*alla apologian*). The NIV appropriately paraphrases the term *apologian,* the usual word for a legal defense (see Acts 25:16; 1 Tim 4:16). Here the term simply means that they are eager and ready to clear themselves from blame in the matter (see Phil 1:7, 16; 1 Pet 3:15). ***Yes, and what a defense!***

Paul seems to refer obliquely to the humiliating circumstances that led to his hasty departure from Corinth after his painful visit (see 2:1; 7:12). Their eagerness to make the matter right may explain Paul's third noun. They have finally expressed their **indignation** toward the troublemaker who injured Paul. And perhaps they are now indignant about their own slowness to defend their apostle.

Their present **alarm** (*phobon, **fear***) was about how the unfortunate situation would affect their relation to Paul and the future of the church. Perhaps, they dreaded his coming to discipline them (see 1:23; 13:1-2; 1 Cor 4:21).

Paul's language is legal. He adopts the terminology of the court of law. Paul, the accused defendant, presents himself as instead the prosecutor and judge of the Corinthians (McCant 1999, 72). Nevertheless, Paul views his relationship with the Corinthians fully in personal terms.

The three remaining nouns—**what longing, what concern, what readiness to see justice done**—indicate that the Corinthians long to be fully reunited with their apostle. They are zealous to defend the honor and authority of Paul against those who have dishonored him. They have adequately disciplined the one who had so grievously offended him (2:6; 7:12).

The first of these last three terms probably express the Corinthians' ***desire*** (*epipothēsin*) to experience their restored relationship with Paul in person. The second term indicates their ***zeal*** (*zēlon*) to respond positively to Paul. The third term describes their "vindication" (*ekdikēsin,* NASB). This may refer to their desire **to see justice done** or to the actual administration of **justice**—the appropriate "punishment" (NRSV) of the wrongdoer.

More difficult to understand is "how" they established their innocence. Paul writes, **At every point you have proved yourselves to be innocent in this matter. Innocent** (*hagnous*) was originally a cultic word meaning ***"pure, holy"*** (BDAG 2000, 13; see 11:2; Titus 2:5; 1 John 3:3). Here it has the forensic sense of "guiltless" (NRSV) or **innocent.**

Had they been completely **innocent** in the particular **matter** (*pragmati*) from the very beginning? Paul had not wrongly judged them guilty earlier, had he? If they had always been innocent, what was their need for **repentance** (vv 9-10)? Most likely Paul means that they overcame their previous complacency, complicity, or acquiescence in the wrongdoing. By disciplining the wrongdoer, they have taken the action that has **proved** (*synestēsate, **demonstrated***) their present innocence in relation to the instigator of the problem in the church. Thus, their conduct is now *right* (Martin 1986, 236).

■ **12** In v 12, Paul explains why (and why not) he wrote the sorrowful letter (see v 8). He wrote that their ***earnestness*** (*spoudēn,* earnest care; see v 11) might be made clear to them. That is, they needed to come to appreciate their own real feelings of devotion to Paul **before God** (see 4:2).

No doubt the painful incident in Corinth was one occasion for writing the sorrowful letter. But Paul did not write to call attention to the wrongdoer or to protest the wrong he had done to Paul. There was a more important issue underlying it all than just **the one who did the wrong** and **the injured party.**

Paul speaks for himself and of himself. He had been wronged. But it was their spiritual integrity in the matter of their relation to the apostle that was at stake. The trouble in the church had cast a cloud of disloyalty and disrespect over the Corinthians' attitude toward their spiritual father. Thus, the Corinthians needed to be reminded that their relationship with God and their relations with Paul were inseparable.

■ **13*a*** **By all this we are encouraged** (*parakeklēmetha,* "find comfort," NRSV). The perfect tense of the verb stresses Paul's present state of mind that resulted from the coming of Titus (see 7:5-7). The verb used picks up the language of conflict and resolution from 7:6-7 and 1:3-7.

As their father in the faith, Paul is so concerned for their ultimate spiritual well-being that (1) he does not hesitate to cause them pain, even though he is no less pained for doing so (vv 8-9). (2) Such pain when used by God produces the kind of repentance that leads *(a)* to salvation and *(b)* to the correction of the difficulties within the church (vv 10-12).

7:12-13*b*

6. The Experience of Titus in Corinth (7:13*b*-16)

Paul has already expressed his reaction to the report of Titus (7:5-9). And he has considered the Corinthians' response to the sorrowful letter (7:9-12). But here, Paul picks up again the thought of vv 6-7. He gives renewed attention to the experience of Titus in Corinth. Earlier Paul focused his attention on the comfort Titus had given him. Now, he describes the favorable effect Titus's positive reception in Corinth had on his delegate. And Paul commends them for their behavior in the matter. This has only strengthened the apostle's faith in the church. In these closing verses of the first part of the letter, Paul prepares the way for Titus's return to Corinth on another mission that Paul will explicate in chs 8 and 9.

■ **13*b*** **In addition** (see BDAG 2000, 365 s.v. *epi de*) marks Paul's emotional progression from **encouragement** (*paraklēsei:* "comfort," NRSV) to joy. The apostle "rejoiced [*echarēmen*] still more at the joy [*epi tēi charai*] of Titus" (NRSV). Paul's joy, a recurrent theme in ch 7 (see vv 4, 7, 13), indicates the major movements within the chapter.

Paul was **especially delighted to see how happy Titus was** after his visit to Corinth. Titus's joy gave Paul ***even much more*** (*mallon*) joy than Titus's comfort had comforted him (see 7:6-7). Given Paul's treatment during the painful visit and the contents of the sorrowful letter he carried, Titus had reason to be concerned about the reception he might receive in Corinth. No wonder his warm welcome gave him comfort and joy!

Paul's joy increased when he learned that Titus's **spirit** was **refreshed by all** the church. Titus was happy because the church had "set his mind completely at rest" (NEB; see 2:13). Paul uses **spirit** (*pneuma*) here as in 2:13 to refer to his inner disposition. Only there, the situation was quite different: "I had no rest for my spirit" (NASB; see 7:5). The joy of the moment can explain Paul's sweeping reference to **all of you** (*pantōn hymōn*), conveniently ignoring the lingering problems in the Corinthian church acknowledged in 6:14—7:1. But it is more difficult to reconcile this all-inclusive treatment of the church in light of chs 10—13. Perhaps the more negative situation reflected there had not yet developed when Paul wrote this part of the letter. But if the situation significantly deteriorated, one wonders why Paul did not simply scrap the first nine chapters of the letter and send only 10—13. (See the Introduction to the commentary and Harris 2005, 549.)

■ **14** Paul offers a further reason for his rejoicing over Corinth's reception of Titus. The apostle had not been **embarrassed** (*katēischynthēn*, ***dishonored, disgraced, shamed;*** BDAG 2000, 517) by his somewhat qualified (*ti*) boasting to Titus about how the Corinthians would receive him. His assurances had not been overly optimistic. **But just as everything we said to you was true, so our boasting about you to Titus has proved to be true as well.** The truth of Paul's Spirit-inspired love for them had penetrated to the genuineness of their care for him (vv 11-12). Paul was never one to despair of the grace of God in his converts. And he believed his boast about them would continue to be vindicated (see 8:24).

Far from being shamed by braggadocio, ***on the contrary*** (*alla*, **But**), Paul's boast about them proved to be true. But Paul insists that he always spoke ***all things*** to them ***in truth.*** He takes for granted here what he had been constrained to defend earlier in the letter. After all, the Corinthians' conduct was a testimony to the consistency of the apostle's character and the reliability of his work among them.

■ **15** When Titus **remembers** the Corinthians' ***obedience*** (see 2:9) to Paul and to himself in their reception of him, **his affection for** them **is all the greater.** As in 6:12, **affection** (*splanchna*), as the seat of human emotions, could just as well be translated "heart" (NRSV).

Significantly Paul describes their reception of Titus as **with fear and trembling.** In the NT, this phrase is used only by Paul (1 Cor 2:3; Phil 2:12; Eph 6:5). The OT background of the phrase is twofold. It can refer to the proper human stance before the divine majesty (Ps 2:11). Or, it can refer to the human reaction to God's protective power (Exod 15:16; Deut 2:25; 11:25; Isa 19:16; see Harris 2005, 532; Hafemann 2000, 316). Here it is the reaction of the Corinthians to the presence of Titus in their midst as the delegate of the apostle. Paul may allude directly to Isa 19:16. There it refers to the terror Egypt will experience when it becomes aware of God's "uplifted hand . . . against them." This would lend additional support to the assumption that Paul understands Isaiah's proclamation of a "second exodus" as fulfilled in the gospel ministry (see 6:2, 17; 5:12).

The Corinthians' **fear and trembling** was due ultimately to their recognition of Titus as not only the authoritative representative of the apostle, but as a divine messenger. Paul began his ministry in Corinth "in . . . fear, and with much trembling" (1 Cor 2:3), because he sensed his awesome responsibility before God. It was now appropriate that the hesitant congregation in Corinth should experience **fear and trembling** when it faced up to its responsibility to those who proclaimed the will of God to them.

■ **16** Here again Paul uses the recurring theme of joy (see vv 4, 7, 13) to affirm that his reconciliation with the Corinthians is effective and satisfactory. **I am glad** [*chairō:* "I rejoice," NRSV] **I can have complete confidence in you.** Paul rejoices *hoti,* either "because" (NRSV) or "that" (NASB) he has **complete confidence** in them. Paul asserts that ***in everything*** (*en panti*) he now finds himself able to depend (*tharrō;* BDAG 2000, 444) on the Corinthians.

With persuasive rhetoric, Paul has intentionally laid the groundwork for the requests to follow in chs 8—9. Perhaps, he looks forward to a "joyful visit," in contrast to his previous "painful visit." But to what extent was Paul's **complete confidence** misplaced? We know from 2 Cor 10—13 that there were still problems to be faced (see the commentary Introduction). Nevertheless, strong

hints in Romans (15:23-28; 16:1) suggest that Corinth apparently did rise to the occasion and support Paul's collection scheme, which is his concern in 2 Cor 8—9.

Paul closes this first section of the Epistle (1:12—7:16) on a positive note. Hughes describes 7:16 as "the delicate pin around which the whole of the epistle pivots" (1962, 282). It serves as a transition to what follows in the rest of the letter. His confidence in the Corinthians has been sorely tested. But it holds steady. It gives Paul the courage to bring up the matter of their responsibility to other Christians in need in chs 8—9. And it gives him the confidence to denounce those false apostles who have been undermining his authority in the church in chs 10—13. We cannot state the second point too strongly, since there seems to have been a time gap between his writing of chs 1—9 and 10—13.

The apostle's sense of joy (7:13*b*-16) is intimately tied to the total well-being of those with whom he is lovingly concerned, whether it is (1) his fellow worker (vv 13-14), or (2) his converts to the faith (vv 15-16). Paul's confidence in the Corinthians (6:11—7:16) arises from (1) the openness of his heart and life to them (6:11—7:4); (2) the continued operation of the grace of God in the lives of the Corinthian believers (7:5-12); and (3) his conviction of their real attitude toward him when undisturbed by sinister outside influences (7:13-16).

Barclay comments that Paul has experienced the three great human joys, "the joy of reconciliation," "the joy of seeing someone in whom you believe justifying that belief," and "the joy of seeing someone you love welcomed and well-treated" (Barclay 1956, 252). On Paul's side the reconciliation (1:12—7:16) has been effected by completely laying open (1) the details of his relations with them (1:12—2:14); (2) the Christlike motives of his ministry among them (3:1—6:10); and (3) the depth of his affection toward them (6:11—7:16).

FROM THE TEXT

Is it appropriate to use the designations "Father" and "children" for the relationship between pastor and people? The Apostle Paul speaks to the Christians in Corinth as "my children" (6:13). The language of personal feeling characterizes 6:11-13 and 7:2-16 with an intensity of affection seldom seen elsewhere in Paul's letters. In between the two expressions of affection is a strong exhortation to a separated or holy life (6:14—7:1). In this lengthy parenthesis Paul employs an OT quotation (2 Sam 7:14) affirming that God relates as a Father to his children (6:18), the people of God, the church.

How are we to combine Paul's apparently stringent call to holiness with the tender and intimate relationship he desires with the Corinthians? Do these two inherently go together in the ministry of the local church? What can we learn from Paul about how pastor and people are to relate to each other in the life of the congregation?

We suggest at least three primary areas of relevance to the present life of a healthy and effective church: First, *pastor and people are to cultivate an atmosphere of mutual openness and love* (6:11-13). Second, *pastor and people are to maintain a relationship of trust and confidence in each other* (7:2-16). And third, *pastor and people are to devote themselves as one to holiness of heart and life* (6:14—7:1). The first two surround the third, and the third is at the heart of the integrity of the first two. The responsibility of the "are to" rests equally on pastor and people—*cultivate, maintain,* and *devote.* We look briefly at the first two, before engaging in a more extensive discussion of the third, concerning *holiness.*

First, *pastor and people are to cultivate an atmosphere of mutual openness and love* (6:11-13). Paul's language at this point is vivid, for his metaphors are those of an open mouth, an enlarged heart, and a visceral affection. John Chrysostom (344/354-407) explains: "Paul means by this that he talks to the Corinthians freely, as he would to people whom he loves. He holds nothing back and suppresses nothing. Nothing is wider than Paul's heart, which loved all the believers with the passion which one might have toward the object of one's affection" (ACCS NT 7:260). Paul's expressions suggest that the characteristics of the atmosphere within which an effective ministry of pastor and people can thrive must be open not closed, deep not shallow, spacious not narrow, honest not deceitful, and other- rather than self-seeking. Oscar Reed was correct when he wrote that "the success of a Christian minister depends, to a large extent, on his love and compassion for his people" (1976, 237). Freedom of speech and wideness of heart are the ocean upon which grace can sail unrestricted.

Second, *pastor and people are to maintain a relationship of trust and confidence in each other* (7:2-16). The metaphor continues from 6:13 to 7:2: **Make room for us in your hearts.** If the people are to do this, then the pastor must in no way take advantage of them. Paul envisions a pastor who does not seek to wrong, corrupt, or exploit anyone in the congregation. Such pastoral care for their people is genuinely imbedded in the gospel of the death and resurrection of Jesus for such ministers. Thus, Paul's profession is characteristic: "you are in our hearts to die together and to live together" (7:3 NASB).

Such a minister "is a proclaimer of the gospel, not a motivational speaker" (Hafemann 2000, 317). The authority of ministers is in their message to the degree that they faithfully represent the gospel of Christ. When Paul wrote, he had just been "greatly encouraged." Therefore, he freely expressed the **confidence** and **pride** he had in the people and the **joy** he felt in relation to them (7:4).

It is significant that the implications of discipline appropriate to a father and his children are present in the situation (7:5-16). Mutual trust and confidence between pastor and people take careful maintenance. Issues that create discord must be faced.

In Corinth Paul had to deal with a problem in his relationship with the church. Damage control and restoration needed to take place. And Titus had to be sent with a disciplinary letter to heal the wounds. Paul speaks prophetically as an apostle and a spiritual father—that is, as a true minister.

We understand why Paul experienced such deep distress as he waited for the return of Titus. But we also understand why with his return, Paul was so greatly comforted by the joyful news of the Corinthians' reception of both Titus and the corrective letter he delivered. Their attitudes and behaviors had changed. That is, **repentance** had occurred. And the Corinthians' true desire to be at one with Paul, their father in the faith, was again fully evident. The apostle's **confidence** in the church is now **complete,** and the love they have for each other renewed.

Paul's use of the word **repentance** in the phrase ***repentance unto salvation*** is significant. It indicates that serious issues in the spiritual welfare of both pastor and people are at stake in their relationship. The contrasting phrases **godly sorrow** and **worldly sorrow** (v 10) are also significant. James Denney observed more than a century ago: "want of love and confidence between the minister of the Gospel and those to whom he ministers has great power to frustrate the grace of God" (1943 [repr.], 5:775). But when pastor and people value and give sincere attention to preserving their trust and confidence in each other, joy will permeate the life of the church. More importantly, grace will flow freely in their lives inside and outside the church.

Third, *pastor and people are to devote themselves as one to holiness of heart and life* (6:14—7:1). It is theologically significant that a passage about the integrity of the church as "the temple of the living God" (6:16) is placed between passages dealing with the integrity of relationships within the church. The holy God seeks to live in the individual lives and in the corporate fellowship of his people: "I will live with them and walk among them, and I will be their God, and they will be my people" (6:16). If nothing else, this means that the divine call to holiness of life and heart is of utmost and decisive importance for the people of God.

Without the reality of what biblical holiness means, the mutual openness, love, trust, and confidence that characterize the church as the church of God becomes impossible. The divine dimension, not common tastes and preferences or compatible personalities, constitute human relationships as truly Christian. The church as a true fellowship (*koinōnia*) is by biblical definition a horizontal sharing together in a vertical reality: "fellowship with us" entails "fellowship . . . with the Father and with his Son, Jesus Christ" (1 John 1:3; see 1 Cor 1:9; 10:16; 2 Cor 6:14; 13:13; Phil 2:1; 3:10; Acts 2:42). Fellowship in the gospel and in ministry is by definition mutual participation in the redeeming and sanctifying presence and mission of God.

It is imperative that we pay careful attention to the apostolic presentation of the call to holiness. Second Corinthians 6:14-18 tells us that it is a call *from* something and a call *to* something. It is a call from unethical and immoral living to ethical and moral living, from a clouded vision to an enlightened vision, from the domination of Satan to the lordship of God in Christ, and from unbelief and doubting to belief and trust. It is all summed up as a call *from* the worship of false gods *to* all of life found in the very sanctuary of God. Simply put, as Christians we are to be done with all forms of idolatry that confront us in so many guises. In view are those aspects of our lives that take the rightful place of God and contradict the "clean" or holy character of God, we hear the exhortation: "touch no unclean thing."

Barclay points out that "in first century Corinthian culture to be a Christian could mean that a person gave up their *trade,* or *social life,* or even *family ties"* (1956, 248). This is tragically still true in some areas of the world today. Profoundly put, we are privileged to live in the assurance that we are God's people, God's sons and daughters, with whom he lives and walks as our Father. The motivation to respond to such a call is twofold, both "from" and "to." Holiness is a deliverance and a gift!

In 7:1, Paul offers criteria by which to judge what the "unclean thing" is for us who walk with God. He states it clearly: "everything that contaminates body and spirit" or "all defilement of flesh and spirit" (NASB).

Two things are obvious: First, holiness is a matter of both the inner and the outer life. What we do with and to our all-too-human bodies is consequential. And what we allow to fester in our thoughts, motives, and feelings has consequence. Our whole persons and the whole of our lives are involved. Both flesh and spirit are to be kept holy!

Second, equally obvious is the test we apply throughout the day. We must seek to live moment by moment in the presence of God. As we do, we must ask: Does this action or thought defile or contaminate me, does it harm me physically, and does it darken my mind and heart? In the words of Scripture, Does our heart "condemn us" (1 John 3:20)? Has it left me feeling unkind, small, dirty, or estranged? If so, this thing, this thought, this attitude, this action, this emotion is not to be touched or admitted into our lives. It is to be denied any continuing access. We must no longer allow it to influence our living. This is the kind of living Paul describes as "perfecting holiness out of reverence for God." As Bengel (1687-1752) put it centuries ago, "It is not enough to begin; it is the end that crowns the work" (1895, 3:391).

This implies that the call to holiness is a *decisive* call to lifelong transformation. This is anticipated in 3:18: "we . . . are being transformed into his likeness with ever-increasing glory." The Benedictines speak here of the continuing "conversion of life" (*conversatio morum*). Holiness is obviously ethically progressive and thus processive. But as the term "decisive" suggests, it is also relationally definitive. We enter into an intentionally established relationship with a holy God within which we live henceforth.

How do we define a relationally definitive faith-moment that sets the course for the progressive transformation of the Christian into the likeness of Christ? The context provided by 6:14-18 indicates that Paul is speaking decisively in 7:1. The aorist tense of the exhortation is less concerned with a point in time than a point of fact. Whether in an instant or through a long, agonizing process, we must respond to the call: *Let us cleanse ourselves* in a faith commitment to a life of *perfecting holiness in the fear of God*. We take a clue from John Wesley with a "holiness hermeneutic" that works from "the privilege of grace to the crisis of faith."

The biblical presentation of holiness or the sanctification of life as applied to persons is essentially a quality of life flowing from the grace of God in Jesus Christ. The scriptural concern in relation to sanctification possesses the following hierarchical order:

- first, sanctification as a grace relationship to God in Jesus Christ
- second, sanctification as an ethic or response in life enabled by the Holy Spirit consistent with the nature of that relationship
- third, sanctification as a faith-decision through which one enters into a perfected or thoroughgoing grace relationship to the Christ of the cross and the resurrection

We interpret and apply the biblical materials from the nature and privilege of the life in grace to our experiential need for some kind of a decisive "faith crisis," which is fully realized in day-to-day discipleship.

The primary necessity for this "crisis" flows from the gospel's presentation and call to the life of grace. The holy life is initially the privilege of living as those who belong to the Holy One. This approach is fully applicable to the Pauline text at hand: "Since we have these promises, dear friends, let us purify ourselves from everything that contaminates body and spirit, perfecting holiness out of reverence for God" (7:1).

As a fruitful holiness hermeneutic, "the privilege of grace to the crisis of faith" can be applied throughout the biblical record from the great commandment (Deut 6:4-5; Mark 12:28-31) to the Johannine presentation of "God is love" (1 John 4:8, 16). These texts thus give biblical integrity to John Wesley's crucial definition of holiness as "love excluding sin" (Outler 1985, 160).

A Theology of Christian Experience

Paul's theology of *law* and *flesh* in contrast to *grace* and *Spirit* opens up a way of understanding "the privilege of grace to the crisis of faith" theologically. It also has some possibilities for articulating it psychologically. A helpful way to see this is to apply these categories to an often cited holiness proof-text in Acts. This is a text directly related to the disciples' experience of the Holy Spirit at Pentecost. We may interpret it from the viewpoint of Pentecost as primarily and theologically a defining event, inaugurating the NT era.

In the context of the Jerusalem council Peter speaks in Acts 15:8-9 about the coming of the Holy Spirit on the Roman centurion Cornelius (reported in Acts 10:34-48): "And God, who knows the heart, testified to them, giving them the Holy Spirit, just as He also did to us; and He made no distinction between us and them, cleansing their hearts by faith" (NASB). There were those in the church who wanted to compromise the freedom of the gospel of grace by a return to circumcision and the law of Moses (15:1, 5). The church assembled at Jerusalem to address the issue. During the proceedings, Peter brings the experience of his ministry to Cornelius to bear on the problem.

In its literary context Peter's speech functions as a miracle-authenticated call to discipleship (see Mark 10:46-52) in its understanding of the gospel as experienced and understood in the Gentile mission. Peter saw in the miracle of the gift of the Holy Spirit to his Gentile friends the evidence that the nature of every believer's relationship with God is one of unadulterated grace: "We believe it is through the grace of our Lord Jesus that we [Jews] are saved, just as they [Gentiles] are" (15:11).

From this perspective, we can understand the cleansing of the heart by faith theologically as that operation of the Holy Spirit in our Christian lives that cleanses our hearts "all the way to grace." Involved is a cleansing of the will from all trust in the flesh before God. That is, we must surrender all confidence in our spiritual self-sufficiency. An "all the way to grace" cleansing removes all vestiges of confidence in what humans can do so that we learn to depend wholly on what God alone can give. The extent to which and precisely when persons can fully realize this in their lives is a matter of the chronology of their own personal experience.

When the cleansing work of the Holy Spirit in the heart is interpreted in Pauline language, it has primary reference to the issues of law and grace in salvation (see Acts 15:1, 5, 11). The "cleansing" of the heart is *from* all reliance on any human performance *to* an utter dependence upon divine grace in salvation. It is *from* any confidence in the power of the flesh *to* a singular trust in the presence of the Spirit for spiritual adequacy. *Potentially* to be "filled with the Holy Spirit" (Acts 2:4) we understand as having been brought by the cleansing presence of the Spirit *"all the way* to grace" in one's relation to God and fellow persons as a Christian.

The above is presented primarily as a "theology of Christian experience" rather than as a "psychology of Christian experience." We describe what the full faith-apprehension of the privilege entails rather than the chronological process that leads to it.

To speak psychologically out of this theologically defined context, a second crisis of faith (in Wesley's terms, entire sanctification) can be that moment in one's Christian pilgrimage when the Holy Spirit leads one "all the way to grace." This takes place in a moment of conscious faith-commitment as one decisively and once for all shifts from reliance on human strength and wisdom in "Christian" living to a sole dependence on the Spirit of Christ for a holy life. One moves from a confused and partially flesh-based spiritual life to a full commitment to a Spirit-grounded existence. One moves from notions of achievement to total dependence on God's gift—grace. Again, depending on the uniqueness of persons, this may occur almost without conscious awareness in an obedient walk with Christ. But it may also occur in a moment of deep struggle of soul.

Thus, if it is properly qualified, biblically, theologically, and psychologically or experientially, there can be a point in our Christian walk that can reasonably be called a crisis-of-faith moment. This is a decision in which the foundation for all subsequent Christian life is clearly and decisively laid. It is a faith-point that determines once for all the direction, motivation, and source of our spiritual living. We, so to speak, drive a stake down in heart, mind, and will as our final appeal. How the Holy Spirit leads us to and through this point is an open question. But we will know its reality when we arrive.

To this quality of relation and life the apostolic ambassador of Christ called the Corinthians, and to this the true minister of the gospel, the spiritual father of a people, will clearly, faithfully, and inescapably call his children. This is the apostolic, indeed the divine, call to holiness that is at the heart of the Wesleyan heritage.

Further Reading on Holiness of Heart and Life

Carver, Frank G. 1987. "Biblical Foundations for the 'Secondness' of Entire Sanctification." *Wesleyan Theological Journal* 22, 2:7-23.

Outler, Albert E., ed. 1985. "The Scripture Way of Salvation." Pages 34-70 in *The Works of John Wesley*. Vol. 2: *Sermons II*. Nashville: Abingdon Press.

Staples, Rob. 1972. "Sanctification and Selfhood: A Phenomenological Analysis of the Wesleyan Message." *Wesleyan Theological Journal* 7:3-16.

Wesley, John. 1966. *A Plain Account of Christian Perfection*. Kansas City: Beacon Hill Press of Kansas City.

III. THE GRACE OF CHRISTIAN GIVING: 2 CORINTHIANS 8:1—9:15

Like 2 Cor 6:14—7:1, these chapters appear to take the form of a digression. But they express the practical point of the letter as a whole. And as such, they are significant for Paul's theology (Hafemann 2000, 358). More specifically, they are relevant to Paul's relation to the church at Corinth as a part of his overall argument in defense of his integrity as an apostle. Ben Witherington calls them "a daring rhetorical move" (1995, 411).

Paul has been "walking on eggshells" in his relationship with the Corinthians. And their most recent misunderstanding has just been resolved. But the apostle is willing to risk it all in the interests of his larger vision for the relationship between his Gentile churches and the Jewish mother church in Jerusalem. In chs 8—9, Paul offers the Corinthians another opportunity to demonstrate their genuineness and their confidence in him by responding to his urging to complete the long-delayed offering for the poor saints in Jerusalem.

So in chs 8—9 Paul turns to the collection that he has been promoting among his missionary churches in Galatia, Achaia, Asia, and Macedonia for the aid of the poor among or relief for the economic situation in the Jerusalem Christian community (Rom 15:22-28; 1 Cor 16:1-4; see Gal 2:10). This offering appears to have been very significant in Paul's apostolic ministry, for he persisted in its personal delivery in spite of the dangers he knew awaited him in Jerusalem (see Acts 20:3, 23; 21:4, 10-15; Rom 15:30-32). Further, it was accompanied by a delegation (2 Cor 8:16-24; 1 Cor 16:3; see Acts 20:4) that probably outweighed the size of the offering.

As Paul sought to fulfill his promise of financial aid to the mother church, the collection project was in continuity with the OT covenant ethic (Lev 19:17-18 and Mic 6:8) and the practice of charity in Judaism (Matt 6:2; Acts 3:2). It was also in agreement with Jesus' teaching on assistance to the poor (Matt 5:42; 6:2; 25:43-46; Mark 10:21; Luke 19:2-9; John 13:29). Jesus' teaching about the nature of mutual relations between disciples (Matt 20:24-25; Mark 10:42-45; Luke 22:24-27) came to striking fruition in the "everything in common" commitment of the earliest church (Acts 2:44; 4:32; see 6:1-8).

Paul kept such spontaneous brotherly love, effected by a new relation to God through the Holy Spirit, at the heart of the Christian ethic (Rom 12:8-13; 13:8-10; Gal 6:6; Phil 4:14-17). Paul's concern for the needs of fellow believers was an expression of the unique fellowship they all enjoyed "in Christ."

Beyond this basic practical significance, the collection was theologically significant for Paul. It would be a theological demonstration of the solidarity of the church made up of both Jewish and Gentile believers. Their interdependence, the spiritual indebtedness of the Gentiles to the church in Jerusalem, and the unity and equality of Jew and Gentile in Christ would be concretely evidenced.

Paul probably hoped the collection would allay Jewish suspicions concerning the Gentile mission. Yet it was not a kind of Christian "temple tax," an implicit recognition of the superiority of the mother church. Nor was it primarily an eschatological pilgrimage of Gentile Christians to Jerusalem to confront unbelieving Jews with the reality of the divine gift of salvation to the Gentiles, and so to move them through jealousy to accept the gospel (so Munck 1959, 303-8; and Nickle 1966, 129-42; but see Harris 2005, 87-101).

Paul believed that the Gentiles, who shared in the spiritual blessings of the Jews, had an obligation to be of service to them in material blessings (Rom

15:26-29). And he hoped that the church in Jerusalem would be moved to glorify God (9:12-14) for the genuineness of the Gentiles' faith in Christ. The collection had the potential to compel them to see the reality of the bond of fellowship between them as equally privileged members of the body of Christ. Paul will ask the Romans to pray with him that the offering, complete by the time he writes, will be accepted in this spirit (Rom 15:30-31). Furthermore, Romans suggests that the Corinthians cooperated fully in the collection (15:23-28; 16:1). Luke's account in Acts 21:17-20 appears to indicate that it was accepted with gratitude (compare Acts 21:20*a* with 2 Cor 9:13).

Instructions concerning the collection were given in 1 Cor 16:1-4, and it may have been mentioned in "the previous letter" (1 Cor 5:9, 11). Whether or not the Corinthians had made any progress in raising the funds Paul requested is not known. But if so, progress no doubt ceased with his "painful visit" (2:1; 13:2). Apparently, a ringleader in the church rose up in arrogant defiance against Paul (2:5-8; 7:12). And the church sided with Paul's opponents, forcing Paul to return to Ephesus. From there, Paul sent Titus with the sorrowful letter to correct the situation. Titus returned with news of his success in correcting the situation (7:6-16). So Paul immediately returns to the issue of the collection in these chapters. He urges the soon completion of the collection. And it was eventually successful: "For Macedonia and Achaia were pleased to make a contribution for the poor among the saints in Jerusalem" (Rom 15:26).

BEHIND THE TEXT

Caught up in Paul's larger forensic purposes, these two chapters are deliberative arguments. They are designed to call for a particular action on the part of the readers. Such arguments assume that Paul's Corinthian audience accepts the credibility of his character. It also assumes that he knows the essential character of his letter's recipients. Both of these assumptions were risky, given the recent misunderstanding between them. Paul's fund-raising efforts were also a matter of considerable risk, because of Paul's refusal of patronage from the Corinthians, which appears not to have set well with them (11:7-11).

The deliberative rhetoric then, although directed to the collection, also serves the interests of his credibility with the Corinthians—both Paul's innocence and honesty and the Corinthians' confidence and trust in him. The completion of the collection by the Corinthians would demonstrate both (Witherington 1995, 335-36, 411-13).

In the social and economic relationships of Paul's day, patronage often took place between people of unequal social status because of financial need. Lending institutions were nonexistent, and the social safety nets we take for granted were not often in place. Thus, personal patronage was a practical necessity, much like various guarantees of job security today.

For all of the economic benefits accompanying patronage relationships, there were social consequences. Issues of honor and shame were also involved in such patron-client relationship (Witherington 1995, 414-19). The giving and acceptance of gifts or favors placed their recipients in an inferior role and under obligation to respond to their patrons with gratitude and honor. Some such relationships were called friendships, as if between equals. But the label was often a polite covering for what was really a patron-client relationship.

Paul seems to have concluded that he could not take financial help from the Corinthians as he did from the Philippians (4:13-19). To have done so would have placed him in a socially inferior power relationship, under the domination of his wealthy Corinthian patrons. So he refused their support and worked at his trade in Corinth (1 Cor 9:12, 18; see 2 Cor 11:9; 12:14). He also preferred this bivocational approach to ministry in Thessalonica (2:9), but perhaps for a different reason—a recognition of "their extreme poverty" (2 Cor 8:2).

The terminology of these chapters reflects some features of ancient administrative letters, which often accompanied royal envoys. Paul has "Christianized" their language and used it more for motivation than for recommendation (Hafemann 2000, 330, 333; see Betz 1985, 46, 133).

IN THE TEXT

Based on the reconciliation and personal warmth evidenced in 7:4-16, the apostle seeks to motivate the Corinthians to complete their part of the offering for the Jerusalem church. As Paul applies "the grace of Christian giving" to their situation, he divides his plea into three phases. Paul:

1. subtly asks for the offering to be completed (8:1-15)
2. makes adequate provision for the offering to be delivered to Jerusalem (8:16—9:5)
3. emphasizes the blessings of such generosity in giving (9:6-15)

As part of his rhetorical strategy, Paul plays on the Greek word for **grace** (*charis*), throughout these two chapters. He uses *charis* with differing denotations, which we will note as we proceed (8:1, 4, 6, 7, 9, 16, 19; 9:8, 12, 14, 15). He uses it to form an *inclusio*, placing it like literary bookends at the beginning (8:1—*charin*, **grace**) and end (9:15—*charis*, **Thanks be**) of the passage. Significantly, all of Paul's letters include some form of *charis* at their beginning and ending.

A. Paul Encourages the Completion of the Offering (8:1-15)

When the pillar apostles in Jerusalem recognized Paul's mission to the Gentiles as of equal validity with theirs to the Jews, they gave him "the right hand of fellowship" (*koinōnias*). They asked only that he "remember the poor" (Gal 2:9-10). Because of a famine in Jerusalem, Paul had already, along with

Barnabas, brought a relief contribution from Antioch to Jerusalem (Acts 11:27-30). Now on his third journey Paul undertakes a much more ambitious offering occasioned by the need among the Christians in Judea.

Murray Harris suggests several factors that may have contributed to economic hardships of Christians in Judea (2005, 88-89):

1. The constant influx of Jewish converts to Christianity may have led to the experience of social ostracizing and economic persecution.
2. The continuing results of the famine would affect the poor more than the rich; and there were probably few rich and many poor in the early church.
3. It was expensive to live in Jerusalem during the first century.
4. Everyone faced crippling twofold taxation, civil by the Romans and religious by the Jews.
5. Their capital resources may have been depleted as a result of their voluntary sharing of goods and property (Acts 2:44-45; 4:34-35).
6. The money needed to support a proportionately large number of teachers in the mother church overextended their resources (see Acts 6:4; 1 Cor 9:4-6).
7. The social obligation of extending hospitality to frequent Christian visitors to Jerusalem contributed to their poverty (see Rom 12:13; Heb 13:2; 1 Pet 4:9).

At least a year prior to the writing of 2 Corinthians, Paul had asked the Corinthians to contribute to the offering week by week and to prepare a delegation to accompany him to deliver the offering (1 Cor 16:1-4). Due to the difficulties between them, the church had not made much more than a start (2 Cor 8:10; 9:2). Paul seeks to reactivate the project among them.

Paul's primary concern in chs 8 and 9 is to motivate the Corinthians to contribute to the cause. As he begins his appeal he bases it on the example (1) of other churches who "urgently pleaded with us for the privilege of sharing in this service to the saints" (v 4; see vv 1-5), and (2) of their mutual Lord (v 9).

1. The Liberality of the Macedonians (8:1-7)

■ **1** The apostle moves delicately to the new and touchy subject of money. As we have already indicated, Paul's perspective is that of **grace** (*charis:* vv 1, 4, 6, 7; see vv 9, 16, 19; 9:8, 14, 15), his leading theme in the discussion that follows (Matera 2003, 185).

Paul identifies his subject as ***the grace of God*** (a subjective genitive or genitive of source). This **grace *had been given*** [*dedomenēn*] ***by God*** to **the Macedonian churches.** The perfect tense indicates that it was still operative among them. From Acts (16:9—17:15; 19:21-29; 20:1-6; 27:2), we know that Paul planted churches in the northern Greek province of Macedonia—in Philippi, Thessalonica, and Berea. Three of his preserved letters were directed to churches there: 1 and 2 Thessalonians and Philippians.

Paul appealed to the example of the Macedonian Christians as models for the Corinthians. He writes so that the "brothers and sisters" (NRSV; Greek: *adelphoi*) in Corinth may **know** in their own experience ***the grace of God*** that motivated and enabled **the churches of Macedonia** to give generously and enthusiastically toward the collection.

Grace, as God's freely offered gift of salvation in Christ (8:9; 9:8, 14; Rom 3:24), is at the heart of Paul's theology. All else flows from this. Paul's theology is above all a theology of grace, a theology that informs even the most practical of his writings. Paul's greeting in the letter opening includes "grace . . . to you from God our Father and the Lord Jesus Christ" (1:2); his farewell prayer was, "may the grace of the Lord Jesus Christ . . . be with you all" (13:14).

■ **2** After announcing the theme of **grace** in v 1, Paul explains in vv 2-4 how grace was evident among the Macedonians. He describes the situation within which the churches in Macedonia received grace (v 2): in the midst of ***a severe ordeal*** caused by ***affliction*** (see Phil 1:29-30; 1 Thess 1:6-7; 2:14; 2 Thess 1:4-10; Acts 16:11—17:15) and "deep poverty" (NASB). Paradoxically (see 2 Cor 8:9), in this situation they experienced ***the abundance of their joy*** and "overflowed in the wealth of their liberality" (NASB). In the Macedonians persecution produced **joy** (see 7:4) and **poverty** produced **generosity.** How so? Another power, **grace** (v 1), was at work.

The extent of the **poverty** of the Macedonians was probably due to the social ostracism and harassment they experienced because of their Christian faith as well as the general economic condition of Macedonia (Betz 1985, 43, 50-51; Thrall 2004, 522-23).

The translation of *haplotētos* as **generosity** here is an interpretation unique to certain Pauline contexts (8:2; 9:11, 13; Rom 12:8). Its normal meaning is ***"simplicity, sincerity,"*** or ***"frankness"*** (BDAG 2000, 104), as elsewhere in the NT (2 Cor 1:12; 11:3; Eph 6:5; Col 3:22). Thus, **generosity** here is, at best, an extended meaning (Thrall 2004, 523-24; see Harris 2005, 563). Bauer considers "sincere concern" a more appropriate translation (BDAG 2000, 104). Certainly, Paul refers, not to the size of their contribution, but to the attitude that prompted their participation in the collection. It was the uncalculating spirit of their giving as vv 3-5 indicates.

Here was unquestionable evidence of the genuineness of grace at work among the Macedonians. It was producing in them a likeness to Christ (v 9; see Mark 12:41-44). The result was, of course, their **generosity** or ***liberality:*** "Simplicity renders men liberal" (Bengel 1895, 3:399).

■ **3** Paul interjects his personal observation: **I testify** [*martyrō*] **that** the liberality of the Macedonians was evidenced (*hoti*, **For/*Because***) in four ways (vv 3-5).

First, **they gave as much as they were able, and even beyond their ability.** There is no explicit verb in Greek, but **gave** (*edōkan*) is implied from v 5. The Macedonians gave beyond what their limited resources would normally allow.

Second, **they gave . . . entirely on their own** (BDAG 2000, 150 s.v. *autairetos: "**of** [their] **own accord**"*). This understands *authairetoi* as referring to "giving" (NASB, NRSV) rather than to "pleading" (NIV, NEB) on contextual grounds. Paul uses the word only here and in 8:17, where it describes Titus. Apart from any coercion on Paul's part, the Macedonians "voluntarily gave" (NRSV) in two senses—on their own initiative and of their own free will (see Rom 15:26-27).

■ **4** Third, the Macedonians had **urgently pleaded** with Paul **for the privilege** [*charin:* ***grace***] **of sharing in this service to the saints.** Paul's words are carefully chosen, "dense but significant" (Matera 2003, 187). The word **urgently** ("earnestly," NRSV; see NASB) paraphrases the Greek words *meta pollēs paraklēseōs—**with great encouragement.***

Thus, Paul repeats here the terminology prominent in the introduction to 2 Corinthians (1:3-7; see 7:4, 6-7, 13; 8:17). Appearing also is the Greek term for "grace," but used in a second sense, now as a **privilege** or "favor."

Paul defines this "favor" as **sharing** (*koinōnian*) in the relief of the needs of the poor **saints** in Judea. *Koinōnia* carries with it the connotation of ***participation*** in the resurrection life of Christ, which constitutes the Christian community (see 13:14; Acts 2:42; 1 Cor 1:9; 10:16; Phil 1:5; 3:10; Phlm 6; 1 John 1:3-7; see also *koinōnoi* in 2 Cor 1:7; see Nickle 1966, 105-6, 122-25; Thornton 1950, 5-33).

As applied to the collection, *tēn koinōnian* means taking part in the offering. Significantly, it implies their common relationship "in Christ." This motivation gives their gift theological integrity.

Added to these significant words—*paraklēsis, charis,* and *koinōnia*—Paul refers to the collection as *tēs diakonias,* **this service** ("this ministry," NRSV). This is Paul's favorite designation for his own "new covenant" ministry (3:6; see 4:1; 5:18; 6:3-4; 11:8, 23; see Mark 10:43-45).

The early church used the term *diakonia* for their charitable work within and between congregations (see Acts 6:1; 11:29; 12:25; Rom 15:31). By referring to the collection as **service** (*diakonias*), Paul suggests that he considered it an act of Christian fellowship fulfilled in the service of the Lord (9:1, 12; Nickle 1966, 106-9). It was, indeed, a ministry, an essential part of his apostolic ministry of the new covenant.

Paul selected another theologically loaded term to designate the intended recipients of the collection. By referring to **the saints** (see 1:1), he suggests that the offering was for the church at Jerusalem as a whole, among whom some were economically "poor" (Rom 15:26; Gal 2:10).

The term **saints** is not to be simply equated with the "poor" in Rom 15:26 and Gal 2:10. Paul does not mean only "the poor among the saints." Nor does he merely equate the "poor" with **the saints**—the Jerusalem Christians (see Thrall 2000, 506-9; Harris 2005, 89-91). Nor is **saints** simply an "honorific religious title" given those who surrendered their personal property for the sake of the early Christian community (Acts 2:44-45; 4:34-35; Shillington 1998, 175).

■ **5** The fourth evidence of the Macedonians' liberality was that they did more than Paul had **expected** (*ēlpisamen;* BDAG 2000, 319). They exceeded his expectations both in the amount they gave and in the manner of their contribution. Paul explains: **they gave** [*edōkan*] **themselves first to the Lord and then to us in keeping with God's will.** The literal wording—*prōton tōi kyriōi kai hēmin: **first to the Lord and to us***—makes for an awkward but bold expression (Matera 2003, 187).

By **first,** Paul refers primarily to the priority in importance and only secondarily to the sequence in time. Both actions were as God intended—***by*** [*dia: **through the instrumentality of***] ***the will of God.*** His point is not that God gave them extraordinary, special guidance. They merely did what was consistent with the grace of God in Christ (see 1:1, 9).

Their self-gift involved "putting themselves at the disposal of" God and Paul. They dedicated themselves to the Lord for the specific task of the offering. And they spontaneously and generously responded to the appeal of Christ's apostolic representative to contribute to the collection. Paul considered this the direct result of their commitment to Christ.

It may be going too far to say that Paul's lavish praise of the Macedonians (vv 1-5) deliberately played on the ethnic and political rivalry between the Corinthians and the Macedonians (Betz 1985, 48). Yet his example of the Macedonians surely exerted subtle pressure on the Corinthians to do as well as or better than the Macedonians. The apostle's rhetoric was calculated to motivate them to allow the same grace to work in their lives, so that they, too, would give themselves to the completion of the collection (v 7).

■ **6** Paul's appeal to the Corinthians is twofold. First, he refers to the example of the generosity of the Macedonians in vv 1-5. Second, here he mentions his fervent request (*parakalesai: **encouragement;*** see v 4) to **Titus** (see 7:13-15). He **urged** him **to bring also to completion this act of grace on your part.**

The expression **act of grace** is simply *tēn charin tautēn, **this grace.*** The term takes on its third sense within this passage. Here Paul equates it with the offering itself ("this generous undertaking," NRSV). Interestingly, he never uses the ordinary word for collection (*logeia*) in 2 Corinthians as he did in 1 Corinthians (16:1).

Titus **had earlier made a beginning** (see v 10) on the collection. This was probably after the delivery of 1 Corinthians (see 16:1-4). It is less probable that the **beginning** took place when Titus was sent to Corinth with the sorrowful letter (2:3-10). The word **also,** however, probably refers to this successful visit of Titus to Corinth.

What is impressive is how Paul uses all the resources of language to set the offering within his theological understanding of the gospel of Christ. To participate in the collection is a ministry that participates in God's grace, a perspective that Paul will unfold again in 9:6-15.

■ **7** Verses 1-6 are one sentence in Greek. Verse 7 serves as a transition to vv 8-15. It can be viewed as an appropriate conclusion, making explicit the main point of the example of the Macedonians. Or it can be seen as emphatically introducing an exhortation, strengthening the command that follows in v 8. As transitional, we take it as fulfilling both functions. On grammatical and contextual grounds, it is most closely associated with vv 1-6. Paul begins to urge the Corinthians to respond to what he has just written.

Paul urges them to give based only partly on the example of the Macedonians. More importantly, he emphasizes that the Corinthians are also abundantly supplied with the gifts of divine grace (v 7; 9:14; 1 Cor 1:4-5; see chs 12—14). He claims hyperbolically: **you excel in everything.** Paul appeals specifically to the gifts of **faith, . . . speech, . . . knowledge, . . . complete earnestness and . . . love for** Paul.

The first three gifts seem to refer to the charismatic spiritual endowments Paul discusses at length in 1 Corinthians (1:5; 12:8-10; 13:2; see Rom 12:6-8). If so, **faith** does not refer to saving faith, but to faith that is active in all of life. It refers to their willingness to trust God to supply their every need, to trust one another, etc. **Speech** and **knowledge** comprise the gifts that deal with the perception and declaration of the truth of the gospel.

In 8:16, Paul will use the term **earnestness** to refer to something "God . . . put into the heart of Titus." God made him as eagerly committed to assist the Corinthians as Paul was. Here, **complete earnestness** (*pasēi spoudēi;* literally, "all haste") refers either to "every kind of" earnestness or to a high degree of earnestness ("utmost eagerness," NRSV). The evidence of their ***"eagerness, earnestness, diligence, willingness, zeal"*** (BDAG 2000, 939) is, no doubt, based on the Corinthians' recent favorable reception of Paul's sorrowful letter and his delegate who delivered it (7:11). They needed no coercion; they were quick to cooperate.

The last endowment of grace Paul mentions might be translated either **your love for us** or "our love for you" (NRSV). The difference arises from the translators' choice of variant readings in the Greek manuscript traditions—whether *hymōn en hēmin* (***the love from you in us***) or *hēmōn en hymin* (***the love from us in you***). Does Paul refer to the love *he* "inspired" in the Corinthians for him (NASB) or to the love the *Corinthians* inspired in Paul for them? Textual scholars and translators divide evenly on the choice.

In favor of the first reading is that it lists spiritual qualities the Corinthians possess. The second reading, however, makes more sense in the context of the letters. Paul would normally speak of "love which came from us and dwells in you" (Betz 1985, 37), not "love which came from you and dwells in us." The Greek may mean that Paul's open affection for the Corinthians has been reciprocated in the affection with which Paul is now held in their hearts (6:13; 7:2-7).

Paul's point is that those as gifted as the Corinthians should be expected to give in kind. The generous giftedness of the Corinthians should lead them to be generous in giving to the collection. Paul is not reluctant to resort to sincere flattery.

Does Paul write **just as you excel in everything, . . . see that you also excel in this grace of giving** as a wish or as a command? The NIV translates the conjunction *hina* as **so that,** giving his statement the force of an imperative (with many interpreters: e.g., Harris 2005, 575; Turner 1963b, 95). Yet the opening words of vv 7 and 8 may be an indicative wish.

The expression **this grace of giving** (*en tautēi tēi chariti*; literally, "in this grace") represents yet another meaning for the Greek *charis*. Here it describes the quality of the very act of participating in the collection.

For the apostle, even the mundane matter of taking an offering has theological significance. He cannot escape the comprehensive reality of ***grace*** as it penetrates his own life and ministry and the life of the church. The grace of God undergirds all, motivates and enables all, and defines the activity and concrete acts of the body of Christ. But Paul is not yet finished writing about grace. In soaring theological terms he will continue his appeal to the practical outworking of grace in the lives of the Corinthians.

2. The Challenge of the Liberality of Christ (8:8-15)

Paul's challenge to the Corinthians to complete the offering for the church at Jerusalem continues in vv 8-15. The apostle links the manner in which he seeks to motivate their "grace of giving" (v 7) directly and intrinsically with the gospel he proclaims. As such, he presents us with the standard of all Christian giving. Paul does this with an appeal to an even more inspiring example of giving as he draws out its implications for the concrete task at hand.

■ **8** Paul writes ***not as a command*** (v 8). Instead, he appeals to the model of the **earnestness** [see v 7; 7:11-13] **of others,** specifically the Macedonians (vv 1-7), in the matter. He hopes their example will motivate the Corinthians to ***prove*** the "genuineness" (NRSV) of their **love** (see 8:24).

The translation of *dokimazōn* as **test** (in the NIV and NRSV) suggests that this is the second of three great tests the Corinthians must pass (see 2:9 and 13:1-2; Matera 2003, 191; see 1 Cor 11:28-29). Paul seems to presume that his authority as an apostle (1:1) gives him the right to enforce the completion of the offering (see 8:11). But he does not exercise his right. Instead, he appeals to another example, that of "our Lord Jesus Christ" (v 9).

The apostle may be saying only that he does not have a direct command from the Lord concerning the offering (see 1 Cor 7:6, 25; see Rom 16:26). But this is contextually questionable. Another alternative leaves his apostolic right to command fully intact (Hafemann 2000, 336-39, 343-44). Another removes every authoritative obligation except love as a motivation for their participation. This prevents them from contradicting or compromising the nature of their giving as a response to grace (Barnett 1997, 405-6).

Murphy-O'Connor comments that "one cannot be 'bound' by a precept and free at the same time" (1991, 82). Obviously, Paul is not using dictatorial tactics (see 1:24). Instead, he stresses the voluntary nature of Christian giving (see 8:3; 9:5, 7). Betz suggests that in the deliberative rhetoric Paul uses in 8:1-15, commands are out of order (Betz 1985, 59). Paul does not seem prepared to abandon his apostolic authority. It finds its credibility in his message, as v 9 indicates. What he writes always carries with it the integrity and power of his gospel.

Paul intends the example of the Macedonians' **earnestness** to activate the **sincerity** (*gnēsion:* "genuineness") of the Corinthians' **love** so they will get on with the task of the collection. The term *gnēsios* referred originally to the importance of "belonging to a race" (*genos*). It identified one as *"born in wedlock, legitimate"* (BDAG 2000, 202). Real love takes action.

By referring to the example of the Macedonians, Paul prepares for an appeal to an even greater, indeed the ultimate, example in v 9. No wonder Paul feels no need to dictate. He can crown all other incentives (vv 7-8) with an appeal to the essence of the apostolic message (v 9).

■ **9** With **for you know the grace of our Lord Jesus Christ,** "Paul's key word *charis* reaches its apex of significance" (Shillington 1998, 178). Paul "hammers" on the supreme reason (*gar,* **For**) why the Corinthians should "excel in this grace of giving" (v 7). I once heard James S. Stewart remark, "Paul is using a sledgehammer to crack a nut!" (1959, classroom memory).

In this instance, the "grace of God" (v 1 NRSV) is God's lavish favor displayed in **our Lord Jesus Christ.** Paul is confident that his example will motivate and enable the Corinthians to participate in the collection. Understanding **the grace of our Lord Jesus Christ** as a subjective genitive indicates that the **Lord Jesus** gives this grace. All that follows defines *charis* (**grace**): **that though . . . become rich.** The Corinthians **know** all this was **for** their **sakes** (*di' hymas:* ***for you***). Paul makes a point of emphasizing this by placing *di' hymas* in the first position in the clause.

What is the precise reference of Paul's fascinating references to Christ's wealth and subsequent poverty in contrast to the Corinthians' poverty and subsequent riches? Literally, Paul wrote: ***For your sakes he became poor, being rich, in order that you by that one's poverty might become rich.*** The final **rich** obviously refers to the spiritual enrichment of the Corinthians. But what about the initial **rich** and the contrasting **poor/poverty** descriptive of Christ? Scholarly opinion is varied.

Some interpreters exclude any reference of **rich** to the preexistent state of Christ (see Dunn 1998, 291-92). They see "the underlying thought . . . of 5:21" being that the earthly Jesus "became 'poor' by accepting the radical impoverishment of a degrading and humiliating death in which everything was taken from him" (Murphy-O'Connor 1991, 83).

We, however, find the traditional view compelling. Christ's heavenly preexistence is implied in **he was rich.** The concessive interpretation of the adverbial participle, **though he was rich** (emphasis added), however, presumes that generosity is out of character for Christ. But if this verse is a summary variation of Phil 2:6-11, the participle might be translated causally: ***For your sakes he became poor, because he was rich*** (see Flemming 2009). The words **he became poor/his poverty** refer to the whole of his incarnation, life, crucifixion, and resurrection (see Thrall 2004, 532-34; Harris 2005, 578-80). Paul has translated the "theology of the cross into the language of benevolence" (McCant 1999, 84).

Our Lord's descent from the height of riches to the depth of poverty (see Matt 8:20) was more than a general display of divine grace. Paul directly appeals to the Corinthians' personal experience of Christ's saving love. Grace expressed itself through the **poverty *of that one*** [*ekeinou*] ***in order that you*** [*hymeis*, an emphatic nominative pronoun] **might become rich** (1 Cor 1:5). Such **grace of our Lord Jesus Christ** is likewise at the heart of Paul's own ministry (see 6:10). Thus, in a sense Paul "becomes a second Christ to the Corinthians" (McCant 1999, 76). This should certainly be an adequate motivation for the Corinthians.

Christ's love makes human love possible and genuine in a practical project. Paul, as usual, unites theology and ethics; it is impossible for him to separate them. The most profound doctrines of all, the incarnation and atonement, belong at the heart of the daily practice of every Christian. The center of our faith must be applied to the circumference of our lives or we are unfaithful servants.

■ **10** Rather than **commanding** (v 8), Paul's approach here is to give **advice** (*gnōmēn:* "judgment"; BDAG 2000, 202). This is "serious apostolic counsel" (Furnish 1984, 405) under the Spirit's guidance. ***For this*** (*touto gar*) matter at hand, Paul's counsel seems to be **what is best** ("appropriate," NRSV) for the Corinthians.

They began to participate in the collection **last year,** perhaps over a year before Paul writes 2 Corinthians (see 1 Cor 16:1-4; Harris 2005, 582-83; Furnish 1984, 405-6). He describes their initial enthusiasm for the project. They **were the first** of his churches to give, but also the first to express their willingness to participate in the collection.

The present tense of the infinitive ***to will*** (*to thelein*) refers to the Corinthians' long-standing **desire** to participate in the collection. The aorist tense of the infinitive ***to do*** (*to poiēsai*) points to the fact that they did begin **to give,** but had abandoned the project. The unexpected word order, **to give** before **the desire,** highlights the priority of their motivation in both time and importance (Harris 2005, 582). So Paul appeals to their already avowed determination to carry through on the offering (Martin 1986, 265). The apostle "praises what can be praised (their willingness), and permits the Corinthians' self-respect to function as an internal incentive." This is "Paul at his best in terms of religious leadership" (Murphy-O'Connor 1991, 84).

■ **11** So **now** they should **finish the work.** They are to bring their ***doing*** (*to poiēsai*) to its appropriate conclusion. The purpose is that the **completion** of the collection might demonstrate the Corinthians' original enthusiasm. Paul's boasting of this to the Macedonians (see 8:2-5) had helped motivate their participation.

The NIV correctly interprets the intended sense of *hopōs . . . houtōs kai* (***in order that . . . so also***) with **so that . . . may be matched.** The Greek lacks the connecting verb. The expression of the Corinthians' **eager willingness** (*prothymia tou thelein:* "readiness to desire," NASB) is a Greek idiom in use since Plato (Laws 3.697d). It conveys a flavor of intensity in a consecutive or final sense (Turner 1963b, 141). That is, the Corinthians fully intended to complete what they had started.

Paul adds that their giving should be **according to** their **means.** He does not ask the Corinthians to give as heroically as had the Macedonians—"beyond their ability" (8:3). Paul displays a pastoral sensitivity in relation to the situation at Corinth. He does not want to take advantage of or risk the Corinthians' recent reconciliation with him.

■ **12** Paul insists that their **willingness** must be present for their contribution to be **acceptable** (6:2; Rom 15:16, 31; see 1 Pet 2:5). God judges **according to what one has, not according to what he does not have** (see Mark 12:43-44). Thus, in giving, it is not the size of the gift that counts. Rather it is goodwill, the eagerness to give, that matters. The amount of their gift should be in proportion to their resources. That is, it is not a certain percentage or tithe of what they possess, but according to the measure of God's grace. They are to be gracious in proportion to how God has graced them.

■ **13-14** The intent of the collection is not to ease the distress of the Judean Christians to the impoverishment of the Corinthians (vv 13-15). Rather it is a matter of **equality** (vv 13-14). One section of the church is not to **be relieved** by leaving another section **hard pressed.**

Paul appeals to the well-known principle of **equality** (*isotētos:* "fairness," BDAG 2000, 481; see Col 1:4) in the world of his day. The Corinthians were, no doubt, committed to this principle (see Furnish 1984, 407; Harris 2005, 590). Paul's object is that the Corinthians, in their **present time** of **plenty** should **supply** the **need** of the Jerusalem Christians. Should situations reverse and the Corinthians become the ones in **need** (v 14), they can expect to receive from the plenty of others.

As with most translations, the NIV properly adds to the Greek text the first verb **supply,** an implied omission. The obvious, but by no means certain, reference of the parallel construction, **supply . . . need . . . supply . . . need,** is to material resources. Some interpreters suggest that the Jerusalem Christians will furnish spiritual benefits for the anticipated need of the Corinthians (see Rom 15:27; Hafemann 2000, 340; Matera 2003, 193).

Interpreting through the lens of Rom 9—11, Martin proposes that Paul has in mind the reciprocity of both spiritual and material benefits between Gentile and Jewish Christians (Martin 1986, 267-70). But his hypothesis has not met with general acceptance (Thrall 2004, 541-42). Once again, Paul emphasizes his concern for balance; he seeks to establish the **equality** of all Christians in all matters. Here **equality** refers to the relief of want, not to equitable wealth redistribution.

■ **15** Paul appeals to an OT illustration for this mutual reciprocity of resources, the "equality" that expresses the nature of the Christian church. He refers to the daily gathering of manna by the Israelites in the wilderness, quoting Exod 16:18: **He who gathered much did not have too much, and he who gathered little did not have too little.** The story was, no doubt, familiar to the Corinthians. Paul is confident that the "present abundance" (v 14 NRSV) of the Corinthians, like the manna from the Lord, will be enough to provide relief for the necessities of the Judean Christians.

Hoarded wealth, enjoyed at the expense of those in real want, can become corrupt like stored manna and lead to inequalities contrary to the constitution of the Christian community. Dare one say that there is no place for elegance in the fellowship of the church, just as there is no room for hunger and nakedness that can be relieved (see Prov 3:27-28; Matt 25:31-46; Acts 4:34)?

The single point of the quotation from Exodus is the principle of "equality" that should exist among Christian communities. Paul appeals to fairness to motivate the completion of the offering for the Jerusalem church on the part of the Corinthians (see Ellis 1957, 134).

Paul uses his favorite formula for introducing OT quotations, **as it is written** (4:13; 9:9). It occurs twenty-nine times in his letters. Here, the example of

Scripture (vv 12-15) rhetorically furnishes an ending bracket to his appeal to the Corinthians. This furnishes rhetorical balance to the opening bracket, which refers to the examples of the Macedonians and of Jesus (8:1-10).

The criteria for Christian giving that Paul applies in these verses includes (1) the reach of the grace of Christ (vv 8-9); (2) the extent of personal resources (vv 10-12); and (3) the mutual needs of the body of Christ (vv 13-15).

B. Paul Chooses Messengers (8:16—9:15)

Paul continues to emphasize the spiritual nature of the collection as he further develops his appeal for ***the grace of partaking in the ministry to the saints*** (8:4). Paul expands the basis of the request to the Corinthians to include the plans for the organization of the collection (8:16—9:5), and the benefits of ***this gracious gift*** (*tēi chariti tautēi*, v 19] for both the givers and the recipients (9:6-15).

1. The Recommendation of Titus and His Companions (8:16-24)

In this second part of his appeal, Paul authorizes three men to go to Corinth to collect the offering. Titus and the two "brothers" (see vv 17, 22) are to safeguard the integrity of the enterprise. The apostle calls attention to the eagerness of Titus, followed by the introduction and commendation of the unnamed pair who will travel with him. These verses constitute and function as a letter of commendation. Although Paul did not need such letters (see 3:1), his envoys did, as they approached their delicate task.

■ **16** Paul gives ***thanks*** [*charis*] ***to God*** (see 2:14) for the extraordinary way God used **Titus** in relation to the church at Corinth (see 2:13; 7:6, 13-16). The apostle uses the "grace" word (*charis*) again with another nuance (see vv 1, 4, 7, 9). **God** graciously put **the same concern** (*spoudēn:* "eagerness," NRSV; see 7:11, 12; 8:7-8) for the Corinthians into **the heart of Titus** as Paul himself felt. Paul stresses the strong bond between himself and his principal representative to the church at Corinth.

■ **17** Like Paul, Titus's coming to the Corinthians concerns much more than meeting the material needs of the Jerusalem poor. Paul offers two manifestations of the eagerness he shared with Titus (v 17).

First, Titus's Spirit-motivated care was such that **he welcomed** Paul's **appeal** (*paraklēsin*). Second, Titus was "more eager than ever" (NRSV) to see the Corinthians. And he "is going to [them] of his own accord" (NRSV; **on his own initiative**). His initiative was like the Macedonians' generous giving (v 3). He implies that the Corinthians should participate in the collection on their own initiative, without coercing from Paul. Titus was going to Corinth on his own, but also in response to Paul's request and with his full apostolic support.

■ **18** Throughout vv 16-24, Paul uses the aorist tense to describe events that were in the future at the time he wrote. These are examples of the epistolary aorist. The described actions would be past by the time the letter was read to the Corinthians (Turner 1963b, 72-73).

The apostle writes, **we are sending along with** Titus a certain, unnamed **brother** (v 18; see 1:1). He uses a compound form of his usual term (*synepempsamen*) for sending representatives to the churches (see 1 Cor 4:17; 16:3; 2 Cor 9:3). The designation *adelphon*, **brother,** could indicate merely a fellow Christian or a colleague in ministry. It is probably the latter here (Ellis 1970-71, 447 n 2).

Paul highlights two qualifications of this **brother.** First, he is **praised by all the churches *in the gospel*** (*en tōi euanggelōi*), most probably for "his proclaiming" (NRSV) of the gospel (see Rom 1:9; 1 Cor 9:18; 2 Cor 10:14; 1 Thess 3:2). Paul leaves this famous, well-respected preacher anonymous.

■ **19** Paul identifies a second qualification with the words **What is more,** literally: ***and not only, but*** (*ou monon de, alla;* see 8:10). Titus's companion, more importantly, was qualified by the fact that he **was chosen by the churches to accompany** them in ***this grace*** (*chariti*). Here ***grace*** appears to designate the collection itself.

To accompany translates the noun *synekdēmos*, "traveling companion" (BDAG 2000, 968), with the connotation of "fellow missionary" (Young and

Ford 1987, 170). Which **churches** were involved in his selection is uncertain. But most probably, they were those in Macedonia, although Asia and Judea have been suggested.

The verb used for the brother's selection is *cheirotonētheis*, **chosen.** It originally meant "to elect by a show of hands" in Greek assemblies. It came to mean simply "to elect" by any means or "to appoint," as in its only other NT occurrence in Acts 14:23 (Furnish 1984, 422; Harris 2005, 602).

The **offering *administered*** by Paul has two purposes (*pros*, "for," **in order to**). It is, first, **to honor the Lord** (*pros tēn [autou] tou kyriou doxan: **for the glory of*** **the Lord himself**). Generous giving manifests the very glory of God (8:9). Second, it is **to show** Paul's **eagerness to help** (*pros tēn . . . prothymian hēmōn: **for our eagerness***). All these arrangements demonstrate how willing and ready Paul and his fellow workers were to assure the success of **the offering** (see Gal 2:10).

Neither this "brother" nor the second one mentioned in v 22 are named by Paul. We do not know who they were or why Paul omits their names. But this has not precluded considerable scholarly speculation as to both who and why (see, e.g., Betz 1985, 73; Furnish 1984, 435; and Thrall 2004, 557-62). Luke has frequently been honored as the first brother (v 18; see Plummer 1915, 248; Hughes 1962, 312-16). But the evidence offered is far from conclusive.

■ **20** When it came to financial matters, Paul was extremely careful. He shared with others the responsibility of administering the offering so as to avoid even the appearance of impropriety. He expresses his caution first negatively (v 20) and then in positive terms (v 21).

First, the negative form is translated literally: "taking precaution [*stellomenoi: **avoiding,*** see NIV and BDAG 2000, 942] so that no one will discredit us in our administration of this generous gift" (NASB). Paul takes precaution to avoid **criticism,** that is, that no one should "blame" (NRSV) him for mishandling **this liberal gift** (*hadrotēti*). The noun *hadrotēs* appears only here in the Greek Bible. It means ***"abundance"*** or lavishness, thus a *"lavish gift"* (BDAG 2000, 21; "generous gift," NRSV).

Significantly, the verb **administer** (*diakonoumenēi*, see v 19) here is his normal term for "minister" (3:3; see 3:7-9; 4:1; 5:18). The collection was a ministry motivated by and partaking of the apostolic ministry of Paul and his associates.

Paul took satisfaction in his financial independence from the Corinthians (11:9-12; see 1 Cor 9:12-18). Thus, he wants to preempt any possible accusation that he might gain personally from the collection project. By calling the offering a **liberal gift** (*hadrotēti*), he stresses its abundance. This is consistent with his expectation that their giving will be most generous. Paul both compliments their intentions and indirectly motivates them not to disappoint him (see 8:2).

■ **21** Second, Paul expresses his precautionary concerns in a positive form:

For we are taking pains to do what is right, not only in the eyes of the Lord but also in the eyes of men. Paul's language is that of forethought, "we think in advance" (*pronooumen*). His words echo the LXX of Prov 3:4: *pronoou kala enōpion kyriou kai anthrōpōn:* ***take thought for what is good in the sight of the Lord and human beings*** (see Rom 12:17).

By citing proverbial wisdom, Paul recognizes that in this situation it is not enough to be **right** or ***honest*** [*kala:* ***good***] ***in the presence of the Lord.*** One must also take pains to be and to be perceived as ***honest***/"honorable . . . in the sight of men" (NASB). Charles Hodge comments that "it is a foolish pride which leads to a disregard of public opinion" (1866, 210). The precautions Paul takes may well be due in part to earlier criticisms voiced in Corinth (see 12:16-18).

■ **22** The second delegate, **our brother** (v 22), whom Paul sends to accompany Titus to Corinth, is less renowned than the first (v 18). But he may have had a closer relationship with Paul than the other, as indicated by the possessive pronoun **our.** Paul had "often tested and found [this brother] eager in many matters" (NRSV). This **brother** was ***now*** [*nyni de*] ***even more eager*** (*spoudaioteron;* see 8:7-8, 16, 22; 7:11-12) for his new assignment in Corinth.

This **brother** had **great confidence** in the Corinthians. Perhaps this emerged as he worked with Paul during his difficult relations with the church at Corinth. In any event, he is as enthusiastic for the task they face as the first brother.

Perhaps, **our brother** here is the same one mentioned with Titus in 12:18. Whether the churches chose him or Paul appointed him is not stated. If Paul was responsible, the brothers sent with Titus provide a balanced delegation—one elected by the churches and the other a proven associate of Paul. But Paul describes both as "representatives of the churches" (v 23).

■ **23** Paul sums up his recommendation of the three delegates in v 23. He makes his final appeal in their behalf in v 24.

The apostle commends **Titus** as the presumed leader of the delegation (v 23). The Greek construction here, particularly the use of *hyper,* is similar to the authorization formula in legal and administrative texts of the day (Betz 1985, 79). The presence of *hyper* with **Titus** and its absence before **our brothers** may indicate two kinds of authorization, with Titus having the higher (Shillington 1998, 183).

Paul clearly names Titus as his **partner and fellow worker among** the Corinthians. Thus, he distinguishes him from the two anonymous **brothers,** whom he describes as **representatives of the churches.** Titus is Paul's **partner** (*koinōnos;* see on 8:4) in the gospel ministry generally. That is, they share a common (*koinos*) task. He is also Paul's **fellow worker** (*synergos*) in his service to the Corinthians.

Paul's Coworkers

Paul applies the specific designation **fellow worker** to seventeen associates in ministry: Priscilla and Aquila (Rom 16:3); Urbanus (Rom 16:9); Timothy (Rom 16:21; 1 Thess 3:2); Apollos (1 Cor 3:5-9); Titus (2 Cor 8:23); Epaphroditus (Phil 2:25); Euodia, Syntyche, Syzygus, and Clement (Phil 4:2-3); Aristarchus, Mark, and Jesus-Justus (Col 4:11; Phlm 24); Philemon (Phlm 1); and Demas and Luke (Phlm 24). But this only scratches the surface of those who seem to have been a part of Paul's colleagues in ministry.

> In Acts and the Pauline letters some one hundred individuals, under a score of titles and activities, are associated with the apostle at one time or another during his ministry. They are participants in his preaching and teaching and in his writing, and they define the apostle's work as a "collaborative ministry" (Harrington). (Ellis 1993, 183)
>
> The total number of Paul's coworkers has been placed at ninety-five (Redlich) or eighty-one (Pölzl), depending on how broadly one defines the term. When the names mentioned only in Acts and those with unspecified and general relationships to Paul are eliminated, thirty-six coworkers under nine designations can be identified with considerable probability. (Ellis 1993, 183; see 183-88)

The two associates Paul designates as **our brothers** are ***apostles*** [*apostoloi*, **representatives** or "messengers" (NRSV)] ***of the churches.*** But they are
8:23-24
not apostles of Christ in the same sense that Paul was. They had not seen the risen Christ and been commissioned as his agents, as Paul had (1:1; 1 Cor 9:1; 15:5-9; see Matt 10:2). Yet they are sent with the full authority of those who commissioned them (see Phil 2:25). They were official envoys of the churches.

Paul names them further as **an honor to Christ,** literally, ***the glory of Christ*** (v 23; see 4:4). The precise sense of this phrase is difficult to determine. The precise force of the genitive construction *doxa Christou* is ambiguous. We take it to mean that the **brothers** are messengers through whose lives Christ shows his glory. Therefore, their ministry is a reflection of Christ's glory (v 19; 4:6; see 2:15; 3:3-11, 18; 9:13). In short, Paul recommends them as a glowing credit to Christ. In vv 16-23, those Paul sends to Corinth possess an authorization that is *personal, ecclesial,* and *christological.* That is, they represent Paul, the churches, and Christ himself (Harris 2005, 595-96).

■ **24** In vv 16-22, Paul prepares the way for his summary commendation of his delegates in v 23. In v 24, he makes a concluding appeal to the Corinthians to complete their participation in the offering. This renews the appeal of 8:7-15. Paul's exhortation is twofold, carried by an imperatival participle (*endeiknymenoi*) translated simply as **show.**

First, **therefore** (*oun*), the Corinthians are to demonstrate to these messengers the **proof** (*endeixin*) of their **love** (see v 8).

Second, they are to **show** the validity of Paul's **reason for . . . pride in** or ***boasting about*** them (see 9:2). He expects the Corinthians to offer a warm and hospitable reception to the delegates. The church is to give a positive response to their request concerning the collection.

The twofold demonstration is to be **so that the churches can see it.** Paul writes literally: "in the face of the churches." Paul expects the Corinthians to respond to the visit of Titus and the two brothers as if the congregations they represent are present and overseeing the reception. In a sense this is the case, since the delegates will report back to their respective churches what they have seen and heard in Corinth (Plummer 1915, 251). In fact, the reception of Paul's representatives "will be officially reported throughout Christendom" (Denney 1943, 5:784) to the universal church of that day.

Paul encourages the Corinthians to participate fully in the offering. (1) He did this by handling the project in a manner that left no room for suspicion. (2) This he did by delegating a share of the responsibility for the collection and its oversight to others. (3) Among these, Paul chose spiritual men, adequately qualified to represent him and the churches who sent them.

2. The Sending of the Brothers (9:1-5)

The literary integrity of these verses in their present context has been questioned (see the Introduction). But they are connected closely both grammatically and in thought with the preceding verses (see Matera 2003, 199-200; Harris 2005, 617-18). The opening phrase in v 1, *peri men gar* (***For, on the one hand, concerning***), almost never functions as an introduction. The clarifying conjunction *gar*, ***for,*** omitted by the NIV, looks back to 8:24. The particle *men* anticipates the *de* in v 3, as part of an "on the one hand, but on the other hand" construction.

Paul again expresses confidence in the Corinthians. But he apprehensively explains why the delegation is being sent and why he wants them to go. He urges the church to respond positively to the delegation by having the collection ready when he pays his next visit to Corinth. Paul wants to avoid disgrace for himself and the Corinthians. He does not want those he bragged about to the Macedonians or himself to be embarrassed by their being unprepared should any Macedonians accompany him (see 8:24; 9:4).

■ **1** Paul admits that **There is no need** (***it is superfluous*** or "redundant," Betz 1985, 87) for him **to write** more about **this service** [*diakonias*, ***ministry***] **to the saints** (see the commentary on 8:4). But he proceeds to do just that (see Heb 11:32-38). This is an example of a familiar epistolary or rhetorical device called *paraleipsis* ("a passing over"). Writers and speakers use this when they profess to pass over a subject only to mention it all the same (BDF 1961, 495; Betz 1985, 90-91). Thus, professors have been known to say, "I need not remind you that the final exam will be comprehensive." By saying this, the reminder has been made.

Perhaps Paul thinks his readers are becoming bored with the topic or that resuming it indicates that he lacks confidence in their generosity (Thrall 2004, 564). But his repetition reminds the Corinthians that they need to get on with the project (8:6).

■ **2** In v 2 Paul offers the reason why (*gar,* **For**) he does not **need . . . to write** (v 1) further about the collection. He is aware of the Corinthians' willingness to participate (*prothymian;* see 8:11-12). In fact, he has been boasting to the Macedonians of their **eagerness to help** . . . **since last year** (8:6, 10). News that those **in Achaia were ready to give . . . stirred most of them to action.**

Achaia was the Roman province in southern Greece. Paul included this provincial name in his address of the letter to Corinth (1:1; see 11:10; 1 Cor 16:15). Corinth, the capital of Achaia, certainly contained most of the believers in Achaia. No doubt, Paul had in mind primarily the church there in his reference to Achaia here. We know there was a church in nearby Cenchrea, the Aegean (eastern) port of Corinth (Rom 16:1). Perhaps, Paul uses Achaia in parallel to his mention of the province of Macedonia (Matera 2003, 202; Rom 15:26). Perhaps, he uses it to flatter the Corinthians by identifying the province with their city (Harris 2005, 619).

What did Paul mean by suggesting that the Corinthians had been ready for a year? The perfect tense of *pareskeuastai,* **were ready,** normally suggests a present state resulting from a past event. But vv 3-4 indicate that the offering was not ready (*aparaskeuastous,* **unprepared**). The apparent discrepancy disappears *if* one can accept the NIV translation **ready to give** (see 8:10-11).

Paul says that the Corinthians' **enthusiasm** (*zēlos;* "zeal," NRSV) to begin preparations for the offering had **stirred most of** the Macedonians **to action.** But the intended progress on the collection had been hindered by the conflict that had developed between Paul and the Corinthians. Paul was sending the three-man delegation to help with the execution of the task.

■ **3** With the first three of four purpose clauses (*hina . . . hina . . . mē pōs ean . . . hina*) in one sentence, Paul gives a negative, a positive, and another negative reason for **sending** (an epistolary aorist) **the brothers** (v 3; see v 5). Titus is probably now included (see 2:15).

The adversative *de* (**But**) joins v 3 with vv 1-2. Paul now gives us the other side of the story (Thrall 2004, 567). He must broach the subject again **in order that** his own **boasting about** the Corinthians to the Macedonians (see v 1) **should not prove hollow** (*kenōthēi en tōi merei toutōi;* see 6:1; 2 Cor 1:17; 9:15). That is, he does not want his use of the example of the Corinthians' eagerness to motivate the Macedonians to appear to have been an empty, manipulative ploy. So he urges the Corinthians to have the offering fully ***prepared*** (*pareskeuasmenoi;* **ready,** see v 2) to send when the delegation arrives.

■ **4** In v 4 Paul gives his second negative purpose for repeating the arrangements for the collection. This is his most significant reason, expressed in a tentative and apprehensive manner. It is *mē pōs ean, "so that . . . (perhaps) not, lest* *somehow"* (BDAG 2000, 901; see 2:7) he might not be "humiliated" (NRSV) by their failure to follow through.

As in v 1, Paul again resorts to *paraleipsis*. He reminds the Corinthians that their failure to deliver on their promise will humiliate not only him but them as well. While professing **not to say anything about** the Corinthians' shame, he alludes to it nonetheless. In the honor-shame society of the ancient Mediterranean, failure to keep one's word meant embarrassment and serious loss of esteem in the eyes of others. Unlike people in the modern West, the experience of shame, contempt, disrespect, disgrace, or public humiliation was a fate worse than death.

Further Reading on Honor and Shame in Mediterranean Society

Carter, T. L. 2002. *Paul and the Power of Sin: Redefining 'Beyond the Pale.'* Cambridge: Cambridge University Press.

deSilva, David A. 2000a. "Honor and Shame." In the *Dictionary of New Testament Background*. Downers Grove, Ill.: InterVarsity Press.

_________. 2000b. *Honor, Patronage, Kinship and Purity: Unlocking New Testament Culture*. Downers Grove, Ill.: InterVarsity Press.

Gilmore, D. D., ed. 1985. *Honor and Shame and the Unity of the Mediterranean*. Washington: American Anthropological Society.

Malina, Bruce. 1981. *The New Testament World: Insights from Cultural Anthropology*. Atlanta: John Knox.

Moxnes, Halvor. 1988a. "Honor and Righteousness in Romans." *Journal for the Study of the New Testament* 32:61-77.

_________. 1988b. "Honor, Shame, and the Outside World in Paul's Letter to the Romans." Pages 207-18 in *The Social World of Formative Christianity and Judaism*. Edited by Jacob Neusner, Peder Borgen, Ernest S. Frerichs, and Richard Horsley. Philadelphia: Fortress.

_________. 1996. "Honor and Shame." Pages 29-40 in *The Social Sciences and New Testament Interpretation*. Edited by Richard L. Rohrbaugh. Peabody, Mass.: Hendrickson.

Paul is sending "the brothers" to administer the details of the collection so that neither he nor the Corinthians will lose face "in this undertaking" (NRSV). This latter phrase, *en tēi hypostasei tautēi*, may also be translated "by this confidence" (NASB). This justifies the NIV paraphrase: **having been so confident** (see 11:17; see Heb 11:1).

The word *hypostasis* may mean substantial nature or essence (Heb 1:3), realization, plan or endeavor, situation or condition (see BDAG 2000, 1040). But in the present context, *en tēi hypostasei tautēi* probably means "in connection with this undertaking" (see Furnish 1984, 427-28; Thrall 2004, 568-70; Harris 2005, 626). Here, "this undertaking" (NRSV) refers to the collection plan or project. As elsewhere in chs 8—9, Paul avoids using monetary terms to refer to the collection.

■ **5** The inferential particle *oun,* **So** or ***therefore,*** looks back to vv 3-4, further explaining his reasons for sending the delegation ahead of his third visit to Corinth. Paul **thought it necessary** to conclude with an appeal to **the brothers,** again including Titus (see 8:6), to proceed to Corinth **and finish the arrangements for the generous gift** they **had promised** in advance of Paul's arrival.

Paul repeats three verbs with the alliterative use of the prefix *pro-* (*proelthōsin . . . prokatartisōsin . . . proepēngelmenēn:* ***precede*** *. . .* ***prepare*** *. . .* ***promise***) to embellish his style. He stresses his coming visit, subtly reminding the Corinthians of the threat to their honor should he arrive and find them unprepared. The fulfillment of a promise was a primary responsibility in the Greco-Roman world (Thrall 2004, 570; McCant 1999, 91).

The phrase **generous gift** twice translates *eulogian* (literally, "good word," normally meaning ***blessing***). Thus, we have yet another nonmonetary word applied to the collection. In 1 Cor 16:1 *logia* designated the collection itself. This, *eu-logia,* "really fine collection," will be a blessing—an expression of love that will bless its recipients. The term *eulogia* as blessing ordinarily reflects the relationship between God and humans (see Eph 1:3). But it is directed here to human motivation, perhaps understood as flowing from the experience of God's blessing (Hafemann 2000, 365).

Paul wants the Corinthians to finish the collection before his arrival (***in this way,*** *houtōs*). Despite his various persuasive tactics, the apostle wants the offering to be **ready as a generous gift, not as one grudgingly given** (*pleonexian*). Thus, the words *eulogia* and *pleonexia*—***blessing*** vs. **extortion** (see BDAG 2000, 824)—are used as polar opposites. The money may be the same; the difference is in the motives of the giver. Are they giving generously or only out of avarice or greed? Are they participating freely or only because Paul coerced them to do so? Only if their participation is a free act of Christian love can their gift be a vehicle for blessing. "Paul wants a blessing, not an extortion" (McCant 1999, 91). He develops this thought in the next paragraph (9:9-15).

Paul seeks to insure the Corinthians' appropriate response to the mission of the delegation:

1. by reaffirming his confidence in their eagerness to participate (vv 1-2)
2. by reminding them that he had staked the honor of his word—and theirs—on their performance (vv 3-4) and
3. by using terms that highlight the spiritual character of the financial undertaking (v 5)

3. The Blessings of Liberality (9:6-15)

In preparation for his third visit to Corinth, Paul is sending delegates ahead to ensure that the collection will be complete by the time he arrives.

Still seeking to motivate his readers, he expands on the theme touched on in the last clause of v 5. His concern moves from the need to finish the project to how giving can be a matter of joyful generosity. He encourages the Corinthians' liberal giving by explaining the benefits of liberality (1) in God's enrichment of the givers (vv 6-11) and (2) in its impact on the recipients (vv 12-15).

In Paul's mind the theological language of benevolence and the Corinthians' loyalty to their apostle are connected as "the testing of this ministry" (9:13 NRSV). McCant (1999, 93-98) identifies five theological affirmations underlying the practice of generous giving:

1. One should give from the heart (9:7).
2. God is the source of all giving (9:8).
3. Giving enriches the giver (9:9-11).
4. Giving evokes the worship of thanksgiving to God (9:12).
5. Giving honors God (9:13-15).

■ **6** Paul logically, carefully, effectively, and subtly proceeds to construct his exhortation to generosity. **Remember this** in Greek paraphrases *touto de*, ***now this*** ("the point is this," NRSV; "now this I say," NASB). This elliptical linking expression introduces the agricultural proverb that follows (see 1 Cor 7:29; 15:50; Gal 3:17). The maxim resumes the concluding idea of 2 Cor 9:5, an image familiar in both Jewish wisdom tradition and the Greco-Roman culture of Paul's time (see Harris 2005, 634; Thrall 2004, 574-75; Furnish 1984, 440).

Proverbs 11:24-25 may represent this wisdom principle: "Some give freely, yet grow all the richer; others withhold what is due, and only suffer want. A generous person will be enriched, and one who gives water will get water" (NRSV; see 19:17; Job 4:8; Gal 6:7-10). Paul crafts his version of the axiom as a double chiasm (abb'a' . . . abb'a'): ***sows sparingly, sparingly reaps*** and ***sows generously, generously reaps.***

The Greek expression twice translated **generously,** *ep' eulogiais*, in v 6 provides a linguistic link to the twofold "generous gift" (*eulogian*) of v 5. To sow expects a harvest in kind. As applied to the Corinthian situation, the harvest does not await the end of the age. Paul encourages his audience to expect spiritual and perhaps even material blessings in their present hearts and lives. One who **sows generously** is sowing on the principle of blessings and on this basis reaps (see Luke 6:38).

■ **7** Consistent with and basic to this principle is another with its biblical and cultural precedents. This kind of giving must be done by "each one" (NASB)—individually, freely, and privately. Each must do as he or she **has decided** from the **heart** ahead of time (8:3; see Acts 4:32). This kind of giving cannot be done either **reluctantly or under compulsion**.

The first term, **reluctantly** (*ek lypēs*), is literally ***from pain*** or ***sorrow*** (see 2:1-3). Paul's terminology echoes Deut 15:10 (LXX), where the Law requires that the debts of the poor be canceled in the seventh year "without a grudging heart" (*ou lypēthēsei tēi kardiai*) so that God may "bless" (*eulogēsei*) their creditors.

The second term, **under compulsion** (*ex anankēs*), indicates pressure from the inherent nature of things, perhaps as merely a social necessity (BDAG 2000, 60-61).

The positive counterpart of these mistaken kinds of giving follows. That **God loves a cheerful giver** alludes to Prov 22:9 (LXX; see v 11). There it is said that God blesses those who are both generous givers and cheerful about it.

The Greek term translated **cheerful** here is *hilaron,* the source of the English word "hilarious." Paul substitutes **loves** (*agapai*) for the LXX "blesses" (*eulogēsei*), perhaps to suggest that God not only "approves" or "values" such generosity, but positively directs his love toward cheerful givers in some special sense. The Greek places both **cheerful** and **God** in the emphatic first and last positions in the sentence. Truly Christian giving is inspired by grace, motivated by love, and has blessing as its goal (see 8:1; 9:8).

■ **8** Verses 8 and 9 pick up the whole of the preceding exhortation and begin Paul's commentary on v 6*b* (vv 8-14). They also connect directly to v 7*c,* explaining why God loves cheerful givers.

The literary construction of v 8 is fascinating. Alliteration (repeated initial consonant sounds), paronomasia (wordplay), and anaphora (repetition) give it a rhetorically attractive style and emphasis (McCant 1999, 94). Most striking are the "all" words, each beginning with *pan* or *pas*. *Pasan . . . panti pantote pasan . . . pan* are set within the repetition of the verb **abound** (*perisseuō*).

Paul's key word continues to be **grace** (*charin*)**: God is able to make all grace abound to you** (v 8). Grace is the motivating concept that underlies Paul's entire treatment of the collection (8:1, 9; see 8:4, 6, 7, 9, 16, 19; 9:14, 15; 1 Cor 16:3). It reaches out to encompass both spiritual and material benefits (Harris 2005, 637). The abounding of **grace** is probably not about repayment, but simply harvest or intrinsic reward (Thrall 2004, 577-78).

The result of the Corinthians' generosity in the context of the grace of God is **that in all things at all times,** they will have **all that** they **need** so they can provide for others. Paul's words are literally: "always having all sufficiency in everything" (NASB). The Greek term *autarkeian,* "sufficiency," is a favorite virtue among the Cynic and Stoic philosophers denoting self-sufficiency or inward contentment. In its only other NT occurrence, in 1 Tim 6:6, it means contentment (see Phil 4:11—*autarkēs;* BDAG 2000, 152). Here, however, Paul uses "sufficiency" to refer to the resources God will supply the Corinthians to enable them to **abound in every good work.**

Paul is not thinking of "good works" generally, but of the continuing **work** of generous giving. Cheerful givers not only have the grace to do with less but also are divinely resourced with more to give others. Paul says, in effect, that God's gift of grace will supply all the Corinthians need—spiritually and materially—so they can continue to be generous in blessing others. God's grace is a giving grace, able to fatten the leanest and meanest of souls.

■ **9** Paul resumes the agricultural metaphor of "sowing," introduced in v 6, to illustrate his point with a scriptural citation (v 9). **As it is written** (see 8:15) introduces his quotation of Ps 112:9. Those who serve the Lord scatter (*eskorpisen*) their wealth, like the farmer scatters seed, by giving **to the poor.**

The psalm describes the person "who fears the LORD," delights "in his commands" (v 1), prospers (vv 2-3), is "gracious and compassionate and righteous" (v 4), is just and stable (vv 5-8), and lavishes gifts on the poor (v 9). Such persons are honored and remembered (vv 6, 9); their **righteousness endures forever** (vv 3, 9). Some interpreters claim that Paul uses this quotation with God as the subject, as in v 8 (Betz 1985, 111-12). But the contexts of both the psalm and 2 Cor 9:9 suggest that it is the Corinthian giver.

Here, the **righteousness** that **endures forever** is not God's faithful character, but that of the human giver. **Righteousness** probably refers to the moral character of the Corinthian givers as expressed in their generosity (see v 10). That it **endures forever** has the biblical sense of being "remembered" (Ps 112:3), which parallels "forever" in vv 6 and 9 of the psalm. Thus, their generosity continues as a reality in the present and future. It can stand the test of judgment. Scripture indicates that the Corinthians' "good work" will have a continuing impact. They will never lack the resources to be generous. God will see to that (v 8; see vv 10-11).

■ **10** Paul's point in vv 6-9 is clearly expressed in v 10. It expands on v 8 by employing the agricultural imagery introduced in vv 6 and 9. He has reinforced his point by appealing to Scripture (v 9). Now he nails it down, identifying God as the primary actor in an adaptation of Isa 55:10:

As the rain and the snow
come down from heaven,
and do not return to it
without watering the earth
and making it bud and flourish,
so that it yields seed for the sower and bread for the eater.

Paul adds to his biblical foundation for generosity. In his adaptation of Isa 55, instead of "the earth," he implies that God is the one **who supplies seed to the sower and bread for food. Food** (*brōsin*) refers to the act of ***eating*** (BDAG 2000, 184) in parallel to ***the one sowing*** (*tō speironti*). The God who supplies the seed and the strength to sow will also **supply and increase** the Corinthians' **store of seed.** Paul refers twice to **seed** (*sporon*), first literally, and then figuratively. He continues to avoid explicit references to money, using the imagery of seeds to refer to their resource for giving (see Prov 11:24). God is the source of their liberal giving.

Paul picks up the word **righteousness** from his quotation of Ps 112:9 to expand the divine promise to the Corinthians. He adds: God **will enlarge the harvest** [*genēmata*] **of your righteousness.** Again he alludes to Scripture, this time to Hos 10:12 (LXX): "Sow for yourselves righteousness, reap the fruit [*genēmata*] of unfailing love." By the harvest or "fruits" of the Corinthians'

righteousness, Paul means the results of their generosity in the form of both material and spiritual blessings for them and the saints in Jerusalem.

God will enlarge the harvest of the Corinthians' generosity. That is, he will continue to supply them with the means to meet the needs of the recipients. Their **righteousness** is "the manifestation of God's righteousness" (Hafemann 2000, 368, 370). God is able to make every grace abound in and through the Corinthians (v 8). With the vivid imagery of a farmer planting and harvesting in dependence on God, the apostle portrayed the generosity of Christians.

■ **11** In v 11, Paul summarizes what he has been saying in vv 6-10, while providing a transition to what follows. The Corinthians **will be made rich in every way *for every kind of generosity*** (*haplotēta;* see on 8:2). God is the implied "subject" of the present participle *ploutizomenoi,* ***being made rich.*** The same grace of God that is enriching them will continue to enrich them, as it enabled the impoverished Macedonians to give liberally (8:1).

Perhaps Paul accents the present to motivate the Corinthians. He goes on to say that such selfless giving in behalf of others ***is producing*** (*katergazetai,* present tense) or **will result in thanksgiving to God** (see NASB, NRSV). Here selfless giving has its concrete form in the collection being raised and delivered through Paul and his associates to the saints in Jerusalem. Perhaps he says that the greatest benefit of the Corinthians' giving is the thanksgiving that will be given to God by the saints in Jerusalem when they receive the collection. Paul's main point, however, is that the collection is God's work from start to finish. It begins with God's grace and ends in thanksgiving to God (Matera 2003, 208). It is noteworthy that **thanksgiving** (*eucharistian*) has "grace" (*charis*) at the heart of it.

■ **12** In v 12, Paul expands on and explains v 11 (*hoti, **for***), restating the reasons for and results of the offering. His ***not only . . . but also*** (*ou monon . . . alla kai*) construction indicates that the second purpose for the collection is the more significant.

The first and most obvious historical purpose was **supplying the needs of God's people** (*tōn hagiōn, **the saints***). The second purpose, **overflowing in many expressions of thanks to God,** is a distinctly theological aim (Harris 2005, 650). Paul employs here yet another descriptive designation for the collection: ***the ministry of this service*** (*diakonia tēs leitourgias tautēs:* **this service that you perform**).

Paul has used the term *diakonia* previously in connection with the offering (8:4; 9:1, see v 13). But the second term, *leitourgia,* occurs in Paul's letters only here and in Phil 2:17 and 30. Both terms carry the general meaning of "service." Two issues face us: First, what kind of relation between the two terms does the genitive case indicate? And second, is the sense intended non-technical/popular or religious/cultic?

Scholarly opinion on the first question is divided. If *tēs leitourgias* is an epexegetic (explanatory) genitive, it defines *diakonia* more precisely as "the charitable act of this public service" (Betz 1985, 87). If it is an objective genitive, the first term indicates the action performed on the second. Thus, it has the meaning of "the execution of this act of public service" (Barrett 1973, 239; see Martin 1986). This is the force of the genitive implied by the NIV and NRSV translations. It is probably to be preferred because the emphasis falls on *leitourgias.*

The second question concerns the precise meaning of the term *leitourgias*. The NIV translates *tēs leitourgias tautēs* as **this service.** But this can be taken in any one of three senses:

- "public service" performed for the community in mind
- a priestly (liturgical) or "holy service"
- "service" in a popular or generic sense

The Greek word *leitourgos,* ***minister,*** is the source of the English cognate "liturgy." The term is a compound of two words referring to "people work." In the NT those who render such service are often not merely civil servants, but leaders of considerable status (BDAG 2000, 591).

In Rom 13:6, Paul refers to government "authorities" as also "God's servants [*leitourgoi*]"—secular ***ministers*** (as in the British parliamentary system). In Rom 15:16, Paul describes himself as "a minister [*leitourgon*] of Christ Jesus to the Gentiles with the priestly duty of proclaiming the gospel of God." In other letters, he refers to certain church workers using the same title (Phil 2:17, 25, 30).

In the LXX the *leitourg-* word family applies to the cultic service of Israel's priests and Levites (Num 8:22; 1 Chr 16:4, 37; see Luke 1:23; Heb 8:2). Paul uses *leitourgia* in this religious sense (metaphorically) in Phil 2:17 (alongside "sacrifice," *thysia;* see Flemming 2009). But it refers only to personal financial assistance in Phil 2:30.

Paul's language for the collection (*leitourgeō* in Rom 15:27) throughout chs 8 and 9 implies that *diakonia tēs leitourgias tautēs* connotes more than merely public service. It has cultic overtones (Matera 2003, 209; see Furnish 1984, 451). For Paul, here as elsewhere, what is done for the sake of the gospel and the church in the name of Christ partakes of the character of Christ's own sacrificial service. The collection is "an essential part of the ministry of the gospel and a genuine expression of worship" (Hafemann 2000, 370).

The offering will be a ***filling up*** (*prosanaplērousa,* **supplying**) of the needs of the saints in Jerusalem. The Corinthians were merely "adding to" the total collection; other churches were contributing as well. More importantly, their **service** will also overflow **in many expressions of thanks to God.** The participles **supplying** and **overflowing** suggest that the offering will be sufficient for or exceed the need. God blesses those who give and those who receive; others in turn "bless" God! In vv 13 and 14 Paul explains why and how there will be ***many thanksgivings to God.***

■ **13** Verses 13-14 contain many of the spiritually "loaded" terms Paul has used throughout chs 8 and 9 to refer to the collection—*dokimē, diakonia, haplotēs, koinōnia, charis*. A new combination of these terms appears in **the obedience that accompanies your confession** (*tēi hypotagēi tēs homologias hymōn*). Its meaning is crucial to the interpretation of vv 13 and 14.

Paul communicates his central thought in v 13 with the adverbial participle phrase *doxazontes ton Theon*. This is probably best translated ***people will glorify God.*** Some interpreters, however, consider the Corinthians ("you," NRSV) the implicit subject, as in v 11 (see Matera 2003, 210). But the context indicates that Paul has changed the focus from the Corinthians to the recipients of the collection, who ***will glorify God.***

The reason (*dia*, **Because**) for their glorification or **praise** of God is **the service by which you have proved yourselves** (literally, ***the proof of this ministry:*** *tēs dokimēs tēs diakonias tautēs*). The NRSV translates *dokimēs* here as "testing" (see 8:2). But, as in 13:3, it is better taken as "approved character" (BDAG 2000, 356). The successful completion of the offering by the Corinthians will give the Jerusalem Christians evidence of the Corinthians' genuineness as Christians. They **will praise God for** [your] **obedience . . . and for your generosity** (*epi . . . kai*, emphasis added).

The first ***proof*** is **the obedience that accompanies** the Corinthians' **confession of the gospel of Christ.** If we take *tēs homologias* (***of the confession***) as a subjective genitive, their **confession of the gospel of Christ** produces their **obedience.** Etymologically, the verb *homologeō*, confess, is a compound of two Greek words meaning "I say the same thing." Thus, confession here implies that the Corinthians demonstrate their agreement with God's assessment of Jesus as good news. Their **confession** refers to the call and claims of **the gospel,** the source and content of which is **Christ.** That is, by participating in the collection, the Corinthians practically acknowledge the good news about Christ. This concrete confession of faith is at once an expression of their obedience to Christ.

Betz, however, takes **confession** here as referring to a legal agreement by which the Corinthians acknowledge the authority of Jerusalem as the mother church. This submission is to be demonstrated in their offering for the saints (1985, 122-24). Thrall (2004, 589-90) and Harris (2005, 654) offer effective arguments against this view.

The tangible expression of the Corinthians' **obedience** here refers specifically to their cooperation in the collection. The first ***proof*** of their obedience in "confessing the gospel finds expression in obedient subjection to its requirements" (BDAG 2000, 709). We need not repeat here our earlier comments on the cluster of theological terms Paul uses to refer to the collection (see the commentary on *dokimē* in 8:2; *diakonia* in 8:4; 9:1, 12; *haplotēs* in 8:2 and 9:11; and *koinōnia* in 8:4).

The second ***proof*** of the obedience of the Corinthians visible to the

Jerusalem church is their **generosity in sharing with them and with everyone else** (*haplotēti tēs koinōnias eis autous kai eis pantas*). This is literally ***the sincerity of communion to them and to all.*** By **everyone else** Paul refers to their active concern for the needs of others (see Gal 6:10). The word "contribution" (NASB; see Rom 15:26) is not the best translation of *koinōnia* here. What Paul seems to have in mind is more like equal "partnership" with the Jerusalem church.

■ **14** Paul continues to stress his concern for the ties of mutual recognition and love between Gentile Christians and the believers in Jerusalem. He expects that the Jerusalem Christians will remember the Corinthians **in their prayers** (*deēsei*). As they do, **their hearts will go out to** the Corinthians. The adverbial participle phrase *autōn deēsei hyper hymōn epipothountōn hymas* (literally, ***their desiring you in prayer for you***) is a genitive absolute construction. Thus, it is an independent assertion of an action that will accompany the Corinthians' generosity (v 13). The Judean saints, who will receive the collection, will "long" (NRSV) or "yearn" (NASB) for its Gentile donors. That is, it will demonstrate the solidarity of Jewish and Gentile Christians and contribute to the unification of the church.

In Rom 15:26-27, Paul offers another explanation of his understanding of the collection. It was something the churches of Macedonia and Achaia had contributed as a gesture of solidarity (*koinōnian*, ***a sharing***) with one another and with "the poor among the saints in Jerusalem" (v 26). By referring to the collection as *koinōnia*, he emphasizes that it is not an act of charity but an expression of the commonality of the churches involved—both those giving and receiving aid.

In 2 Cor 9:14, the dative *deēsei* (**in their prayers**) may signify the metaphorical location where the longing of the Jerusalem Christians for the Corinthians will be expressed. It might also be translated instrumentally as ***by praying*** or as an attendant circumstance—"as they pray" (Harris 2005, 657).

Paul is confident the offering will meet with a positive reception **because of the surpassing** [see 3:10; Hafemann 2000, 371] **grace God has given** the Corinthians. The NIV interprets the expression ***the grace*** [*charin*] ***of God*** as a subjective genitive: God gives grace. Grace, as the manifestation of God's "surpassing glory" (3:10), has now enclosed the entire discussion of the collection (8:1; 9:14; see 8:4, 6, 7, 9, 16, 19; 9:8,15). Here, no doubt, **grace** refers to God's freely given inspiration for and provision of resources for the offering.

It is a long way from Jerusalem to Corinth, but Paul is convinced that prayer and intercession can span the distance. With all this, of course, the apostle intends to encourage the Corinthians to complete the collection. As we noted at the beginning of our comments on these chapters, the apostle offers here his eschatological vision of a profound unity between his Gentile congregations and the Jewish church of Jerusalem (Matera 2003, 209; so Munck 1959, 303-8; and Nickle 1966, 129-42; but see Harris 2005, 87-101). Did Paul see the delivery of the collection as (at least) a partial fulfillment of prophetic expectations that in the eschaton the wealth of the Gentiles would flow into Jerusalem (see Rom 9:26; 15:22-29; Isa 45:14; 60:5–17; 61:6; Mic 4:13; Tob 13:11)?

■ **15** Paul ends his discussion of the collection with a liturgical and prayerful outburst of gratitude: **Thanks [*charis*] be to God for his indescribable gift.** What he implies is: "Let us all give thanks to God." Here is yet another use of the thematic word for "grace" (see the introduction to the IN THE TEXT section on 8:1—9:15; 8:16; see Rom 6:17; 7:25; 1 Cor 15:57).

But what is the nature of God's **gift** (*dōreai*)? Is it the grace of God operative in the collection as the context might suggest? Is it the whole redemptive work of God as in Rom 5:15-17 (see Eph 3:7 and 4:7)? Or is it simply God's gift of himself in the person of his Son?

The latter is certainly feasible. The adjective **indescribable** (*anekdiēgētōi*) occurs only here in NT. Paul certainly implies (8:9; see Rom 8:32) that what God has done in Christ is the supreme motivation for his lengthy appeal to the Corinthians. Second Corinthians 9:1-15, as Matera suggests, "present an exalted vision of the collection" (2003, 207). Is it possible that Paul could not distinguish completely the three understandings of God's gift delineated in the previous paragraph?

Whatever he meant precisely, we know that the Corinthians were moved to action by Paul's impassioned rhetoric. The apostle's grand appeal proved successful, for a few months later he wrote from Corinth to the Romans: "Macedonia and Achaia were pleased to make a contribution for the poor among the saints in Jerusalem" (Rom 15:26).

In 2 Cor 9:6-15, Paul gives three valid motives for generous and joyous giving.

1. To give with a right spirit is a sowing that ensures a harvest (vv 6-7).
2. God is able and willing to grant all that one needs within and without for a loving sharing with others (vv 8-10).
3. What is given does more than meet material needs; it can have thrilling spiritual implications—blessings all around (vv 11-15; Plummer 1915, 257).

Paul begins chs 8—9 by reporting how the grace of God manifested itself in the generosity of the Macedonians. This leads into his exhortation to the Corinthians to resume what they began a year before in the interest of equality among the churches (8:1-15). The chapters conclude with Paul's exhortation to the Corinthians to give generously so that others will be able to praise the same grace in them (9:6-15). Along the way, he commends the delegation headed by Titus, which will make preparations for this gracious gift (8:16—9:5). Although the appeal is for money, a theology of grace underlies it all. The grace God revealed in Christ enables people to be generous to one another (Matera 2003, 210-11).

If one gathers all the significant terms Paul applies to the collection in chs 8—9, Christian giving is described as:

1. an expression of grace (*charis;* 8:1, 4, 6-7, 9; 9:8, 14)
2. sincerely motivated generosity (*haplotētos;* 8:2; 9:11, 13)
3. the implementation of Christian fellowship and partnership (*koinōnia;* 8:4; 9:13-15; Rom 15:26-27)
4. an indispensable part of Christian ministry (*diakonia;* 8:4, 19-20; 9:1, 12-13)
5. a liberal gift (*hadrotēs;* 8:20)
6. a means of spiritual blessing (*eulogia;* 9:5-6)
7. a sacred service (*leitourgia;* 9:12).

Using these religious and theological terms Paul expresses a theology of giving. It is at once a theology of "the grace of our Lord Jesus Christ" (8:9). "The grace of Christian giving" is simply the Spirit-empowered following of his lead.

FROM THE TEXT

In these chapters, the Apostle Paul uses terms of rich theological significance to impress on the Corinthians that their participation in the offering was integral to their very being as Christians (Murphy-O'Connor 1991, 76): "For you know the grace of our Lord Jesus Christ, that though he was rich, yet for your sakes he became poor, so that you through his poverty might become rich" (8:9).

In his apostolic ministry, Paul sees a living connection between giving and theology. Dare we then say that "Christian" givers are theologians, that there is such a thing as "a theology of Christian giving"? What does theology have to do with giving? Everything! So we ask, What do chs 8—9 contribute to such a theology, a theology that informs who *we* are and what *we* do *as* Christians?

We must put together all the spiritually pregnant terms Paul applies to the collection. Christian giving may be viewed from various perspectives. It is grace (*charis*), generosity (*haplotētos*), partnership (*koinōnia*), ministry (*diakonia*), a liberal gift (*hadrotēs*), a blessing (*eulogia*), and a service of worship (*leitourgia*). Paul's choice of words expresses a profound understanding of giving, one informed by a theology of grace. It originates in the graciousness of the God revealed in his Son Jesus the Christ. He "graces" people to be gracious and generous in ministry to one another in his name. The witness of 2 Corinthians to "a theology of Christian giving" is expressed in (1) *a theology of grace* and (2) *a theology of ministry.*

First and foremost, "a theology of Christian giving" is *a theology of grace.* The language of "grace" permeates all the letters of Paul. It both opens (8:1) and closes (9:15) the present passage and occurs no less than ten times in his appeal to the Corinthians to complete "the collection for God's people" in Jerusalem (1 Cor 16:1, 3).

When Paul uses "grace" (*charis*) in direct reference to the offering itself, *charis* is a "privilege" (8:4) or "favor" (NASB), an "act of grace" (8:6) or a "generous undertaking" (NRSV), and simply "the offering" (8:19) or a "gracious work" (NASB).

When the apostle urges the Corinthians to be generous and cheerful givers, "grace" is offered as their fully adequate resource, which enables them to serve others. "And God is able to make all grace abound to you, so that in all things at all times, having all that you need, you will abound in every good work" (9:8; see vv 6-11).

Paul's life and apostolic ministry was totally within the embrace of the grace of God in Jesus Christ from whom he "received grace and apostleship" (Rom 1:5). He testified: "By the grace of God I am what I am" (1 Cor 15:10). His ministry was conducted "not according to worldly wisdom but according to God's grace" (2 Cor 1:12). He realized that he was able to fulfill his apostolic calling only through grace. In his unrelieved pain, he learned from God: "My grace is sufficient for you, for my power is made perfect in weakness" (2 Cor 12:9). Supremely for Paul, the reality of his life and ministry was "this grace in which we now stand" (Rom 5:2). He understood this christologically as "the grace of our Lord Jesus Christ" (8:9; see Rom 5:15-21). Thus, he urged the Corinthians "not to receive God's grace in vain" (2 Cor 6:1).

Paul applies his understanding of grace to the task of the collection. God's grace revealed in Christ provides the standard by which giving is to be measured. Paul takes into consideration the entire scope of God's revelation in Christ from the incarnation to the resurrection. In Charles Wesley's lines:

All-wise, all-good, almighty Lord,
JESUS, by highest heavens adored,
Ee'r time its course began,
How did Thy glorious mercy stoop
To take the fallen nature up,
When Thou Thyself wert man!
—Wesley 1991, Hymn XV, 36

As their measure of giving, Christians are to look to Christ who "became obedient to death—even death on a cross!" (Phil 2:8). Look to him who, Paul writes, "that though he was rich, yet for your sakes he became poor, so that you through his poverty might become rich" (2 Cor 8:9). Poverty can be "productive of great wealth" observed John Chrysostom (344/354-407, ACCS NT 7:272). Here is the very heart of "a theology of Christian giving." Before our eyes the pattern of the giving of Christ remains "the fountain of an inspiration as strong and pure to-day as when Paul wrote these words" (Denney 1943, 5:782).

Paul uses two very similar words to stress that *a theology of grace* involves sincere and generous giving. The genuinely received grace-generosity of God in Christ results in the graced generosity of God's people. Thus Paul calls the offering "this liberal gift" (*hadrotēs;* 8:20) or "this generous gift" (NRSV). Similarly, he uses *haplotēs*, "simplicity" or "sincerity," to mean "generosity" (NIV,

NRSV) or "liberality" (NASB). Thus, Paul speaks of the "rich generosity" (8:2) of the impoverished Macedonians. And he assures the Corinthians: "You will be made rich in every way so that you can be generous on every occasion" (9:11; see v 13).

Consistent with the grace-character of Christian giving is the apostle's insistence that he is "not commanding" (8:8) the Corinthians' participation in the collection. Rather, grace means that "Each of you must give as you have made up your mind, not reluctantly or under compulsion, for God loves a cheerful giver" (9:7 NRSV; see Phlm 14). Implicit in what Paul writes to the Corinthians is that all "Christian" giving takes place within the realm of grace and looks to the resources of that realm for its enabling. As Johannes Bengel (1687-1752) saw centuries ago, "When anything is well done, there is *grace* to those, who do it, and also *grace* to those to whom it is done" (1895, 3:399).

Flowing inherently from this *theology of grace* is *a theology of ministry.* Paul's apostolic ministry is the practical concern of 2 Corinthians: "through God's mercy we have this ministry" (4:1; see 6:3). He defends his ministry as "a new covenant . . . a ministry of the Spirit" (3:6, 8), in contrast to the old covenant of "the letter." He is a minister of this new covenant (3:6-11). He describes his ministry in terms of "the light of the knowledge of the glory of God in the face of Christ" (4:6).

Consequently, Paul's ministry shares in and reflects the death and resurrection of Christ. Thus, "we who are alive are always being given over to death for Jesus' sake, so that his life may be revealed in our mortal body" (4:11; see vv 7-12; 6:4). The apostolic ministry, although a "treasure in jars of clay" (4:7), is grandly "the ministry of reconciliation." In his ministry, God is "reconciling the world to himself in Christ" (5:18-19).

These are the theological assumptions that stand in the background of Paul's designation of the offering as a "ministry to the saints" (8:4 NRSV; 9:1; see 9:12-13). All four occurrences of *diakonia* in chs 8—9 are translated "ministry" in the NRSV. Paul describes the participation of the Macedonian churches in the collection in these terms: they "gave themselves first to the Lord and then to us" (8:5). He affirms the Corinthians' "eagerness to help" in the planned collection (9:2). Their participation both supplies "the needs of the saints" (9:12*a* NRSV) and overflows "in many expressions of thanks to God" (9:12*b*). By "this ministry" the church at Corinth will "glorify God by [their] obedience to the confession of the gospel of Christ" (9:13 NRSV).

One cannot escape the biblical conviction that "Christian giving" is an expression of the ministry of God in Christ. Divinely motivated and directed giving is as much a ministry as anything else we do in the name of Christ.

Other key terms Paul employs further unfold the implications of "a theology of Christian giving" as *a theology of ministry.* The Corinthians' "sharing" (8:4; 9:13) in the offering is expressed by *koinōnia.* The term involves a participation in a common task, here in "this act of grace" (8:6) or "this liberal gift"

(8:20). Elsewhere in his letters Paul uses *koinōnia* for the believer's participation in the divine dimension, in "the Holy Spirit" (13:14; Phil 2:1; see Acts 2:42) and even in "his Son Jesus Christ our Lord" (1 Cor 1:9; see 10:16). These overtones may also be present in his reflections on giving.

The theme of giving as blessing appears with the fourfold use of *eulogia*. Blessing indicates both the proper motivation for giving and the consequences of generosity. It is to be a "generous gift" so that the one who so gives will "reap generously" (9:5-6). Paul can speak of the giving of his time and talents in a church visit as coming "in the full measure of the blessing [*eulogias*] of Christ" (Rom 15:29; see Gal 3:14).

The principle of blessing, the blessing of God in Christ, is involved in generous giving, both for the giver and for the recipient. As the apostle expands this idea in 9:8-11, the question arises as to how far we can push the promise of material blessing. What does Paul's language imply in these verses?

Spiritual blessings are obvious. And it is also plain that God promises to enable givers to give, and that generously. Nevertheless, he calls for giving "according to what one has, not according to what he does not have" (8:12).

When my wife and I visit retired friends who must live on an extremely limited fixed income, I am amazed that every time they give us something, even if it is nothing more than a fresh flower. They are always grace-enabled to find a way to "abound in every good work" (9:8).

There is no ammunition for the proponents of the prosperity gospel here! Paul is presenting a prosperity that is far more "true" to the gospel than that. Generosity from the heart for the needs of others, not personal wealth, is his point. When given, riches are to be "applied to [God's] glory, and the good of men" (Clarke 1854, 2:353).

Further, the apostle characterizes generous giving as a *ministry* that is being "administered" (*diakonoumenēi*) in order to make known "the glory [*doxan*] of the Lord himself" (8:19 NRSV). The representatives Paul sent ahead to collect the offering are described as "the glory of Christ" (8:23 NRSV). Therefore, the Corinthians' participation in the offering is not only a work of ministry (*diakonia*) but also an act of worship (*leitourgias*) that is "overflowing in many expressions of thanks to God" (9:12).

Another expression employed by the apostle appears to contribute to giving as *a theology of ministry*. The term *hypostasei* can designate the substantial nature of something (9:4; see Heb 1:3). But in the present context, it has the primary sense of an endeavor or "undertaking" (NRSV). Giving is something significant in the exercise of ministry to others for the glory of Christ.

A final characteristic of giving in the context of Christian ministry is implicit in all the apostle writes about the collection. Significantly, it occupies nine verses: we must handle the Lord's money with complete integrity to ensure that it gives glory to God.

The appointment of delegates respected in the churches and fully trusted by Paul indicates the almost extreme importance he attached to this aspect of the offering. As Murphy-O'Connor puts it, "To be honest was not enough; he had to be seen as honest, and this is where the envoy came in" (1991, 87). Denney bluntly reminds us that "many a man has ruined himself—not to speak of those who trusted him—by too blind a belief in his own integrity" (1943, 5:784).

There is nothing more important in the life of the church and in the work of the minister than the transparency of handling the funds contributed by God's people. As has been evident in our time, failure at this point happens all too often. So we affirm with the Apostle Paul that "we want to avoid any criticism of the way we administer this liberal gift. For we are taking pains to do what is right, not only in the eyes of the Lord but also in the eyes of men" (8:20-21). God's people must take extreme care that they leave no room for suspicion.

A surprising comment describes a recent trend in the search for meaning in contemporary culture: "We're such a hyperaffluent society, what else is left for us to do than take things away from our lives?" (Yabroff 2007, 84). More than we know, our highly technical, thoroughly materialistic, and affluent culture can subtly, and not so subtly, subvert the Christian culture of the local and general church. Indeed, it can infiltrate the moral and spiritual perspectives of the individual Christian. To this issue the biblical text is penetratingly and critically relevant. It proclaims a Pauline theology of "Christian giving" as an enabling theology focused in *a theology of grace* and *a theology of ministry.*

Such a theology of the "economy of God" (Young and Ford 1987, 178) calls for discernment. We must clarify our values, put our "wealth" in perspective, and purify the manner and motives of our giving. "Christian giving" is foundational to the stewardship of our resources. It may serve as an antidote to the dark side of North American culture—our tendency to overvalue material wealth, at times even to grant it ultimate value. Because this is true, far too many of us sacrifice our moral and spiritual character to obtain and hold on to it.

Sadly, this is not a new problem for supposed Christian believers whose lifestyles define them as "enemies of the cross of Christ" (Phil 3:18). To what extent did professing Christians contribute to the 2008 implosion of the world economy by their greed, consumerism, spending beyond their means, abuse of easy credit, and willingness to incur heavy indebtedness? How might our lives be different, if we truly sought to base our lives on the economic values inculcated in 2 Cor 8—9?

Many Wesleyans are surprised to learn that about ten percent of John Wesley's preserved sermons treat the subject of money at length. Fourteen of his one-hundred-forty-one sermons devote at least several pages to money. The following five are devoted entirely to the subject: "The Use of Money," "The Good Steward," "The Danger of Riches," "On Riches," and "On the Danger of Increasing Riches." He sadly learned that, in general, "the more people increase in goods, the more they decrease in grace" (Wesley 1979, 4:303, "Journal" entry for April 25, 1785).

When Wesley was 83 (in 1786), he wrote in frustration:

> I am not afraid that the people called Methodists will ever cease to exist. But I am afraid, that they will exist only as a dead sect, having the form of religion without the power. And this undoubtedly will happen, unless they hold fast to the doctrine, spirit, and discipline with which they began.
>
> I fear because I have seen that wherever riches have increased, with but few exceptions, the essence of religion, the mind that was in Christ, has decreased in the same proportion. Therefore, I do not see how it is possible, in the nature of things, for any revival of true religion to continue long. For religion must necessarily produce both industry and frugality; and these cannot but produce riches. But as riches increase, so will pride, anger, and love of the world in all its forms.
>
> How, then, is it possible that Methodism as a religion of the heart should continue long? For the Methodists in every place grow diligent and frugal; consequently, they increase in goods. Hence they proportionately increase in pride, in anger, in the desire of the flesh, the desire of the eyes, and the pride of life. So, although the form of religion remains, the spirit is swiftly vanishing away.
>
> Is there no way to prevent this continual decline of genuine religion? We ought not to forbid people to be diligent and frugal. We must exhort all Christians to gain all they can, and to save all they can. But to do so is, in effect, to urge them to grow rich! So how can we avoid letting our money send us to hell?
>
> There is one way, and only one, under heaven. If those who "gain all they can," and "save all they can," will likewise "give all they can," then the more they gain, the more they will grow in grace. (Paraphrased from Wesley 1979, 13:258, 260-61, §§1, 10-12, "Thoughts on Methodism")

IV. THE VINDICATION OF PAUL'S APOSTOLIC AUTHORITY: 2 CORINTHIANS 10:1—13:14

With a sudden shift in tone and rhetoric, Paul takes up the theme of the legitimacy of his apostleship with renewed vigor. He turns his attention to countering the personal attacks primarily of intruding "false apostles" (11:13) and the ill effects of their influence on the church. Some Corinthians have turned against Paul. A stern note of warning permeates the passage directed primarily toward those who have sinned and not yet repented (12:20-21; 13:1-2). As Paul prepares for a third visit to Corinth, he expounds further upon the character of a true apostolic ministry. His identification of himself with his gospel, implicit in earlier chapters, becomes more explicit. As Witherington comments, "What has been simmering on a back burner in chs. 1–9 is brought to a roaring boil in chs. 10–13" (1995, 431). We are faced with an abrupt transition between chs 1—9 and 10—13.

The past governs chs 1—7, where Paul explains his recent travel conduct, describes the nature of the new covenant, and, therefore, of his apostolic ministry. The appeal of chs 8—9 is to the present, as he seeks to complete the offering for saints in Jerusalem. Paul's focus to this point has been on the Corinthians themselves. His attention now turns to his opponents in chs 10—13, where the future perspective takes over as Paul defends his apostolic authority in preparation for his third visit.

As noted in the Introduction to the commentary, many scholars adopt one of several partition theories to help explain the difficult transition from chs 1—9 to 10—13. Some suggest that chs 10—13 comprise a separate letter, either part of the earlier (apparently lost) sorrowful letter (2:3-9) or a later letter to Corinth distinct from chs 1—7. We concede the hypothetic possibility. But we hold to a literary unity of 2 Corinthians for the purposes of our exposition. We take the position that chs 10—13 belong to the letter where they are, but were written later. This allows time for a fresh situation to have developed in the church and for late word of it to have reached Paul. The chapters assume a worsening situation has come to his attention.

These chapters fall into three discernible parts. In 10:1-18 Paul directly confronts his opponents in Corinth in defense of his integrity as an apostle. In 11:1—12:13 he feels compelled to play the part of a fool in his boasting. Finally, in 12:14—13:10 Paul admonishes the church to set itself in order in preparation for his third visit to Corinth. Otherwise he will be forced to act with severity when he comes. The letter concludes in 13:11-14 with a final exhortation and a benediction.

A. Paul Answers His Opponents (10:1-18)

The intruders who opposed Paul's authority in Corinth were Jews (11:22), advocating that Gentile Christians adopt Jewish practices, while claiming to be apostles of Christ (11:13). They entered the church at Corinth, worked there for a short time, and proceeded to take credit for all that had been accomplished there (10:12-18). They were apparently arrogant, tyrannical, and boastful men (10:12; 11:18, 20). Some Corinthians sided with them. Others, with gnostic tendencies, as we have seen, had their own differences with Paul, especially in their understanding of the gospel and its ministry (see Introduction).

The apostle faced his various opponents' charges, both direct and indirect, with the basic assertion: "we do not war according to the flesh" (10:3 NASB). In his ministry as an apostle, Paul's weapons are spiritual (vv 1-6), his authority is consistent (vv 7-11), and his boasting is legitimate (vv 12-18).

Paul does not name his opponents, but he, no doubt, does know who they are. Perhaps, as Shillington suggests, he does not name them because "the technique of not naming was already recognized as a way of diminishing an opponent's status" (1998, 207-8; see Thrall 2004, 641). Paul does name his friends and associates!

BEHIND THE TEXT

The rhetorical character of 10:1-18 is one with chs 10—13. The mood is defensive and belongs to the larger genre of forensic/judicial rhetoric, which has the setting of the law court, as do chs 1—7. Intent on persuading his readers, Paul writes within the persuasive tradition of Greco-Roman rhetoric. As an educated man of his time, he probably does this naturally rather than self-consciously. The forensic note dominates his defense of his apostolic authority and his gospel.

As part of the larger *probatio* and *refutatio* (3:1—13:4), Witherington describes 10:1—13:4 as a rhetorical *synkrisis.* That is, it compares Paul with the false apostles in Corinth with strong emotional appeal (1995, 336).

As already noted (see Introduction), a somewhat new situation appears to have developed between the writing of chs 1—9 and chs 10—13. This would, no doubt, affect Paul's rhetorical strategy (see Crafton 1991, 103-4). Thus, along with others, Peterson sees especially chs 10—13 as a rhetorical unit in line with the guidance of Hellenistic rhetorical handbooks (1998, 75; see Betz 1972).

Peterson identifies 10:1-6 as the *exordium*, 10:7-11 as the *propositio,* and 10:12-18 as the *narratio.* The *exordium* functions as an introduction and is designed to gain the attention of the readers. The *propositio* seeks to make clear the main points or point under dispute. The *narratio* persuasively attempts to inform the readers of the facts of the matter (1998, 75, 87, 93-94).

Peterson identifies 11:1—12:18 as the *probatio* (proof) in three confirming arguments (11:1-15; 11:16—12:13; and 12:14-18). That leaves 12:19—13:10 as the *peroratio* (conclusion), which summarizes the proofs and appeals to the emotions (Peterson 1998, 75-139).

To deal with his adversaries and the danger they presented his converts in chs 10—13, it was "rhetorically obligatory for Paul to resort to pathos, irony, invective, sarcasm, parody and the like" (Witherington 1995, 431). McCant observes that "nowhere is the proliferation of genres more evident than in 2 Cor 10—13" (1988, 551).

IN THE TEXT

1. The Spiritual Nature of Paul's Weapons (10:1-6)

Paul implores the Corinthians not to make it necessary for him to assert his authority boldly when he next comes to visit them. The apostle appears to respond to a view of himself held by some in Corinth. John Calvin vividly describes it: "'See,' they were saying, 'here is a man who, well aware of his inferiority, is in our presence so very modest and timid, but now when he is far away, he bursts out into fierce attacks upon us. Why is his speech less bold than his letters?" (1964, 10:126).

In his critics' minds, Paul's personal presence did not correspond to the authority he displayed in his letters (see v 10). They misinterpreted Paul's reticence to exert his apostolic authority because they did not accurately discern the spiritual nature of apostolic ministry. Their lack of understanding of Paul's "warfare" reflected on their perception of the gospel itself and, therefore, of its Christ. All was perverted for them.

■ **1** Paul opens this section of his letter with an emphatic personal appeal that rings with an air of authority: "I myself, Paul, appeal" (NRSV; *autos de egō Paulos parakalō*). This forceful self-designation occurs only here in Paul's letters. He combines the similarly assertive expressions in Gal 5:2, "I, Paul" (*egō Paulos*), and 2 Cor 12:13 and Rom 7:24, ***I myself*** (*autos egō*). Paul may perhaps want to distinguish himself from his co-sender Timothy (2 Cor 1:1) and other coworkers. The point is, however, that he "is preparing to assume a mantle of authority" (Martin 1986, 302). Paul faces personally the challenge to his authority as an apostle.

Yet Paul somewhat softens the proposed exercise of his apostolic authority. He expresses it not as a command, but as an appeal, **I appeal** [*parakalō*] **to you** (see Rom 12:1; 15:30; 1 Cor 1:10). In 1967 Carl J. Bjerkelund made a detailed study of clauses with *parakalō* in the letters of Paul. He observes that the use of the verb at 10:1 marks the transition from the milder to the sharper part of the letter. Yet it maintains what he identifies as the *eucharistō-parakalō* style and functions as it normally does in Paul (see Phlm 4, 9-10).

Some see 10:1, however, as the opening of a separate letter (see Introduction). With *parakalō*, Paul speaks to the congregation as fellow believers, certain that they will acknowledge him as an apostle (Bjerkelund 1967, 154-55, 188). This is confirmed by Paul's qualification: **by the meekness and gentleness of Christ.** The continued *parakalō* appeal takes an even lower tone in v 2 with *deomai*, **I beg** (see Gal 4:12; Martin 1986, 302; but see Lambrecht 1996, 408; 1999, 154). Interestingly, *parakalō* and its cognates do not appear in Galatians.

Paul's authority is affectionately exercised in the spirit of Christ, who commissioned him to serve. Some think Paul is also indirectly appealing to the Corinthians to act in this way. The context, however, puts the emphasis on Paul (Thrall 2004, 600). Christ's character as defined by **meekness and gentleness** is the manner and agency (*dia*, **By**) of Paul's appeal (BDAG 2000, 224; see 5:20; Rom 12:2; 14:30; 1 Cor 1:10). The two terms are often found together in ancient texts, including other early Christian texts (see Furnish 1984, 455).

The same question applies here as in 8:9, which referred to Christ becoming poor. Does Paul's reference to Christ's **meekness and gentleness** describe the preexistent Christ, who in his incarnation took upon himself the lowliness of humanity (Leivestad 1965-66, 161; Furnish 1984, 460; Bultmann 1985, 182)? Thrall suggests that these qualities also apply to Jesus' humiliating death (2004, 600; see Phil 2:7-8). Does Paul refer to characteristics displayed in the historical life of Jesus, who claimed, "I am gentle and humble in heart" (Matt 11:29; Plummer 1915, 273; see Lambrecht 1996, 413-14)?

Some interpreters seek to decide on the basis of a careful study of the words **meekness** (*praytētos*) and **gentleness** (*epieikeias;* Leivestad 1965-66, 157-64). Although both terms can mean "gentleness," they are not simply synonyms. Together **meekness and gentleness** form what grammatically is called hendiadys. In this figure of speech, one abstract noun qualifies the other, as if it were an adjective. Similarly, in Rom 1:5 "grace and apostleship" is the privilege of being an apostle.

In 2 Cor 10:1, the more familiar term *praytētos* (**meekness**) probably defines *epieikeias* (**gentleness**). Thus, Paul refers to "gentle restraint" (Young and Ford 1987, 271; see Leivestad 1965-66, 159-60). In the only other NT occurrence of *epieikeias* in Acts 24:4, Felix the governor is courteously requested to hear the charges against Paul: "be kind enough to hear us." That both terms signify character traits leads Harris to conclude that they describe Christ's "gentle demeanor throughout his earthly life," including "his non-retaliation during his passion" (2005, 668; see 1 Pet 2:21-24).

Meekness (*praytētos;* "gentleness, humility" is "the quality of not being overly impressed by a sense of one's self-importance" (BDAG 2000, 864). Put another way, *praytēs* as used in Scripture "denotes the humble and gentle attitude which expresses itself in particular in a patient submissiveness to offence, free from malice and desire for revenge" (Leivestad 1965-66, 159). As such it is one of the fundamental Christian virtues (1 Cor 4:21; Gal 5:23; 6:1; Eph 4:2; Col 3:12; 2 Tim 2:25; Titus 3:2; Jas 1:21; 3:13; 1 Pet 3:16; see LXX Zech 9:9; Matt 11:29). **Meekness** (*praytētos*) is that grace-imparted disposition by which one accepts without resistance the disciplines of God, just as Jesus submitted to the disciplines of his ministry as a suffering Servant (see Heb 5:7-9; 12:10; 1 Pet 2:21-23).

Gentleness (*epieikeias*), employed only here and in Acts 24:4 in the NT, is translated by Plummer as "unfailing fairness" (1915, 270). It includes the sense of "graciousness" and "forbearance"—the quality that makes allowances when the facts of the situation might call for a different reaction (BDAG 2000, 371). In the LXX, the word family describes God's character of gracious forbearance (Harris 2005, 668). With this term Paul is pointing out "that nothing lies nearer his heart than gentleness, which becomes a minister of Christ" (Calvin 1964, 10:127; see Matt 11:29-30). Paul's severity when exercised in his ministry, like that of his Lord, rises out of deep compassion for those whom he serves (see 4:5). Harris see this first clause in 10:1 functioning as a rubric for all of chs 10—13 (2005, 669).

In light of the charges against him, Paul describes himself with a note of irony. He is one who is **"timid"** [*tapeinos*] **when face to face with** the Corinthians, **but "bold"** (*tharrō*) toward them (*eis hymas*) **when away!** Paul's critics in usual fashion have distorted a truth (see 1 Cor 2:1-5) into an untruth—interpreting Paul's gentleness as weakness (see 10:10). Adam Clarke paraphrases their thought: "This apostle of yours is a mere braggadocio; when he is among you, you know how *base* and *contemptible* he is; when absent, see how he *brags* and *boasts*" (1854, 2:335).

The Greek term *tapeinos* elsewhere in the NT means "lowly" (7:6; Jas 1:9) and "humble" (Matt 11:29; Jas 4:6; 1 Pet 5:5). Here it takes on a negative or pejorative sense that is unusual in the NT—being servile or "demeaned" in manner (Furnish 1984, 454). Paul speaks in irony. Thus, the NIV has set **"timid"** in mock quotation marks. This more negative connotation is consistent with the common use of the term in the larger Hellenistic world as known by the Corinthians. Paul, following the model of his incarnate Lord, paradoxically affirms the term.

The relative pronoun **who** (*hos*) is ambiguous at first glance. It could refer to Christ. But it is clear by the end of the verse that Paul is in view. Thus, in a real sense 10:1 sets up the whole of chs 10—13.

■ **2** With a different and softer verb, **I beg** (*deomai*), Paul resumes (*de*) the appeal of v 1 by specifying its content. He asks the Corinthians to set things in order so that when he comes he will not need **to be . . . bold.** Paul describes his boldness as displaying "the confidence with which [he] propose[s] to be courageous" (NASB). The verb "to be bold" (*tolmēsai,* here and in 10:12 and 11:21) was employed ironically in Greek philosophical rhetoric as "to be audacious" (Betz 1972, 67).

The NIV smooths out Paul's decisively put statement, paraphrasing it: **I may not have to be as bold as I expect to be.** If his third visit to Corinth is not to reprise his second painful visit (see 2:1), those who regard him as living **by the standards of this world** must change. Paul advises the Corinthians that it would be to their advantage to address their internal problems before he arrives, so he won't have to take more severe measures than he would like. This behavioral expectation is in keeping with the normal use of *parakaleō* ("I appeal") with *dia* ("By") in Pauline usage. But the scope is narrower than normal (see Rom 12:1; Lambrecht 1996, 404-8).

Paul answers critics who regard (*tous logizomenous*) him ***as walking according to the flesh*** (*hōs kata sarka peripatountas;* see 1:12; 5:12). It is difficult to discern whether flesh here takes on a sinful sense (Rom 8:4-8) or refers merely to a human manner (5:16). Most interpreters take it as the latter, translating flesh as **the standards of this world** or "human standards" (NRSV). The two can hardly be entirely separated. Paul's normal metaphorical use of the verb *peripateō,* ***I live,*** includes his whole life and moral conduct. Its particular sphere (*en*) or norm (*kata*) is usually indicated by the accompanying preposition (Harris 2005, 674).

The focus is, no doubt, on Paul's relation to the Spirit (see Rom 8:3-9). Paul concedes that his behavior and presence are weak throughout the letter (see 1:12-18; 2:17; 4:2, 7). This indicates to his critics that he is devoid of the Spirit's power and gifts. The primary issue may have been that the "weapons" of his ministry seemed to lack "divine power" (v 4). Paul lacked the expected apostolic charisma (Thrall 2004, 607). His opponents thought he acted in dependence on merely human ability according to the world's criteria, and that he was motivated by expediency and self-seeking. They viewed his ministry as conducted primarily in reliance on human ingenuity, eloquence, or the charm of his personality. To conduct one's ministry in such a manner would, of course, for Paul be sinful.

■ **3** Paul denies conducting his life *kata sarka* (v 2), but concedes here that he lives *en sarki*. Flesh is not the source or orientation of his life and ministry. But he does necessarily live on human terms. He lives in the human world with its limitations and subject to human weakness.

In answer to his critics, Paul changes from a moral to a military metaphor. **For** [*gar*] **though we live** [*peripatountes*] **in the world** [*en sarki*], **we do not wage war** [*strateuometha*] **as the world does** (*kata sarka*). The contrast between life ***in the flesh*** and war ***according to the flesh*** justifies the concessive translation (**though**) of the adverbial participle ***walking.***

What follows in v 4 is Paul's most extensive use of military imagery in his letters—making war, weapons, warfare, strongholds, high things, taking captive, state of readiness. These metaphors were familiar from both Jewish scriptures and Greco-Roman rhetoric (McCant 1999, 106; see 2:24; 6:7; Rom 13:12-13; 1 Cor 9:7; Eph 6:10-17; 1 Thess 5:8; Phil 1:30; 2:25; 1 Tim 1:18; 6:12; 2 Tim 2:3-4; 4:7; Phlm 2). Thus, Paul may have known more about rhetorical conventions than about Roman military strategy. But Harris suggests that in vv 3-6 Paul draws on the technical vocabulary of siege warfare (2005, 676).

■ **4** In v 4, Paul explains (*gar;* "for," NRSV) the important difference between living in the flesh and warring according to the flesh. He expands and extends the military imagery to prove his point, insisting that **the weapons** [*hopla*] ***of*** [his] ***warfare*** are not those of the enemy. Rather, they are "weapons of righteousness" (6:7), "the armor of light" (Rom 13:12), with "faith and love as a breastplate, and the hope of salvation as a helmet" (1 Thess 5:8; see Eph 6:11-17). In true apostolic ministry, as Calvin aptly phrases it, "the kind of weapons correspond to the kind of war" (1964, 10:129). Paul's **weapons** are not ***fleshly*** (*sarkika*) or merely human resources—**the weapons of the world.**

Fleshly (*sarkika*) picks up *kata sarka* from v 3. As Paul uses it here, it can be defined primarily in contrast to the descriptive having **divine power** (*dynata tōi theōi*) that follows. The dative *tōi Theōi*, is translated by the NIV as a Hebrew intensive (so also NASB: "divinely powerful"). But ***powerful to/for God*** is better taken as a dative of advantage, "in God's cause" (JB) or "in God's service" (Harris 2005, 679; see Furnish 1984, 457; Thrall 2004, 609). Lambrecht suggests that the phrase could be seen as "spiritual" as the opposite to "fleshly" (1999, 155).

Paul's **weapons** are thus the Christlike life he lives and the gospel of Christ he proclaims. The gospel is the **divine power to demolish** or ***tear down*** [*kathairesin*] **strongholds.** Paul pictures himself here, no longer as a captive in God's triumphal procession (as in 2:14), but as a soldier armed with the Spirit-empowered weapon of the gospel. He assaults first the powerful "fortresses" (NASB) of those who attack his ministry with their false teaching and misleading reasoning (Matera 2003, 223). But he probably has more in mind than these.

Paul is armed, writes Denney, with the "tremendous sense of what the Gospel was—the immensity of grace in it, the awfulness of judgment; and it was this which gave him his power, and lifted him above the arts, the wisdom, and the timidity of the flesh" (1943, 5:788). Paul sought only to declare the truth openly (4:2). He comes armed with weapons ultimately dependent on the power of the Spirit, not on human strength and talent (see 4:7; 1 Cor 2:1-5).

■ **5** The apostle expands the military metaphor with three participial expressions. All perhaps point back loosely to the finite verb in v 3—*strateuometha*, "we . . . wage war." Each speaks to a phase of his warfare. Paul's threefold depiction of his warfare is similar to the description in 1 Macc 8:9-10 of a Roman battle against the Greeks. They successively destroyed their strongholds, took their wives and children captive, and made them slaves (Matera 2003, 223-24).

First, Paul speaks of ***demolishing*** [*kathairountes*] **arguments and every pretension that sets itself up against the knowledge of God** (v 5; in Greek, the first phrase is in v 4). The word **arguments** (*logismous*) echoes the negative use of the cognate verb *tous logizomenous* ("some people who think") in v 2. So Paul refers to the specific criticism in v 2, the other **arguments** of his critics in Corinth, as well as deceptively subtle ***"reasoning"*** or *"sophistries"* in general (BDAG 2000, 598).

Alongside **arguments,** Paul names as the target of his demolition **every pretension** (*pan hypsōma*) or "proud obstacle" (NRSV) **that sets itself up against** the gospel. He identifies the gospel here as **the knowledge of God** (see 2:14; 4:6; 6:6), an objective genitive (i.e., "you know God"; see Gal 4:9).

The word **pretension** (*hypsōma*) is literally a "high thing" (KJV). Here the high-minded attitude of his opponents is ***"arrogance"*** (BDAG 2000, 1046). Thus, Paul adds to his military metaphor lofty defensive bulwarks, the pridefully arrogant mentality of his opposition. The gospel will tear down all defiant walls and towers of the human will and intellect (see 1 Cor 1:18-25; 8:1). There is no fleshly or worldly shortcut to inward loyalty (see Matt 4:1-11).

We turn now to the second participial expression that expands the military metaphor describing Paul's gospel ministry. It is ***taking captive*** [*aichmalōtizontes*] **every thought to make it obedient to Christ** (see 1 Cor 2:16). By **thought** (*noēma;* see 4:4; 11:3) he refers to designs or schemes employed by human minds to evade the truth and claims of the gospel (see 2:11;

BDAG 2000, 675). Captivity in this war leads rebels to ***the obedience of Christ*** (*tēn hypakoēn tou Christou*). That is, Paul persuades people to obey Christ (an objective genitive).

Paul pictures the captured rebellious defenders of a fortified city, wherever it may be, reduced to serving Christ (see Phil 2:9-11). He directs his offensive (his apostolic ministry) first against the defenses of the unbelieving world. The gospel as the power of God (Rom 1:16-17) is able to break down barriers in human minds and hearts. What would otherwise be captivity in the worldly realm is transformed into radical liberation by virtue of the character of the conqueror (see 2:14). Hafemann suggests that Paul's mention of God and Christ in v 5 underscores "once again the identification of his own person and message with the knowledge of God and Christ being revealed through them" (2000, 397).

■ **6 We will be ready** contextually translates Paul's third participial expression (*en hetoimōi echontes;* see BDAG 2000, 401 s.v. *hetoimōs*). This completes his use of military imagery to describe his apostolic ministry. Harris, with most translations, treats the three participles, *kathairountes . . . aichmalōtizontes . . . echontes*, as finite verbs. They function as indicative verbs, grammatically independent of v 3 (2005, 681, 684).

So third, Paul is **ready to punish every act of disobedience** (*parakoēn;* only here and in Rom 5:19 in Paul). He refers to the remaining insurgents in the Corinthian church, not exclusively to the intruding "false apostles."

Paul patiently waits to impose apostolic discipline until (*hotan:* **once,** ***whenever***) the **obedience** (*hypakoē;* see 2:9; 7:15) of the Corinthians **is complete.** Note the wordplay of **disobedience** (*parakoēn*) and **obedience** (*hypakoē*). The **obedience** Paul expects is first of all to Christ (v 5) and by implication to him as Christ's apostle.

Paul leaves unspecified the precise nature of the punishment (*ekdikēsai,* **to punish**) he has in mind. But he probably refers to the apostolic prerogative of excommunication from the fellowship of the church, as it fits his waiting for their **obedience** (see 1 Cor 5:3-5; Gal 4:30; 5:12; 2 Thess 3:14-15). Some interpreters propose other, less likely possibilities (see 12:20-21; 13:2; Thrall 2004, 615). Paul gives the congregation time to solve its own problems before interjecting his apostolic authority.

Paul apparently hopes that the Corinthians will so understand the true character of his apostolic authority that he will not need to be a disciplinarian during his next visit. Yet for the welfare of the church he is willing to act as boldly as necessary, for his ministry is grounded in the power of the gospel. The gospel, as the knowledge of God, is powerful enough to destroy the towering strongholds humans construct to barricade themselves against obedience to Christ.

To wage Christian warfare with spiritual weapons we must: (1) never rely solely on the methods the world uses to capture human minds and hearts (vv 3-5); and (2) always submit to the Spirit of Christ in the defense of the truth (vv 1-2, 6).

2. The Consistency of Paul's Authority (10:7-11)

Having briefly described his ministry in the imagery of warfare (vv 3-6), Paul now addresses the Corinthians personally. In vv 7-11, he explains how he will exercise his apostolic authority among them. He insists that once the Corinthians take proper account of the character and purpose of his authority, they will discover that he is in person what he appears to be in his letters. As a servant of Christ there is no inconsistency between Paul's written word to them when away and his conduct when present with them. The problem is that some have mistakenly judged him by worldly criteria. In response to their charges, Paul gives an answer and a warning.

■ **7** Do the opening words of v 7—*Ta kata prosōpon blepete*—make a statement, ask a question, or issue a command? The NIV has: **You are looking only on the surface of things.** The KJV: "Do ye look on things after the outward appearance?" The NRSV ("Look at what is before your eyes") and NIV margin ("Look at the obvious facts") translate them as an imperative.

Although each option has some support (see Harris 2005, 686-87; Hafemann 2000, 397), the third seems preferable. Elsewhere in Paul's writings *blepete* is always used as an imperative (Thrall 2004, 618-19). It also fits with the logic of the apostle's thought to exhort his readers to take a look at ***the things*** (*ta*) that are obvious, right before their eyes.

He asks them to note that in his ministry among them he ***also*** (*kai hēmeis*) belongs **to Christ.** Does this indicate that *Christou einai* (***to be Christ's***) was a self-designation of Paul's opponents? The genitive is possessive, to **belong to Christ** in some particular sense.

A clue as to how Paul understood the designation may be found in v 8. There Paul's "authority . . . for building . . . up" the church appears to be at issue. More is at stake than his status as a Christian **just as much** [*kathōs*] as **anyone** [*tis*], whoever that is. It is implausible that *Christou einai* means "simply Christian." Those who used the phrase in 1 Cor 1:12 belonged to the "Christ party" or had a special relationship to the earthly Jesus (see Harris 2005, 688; or Thrall 2004, 620-22).

Most likely Paul's opponents claim in some superior sense to be "servants of Christ." Thrall suggests that *Christou einai* is "a kind of shorthand" for servant or "apostles of Christ" (11:13; Thrall 2004, 621). This would include, in Paul's usage of the phrase, his being with the Corinthians a full member of the new covenant community (3:4-6). Paul's opponents discredited him on both accounts. As Pelagius remarks, "No one is more foolish than the person who thinks that he alone belongs to Christ" (ca. 354-420, ACCS NT 7:285).

Paul's reference to **if any** (*ei tis*) may point to the ringleader of the intruders. To assign one's opponents to anonymity was the ultimate insult. But Paul's reference is probably more representative than specific. This typical opponent is ***self-confident within himself*** (Bultmann 1985, 1878) **that he belongs to Christ.** Such a person should "consider this again within (or 'by') himself (*eph' heatou*), that just as he is Christ's, so also are we" (NASB). ***By himself*** could indicate that this one should not wait for a face-to-face confrontation with Paul (Peterson 1998, 90). Paul's point is to disallow any claim of his opponents to a distinctive relationship to Christ. Paul denies them a superior spirituality that by their criteria would discredit him as an apostle (see 11:5).

The plain fact in the ***face*** (*prosōpon*) of the Corinthians was that Paul was an apostle. As such he had as much right to claim to belong to Christ as anyone. Was it not his ministry that first brought the gospel to Corinth? Are not the Corinthians themselves Paul's letters of commendation (3:1-3)? The genuineness of the Corinthians' relationship to Christ validated Paul's ministry in their midst as an apostle. He is their father in the faith (1 Cor 4:15). For Paul the integrity of his relationship to Christ was intimately connected to the question of the legitimacy of his apostleship.

■ **8** The ministry of Paul among the Corinthians, he writes, speaks for itself. **For** (*gar*) it validates that he belongs to Christ by virtue of his apostolic authority. He apologizes in advance for asserting this authority. He may **boast somewhat freely about the authority** [*exousias hēmōn*] **the Lord gave** him (see 13:10; 1 Cor 9:4-6, 12, 18). Paul's apostolic *exousia* is designated "my" only in 13:10 (*moi, **to me***) and in 1 Cor 9:18 (*mou*, "my"). But here, even between singular verbs (**I boast . . . I will not be ashamed**), he emphasizes his (i.e., *hēmōn, **our***) shared **authority** (Plummer 1915, 280). Although the mixture of singular and plural continues for a while, by chs 11—13 the singular prevails.

The verb *kauchaomai* (**boast**) appears here for the first time since 9:2. The force of the comparative adjective *perissoteron* with **boast** (*kauchēsōmai*) has an adverbial sense, "I boast a little too much" (NRSV; see Harris 2005, 692). Paul's point is that **even if** (*ean te*) he appears to be boasting too much, he will **not be ashamed.** Paul says, as Wesley put it, I have said no "more than I can make good" (1950, 668). The source and purpose (*eis*, **for**) of his **authority** back up his boast. **The Lord** gave him his apostolic **authority** "for building . . . up and not for tearing . . . down" (NRSV), "for edification, and not for . . . destruction" (KJV; see 13:10; 5:18-21).

The shift of tenses and moods is noteworthy: ***For even if I were to boast*** [*kauchēsōmai*—an aorist subjunctive] ***somewhat concerning the authority, which the Lord gave us for your construction and not your destruction, I will not be put to shame*** (*aischynthēsomai*—a future indicative). With **boast** (used earlier in 1:12; 1:14; 5:12; etc.), we encounter a key term in chs 10—13 (see 10:13, 17; 11:10, 16-18, 30; 12:1, 6, 9). The apostle, however, is uneasy that this situation may drive him to **boast somewhat freely,** that is, more than he considers appropriate (see 11:16; 12:6). Even so, the quality of his labors and the character of his ministry will protect him from disgrace.

As the source of Paul's apostolic calling, **the Lord** refers primarily to Christ (1 Cor 1:17; Gal 1:1; see Gal 1:15-16). The aorist verb **gave** (*edōken*) points to Paul's apostolic commission at the time of his conversion (Plummer 1915, 281; see Acts 9:6, 15; 22:15; 26:15-16).

The imagery of **building . . . up** (*oikodomēn*) vs. **pulling . . . down** (*kathairesin*) draws upon common OT motifs. These appear particularly in Jeremiah (24:6; 1:9-10) where the corresponding verb forms are employed (31:28; 42:10). Paul may echo the language of Jeremiah's call (1:5-10) and apply it to his own sense of calling (compare Gal 1:15-16 with Jer 1:5). Both Paul and Jeremiah were to act under divine authority, but with a difference. Jeremiah's commission was primarily to tear down; Paul's was to build up (Harris 2005, 695).

Paul normally uses the noun *oikodomē* to refer to the edification of an existing Christian community (12:19; 1 Cor 3:9-10; 14:3, 5, 12, 26). But here he probably also thinks of the authority that brought him to Corinth. He was the one who first proclaimed the gospel on which the church was founded (Furnish 1984, 467).

Paul adds to this positive purpose, a negative one: ***not for tearing you down*** (*ouk eis kathairesin hymōn*). He assures the Corinthians that the goal of the exercise of his authority among them was ultimately their edification, not their destruction. Perhaps he adds it in order to contrast his tactics with those of his rivals, who have brought strife and division into the community (11:20). They tore up the fellowship of love that is the body of Christ (12:20). By way
10:8 of contrast, Paul was committed to their spiritual strengthening (12:19) and to the promotion of harmony and unity (1 Cor 1:10; Harris 2005, 694).

Paul's identical vocabulary in 10:4 and 8 seems contrived to make explicit what he was and was not to destroy. According to 10:4, Paul was empowered by God ***for*** [*pros*] ***the destruction*** [*kathairesin*] ***of strongholds,*** **by destroying** (*kathairountes*) "the conceits of men, every barrier of pride which sets itself up against the true knowledge of God" (Knox 1944, 10:4-5). But he was not authorized ***for*** [*eis*] ***the destruction*** [*kathairesin*] ***of*** the Corinthian church (= *hymōn*, **you;** v 8).

Boasting

The verb *kauchaomai* ("boast") and the nouns *kauchēma* ("pride") and *kauchēsis* ("boasting") appear about sixty times in the NT. Of these, fifty-four or fifty-five (1 Cor 13:3 has a textual variant) appear in the Pauline letters. The word group can have a negative (braggadocio) or positive (taking pride/rejoicing) connotation. The difference for Paul depends on what one boasts about and why one boasts. Boasting in divine accomplishments is an appropriate expression of praise to God. But boasting in human accomplishments is always unjustified. Paul, however, considers it acceptable for Christians to boast in their human weakness and suffering, since it leaves room for the power of God. (For a more thorough treatment, see Zmijewski 1990.)

■ **9** The precise meaning of v 9 depends on how it relates to the previous verses. Its opening conjunction (*hina*) indicates purpose or result. But of what? The suggested solutions are many. The best guess appears to be that an intermediate thought remains unexpressed. The opening phrase (*hina mē doxō hōs an ekphobein hymas*), ***that I may not seem as to frighten you,*** is elliptical. Both the NIV and NRSV paraphrase it, assuming an unexpressed "I want": **I do not want to seem.** It may be better to insert an assumed "I say this" and translate the verse with Harris: "I say this so that I may not seem as if I am trying to terrify you" (2005, 696, 697; so Thrall 2004, 626-28).

The compound form of the infinitive is intensive, **to frighten** (*ekphobein*) or "terrify" (BDAG 2000, 312). This form of the verb, common in the LXX (see Lev 26:6; Deut 28:26; Judg 16:25; Ezek 34:28; 39:26; Mic 4:4; Zech 3:13; Nah 2:11), occurs only here in the NT.

What Paul identifies as potentially frightening are his **letters** (*dia tōn epistolōn, **by the letters***). In 7:8 he notes that the sorrowful letter Titus delivered caused the Corinthians **"severe mental or emotional distress"** (BDAG 2000, 604 s.v. *lypeō*). In 10:1, he refers to their charge that he was "timid" in person, but "bold" when absent. Here he implies that the letters he writes while away from the community not only are considered more forceful than he is face-to-face but are even terrifying.

■ **10** In v 10, Paul returns to the accusation he faced in 10:1-6. He assures the Corinthians that his letters were not intended to terrify them into submission to his authority. To tear them down in this way would be contrary to his apostolic commission to build them up (see v 8). Paul mentions what some in Corinth are saying about his **letters** in order to make the accusations specific.

Some say (*phēsin, **he says***) is singular. It may refer to a specific person, a representative of Paul's rivals. This seems to be the function of the singular *toioutos* (***such a one***) in v 11 (Barrett 1973, 260; Martin 1986, 311; Thrall 2004, 629-30). Most interpreters take *phēsin* in an impersonal sense, "it is said" (**some say;** "they say," NRSV and NASB), referring to anyone in the group (Furnish 1984, 468; Harris 2005, 698). This use of *phēsin* is typical of the ancient diatribe style (BDF §130.3). The translation of *phēsin,* however, as: ***such a one says*** appears best to fit the context.

The accusation falls into two parts in reverse order from that in 10:1. One refers to Paul's **writing** while absent; the other, to his **speaking** while present (see v 11). The precise nature of the contrast indicated by *men . . . de* ("on the one hand . . . on the other hand," BDAG 2000, 629 s.v. *men*) remains unclear. The latter part of what is being said about Paul in Corinth is certainly negative—**"he is unimpressive and his speaking amounts to nothing."** But the first part of the quotation, **"His letters are weighty and forceful** [*bareiai kai ischyrai*]," might be intended as a compliment, even if "backhanded" (Shillington 1998, 209). Is he accused of being inconsistent—authoritative in his letters, but inconsequential in person (see v 1) as most seem to take it (see NRSV, NASB)?

But would the apostle's opponents have paid him any kind of compliment? Harris thinks not. His different interpretation emphasizes Paul's use of *ekphobein* ("to terrify") to describe his letters. He translates the first part of the accusation as "his letters are tyrannical and aggressive" (2005, 698; see BDAG 2000, 167, 484, s.v. *ischyros*). The charge against Paul would then be negative on both counts. Inconsistency on Paul's part is an issue in Corinth. But it is hard to escape a negative tone in the reference to his letters.

In contrast to his letters, Paul **is unimpressive** face-to-face. Literally, he writes, ***his bodily presence is weak*** (*hē . . . parousia tou sōmatos asthenēs*). Does this refer to Paul's physical appearance as some later and apocryphal descriptions suggest (Furnish 1984, 468; Martin 1986, 312)? The apocryphal "Acts of Paul," describe him as:

> a man small of stature, with a bald head, and crooked legs, in a good state of body, with eyebrows meeting and nose somewhat hooked, full of friendliness [grace]; for now he appeared like a man, and now he had the face of an angel. (Schneemelcher 1965, 354)

This description, dated between 185 and 195 (Schneemelcher 1965, 351), must be read in the context of ancient, not modern notions of physical attractiveness (see Witherington 2001, 42-44).

According to the ancient philosopher Epictetus (Dissertationes 3.1, 22.86-88), physical appearance was important to Cynic philosophers and was a means of impacting audiences for students of rhetoric (see Thrall 2004,
10:10 631). We do not know what importance personal appearance may have had for the Corinthians. But more was at stake than the features of Paul's face. In what sense did the apostle cut a sorry figure in person (Furnish 1984, 468)? The more likely reference of *tapeinos* comprehends his total person. His critics dismiss his personality as ***"lowly, undistinguished, of no account,"*** **"servile in manner, . . .** ***abject," "humble"*** (BDAG 2000, 989; of v 1).

Compatible with this understanding is the additional charge: *ho logos exouthenēmenos*, Paul's **speaking amounts to nothing**/his "speech contemptible" (NRSV). Paul's letters evidence an effective use of rhetorical devices (see v 6; Peterson 1998, 86), and he describes his first preaching at Corinth as "with a demonstration of the Spirit's power" (1 Cor 2:4). But perhaps he lacked the expected power of speech (2 Cor 11:6) of a competent orator. He acknowledges as much in 1 Corinthians: "I came to you in weakness and fear, and with much trembling [for] my message and my preaching were not with wise and persuasive words" (1 Cor 2:3-4).

Perhaps Paul was not gifted in extemporaneous rhetoric or "spiritual" spontaneity, thus, failing to satisfy their criteria for the possession of the divine Spirit. While *logos* in 1 Cor 2:4 indicates Paul's message, "Jesus Christ, and him crucified" (1 Cor 2:2), here *logos* refers to his **speaking.** Calvin comments, "By speech he means not the substance of his teaching but simply its form and outward shell, for he would have been more vehement in defending his doctrine" (1964, 10:134). This verse provides significant clues for the interpretation of 10:1-11 (McCant 1999, 108).

■ **11** In response to his critics, Paul straightforwardly denies that he behaves as two different people in relation to the Corinthians. **Such people should realize** is literally ***let such a one consider*** (*logizesthō ho toioutos*). He allows an anonymous person to represent his rivals (see the commentary on *phēsin* in v 10).

The sentence begins with an emphatic ***This*** (*touto*), anticipating the content of the following *hoti* clause, **that . . .** What his critics are to **realize** is this: When Paul (**we**) comes next to Corinth, he will be as resolute in his **actions** (*tōi ergōi*, ***in deed***) as he is in his **letters** written at a distance from them. Paul's disposition of gentleness and patience (v 1) will not prevent him from bold, decisive action, if need be (see on v 6), on his third visit to Corinth (see 13:2, 10). In v 6 he has already described the action he will take as disciplinary, punitive. The twofold use of ***when present*** (*paron . . . parontes*) in vv 2 and 11 and of ***when absent*** (*apōn . . . apontes*) in vv 1 and 11 form an *inclusio*, a literary frame enclosing the passage.

The issue throughout 10:1-11 is Paul's alleged inconsistent behavior in relation to the Corinthians. Paul counters this in vv 7-11. He insists that his consistency ought to be obvious to them. It can be seen (1) in his commitment to Christ (v 7); (2) in his commission from the Lord to build up and not to tear down (v 8); and (3) in his conduct among the Corinthians (vv 9-11).

Whether present or absent, Paul's authority is from Christ (v 8). He is armed with the powerful weapons of the gospel (vv 4-5). And he is ready to act with boldness (vv 6, 11). His detractors have misinterpreted his mild demeanor as worldly-weakness. His gospel-weakness is at the heart of the defense of his apostleship in the letter. Leivestad observes that "clearly he is not prepared to deny the charge of weakness, but rather to demonstrate its relevance to the Christian paradox. His weakness is, in fact, the only thing he can rightly boast of!" (1965-66, 162). Paul's weakness is "the meekness and gentleness of Christ" (v 1), his humility and his forbearance.

3. The Legitimacy of Paul's Boasting (10:12-18)

In the minds of Paul's rivals, he is disqualified from being an apostle by his weakness (10:10). By their criteria, they are the ones who possess the right to exercise apostolic authority in Corinth. These challenges from Paul's opponents force him to defend his apostleship in Corinth. He writes with emotional intensity as he takes on the invaders to his church there. This makes his syntax difficult to translate; and, therefore, not easily interpreted precisely.

The legitimacy of Paul's boasting is at stake. He is compelled to boast about his apostolic authority in the Corinthian church, as he has already hinted in 10:8 and fully spells out in ch 11. He defends the nature of his apostolic activity and presence to the Corinthians (10:1-11). He has the right to fully exercise his authority. The issue of self-commendation opens and closes the paragraph in a ring composition (*inclusio*). For the sake of the church, Paul seeks to demolish the self-proclaimed superiority of his opponents. In the process, he carefully sets the limits of his own boasting.

■ **12** Paul begins with "strong irony" (Wesley 1950, 668): **We do not dare** (see v 2, 11:21). The NIV and NRSV fail to translate the conjunction *gar* ("for"). With what has been said in the preceding context, Paul's ironic meaning is clear enough. Paul is prepared to act boldly against his critics (v 2). Yet, with sarcasm and "mock humility" (Martin 1986, 318), he admits he is still a coward because (*gar*, ***For***) he does not have the courage to **classify or compare** himself **with some who commend themselves.**

The Greek wordplay (*enkrinai ē synkrinai*) is brought out by Plummer with "'pair' and 'compare'" (1915, 286). Occurring only here in the NT, *enkrinai* means to judge as being within the same class as someone/something else. *Synkrinai* means to judge with someone or something else. Both terms mean to compare in order to classify (Hughes 1962, 364).

In antiquity the rhetorical encomium was a comparison used to amplify the virtues of the one praised in order to depreciate others (Lambrecht 1999, 165; see Betz 1972, 119-20). Sophistic teachers often used self-*synkrisis* to attract students away from their rivals (Harris 2005, 707; see Furnish 1984, 469-70, 480). Paul's rivals in Corinth were making comparisons flattering themselves at Paul's expense. He stoops to imitate their practice, but only "as a fool" (11:17, 21; see 11:21*b*—12:11).

10:12-13 **Some who commend themselves** probably refer to those nameless intruders who "write their own references" (JB; see 3:1; 5:12), not Paul's Corinthian critics. The issue is self-praise, for they are **measur**[ing] **themselves by themselves and compar**[ing] **themselves with themselves.** "The old proverb is true," writes Calvin, "'Ignorance is bold'" (1964, 10:135-36). There are always some taken in by the arrogant, the bigoted, and the dogmatic. Paul chooses not to compete with this kind of illegitimate self-commendation. He does not object to their boasting, but to the criteria they used. He considers such "superior" people completely out of his class! (see Thrall 2004, 639, 641).

Paul illustrates and emphasizes his ironic point. **When** (*alla*, ***but***) his opponents employ only their own standards to validate their ministries in the eyes of the church, **they are not wise** (*ou syniasin:* "they do not show good sense" [NRSV]; "they have no understanding" [Furnish 1984, 465]). They have refused any worthy standard of comparison, for external criteria are always needed for credible evaluation.

Some early Greek manuscripts omit both *ou syniasin* in v 12 and *hēmeis de* (**We, however**) in v 13. A few interpreters prefer this shorter text (e.g., Bultmann 1985, 192). But most (see NIV, NRSV, and NASB) favor the longer reading on both internal and external grounds (see Furnish 1984, 470-71; Thrall 2004, 636-39; Harris 2005, 705-6).

■ **13** "Paul disavows 'self-praise,'" yet he "seems unable to avoid it" (McCant

1999, 111). So he will boast, but with careful qualification. This is consistent with the practice of ancient orators. They viewed self-praise as offensive and dangerous, but necessary under certain conditions (see 1 Cor 15:10; McCant 1999, 111; Thrall 2004, 643). The apostle contrasts (*hēmeis de:* **We, however**) his conduct with that of his rivals. He is not going to **boast beyond proper limits** (literally, in things "immeasurable," *ta ametra,* only in vv 13 and 15 in the NT; BDAG 2000, 53).

Paul formulates his criterion for boasting as ***according to the measure of the rule*** [*kata to metron tou kanonos*] ***that God has assigned to us as a measure*** (*hou emerisen hēmin ho Theos metrou*). The genitive expression ***the measure of the rule*** is "notoriously difficult to interpret" because of complex lexical and grammatical issues (Harris 2005, 710-16; see Furnish 1984, 471-72; Thrall 2004, 644-47). How do the terms ***measure*** (*metron*) and ***rule*** (*kanōn*) relate to each other? Are they simply synonymous (epexegetical)? Which of the various possible meanings of each Greek term best suits the present context? How do these terms relate syntactically to the rest of the sentence?

Metron is the source of our English word "meter." It generally means "that by which anything is measured." It can refer to **"an instrument for measuring, *measure*"** or **"the result of measuring, *quantity, number*"** (BDAG 2000, 642).

Kanōn originated as the designation of a "straight rod" used for measuring. It may mean **"a means to determine the quality of someth**[ing]**, *rule, standard*"** (as in Gal 6:16 and Phil 3:16); or a **"set of directions or formulation for an activity, *assignment, formulation.*"** In the second century in the Christian church *kanōn* came to stand for revealed truth, ***"rule of faith"*** (BDAG 2000, 507-8).

We translate v 13 as follows: ***Yet we will not boast beyond the proper limits, but only in accord with the limit of the jurisdiction that God has assigned to us as our limit, to reach even as far as you.*** This anticipates exegetical conclusions reached in our treatment of v 14.

■ **14** The first consideration toward a solution is the probability that the infinitive phrase ***to reach even as far as you*** functions epexegetically to explain *kanōn.* Paul was "the first to come even as far as you in the gospel of Christ" (NASB). That is, God commissioned Paul to found the church in Corinth.

The second consideration concerns vv 15-16. They refer to Paul's intention to expand his appointed ministry in the Gentile world into "the regions beyond" Corinth. This apparently applies the aorist verb ***assigned*** (*emerisen*) in v 13 to Paul's initial call to preach the gospel to Gentiles (Gal 2:8-9).

Taking the genitive relation between *metron* and *kanonos* as epexegetic (mutually explanatory) with these two contextual considerations leads to translations such as "the measure of the jurisdiction" (Furnish 1984, 465, 471) or "a limit . . . the assignment" (Harris 2005, 709; see BDAG 2000, 507).

Paul's apostolic authority in relation to the church at Corinth derives from his divine assignment as a missionary to the Gentiles. Thus, it was within the bounds of his God-given commission that he founded the church there.

The Corinthians are Paul's "letters of recommendation," "a letter from Christ, the result of [his] ministry" (3:1-2). The Corinthian church is itself his standard or measure of boasting. It goes almost without saying that Paul's gospel is always the underlying issue at stake in his relation to them.

The ***limits*** Paul mentions in v 13 include a geographical reference. But the meaning is more theologically profound than that. The ***limits*** of Paul's assignment refer to the specific task and the particular grace God gave him (Acts 9:15; Gal 2:9; Rom 1:5; 15:20). This task and grace are demonstrated and confirmed by the fruitfulness of his missionary labors among the Corinthians (1 Cor 15:10; see Hafemann 1990a, 79).

In v 14 Paul emphasizes that he is not ***overextending*** (*hyperekteinomen*, only here in the NT) himself in relation to the Corinthians. His attitude toward them is not presumptuous. In almost identical opening clauses in the preceding and following verses (vv 13, 15), Paul insists that he is not boasting beyond his proper limits. Although he does not use the word for **boasting** in v 14, his point is similar. He is not acting as **if** [he] **had not come to** [them]. Rather, he **did get as far as** [them] **with the gospel of Christ.**

The verb *ephthasamen* in classical Greek often has the idea of "coming first" (see 1 Thess 4:15). This meaning is supported by the present context. So the NRSV translates, "we were the first to come all the way to you." Thus, v 14 supports (*gar*, "For," NRSV) what Paul wrote in v 13. It also prepares for what he is about to say in vv 15-16. His apostolic authority, his **boasting** about the Corinthians is fully justified. Paul is "not overstretching" his "commission" (NEB, see 1 Cor 4:15) in relation to the church at Corinth. His relation to the Corinthians is unique. Paul's opponents, however, are out-of-bounds. They are trespassing on his divinely assigned territory. They are disqualified as the apostle's competitors in Corinth.

■ **15** Unlike them, Paul is not boasting in things "immeasurable" (*ta ametra*). He is ***not boasting beyond limits, in the labors of others*** (see Rom 15:20). He implies that this is exactly what the intruders who oppose him in Corinth have done. Calvin calls them "men who stretch out their hands to reap another man's harvest and who yet dare to revile those, whose sweat and labor had prepared the place for them" (1964, 10:137).

Despite his concern about the Corinthians' attention to the outsiders, Paul sounds a positive note. His confident **hope** is "a genuine Pauline gem" (Sampley 2000, 144). He ***has*** **hope** (*elpida de echontes*) that their **faith** will ***keep growing*** (*auxanomenēs*). And as it does so, his hope is that his apostolic ministry ***will be enlarged*** (*megalynthēnai*) as well.

What is the meaning of Paul's biological imagery applied to **faith**? How does faith **grow—"become greater in extent, size, state, or quality"** (BDAG 2000, 151 s.v. *auxanō*/*auxō*)? The present tense of the participle implies that their faith is already growing. But in what sense? Does he have in mind their increased capacity to trust God? Or, does he refer to their becoming more trustworthy? Does he refer to their ability to believe God more fully or intensely? Do they believe in more things than they did previously? Given Paul's normal use of the **faith,** it seems unlikely that he refers to their growing faith in their apostle. We cannot be certain, since this is the only place in Paul's letters that explicitly refers to growing faith. What he writes of Abraham in Rom 4:20, "he grew strong in his faith" (NRSV), employs a different verb: he "was strengthened [*enedynamōthē*] in his faith."

What does Paul mean by the accompanying "greatly enlarged" (*megalynthēnai*) "sphere of action" (NRSV)? The apostle takes considerable satisfaction in what God has done to advance his mission (see Rom 11:13). Paul's reference to his activity **among you** (*en hymin*) Corinthians could also be "by you" (NASB). If he means "by you," he looks forward to v 16, referring to the geographical expansion of his pioneer ministry with the aid of the Corinthians. If he means **among you,** he looks backward to **grow,** indicating how his ministry in the church added to the numbers of believers or increased the quality of their faith. As the Corinthians fully obey the gospel, Paul's ministry will expand. The Corinthians can liberate the apostle to a greater usefulness.

■ **16** Verse 16 explains the purpose (*eis* + infinitive) Paul has in mind for his "greatly [*eis perisseian,* ***to abundance***] enlarged" (NRSV) ministry among the Corinthians (v 15): **so that** [*eis*] **we can preach the gospel** [*euangelisasthai,* ***to evangelize***] **in the regions beyond you.** Harris's translation clarifies the contextual meaning of *eis perisseian:* "our work may be enlarged . . . until it overflows." "The phrase is expressive of Paul's hope in God, not simply his confidence in the Corinthians" (2005, 705).

Regions is added by English translations to the term *hyperkeina* (only here in the NT), which simply means **beyond** (BDAG 2000, 1032). Paul wants to evangelize in lands beyond Corinth. From Romans, we learn that he had long-cherished plans to visit Rome en route to a mission to Spain (Acts 19:21; Rom 15:22-24).

Paul does **not want to boast about work already done in another man's territory** or assigned area (*kanoni*). The expected result of his "hope" is defined by "expand" and **preach the gospel.** His boast will be in his successful evangelism in previously unevangelized areas beyond Corinth. As a result, Paul has no need **to boast** in ***the accomplishments*** (*ta hetoima*) of others (see BDAG 2000, 401).

But this is the only boast Paul's opponents in Corinth can make. Because they are poaching on his territory, their boasting is totally illegitimate. At this point, Paul does not reproach the community for listening to the vain boasts of his opponents. He is counting on the Corinthians to contribute to the unlimited extension of his apostolic ministry.

■ **17** The situation in Corinth has forced the apostle to engage in boasting, contrary to his personal preferences. In v 17, he explains what distinguishes inappropriate from appropriate boasting. Paul's principle for legitimate boasting depends on the LXX of Jer 9:24: **"Let him who boasts boast in the Lord."** He used the same citation in 1 Cor 1:31 to counteract pride in human strength and wisdom. In both passages Paul reformulates it into a maxim. But here he omits the citation formula, "It is written."

Legitimate boasting, he wants it understood, can only be strictly **"in the Lord"** (*en kyriōi*), in what the Lord has done. Here Paul refers to Christ rather than to God as **the Lord,** unlike 1 Cor 1:31. This is the normal practice for this phrase in his letters (Rom 15:17-18; but see Lambrecht 1999, 167).

Permissible or legitimate boasting for Paul has two necessary characteristics. First, it is not about personal accomplishments or status, but about who the Lord is and what he has accomplished. Second, boasting must be confined to the Lord's accomplishments within one's divinely allotted assignment (Harris 2005, 726). Ambrosiaster (ca. 366-384), inspired by Paul, wrote three centuries later, "Someone who has confidence in the power of the gospel has confidence in the God who enables it" (ACCS NT 7:288).

■ **18** Paul returns to the terminology with which he began the paragraph (vv 12-18). He adapts the language of Jeremiah to explain (*gar,* **For**) the basic principle of his apostolic ministry: **it is not the one who commends himself who is approved, but the one whom the Lord commends** (see 4:5; 5:9; 1 Cor 4:15).

An *inclusio* (literary bracket) is formed by "some who commend themselves" in v 12 and **one who commends himself** in v 18. This links the paragraph with all Paul has said previously in the letter about self-commendation and proof of authentic ministry. Hafemann calls this verse "the *crux interpretum* for understanding how Paul himself judged his own apologetic, as well as that of his opponents" (1990a, 74).

Paul's phrase, **one who commends himself** (*ho heauton synistanōn*), describes those who praise and promote themselves out of personal ambition. Undoubtedly he excludes the type of commendation he has reluctantly felt compelled to engage in to defend his own ministry (see 4:2; and 6:4: "as servants of God we commend ourselves in every way").

In contrast to **one who commends himself,** Paul refers to ***that one*** [*ekeinos*] **whom the Lord commends.** It is the latter **who is approved.** To be **approved** by the Lord, one must pass the test of genuineness [*dokimos;* see 13:7]. The cognate family—*dokimazō, dokimē, dokimos*—is both frequent and significant for Paul's argument in 2 Corinthians (see 2:9; 5:8; 8:2, 8, 22; 9:13; 10:18; 11:16; 12:10, 19; 13:3, 5, 6, 7).

Divine approval was Paul's goal and desire (5:9-10). For him God's recommendation was the only mark of genuineness. Paul's boast is not that he is an apostle but that God has made him one (1 Cor 15:8-10). As the servant of Christ, Paul can boast only of what God has done, is doing, and has promised to do through him for God's glory. The fact that the Corinthians came to Christ through Paul's ministry is for Paul divine commendation of his ministry among them (1 Cor 2:1-5; 9:1-2).

In 2 Cor 10:12-18 Paul offers three criteria that discredit the boast of his opponents and define the limits for legitimate boasting as servants of Christ. These are: (1) a standard external to one's own immediate frame of reference (v 12); (2) the nature and extent of the commission as personally received from God (vv 13-16); and (3) the commendation of the Lord himself (vv 17-18).

FROM THE TEXT

Paul's penetrating glimpse into the nature of a truly Christian ministry is still significant for our day. This is despite their origin in the apostle's answers to those who have attacked the legitimacy of his ministry in the church at Corinth. Whether we are lay or clergy, whenever we seek to serve others as Christians, our ministry flows within the same stream of spiritual life as Paul's. This is because Paul sought to imitate Christ in his ministry (1 Cor 11:1).

Second Corinthians 10:1-18 reveals the integrity of a Christlike ministry in its consistency. A Christian ministry is *consistent:*

1. *with the cross of Christ in its manner and methods, when its weapons are spiritual* (10:1-6)
2. *with one's calling in Christ, when its authority is that of its Lord* (10:7-11)
3. *in an attitude of humility that labors only in obedience, giving all credit for its success to the Lord, when its boasting is legitimate* (10:12-18)

Obviously, a Christian ministry is *consistent with the cross of Christ in its manner and methods, when its weapons are spiritual* (10:1-6). In ministry to others, Christian behavior partakes of **the meekness and gentleness of Christ** (v 1). Ministry, as Oscar Reed expresses it, is penetrated with the "attitudes of the Cross" (1976, 263). These "attitudes of the Cross" Jesus displayed for us throughout the whole of his life and ministry. They were evident from his conduct throughout the events of his passion. He who was "gentle and humble in heart" (Matt 11:29) as he ministered in life to others was one who in death "did not retaliate . . . when he suffered" but "entrusted himself to him who judges justly" (1 Pet 2:23).

Likewise we are gentle and forbearing in our dealings with others. We are "most reluctant to use methods and attitudes which bear the stamp of severity" (Reed 1976, 264). As the Apostle Peter translated the cross of Christ into life for those facing persecution, we have a word for Christians in ministry in 1 Pet 3:15-18:

> In your hearts set apart Christ as Lord. Always be prepared to give an answer to everyone who asks you to give the reason for the hope that you have. But do this with gentleness and respect, keeping a clear conscience, so that those who speak maliciously against your good behavior in Christ may be ashamed of their slander. It is better, if it is God's will, to suffer for doing good than for doing evil. For Christ died for sins once for all, the righteous for the unrighteous, to bring you to God. (See Carver 1987, 95-103)

Gentleness with Paul should not be confused with timidity. As he makes clear, there are times when we must assert the authority of our faith. James Denney warns us that this can be difficult to do without sin: "It is an exhilarating sensation to human nature to be in the right, and when we enjoy it we are apt to enlist our temper in the divine service, forgetting that the wrath of man does not work the righteousness of God" (1943, 5:787). Ministry in anger is hardly consistent with **the meekness and gentleness of Christ** (2 Cor 10:1).

In ministry we are confined to "the strategies of the Cross" (Reed 1976, 264). **The weapons we fight with are not the weapons of the world** (10:4). In Paul's terminology, although we live our lives "in the flesh," we do not conduct our ministries "according to the flesh" (10:3 NASB), as people usually do. "Social life 'in the world,'" remarks Murphy-O'Connor, "is dominated by a false value system, which makes the individual the focus of all his or her striving" (1991, 101).

The focus of ministry is not our own exaltation and our own ability and talents. We always fight a losing battle in the realm of the Spirit when we fight in our own strength (Zech 4:6). Understood in the context of God's purposes and power, gentleness, compassion, kindheartedness, and a readiness to forgive are not symptoms of weakness. Rather they are an occasion for the invasion of the divine presence and action—the power of the resurrection.

The weapons of a Christian ministry, "the strategies of the cross," **have divine power to demolish strongholds** (2 Cor 10:4; see Eph 6:10). Only in such a manner and with such methods, insists the apostle, are we in a position to **demolish arguments and every pretension that sets itself up against the knowledge of God** (2 Cor 10:5*a*), that is, against the gospel of Christ. In view is the intellectual and moral mind-set of fallen humanity formed by its failure to honor God as God (see Rom 8:18-32).

Only the resurrection power of God, released through faith-identification with and obedience to the way of the cross, is able to **take captive every thought to make it obedient to Christ** (2 Cor 10:5*b*). If so, how much of what we do as we "do church" is simply not Christian? The law of unintended consequences is always at work. No matter what our intention, our actions produce effects consistent with their nature. We do not attract people to Christ with methods that contradict who and what he is.

Second, the Apostle Paul would emphasize that a Christian ministry *is consistent with one's calling in Christ, when its authority is that of its Lord* (vv 7-11). The integrity and quality of our ministries possess a twofold limitation, that of "presence" and that of "task." "Presence" means that we have no true authority but Christ, no authority apart from the presence and power of the Spirit of Christ, making use of our weakness. We have only **the authority the Lord gave us** (v 8). There is an authority of presence, our presence as an instrument of his Presence (Rom 1:11-12).

The apostle insists, **we belong to Christ** (2 Cor 10:7). We are limited to "who" and to "what" Christ is. What a limitation! What freedom! Our authority functions only in and through our obedience to what Christ has called us to be and do, in particular our task in relation to those whom we serve. We are not called to be and do everything—to pitch and play first base at the same time!

We have no authority in ministry outside our calling. We cannot be like the psychologist who tries to speak authoritatively as a theologian, or the theologian who attempts to speak authoritatively as a scientist.

Clear from this passage as well is that in ministry we belong to Christ along with others. We do not have a monopoly on the Lord's mind and presence. We are not alone or unique in the Lord's service. Our possession of truth of the gospel is not as exclusive as our human nature might prefer. Christ exercises his authority through whomsoever he chooses and however he wishes. The Spirit (*pneuma*) is like the wind; "the wind [*pneuma*] blows wherever it pleases" (John 3:8). Pride in ministry, as Paul will indicate (2 Cor 10:10-12), has to be carefully defined.

Our common task is to build up others, not to tear or put them down (v 8). It is to edify the Christian community, not to divide it (see 1 Cor 3:16-17), to encourage and enlarge their vision, not to serve our prideful view of the "right." And if our anointed conduct and speech is of the Lord, we remain essentially the same whether present or absent from those whom we serve. We are not politicians whose manner and message change with the expected voter winds and campaign contributions—or celebrity attention! Whether our role is on the public platform to the gathered many or one-on-one in private, it is the same Lord who makes himself known in every circumstance through our submission in faith to Christ's death and resurrection in ministry. With Paul, "So then, death is at work in us, but life is at work in you" (4:12).

In this passage Paul opens up a third aspect of our ministries in the Lord's name. Here we see that a Christian ministry *is consistent in an attitude of humility that labors only in obedience, giving all credit for its success to the Lord, when its boasting is legitimate* (10:12-18). Paul's antagonists in Corinth are apparently involved in some kind of self-commendation: **they measure themselves by themselves and compare themselves with themselves** (v 12). Thus, "they do not show good sense" (NRSV), by evaluating themselves only by comparison with those within their closed circle of understanding of the gospel and its ministry.

Our temptation to "exclusive superiority" may be in our doctrinal heritage—whether Wesleyan, Reformed, Lutheran, Orthodox, or Catholic. Perhaps it is in our church polity—from hierarchal to congregational; our manner of worship—from high to low. It could be in our cultural ethos as defined by education, wealth, or national origin.

Yet Paul dares to write about his boasting, his satisfaction, his pride in his apostolic ministry. And he insists that he has a right to boast! Does that mean that there is a rightful place for personal satisfaction and pride in what we do in the interests of the gospel of Christ for others? Is it ever OK to boast? Is human ego satisfaction not all bad? Apparently.

But how can boasting be legitimate? Paul states two qualifications: First, it must be within **proper limits** (v 13). That is, it must be related to the fulfillment of one's specific assignment, an expression of the particular grace God has granted. Paul's boast is limited to the Corinthians whom he was allowed to be the first to evangelize. By boasting in the Christians at Corinth he was not overstepping his limits. If he were to boast in work done by others, he would be out of line.

Paul's assignment is to virgin territory; so it includes **regions beyond** Corinth. He refuses **to boast about work already done in another man's territory** (v 16). Simply put, our satisfaction is to be found in that which God has specifically assigned to us. We may take personal pride in those he has providentially placed in our care, that is, in those to whom God has given us the grace to minister. It is in their growth in faith and the resultant enlargement of our ministry that is our legitimate boast. We boast only in others in whom the Lord is at work!

Paul's second qualification is scriptural: **Let him who boasts boast in the Lord** (v 17). Making use of Jer 9:23-24, he concludes that the Lord's commendation is the only valid seal of approval. We find satisfaction in and our commendation from what the Lord is accomplishing in and through us in behalf of others (see Rom 1:11-12). As we are obedient within the sphere to which God has placed and called us, we give him the credit for his work. Only on this basis may we feel good about ourselves and take pride in our ministries.

Self-esteem is legitimate so long as we depend on and boast in the Lord's commendation, rather than on human approval. When the latter does come, we are grateful to the Lord—to "grace as both the figure and the ground of our lives" (Douglas 2008, 9).

The boundary within which pride is allowed us is humble obedience to our assignment and the Lord's approval of our faithfulness to depend on his resources. Our boast is in others (1:14; 7:14), not in our abilities, talents, or charismatic personality. It is in the power of God's grace at work through us for and in others. Thus we give glory to God.

B. Paul Boasts in His Foolishness (11:1—12:13)

Here Paul begins the sharpest polemic to be found in any of his writings. He wields masterfully the weapon of irony tempered by the truth of the gospel. The catchword "boast," present in 10:12-18, continues here. Paul's boast becomes more specific and, thus, more dangerous in light of what he has just written, "Let him who boasts boast in the Lord" (10:17).

Paul asks the Corinthians to endure his foolishness (11:1-4, 16-21*a*).

They have driven him to it; and it has made him a fool (12:11). Paul's boast, however, is not an empty one, for he is in no way inferior to the intruding apostles (11:5-15).

Following his extended introduction, Paul boasts (11:21*b*—12:10) in his lineage, his sufferings, and his personal revelations. These he ultimately sums up in a declaration of his likeness to his crucified and risen Lord, "When I am weak, then I am strong" (12:10; see 13:4). In a concluding epilogue, although admitting the foolishness of his boasting, Paul presents his actual conduct in Corinth (12:11-13) as the basis upon which he has demonstrated the authenticity of his apostleship.

Ironically imitating his opponents in a form of self-commendation, Paul really boasts in Christ, his Lord. The contradiction between the fool's mask of his boasting and his actual boast in his ministry gives this whole passage a unique literary charm and captivating force. But most significantly, it reveals both Paul's weakness in his sufferings and the nature of his "visions and revelations from the Lord." These admissions were wrung from him in the struggle with the opposition at Corinth. Without it, we would have missed his "power in weakness" testimony.

BEHIND THE TEXT

With all of chs 10—13, the rhetorical character of 11:1—12:13 remains the umbrella genre of forensic or judicial rhetoric. The setting of this rhetoric is the court of law as in chs 1—7. The forensic note dominates as Paul defends his apostolic authority and thereby his gospel with strong emotional appeal.

Peterson identifies 11:1—12:18 as the *probatio*. It is the principal evidence supporting the case confirming Paul's authority among the Corinthians, introduced in 10:8. In 11:1-15, his first argument, common in rhetoric, is a plea for his audience to put up with what he is about to say. His second argument, in 11:16—12:13, deals with the actual boasting (Peterson 1998, 104-5, 112).

Scholarly judgments vary as to the rhetorical character of "the fool's speech" (11:1—12:13). How does it relate to distinct literary forms known in Paul's day? All admit that the speech is penetrated with irony and parody. Some, influenced by Betz, view it specifically as a model of Socratic irony (Betz 1972, 75-76; Crafton 1991, 109-16; McCant 1988, 557-58). As such, it is not to be taken seriously, but as "a parody of self-praise," used in debates between sophists and philosophers.

Plutarch's *On Self-Praise Without Offending* provides the rhetorical model for this (Martin 1986, 358; see 328-31, 358-60). Plutarch (ca. 46-122), a late contemporary of Paul, reflects cultural precedents that may predate the apostle. If Paul consciously used this cultural model, the autographical data reflected in his "fool's speech" is of diminished value. It would tell us more about what was expected in such speeches than about the apostle's actual experiences. Paul does use some of the standard rhetorical vocabulary. But his speech does not seem to depend on Hellenistic authors so much as it demonstrates his awareness of his culture and rhetorical conventions (Barnett 1997, 494-95).

Paul narrates his actual experiences in 11:23—12:5, even if the narrative conforms to cultural precedents. His boasting is foolish and dangerous; but he meant it to be taken seriously. Matera concludes: "It seems unlikely that Paul is *merely* parodying the boasting of his opponents, since what he narrates is true (12:6)" (2003, 238). Nonetheless, Witherington points out that irony is an important feature of this passage from a rhetorical point of view (1995, 442-43).

Self-deprecating irony in the Greco-Roman culture of Paul's day was used to pretend to be less than one was, to say one thing and mean another. Irony, appropriate in forensic oratory, was viewed as an "effective means of stealing into peoples' minds." Paul certainly uses it throughout this discourse. Witherington concludes that Paul "sees his life as characterized by irony, . . . [as] a suffering sage . . . , hence the catalogs of his apostolic experiences and the disclaimer about his oral rhetoric" (1995, 443).

IN THE TEXT

1. An Appeal to Bear with Paul's Foolishness (11:1-6)

The apostle introduces an awkward type of self-defense for which he has no appetite with an "anticipatory correction." The literary device of prodiorthosis begs one's hearers' indulgence in advance for what the speaker feels may offend them (BDF 1961, §495.3). Paul asks the Corinthians to put up with his "foolishness" (v 1)—a foolish boasting necessitated by his intense concern and affection for their spiritual welfare (v 2). Paul is fearful that the Corinthians may be theologically seduced. He is anxious that those who would preach "a Jesus other than the Jesus [he] preached" may turn them away from their faithfulness to Christ (vv 3-4). Paul considers himself in no way inferior to these subversive intruders (v 5). Even though he is not a professional orator, the Corinthians know that he effectively conveyed knowledge to them (v 6). Paul implores the church to tolerate his brand of self-commendation.

Harris sees the dilemma Paul faced in relation to the Corinthians—"to boast or not to boast"—illustrated in Prov 26:4-5:

> Do not answer a fool according to his folly,
> or you will be like him yourself.
> Answer a fool according to his folly,
> or he will be wise in his own eyes.

The juxtaposition of contradictory advice about answering/not answering fools indicates that the truth lies in both proverbs considered together. "Both ignoring the fool and trying to answer the fool are procedures fraught with danger" (Harris 2005, 729-30).

Paul risks losing the Corinthians to a false gospel (2 Cor 11:4), if he refuses the tactics of his adversaries and refrains from foolish boasting. But if he chooses to indulge in such boasting, he runs the risk of being misunderstood by the Corinthians. Paul deems the first risk greater. And so with dripping irony, Paul adopts the technique he judges most apt to alert the Corinthians to the reality of their situation (Harris 2005, 730).

■ **1** Paul begins v 1 with a wish whose end is yet to be attained. **I hope/*wish*** [*ophelon*] **you will put up with a little of my foolishness.** Bengel (1687-1752) calls this "an anticipatory apology for what he is about to say, which might seem inconsistent with modesty on his part" (1895, 3:415). Paul requests that the Corinthians "bear with [him] in a little foolishness" (NRSV).

The position of *mou* (= ***of me***) directly following the verb in the second clause of the verse favors the NRSV's translation "bear with me," rather than the NIV's **a little of my foolishness**. The verb *anechō* may take genitive objects, here *mou*. It belongs with the preceding verb rather than with the following noun expression (*mikron ti aphrosynēs*).

The word **foolishness** is rooted in the OT wisdom tradition (e.g., Job 1:22; Ps 14:1; Prov 9:13-18; Isa 32:5-6). Paul utilizes it to inform his audience that he is playing the fool. It is not because he is foolish but because he is mocking his opponents by imitating (in parody) their indulgence in self-praise (see 11:16-17, 19, 21; 12:6, 11). Thus Paul's boasting is "a little foolishness" (NRSV) he hopes they will be able to see through and continue to **put up with,** to their profit.

The context suggests that the verb *anechesthe* should read as an imperative ("Do bear with me!" [NRSV]) rather than an indicative ("you are bearing with me" [NASB; see NIV]). The following verses explain why the Corinthians *should* listen to Paul, not why they *are* listening to him (Peterson 1998, 105). McCant considers the verb indicative but takes Paul's statement as a teasing ironic taunt that they are not putting up with him! (1999, 117).

In vv 2-4, Paul offers three reasons (*gar*, ***for***) motivating his request that the Corinthians ***bear*** (*anechesthe*) with his foolishness. Each reason is introduced with *gar*, which is not always clearly evident in the translations. These reasons are:

1. Paul's **godly jealousy** in relation to the endangered faith of the Corinthians (vv 2-3)
2. The church's willing acceptance of those who come to them with a message contrary to that of the apostle (v 4)
3. Paul's noninferiority to "the most eminent apostles" (NASB) to whom the intruders in Corinth were apparently appealing (v 5)

■ **2** The first motivation for Paul's plea for the Corinthians to tolerate his **foolishness** flows from his *Theou zēlōi* (**godly jealousy**). He shares the same deep concern for them that God has for his people. Thus, the genitive *Theou* (= "of God") is qualitative. But the idea of origin (subjective genitive = "from

God") is not far off. Some interpreters prefer the possessive genitive (= ***God's***), the jealousy God himself possesses (see Exod 20:5; 34:14; Deut 4:24; 6:15; Josh 24:19-20; Ezek 23:25; Nah 1:2). Whatever the precise nuance, Paul's point is that in some strong, more than merely human, sense, God is intimately involved in his depth of feeling for the church at Corinth (see Furnish 1984, 486; Harris 2005, 734). As "lovers seem to be out of their wits" (Bengel 1895, 3:416), so Paul plays the fool.

The metaphor Paul employs to explain his **godly jealousy** is one familiar from Scripture: **I promised you to one husband, to Christ, so that I might present you as a pure virgin to him.** The verb **promised** (*hērmosamēn*), only here in the NT, means "to bring into close association, to join" (BDAG 2000, 132). It is used here for "betrothal" in the context of traditional Jewish marriage customs.

The background of Paul's imagery is the OT. Israel's prophets frequently picture God as the bridegroom of his people (Isa 50:1-2; 54:1-8; Jer 3:1; Ezek 16:23-33; Hos 2:19-20) and Israel as God's bride (Isa 49:18; 54:5-6; 62:5). The figure illustrates the nature of the covenant bond between them.

Jesus often spoke of the messianic consummation in terms of a marriage feast (Matt 22:2; 25:1; see Eph 5:23-32; Rev 19:7-9; 21:2, 9) and of himself as the bridegroom (Mark 2:18-20; see John 3:27-29). Paul uses the analogy of marriage for the entire Corinthian church as the bride of Christ, "regarded corporately and as representative of all believers" (Harris 2005, 737). Paul be-
11:2 trothed them (*hymas*, **you** [plural]) **to one** [singular] **husband,** an exclusive relationship. According to Jewish custom, betrothal was a formal contract in which the engaged couple were legally husband and wife, although there was a year's interval before the wedding festivities. Only at that time did the woman leave her parents' house to take up domestic and sexual relations in her husband's home (Deut 22:23-24; Matt 1:18-24; Harris 2005, 735-36).

Although other options are possible (marriage broker or friend of the bride, see Harris 2005, 736), Paul seems to present himself metaphorically as the father of the bride (12:14; 1 Cor 4:15), who arranged the betrothal. This is consistent with Paul's imagery, since the father was responsible for protecting the sexual purity of the bride until the marriage was consummated. The apostle is the one who fathered and nurtured the church at Corinth by his evangelistic preaching and ministry (explicit in 1 Cor 4:15). As such, he guards them with a **godly jealousy** against all rivals to the purity of their faith until he can present them (*hymas*, **you** [plural]) **as a pure virgin** (*parthenon hagnēn* [singular]) "to One as husband" (Lenski 1937, 1235), that is, **to Christ.** No rivals can be tolerated.

Paul's singular point is the preservation of the chastity of the bride, the Corinthians. Chrysostom (344/354-407) notes that "in the world a woman is a virgin before her marriage, when she loses her virginity. But in the church, those who were anything but virgins before they turned to Christ acquire virginity in him. As a result the whole church is a virgin" (ACCS NT 7:290). **Virgin** (*parthenon*) here, as emphatically qualified by **pure** (*hagnēn*), refers to a female of marriageable age, as always in the NT, "who has never engaged in sexual intercourse" (BDAG 2000, 777).

In keeping with the figure, the marriage consummation at which Paul is to present the Corinthians **to Christ . . . as a pure virgin** is, no doubt, the day of messianic fulfillment, the Parousia at the end of the age (see 4:15 and comments on 5:1-10). The apostle's concern here is one he often expresses in his letters: that his converts "may be pure and blameless until the day of Christ" (Phil 1:10; see 1 Cor 1:8; Eph 5:27; Col 1:22; 1 Thess 5:23). Paul expects the church and Christians to live "in between the times" with the loyalty and purity of an eager and anxious bride. Paul's function is "to preserve the virginity of the infant church right up to her wedding day" (Harris 2005, 738).

■ **3** Moved by his responsibility for his spiritual children in Corinth, Paul is convinced that the intruders present a serious threat to their faith. His ministry in Corinth may come to naught with dire consequences to the Christians there. He is **afraid** with a pastoral fear. Such fear is "not only not contrary to love, but . . . a property of love" (Bengel 1895, 3:416).

Paul's fear is that the Corinthians, **just as Eve was,** may be completely **deceived** [*exēpatēsen*—a compound verb intensifying the meaning] **by the serpent's cunning** (v 3). According to Augustine (354-430), the serpent destroyed "her virginity of heart" (ACCS NT 7:290). The serpentine **cunning/*craftiness*** (*panourgiai;* "deception" in 4:2; "crafty fellow" in 12:16; 1 Cor 3:19), literally the "readiness to do anything" (BDAG 2000, 754), is the "deception" Paul had renounced in 4:2. Paul's twofold fear is expressed by an unusual verb, used only here in the NT: *phtharēi . . . apo* ("corrupted . . . from"—**led astray from**).

His first fear is the corruption of the Corinthians' **minds** (*noēmata hymōn*). That is, he is concerned that their intellectual or thinking processes should not be deceived (see see v 4; 3:14; 4:4). In short, he is afraid that they will accept "a different gospel" (v 4).

Paul's second fear is that their deception will lead them to depart from their **sincere and pure devotion to Christ.** The NIV translates the meaning adequately enough. But the Greek is far more emphatic: ***that simplicity*** [*tēs haplotētos*] ***and that purity*** [*kai tēs hagnotētos*] ***that is unto Christ*** (*tēs eis ton Christon*).

Theology, how one thinks about one's faith, is important, not merely a matter of indifferent private opinion. Theological deception can lead people to be "corruptly diverted from" (Thrall 2004, 656) single-minded and exclusive commitment to Christ.

Some Greek manuscripts do not contain the phrase *kai tēs hagnotētos.* But the strength of the external manuscript support favors the inclusion of both descriptive nouns. Both relate neatly to Paul's imagery in v 2, continuing the marriage metaphor. The noun *haplotētos* ("singleness," BDAG 2000, 104) takes up *heni andri* ("one husband"), while *hagnotētos* (***"purity,"*** BDAG 2000,

13) picks up on the motif of *parthenon hagnēn* ("pure virgin"; Thrall 2004, 663).

Eve is mentioned elsewhere in the NT only in 1 Tim 2:13-14. With her mention here as **deceived by the serpent's cunning,** "the reference to the fall of Adam reveals just how serious the danger facing the Corinthians really is" (Hafemann 2000, 427).

It is uncertain whether Paul was familiar with speculation about the story of Adam and Eve in contemporary Judaism (Wis 2:23-24; *2 En.* 31.6; see Thrall 2004, 662). But it seems clear that the image of the serpent suggests that he sees Satan (the equation is explicit only in Rev 12:15) at work (see 2:11) in the presence of the false apostles in Corinth. Paul explicitly identifies their methods as satanic (2 Cor 11:13-15). There is no compelling reason for the suggestion that Paul alludes to the rabbinic tradition that the serpent sexually seduced Eve (see Harris 2005, 741).

Paul probably intends his readers to recognize three parallels between the account of Eve's temptation by the serpent in Gen 3:1-13 and what he faces in the church at Corinth (Harris 2005, 740-42).

1. Eve was deceived and the church was at risk of being deceived, both endangering their innocence, that is, their relation to God/Christ.
2. The deception is carried out by an agent—the serpent, who is Satan in disguise—"Satan himself masquerades" (v 14).
3. The means used in both cases was cunning or craftiness: "Now the serpent was more crafty than any of the wild animals the LORD God had made" (Gen 3:1).

For the Corinthians to be influenced by such false apostles would be to violate their betrothal pledge to Christ and sacrifice their virginal relation to him. As their father in the faith, this was what Paul was concerned to protect, lest their **minds** would **somehow be led astray from** their **pure devotion to Christ.**

■ **4** Paul clearly states his first reason for asking the Corinthians to put up with his foolishness in vv 2-3. In v 4, Paul states his second reason. The conjunction **For** (*gar*) connects his thought back with v 1 (since Paul justifies his fear in v 3).

Paul's apparently hypothetical reference, **if someone comes** (*ei . . . ho erchomenos*), actually points to the boastful interlopers. They came to Corinth with a message different from the one Paul brought. The apostle chides the Corinthians: **you put up with it easily enough.** The unspoken thought in Paul's mind, which his readers could not miss, is: "Why should you not put up with me then?" (see v 1). If they could tolerate so readily one who preaches ***another*** [*allon*] **Jesus**—one other than the Jesus crucified and risen whom Paul had **preached** to them, surely his "little foolishness" (NRSV) would be no burden to them.

What was different about the preaching of Jesus by Paul as compared to the false apostles? Paul does not say. But some interpreters plausibly suggest here a specific reference to their omission of Jesus' humiliation and suffering culminating in his death by crucifixion (Lambrecht 1999, 174).

Paul expands his apparently hypothetical description of the Corinthians' openness to ***another Jesus*** with two more. Both are introduced with the alternative particle (*ē*, **or**). The constructions are parallel, although the conditional particle (*ei*, **if**) appears only with the first.

Paul's second decription of the Corinthians' deception follows: **or if you receive** [*lambanete*] **a different** [*heteron*] ***Spirit*** **from the one you received** (*elabete*). Although English versions prefer to translate *pneuma* as **spirit** (NIV, NRSV, NASB, KJV), consistency with Paul's declared message would signify here the gift of the Holy Spirit. This would be consistent with his earlier reference to ***another Jesus.*** For Paul the **spirit** most often designates the Spirit of God or Christ (see 3:17; 1 Cor 2:12; Rom 8:16; 14:17), who is the pledge of future fulfillment of God's promises (1:22; 5:5; see Eph 1:13-14). The parallel of ***another*** **Jesus** and **a different *Spirit*** suggests that Paul presumes that the false apostles promoted a different understanding of the Holy Spirit than his.

Third, Paul completes the picture by adding that the Corinthians had been deceived by **a different** [*heteron*] **gospel** [see Gal 1:6] **from the one** [they] **accepted** (*edexasthe*) when he founded their church. The false apostles apparently used the same terms—**Jesus, *Spirit*, gospel**—for their message. But the message they proclaimed was different. It was not only different in emphasis from what Paul had originally preached but also so "other" that it could only be described as false.

Many interpreters have attempted to identify the message of the intruding false apostles more specifically than this. But it is difficult to say more with certainty (see Furnish 1984, 500-502; Thrall 2004, 667-70; Harris 2005, 744-45), since Paul doesn't. And the Corinthians knew well enough. The general tenor of the letter and 11:20-30 in particular, however, suggest that their teaching involved an interpretation of the ministry of Jesus that discredited the apostolic status of Paul, whose "power is made perfect in weakness" (12:9). Thus, the intruders are proclaiming **a different gospel,** redefining the apostolic ministry as one whose methodology is not grounded in the weakness of the crucifixion and the resultant power of the resurrection (see 13:4).

With **Jesus, *Spirit,*** and **gospel** Paul gives us a three-word summary of Christianity. Christianity for him consists of "Jesus—the New Creation; Spirit—the new Life in which to live in this Creation; Gospel—the instrument for spreading this life in this Creation" (Hanson 1954, 81).

■ **5** Verse 5 presents Paul's third reason for his request in v 1 that the Corinthians should bear with his foolishness. He does not consider himself **in the least inferior to those "super-apostles."** The crucial interpretive issue is: "Who are the **'super-apostles'**"?

The NIV translates the conjunction *gar* as an adversative, indicating contrast. **But** is a highly unusual translation for *gar*. The NIV translation of the ironic *tōn hyperlian apostolōn* as <u>**those**</u> **"super-apostles"** (emphasis added; similarly NRSV) identifies them with Paul's opponents in v 4 (see vv 13-15). Other interpreters prefer the more common causal force of *gar* ("For," NASB). Others also argue that Paul's reference to "the most eminent apostles" (NASB) intends the pillar apostles (see Gal 2:9) or simply the Twelve, both here and in 12:11. Detailed arguments can be found for both interpretations. Thrall has recently defended the first understanding of the **"super-apostles"** (2004, 671-76); Harris, the second (2005, 75-76, 746-47).

If the second interpretation is correct, Paul is comparing himself here, not with the opposing "false apostles" (v 13), but with the original apostles. The translation of *tōn hyperlian apostolōn* could be "the very chiefest" (KJV), "superlative" (RSV), or "most eminent apostles" (NASB). These translations could reflect the description of the original apostles regularly used by Paul's opponents to disparage him by comparison. Or, "more probably, [this reflects] the apostle's ironic description of the exalted view of the Twelve held by the 'false apostles'" (Harris 2005, 76).

The implication for the Corinthian readers is that they are in danger (vv 3-4), if they buy into the message of Paul's opponents. If the second interpretation is correct, Paul argues that he is in no way inferior in status or authority with the church's premiere apostles. He, too, authentically represents the apostolic tradition (Hafemann 2000, 431). Thus the third reason the Corinthians need to put up with Paul's foolishness (v 1) is that he "supposes" himself "not a whit behind the very chiefest apostles" (KJV).

Nevertheless, the obvious reference to the intruders in vv 13-15 argues for the first interpretation, identifying the **"super-apostles"** with the intruders. If this view is correct, Paul insists that he is not inferior to the intruders, who are exalting themselves as **"super-apostles"** by depreciating him and his weakness as an apostle.

■ **6** Paul immediately qualifies his assertion in v 5 with a concession and a new assertion, introduced by ***And even if*** [*ei de kai*]. First, he concedes that he **may not be a trained speaker** (see on 10:10; 1 Cor 2:1-4). What he says literally is that he is *idōtēs tōi logōi*, ***an amateur in rhetorical discourse*** (BDAG 2000, 468). He admits that he is "untrained" (NRSV), but not "unskilled" (NASB; so Peterson 1998, 109).

Second, Paul asserts with an emphatic double *all'* ("but") that he is not *idōtēs*, an amateur, in **knowledge** (*tēi gnōsei*). The double *all'* can be translated: "but . . . certainly" (NRSV) or "certainly . . . on the contrary" (Harris 2005, 748; see BDAG 2000, 45 s.v. *alla* 4a).

The gospel he preaches (2:14) and defends (10:5) demonstrates that his knowledge of God through Christ (4:6) is comprehensive (see 1 Cor 2:6-16; Eph 3:3-5; Col 2:3). He considers this obvious even to his uncooperative converts in Corinth. Thus, he stresses, "certainly [*all'*] in every way [*en panti*] and in all things [*en pasin*] we have made this evident to you" (NRSV). Both in word and deed, in his preaching and in his apostolic life (4:7-12; 6:3-10), Paul displays his knowledge of the gospel's essence (see 2:14). His communication of the divine truth to the Corinthians has been comprehensive in both means and extent. "The depth of Paul's spiritual insight should have been clear to the Corinthians in every dimension and detail of his ministry among them" (Furnish 1984, 491).

Paul's subject matter was more significant than his manner of delivery. His substance was more consequential than his style. His accurate knowledge of the gospel mattered more than his eloquence in proclamation. Calvin asks, "And is it not true that the efficacy of the Holy Spirit appears more clearly in bare unpolished words than under the guise of eloquence and ornament?" He adds an old Latin proverb, "Let others have the word but give us the reality" (1964, 10:143). In the very faithfulness of Paul's witness to the gospel of Christ to the Corinthians, they possess incontrovertible evidence of the genuine character of his apostleship.

The rationale for the foolishness Paul feels he must indulge in confronts us with our stewardship of the gospel of Christ. Like Paul, we should be:

1. fully cognizant of our human limitations (v 6)
2. confident in our conviction of divine truth in the gospel (vv 5-6)
3. concerned for the spiritual welfare of those to whom we minister in the faith (vv 2-3)

Under and through it all remains the vital question: Who is the Jesus we worship and serve? Is he the Jesus witnessed to by the apostolic tradition we find in the NT, and to which Paul is faithful?

2. The Self-Support of Paul's Mission (11:7-15)

Paul's opening paragraph (vv 1-6) is considered by some interpreters an introducion to the entirety of "the fool's speech" (see Thrall 2004, 682). Following this, in vv 7-15, Paul takes up another matter in which he feels himself not in the least inferior to the "superlative apostles" (RSV).

In addition to defending his "knowledge" (11:6), Paul seems concerned to defend his refusal to be financially dependent on the Corinthians. They seem apparently to have taken offense at this. Among the possible reasons for their criticism are:

1. Manual labor is beneath any apostolic status and undercuts apostolic authority.
2. Paul violated the conventions of the patron-client relationship by which the wealthy supported their visiting teachers.
3. Most probably, he was operating on a double standard by accepting financial aid from the Macedonians (see Harris 2005, 751-52), while refusing it from them.

The self-appointed "apostles" who had invaded the church at Corinth did accept pay for their services. They are, no doubt, using this fact to denegrate Paul in the minds of his Corinthian converts (see 11:3). How could Paul simply ignore the Lord's command "that those who preach the gospel should receive their living from the gospel" (1 Cor 9:14)? If those who preach and teach well in the church "are worthy" to be paid (1 Tim 5:17-18), was Paul unworthy? The apostle draws a clear contrast between his motives and the motives of those he calls false apostles in vv 13-15.

■ **7** Paul tackles the issue of financial support with an exaggerated rhetorical question. Its formulation forces a negative response: **Or** [*ē*] ***did I commit a sin by lowering myself in order that you might be exalted, because I preached the gospel of God to you free of charge?*** Paul appears to write with stinging irony, "at its most bitter" (Barrett 1973, 281) and "brutal" (McCant 1999, 121). Paul's rhetoric here follows the conventions of Hellenistic polemical discourse (Betz 1972, 100-101).

Paul does not admit that his financial arrangements with Corinth were sinful. His formulation suggests that this only reflects how the Corinthians saw Paul's "renunciation of their status as a patron congregation" (Furnish 1984, 508; see Thrall 2004, 683). Paul admits that he preached **the gospel of God** to the church at Corinth **free of charge** (*dōrean:* literally, "without money," as in [LXX] Exod 21:11 and 2 Thess 3:8). This was Paul's consistent practice in his missionary endeavors in Corinth (1 Cor 9:12-18). Freely he had received; freely he would give (Matt 10:8).

Paul fully recognized that "the Lord has commanded that those who preach the gospel should receive their living from the gospel" (1 Cor 9:14; see Deut 25:4; 1 Tim 5:18; Did. 13:1-2). But Paul's preaching did not so much incur a debt as it discharged one: "I am obligated" (Rom 1:14; 1 Cor 9:16). He considered the gospel an apostolic commission entrusted to him: "If I proclaim the gospel, this gives me no ground for boasting, for an obligation is laid on me, and woe to me if I do not proclaim the gospel!" (1 Cor 9:16 NRSV). Paul did not take up the task voluntarily. Therefore, his reward could not be in mere obedience (see Luke 17:10). His reward must be "just this: that in my proclamation I may make the gospel free of charge, so as not to make use of my rights in the gospel" (1 Cor 9:18 NRSV).

Paul had explained his financial principles and practice in 1 Corinthians. Did the Corinthians fail to understand or accept them as persuasive or sincere? Or, had the intruders offered them another explanation for Paul's arrangement that cast him in a negative light?

Because (*hoti*) Paul had preached ***the gospel of God*** to the Corinthians **free of charge,** he had lowered or "humbled" himself in their eyes. Four kinds of financial support were standard practice among teachers in the Hellenistic age: charging fees, entering a rich patron's household and receiving wages, begging, or self-support from working at a skilled or unskilled job (Hock 1980, 52-56). Some of Paul's contemporary teachers justified their demand for pay by claiming that if they taught for free, it would suggest that their teaching was worth nothing (McCant 1999, 122).

Only laboring at a trade fits Paul's apostolic modus operandi. This, along with his renunciation of the apostolic right to support and his contentment with the frugal lifestyle of a first-century artisan (Phil 4:11-12), constituted his "humbling" himself (NASB and NRSV; Harris 2005, 754). To make his living as a tentmaker (Acts 18:3; 20:34; 1 Thess 2:9; 2 Thess 3:8; see Hock 1980, 20-25) was **to lower** himself. Manual labor, even that of a craftsman, was considered demeaning in the social world of Paul's day. It was thought to be the least acceptable way for a philosopher or a teacher to provide for life's necessities (Furnish 1984, 506-7; see Hock 1980, 40-65).

What Paul's critics and the Corinthians may have regarded as an apostolic negative, Paul viewed as an apostolic positive. **Preaching the gospel of God . . . free of charge** was for him a sign of the authenticity of his calling. Like Christ, he chose **to lower** [himself] **in order to elevate** them (see 4:12; 6:10; 8:9), for their spiritual enrichment (9:11). He kept his ministry to them consistent with the freedom of the gospel he preached to them (see 4:5-12). Thus, his question, ***Did I commit a sin?*** is ironic.

■ **8** In shockingly vivid language Paul appears to rub it in: he has not sinned in financial matters. Rather, as he writes with obvious irony, **I robbed other churches by receiving support from them so as to serve you.** Paul's imagery is military; he takes ***wages*** (*opsōnion*). As used here in relation to **robbed** (*esylēsa, "sacked";* BDAG 2000, 955), *opsōnion* functions as a metaphor for taking booty in war, which then takes on the meaning of a soldier's pay.

By the military metaphors, Paul may have sought to dispel suspicions that he rejected benefactors in Corinth to become a client of other Christian patrons (Thrall 2004, 684). Instead, by allowing other churches to contribute to his support, Paul, in effect, ***plundered*** others. He explains that he did this in order **to serve** the Corinthians "free of charge" (*dōrean,* ***"as a gift,"*** BDAG 2000, 266; v 7). The expression **to serve you** translates *pros tēn hymōn diakonian* (literally, ***for your ministry***). Although *diakonia* appears frequently in chs 1—9, it appears only here in chs 10—13.

Paul does not identify the **other churches** from which he accepted support. In v 9 he mentions support from "the brothers who came from Macedonia." We know that the church in Philippi had a unique and ongoing financial partnership with Paul (Phil 1:5; 4:15-16). The **other churches** perhaps also included those in Thessalonica (but see 1 Thess 2:9; 2 Thess 3:7-9) and Berea. Acts 17:14-15 implies that the Bereans sent Paul on his way with adequate provisions for his journey and continuing ministry.

■ **9** When Paul was with the Corinthians, he was unable to support himself entirely through practicing his trade. He apparently exhausted what he **needed** in the way of food, clothing, and shelter. Still, he refused support from the Corinthians. Artisans normally had to work long and hard for their daily bread. Paul reminded the Thessalonians: "we worked night and day in order not to be a burden to anyone while we preached the gospel of God to you" (1 Thess 2:9; see 1 Cor 4:12; 2 Cor 11:27; Hock 1980, 34-35).

Likewise, in Corinth he refused to be **a burden to anyone.** The verb Paul uses here (*katenarkēsa*) was originally a medical term meaning "grow numb" or "be anesthetized" (12:13, 14, 16). Here it has the figurative sense of "be a burden to" (BDAG 2000, 522), with no difference in meaning from *katebarēsa* in 12:16 (see *abarē* in 11:9; Gal 6:1-6).

Rather than accept Corinthian support, funds for Paul's physical needs were "fully supplied" (NASB) by **the brothers who came from Macedonia.** The occasion could have been the coming of Silas and Timothy with gifts at least from the church at Philippi (4:16). Acts reports that subsequently Paul, who had been working at his tentmaking trade in Corinth, "devoted himself exclusively to preaching" (Acts 18:3-5; see Harris 2005, 762).

Through the generosity of others, Paul has been able to keep himself **from being a burden** (*abarē*, only here in the NT) to the Corinthians **in any way.** This he intends to **continue to do** in the future. When ministering to the Corinthians, he is not indecisive (an earlier accusation; see 1:17) as to his financial independence.

Paul's financial relationship with his churches was governed by two principles. Apparently, there were early Christian "missionary rules" operative in the mission of the early church (see Furnish 1984, 506). One was the missionaries' right to be supported by those to whom they were sent. Paul recognized this right: "the Lord has commanded that those who preach the gospel should receive their living from the gospel" (1 Cor 9:14; see Deut 25:4; 1 Tim 5:18; Did. 13:1-2). Another "missionary rule" appears to be that the gospel must be given to the hearers without cost (Matt 10:8; Did. 11:3-6, 8-9, 12). Paul apparently adopted this second rule, especially in Corinth.

Paul saw himself as a special, unique case—an apostle "abnormally born" (1 Cor 15:8), "unfit to be called an apostle" (1 Cor. 15:9 NRSV). His compulsion to apply to himself such stringency in financial dealings may arise directly from his Damascus appearance—"an obligation is laid on me" (1 Cor 9:16 NRSV; see Rom 1:14).

Paul's application of the second missionary rule took two expressions. His first principle was not to take financial aid from those to whom he was ministering at the time. Primarily, he did not want to be a burden to his converts (11:9; 2:13-14, 16; 1 Thess 2:9). Other reasons may have included consistency with his gospel of free grace (see 2 Cor 6:3; 1 Cor 9:12; 1 Thess 2:5) and avoidance of any appearance of a patron-client relationship (Furnish 1984, 507-8). In Corinth, an additional desire could have been to maintain an advantage over his rivals, who took payment for their services. Furthermore, he may have been more eager that the Corinthians complete their contribution for the collection (chs 8—9) than for his own support.

Paul's second principle was his willingness to accept gifts from distant

Christians (11:8-9; Phil 4:16). He was also willing to be helped on his way as he left one area to evangelize in another (2 Cor 1:16; 1 Cor 16:6; Rom 15:24). The apostle's concern not to be a burden when with the Corinthians apparently does not mean that he would not accept hospitality from anyone while there (see Acts 18:3; Rom 16:23). Nor does he say anything about not accepting aid from them for ministry outside of Corinth (Harris 2005, 765-66; see Thrall 2004, 699-708).

■ **10** In v 10, Paul explains his intention not to be a "burden" to the church in Corinth. He affirms it with an oath: **As surely as the truth of Christ is in me** (Barnett 1997, 518-19; see Thrall 2004, 687-88). Paul is not reluctant to appeal to God to guarantee the truth of what he says (see 1:18, 23; 11:11, 31; 12:2-3; Rom 1:9; 9:1; Phil 1:8; 1 Thess 2:5). Here his appeal to Christ makes a similar point. It goes beyond simple "truth-telling" as in 2 Cor 7:14 and 12:6 (Furnish 1984, 493).

Commenting on the absence of the article in the expression *alētheia Christou*, **truth of Christ,** Bengel says it "refers to a special truth" (1895, 3:419). If Paul is not taking an oath, he is using at least a *"solemn form* of *asseveration."* He asserts, "I speak as becomes a Christian man, and as influenced by the Gospel of Christ" (Clarke 1854, 2:361; see Harris 2005, 763). Paul speaks theologically of the truth given to him by Christ (subjective genitive), just as he could speak of having "the mind of Christ" (1 Cor 2:16; see Rom 8:9).

The content of Paul's solemn affirmation is that **in the regions of Achaia,** literally, ***this boasting will not be stopped in regard to me.*** Considering the translation possibilities of *phragēsetai* and *eis eme* (see Harris 2005, 764-65), the meaning appears to be that Paul will allow nothing to stifle him (Lambrecht 1999, 172) nor anyone or circumstance to bar him from (Thrall 2004, 656) his boast in relation to his ministry in Achaia—that is, Corinth.

With either force of the expression the general import is the same: his policy regarding financial aid stands. The boast is obviously Paul's, not those in Achaia. His conduct in the matter is linked with who he is as a Christian. That is, he considers this a matter of the integrity of his calling as an apostle. It is **the truth of Christ** in him that he will not allow to be compromised away. It is no idle boast.

■ **11** If Paul's questions mirror Corinthian accusations, they had apparently taken his refusal of support from them as an unfriendly act. Their misunderstanding of his motives were perhaps reinforced by the accusations of the intruders: "You do not truly love us!" Paul denies this with another oath-like exclamation (see 11:31). His question and answer explain why he had refused their financial support. **Why? Because I do not love you? God knows I do!**

Paul employs the literary device of *litotes* (understatement; McCant 1999, 124). He must leave his vindication to God, to whom he has always been open (5:11) and who alone knows the heart (Acts 15:8). It is not unusual for the apostle to call upon God to witness to the truth of his claims (see 1:23;

2:17; 11:31; 12:19; Rom 1:9; 9:1; Gal 1:20; Phil 1:8; 1 Thess 2:5, 10). This is not because he is usually an untrustworthy liar but because the claims he makes under oath are impossible to validate. God alone can vouch for his claim to love the Corinthians. If the Corinthians are not aware of his love for them, God is. This is Paul's assurance.

■ **12** Having denied that any lack of affection for them governs his actions, Paul now gives a positive reason for refusing support from the church. This is his second answer to the "Why?" of v 11. This time, he does not explain his reason, but his purpose. He refuses support, he says: "so that [*hina*] I may cut off [*ekkopsō*] opportunity [*aphormēn*] from those who desire an opportunity [*aphormēn*] to be regarded just as we are [*kathōs kai hēmeis*] in the matter about which they are boasting" (NASB).

Paul is passionate in his resolve. He **will keep on doing what** [he is] **doing.** His opponents apparently want to bring him down to their level of financial dependence. He explains his objective with a clever play on words. The verb translated "cut off" means literally to cut down a tree (Matt 3:10), cut off a branch (Rom 11:24), or amputate a limb (Matt 5:30). But Paul uses it here in a figurative sense with *aphormēn* to indicate his intention **to cut the ground from under** the **boast** of his opponents. Their **boast** was in their claim to financial support, which they viewed as proof of their apostolic rights (1 Cor 9:14).

Paul intends to eliminate the "assets" of those who desire such "assets" (McCant 1999, 125). What his opponents consider an apostolic right, he claims as well. But he insists on willingly foregoing this right in the interests of the gospel and the Corinthians (1 Cor 9:3-18). His opponents want to goad Paul to accept the asset he has refused: to be like them and receive support from the Corinthians. This would allow the intruders "opportunity to be recognized as [his] equals" (NRSV), thus removing Paul's advantage over them. They were too mercenary to rise to his level. Paul knew the spot he had them in; and he meant to keep them there. He was not deceived by their tactics. His bantering tone has become intensely ironic.

■ **13** Paul now plainly states what he has been implying. He sharpens his differences with his opponents in Corinth. In apparent anger, he describes them with "remarkable severity of language" (Bengel 1895, 3:420). Perhaps, he is a little too uncompromising and excessive in his severity (v 13; see vv 22-23).

Referring to his Corinthian opponents as **such men** (*hoi toioutoi*), Paul describes them as **false apostles, deceitful workmen, masquerading as apostles of Christ.** He presents them in the worst possible light. With a word, apparently of his own invention—it appears only here in the NT—Paul labels them **false apostles** (*pseudapostoloi*). He denies their claim to be genuine apostles. From Paul's perspective, they are false in the message they brought to Corinth. They proclaimed a "different" Jesus, Spirit, and gospel than what Paul proclaimed to them (11:4). And they are false as well in the methods they employ, as he indicates in vv 13-15 (11:3; see 4:2).

Thus, they are **deceitful *workers,*** their activities in Corinth are deceitful, treacherous, and cunning. Lenski points out that the noun *doles* (a cognate of *dolios*, **deceitful**) originally meant "bait." Bait was put out to catch victims; "the connotation is a deception that kills" (1937, 1256). Although ***workers*** (*ergatai*) appears to have been used as a technical term in the church for those in missionary service (Matt 9:37-38; Luke 10:2; Did. 13:2; see Matt 10:1-10; Luke 10:7), Paul employs it for his opponents only in the sense that they were "at work" in Corinth.

The opponents were only **masquerading** [*metaschēmatizōmenoi*] **as apostles of Christ.** Like ***workers*** (*ergatai*), **apostles of Christ** was probably one of their preferred self-designations. But Paul insists that it was a masquerade, a disguise, a pretense. He calls them **false apostles** (*pseudapostoloi*). The Greek verb translated **masquerade** (*metaschēmatizō*) is a catchword in vv 13-15. Its threefold appearance binds the verses together. It presumes here a deceptive change in external appearance only (contrast Phil 3:21), a superficial or pretended transformation. They were not what they seemed.

■ **14** In diatribe-like language, filled with irony, the apostle continues. He insists that there is nothing incredible about this: **no wonder** [*ou thauma*], **for Satan himself masquerades as an angel of light.** With the description of **Satan** as an **angel of light** Paul may reflect acquaintance with certain Jewish legends (see Furnish 1984, 494-95; Thrall 2004, 695).

In the pseudepigraphal *Life of Adam and Eve* (9:1), Satan "transformed himself into the brightness of angels" as he went to deceive Eve. According to the *Apocalypse of Moses* (17:1), Satan entices Eve over the walls of paradise "in the form of an angel and sang hymns like the angels" (APOT).

But the precise expression, *angelon phōtos,* is unique to this Pauline context. Although Harris cites the Jewish documents, he considers the expression Paul's own formulation (2005, 774-75; see Plummer 1915, 309-10). It could arise from the popular association of Satan with darkness (2 Cor 6:14-15) and deception (4:4), and in contrast to the linking of Christ with light (4:6). Paul's own observation of Satan's schemes and tricks would be in his mind as well (2:11). Chrysostom (344/354-407) observes that "an angel of light is one who is free to speak because he stands close to God. This is what the devil pretends to be" (ACCS NT 7:294).

Adam Clarke notes that Satan sometimes tempts in the forms of a *subtle serpent* and a *roaring lion.* But he adds, Satan "often, as the *angel of light,* persuades men to do things under *the name of religion,* which are subversive of it" (1854, 361). Furnish observes that "no more serious charge can be brought against the false apostles, for if they really are Satan's ministers," they are not merely opponents of Paul, but of Christ and his gospel. This is a severe condemnation indeed (1984, 510; see 1 John 4:1-3).

■ **15** With another *litotes* (understatement, see v 11), Paul introduces an argument from the greater to the lesser (*argumentum a majori ad minus*). **It is**

not surprising [*ou mega*, ***no great thing***], **then, if his servants masquerade as servants of righteousness.** If Satan, the "great" one, takes on a disguise, "it is not strange" (NRSV) that the "lesser," **his servants,** also disguise themselves as something different from what they really are.

Servants (*diakonoi*) or "ministers" (NRSV) has been significant language throughout the letter (see 3:3, 9; 4:1; 5:18; 6:3). The phrase **servants of righteousness** (*dikaiosynēs*, an objective genitive = they serve righteousness) has been variously interpreted (see Thrall 2004, 696-98). Most interpreters take it in the general sense as referring to "servants of God" (6:4) or "servants of Christ" (11:23). It seems to be synonymous here with "apostles of Christ" (v 13).

But **righteousness** (*dikaiosynēs*) may bring with it the flavor of Paul's distinctive usage (5:21; see Rom 1:16). His point, however, seems to be to label the intruding "false apostles" (v 13) as deceptive and satanic in character. They are not righteous or just before God. They are unrighteous pseudo-gospel-mercenaries. These are strong words, indeed. Yet such words deserve consideration by those of us who "receive [our] living from the gospel" (1 Cor 9:14)!

Of those who sell the gospel for money (see 2:17) the apostle can only say that **their end will be what their actions deserve** or "according to their deeds" (NASB; see Rom 3:8; 1 Cor 3:17; 4:5; Phil 3:19; 1 Thess 2:16; 4:6; 2 Thess 1:8). The threat of divine judgment, though unspecified, is real (see 2 Cor 5:10). Could it be said that one's ministry may very well turn out according to the motives one brings to it?

11:15-21*a* Paul's behavior was more than apostolic strategy. It flowed from the fountain of his deepest motives, from his knowledge and experience of the gospel of Christ. For Paul "the ultimate justification of his attitude was Christological" (Lambrecht 1999, 186). It was grounded/rooted in who he was as informed and transformed by the truth of Christ. From this reality the apostle could not be separated, even by treacherous means. With Paul the practice of all Christian ministry, authentic service in the name of Christ to others, is controlled by the very nature of its Christ. It is molded by the truth of the gospel that is proclaimed. The ministry cannot be a masquerade by which we deceive ourselves and others.

3. Renewed Appeal to Bear with Paul's Boasting (11:16-21*a*)

Paul's rivals in Corinth employed boasting as a weapon to gain the Corinthians' favor (v 18). Their acceptance of such tactics leads Paul in desperation to use the means of boasting as well. But before he will boast as "the world does" (v 18) in vv 21*b*-23, he makes it clear in vv 16-21*a* just how foolish such boasting is. Yet since the Corinthians appear to tolerate fools gladly (vv 19-20), Paul will proceed to play the fool (vv 16, 17, 21; see 11:1; 12:11).

Calvin is probably correct when he suggests that Paul's rivals were probably—as charismatic personalities usually are—"not merely tolerated by the Corinthians but [were] received with great applause" (1964, 147). As Paul dons the mask of the fool he creates a parody of his opponents, intended to expose the falseness of their so-called apostolic authority as compared to his (vv 20-21*a*).

Paul returns (*inclusio*—in the pattern of a literary ring or frame) to the request he made in v 1. In v 16, he again asks for the Corinthians' indulgence as he plays the **fool.** The appeal concludes with Paul's ironic admission of his weakness that leads into his theme of boasting in weakness.

■ **16** Paul writes simply, **I repeat** (*palin legō*, ***I say again***), looking back to v 1. But his focus shifts from a plea to tolerate his "foolishness" to an appeal for an acceptance of his **boasting** as a **fool.** He does not want them to misunderstand what he is doing: **Let no one take me for a fool.** Paul is no fool; and he does not want to be thought of as such. He knew full well how suspect self-praise was in Greco-Roman culture (see McCant 1999, 128; Forbes 1986, 8-10).

But if [the Corinthians] **do** think him foolish, the apostle concedes, then they should just receive him ***even as foolish*** (*kan hōs aphrona*) so that he **may do a little boasting.** The expression *ei de mē ge* (literally, "But otherwise"; **But if you do**) appears only here in Paul.

Paul concludes that the situation in Corinth compels him to boast. But he does so reluctantly nonetheless. He can indulge in this kind of self-praise only "as a fool" (v 17). The Corinthians have apparently compared him to his opponents. So he asks them to grant him the privilege of boasting as his opponents have exercised (v 18).

Paul insists that for him to boast like his opponents will be foolishness. Thus, his concern will be to boast in a manner that distinguishes him from the intruders. Paul asks only for a fair hearing. All he asks is that they **receive** [him] **just as** [they] **would a fool.** He risks being misunderstood as actually foolish, if need be, to make the issues clear. This will point out who is *really* foolish!

■ **17** Verse 17 calls for a literal translation: ***What I am saying I say not according to the Lord, but as in foolishness, in this matter of boasting.*** Paul guards against being misunderstood. When he boasts, he speaks *ou kata kyrion,* **not . . . as the Lord would** (see 10:1). That is, he does not speak "with the Lord's authority" (NRSV), "as a Christian" (NEB; see 2:17; 12:19), or as "prompted by the Lord" (JB). The differences between these are slight, but the last is best. Paul boasts by his own choice, not at the Lord's direction (so Harris 2005, 780).

Second, the apostle boasts ***as in foolishness*** (*hōs en aphrosynēi*). That is, Paul is only "playing" the fool; but his intention is serious. He seeks to expose the folly of his rivals and to reestablish his own apostolic standing in Corinth. As a result, "Paul does not find it easy to make clear how far he is serious, how far ironical" (Barrett 1973, 290).

In the final phrase, ***in this matter of boasting,*** *hypostasei* ("confidence" in the NASB, NRSV, and NIV), is better understood as in 9:4: "in this undertaking" (NRSV). Here, it has the meaning "in this boasting project of mine" (BDAG 2000, 1041).

■ **18** Paul excuses his boasting: "Everybody's doing it." His reference to the **many** (see 2:17) may contemptuously refer to his rivals. Or it may have a wider reference to all boasters, including some Corinthians. So Paul will join them, **boasting in the way the world does** (i.e., *kata sarka:* ***according to the flesh;*** see 5:16; 10:20-23).

To boast *kata sarka* stands in antithetical contrast to *kata kyrion* but parallel to *en aphrosynēi,* ***in foolishness*** (both in v 17). His emphasis is on the manner, not the content of his boast. That is, he stresses the way he will boast, and only to a lesser extent what he will boast about. As an inescapable necessity (12:11, 1), Paul **too will boast** as his opponents **are boasting.**

Paul does not repeat *kata sarka* as the syntax anticipates. The Corinthians had accused him of making plans *kata sarka* (1:17; see Rom 8:4-8, 12-13). He will imitate the foolish human approach to boasting to point out its folly. Paul's ironic boasting reveals its essential contrast to that of his opponents.

■ **19** With "beautiful irony" (Wesley 1950, 671) Paul offers a reason (*gar,* "For," NRSV) why the Corinthians should accept him "as . . . a fool" (v 16): **You gladly put up with** [*anechesthe;* see v 1] **fools since you are so wise!**

Paul heightens his irony with an emphatic **gladly** (*hēdeōs*) and a sarcastic **you are so wise,** referring to the Corinthians' boast of wisdom (1 Cor 3:18-20; 4:10; 6:5; 8:1-7; 13:2; McCant 1999, 129). He is confident that they will have no difficulty putting up with him. After all, in their "wisdom," they are amazingly tolerant of fools. So he, too, will speak as a fool. But, unlike the intruders, Paul knows such speech is not *kata kyrion.* The intruders are unaware that they are speaking *kata sarka.*

■ **20** In v 20, Paul unmasks his biting irony, just in case they missed it. They not only "suffer fools gladly" (v 19, KJV), but Paul continues to explain (*gar,* "For," NRSV): **In fact, you even put up with** [*anechesthe;* see vv 1 and 19] **anyone . . .** He repeats *anechesthe* from 11:1 and 19, mentioning five examples of intolerable abuse the Corinthians tolerate.

Paul makes his intention clear with the hammer-blows of five verbs, each building on the preceding. "Each clause of this splendid series [operates] as a whiplash" (Windisch 1924, 347). Scholars debate whether Paul intends to be taken literally, metaphorically, or rhetorically (Martin 1986, 364). The metaphorical reading seems most natural; but each verb should be considered on its own. The fivefold anaphoric (literary repetition) use of ***if anyone*** (*ei tis*) intensifies the passion of Paul's characterization of the Corinthians' absurd submission to the intruders. They "put up with it" (NRSV):

First, ***if anyone*** **enslaves** (*katadouloi,* ***dominates***) them. Paul says that the Corinthians allow the intruders to exercise undue authority over their faith.

His only other use of this verb is in Gal 2:4. There he reports that "some false brothers . . . infiltrated [the Jerusalem church] to spy on [their] freedom . . . in Christ Jesus and to make [them] slaves."

Second, ***if anyone*** **exploits** (*katesthiei;* see Gal 5:15) them. That is, the Corinthians allow the outsiders to "devour" or "eat them up" (BDAG 2000, 532). Perhaps Paul refers to aggressive behavior on the part of the false apostles. He hints that they prey upon and plunder the Corinthians' resources like parasites in their dependence on the church for support. By way of contrast, Paul is willing to expend himself for them (12:14-15; see 2:17; 6:4-5).

Third, ***if anyone*** **takes advantage of** (*lambanei*) them. This least descriptive of the five verbs simply reinforces what Paul has just said. In 12:17-18, he denies the charge that he has taken advantage of them. In 12:16, the same verb is translated, "I caught you by trickery" (*dolōi . . . elabon*). The metaphor of hunting or fishing lies in the background (see Luke 5:5).

Fourth, adds Paul, ***if anyone*** **pushes himself forward** (*epairetai:* "puts on airs," BDAG 2000, 357). He describes the false apostles' presumptuous and arrogant treatment of the Corinthians. He uses the same verb in 10:5, writing: "We demolish arguments and every pretension that sets itself up [*epairomenon*] against the knowledge of God." Paul "lowered" himself (11:7) in order "to lift up" the Corinthians. The intruders had **enslaved** them in order to "put on airs" (NRSV).

Fifth, ***if anyone*** **slaps** [them] **in the face.** Paul describes the abuse the Corinthians willingly endured in the terminology of physical violence and contempt. A slap on the cheek, especially the right cheek, was intended to humiliate (see Matt 5:39). Paul's language may be no more than a figurative description of a verbal attack; the intruders insulted the Corinthians. But he may allude to an instance of actual physical assault. In that day, those in authority, even ecclesiastical authority, considered themselves free to strike offenders for their insolence and impiety (Hughes 1962, 400; Harris 2005, 786; see John 18:22; Acts 23:2; 1 Cor 4:11; 1 Tim 3:3; Titus 1:7). 11:20

The five implicit charges Paul lodges against the interlopers are similar. In fact, the last four could be merely illustrations of the first; all were forms of enslavement or domination. Alongside their different Jesus, Spirit, and gospel (see 11:4), their view of apostolic leadership is strikingly different from Paul's (see 1:24; 4:5; 11:3; 12:14-15). Paul was their *doulos* (***slave***), not their *kyrios* (***lord;*** 4:5).

In contrast to the false apostles, Paul "had remained financially independent (11:7-12); he had refused to act with unscrupulous cunning (4:2); he did not lord it over them and their faith (1:24); he was committed to protecting them from spiritual violation (11:2)" (Harris 2005, 787).

"The fault of the Corinthians was that they had accepted this indignity as though coming from men of apostolic authority, without discerning how utterly incongruous it was with the true spirit of Christ and His apostles, and thereby dishonoring Paul . . . and the gospel which he had preached to them" (Hughes 1962, 401). Ironically, by tolerating the intruders, the Corinthians contradict the very gospel they received in becoming a church.

■ **21*a*** With 11:20*a* Paul's "irony becomes sarcasm" (McCant 1988, 558). He probably responds to a charge leveled against him in Corinth. He admits that he did not exercise his authority as they expected. He did not abuse them as the intruders were doing: **To my shame I admit that we were too weak** [*ēsthenēkamen*] **for that!**

Some interpreters take the **shame** as belonging to the Corinthians. That is, perhaps he refers to their shaming of him. The opening clause is literally ***according to dishonor I speak*** (*kata atimian legō*). But it is more natural to refer it to Paul's own shame. If his opponents display the marks of true apostolic authority, then, to his ***dishonor,*** he confesses that by comparison he is indeed a weak failure (see 10:10; see 10:1). Paul has not lorded it over them as have his rivals.

Paul's understanding of weakness differs radically from that of the false apostles. His highly ironic mention of weakness here anticipates his paradoxical boasting that will follow. He will boast of his weakness (11:23-30; 12:1-10). The incongruity of Paul's apostleship is that when he is weak, then he is strong (12:10) because of the power of Christ (12:9).

The adjective "weak" (*asthenēs*) appeared in 10:10 for the first time in 2 Corinthians. But this is the first occurrence of the verb *astheneō*, "be weak" (11:21, 29; 12:10; 13:3, 4, 9). The noun *astheneia*, "weakness," also occurs for the first time in ch 11 (11:30; 12:5, 9, 10; 13:4). From this point on, the *asthen-* cognate group plays a key role in Paul's presentation.

The basic thought, however, has already appeared in other terms throughout the letter (recall "jars of clay" in 4:7-12; "wasting away" in 4:16; and Paul's table of circumstances in 6:4-10). Paul may be weak, but he is bold enough to counterattack effectively!

In the course of his embarrassing apology for the boasting that is to follow, Paul finds its legitimacy in (1) the realization of its true character—foolishness; and in (2) the recognition of the particular nature of the situation that has made it necessary. Now placed in sharp relief is the direction in which a valid understanding of ministry is to be found. This is what he prepares to present in his own defense. His ministry is grounded in weakness. Thus, its nature and power is not *kata sarka* but *kata kyrion*. It does not follow human patterns, but that of the Lord Jesus.

4. The Boasting of the Apostle (11:21*b*—12:10)

The apostle now boldly launches into the "boasting" he has been threatening since 11:1 (see 11:16-18), but so far he has been hesitant to indulge in. Once again (11:1, 16, 17, 19) he emphasizes that he intends only to parody his opponents: **I am speaking as a fool** (v 21) and ***as a madman*** (v 23; see Furnish 1984, 533).

The remark in v 21*b*—**I am speaking as a fool**—introduces all that follows through 12:10. In the course of his boasting Paul subtly compares himself to and contrasts himself with the intruders. He presents his unique credentials as an apostle (11:21*b*-33) and brings to light his "visions and revelations from the Lord" (12:1; see 12:1-10).

Paul's mock boasting perhaps reflects the specific claims of his rivals. His goal is to unmask the duplicitous behavior of the intruders. He boasts genuinely in what his opponents deplore—his weakness. And he boasts foolishly in what they admire—his ethnic heritage and spiritual experiences. Both boasts are an indictment of their boast.

a. The Credentials of an Apostle (11:21b-33)

Paul's boast moves through several stages. The first is his catalog of what he has endured for the sake of the gospel (vv 21*b*-29). The second is a dramatic illustration of his weakness (vv 30-33).

The first stage develops his catalog in 6:4-10. But it is a richer, more comprehensive, and intensely passionate presentation. To the privileges of his birth and training Paul adds a full account of his apostolic sufferings and perils. He displays his divine empowerment as a servant of Christ to overcome considerable hardships. In the process Paul presents himself as both equal (vv 21*b*-22) and superior to (vv 23-29) his opponents.

■ **21*b*** Paul is on the offensive; ready now to match boldness with boldness, to play the same game on the same playing field as his rivals. Yet he remains consciously apologetic about his boasting, adding again (see 11:1, 16, 17, 19): **I am speaking as a fool.** This indicates that his mood of irony continues; he is not indulging in behavior his readers are to emulate.

On the contrary, Paul is forced to boast for the sake of the Corinthians. Therefore, he writes, "I am just as bold myself" (NASB). The NIV and NRSV add **boast** to the explicit verb to complete the thought: **I also dare to boast about** (*tolmō kagō*). This is the third of his sixfold use of *kagō*—***I also***—in vv 16-22 (vv 16, 18, 21, 22 [3 times]). Paul uses this to express his parity in "boldness to boast" with his opponents (see 10:2, 12).

■ **22** With a series of questions Paul specifies the claims of his rivals: **Are they Hebrews? . . . Are they Israelites? . . . Are they Abraham's descendants?** To all three questions he answers emphatically, **So am I** [*kagō*]. Together these designations stress the full Jewishness of Paul and his rivals.

A progression of privilege in ascending order appears to be indicated (Harris 2005, 796). In Acts 6:1, **Hebrews** (*Hebraioi*) designates the Aramaic-speaking Jewish Christians of the Jerusalem church who attended Hebrew-speaking synagogues and represented Palestinian orthodoxy. This designation distinguished them from the Hellenists, who could speak only Greek and attended Greek-speaking synagogues (Acts 6:9).

In Phil 3:5 Paul describes himself as "a Hebrew of Hebrews" (*Hebraios ex*

Hebraiōn). Here, **Hebrews** indicates both his nationality and his descent from a Palestinian (probably Hebrew-speaking) family. Paul could read and study the Jewish Scriptures in the original Hebrew. But if his formative years and education took place in Jerusalem, his mother tongue was Aramaic (Acts 21:39—22:3; Van Unnick 1962, 52). Some scholars hold that Paul did not come to Jerusalem until he was in his teens. His letters certainly suggest a native-command of Greek.

The invaders in Corinth were no doubt also Aramaic-speaking Palestinian Jews who were attempting to use their descent and heritage to put the apostle, born on foreign soil—in Tarsus of Cilicia (Acts 22:3)—in an unfavorable light.

Are they Israelites? So am I. Like the Corinthian interlopers, Paul, too, was a descendant of Abraham, Isaac, and Jacob—later renamed "Israel" (Gen 32:28). The apostle was not a convert to Judaism, but "of the people of Israel, of the tribe of Benjamin" (Phil 3:5; see Rom 11:1).

Paul takes pride in Israelite ancestry. He belonged from birth to the chosen covenant people of God, God's particular instrument for the salvation of all humanity. They were "Israelites, to whom belongs the adoption as sons, and the glory and the covenants and the giving of the Law and the temple service and the promises, whose are the fathers, and from whom is the Christ according to the flesh" (Rom 9:4-5 NASB).

The faith of the people Israel was fully his, too; for, like Nathanael, Paul was "an Israelite indeed" (John 1:47 NASB). As a term for the Jewish people, unlike the frequent *Ioudaios* ("Jews"—195 times in the NT), *Israēlitēs* is used only nine times in the NT, three in Paul's letters (Rom 9:4; 11:1; 2 Cor 11:22). Two of these occur with the next term, ***the seed of Abraham*** (*sperma Abraam*).

Are they Abraham's descendants? So am I. Paul was "a descendant of Abraham" (Rom 11:1), to whom the promise of an everlasting covenant was given and through his descendants the promise of blessing to all nations (Gen 12:1-3; 17:7; 22:18).

Paul was a member not only by race but also by faith of **Abraham's descendants** (see Gal 3:8). The seed of Abraham was Christ (Gal 3:16), and in Christ the blessing of Abraham had come upon all, wrote Paul, "that by faith we might receive the promise of the Spirit" (Gal 3:14). As a Christian Paul remained more than ever a member of Abraham's family.

The apostle's opponents had nothing on him. He was a Jew in the fullest sense of the term: "according to the strictest sect of our religion, I lived as a Pharisee" (Acts 26:5; see Phil 3:5-6). Yet Paul could count it all as "a loss compared to the surpassing greatness of knowing Christ Jesus [his] Lord" (Phil 3:8).

■ **23** The formulation of Paul's question continues as before in v 23. But the form of his answer changes with this final question: **Are they servants of Christ?** Although similar to the preceding three, this question transcends them and reveals the crucial issue. All four designations appear to take up the boasts of his opponents in Corinth. But this final claim is the preeminent one.

Paul uses *diakonos*, "servant/minister," twenty-one times in his letters, applied to himself and other ministry colleagues. But he can also use the term to refer to government officials (Rom 13:4) and agents of Satan (2 Cor 11:15). The singular formulation, "servant of Christ," occurs twice in the Pauline letters (Col 1:7; 1 Tim 4:6 NASB). But this is the only instance of the plural *diakonoi Christou* (see 2 Cor 3:6; 6:4; Phil 1:1; 1 Tim 3:8, 12). In 2 Cor 11:13, Paul insists that his rivals are "false apostles, . . . masquerading as apostles of Christ." Thus, we might expect him here to answer his question, No; or to claim that they are only masquerading as **servants of Christ.** But this is not what he says.

There may have been no distinction between Paul and his rivals with respect to their Jewishness. But as **servants of Christ** there emphatically is. Paul's answer to his question is no longer **So am I** (*kagō*, v 22), but **I am more** (*hyper egō:* "I am a better one," NRSV). This is the only adverbial use of the preposition *hyper* in the NT.

To make this claim is for Paul to talk "like a madman" (NRSV). He seems to apologize for making such a comparison: **I am out of my mind** [*paraphronōn*] **to talk like this.** Here *paraphronōn*, to "be beside oneself" (BDAG 2000, 772), is a stronger word than *aphron*, translated "fool" in vv 16 and 19. Paul considers boasting about so sacred a matter as the service of Christ simply insane (Plummer 1915, 321).

Nonetheless, in vv 23-28 Paul catalogs an avalanche of occupational hardships he faced, which ironically demonstrate his superiority as a minister of Christ. He is superior to his rivals in that they have had far fewer "weaknesses" than he (11:23—12:10; 1 Cor 4:10-13).

If there are apostolic credentials *kata sarka* (v 18: "according to human standards," NRSV), they are to be found, not in the strength of the flesh, but in its "weakness" (12:5). Paul seeks to outboast the boasters (McCant 1999, 132). But he boasts of experiences that would disqualify him in their eyes. But by the proper measure of an apostle, Paul is "not . . . in the least inferior to those 'super-apostles'" (11:5; 12:11). His ministry was in fulfillment of the words spoken by the Lord of him to Ananias, "I will show him how much he must suffer for my name" (Acts 9:16; see Matt 10:24 and the commentary on 1:5-10; 4:7-12; and 6:4-5).

The extent to which Paul is beyond his opponents is brought out by an advance guard of four *en* (literally, "in" or "with") prepositional phrases, each modified with an adverb. Lenski suggests that "these four are used to indicate rhetorical completeness and are arranged in an ascending scale" (1937, 1271). Together they form a climax with the fourth the most serious (Plummer 1915, 322): "labors . . . imprisonments . . . floggings . . . death" (NRSV).

The words **much harder** and **more frequently** translate the same Greek comparative adverb—*perissoterōs*, perhaps with a superlative force. Paul worked the hardest (see 1 Cor 15:10) and was imprisoned the most.

The next two adverbs, **more severely** (*hyperballontōs*) and **again and again** (*pollakis*), probably have a superlative force (see Harris 2005, 799; Thrall 2004, 735-36). The NRSV translates: "with countless floggings, and often near death." Thus, Plummer entertains the possibility that after **I am more** the thought of comparison should be banished from consideration (1915, 322). Regardless of the grammatical considerations, Paul's emphatic use of *hyper egō* implies that he possesses superior credentials as compared to his rivals.

As a minister of Christ, Paul surpasses his opponents most significantly because, as he says, **I have worked much harder,** or ***with far more*** or "greater" (NRSV) ***labors.*** The term ***labors*** (*kopois*) probably refers to his numerous and arduous evangelistic campaigns. Furnish, however, attempts to make a case for his manual labors as a craftsman citing v 27 (1984, 515, 536).

In vv 23-28 Paul offers the longest of his four lists of sufferings in this letter (4:8-9; 6:4-5, 8-10; 11:23-28; 12:10). This catalog of suffering experienced in the course of his apostolic ministry begins with "far more imprisonments" (see, e.g., Acts 16:23-40) and "countless floggings" (NRSV; or **flogged more severely;** see Gal 6:17).

In climactic order Paul comments that he has been **exposed to death again and again,** a frequent theme in the letter (1:8-10; 4:11; 6:9; see 1 Cor 15:31-32). As Harris comments, "Death was Paul's daily companion, constant-
11:23-25 ly at his side" (2005, 800). Thus, he enlarges on this in 2 Cor 11:24-25.

Paul implies that these painful experiences from his life poured out for the gospel were totally foreign to the so-called ministry of his opponents. They had hardly worked, much less labored. They had never been in prison or beaten or faced death for Christ's sake. Paul shows up these so-called ministers of Christ. They might have been able to equal Paul in the first three boasts related to their Jewish identity (v 22). But here it ends. Paul moves on a different plane where ministry is concerned.

■ **24-25** In vv 24-25, Paul amplifies his sufferings with numerical specificity: **Five times . . . Three times . . . once . . . , three times.** This is typical of other ancient lists of the exploits of notable persons (McCant 1999, 135).

At the hands of **the Jews,** probably for blasphemy, Paul records that **five times** he received **forty lashes minus one,** the most severe beating allowed by Scripture (Deut 25:1-3). More would be degrading. The Jewish practice was to stop at 39 lashes lest a miscount should lead to an infringement of the Law, for which the administrator would be liable (Josephus, *Ant.* 4:238, 248; *The Mishnah* tractate *Makkot* ["Stripes"] 3:10; see Harris 2005, 801). Harris notes that the whip had three straps, so thirteen strokes would be the maximum (2005, 801).

This brutal scourging took place in the synagogues, fulfilling Jesus' warning that his disciples would be scourged by the Jews (Matt 10:7; Mark 13:9; Luke 12:11). Before his conversion-call, Paul had persecuted Christians in this way (Acts 22:19; 26:11). The precise occasions of the five scourgings suffered by Paul cannot be identified. But their mention reflects the persistent and bitter hostility of the Jews toward him. That he received these floggings at all indicates that he maintained his ties with the synagogue even after his conversion and, more importantly, that he submitted to its discipline. He might simply have avoided synagogues.

Three times Paul was **beaten with** wooden **rods.** This was the punishment administered by local Roman magistrates, such as those in the Roman colony of Philippi (Acts 16:22-23). As a citizen of Rome, Paul was protected from such treatment from the authorities; but pressure from an aroused populace meant that this exemption was not always observed in the provinces. Why Paul, as in Philippi, did not inform the authorities of his status, we can only conjecture (for the possibilities, see Thrall 2004, 739-42).

The one time Paul **was stoned** is recorded in Acts 14:19-20, where after the experience he was given up for dead at Lystra. Shortly before this he had barely escaped being stoned at Iconium (Acts 14:1-7).

Acts does not mention the three shipwrecks that the apostle suffered prior to the writing of 2 Corinthians. The one it reports had not occurred yet when he wrote. As Ambrosiaster (366-384) remarked, however, "Someone who sailed as much as he did would easily have been shipwrecked three times" (ACCS NT 7:298; see Acts 9:30; 13:4, 13; 14:25-26; 16:11; 17:14; 18:18).

As a result of one of these shipwrecks, Paul **spent a night and a day in the open sea,** twenty-four hours adrift ***in the deep*** (*bythōi*). In the world of Paul's day all sea voyages were considered potentially life-threatening. A safe voyage was always an occasion of thanks to the gods. These two verses form "a parenthesis of particularity" (Hughes 1962, 408). Verses 24 and 25 are both preceded and followed by more general descriptions of Paul's hardships.

■ **26** Heading an emotion-provoking list is *hodoiporias pollakis*, ***on frequent journeys,*** which the NIV paraphrases: **I have been constantly on the move.** Paul introduces the dangers he faced in the course of his frequent missionary travels in the Mediterranean world of the first century.

Arranged for rhetorical effect, the first two, dangers from **rivers** and **bandits,** would be common to all travelers. The second two, dangers **from my own countrymen** and **Gentiles,** were more specific to Paul's missionary endeavors. The next three, dangers from **the city, the country,** and **at sea,** define the areas in which Paul was at risk. Placed last for emphasis is the apostle's threat of **danger from false brothers** (Thrall 2004, 743-44). Even supposed fellow believers betrayed him and put his life in jeopardy.

Lenski emphasizes that Paul's travels (***journeys***, *hodoiporias*) are grammatically dependent on "I am more" (v 23). Thus, they are parallel to the *en* clauses of v 23 (1937, 1276). Consequently, every time the apostle went out in obedience to his apostolic commission, he took his life in his hands. He was "always being delivered over to death for Jesus' sake" (4:11). Paul survived his missionary travels, not as a private citizen, but only as a servant of Christ (11:23).

Paul faced **danger from** unbridged **rivers** that he may have had to ford, especially at floodtimes. Dangers **from bandits** undoubtedly occurred in the uninhabited regions he had to pass through.

Paul's life was in danger from his **own countrymen**—his fellow Jews (see 1 Thess 2:14-16). They hated him for accepting a crucified Messiah (see Acts 9:23; 24:7) and for his evangelistic successes among both Jews (Acts 24:7) and Gentile "God-fearers" (Acts 13:26; 14:16; 17:4).

Occasionally even **Gentiles** rose up against him (Acts 16:16-24; 19:23—20:1; see 14:6). As from everyone—Jew and Gentile, so from no area was Paul free from peril.

In the city mobs were incensed against him (see Acts 14:4-7; 16:19-24; 17:5, 13; 19:23-41). And **in the country** (*erēmiai, **desert***) there was the savagery of man and beast. And, of course, **at sea** storms could break the calm and wreck the small vessels of that day, not to mention other dangers on board ship.

Worst of all, in a class by itself, was **danger from false brothers** (*pseudadelphois;* see Gal 2:4). Other dangers could threaten life, limb, and property, but this one, under the mask of fellow believers, was treacherous and insidious and could undermine and ruin the ministry of the apostle. Harris reasons that, since Paul calls his rivals at Corinth *pseudapostoloi* (v 13), he may have included them among these *pseudadelphois*. But the latter term would have a wider reference in this context (2005, 808). The Christian church has never been free from treachery within. Even Christ had his Judas.

■ **27** In v 27, the apostle characterizes his ministerial life as he founds and establishes churches. The consequences of his practice of self-support are, no doubt, reflected in these descriptions. Although hidden in the NIV's periphrastic translation and obscured somewhat in others, this verse is structured with five phrases, four of which are introduced by the preposition *en*. Each has a locative ("in"—place) or circumstantial ("with") meaning.

The first phrase has no preposition. The words "labor and hardship" (NASB) are parallel to ***on frequent journeys*** (v 26). They depend, like them, on "I am more" in v 23. This serves as a general heading for the four descriptions that follow:

"Labor [*kopōi*] and hardship [*mochthōi*]" include the manual toil by which Paul supported himself while preaching and teaching in his evangelistic ministry (1 Thess 2:9; 2 Thess 3:8; see on 2 Cor 11:23). The two terms are probably used synonymously. Plummer, however, sees in *kopōi* a passive force indicating the fatigue resulting from prolonged exertion. The term *mochthōi* has a more active meaning, denoting the actual struggle involved in the exertion (1915, 327).

The resulting hardships Paul faced in his ministry are nouns adequately paraphrased by the NIV as brief descriptive phrases. Paul boasted: I **have often**

gone without sleep; I have known hunger and thirst and have often gone without food; I have been cold and naked.

Paul's "sleepless nights" (*agrypniais;* BDAG 2000, 16; see 6:5) were probably due to the long hours required by his bivocational ministry. He worked to support himself and his missionary party. He had letters to write and books to study (see Acts 20:7-11; see Plummer 1915, 328). Perhaps he also observed prayer vigils.

Paul worked in **hunger and thirst.** This may have been because he was unable at times to obtain proper food and drink, due to his refusal of financial support. That he had **often gone without food** may suggest voluntary fasts. He went without meals in order not to interrupt his work as a minister of Christ, or perhaps his manual labor.

Finally, in the course of his ministry, Paul had endured being **cold and naked** as a craftsman working in unheated quarters (see Hock 1980, 84 n 94). He probably faced unpleasant conditions during his travels, when at times his clothing was inadequate to the weather. Martin notes that this pair "go together as marks of extreme loss, including a loss of dignity and self-esteem" (1986, 380). Present as an undertone at least could have been a sense of shame that characterizes the nakedness of the afflicted and disgraced in Scripture (Gen 2:25; 3:7-11; Ezek 16:8; Nah 3:5; Mic 1:11; Rev 3:18; see 1 Cor 4:11; Rom 8:35).

■ **28** Paul's list of privations is by no means exhaustive. He writes, **Besides everything else** [*chōris tōn parektos*], **I face *the day by day*** [*kath' hēmeran*] **pressure of my concern for all the churches.** Paul may refer by *tōn parektos* back to the "external things" (NASB) he has just enumerated. Or he may refer to what follows. But most recent interpreters see it as a reference to a list of ***other things*** that he has not and will not mention (e.g., Hafemann 2000, 441; Harris 2005, 810-11). Leaving these unmentioned, the apostle's catalog of sufferings reaches its climax in the weight of his anxious **concern for all the churches.**

It is uncertain whether *epistasis* refers to the **pressure** Paul feels **daily** or to the load of "responsibility" (NEB) he continually carries for the churches. Thrall combines the two options, referring to "the daily pressure of responsibility" (2004, 749) Paul defines as his **concern for all the churches.**

The word **concern** (*merimna*) refers to the sense of "anxiety, worry, care" (BDAG 2000, 632) Paul has already expressed for the Corinthians (11:2-3). All his other sufferings were secondary to the weight of this **concern.** This his opponents did not share. On the contrary, they contributed to it. Paul's anxious care for the churches he planted does not exclude care and prayerful concern for other Christian congregations (see Rom 1:8-15; Col 2:1).

In Phil 4:6, Paul orders: "Do not be anxious [*merimnate*] about anything." But in Phil 2:20, he recognizes Timothy's "genuine interest in [*merimnēsei*]" the Philippians welfare as worthy of honor (Phil 2:29). Thus, he uses the same verb both negatively and positively. But he only seems to contradict himself. Obviously, fretful self-preoccupation—anxiety and worry—are counterproductive. But Paul recognizes the need for appropriate concern about and care for others and their needs. In fact, he seems indirectly to criticize his opponents for their lack of care for the Corinthians.

■ **29** Paul's expression of concern for the individuals in the churches brings his list of hardships to an oratorical climax in two rhetorical questions: **Who is . . . ? Who is . . . ?**

With the corresponding **I do not . . . I do not,** the expected answer is "no one." Paul cannot hide his sympathetic, passionate, pastoral love and care. Chrysostom (344/354-407) remarked, "What wonderful affection in a pastor!" (ACCS NT 7:299). There are three interpretive issues here.

First, what does Paul mean by **Who is weak** [*tis asthenei*] . . . ? as applied to the Corinthian Christians? Is he referring to those who are weak in conscience in regard to eating food that has been sacrificed to idols as in 1 Cor 8:7-13? Or is he thinking of the overscrupulous concerning Mosaic food regulations as in Rom 14:1-2? Both verbs in Paul's questions here, *astheneō* ("be weak") and *skandalizouai* ("made to stumble," NRSV) also occur in 1 Cor 8:11-13. Does he refer simply to physical difficulties—sickness and accidents? Or does he refer to human inadequacies and inadvertent failures?

It would be consistent with the picture Paul paints of himself in chs 10—12, that he empathetically identified "with his fellow believers in their weakness, whatever its precise nature—physical, psychological, social, or spiritual" (Harris 2005, 814; see Thrall 2004, 750-52). In his "fool's speech"

(11:1—12:13), Paul emphasizes his unimpressive and noncharismatic *persona* and presence in Corinth. He is **weak** as one who identifies with those to whom he has been sent with the gospel. For him "the mark of a true apostle is his willingness to suffer for his people as representative of the crucified Christ" (Hafemann 2000, 442). Far from caring for or suffering for the Corinthians, the interlopers are destroying and scandalizing them.

In Paul's second question the NIV has translated *skandalizetai* with the preferred, **Who is led into sin . . . ?** rather than the possible "who is offended" (Barrett 1973, 301; see 1 Cor 8:13; Rom 9:33). The NRSV is closer to the image implied in the verb: "who is made to stumble . . . ?" The figure is that of being caught in a trap (see 2:11). This image sets up Paul's expression of blazing indignation, or even anger, at those who would seduce any of his converts into sin: **Who is led into sin, and I do not inwardly burn?** What he says by way of metaphor in *pyroumai* is ***I am on fire.***

Origen preserves a saying of Jesus that reads: "He that is near me is near the fire" (Jeremias 1958, 54; this saying may be genuine, for it echoes Mark 9:49 and 12:34). Paul's "weakness" is balanced by his "burning" passion over those who are led astray. Without moral indignation Christian love is often deficient. Flowing naturally from v 28, the context of Paul's two affirmations about himself is the work and burden of his ministry. He identifies with individuals in their weakness and failure. He is intensely concerned about their spiritual welfare. Thus, fire describes the suffering Paul experiences as an essential credential of his apostolic calling.

■ **30** A new paragraph begins with v 30. Paul continues to discuss the hardships accompanying his ministry. Now he defines them as **weakness.** If he must boast, it is more fitting to boast of these. The Greek impersonal verb *dei*, "It is necessary" (NRSV) appears in 11:30 and 12:1 (see 12:5, 9, 10; 13:4).

It becomes clear, says Paul, **If I must boast** [*ei kauchasthai dei;* literally, ***If it is necessary to boast***], **I will boast of the things that show my weakness** (*ta tēs astheneias mou;* literally, ***the things of my weakness***). Is he referring to examples, evidence of, results of, or simply the things that make up his weakness? Paul is entering the realm of his opponents. He boasts in order to counter their claims, yet "paradoxically he parades the very evidence his opponents would ridicule" (Martin 1986, 383).

They cannot and will not match Paul's boast. His pride is in the weakness of human instruments, in their humiliations and sufferings as they become the occasion for displays of the grace and power of the God of the resurrection (see 1:8-10; 4:7-12; 13:4). The letter is moving rapidly to its climax, which comes with 12:9-10. Paul is about to express with vivid clarity the theme of power through weakness, which threads throughout the entire letter. 2 CORINTHIANS

■ **31** In v 31, Paul combines the elements of a doxology (see Rom 1:25; 9:5) and an oath formula (see Gal 1:20; Rom 9:1). He solemnly affirms that all he has said and is going to say in relation to his boast in weakness will be the truth: **God . . . knows that I am not lying** (see 11:10-11 and 1:13). 11:29-33

As always when faced with those who might doubt his veracity, Paul appeals to God, before whom he lives an open life (see 1:23; Rom 9:1; Gal 1:20; 1 Tim 2:7). The God to whom he appeals is both the **God and** [the] **Father of the Lord Jesus** (see the commentary on 1:3). He is the God whom Paul knows intimately through the one who is also the Son of God, **Jesus.** Because "in Christ" God made his way into Paul's life, God is ***he who is blessed forever*** (*ho ōn eulogētos eis tous aiōnas;* see Mark 14:61; Rom 1:25; 9:5).

■ **32-33** Some earlier scholars (Windisch 1924, 363-66) considered this a later gloss. And it does seem strange, at first, that Paul purposely drops in an account of his harrowing escape from Damascus (see Acts 9:23-25).

Among the many reasons suggested for why he might have done so (see Thrall 2004, 763-66), the most likely explanation is that Paul mentions this as a humiliating incident. It highlights the theme of weakness on which he now focuses his boast. Shillington sees it as bringing Paul's list to a dramatic climax. The Damascus incident, with "its motif of *descent,*" provides "a bridge to the empty boast about ascent that follows" in the fruitless rapture to paradise (12:1-6; Shillington 1998, 228).

Some see the episode as a reversal of the Roman *corona muralis* (wall crown). Like a medal of valor, it was awarded by the emperor for the bravery of the first soldier to scale a city wall. Far from a conquering hero, Paul narrowly escapes to avoid capture. Thus, Paul's account may serve as a parody of such tales of heroism, turned on their heads. If his was in the background of Paul's mind, it helps explain its placement in the letter (Furnish 1984, 542; McCant 1999, 141).

Several historical questions surround Paul's mention of **the governor under King Aretas.** He ruled the desert kingdom of Nabataea from 9 B.C. to A.D. 40 (see Gal 1:7). Most pertinent is the question: Who was **the governor** (*ho ethnarchēs*)? He was probably in charge of Damascus as a representative of the king (Thrall 2004, 766-70). But Harris limits the title to the head of a colony of Nabataeans in Damascus (2005, 821-23).

As one with full authority, **the governor . . . *was guarding*** [*ephrourei*] ***the city.*** Since he did not do so personally, it is probably better to paraphrase: He **had the city of the Damascenes guarded in order to arrest** the fledgling apostle. In order to escape with his life, Paul **was lowered . . . from a window in the wall.** His friends lowered him **through** (*dia*) an opening in the city wall. By this cowardly means, he **slipped through** the **hands** of *ho ethnarchēs*.

This experience no doubt held a particular significance for the apostle. Hughes suggests three reasons: First, it was Paul's first apprenticeship, his initiation as a raw recruit into the front line of gospel warfare.

Second, it emphasized for him the frailty and the humiliation that were to characterize his total apostolic ministry. The contrast is striking. Before his conversion, the mighty Saul of Tarsus arrogantly approaches Damascus to destroy believers there. On the way there, however, he meets the risen Christ. Afterward, he enters Damascus weak, stricken, and blind. And later he is forced to flee the city for his life, under the cover of darkness. No wonder this was a city he would never forget!

Third, Paul may be presenting it as a contrasting and effective prelude to the experience that he will soon describe in 12:2-4. The rapturous ascent into the third heaven was experienced by the same person who suffered the ignominious descent through a window in the Damascus wall (1962, 422).

Paul's reference to his high spiritual experience is kept between the narration of an unpretentious escape and the mention of his humiliating "thorn in my flesh" (12:7; see vv 7-10). Paul intends to keep himself and his ministry in true perspective—a frail instrument utterly dependent on the transcendent power of God.

Out of necessity Paul is forced to present his credentials as an apostle of Christ (vv 21*b*-33). They can be viewed as consisting of:

1. not primarily a privileged heritage (v 22), but rather
2. in part, those indignities and hardships most contrary to human exaltation, comfort, and ease (vv 23-27). They include, most centrally,
3. a burdened concern for those for whom he is responsible before God (v 28). These all flow from the principle that
4. the human foundation of a true ministry of Christ is the recognition and acceptance of human weakness (vv 29-33).

b. Paul's Revelations from the Lord (12:1-10)

Paul begins the second phase of his "foolishness of boasting" (see 11:16-30) with an introduction of the theme of "visions and revelations." Compelled by the situation to boast involuntarily (12:1), he moves from the description of his sufferings for Christ's sake to an account of a heavenly experience granted to him (vv 2-6). Paul does this perhaps because such experiences figured significantly in his opponents' boasting.

Paul places his great ecstatic experience and revelation (vv 1-6) ironically between the great humiliation of his hurried escape from Damascus (11:32-33) and his unrelieved weakness as exhibited by his thorn in the flesh (12:7-10). The thrust of the accounts as Paul tells them is that Paul's strength as an apostle comes through the admission of his weakness for the sake of the power of Christ in his life.

There are other noteworthy differences between vv 1-6 and 7-10. In vv 1-6, Paul describes his experience in the third person about an unnamed **man.** He narrates vv 7-10 in the first person—**I, me, my.** The first narrative is an opaque description about which he seems unable to speak. The second is a specific declaration about which he speaks openly and even quotes Christ verbatim (Hafemann 2000, 461).

The rhetorical intent of Paul's approach was to unmask the boast of his opponents before the Corinthians. Had the intruders boasted all the more because of Paul's **thorn**? Or, had they ridiculed him "for his thorn" (Martin 1986, 393)? Paul seems to play the role of the wounded healer, unhealed himself in the interests of others (Witherington 1995, 444).

■ 1 The apostle feels he **must** (*dei*) continue to boast, but does so with great reticence. Most often in the NT, the impersonal verb *dei* implicitly suggests that what must be done is God's will (BDAG 2000, 213-14). His opponents and the church have left him no alternative: **I must go on boasting.** But he quickly adds, **there is nothing to be gained** (i.e., "it is not profitable," NASB; see 1 Cor 6:12).

Paul moves quickly to a new theme: **I will go on to visions** [*optasias*] **and revelations** [*apokalypseis*] **from the Lord.** Among the host of exegetical questions interpreters face in this passage is the force of the genitive *kyriou* (***of the Lord***). Is it a subjective genitive indicating the source of the **revelations** as **from the Lord,** or is it an objective genitive designating the content of the **visions and revelations** as being **the Lord?** The NASB and NRSV leave the question open.

The argument for the objective genitive points to other instances where *apokalypsis* is followed by a genitive (Rom 2:5; 8:19; 1 Cor 1:7; Gal 1:12), which identifies the content of the revelation (Thrall 2004, 775). Paul's revelation at the time of his conversion and call involved seeing the risen Lord (1 Cor 9:1; 15:8; Gal 1:16; Lambrecht 1999, 2000).

Most commentators, however, take the genitive here as subjective (Harris 2000, 832-33; see, e.g., Furnish 1984, 525; Martin 1986, 397). Plummer, who prefers the subjective, observes that "where either objective or subjective makes good sense, it is sometimes difficult to see on which side the balance of probability lies" (1915, 338). In the present context, we proceed on the assumption that this is a subjective genitive (of source).

There is not a great difference between the terms **visions** (*optasias*) and **revelations** (*apokalypseis*). But the latter is the broader and more significant word; not all visions reveal something, and not all revelations require visions (Plummer 1915, 338). Here, in vv 2-4, Paul indicates that the vision is the source of the revelation (Martin 1986, 397).

The singular noun "revelation" was an important word for Paul in connection with his call and commission (Gal 1:12; 2:2). It was an apocalyptic event, marking the turning or dawning of the end of the age. But his use of the plural here probably gives it a general or topical force, since he feels it appropriate to report only one such experience rather than several (see Lincoln 1981, 72, 76). Acts 18:9-11 and 22:17-21 (see 23:11; 27:23-24) report that Paul had visionary experiences of Christ, but his letters mention only the resurrection revelation in 1 Cor 9:1 and 15:8.

So with hesitancy, Paul speaks of an ecstatic experience. Recall that Corinth was inclined to overplay the significance of such manifestations (see 1 Cor 14:1-5). Of course, this experience is not comparable to his revelation encounter with the risen Christ on the road to Damascus. Perhaps it is more in continuity with his experiences recorded in 1 Cor 14:18-19.

The reticence with which Paul speaks of his extraordinary religious experience is instructive. He deliberately discounts it as an argument and describes any such use of it as boasting. It is irrelevant as validation for his ministry. It neither authenticates his ministry nor benefits the community (Murphy-O'Connor 1991, 118).

Paul does not belittle religious experience. But he always attempts to keep it in proper perspective and balance. The yardstick of all ecstatic experiences and emotional demonstrations is "whether they proclaim Jesus as Lord, or in other words, whether they build up the church" (Schweizer 1965, 31).

■ **2** Verses 2-4 give two parallel descriptions of the heavenly journey (v 2 and vv 3-4). Some take these as two distinct accounts (Plummer 1915, 344). McCant, however, suggests that **and** (*kai*) in v 3 is probably ascensive (i.e., it means ***even***). Thus, the parallel structure functions like Hebrew synonymous parallelism, in which repetition in slightly different ways makes for emphasis (1999, 142).

Second, some see Paul's report as merely a fictional literary construct, like the accounts of heavenly raptures in the Jewish apocalypses (see Thrall 2004, 776). Others take it as a self-parody of heavenly journeys and healing miracles. Paul employs it to expose the absurd pretensions of his rivals (Betz 1972, 72-73, 82-85, 89-95; see McCant 1999, 142). But most interpreters judge it to be a serious account of a real and personal religious experience of the apostle.

In this account of ascent into heaven Paul speaks in this order:

1. of the person involved: **a man in Christ**
2. the time it occurred: **fourteen years ago**
3. the circumstances: **in the body or out of the body I do not know—God knows**
4. its destination: **caught up to the third heaven**

First, Paul uses the third person—**I know a man in Christ**—to speak of himself. He is simply a Christian, in union with Christ, ***a human being*** (*anthrōpon*) overwhelmed by a gracious moment in the divine presence of Christ. The Socratic tradition taught "that one must not boast about oneself, but if necessary this may be done by someone else" (Lincoln 1978, 208-9; see 1981, 73-76). Paul may have followed this convention here. Admittedly, this leaves unexplained why he retains the first person perspective in vv 7-10.

Second, attempts have been made to identify the **fourteen years ago** with a previously mentioned event, but none are convincing (see Martin 1986, 399). The best that can be said is that it occurred during the period of Paul's activities in Syria and Cilicia, around A.D. 43. Beyond confirming the fact of his experience, Paul probably dated it only to draw attention to his long silence about the episode. Perhaps it also suggests the infrequency of such incidents in his experience. Obviously, the episode was of little importance for his ministry. Possibly, he also wanted to accent how long he had struggled with his debilitating "thorn in the flesh" (see Harris 2005, 835-37). Some suggest that Paul makes an intentional parallel with the dating of similar events in the prophetic writings (Isa 6:1; Jer 1:2; Ezek 1:1; see Furnish 1984, 524).

Third, Paul's report is ambiguous as to the circumstances of his experience, **in the body or out of the body I do not know.** Interpretive judgments vary as to how his description may have been understood by his readers in relation to Greek and Jewish traditions (see Thrall 2004, 785-78; Furnish 1984, 525; Lincoln 1981, 83-84).

Paul stresses his ignorance as compared with God's knowledge. The apostle does not know how or whether he was (actually) transported **up to the third heaven.** Was this merely a visionary experience, or was his body (*sōma*) transported to paradise? He concedes: only **God knows** (see 11:11). Why Paul gives such a brief and enigmatic description is open to speculation; perhaps it is lest he say too much.

Fourth, how do we understand the destination of his journey—**caught up to the third heaven**? The same verb (*harpazō*) is used in Acts 8:39, where it is reported that "the Spirit of the Lord snatched Philip away" (NASB). The same verb appears also in 1 Thess 4:17, in which Paul writes that at the Parousia living believers "will be caught up . . . in the clouds" with resurrected believers "to meet the Lord in the air."

The passive voice of the verb, "to be caught up," is probably a "theological passive." That is, God is the unnamed actor; Paul, the one who suddenly ascended (in contrast to Jesus' slow departure at his ascension? see Luke 24:51; Acts 1:10).

Paul was swiftly **caught up to the third heaven.** Bengel writes that "the first heaven is that of the clouds; the second is that of the stars; the third is spiritual" (1895, 3:426)—the earth's atmosphere, outer space, and the realm where God dwells. Some nearly contemporary Jewish apocalypses refer to seven or more heavens. Sometimes they locate **paradise** (see v 4) at a level lower than the residence of God. Paul's point is surely that his destination was the highest level imaginable.

Calvin suggests that "the number three is used as a perfect number to indicate what is highest and most complete" (1964, 10:156). Paul emphasizes the "high" character of his experience, and appears to identify the third heaven with paradise (v 4). He is almost certainly thinking in a general sense of "the highest heaven," where God dwells (echoing 1 Kgs 8:27; see 2 Chr 2:6; 6:18). Although Paul may use the terminology, he does not have the schemes of Jewish apocalyptic cosmology in the forefront of his mind.

The Third Heaven

The Testament of Levi refers to three heavenly realms, with the third heaven being where Levi stands in the presence of the Lord and his glory (*T. Levi* 2:7-10; 3:1-4). Jewish apocalyptic writings that contain speculations about cosmology speak of multiple levels of heaven. Some mention only one heaven, some two, others three, five, seven, and even ten. Third Enoch conceives of 955 heavens above the seventh heaven! (See documentation in Lincoln 1981, 78-79; and Furnish 1984, 525-36.)

The origin of much of this speculation can probably be traced back to OT texts like Deut 10:14, which refer to "the heaven, even the highest heavens" (see 1 Kgs 8:27; 2 Chr 2:6; 6:18). The Hebrew in literal translation reads "the heavens, the heaven of the heavens" (*haššāmayim ûššmê haššāmayim*). The NT does not contain the expression "the highest heaven" (or "the heaven of the heavens"). It offers no speculation as to the number of heavens, apart from the possible exception of this reference by Paul of the third heaven.

It must have been a sublime experience to enter into the heavenly presence of Jesus. Like Peter, James, and John on the Mount of Transfiguration, Paul is granted a glimpse of the glory to be revealed at the Parousia (see 4:14—5:10). By it he is strengthened for the sufferings that await him in the course of his mission to the Gentiles: "I consider that the sufferings of this present time are not worth comparing with the glory about to be revealed in us" (Rom 8:18 NRSV). Only the **man in Christ** has this anticipation. Of him Paul will only speak in the third person, "the rarest of all examples: a boastless boast" (Lenski 1937, 1292).

■ **3-4** Since Paul dates it only once, he must be describing the same revelation, now enhanced by repetition. At first the terminology is almost identical: **I know that this man—whether in the body or apart from the body I do not know, but God knows—was caught up** (*hērpagē*). But here he identifies "the third heaven" as **paradise,** which appears just twice more in the NT.

Paradise

In Luke 23:43 Jesus says to the thief on the cross, "today you will be with me in paradise." With an allusion to the Garden of Eden in Rev 2:7, the church at Ephesus is promised: "To him who overcomes, I will give the right to eat from the tree of life, which is in the paradise of God." The word is used in the LXX for the Garden of Eden (Gen 2:8; 13:10; Isa 51:3).

Paradise appears with eschatological overtones in the NT. The first paradise reappears at the end, so it exists as hidden in the present. This may be in the background of Paul's mind in 2 Cor 12:2-4. The LXX also uses paradise for the abode of God (Ezek 28:13; 31:8). Harris concludes that, by the "hidden" **paradise,** Paul refers to the dwelling place of the righteous dead located within the third or highest heaven, the abode of God (2005, 845; see 2 Cor 5:8; Phil 1:23). The word is of Persian origin, meaning "walled garden." As found in Greek, it refers to the parks belonging to Persian kings and their nobles.

Barclay writes illuminatingly that "when a Persian king wished to confer a very special honour on someone who was specially dear to him he made him a *companion of the garden,* and gave him the right to walk in the royal gardens with him in close and intimate companionship" (1956, 286; see Lincoln 1981, 79-81, for documentation).

Paul was granted for an indescribable moment intimate companionship with the Lord within the courts of heaven itself. For an instant he was "at home with the Lord" (5:8). While there Paul emphasizes not what he saw, but what he heard—**inexpressible things.** This is an oxymoron in both English and Greek; the expression *arrēta rēmata* means literally "unutterable utterances."

This is all he tells us. His account of a revelation contains no revelation! And what's more, what he does hear "no mortal is permitted to repeat" (NRSV). A tradition of a sealed revelation was known in the OT (Isa 86; Dan 12:4). Secret revelation is a standard feature of apocalyptic literature, rabbinic Judaism, and the mystery religions (Lincoln 1981, 82).

Whatever the precise background, the question here is: Did Paul hear words he did not understand, words beyond his power to express, or words that God forbade him to speak? Opinions vary; and most interpreters leave the question open. Some put the primary emphasis on the latter; Hafemann insists that God's prohibition is the only plausible meaning (2000, 460).

Paul, however, is silent not only about what he saw but also about the identity of the speaker and the content of the words. Suggestions have varied from angelic singing to veiled secrets (see Thrall 2004, 794-97). Lincoln sees Paul's visionary experience as a part of the charismatic manifestation of the Spirit in the Christian community (1981, 85; so Dunn 1975, 212-15). Whatever he saw and heard, two things *are* clear from this account.

First, the influence of this and other like experiences upon Paul's ministry must have been incalculable for his own personal encouragement and strength to carry on his strenuous ministry. The experience was sacred between him and God; it was for him alone. For "a man who had awaiting him troubles hard enough to break a thousand hearts needed to be strengthened in a special way to keep him from giving way and to help him persevere undaunted" (Calvin 1964, 10:157). What he heard was not meant to edify the church; and thus was not a credential for ministry. Could the secret of Paul's power lie in his hesitancy to speak of such private revelations?

Second, if his opponents emphasized such experiences to validate the superiority of their ministry, Paul's parody was a telling critique of them. Murphy-O'Connor observes, "If their experience was the same as Paul's, it contributed nothing. If their experience was something they could talk about, it was less ineffable than his" (1991, 118).

■ **5** In order to introduce what he has to say in v 6, Paul returns to the theme of boasting (v 1). But he will not boast in his personal rapture to paradise. He will speak of that experience only in a detached way—in the third person of "a man in Christ." It is not his claim to fame; he assigns full credit to his Lord (vv 2-3).
12:3-6 Paul **will boast** "on behalf of such a one [*toioutou*]" (NRSV). But he **will not boast about** *himself* in such a manner, **except,** he says**, about my weaknesses.**

Insisting on this technical distinction between himself and "such a one," Paul returns to his theme of boasting in weakness (11:30). His real boast is only of "a man in Christ." He boasts not of *himself* as a Christian, but of himself as a *Christian*. When Paul must speak of himself, he will boast only of his **weaknesses.** By this means he intends to draw attention to his Lord and his provision for human weakness. Paul wants the Corinthians to recognize the foolishness of the opposition's boast in their strengths. Realizing this may "reignite the flame of the Corinthians' undivided loyalty to Christ (11:2-3) and to Paul himself (2:13; 10:6; 12:15)" (Harris 2005, 847).

■ **6** Paul could boast of impressive experiences and achievements if he wanted to (*thelēsō*). This is clear from the apodosis of his unreal conditional sentence: ***For*** [*gar*] "if I wish to boast, I will not be a fool" (NRSV). On the contrary, he **would be speaking the truth.** Does he also imply that the veracity of the false apostles' claims are in doubt? Are their stories of heavenly journeys pure fiction or pious imagination?

In v 6, Paul switches to a different meaning of the word **fool** (*aphrōn*) than usual in the fool's speech (see 11:16). Here *aphrōn* refers simply to boasting without substance, to foolish lying. Only a fool brags beyond the truth.

Paul refrains from boasting about his rapture to paradise on purpose. He does not want anyone to form an estimate (*logisētai*) of him beyond (*hyper*) what can actually be seen in him or heard from (*ex*) him. *Logizomai* was often used in commerce meaning to credit one's account with something. Thus, we could paraphrase the clause: ***so that people will not give me credit beyond what they see me doing or hear*** [*akouei*] ***me saying.***

The phrase ***what one sees me doing*** (*ho blepei me*) could also be interpreted as ***what one sees me to be.*** The verbs *blepō* ("I see") and *akouō* ("I hear") may encompass the two primary ways we evaluate persons—by observing their conduct and by listening to what they say (see Mark 8:18; Matt 11:4; Acts 8:6; Rom 11:8). The apostle does not want to be venerated based on reports of spectacular spiritual experiences—visions or revelations (see v 7). But this is not because he would have nothing to report (see 1 Cor 14:18-19). Nevertheless, he chooses to be judged only by the visible conduct of his ministry.

Paul wants his apostleship to be evaluated only on the basis of the changed lives of his converts and the stark realities of his life in the service of the gospel. His concern is not to impress admiring crowds. It is, "does his ministry measure up to the standard of the crucified Christ?" (Shillington 1998, 231). Lenski's comment is still apropos: "however highly the Lord favors and blesses his ministers, for his work among men he is able use none unless they be lowly as he himself once was when he walked on earth . . . (4:7). The vessels dare be earthen only" (1937, 1298).

■ **7** Several interpreters (e.g., Furnish 1984, 513; Young and Ford 1987, 274), like the NRSV, treat the opening phrase of v 7 as the conclusion of v 6: "even considering the exceptional character of the revelations."

The strongest argument for this is that it makes the following *dio* (***"therefore, for this reason,"*** BDAG 2000, 250) the first word in the new sentence, its usual position in Paul's letters (1:20; 2:8; 4:16; 5:9; 6:17; 12:10). Many ancient scribes apparently attempted to solve the problem by omitting *dio.* The inclusion of *dio* remains the preferred reading (see Thrall 2004, 803).

The NIV reverses the order of the first two clauses in v 7. Thus, its translators either reject *dio* as a secondary reading or leave it untranslated: **To keep me from becoming conceited because of these surpassingly great revelations . . .**

With Harris, however, it seems preferable to translate *dio* as looking back to the preceding phrase and to begin a new sentence with v 7 as in NASB: *"Because of* the surpassing greatness of the revelations, *for this reason . . ."* (emphasis added; Harris 2005, 852-53).

The reason Paul narrates his ascent to paradise is to expose and explain his greatest disability. He calls this metaphorically **a thorn in my flesh.** He emphasizes the purpose of his **thorn,** by twice repeating the clause *hina mē hyperairōmai,* ***in order that I may not be exalted*** (see 4:7). The NIV omits the repetition.

In v 7, Paul introduces the second illustration of his reluctant willingness to boast in his weakness (11:30; 12:10; see 11:31-32). The tormenting condition occasioned by the **thorn** apparently dates from the time of his rapture to paradise, "fourteen years ago" (v 2). Perhaps Paul's opponents guaranteed that he would not become too **conceited** by ridiculing him for his thorn (Martin 1986, 393). If so, their hypocrisy is now revealed to the gaze of all. Most significantly, his **thorn** was **given** (*edothē*) to him as John Wesley observes, "by the wise and gracious providence of God" (1950, 673).

The passive verb allows for the possibility that **Satan** was its source. Paul does identify it as **a messenger of Satan** (*angelos satana*). He uses the conjunction *hina*, which usually indicates either purpose or result (BDAG 2000, 475-77), three times in v 7. And he assigns the thorn once a negative—**to** [*hina*] **torment** [*kolaphizēi*] **me**—and twice a positive role—**To** [*hina*] **keep me from becoming conceited.**

Typically, however, Paul's use of the passive voice follows Jewish precedent with God as the implied agent (as in 12:2 and 4). This has been called the "theological passive." It would not be exceptional for a "gift from God" to be used by Satan (see 2:11) **to torment** Paul (see Job 1:8-19; 3:3-7; Luke 13:16; 1 Cor 5:5). The early church father Tertullian (155/160-225/250) recognizes that "the right to tempt a man is granted to the devil" (ACCS NT 7:304) by God.

The verb *kolaphizēi* in the present tense, if taken literally, refers to a continual repetition of blows struck with a closed fist (Matt 26:67; see 1 Cor 4:11). But it also has the figurative meaning of causing **"physical impairment, *torment*"** (BDAG 2000, 555). Paul expresses himself paradoxically. What Sa-
12:7 tan was allowed to use against him as an instrument of torture, God in his providence used to serve his divine purpose in Paul's life: "to keep [him] from being too elated" (NRSV).

The classical meaning of *skolops*, **thorn,** is "stake," a sharpened wooden shaft. But it is commonly used in the LXX and the papyri for thorns, splinters, or slivers (Moulton and Milligan 1949, 578; see BDAG 2000, 930-31). In antiquity the military used "stakes" as fences around walls and on earthworks, to serve like modern landmines in hidden pits, or as means of execution by impalement (Thrall 2004, 806-7; see Hughes 1962, 447). The LXX uses the term metaphorically, usually for people who are causing difficulty (Num 33:55 and Ezek 28:24; Hos 2:6).

Paul labels this instrument of pain and humiliation **a thorn in/*for the* flesh** (*skolops tēi sarki*). The dative case of **flesh** may have a locative ("in") force, referring to the place of Paul's torment. Thus, **in *the* flesh** would refer to a physical disability of some kind (see Gal 4:14: *en tēi sarki*). But, it may be a dative of (dis-)advantage ("for"). In this instance, the reference could be either to something strictly physical or something that affected his whole physical life so as to cause him serious "pain" in his ministry. Across the centuries of biblical interpretation, the speculative guesses as to the precise identification of Paul's thorn have been legion.

Paul's Thorn in the Flesh

The earliest known interpretation comes from Tertullian (155/160-225/250). He explained Paul's *skolops* as severe headaches, consistent with the verb *kolaphizō* ("to beat"). His view was accepted by Jerome (347-420). Chrysostom (344/354-407) identified the thorn as Paul's named opponents (2 Tim 2:17; 4:14) and all opponents of the gospel. This view was accepted by other Greek fathers as well as by Augustine (354-430).

An interpretation current in the Middle Ages was suggested by the Vulgate translation *stimulus carnis:* "sting of the flesh." Aquinas (1224/25-1274) adopted this view—that the **thorn in *the* flesh** referred to sexual temptation.

This approach was rejected by the Protestant Reformers Luther and Calvin. They preferred to identify it with spiritual trials, such as the temptation to despair or to be lax in ministry (see Thrall 2004, 809-14). Calvin wrote, "this phrase is meant to sum up all the different kinds of trial with which Paul was exercised" (1964, 10:159).

Modern interpreters have only added to the array of suggestions as to the specific identification of Paul's **thorn.** We cannot discuss them all in detail here. Space constraints allow us only to sketch the range of explanations from the least to the most likely.

First, it was some spiritual anxiety or psychological condition. Specific suggestions include pangs of conscience about his role as a persecutor of Christians or anguish over his inability to win the Jews.

Second, following Chrysostom, it may be identified with opposition to Paul. These, too, vary. Some posit opponents in general, such as a Judaizing anti-Paul movement. Others presume Paul referred to a single opponent or to the false apostles at Corinth. McCant identifies Paul's thorn as the minority within the Corinthian church who rejected his apostleship (McCant 1988, 550-72; 1999, 144-53). This view has not won general acceptance, because Paul seems to date the "gift" of the thorn to fourteen years earlier.

Third, the most widely accepted view is that Paul's thorn was some kind of physical malady. His letters indicate that his physical condition gave him difficulty at times. But, on the positive side, he reminded the Galatians that his preaching to them had been occasioned by "an illness [*astheneian tēs sarkos*]" or a "physical infirmity [*en tēi sarki mou*]" (NRSV, Gal 4:13-14).

Some interpreters leave the malady unspecified. Others suggest fever (malaria), headaches (migraine), or defective vision or an eye disease (speculating on Gal 4:15 and 6:11). Harris concludes that some kind of physical ailment best fits Paul's description (2005, 857-59; see Hafemann 2000, 462; and Thrall 2004, 797-818).

At the end of the day we must admit that we do not and cannot know precisely what the apostle meant by his **thorn in *the* flesh.** This may be beneficial for those of us in ministry. We learn from Paul that, in spite of his heavenly rapture, God gave him "something to keep him weak, and that his weakness . . . becomes the 'criterion of ministry'" (Martin 1986, 393). We all know our own particular **thorn.** Like Paul, we can trust God to grant us a perspective from which to handle whatever plagues our outward nature—whether physical or emotional affliction, the actions of others, or unrelieved circumstances that humiliate us.

Lenski writes: "Paul tells about this thorn for the flesh just as he tells about his *raptus* into paradise for the first time. In both he bares intimate secrets of his personal life which were never bared to the Corinthians before and are now bared only under compulsion" (1937, 1301). But what Paul conceals about these experiences is as intriguing as what he reveals.

■ **8** Whatever his troubling "thorn" (v 7), the apostle wanted to be rid of it. Not immediately realizing its intended purpose, Paul prayed earnestly or **pleaded** [*parekalesa*] **three times** for **the Lord** to **take it away.**

In Greek the verse begins with *hyper toutou,* ***Concerning this.*** Some interpreters read the ambiguous genitive *toutou* (***this***) as masculine, referring to "this one," rather than neuter, "this thing." They identify its antecedent in v 7 as the "messenger of Satan," not the "thorn" (Hughes 1962, 441; Barrett 1973, 316; Lambrecht 1999, 203; see against this view Harris 2005, 859).

The Lord with whom Paul **pleaded** is the risen Christ (v 9). Since prayer in the NT is usually addressed to God the Father, that Paul directed his request to Christ implicitly suggests that he equated Christ with God as the recipient of prayer.

As to why Paul prayed **three times,** interpreters point to the influence of Jewish custom, Greek religion, or even Hellenist healing stories (Thrall 2004, 818-19). Chrysostom takes three times, not as a precise number, but "repeatedly" (ACCS NT 7:306). Others identify a threefold prayer as particularly intense or complete. But the use of **three** (*tris*) may simply have its natural meaning of three different occasions (Harris 2005, 861). Like Jesus in the Garden of Gethsemane (Matt 26:44; Mark 14:41), Paul petitioned three times. And the results were similar (see Matt 26:39). Like Jesus, Paul knew the experience of not having his prayers answered as he desired.

Pelagius (350/354-420/425) remarked: "we learn from this that even a wrong prayer will receive an answer, even if it does not get what it wants" (ACCS NT 7:307). Augustine (354-430) surmises that "not everyone who spares is a friend, nor is everyone who strikes an enemy. . . . Love mingled with severity is better than deceit with indulgence" (ACCS NT 7:306). Ambrosiaster adds that Paul's request was denied because his plea "was against his own best interests" (ACCS NT 7:306).

■ **9** In contrast (*kai,* **But**) to Paul's request, the response is reported as a direct quotation: **he said to me.** The apostle does not indicate whether he heard an audible voice, sensed the Spirit's witness, or came to this insight by meditation on the cross and resurrection of Jesus. What is emphasized is "the depth of the personal relationship with Christ which Paul felt himself to enjoy" (Thrall 2004, 821). The perfect tense of Christ's answer indicates that his decision stands. Thus, Paul's praying (in the aorist tense) on this matter is over.

Paul's prayer did not go unanswered. Christ promised: **My grace is sufficient for you.** John Wesley aptly called this a "tender . . . repulse" (1950, 674). John Cassian (360-435) identified this promise as the answer to unanswered prayer (1958, 321). E. Glenn Hinson suggests that here **grace** "means God's gift of Godself, the Holy Spirit. 'My *Shekinah*, my Presence, is enough for you'" (2008, 39).

Christ explains (*gar*, **for**) his denial of Paul's request: **my power is made perfect in weakness.** In this "shining centerpiece of the Fool's Speech" (Shillington 1998, 231), **power** (*hē dynamis*) now defines **grace** (*hē charis*). Both **grace** and **power** are gifts of the resurrected Lord (**my . . . my**). Both are governed by verbs in the continuous present tense: **is sufficient . . . is made perfect** (*arkei . . . teleitai*). As such, they are an enduring reality to be experienced as needed.

It is in relation to Paul's **weakness** that the **grace** and **power** of Christ find their *"consummation"* or reach *"perfection"* (BDAG 2000, 997 s.v. *teleioō*). That is, they fulfill their intended purpose when they encounter *astheneiai*—**"debilitating illness, *sickness, disease* . . . incapacity . . . limitation, *weakness* . . . lack of confidence or feeling[s] of inadequacy"** (BDAG 2000, 142).

The preposition *en*, **in**, interpreted in a local sense (i.e., as a literal or metaphorical place), makes **weakness** and **power** simultaneous. It is **in** the throes of Paul's **weakness** that he will know the **power** of the resurrection. This was true of his Lord, who "was crucified in weakness, yet he lives by God's power" (13:4). **Weakness** becomes both "a prerequisite and a concomitant of Christ's power" (Harris 2005, 864).

Paul is not merely resigned to his **weaknesses;** he boasts **all the more gladly** in his **weaknesses, so that** [*hina*] **Christ's power may rest on** him. The expression **all the more** invites comparison. **More** than what? The possibilities are in contrast (1) to complaining about them, (2) to praying for their removal, or (3) to boasting about anything else, such as his ascent to paradise (see v 5). The last seems to fit the context best (Thrall 2004, 826).

The conjunction *hina*, **so that,** does not imply that Paul's boasting in his **weaknesses** is a prerequisite to the presence of **Christ's power.** Rather, it indicates the divine purpose behind or the result of his weakness as an apostle of Christ (Thrall 2004, 827). Harris considers an *acknowledgment* of weakness "a precondition for the exercise of Christ's power" (2005, 865). Paul learns that the divine power in his life needs constant renewal.

In the Greek sentence **Christ's power** is placed in an emphatic position (final). As such Paul says it is to **rest on** him (*episkēnōsēi ep' eme*). The compound verb *episkēnoō* appears only here in biblical Greek, although the simple form *skēnoō* occurs in the LXX and in the NT in John 1:14 and Rev 7:15;

12:12; 13:6; and 21:3. John 1:14 is most familiar: "The Word became flesh and made his dwelling [*eskēnōsen*] among us." In the light of Paul's use of tent (*skēnous*) imagery in 5:1, the image is of **power** "pitched like a tent over" him (Young and Ford 1987, 274).

The basic meaning of the verb is ***"live, settle, take up residence"*** (BDAG 2000, 929 s.v. *skēnoō*). Some interpreters see an allusion to the Shekinah glory that rested on the ancient tabernacle in the wilderness (Exod 40:34-35; see Luke 9:34). Paul's use of Exod 34:29 in 2 Cor 3:7-16 suggests that he was familiar with the thought of *Shekinah* (Exod 34:34-35). But the evidence is far from certain (Furnish 1984, 531).

We are confronted in vv 7-10 with a quite different revelation than in 12:1-4. There it was a matter of a vision of paradise and inexpressible words. Here it is the word of grace in personal encounter that gives the meaning of suffering and aid for the sufferer.

The life of the apostle was bound up with the heavenly world in a special way. So he was involved in a special way with satanic power at work in his sufferings. This is the paradox of Paul's existence, indeed the paradox of the cross. His ministry as a true servant of Christ necessarily partakes of that of his Lord. There is a sense in which Paul experienced a cure. But it was not in the normal sense of the word. He received the power of Christ that enabled him to continue to minister (Martin 1986, 393).

■ **10** The pinnacle of the letter is reached as Paul brings this account to a conclusion. He relates the account of his thorn in the flesh in order to reveal the key to his ministry. The key, which upsets the conventional wisdom of the world, is the paradox: **when I am weak, then I am strong.** Human inadequacy makes way for the adequacy of the grace and power of God in Christ. **That is why, for Christ's sake,** Paul can **delight in** [*eudokō*] his **weaknesses.**

Eudokō can mean "I am content with" (NRSV) or "I am well content with" (NASB). But Pauline usage favors a stronger translation like "well-pleased" (Rom 15:26-27; 1 Cor 1:21; 10:5; 2 Cor 5:8; Gal 1:15; 1 Thess 2:8; 3:11; see Thrall 2004, 829 n 455). The more difficult question is whether Paul is ***well-pleased*** **for Christ's sake** or suffers **for Christ's sake.** The word order of the Greek sentence suggests the latter. The NIV favors the former: **for Christ's sake, I delight.** The NRSV favors the latter: "calamities for the sake of Christ." The NASB leaves the question open. Most interpreters conclude that "it is for Christ's sake that Paul can take pleasure in his sufferings" (Thrall 2004, 830; see Plummer 1915, 355; Furnish 1984, 531).

Paul's ministry is secure in the strength of Another. The reason (*gar,* **for**) is, as he says, **when I am weak, then I am strong.** This is his relaxed assurance, his personal paradox of weakness and strength. Paul's **weaknesses,** rather than hindering, actually make room for the strength of the risen Christ to be revealed in his ministry (see 4:7).

To clarify what Paul means by **in** [*en*] **weaknesses,** which heads the list,

Paul inserts a fourth "hardship list" (4:7-10; 6:4-10; 11:23-29; see BEHIND THE TEXT on 4:6—5:10). In this shorter list, **weaknesses** function as the general concept. It is developed by four terms that describe what the apostle endures in his ministry.

- First, **in** [*en*] **insults** (*hybresin*) appears only here in hardship lists. They could be only verbal or also include physical abuse, as in "insolent mistreatment" (Harris 2005, 867).
- Second, paired with **insults** is **in** [*en*] **hardships** (*anangais*) or perhaps "torture" (BDAG 2000, 61).
- The final pair is **in** [*en*] **persecutions *and*** [*kai*] **difficulties.** These refer to **persecutions** (*diōgmois*) of any nature and stressful circumstances (*stenochōriais*) making for "anguish" or "distress" (BDAG 2000, 943).

The revelation of the power of Christ in Paul's weaknesses and his acceptance of the paradoxical nature of his ministry "form the high point of his argument in this passage and, in doing so, provide summary of the theological substructure of 2 Corinthians as a whole" (Hafemann 2000, 465).

As an apostle (11:21*b*—12:10), (1) Paul's credentials consist in his often humiliating sufferings endured for others in the cause of Christ (11:21*b*-33). (2) Any boast he has focuses in his weaknesses in order that his adequacy as a minister of the gospel might reside in the power of Christ alone (12:1-10).

Further Reading on 2 Cor 12:1-10

Barré, Michaell L. 1980. "Qumran and the Weakness of Paul." *Catholic Biblical Quarterly* 42:500-526.

Bowker, John W. 1971. "'Merkabah' Visions and the Vision of Paul." *Journal of Semitic Studies* 16:157-73.

Goulder, Michael D. 2003. "Visions and Revelations of the Lord (2 Corinthians 12:1-10)." Pages 303-12 in *Paul and the Corinthians: Studies on a Community in Conflict, Essays in Honour of Margaret Thrall.* Edited by Trevor J. Burke and J. Keith Elliott. Leiden: Brill.

Heckel, Ulrich. 1932. "Der Dorn im Fleisch. Die Krankheit des Paulus in 2 Kor 12,7 und Gal 4,13f." *Zeitschrift für die neutestamentliche Wissenschaft und die Kunde der älteren Kirche* 84:5-92.

Himmelfarb, Martha. 1993. *Ascent to Heaven in Jewish and Christian Apocalypses.* New York: Oxford University Press.

Leary, T. J. 1992. "A Thorn in the Flesh"—2 Corinthians 12:7. *Journal of Theological Studies* 43:520-22.

Lincoln, A. T. 1978. "Paul the Visionary: The Setting and Significance of the Rapture to Paradise in II Corinthians XII. 1-10." *New Testament Studies* 25:204-20.

_________. 1981. *Paradise Now and Not Yet: Studies in the Role of the Heavenly Dimension in Paul's Thought with Special Reference to His Eschatology.* Society for New Testament Studies Monograph Series 43. Cambridge: Cambridge University Press.

McCant, Jerry W. 1988. "Paul's Thorn of Rejected Apostleship." *New Testament Studies* 34:550-72.

_________. 1999. Pages 144-53 in *2 Corinthians*. "Readings: A New Biblical Commentary." Edited by John Jarick. Sheffield: Sheffield Academic Press.

Menoud, P. H. 1978. "The Thorn in the Flesh and Satan's Angel (2 Cor. 12:7)." Pages 19-30 in *Jesus Christ and the Faith: A Collection of Studies*. Pittsburgh Theological Monograph Series 18. Pittsburgh: Pickwick.

Morray-Jones, C. R. A. 1993. "Paradise Revisited (2 Cor 12:1-12): The Jewish Mystical Background of Paul's Apostolate." *Harvard Theological Review* 86:177-217, 265-92.

O'Collins, Gerald G. 1971. "Power Made Perfect in Weakness: 2 Cor 12:9-10." *Catholic Biblical Quarterly* 33:528-37.

Savage, T. B. 1996. *Power Through Weakness: Paul's Understanding of the Christian Ministry in 2 Corinthians*. Society for New Testament Studies Monograph Series 86. Cambridge: Cambridge University Press.

Schäfer, Peter. 1984. "New Testament and Hekhalot Literature: The Journey into Heaven in Paul and in Merkavah Mysticism." *Journal of Jewish Studies* 36:19-35.

Smith, Neil Gregor. 1959. "The Thorn That Stayed, An Exposition of II Corinthians 12:7-9." *Interpretation* 13:409-16.

Tabor, J. D. 1986. *Things Unutterable: Paul's Ascent to Paradise in Its Greco-Roman, Judaic, and Early Christian Contexts*. New York: University Press of America.

Woods, Laurie. 1991. "Opposition to a Man and His Message: Paul's 'Thorn in the Flesh'" (2 Cor 12:7). *Australian Biblical Review* 39:43-44.

12:11

5. Paul's Behavior in Corinth (12:11-13)

With these verses Paul concludes "the fool's speech" (11:1—12:13), ceases his boasting, and brings his polemic against his opponents to an end. Some, however, extend this section through v 18 (Thrall 2004, 832; McCant 1999, 153). But his tone has changed. In this section Paul:

- reiterates his foolishness
- reasserts his equality with his rivals
- reemphasizes the authenticity of his ministry and
- reminds the Corinthians that he has not mistreated them, except (ironically) by sparing them his financial support

These verses lead into the last section of the letter, in which he will focus on his coming third visit to the church in Corinth.

■ **11** With an *inclusio*, the apostle declares again that he has been **a fool** (see 11:1). The perfect tense indicates a completed state: **I have made** [*gegona*] **a fool of myself.** Throughout the speech Paul indulges in foolish boasting (11:1, 16-18, 21, 30; 12:1) but insists he is no **fool** (11:16; 12:6). With the mask of the boaster removed, Paul now emphatically blames the Corinthians for his folly: **you** [*hymeis*] **drove me to it.** They left him no option.

Paul explains (*gar*, ***for***) how they "forced" (NRSV) him to defend himself: **I ought to have been commended** [*synistasthai*] **by you.** But they instead welcomed the intruders and criticized him. Paul's frequent use of the verb *synistasthai* throughout the letter (3:1; 4:2; 5:12; 6:4; 7:11; 10:12; 10:18) comes to a climax here. Paul considered the Corinthians his apostolic credentials. Their existence as a church was his letter of commendation (3:2-3; 1 Cor 9:1-2). But they had failed to fulfill their natural obligation to their father in the faith (see vv 14-15). Paul was hurt by their ingratitude and disloyalty. To make matters worse, their commendation had gone rather to his opponents, those **"super-apostles"** (see the commentary on 11:5).

Paul insists that he is **not in the least inferior** (*hysterēsa*) to these "false apostles" (11:13). The constative aorist tense probably refers to the whole of Paul's ministry (Harris 2005, 872). This is true, **even though,** as he says, **I am nothing** (*ouden eimi*)**.** Paul accepts as his only boast (11:30; 12:9) what his opponents try to make him out to be—**nothing** (see 6:9). But, if Paul is **not in the least inferior to the "super-apostles,"** and he is **nothing,** what are they? Less than nothing?

Paul may also allude ironically to the Socratic tradition in which the wisdom of true philosophers is ironically *oudena*, **nothing,** as over against the pretensions of the rhetoricians. Familiar in Hellenistic Judaism, this tradition was also linked with the Delphic teaching on self-knowledge. To know oneself enables one to recognize one's own nothingness in the face of divine power (Thrall 2004, 835-37; Betz 1972, 122-28).

If this background was known to Paul, he understands it in an entirely new way. He is speaking quite seriously as one who knows himself, apart from the power of Christ, to be **nothing.** This appraisal of himself is the secret of the evident manifestation of the power of the resurrection in his ministry (see 4:10-12; 1 Cor 2:2-5).

■ **12** In contrast (*men*, untranslated in the NIV, NRSV, and NASB) to his mention of the "super-apostles," Paul speaks of **the things that mark an apostle.** The expression ***the signs of an apostle*** was, no doubt, familiar to the Corinthians (see BDAG 2000, 630). The presence of the article in *tou apostolou* in the present context justifies referring to "a true apostle" (NRSV and NASB; see BDAG 2000, 630). This implication is also captured in the translation of *sēmeia* ("signs") as **the things that mark.**

The word *sēmeia* appears twice in the sentence. Does the first instance refer to something different from the second, in which **signs, wonders and miracles** refer to awe-inspiring deeds **done** through Paul's ministry **among** the Corinthians?

Some interpreters distinguish the two instances. Martin speaks of the latter as "secondary criteria" over against "the primary criterion" (1986, 438). Hafemann distinguishes the three marvels from ***the signs of an apostle.*** The latter are not miracles in the narrower sense of *sēmeia* ("signs"). Rather *ta* *sēmeia tou apostolou* refers to "the outpouring of the Spirit" in "especially the conversion and gifting of believers" (Hafemann 2000, 467).

It seems more plausible, however, to take the second use of **signs** (*sēmeiois*) as an instrumental or epexegetic dative. Within the phrase **signs, wonders and miracles,** the three terms identify some of **the things that mark an apostle** (Harris 2005, 876).

The passive voice of the verb **were done among** (*kateirgasthē*) implies that God, Christ, or the Spirit was the agent (see Rom 15:18-19). Thus, it is a "theological" or "divine passive." Paul regarded himself as only the instrument of the power of God. The ***signs of an apostle*** refer to all the manifestations of the power of Christ visible in Paul's labors in Corinth and elsewhere. Not the least of these were the changed lives of believers (3:2; 1 Cor 9:1), including his own (1:22).

God effected these ***signs*** with ***all*** **perseverance** (*en pasēi hypomonēi*). This phrase qualifies what precedes it. It is not just the first of four signs as Theodoret of Cyr (393-466) assumes within an otherwise apt remark: "Paul rightly puts patience before signs and wonders, because attitudes matter more than abilities" (ACCS NT 7:309). That he was able to conduct his ministry in the face of opposition, persecution, and hardship offered as convincing evidence that he was a genuine apostle as any miracle. This especially distinguished him as "not in the least inferior to the 'super-apostles'" (v 11).

What Paul designates as **signs, wonders and miracles** do not refer to
12:12 three kinds of miracles, but to three different aspects of all miracles. First,
writes Calvin,

> he calls them *signs,* because they are not merely meaningless spectacles but are designed to instruct men. He calls them *wonders* because by their novelty they should arouse and astonish, and he calls them *powers* or *mighty works,* because they are more evidently examples of divine power than those we discover in the ordinary course of nature. (1964, 10:164)

Although **signs** (*sēmeiois*) specifically mean "to authenticate," all three function to authenticate or legitimize Paul's apostolic ministry (see Heb 2:4).

Signs and Wonders

The expression "signs and wonders" (*sēmeia kai terata*) is a common phrase in the LXX (see Isa 8:18; 20:3). It is used especially of the miraculous events surrounding the Exodus (see Exod 7:3; Deut 6:22; 7:19). Found in either order, it is frequent also in the NT, particularly in Acts (see 4:30; 5:12; 6:8; 7:36). The usual word in the Synoptic Gospels for "miracle" is either *dynamis* or *dynameis.* The three terms in 2 Cor 12:12—**signs, wonders and miracles**—are associated four additional times in the NT (Acts 2:22; Rom 15:19; 2 Thess 2:9; Heb 2:4).

Awe-inspiring deeds characterized the ministry of Jesus (Acts 2:22) and that of his disciples (Matt 10:1; Luke 9:1; 10:17). They continued to mark the ministry of the early church (Acts 3:1-9; 5:15-16; 8:13; 9:33-34), including that of Paul (Acts 19:11-12). Acts does not mention any miracles performed by Paul during his stay in Corinth (Acts 1:1-18). But the NT does mention them in connection with Paul's ministries in Galatia (Gal 3:5; Acts 14:3, 8-10), in Macedonia (1 Thess 1:5; Acts 16:16-18), in Corinth (1 Cor 2:4; 2 Cor 12:12), and in Asia (Acts 19:11-12).

Acts mentions miracles more often than do the Pauline letters: "Clearly miracles occurred regularly during the founding of Paul's churches" (Harris 2005, 875). He wrote to the Romans: "I will not venture to speak of anything except what Christ has accomplished through me in leading the Gentiles to obey God by what I have said and done—by the power of signs and miracles, through the power of the Spirit. So . . . I have fully proclaimed the gospel of Christ" (Rom 15:18-19).

As a true apostle, the divine power of God was at work in the ministry of Paul. He considered these signs the mark of the authenticity of his apostleship. They were not the miracles of a man full of supernatural power, but the proof of the power of Christ graciously manifesting itself through his weakness. Suffering and the insignia of an apostle belong together in Paul's ministry.

■ **13** With "a fine, forcible, yet delicate *stroke*" (Clarke 1854, 2:369) Paul asks the Corinthians what more they could have expected of him. His question is rhetorical: **How *then* [*gar*] were you inferior to the other churches?** How had Paul treated them differently than he had treated his other churches? How had he and his rivals treated the Corinthians differently? In view of his patient labors for them and the signs that validated his apostolicity among them, he could think of only one possibility—**except that I was never a burden to you** (see 11:7-10).

Paul's rhetorical question—**How *then* were you inferior to the other churches?**—is followed by an affectionate plea for forgiveness—**Forgive me this wrong!** Both his question and his answers are spoken with irony. We can only guess how the Corinthians may have answered Paul's question about how his ministry disadvantaged them.

Paul's answer returns to a sore point between him and the Corinthian church—his refusal to receive financial support from them. He implicitly denies treating them as inferior to his other churches, adding with mocking irony: "except this, that I never sponged upon you? How unfair of me!" (NEB).

Paul's answer—**I *myself* [*autos egō*] was never a burden to you**—implies that the "false apostles" had asked the Corinthians for financial support. Paul accepts their slighted feelings. What he finds difficult to endure is the way they distort his motives for refusing their support. All he knows to say is, **Forgive me this wrong!** (*adikian*, ***injustice***). Paul's **wrong** was not against God, but he had offended the Corinthians.

Calvin suggests here that "they were being doubly ungrateful." They despised the one to whom they owed so much, and "they were even turning his generosity into a reproach" (1964, 10:164). Paul's reference to not being a burden to the Corinthians recalls his earlier discussion of the issue (11:7-15). It also serves as a transition to 12:14-18, where he will broach the matter again in relation to his next visit to Corinth.

In vv 11-13 we see a true minister of Christ: (1) the minister's humble yet confident character (v 11); (2) the minister's certain yet paradoxical power (v 12); and (3) the minister's despairing yet infinite patience (v 13).

The Accusations Against Paul

As we leave this section it is of benefit to gather the accusations that seem to have been made against Paul by his opponents and others in Corinth. The main charge was that he had no right to call himself an apostle (12:12; 3:2; see 11:5; 12:11). They criticized him from every possible angle to support this slander. Although Paul's letters were admittedly forceful, his personal presence was pitiably weak (10:1, 9-10). He lacked the eloquence and other qualities necessary for a true apostle (11:5-9; 12:11). Paul's conduct aroused suspicion, for he always had some scheme in mind (1:12-13; 3:12-14; 4:1-6; 5:11).

His incessant commendation of himself only indicated his uneasy efforts to stay in the church's favor (3:1; 5:12; 12:19). Paul's refusal to accept from the Corinthians the kind of support he received from other churches revealed his lack of love for the church in Corinth (11:7-12; 12:13). His plans were carelessly changed without regard for the promises he had made to the church (1:15-18). Some considered Paul dishonest in relation to his handling of the collection for Jerusalem. How much of it found its way into Paul's own pocket?

It was Paul's handling of such charges that allows us to gaze so deeply into the heart of the apostle.

FROM THE TEXT

This section of the letter has become known as "the fool's speech" (11:1—12:13). Paul opens with an expression of hope that the Corinthians **will put up with a little of [his] foolishness** (11:1). He closes with the acknowledgment, **I have made a fool of myself, but you drove me to it** (12:11).

The issue that prompts these words and those that fall between is the appearance in the church of intruding **"super-apostles"** (11:5). Paul describes them as **false apostles, deceitful workmen, masquerading as apostles of Christ** (11:13). These interlopers seek to seduce the Christians in Corinth away from their loyalty to Paul. They are undermining the ministry in Corinth of the founder of the church and his message. These apparently charismatic, triumphalist, arrogant, and boastful figures have attacked Paul's person, conduct, and gospel. And many in Corinth seem to have accepted them.

To deal with this situation Paul feels compelled to adopt their tactics and boast about himself. But as he does this, he makes it plain that he does it only as a fool and they are to receive it as such (11:16). In this foolish endeavor, Paul reveals more profoundly than earlier in the letter, the heart of his apostolic ministry.

So we ask, what can this "fool's speech" say to us about our ministry in the world of our day? This biblical text gives insight into who we are as Christians in ministry as it witnesses to (1) our *commitment* (11:1-15), (2) our *character* (11:16-33), and (3) our *conduct* (12:1-13).

1. Our *commitment* (11:1-15) as Christians in ministry is to the spiritual welfare of those who are providentially placed in our charge. This commitment is first expressed as **a godly jealousy** (11:2), the kind of jealousy that God has for his people (Deut 4:24; see Heb 12:28-29). Thus, it is a God-implanted concern, a divinely inspired care, to which we are committed.

The primary content of our God-given pastoral care is that those to whom we minister may possess a **sincere and pure devotion to Christ** (2 Cor 11:3). The apostle pictures this in terms of the betrothal and marriage customs of his day, and echoing the imagery of the OT (see Isa 54:1-8; Hos 2:19-20). He says, **I promised you to one husband, to Christ, so that I might present you as a pure virgin to him** (11:2).

Sincere and pure devotion to Christ (11:3) involves a concern for theological integrity. Theology matters! The intruders were intent on corrupting the faith of the Corinthians. Paul fears that their **minds may somehow be led astray** from "the simplicity and [the] purity" (NASB) of their relation to Christ. Thus, he compares their innocence to that of our first parents, who were deceived by the serpent's cunning. The apostle sees the issue as theological, or more precisely, christological—the preaching of "another Jesus" (11:4 NRSV). He is troubled that the Corinthians willingly countenanced **a Jesus other than the Jesus we preached, . . . a different spirit from the one you received, or a different gospel from the one you accepted** (11:4).

Significantly, Paul defends the conduct of his ministry among the Corinthians at two points. One is the nature of his personal presence, his inadequacy as **a trained speaker** (11:6). According to the standards of the day, he was inferior to his accusers as a charismatic rhetorician. His personal presence was unimpressive. Some contemporary pulpit and television dispensers of simplistic absolutes in our "Christian" culture would similarly have shamed him.

Paul's response was, in effect, "You're right. I lack style. But I make up for it in substance" (see 10:1-11). He insists, **I do have knowledge** (11:6). Paul had come to Corinth in the *"Spirit"* with the **gospel** of the Christ. His God-empowered message had transformed the Corinthians' individual lives and formed them into the church they were. He had preached not "another Jesus" (11:4 NRSV) but the one handed down to him from the first apostles (1 Cor 15:3-4). In him is **the truth of Christ** (2 Cor 11:10). To the Galatian churches, Paul wrote that he was astonished that they were "deserting the one who called [them] in the grace of Christ and are turning to a different gospel—not that there is another" (Gal 1:6-7 NRSV). Then he added, "if anyone proclaims to you a gospel contrary to what you received, let that one be accursed!" (Gal 1:9 NRSV).

Christology, a correct understanding of who Jesus was and is, is crucial in our ministry to others. Over a century ago the Scottish Free Church (Presbyterian) pastor/theologian James Denney in his published sermons reflects on this issue. He proclaims that our conception of the person of Christ determines our conception of the whole of the Christian faith. What we proclaim as gospel and the life we offer folk from it, depends on how we answer Jesus' question, "Who do you say I am?" (Mark 8:29; Denney 1943, 5:794). This has been the church's primary question from the first to the twenty-first century. It never goes away. A second question is implicit; and that is, "Where is Jesus in our world?" Who is he with? (see John 12:26).

Prominent on the current scene is the research into the historical Jesus that has occupied many NT scholars for over a century. Scholarly proposals include those of Albert Schweitzer (1875-1965), who sought to bring "the spirit of Jesus" into the twentieth century. More recently, they include such popular contemporary scholars as

- John Dominic Crossan (1935-), *The Historical Jesus: The Life of a Mediterranean Jewish Peasant* (1991)
- Marcus Borg (1942-), *Uncovering the Life and Teachings and Relevance of a Religious Revolutionary* (2006), and
- N. T. Wright (1948-), *The Challenge of Jesus: Discovering Who Jesus Really Was and Is* (2000)

This is not the place to judge their proposals. But we would do well to recall James F. Kay's caution. Due to the character of the Gospels when taken as merely empirical historical sources, "determining Jesus' self-understanding or faith through historical reconstruction is a highly speculative process" (2007, 103). The "facts" on these criteria are so slim that if they are taken out of the framework of the biblical narrative, any alternative story line "strung between Nazareth and Golgotha by the imagination of the historian, inevitably means that the historical Jesus begins to look and sound rather like the historian who creates him" (Kay 2007, 104).

It is noteworthy that the Gospels never speak of "the faith of Jesus," which plays a significant role in much of current NT and theological scholarship. This key phrase comes from Paul's *dia pisteōs Iēsou Christou,* traditionally translated (as an objective genitive) "through faith in Jesus Christ" (Rom 3:22 NRSV). But it may be translated (as a subjective genitive) "through the faithfulness of Jesus Christ." The implications, however, are not only christological but also soteriological.

So related to this research are several theological perspectives. These began with nineteenth-century liberalism and its entrenched opposition in twentieth-century fundamentalism. These and other perspectives now function within our contemporary postmodern cultural ethos. Each has its hermeneutical presuppositions for understanding who Jesus really is and how he impacts the life of the Christian, the work of the ministry, and the mission of the church.

A significant example of these would be postliberalism, which seeks to read Jesus from the church's scriptures, creeds, and liturgical practices. For the Christian, all theological perspectives need to be judged by their implications for Christology and soteriology.

Further Reading on Postmodernism and Postliberalism

Harink, Douglas. 2003. *Paul Among the Postliberals: Pauline Theology Beyond Christendom and Modernity.* Grand Rapids: Brazos Press.

Truesdale, Albert. 2006. *With Cords of Love: A Wesleyan Response to Religious Pluralism.* Kansas City: Beacon Hill Press of Kansas City.

Each theological perspective, along with the Jesus research, may point up a significant and needed approach. All, however, must be submitted to the test of the apostolic witness—the four Gospels and the Epistles—and this in the light of the wisdom of the church over the centuries.

From the scholarly point of view, none of us can avoid to some degree "reconstructing" our own Jesus as we assimilate the apostolic witness for our lives of faith and service. We must be careful, however, that we are not seduced by a "deconstructed" Jesus, one remade in our own image, who sanctions our chosen behaviors.

At all levels in the church, we must "test the spirits" (1 John 4:1; see 2:20-25). Theology and ethics are inseparable, since there is no meaningful distinction between them in Paul's thought (Hays 1996, 46). Our various views of Jesus for our day sanction our varying conceptions of the mission of the church and various understandings of Christian ethics appropriate for our time. The people of God, the church, can be seriously divided, even torn apart over these issues, as we are currently and painfully aware. The issue boils down to, "Where is Jesus in the cultural settings of our times?" (see John 12:26).

Local churches need to be concerned about:

- the "Jesus" who is proclaimed
- the "spirit" that permeates the worship and life of the church, and
- the "gospel" that informs how its Christians behave in and relate to a hurting world

These are antenna that we must raise when we visit other churches or are seeking a church home.

We must read the whole of the Scriptures reflectively and prayerfully. There we will encounter the "Jesus" about which its pages speak. There we will imbibe the "spirit" of its people from Genesis to Revelation. There we will hear in our hearts its "gospel." We will make our evaluations and our choices.

"Another Jesus" at all levels of the church's life and ministry is an ever-present temptation in our contemporary church culture, mainline and evangelical.

Paul also defends the conduct of his ministry among the Corinthians in relation to church finances. He refused the financial support of the Corinthians, which was his right according to the patronage customs of his day (see the commentary on 11:7-9). His countercultural stance was thoroughly misunderstood. He was accused of lowering himself beneath his true station as an apostle by working as an artisan. At the same time, he accepted support from other churches to serve the Corinthians free of charge. So they questioned the sincerity of his love for them (2 Cor 11:11). Paul's response was the emphatic **God knows I do [love you]!**

2. Our commitment as Christians in ministry is expressed as love for those whom God has placed in our care, even in the face of misunderstanding. It is a love that persists even when we do not satisfy their cultural or prideful expectations of ministry. We will keep on loving them, as Paul did, even when we have lowered ourselves in their eyes and are accused of doing wrong for it (11:7).

Our *character* (11:16-33) as Christians in ministry is that of a servant: **Are they servants of Christ? (I am out of my mind to talk like this.) I am more** (11:23). The intruders in Corinth were apparently boastful in their ministry, proud of who they were and what they conceived themselves to be as apostles. Paul felt compelled to boast to counter their influence in the church. As he saw it, they were **false apostles, deceitful workmen, masquerading as apostles of Christ** (11:13).

And so he plays their game and indulges in the boasting the Corinthians have come to expect from Christian ministers. Paul begs them: Receive me, **just as you would a fool, so that I may do a little boasting** (11:16). Since he has to boast, he will not be **talking as the Lord would, but as a fool** (11:17). His opponents **are boasting in the way the world does** (11:18). So he will say just the opposite of what their culture has conditioned his audience to expect. By this means he subtly reveals the character of a servant (minister) of Christ.

From Paul's "foolish" boasting we learn:

First, our approach to those whom we serve in Christ must always be sensitive to their feelings. It can never be abusive. We respect the dignity and individuality of others. We never put them down or "lord it over" their faith (1:24). The Corinthians allowed the "egomaniacs of the pulpit" (11:21 TM) to take advantage of them. They admired those who put on airs to enslave, exploit, take advantage of, and assault them (11:20). Paul admits, My coworkers and I **were too weak for that!** (11:21). This foolish boast should be ours as well.

Second, we must learn to wear our particular spiritual heritage loosely. There is no room for sectarian pride. **Are they Hebrews? So am I. Are they Israelites? So am I? Are they Abraham's descendants? So am I** (11:22) was the boast that Paul dared **as a fool** (11:21). So what that my mother was a saint, that my grandfather an old-fashioned Methodist preacher! What does that make me? Grateful. Yes, but who am I in the Lord's sight? I am a Nazarene, a Wesleyan, an evangelical, a Protestant. But how like Christ am I? Can a Calvinist Presbyterian be sanctified? Is it possible for Roman Catholics to be Christian? As a Christian in ministry I am simply one who in obedience to the Spirit of Christ serves others in his name.

Third, as servants of Christ we learn that our worth is found in our empathy with those whom we serve. "Who is weak, and I am not weak? Who is made to stumble, and I am not indignant?" (11:29 NRSV). Following Paul's rhetorical question, "Are they servants of Christ?" and his "insane" response, "I [am] more so" (NASB), Paul lists all the hardships and the sufferings he endured in the course of his apostolic ministry. He concludes with, **Besides everything else, I face daily the pressure of my concern for all the churches** (11:28). This is where his superior proof lies, in his sufferings. If he must boast, Paul says, **I will boast of the things that show my weakness** (11:30; see 11:32-33).

The apostle tells the plain truth about his ministry: **The God and Father of the Lord Jesus . . . knows that I am not lying** (11:31). As Christians in ministry an essential aspect of who we are is encapsulated in Paul's confession, **Who is weak, and I do not feel weak?** (11:29). Of Paul here, James Denney wrote long ago,

> The sorrow that pierced the soul of Christ pierced his soul also. . . . This is the fire that Christ . . . longed to see kindled—this prompt intense sympathy with all that is of God in men's souls. . . . This is indeed the apostle's last line of defense. (1943, 5:799)

3. Our *conduct* (12:1-13) as Christians in ministry is to be an open book. Our lives must be transparent and humble before those we serve. **I refrain, so no one will think more of me than is warranted by what I do or say** (12:6). There is no room for pretense, masquerading, attempts to appear to be more than we are, and certainly no room for hidden or duplicitous agendas in the way we conduct our ministries (see 11:13).

The situation in the Corinthian church compelled Paul to adapt at least the appearance of "prideful bragging" (**as a fool** [11:21]). So, he proceeds in two ways:

First, he makes clear what he *will not* boast about. He describes a particularly exalted spiritual experience (12:1-6). His language exudes ecstasy—"caught up to the third heaven . . . whether in the body or apart from the body I do not know . . . caught up into Paradise . . . heard inexpressible things" (12:2-4 NASB). But Paul speaks only in the third person as such having been experienced by **a man in Christ** (12:2). Then he adds emphatically, **I will boast about a man like that, but I will not boast about myself, except of my weaknesses** (12:5).

Paul was obviously no stranger to high spiritual experiences. He considered such a privilege and among his strongest sources of inspiration. But Paul kept much of this to himself. "The world knows little of its greatest men; perhaps we very rarely know what are the great things in the lives even of the people who are round about us" (Denney 1943, 5:801). The great apostle had kept silent about this experience for fourteen years. And when he finally reports it, he is determined to make nothing of it. "There are things too great to allow the intrusion of self" (Denney 1943, 5:801). Paul refrains from "spiritual" self-indulgence, for he wants no one to think more of him than they themselves can actually see of him and hear from him as he ministers to them.

Like the great apostle, we must be extremely modest if we even speak of our subjective spiritual experiences. The danger is twofold: (1) we will be calling more attention to ourselves than to Christ—even exalting ourselves, and (2) we will be speaking beyond what can be corroborated in our conduct. We risk the credibility of our witness if we talk about that for which there is no concrete evidence in our lives. The possibility of obvious discrepancies is real.

Teresa of Avila counseled her sisters, "Believe only those who you see walking in conformity with the life of Christ" (Luti 1991, 82). Perhaps because of her physical and psychological makeup, her background and environment, Teresa was subject to ecstatic or extraordinary experiences. These were often to her embarrassment and shame, when they overcame her in public (Hamilton 1982, 68). Such things as union, raptures, locutions (words heard audibly or by interior impression), and even levitations (rising in the air in defiance of gravitation) would catch her unawares (Teresa 1987, 168, 172-74, 212-23). But in her self-evaluation, their only validation was an increase in love for God and others. She writes in "The Interior Castle" (1.4) that such favors are lost when they "fail to benefit those to whom God grants them." Rather, they should "be delighted and awakened through these favors to a greater love of him" (Teresa 1980, 285, see 319).

Second, since Paul is forced to boast, he gives clear witness to what he *will* boast about (12:7-10). This he states clearly, **I will boast all the more gladly about my weaknesses** (12:9). The premier, yet enigmatic example of this he describes as the **thorn in my flesh, a messenger of Satan, to torment me,** given to him by the Lord (12:7). The nature of this "thorn" is ultimately unknown to us. It was probably a physically and psychologically frustrating handicap or circumstance. And Paul had prayed earnestly for deliverance from it.

He reports that he received an unexpected yet real answer to his prayer. It came to him in the form of a locution, **"My grace is sufficient for you, for my power is made perfect in weakness"** (12:9). As an apostle of Christ, Paul boasted in his human vulnerability. This illuminating insight into his ministry, evident throughout this letter, broke through anew to him in that moment. **That is why, for Christ's sake, I delight in weaknesses, in insults, in hardships, in persecutions, in difficulties. For when I am weak, then I am strong** (v 10). Grace is a powerful force!

We learn from Paul that we must not call attention to ourselves in the course of our witness or ministry. But when we must, it should relate to our condition of weakness in the world. Our human limitations and vulnerabilities, whatever they are, are not an insurmountable obstacle to our ministry to others. They are an indispensable part of them. We do not seek them, but they come sooner or later. Our sufferings, our handicaps, our peculiar humanness become a means to the end that "the power of Christ may dwell" (12:9 NRSV) upon us and in us, and minister through us. The power of our ministry is not in us, for our weakness is really our strength **in Christ.**

Theologically expressed, our identification in ministry with the sufferings and death of Christ is met by the power of the resurrection of Christ. How are we to understand the amazing ministry of Mother Teresa and the presence of God with her, so evident to others? We must realize that identification with the passion of Jesus in her sufferings was a part of her call. She took it as a means in her vocation. Her counsel to her sisters was: "Grab the chance to offer something to Jesus" (Kolodiejchuk 2007, 140).

C. Paul Plans a Third Visit to Corinth (12:14—13:10)

As Paul approaches the end of his letter to the Corinthians, he prepares for his third visit: **Now I am ready to come to you** (12:14). And they, too, must prepare for his coming. To this end Paul begins by laying out the nature of his future conduct consistent with the basic principles of his ministry among them (12:14-18). But he is apprehensive as to the moral and spiritual condition in which he will find them (12:19-21). They may be certain that when he comes he will be as firm in his discipline as their situation demands. They are to repent, for his prayer is for the completion of their faith. Paul appeals again to Christ crucified and risen in relation to his ministry among them (13:1-10).

BEHIND THE TEXT

We come to what can be viewed as Paul's closing arguments. He continues generally with his forensic or judicial rhetoric (i.e., he defends himself and accuses them). But it is now mixed with and served by deliberative elements (i.e., he seeks to change their minds and behavior). He is finished with "the fool's speech" (12:11) and resumes normal discourse. By this means he seeks to clarify a matter that apparently still bothers the Corinthians—his refusal of their financial support (12:14-18). Paul abandons his defensive posture and goes on the offensive. He expresses his fears about the behaviors he may find on his next visit to Corinth (12:18-21). His rhetorical strategy is to put them on the defensive.

Courtroom language and the demand for proof take over in a warning, which concludes with an application of the ministry of Christ to his ministry in Corinth (13:1-4). This section concludes with the *peroratio* (13:5-10). Here, the rhetorical conclusion consists of an emotional appeal. With this, his defense rests. Full reconciliation with the Corinthians has been his aim all along. He has sought to remove all the obstacles to full reunion with them. The greatest asset of Paul is his genuineness as an apostle and the authenticity of his ministry (Witherington 1995, 465-73).

IN THE TEXT

I. Paul's Proposed Behavior in Corinth (12:14-18)

The question of finances must have been a touchy one in Corinth. It always is! Paul must return to his financial policy in relation to the church at Corinth. This played a significant role in chs 11—12. Paul strongly insists on two matters:

- He will not change his method of operation.
- Far from having taken any advantage of them, he loves them to the point of self-sacrifice.

These verses are of an "intensely personal and emotive nature" (Harris 2005, 880).

■ **14** This final phase of the apostle's defense of his ministry concerns his approaching **third** visit. The placement of **ready** (*hetoimōs*) could mean that this is
12:14 the third time Paul has prepared to visit Corinth (see NASB). But 13:1 ("this will be my third visit to you") favors taking **third** with the anticipated visit. On his first visit, he first brought to them the gospel (Acts 18:1-18). His second was the painful visit (2 Cor 2:1), which followed the writing of 1 Corinthians.

He insists that on this third visit, he **will,** as always when he is with them, **not be a burden** (*katanarkēsō*). He repeats the verb *katanarkaō* from 11:9 and 13. Here, as there, his point is that he will refuse their financial support. Paul has been misunderstood at this point before (11:7-12). But his principle of not entering into a client-patron relationship with Corinth stands firm.

Here Paul offers two reasons for foregoing his apostolic right to support (see 1 Cor 9:6-12, 14):

First, what he demands of them is far greater than money: **what I want is not your possessions but you.** Paul continually seeks (*zētō*—present tense) their spiritual welfare (see 13:9). He had previously expressed his desire to present them to Christ as "a chaste virgin" (11:2 NRSV).

Second, it is the normal obligation (*opheilei,* see 12:11) of **parents** to store up (*thēsaurizein*) for their **children,** and not children for the parents. The apostle uses this natural analogy to illustrate why he does not exercise his right as a minister in the gospel to be paid for his service. Paul is their parent in the gospel and they are his "dear children" (1 Cor 4:14).

Paul presents this as a general principle, not a rule applicable without exceptions. After all, he did accept support from some of his spiritual children (11:8-9; Phil 4:15-16; 1 Cor 9:14). And grown children do have obligations toward their elderly parents (see Mark 7:10-13).

■ **15** ***But*** (*de*) for the Corinthians the apostle is willing to go beyond mere obligation. He will do more than share with them his excess. "I will most gladly spend and be spent for you" (NRSV). The English pronoun **you** here is literally ***your souls*** (*tōn psychōn hymōn*). Paul expresses his concern and sacrificial care for their total spiritual well-being.

Paul's **I** (*egō*) here is emphatic. In contrast to typical parents, *he* will exhaust everything he has on his Corinthian children. All his time, money, and strength are freely theirs. He will deplete his health and shorten his lifespan for them (see Phil 2:17). And he will do it **gladly** (*hēdista*) for these ungrateful children. He will "boast all the more gladly [*hēdista*] about [his] weaknesses" (12:9), whereas they "gladly [*hēdeōs*] put up with fools" (11:19). He will "spend [*dapanēsō*] and be spent [*ekdapanēthēsomai*] for [them]" (NRSV), not because he is a fool, but because he loves them.

Paul follows this declaration with a reproach that most interpreters take as a rhetorical question: **If I love** [*agapō*] **you more, will you love** [*agapōmai*] **me less?** It is natural for love to generate love. But their love for him is decreasing even as his affection for them grows. "The warmer his love, the cooler theirs" (Harris 2005, 887).

■ **16 Be that as it may** (*estō: **let it be***) looks back to the previous verse. Paul will continue to love them regardless. And precisely because he loves them, he will continue to refuse their financial support. He has not in the past and will not in the future be **a burden** on them. He would not live among them at their expense.

But they don't understand why not. ***On the contrary*** (*alla*, **Yet/*But***), he implies, they appear to have accused him of behaving deceitfully in relation to them. They suspected that the apostle's sacrificial generosity was just another trick of his foxlike nature.

The participle *hyparchōn* (**am**) can have the sense of "being inherently so" (BDAG 2000, 1027). **Crafty fellow** translates *panourgos*, like its cognate *panourgia* (see 4:2; 11:3), is always used in a negative sense in the NT. Both convey "a readiness to do anything" (BDAG 2000, 754). As such a character, they imagine that Paul took them in (*elabon;* see 11:20). He ***ensnared*** them ***by deceit*** (*dolōi*); or so they appear to have thought.

Were Paul's opponents responsible for causing the Corinthians to assume the worst about his motives? Had they been placed in an embarrassing light by Paul's refusal to accept personal support? Are *they* using crafty lies to suggest that Paul will somehow manage to take advantage of the church by some other means? Have they undermined the confidence of the Corinthians in Paul's apostolic integrity as well as his authority? Verses 17-18 seem to suggest they had.

■ 17-18 Paul answers the suspicions and innuendo trumped up against him with a series of four rhetorical questions. The basic issue, bluntly put, is, "Who, of the men I have sent to you, was used by me to defraud you?" (NEB).

Paul's rhetorical disclaimer is supported by a second denial, **Titus did not exploit you, did he?** Paul had urged (*parekalesa*) **Titus to go to** Corinth. (The phrase **to go to you** is added to the text by the translations to complete the thought.)

These first two questions are asked with the negative particles *mē . . . mēti*. These are formulated as rhetorical questions, which imply "no" as the answer. **Exploit** in both questions, as in 2:11 (see 7:2), has the connotation of "take advantage of" (NRSV).

Paul's second pair of rhetorical questions are introduced with the negative particle *ou*. This indicates that the expected answer is a "yes." "Did we not conduct ourselves with the same spirit? Did we not take the same steps?" (NRSV).

Some interpret **spirit** as the Holy Spirit as in Gal 5:16 where the same verb (*peripateō*, "to walk") is used with "Spirit." In 1 Cor 12:9 the precise Greek expression "the same Spirit" (*tōi autōi pneumati*) also refers to the Holy Spirit. But here the parallelism between ***walk in the same spirit*** and walk ***in the same steps*** make it more probable that the human disposition is meant.

Which visit of Titus to Corinth concerning the collection does Paul have in mind? He mentions one **brother** here, but in 8:16-24 two brothers were sent with Titus to care for the offering. Paul probably refers to Titus's initial visit to begin the offering (see 8:6).

Paul gives no indication how he was alleged to have defrauded or exploited the Corinthians. We can only guess what charges had been lodged against Paul or his colleagues in connection with the collection. Whatever they were, Paul assumes complete responsibility for the collection and joins his integrity with that of his emissaries. As the one who sends, so is the one sent (see 1:18-20). Paul and his coworkers were one in their attitude and in their conduct in Corinth—the **same spirit** and ***the same steps***? There is no evidence to support the Corinthians' suspicions.

2. Paul's Apprehensiveness (12:19-21)

His defense finished, Paul states the real reason for it. Out of his love for them he is writing primarily for their spiritual welfare (v 19). He expresses a threefold fear concerning his coming visit (vv 20-21). Will his third visit be as painful as his second (1:23; 2:1)? Will he find them as *he* wishes? Will they find him as *they* wish? It depends on what they do in the meantime.

■ 19 Paul's opening sentence is probably a question, as the NIV takes it. But it could be taken as an accusing statement: "You suppose all along that we are defending ourselves before you" (Furnish 1984, 557, 560; see NASB). Both the warmth of the verse and the lack of an adversative particle (but) in the third clause favor its understanding as a question (see Thrall 2004, 858-59).

Paul cannot deny that he has been defending himself (*apologoumetha;* see Rom 2:15) throughout the letter. But it is not an *apologia* in the usual sense of a self-seeking discourse. His ultimate object is not to exonerate himself, but to rescue the Corinthians from the interlopers, who are leading them dangerously astray. His goal is to build them up, not exalt himself. His real audience is not the Corinthian church, but God.

Paul insists, My **speaking** is not **to you** (*hymin*), but **in the sight of God as those in Christ** (see 2 Cor 2:17; 1 Cor 4:3). Furthermore, **everything . . . is for your strengthening** (*oikodomēs; **edification;*** see 1 Cor 14:12, 26). Within Paul's structural logic, the antithesis of defending himself (*apologoumetha*) is building them up (*oikodomēs*).

Paul had one aim throughout all (*ta . . . panta*) his life among the Corinthians. It was to speak only as one **in Christ** (12:2; see the commentary on 5:17). The real audience, the judge and jury in the case of his apostolic ministry, is not the Corinthian church, but **God**. How God sees his service is what finally matters (1:23; 4:2; 5:11; 7:12). Paul addresses the folks at Corinth as his **dear friends** [*agapētoi: **beloved***], not his antagonists. His loving concern for their progress as Christians (11:2) drove him to a procedure that he fears they may misunderstand.

2 CORINTHIANS

12:19-20

■ **20 For** (*gar*) introduces a long sentence that explains Paul's concern for the Corinthians' welfare. Only the figure of speech *litotes* (understatement) or euphemism (inoffensive substitute) allows the apostle to describe their need as "strengthening" (v 19). He speaks with fatherly restraint of his concern for his children: **I am afraid . . . I fear . . .** "I am afraid" (*phoboumai . . . mē pōs . . . mē pōs . . . mē;* vv 20-21). Paul expresses his fears of encountering ethically deficient behavior in the church in two ways.

First, he is afraid that he **may not find** them as he wishes and that they might **not find him** as they wish. This is because he intends to exercise stern discipline on the unrepentant. The negative particles (*ouch hoious thelō . . . ou thelete*—emphasis added) are more correctly placed in translation as the kind of people "not as I wish . . . not as you wish" (NRSV; see Harris 2005, 897-98). Paul no doubt refers to only a minority in the church (2:5-6).

Second, Paul lists the negative behaviors he fears he may find when he comes to Corinth. In fact, all of the sins cataloged here were mentioned earlier in 1 Corinthians. He lists these in four mutually interpretive pairs for rhetorical effect (Lenski 1937, 1322; but see Furnish 1984, 567; and Thrall 2004, 863, n 683).

The four pairs are (1) **quarreling, jealousy,** (2) **outbursts of anger, factions,** (3) **slander, gossip,** (4) **arrogance and disorder.** The vices listed are traditional, found elsewhere in the NT and in Hellenistic catalogs (see Gal 5:19-

21; Rom 1:29-31; and 13:13). The first pair are singular nouns, the rest are plural. Thus, the latter refer to "instances of" each vice.

1. *Eris*—**quarreling,** "strife, discord, contention" (BDAG 2000, 392)—is the opposite of peace. It occurs elsewhere in Paul's letters in Rom 1:29; 13:13; 1 Cor 1:11; 3:3; Gal 5:20; Phil 1:15; 1 Tim 6:4; and Titus 3:9. *Zēlos*—**jealousy** or "envy," when used in a negative sense—is often associated with *eris* (Rom 13:13; 1 Cor 3:3; Gal 5:20). The term describes a strong emotion in both its good and bad senses.

2. *Thymoi*—**outbursts of anger** or "explosive tempers" (Furnish 1984, 561; see Luke 4:28; Acts 19:28; Gal 5:20; Eph 4:31; Col 3:8)—is the first vice of the second pair. The second, *eritheiai*—**factions**—is found only in Aristotle before NT times. He uses it to denote "a self-seeking pursuit of political office by unfair means" (BDAG 2000, 392). Its exact meaning here is uncertain. In its six other NT appearances, it means either "strife, contentiousness" or "selfishness, selfish ambition" (BDAG 2000, 392; Rom 2:8; Gal 5:20; Phil 1:17; 2:3). Several interpreters take it in the sense of a party spirit as "fractiousness" (Furnish 1984, 561; Thrall 2004, 857, 865).

3. The next pair—**slander** (*katalaliai, **speaking-against***) and **gossip** (*psithyrismoi*)—refer to sins of speech. The noun *katalaliai* occurs only here and in 1 Pet 2:1. But Paul uses the cognate adjective (*katalos*) substantively in Rom 1:30 (the verb *katalaleō* appears in Jas 4:11; 1 Pet 2:12; 3:16). *Psithyrismoi* (only here in the NT; but see Rom 1:29) is an onomatopoeia word like the English "whisperers." It refers to **"derogatory information about someone that is offered in a tone of confidentiality"** (BDAG 2000, 1098).

4. *Physiōseis*—**arrogance**—is used only here in the NT. It pictures one so "puffed up" (*physioō;* e.g., 1 Cor 4:6) with ***"pride"*** or ***"conceit"*** as to be swelled-headed (BDAG 2000, 1070). *Akatastasiai*—**disorder**—refers to "disturbances" of the public order (see 1 Cor 14:33; Luke 21:9; Jas 3:16).

■ **21** The repeated use of the negative *mē* from v 20 in v 21 suggests that Paul continues to be fearful about his coming visit. His third fear is twofold—another humbling experience in Corinth and grief over the unrepentant in the church.

Paul expresses the first aspect of his fear in an unusual way: **I am afraid that when I come** to Corinth, **my God will *again* humble me before you. Again** (*palin*) seems to refer not to his second coming, but to a second humiliation of the apostle (Plummer 1915, 369). Paul's previous humiliation probably refers to the unpleasant turn of events during his second, painful visit to Corinth. Someone wronged him (7:12; see 2:5-11) and the Corinthians failed to support Paul in the matter.

Paul was humbled before them then. But now, what sort of humiliation does he dread on his third visit? And why does he attribute it to **God**? The disastrous spiritual state of the church he fears he may find (described in vv 20-21) is not at all consistent with his desire for their edification (v 19). This could strike Paul as a shameful failure of his ministry **before** them. As God's coworker (6:1), the apostle was accountable to him (5:11). Calvin comments that the Corinthians' "progress in holiness would have been the honour and glory of Paul's apostleship, but being in the grip of so many faults, they had instead brought disgrace upon him" (1964, 10:167). Enduring such behavior and their refusal to repent, Paul could indeed feel himself humbled before God.

The second aspect of Paul's fear is the result of the first. When he comes he **will be grieved over many who have sinned earlier and have not repented.** The single article modifying both participles (*tōn proēmartēkotōn kai mē metanoēsantōn*) indicates that the two groups are the same. The sequence of perfect and aorist tenses suggests a difference in the time of action. Those **who have sinned earlier** "continued in their sinning" (Furnish 1984, 567). Those who **have not repented** are those who did not repent when given opportunities to do so, either during Paul's visits or in response to his letters. For this he will mourn in sorrow over them and accept it as a humiliation from **God.** Such is indicative of the heart of an apostle.

In these verses Paul appears to refer to two different sets of sins. Verse 20 describes those sins from which no one in the Corinthian church was totally free (1:11; 3:3). Harris sees v 21 as describing "the libertine morals of a 'proto-gnostic' wing of the church" (2005, 904). These behaviors were contaminating the church already when he wrote 1 Corinthians (see 5:1-11; 6:12-20). There were obviously still **many** (*pollous*) basic moral problems in the church.

The three overlapping vices **in which they have indulged** and for which
they **have not repented of** are **impurity, sexual sin and debauchery.** These typ- 12:21
ically Gentile sins appear frequently in Paul's vice lists. They are listed together
in a different order in Gal 5:19-20.

The first, **impurity** (*akatharsiai*) is a general term for "a state of corruption" (BDAG 2000, 34) usually in sexual matters. "God did not call us to be impure [*akatharsiai*], but to live a holy life" (1 Thess 4:7; see Rom 1:24; 6:19; Gal 5:19; Eph 4:19; 5:3; 1 Thess 2:3).

The second, **sexual sin** (*porneiai*), refers to all kinds of illicit sexual activity. Paul had already written to the Corinthians to "flee from sexual immorality" (*porneian;* 1 Cor 6:18; see 1 Thess 4:3).

The third term, **debauchery** (*aselgeiai*), indicates a "lack of self-constraint which involves one in conduct that violates all bounds of what is socially acceptable, self-abandonment" (BDAG 2000, 141). Such animal behavior was the willful defiance of public decency, often in sexual matters (see Rom 13:13; Gal 5:19; Eph 4:19).

Together the three terms "testify to the rampant depravity in the city of Corinth and the clinging pagan background of some of the Corinthian converts" (Harris, 2005, 903-4). For Paul, "there was a fundamental incompatibility between a life-style that is indistinguishable from that of the surrounding culture and the life of God's holy people" (Brower 2006, 67).

3. Paul's Determination to Discipline (13:1-4)

Putting words to his fears (12:20-21), the apostle now gives his final warning to the Corinthians. He seeks to encourage them to change their behavior. When he comes the third time he will be as severe in his discipline as their moral and spiritual condition warrant (vv 1-2). If that is what they truly want, they will have the proof that Christ is speaking in him! His apostolic ministry comes from Christ, from his crucifixion and resurrection, from his weakness and God's power (vv 3-4). With this Paul brings to final expression the theme of weakness that played such a prominent role at the end of his "fool's speech" (see 11:30; 12:7-10).

■ **1** With repetitive emphasis (12:14, 20-21) Paul declares that he is ready to come to Corinth for the **third** time (12:14; Acts 18:1-18; 2 Cor 2:1). He is definitely coming. And when he comes, he will discipline wrongdoers. This will be done according to the legal principle laid down in Deut 19:15, namely: **"Every matter must be established by the testimony of two or three witnesses."**

By metonymy the Greek phrase *epi stomatos* (***on the mouth of***) refers to what the mouth says. This justifies the paraphrase **by the testimony of. Matter** translates *rhēma* (***what is said***), representing the Hebrew *dabar*—"thing, object, matter, event" (BDAG 2000, 905). These considerations justify the legal connotations of the NRSV paraphrase: "Any charge must be sustained by the evidence of two or three witnesses."

The legal requirement of more than one witness was unknown in first-century Greco-Roman law. The prescription of Deut 19:15 was intended to prevent the conviction of a defendant on the basis of only one testimony, lest it be the malicious accusation of a false witness. This principle was accepted in rabbinic jurisprudence. The NT applies it to church discipline (Matt 18:16; 1 Tim 5:19; see John 8:17; Heb 10:28; 1 John 5:8). Did Paul have in mind a church trial in which formal charges would be examined and judged? Was he going to "hold court"? If so, who were the witnesses? Some Corinthians testifying against other Corinthians? (so Hafemann 2000, 490).

Most interpreters since Chrysostom (344/354-407) have taken Paul figuratively. He equated the witnesses with Paul's visits and warnings to the Corinthians (see ACCS NT 7:312). Calvin takes him to mean that his "three comings will take the place of three testimonies" (1964, 169; similarly Harris 2005, 908). Barrett notes that Paul is not using the OT quotation as a proof, but only saying in a general way that they have had ample warning (1973, 333; see Martin 1986, 470).

■ **2** Paul now repeats the warning he had given them on his second visit. The sentence structure is complex, as a literal translation demonstrates: ***I have previously said when present the second time, and now while absent I say in advance to those who have continued in their former sins and to all the rest that when I come again, "I will not spare anyone."*** The perfect participle *tois proēmartēkosin* (**those who sinned earlier**) may refer to a present state resulting from a past action. Otherwise, the NIV gives the meaning clearly enough: **I already gave you a warning when I was with you the second time. I now repeat it while absent: On my return I will not spare those who sinned earlier or any of the others.**

The two visits mentioned here are probably the second painful visit of 2:1 and the third visit Paul anticipates. The first group—**those who sinned earlier**—is almost certainly those mentioned in 12:21 as the "many who have sinned earlier and have not repented." Less clear is the identity of **any of the others** (*tois loipois pasin*). Most interpreters think the apostle refers broadly to those Corinthians "who by their indifference or leniency toward immoral conduct on the part of church members have tacitly condoned it" (Furnish 1984, 570; see 1 Cor 5:1-13). Harris suggests, instead, that Paul refers to all of the rest of the Corinthians, who needed a warning for the sake of deterrence (2005, 910). The two groups in view comprehended the entire church.

Paul's repeated mention of those "who have sinned" (12:21) and the fact of their tolerance by the church remind us how difficult it was for Gentile Christians to break with the sexual laxity characteristic of their environment (see 1 Cor 5:1-2; 6:12-20; 1 Thess 4:3-7). The Christian standard of sexual purity came not from the Greeks but from the OT and Judaism. Paul warns the sexually lax and all the rest so that when he comes he will "not have to be harsh in [his] use of authority" (13:10; see 10:6).

Paul uses the verb **I will not spare** (*ou pheisomai*) absolutely to mean "I will show no leniency" (NEB; see NRSV). He probably assumes an object such as ***anyone*** (see 1:23). The imagery of **not spare** originated in ancient warfare as not killing a defeated enemy (see Rom 8:32). What punishment is Paul threatening? Will he excommunicate the unrepentant from the fellowship of the church and hand them over to Satan for "the destruction of the flesh" (1 Cor 5:5 NRSV; see vv 3-13; Harris 2005, 911)? Will he only temporarily exclude them from the life of the church (2 Cor 2:6-11; see Martin 1986, 472)? Will he call for them to be shunned (2 Thess 3:6; 1 Cor 5:9-11)? Will he call upon God to inflict them with some bodily sickness (Thrall 2004, 878; 1 Cor 5:5; 11:30-32)?

We cannot be certain of the nature of Paul's intended disciplinary action. Murphy-O'Connor helpfully suggests: "if the community did not respond to his admonitions, the only alternative was for him to declare that the quality of their lives, both individually and collectively did not conform to the gospel and they were not in fact Christian." This, he adds, "would be a terrible decision for Paul to take," for they would have fallen back into Satan's realm (1991, 132; see Barrett 1973, 334). Clearly, the apostle could not forever tolerate immoral conduct within the fellowship of the church at Corinth.

■ **3** One reason why Paul will not be lenient when he comes is that the Corinthians are **demanding proof that Christ is speaking through** him. If **proof** (*dokimēn*) is what they want, **proof** is what they will get! But it will assume a form they do not yet understand. The form is in the shape of Paul's final reference in the letter to the interchange of weakness and strength in the apostle of Christ that he has been developing throughout the letter (vv 3-4).

The Corinthians are seeking (*zēteite*) in him *their* expected criteria of genuine apostleship—charisma, polished rhetoric, exalted spiritual experience, and triumphalism in life and ministry, not weakness. They demand this as **proof that Christ is speaking through** (*en*) Paul. Whether the *en* is interpreted as instrumental (***through***) or local (in), the point is that Paul speaks for Christ, an ambassador accurate in his representation.

Lacking their expected criteria, they refused to grant that the power of Christ accompanied Paul's presence with them (see 10:10). Unquestionably, Christ has been **powerful among** the Corinthians (1 Cor 12 and 14). But what does Paul mean by saying Christ is **not weak in dealing with** them?

The church at Corinth will get the decisive **proof** they want. But Christ will not speak through Paul in the way they want. He threatens stern discipline as the sign that Christ **is not weak** toward them through his ministry, but rather **is powerful among** them (see Rom 15:18). "In challenging Paul to come and exert his authority, . . . in presuming on what they called his weakness, they were really challenging Christ" (Denney 1943, 5:806).

■ **4 For *indeed*** (*kai gar*) introduces the christological basis for Paul's claim that Christ is powerful in the Corinthian church (v 3). The pattern of his ministry is simply that of his Lord: Christ **was crucified in weakness, yet** [*alla*] **he lives by God's power.** Weakness and power unite in Christ (Phil 2:8; 1 Cor 1:17-30). And the apostle, united to Christ (*en autōi . . . syn autōi*) in his ministry, is both **weak in him** and lives "with him by the power of God" (NRSV). Paul plays with the terms "weakness" and "strength" throughout 13:1-10, always in that sequence (10:3*b*, 4*a*, 4*b*, 9*a*).

Christ **was crucified** "because of [*ex*] weakness" (NASB). He was actually a mortal human being. His was not only apparent weakness as seen by the world (Thrall 2004, 883; see Furnish 1984, 571). "Yet [*alla*] He lives because [*ek*] of the power of God" (NASB). That is, God powerfully raised Christ from the dead. Christ's death and resurrection may be viewed theologically as one complex event, one continually present (4:10). His death is more than a past event followed by his resurrection. "The Risen One remains the Crucified One and the Crucified One remains the Risen One" (McCant 1999, 162).

In v 4*b*, Paul repeats *kai gar* (***for indeed***) to affirm that the crucifixion-resurrection is *the* death-life in which his apostolic ministry participates. The power of his ministry is at one with God's resurrection power; the weakness of his ministry is at one with the weakness of the crucified Christ.

Out of the reality of this christological affirmation, Paul writes to the Corinthians: **we will live with him to serve you** (*zēsomen syn autōi*). He is not thinking primarily of future eschatological life with Christ. His present apostolic "life" is directed, as he says, ***from*** [*ek*] ***the power of God toward you*** (*eis* *hymas*). The NIV translates *eis hymas* **serve you;** the NRSV, "in dealing with you."

It is because Paul's ministry is defined by Christ that he will act decisively when he returns to Corinth. He **will not spare those who sinned earlier or any of the others** (v 2). The power of God in the gospel of Christ (see Rom 1:16) cuts both ways: It is "to the one an aroma from death to death, to the other an aroma from life to life" (2 Cor 2:16 NASB).

The life-flow of Paul's ministry originates in the ministry of his Lord. This explains the paradox of their shared "strength through weakness" (see 4:10-14). As he characterizes his ministry to the Corinthians in these terms, he speaks with more than an editorial **we** (see the commentary on 1:18). Here, as in 5:18-21 and in the following verses, Paul's **we** includes all his coworkers and, by implication, all who live and minister in the tradition of Christ crucified-and-risen, from Paul's day down though the centuries to ours.

4. Paul's Plea for Reformation (13:5-10)

Paul hopes the Corinthians will correct their situation. When he visits them, he does not want to have to deal severely with them. Since they have asked for "proof [*dokimēn*] that Christ is speaking through" him (v 3), he challenges them to prove (*dokimazete*, v 5) their Christian faith. Their faith is not unrelated to his.

But Paul is also apprehensive that they might refuse his pleas. This is obvious in his key vocabulary. After the occurrence of the noun *dokimēn*, "proof," in v 3, five words from the same cognate family occur as a distinctive feature of these verses (*dokimazō* in v 5; *dokimoi* in v 7; and *adokamoi* in vv 5, 6, 7). Representatives of this significant word family occur thirty of its thirty-six times in the NT in Paul's letters.

■ **5-6** Paul turns the tables on the Corinthians with his new approach. With an emphatic and repeated **yourselves** (*heautous . . . heautous*), he writes that they are to **examine** (*peirazete*) and **test** (*dokimazete*) themselves—not Paul—to determine if they are even **in the faith** (v 5).

Here, the verbs *peirazō* and *dokimazō* are virtually synonymous with a slight difference in emphasis. The former indicates the endeavor to discover the nature of something by testing it; the latter, the critical examination of something to determine its genuineness (BDAG 2000, 792, 255). Here, the Corinthians are to test the evidence that they are true believers. As in 1:24, to be **in the faith** (*en tēi pistei*) entails living in obedience to and trust in Christ.

Paul asks a rhetorical question that expects an affirmative answer: **Do you not realize** [*epiginōskete; **know for certain***] **that Christ Jesus is in you?** Paul seeks to elicit the desired behavior from them by appealing to who they know they are. They are a people in whom **Christ Jesus** lives (*Iēsous Christos en hymin;* see Gal 2:20; Eph 3:17). And if they are, this will manifest itself in their behavior. Thus, the test for the expressions **in the faith** and **Christ Jesus . . . in you** are mutually interpretive. To be **in the faith** includes a correct understanding of **Christ . . . in you.**

Paul adds, **unless, of course, you fail the test** (*ei mēti adokimoi este*). Again, Paul's formulation (*ei mēti*) indicates that he does *not* expect them to fail. Some take this comment as a mildly ironic challenge. Their answer of yes to the test question, "Do you not realize that Jesus Christ is in you?" (NRSV), will also affirm the genuineness of Paul's apostleship, for they came to faith through him.

And so, using similar terminology, Paul expresses his hope (*elipizō*) that they **will discover that** he has **not failed the test** (*ouk esmen adokimoi*). In the same way that the Corinthians verify the presence of Christ in them, Paul hopes they are able to be certain "that Christ is speaking" (v 3) through his ministry to them.

If Paul is apprehensive, he is also confident; his hope is real. He knows and wants them to realize that their genuine faith and his genuine apostleship are inextricably linked. They stand or fall together (Harris 2005, 922).

■ **7** Paul is not preoccupied with himself; his interest returns to the situation of his readers. His prayer **to God** (*pros ton Theon,* see Eph 2:18) for them is for their restoration and edification (see 12:19; 13:10). Some interpreters in the past took *hymas* (**you**) as the direct object in the infinitive phrase *mē poiēsai hymas kakon mēden*. Thus, they concluded that either "we" or "he [God] may do you no harm" (Thrall 2004, 894). But the current consensus is that *hymas* is the accusative subject of the infinitive, as in the NIV: **that you will not do anything wrong** (similarly NASB, NRSV). Paul reports this as the basic content of his prayer. The complementary phrases, doing **wrong** and doing **right,** in this context define what is **wrong** (*kakon*) and **what is right** (*kalon*) in the life of the church in terms of what Paul contends they need to do.

The twofold aim of Paul's prayer is indicated by the two *hina* (***so that***) clauses that follow (Harris 2005, 923). The first states its negative purpose: **Not that people will see that** Paul has **stood the test** (*dokimoi*). He does not pray that his apostolic authenticity will be vindicated during his third visit by taking severe disciplinary action against the obdurate Corinthians.

The second aim of Paul's prayer is positive: ***that*** they **will do what is right.** Paul prays that on their own they will repent and mend their ways. And this, he concedes, **even though we may seem to have failed** (*adokimoi*). Paul will gladly give up the "proof that Christ is speaking" (v 3) through him, if only they make real progress toward restoration (v 9) in the faith. He would rather not have to come to them with discipline (v 10). This is not who he is as their spiritual father.

■ **8** Paul's overriding concern as an apostle of Christ is for **the truth.** This is the reason for his prayer. He states that he is not able to **do anything against the truth** (*kata tēs alētheias*), but only dares act **for the truth** (*hyper tēs* *alētheias*). This may sound "like a general maxim affirming the sovereign power of *the truth*" (Furnish 1984, 579). But for Paul, **the truth** here is to be equated with the gospel (see 4:2; 6:7; 11:10; Col 1:5; 2 Thess 2:12; see Eph 1:13). The gospel not only is to be believed but also is something to be behaved in life. Paul wants the truth of the gospel to be "visibly demonstrated in the lives of the Corinthians" (Thrall 2004, 897).

The apostle is unable to **do anything against the truth** as one in whom "the truth of Christ is" (11:10) and as one through whom "Christ is speaking" (13:3). Paul's desire for personal vindication as a true apostle must give way before **the truth** of the progress of the gospel in Corinth. To exercise his apostolic authority for its own sake would be to prostitute it. The proper reception of the gospel is the great aim of his life to which all else surrenders.

■ **9** In v 9, Paul continues to express his concern for the Corinthians. And he does so from the christological center of his apostolic ministry (see 13:4; 11:30; 12:9). He explains (*gar*, ***For***) that he is **glad** [*chairomen*, ***we rejoice***] **whenever** he is **weak but** they **are strong** (see 4:12).

But why does Paul seek this paradoxical contrast? Is he referring to the broad sense of his weakness, which he has so carefully and profoundly developed (so Thrall 2004, 897)? Or does he use the terms here in "a more specific *primary* sense," following up on v 7? That is, is Paul again expressing his hope for a situation in which he will not need to exercise strict discipline when he comes (Harris 2005, 926)?

Paul probably applies the former understanding to this specific situation (Furnish 1984, 579). Thus, his weakness results from their strength. For them to be **strong** means that they are restored to spiritual health. This would remove the necessity for him to demonstrate his apostolic authority in discipline. In 1 Cor 4:10, Paul was ironically critical of the Corinthians' claim that he is weak and they, strong. Now, with an allusion to the same slogan, he accepts it. But he assigns to the Corinthians' strength a new content—moral maturity rather than charismatic gifts.

"This [*touto*] is what we pray for, that you may become perfect" (NRSV). Paul refers to his prayer for the spiritual well-being of the Corinthian community throughout vv 7-9. Thus, his prayer here is also *pros ton Theon* (**to God**) as in v 7. Although *touto* ("this") could refer back to *dynatoi ēte* (**you are strong,** in v 9*a*), it seems to look forward to what follows. He prays for their *katartisin*, **"the process of perfecting, *maturation*"** (BDAG 2000, 526). Since *katartisin* is in epexegetic apposition to *touto*, it is closely related to the Corinthians' spiritual strength (v 9*a*) and to their not doing **wrong** and doing **what is right** (v 7).

The noun *katartisin* occurs only here in the NT. Its cognate noun *katartismos* occurs only in Eph 4:12, where it has the sense of "equipping" (BDAG 2000, 526). The much more frequent cognate verb *katartizō* appears in 13:11. It can mean to *"restore to a former condition, put to rights"* (as in Mark 1:19; Gal

6:1). Or, it can mean *"put into a proper condition . . . make complete"* (as in 1 Cor 1:10; 1 Thess 3:10; Heb 13:21; BDAG 2000, 526).

In this context, *katartisin* surely comprehends the Corinthians being put right with God, with one another, and with Paul. By this means, they will be "made complete" (NASB) or "become perfect" (NRSV). This is, as Wesley comments (alluding to Gal 5:6), **perfection** "in the faith that worketh by love" (1950, 676). Their "restoration" (Harris 2005, 928) to God, one another, and Paul includes, or at least implies their spiritual ***"maturation"*** (BDAG 2000, 526). In effect, Paul prays that the Corinthians will "purify [*katharisōmen*] [themselves] . . . , perfecting holiness [*epitelountes hagiōsynēn*]" (7:1).

■ **10** With v 10, the apostle concludes the main body of his letter. He explains the reason why (*dia touto*) he writes the letter we call 2 Corinthians: so that the Corinthians will take the necessary steps to avoid his discipline. Paul's mention of writing **these things** (*tauta*) refers back to what he had just written in vv 5-9, perhaps even in 10:1—13:9. But pastoral care motivates and permeates the entire letter.

Paul's conclusion refers back to the charge with which he began in 10:1 and 10—that he is courageous in his letters but cowardly in person. Paul writes as he does **when** he is **absent,** [so] **that when** he comes to Corinth he will **not have to be harsh** [*apotomōs chrēsōmai*, ***deal severely***] in the **use** of his apostolic **authority.** The Greek term for **authority,** *exousian*, appears only once in this verse as in the NRSV translation: "severe in using the authority that the Lord has given me."

Paul is not denying his God-given apostolic authority, only reining it in. The purpose (*eis . . . eis*) of the *exousian* **the Lord gave** him was ***for building up*** (*eis oikodomēn*, ***for edification;*** see 10:8; 12:19) not ***for tearing down*** (*eis kathairesin*, ***for destruction***; see 10:4; 10:8). Paul's concern for the spiritual health of the church has been a dominant concern in all his written and personal dealings with them (see 1 Cor 14:3, 12, 19). And now he is hopeful that they will take his advice.

FROM THE TEXT

Deeply imbedded in the text of 2 Corinthians is a theology of ministry. Paul's dealings with the church at Corinth give profound witness to the nature of his apostolic calling. In the present passage he speaks of its source in Christ crucified and risen. And he describes its sole purpose as *oikodomē*—the "edification" (13:10 KJV), "building up" (13:10 NASB), or **strengthening** (12:19) of the church. "The authority the Lord gave [him] for building [them] up" (10:8) is at the heart of the closing verses of the letter. But retrospectively, it emerges as the concern on which the entire letter rests.

These two motifs—the source and purpose of Paul's apostolic ministry—give life to this section of the letter. But another aspect of his ministry vibrates throughout—apostolic integrity. What do these verses offer for our day on the integrity of the Christian ministry? We see this in:

1. the principles that motivate it (12:14-18)
2. its dedication to the spiritual welfare of the church (12:19-21)
3. its devotion to the truth of the gospel of Christ (13:1-10)

Paul gives expression to all of these as he seeks to bring closure to the issues that face his church in Corinth.

1. We see the integrity of the Christian ministry in *the principles that motivate it* (12:14-18). Paul says it well in 12:14: **what I want is not your possessions but you.** The sticky point between Paul and the Corinthians is the apostle's refusal to accept their financial support (see 11:7-12). They have apparently misunderstood and impugned his motives. They cannot imagine that he has no hidden agenda in the matter of the collection for Jerusalem. Was Paul on the take?

But Paul insists that he took great care in handling the delicate matter of the offering. He sent Titus and another equally trustworthy brother to oversee the project. The Corinthians know that Titus did not **exploit** or take advantage of them. Did not Paul conduct himself **in the same spirit and follow the same course** (v 18)? His behavior, like that of the two brothers, was open to full inspection. Openness in mundane matters that concerned the life of the church, as an expression of integrity, was a motivating principle.

Paul also appeals to the normal custom that parents provide for their children, not children for their parents. As their father in the faith, the apostle insists that his love for them goes beyond such customary care: **I will very gladly spend for you everything I have and expend myself as well** (v 15). The guiding motive of Christian ministers must be the sacrificial giving of themselves for others. It is not what they want from the congregation that moves them to serve. It is who they are as created in the image of God: "I do not seek what is yours, but you" (12:14 NASB).

2. Thus, it follows that we find the integrity of the Christian ministry in *its dedication to the spiritual welfare of the church* (12:19-21). **Everything we do, dear friends,** writes Paul, **is for your strengthening** (*oikodomēs;* 12:19). The Corinthians may think that **all along** the apostle was primarily **defending** himself. But he insists that he has been writing **in Christ,** as one authentically Christian, and as one whose life and motives are open to judgment **in the sight of God** (4:2; 7:12).

In 5:10-11, Paul wrote that in view of "the judgment seat of Christ, . . . what we are is plain to God." In the present context, he assures the Corinthians that everything he does in relation to them, he does for their spiritual welfare as a church—**for your strengthening.** Accountability to God in Christ must govern our concern as ministers for the "upbuilding" (NASB) of the people of God in our charge.

Paul expresses his concern for the spiritual welfare of the church at Corinth in two areas, both ethical. Regarding both he is fearful.

First, he fears that when he comes to Corinth he may not find them as he wants them to be. Paul desires a unified church, a church at one in heart and spirit. He fears that he will find instead a fractured church marked by disruptive behaviors such as **quarreling, jealousy, outbursts of anger, factions, slander, gossip, arrogance and disorder** (12:20). A divided church subverts its own mission.

The integrity of the ministry demands that it bring people together in the manifest presence of a holy God. Ministers must not split people apart, protecting their own egocentric charisma. At stake is the spiritual welfare of not only the "body" but also individual folks for whom Christ died! One could add here that care must be taken to lead the whole church, not just select parts of it. No group should be "left behind" as the minister seeks to mold the church into the latest so-called success model. The church's back door must be carefully guarded lest it become an escape route for the neglected, the disillusioned, and the hurting! Sheep are led; cattle are driven!

Second, Paul is fearful that when he comes to Corinth they will not find him as they wish. He fears that God may humble him before the Corinthians. He dearly wants to come in joyful satisfaction over his ministry in Corinth. Instead, he is afraid he will have to come in mourning over some in the church. His ministry will have failed in the lives of those who **have not repented of the impurity, sexual sin and debauchery** (12:21) of their pagan past. They appear to be still indulging in the impure, immoral, and dissolute behavior depicted by the three terms he employs. Over this behavior on the part of some in the church the pastor's heart is deeply grieved.

What Paul said in 10:8 and will say again in 13:10 is that the Lord has given apostles and ministers "authority" for "building . . . up" the spiritual health of the church. He does not want to have to be "harsh" in using his "authority" when he comes. The integrity of a "called" and "anointed" ministry involves the exercise of a God-given authority. But how and when? The church is called to the mutual love and personal purity of its members! The integrity of the Christian ministry cannot escape a discerning use of that authority in the interest of the spiritual welfare of the church as the body of Christ. This impacts both its corporate existence and the individual lives of its members.

3. As Paul continues with the issue of apostolic authority, we know third the integrity of the Christian ministry in *its devotion to the truth of the gospel of Christ* (13:1-10). Christ **was crucified in weakness, yet he lives by God's power** (13:4). Paul has credibly warned the Corinthians that when he comes he will exercise the appropriate discipline if necessary. He **will not spare** being severe since they **are demanding proof that Christ is speaking** in him. They want convincing evidence that through Paul's ministry Christ **is not weak in**

dealing with them, **but is powerful among** them. He will convince them, but not according to the criteria they prefer.

Paul rests his case, appealing to the christological foundation of his apostolic ministry: Christ who **was crucified in weakness, yet** who **lives by** the resurrection **power** of God. The pattern of his ministry is precisely that of his Lord who speaks through him. Paul is **weak in him, yet by God's power** he lives **with him to serve** the Corinthians.

So it is Christ himself the Corinthians are dealing with in their view of Paul's weakness. And it is Christ they will deal with when his apostle comes in discipline. Like Paul, those in Christian ministry are devoted to the gospel of the weakness and the strength of the crucified and risen Christ. This must be our modus operandi in dealing with the health of the body of Christ.

The crucified and risen Christ is the criterion of ministry and Christian standing. The proof is not in any charisma of triumphalism. Paul calls upon the Corinthians to test themselves to determine whether **Christ Jesus** is really in them.

Paul trusts that they will judge him by the same criterion. Then they will see that he has **stood the test.** For he **cannot do anything against the truth** of this gospel of Christ crucified and risen. Rather he is **glad** whenever he is **weak** and they **are strong,** for his supreme **prayer** is for their **perfection** in the faith. He hopes his prayer will be answered so that when he comes they will have done **what is right,** and he will **not have to be harsh in** his **use of authority.** Paul would prefer to **seem to have failed.**

They want proof that Christ speaks in him. But Paul has no desire to 13:11-14
prove it by disciplining them. He would rather avoid this, if possible, for the good of the church. As he understands it, **the authority the Lord gave** him is for **building up** the church, **not for tearing** it **down.**

The integrity of the Christian ministry in practice depends on the integrity of God himself as embodied in Christ crucified and risen. Christian ministry must be loyal to the truth of the gospel of Christ in both its content and its methodology. Such a theology of ministry passes all tests. It alone is effective for the edification of the church, the body of Christ, and for the perfection of the saints.

In the church Jesus Christ is the only ultimate source of authority. He confers his authority by his presence with his servants. They exercise his authority in their various functions in line with the pattern and presence of their Lord. Such authority authenticates itself in its exercise: "We will live with Him because of the power of God directed toward you" (v 4 NASB).

D. Paul Concludes the Letter (13:11-14)

The apostle brings this difficult letter to a somewhat friendly, perhaps even affectionate (**brothers**), close. He observes the usual pattern found in his letters (see 1 Cor 16:19-24; Phil 4:21-23).

Following his introduction (1:1-11), Paul has narrated the events that call his apostolic ministry into question. In the process, he defines his ministry and affirms his pastoral relation to them (1:12—7:16). He appeals to them to complete the collection for the saints in the Jerusalem church (8:1—9:15). Finally, in preparation for his third visit to Corinth, Paul engages in a vigorous defense of his apostolic integrity (10:1—13:10).

Reflecting back on these chapters, Paul brings the letter to a close with a greeting that contains one final appeal, which seeks to remedy the problems in this contentious church. A "Trinitarian-like" benediction is his final word. Paul's concerns for the church subtly permeate every facet of his closing words, even the benediction.

BEHIND THE TEXT

The conclusion to 2 Corinthians is similar to Paul's other letters. Weima's excellent study of Paul's letter closings concludes that they all relate "in one way or another to the key issue(s) taken up in their respective letter bodies. . . . The closings serve as an hermeneutical spotlight, highlighting the central concerns of the apostle in his letters and illumining our understanding of these key themes and issues" (1994, 238). Although they are similar to the closing formulas of the Hellenistic letter, Paul's letters do not include the conventional wish for good health or the usual Greek word for farewell (*errose;* see Doty 1973, 39-42).

In 2 Corinthians, the customary elements of Paul's letter closings follow rapidly on one another—an exhortation (v 11*a;* 1 Thess 5:27), a promise (2 Cor 13:11*b;* see 1 Thess 5:24; 2 Thess 3:16); greetings (2 Cor 13:12-13; see 1 Cor 16:19-21; Phil 4:21; Phlm 23), and a benediction (2 Cor 13:14; see 1 Cor 16:23; Phil 4:23; Phlm 25). Although limited paraenesis may be found in the endings of Paul's other letters (see Rom 16:17), the five imperatives in v 11*a* are striking. They indicate a specific emphasis or concern of Paul for the church (Martin 1986, 493).

Scholars suggest several different alternatives as to what is being brought to a close in vv 11-14. The decision as to whether it is chs 1—9, 10—13, or the canonical 2 Corinthians (Thrall 2004, 901-2) depends on the scholar's view of the composition of the letter. If chs 10—13 are regarded as a separate letter, it certainly belongs with them. But the closing also reflects the thrust of the entire letter. If one regards 2 Corinthians as a unity, the conclusion can be taken as a suitable ending for the whole letter (Weima 1994, 213; Harris 2005, 930-31).

IN THE TEXT

1. Exhortation and Greeting (13:11-13)

In 12:14—13:10, Paul sought to prepare the church for his third visit. Before his final benediction in v 14, he inserts five summary exhortations (v

11*a*). To these he adds a promise of God's presence (v 11*b*), asks them to greet one another with the holy kiss (v 12), and sends greetings from the church where he writes (v 13).

■ **11** With **finally, brothers** (*loipon, adelphoi*), Paul introduces his concluding comments. This expression often marks a transition to a closing hortatory section (see Rom 16:17; 1 Cor 16:15; Gal 6:17; Phil 4:8; Phlm 20). It often refers, however, to what precedes it. The vocative address, **brothers,** is frequent in 1 Corinthians. But it appears here in 2 Corinthians only for the third time (1:8; 8:1; but see 12:19, where he addresses them as "dear friends" [*agapētoi*]).

Brothers, the usual NT term for fellow Christians (11:9; Rom 8:29), indicates that church members are closely related parts of God's family. It stresses their unity and parity of status within that family, a family in Christ (Harris 2005, 932). Calvin suggests that, with this welcoming address, Paul "moderates whatever sharpness there may have been in the whole epistle, as he wanted to leave their minds not exasperated but calmed" (1964, 176).

The NIV translates the first of the five imperatives with **good-by** (*chairete*). This is normal in English translations; the NRSV has "farewell." But the NASB, with most commentators, prefers the meaning "rejoice." The Greek verb *chairō* is often understood as a greeting (Matt 26:49; 27:29; 28:9; Mark 15:18; Luke 1:28; 2 John 10-11). And it can mean "farewell, good-by" (in Phil 3:1; 4:4; BDAG 2000, 1075). There are, however, good reasons for retaining the stronger sense of "rejoice":

- It has this meaning in 13:9.
- It heads a list of imperatives.
- Its similar position in 1 Thess 5:16 is translated by the NIV "be joyful always" (*pantote chairete*).

In spite of all that has passed between the apostle and the church in Corinth, they are to rejoice in the Lord and in what he has accomplished among them.

The next four exhortations are: **aim for perfection, listen to my appeal, be of one mind, live in peace.** The imperatives are directed toward their communal lives as the body of Christ. They need to realize increasingly their relationship to Christ within the fellowship of the church (12:20-21). Paul's admonitions are all present imperatives implying their need to be constantly putting them into practice.

Aim for perfection (*katartizesthe*) can be understood as "put things in order" (NRSV) or "made complete" (NASB). This is the force of *katartisin* in v 9. Here as there, the stress is on the Corinthians' need for full restoration with God, with one another, and with Paul (see the commentary on 11:9). Their situation demands that they "mend [their] ways" (NEB).

Listen to my appeal (*parakaleisthe*) is taken by most interpreters as an exhortation in the passive voice. Thus, it would have the force "be admonished." But it could be taken as a middle voice: "exhort one another" (Barrett 1973, 342), "be encouraged" (NJB), or "be comforted" (NASB).

Be of one mind (*to auto phroneite*) is literally ***think the same thing.*** Paul exhorts them to "agree . . . in the Lord" (see Phil 4:2; Rom 12:16; 1 Cor 1:10; Phil 2:2).

The previous appeal goes closely with the last: **live in peace** (*eirēneuete*). As in Rom 14:19 and 1 Thess 5:13, Paul calls for mutual well-being. He urges them to enjoy reconciled relationships with "one another" (NASB) and "with everyone" as in Rom 12:18. Reconciliation is the name of Paul's game. Paul combines beautifully similar exhortations in Phil 2:5: "Have the same thoughts among yourselves as you have in your communion with Christ Jesus" (BDAG 2000, 1066). Fitting here also is the admonition of the writer to the Hebrews: "Pursue peace with everyone, and the holiness without which no one will see the Lord" (12:14 NRSV; see 2 Cor 7:1).

Following the admonitions Paul adds an encouraging promise to the Corinthians: **the God of love and peace will be with you.** The two genitives (*tēs agapēs kai eirēnēs*) are descriptive—***the loving and peaceful God.*** They are bound together by one article and are in close continuity with the two preceding imperatives.

The phrase **the God of love** is unique to this verse in the Greek Bible. But **the God of . . . peace** occurs frequently in Paul's letters (Rom 15:33; 16:20; Phil 4:9; 1 Thess 5:23; see Weima 1994, 87-100). The addition of love to his usual benediction speaks loudly to the need of the church. Paul has applied his expanded peace-blessing to the Corinthian context reminding them that **the God of love and peace** will be with them, enabling peace in the life of the church (Furnish 1984, 586; Barrett 1973, 343).

The exhortations do not relate to the promise in a conditional, "if, then" fashion. Instead, it is a promise that **the God** who is characterized by **love and peace** *will* empower them to respond to the exhortations for the healing of the church.

■ **12** With **Greet one another** (*aspasasthe allēlous*), Paul employs the conventional term for greeting in the letters of his day. He adds to this a specifically Christian call to express this greeting **with a holy kiss** (*en hagiōi philēmati*). This is a call for the Corinthians to treat one another as brothers and sisters and intimate friends. What Paul desires to characterize their fellowship is filial love and peace. Paul uses the same formula in Rom 16:16 and 1 Cor 16:16, and a similar one in 1 Thess 5:26.

Exchanging kisses was a widespread custom in the ancient world and in Judaism among family members and friends. It was a common practice in Jesus' day (Mark 14:45; Luke 7:45; 15:20; 22:47), among Paul's Gentile churches (see Acts 20:37), and throughout Christian communities (1 Pet 5:14 urges, "Greet one another with a kiss of love [*en philēmati agapēs*]"). Kisses were exchanged upon greeting and at parting. They functioned as signs of reconciliation and of entering and belonging to a specific group, particularly a religious association (Furnish 1984, 582-83; Thrall 2004, 912-13). After NT times the **holy kiss** became closely associated with the Lord's Supper.

Paul's description of the **kiss** as **holy** (*hagiōi*) appears as new. It is **holy** for at least three reasons (Harris 2005, 936):

- It is exchanged between *hoi hagioi*, "the holy ones" or **the saints** (v 13).
- It is an expression of love (*agapē;* 1 Pet 5:14) or selfless commitment.
- And it is not an insincere kiss of deceit as was Judas's kiss of betrayal (Mark 14:45), but a sincere kiss of genuine fellowship in Christ.

The **holy kiss** in the church expressed love and unity, reconciliation, and forgiveness. It exhibited Christian liberty, for its practice transcended distinctions of status, race, and gender (see Gal 3:28; Hafemann 2000, 497 n 20). Chrysostom (344/354-407) stressed that "we are the temple of Christ, when we kiss each other we are kissing the porch and entrance of the temple" (ACCS NT 7:315).

■ **13** The NRSV and some other versions treat this verse as part of v 12. This follows the versification of the critical Greek texts beginning with Robert Estienne in 1551. The KJV, NASB, NIV, and other translations keep it separate. Thus, they number 14 verses in ch 13. The contents are identical, only their numbering differs. The fourteen verse numbering apparently originated with the Bishops' Bible in 1572 (Thrall 2004, 914).

All the saints [*hoi hagioi;* see the commentary on 1:1] **send their greetings.** Paul probably refers by **the saints** to the Christians who were with him in Macedonia from where he wrote. But it is possible that he had in mind all Christians as in Rom 16:16: "All the churches of Christ send greetings" (see 2 Cor 8:18; 11:28; 1 Cor 7:17; 14:33). If so, Paul reminds the Corinthians that the whole body of Christ, the wider Christian community with whom they are united in Christ, are concerned for their spiritual welfare. They all **send their greetings** to the Corinthians (see 1 Cor 16:19-20; Phil 4:22).

In these verses the apostle points to the behavior required of the Corinthian church. He does so, not only by direct appeal, but also by mentioning a Christian custom and remaindering them of the church as a wider fellowship.

Paul's letter closing is more than a summation of his arguments. Its very structure reveals the tenor and thrust of his theology. The movement in v 11 from exhortation to a benedictory promise indicates that God's presence with his people is linked inseparably to their purified hearts and sanctified lives (see 6:14—7:1). The apostle's prayers for the Corinthians are awesomely reinforced by the following benediction, which brings the letter to its final end.

2. The Threefold Blessing (13:14)

■ **14** What the apostle desires most of all for the Corinthians is their full enjoyment of the blessing of God in all of its ethical implications. This he expresses in a concluding benediction: **May the grace of the Lord Jesus Christ, and the love of God, and the fellowship of the Holy Spirit be with you all.**

This benediction is "trinitarian in form but not in substance." It gives voice to "both the goal of the letter and the means whereby it is to be achieved" (Murphy-O'Connor 1991, 136). Harris adds that "it is a singular paradox that a letter so full of indignation, remonstrance, and gyrating emotions should conclude with the most elevated affirmation in the NT couched in the form of a benediction addressed to all the members of a factious church" (2005, 941).

Paul's benediction has the form of a wish rather than a promise (as in 13:11). The ellipsed form of the verb "to be" (*einai*) added by English translations should make it clear that it is a wish rather than an indicative statement. This is confirmed by the presence of **all** (*pantōn*) that stresses the inclusion of everyone and every part of the church in the blessing. As the ending of the letter, the benediction replaces the more generalized wish for well-being of contemporary letters.

John Wesley properly refers to the closing verse of 2 Corinthians as "this awful [= awe-full] benediction" (1950, 677). It is the most elaborate of all the benedictions in Paul's letters, with the possible exception of Eph 6:23-24. Typical of his shorter closing benedictions is 1 Cor 16:23: "the grace of our Lord Jesus be with you." Here the divine source of blessing is solely the Lord's "grace" (Gal 6:18; Phil 4:23; 1 Thess 5:28; 2 Thess 3:18; Phlm 25; see Col 4:18; 1 Tim 6:21; 2 Tim 4:22; Titus 3:15; see Weima 1994, 78-87).

The form of this shorter benediction may partly explain why "grace"
13:14 (*charis*) appears first in Paul's expanded version (Martin 1986, 504). It is
through the grace of Christ that God's love reaches believers (Rom 8:39; see
8:35). The addition of the two other expressions to the first was due, no
doubt, to the situation in the Corinthian church.

Paul expressed his three-in-one benediction comprehensively in terms of the order of the faith and experience of the early church. The first two phrases are most often and best interpreted in parallel with both genitives being subjective. **The Lord Jesus Christ** (*tou kyriou ʾIēsou Christou;* 1:2; 8:9; 12:9) is the source of **grace,** and the **love** is seen as coming from **God** (*tou Theou;* Rom 5:5, 8). The third phrase with the genitive, *hē koinōnia tou hagiou pneumatos* (**the fellowship of the Holy Spirit**) is ambiguous. If we keep its genitive as subjective in continuity with the first two phrases, then *koinōnia* indicates the fellowship with one another created by the Holy Spirit in the Christian community. This fits the needs of the Corinthian context.

If the usage of *koinōnia* (**fellowship**) with a genitive follows Paul's normal usage (see 8:4; 1 Cor 10:16; Phil 3:10; probably also 1 Cor 1:9 and Phil 2:1), it is an objective genitive. As such it would designate the Corinthians' participation in the life and power of the Holy Spirit. This seems to fit the sense of the benediction best. If so, all three phrases speak of the personal relationship of the believers in Corinth with **Christ** the Son, **God** the Father, and **the Holy Spirit.**

Theologically the three phrases form a parallel and progressing symmetry. **The grace of the Lord Jesus Christ** reveals **the love of God** that Christians experience through their ***participation in the Holy Spirit*** (see the commentary on 8:5). The result is a Trinitarian fellowship, which is constituted and defined by a common sharing in the Holy Spirit (see Acts 2:42; Phil 2:1).

The three terms for deity sometimes function interchangeably in Paul's letters. But here the order—Christ, God, Spirit—reveals the way the gospel came to the Corinthians. Their ***participation in the Holy Spirit*** brings to subjective, experiential reality in the life of the church the objective, redemptive reality resident in the person of Christ by virtue of his crucifixion, resurrection, and exaltation (see 1 Cor 1:9).

The identity between the Son and the Spirit is thus a dynamic one of redemptive action. It is an identity rooted in the fact that the Spirit is the life of the resurrected and exalted Lord (13:4; Rom 1:4; 6:4; 8:11; 1 Cor 6:14; 15:45). The Holy Spirit is likewise the channel of the Lord's life in redemptive action (3:17; 1 Cor 12:3). Implicit in the designation **Holy Spirit** (emphasis added) is the claim that this is the Spirit of the Holy One. Thus, God the Father is likewise involved in human redemption. The word **grace** here, writes Calvin, "stands by metonymy for the whole blessing of redemption" (1964, 176).

Although the vertical dimension of *koinōnia* is primary here, there is no doubt "a surplus of meaning" (Matera 2003, 314). For the term always carries with it the horizontal dimension as well (1 Cor 10:16-17; see Acts 2:42; Phil 2:1; Phlm 6; 1 John 1:3). So the apostle prays for a mutuality of participation in redemption. He seeks an ethical difference in the life of the church.

Paul intends for **the grace of the Lord Jesus Christ, and the love of God** to have a practical realization in the life of the church. As the Corinthians open themselves more and more to the Holy Spirit, he will bring about the "perfection" (13:9) Paul desires for them.

The "fellowship in the Holy Spirit" (NEB) is the common sharing of Christians in the Spirit. The Spirit is both Gift and Giver. He effects the unity and mutual love, which must permeate the ethical life of the church as the body of Christ. In fact, only their common experience of the one Spirit constitutes them as the body of Christ (1 Cor 12:12-13).

Paul gives evidence in his own attitude of that for which he prays. His desire is the same for all in Corinth. There are no reservations in his love, no grudges held. His love for his recalcitrant church transcends all human barriers and longs for the best that God has for them. He expresses their highest good in a breathtaking summary of the Christian faith: (1) the grace of Christ (2) revealing the love of God (3) by their fellowship in the Holy Spirit. This is able to transform the quality of their lives together. With his spiritual hands thus spread above the Corinthians in benediction, the apostle's voice sinks into silence.

The letter has come to an end. Every facet of Paul's closing words reveals his apostolic heart—his final advice (13:11), his attention to the formalities of Christian courtesy (11:12-13), and his benedictory blessing (13:14) are all concerned with the progress of the gospel in Corinth. Because this gospel is authentically at work among the Corinthians, Paul confidently hopes for the spiritual welfare of the church.

Paul trusts that his open and bold witness to the character of his ministry will effectively counter the resistance to his apostolic authority (10:1—12:14). His service to Christ does not depend upon the methodology of a worldly power structure (10:1-18). Rather his boast is in the power of the living Christ, which finds its occasion in what the world calls weakness (11:1—12:13). This is the manner in which he as always will continue to make himself known to the Corinthians (12:14—13:14).

This letter comes to us by way of the agonizing, refining furnace of interpersonal conflict. At stake have been the integrity and authority of Paul's ministry among the Corinthians. An illuminating presentation of the Christian ministry has been torn from his soul by the suspicions of his converts. It is a Christian ministry (1) whose integrity is simply that of the gospel it proclaims (chs 1—7); and (2) whose authority is only that of the presence of Christ (chs 10—13). The focus is on Christ crucified and risen—the weakness of his humiliation and the power of his resurrection. "So then, death is at work in us, but life is at work in you" (4:12).

13:11-14

FROM THE TEXT

Paul's final words are the mountain peak of his letter. They reflect the bright sunlight as they send forth the meaning of the whole, like lightning encased in a peal of thunder. The apostle's pastoral heart, the character of his ministry, the cruciform nature of the gospel, and the power of the Spirit of the resurrection in the lives of even a factious and fractious people, are all here. To end such a letter in such a manner to such a church, as Paul does, simply staggers the Christian imagination. How could he do it? The answer speaks to us in our day, even to churches not unlike that in Corinth. It is profound in its penetrating simplicity: *the gospel and its God!*

The gospel is relevant for us in the apostle's unwavering confidence in the overwhelming power resident in the gospel of Christ for the life of the church. Even as he says good-bye he reminds his readers that what they need as a corporate body will be met by an open-hearted reception of the gospel and its implications (13:11). The message of Christ crucified and risen *is* the power and presence of **the God of love and peace.** The gospel does not need to be made relevant; it *is* relevant when truthfully, clearly, and faithfully proclaimed. The gospel needs neither to be thinned nor trimmed. Nor does it need any additives.

The truth of the gospel of Christ permeates the whole of the letter. Every situation and problem addressed by the apostle in the church is embraced and transcended by the reality of the gospel. Paul appeals to nothing else but the nature and power of the gospel itself in the midst of misunderstanding, tension, and conflict. Ministry in our day needs nothing more than apostolic confidence in the Christ who was crucified in weakness, yet who lives by the power of the God who raises the dead. This is the character of the gospel revealed in the mystery of the Trinitarian God.

The God of the gospel is relevant for us in the God who reveals his power in a "Trinitarian" mystery. The divine economy of salvation is comprehended in terms vibrating with life—**grace, . . . love, . . . fellowship**—as the church experiences them. Each term is theologically overloaded with transforming implications for the ongoing life of the church. And these implications are as relevant to the church in modern cities as in the ancient church at Corinth. All that Paul has said to the church is in essence here. This is who God is for the individual lives and the corporate existence of the people of God in the world.

Just as the divine salvation has a threefold expression, so does the divine person—**the Lord Jesus Christ, . . . God, . . . Holy Spirit.** And all of this is found in a benediction containing the heart of the great apostle for the welfare of a troubled church! The deepest desire of all Christian ministers for the people under their care is expressed in a formula defying reason! Here is the tip of the shining peak of Paul's literarily encased soul-cry for the folk to whom he gave spiritual birth. To what extent can we point here to the mystery of the church's doctrine of the Trinity?

Paul has given voice to a threefold source of apostolic faith both before (1 Cor 12:4-6) and after (Rom 15:30; Eph 2:18; 4:4-6) penning this benediction. He is not alone in the early church in that Trinitarian faith (1 Pet 1:2; Jude 20-21). But nowhere has the formula been expressed so majestically and succinctly as in 2 Cor 13:14.

Certainly it is a first step. But how much more is it? How near is it to the Trinitarian formulas of the ecumenical creeds? It is clear that as Paul summarizes his gospel, those terms most naturally drop into his mind which, when logically developed later, contributed to the classic doctrine of the Trinity.

We can view the continuity between Paul and later Trinitarian doctrine with the analogy of grammar. It is possible for one to speak with perfect grammar without consciously knowing any grammar, for its system is a later development in any language. Theologically speaking, the "grammar" of Paul's prayerful speech about God may well have been correctly understood by later theologians even if their terminology was quite different. That is, Paul, while not knowing it, may refer to God with the grammar of the Trinity (Young and Ford 1987, 256).

Another thought: How close is Paul to what later theologians describe as *perichoresis*? Scholars employ this Greek term "to assert that the divine persons are not individually existent beings and that instead they live in and through each other" (Powell 2008, 333). They each exist by virtue of their relation to one another—the Father to the Son, the Son to the Father, and the Holy Spirit to the Father and the Son. Thus, "the Father and the Son exist together in and with the Holy Spirit" (Powell 2008, 333). Paul may not have been there yet with his primary concern for redemptive history, but he was not "afar off."

In a single sentence he brought the name of Jesus, a mere thirty years after his death and resurrection, together with the Holy Spirit and the name of God in a prayer. In this exalted moment of personal faith and ministerial concern, Paul made his unique contribution to the church's later understanding of a Trinitarian God as rooted theologically in the worship of Jesus Christ, crucified and risen—*lex orandi, lex credenti* (as we pray, so we believe).

The mission of the church in our postmodern age in regard to its faith, its worship, the quality of its life together, yearns for the fulfillment of this benediction. The effective witness of the church and its ministry depends on it.

Gloria Patri
et Filio
et Spiritui Sancto

You Can't Hurry Second Chances

A NOVEL

MICHELLE STIMPSON

The characters and events portrayed in this book are fictitious or are used fictitiously. Any similarity to real persons, living or dead, is purely coincidental and not intended by the author.

Published by Sourcebooks Landmark, an imprint of Sourcebooks
1935 Brookdale RD, Naperville, IL 60563-2773
(630) 961-3900
sourcebooks.com

Library of Congress Cataloging-in-Publication Data

Names: Stimpson, Michelle author
Title: You can't hurry second chances / Michelle Stimpson.
Other titles: You cannot hurry second chances
Description: Naperville, IL : Sourcebooks Landmark, 2026.
Identifiers: LCCN 2025040339 | trade paperback | epub
Subjects: LCGFT: Novels
Classification: LCC PS3619.T56 Y68 2026 | DDC 813/.6--dc23/eng/20250903
LC record available at https://lccn.loc.gov/2025040339

Printed and bound in the United States of America.
VP 10 9 8 7 6 5 4 3 2 1